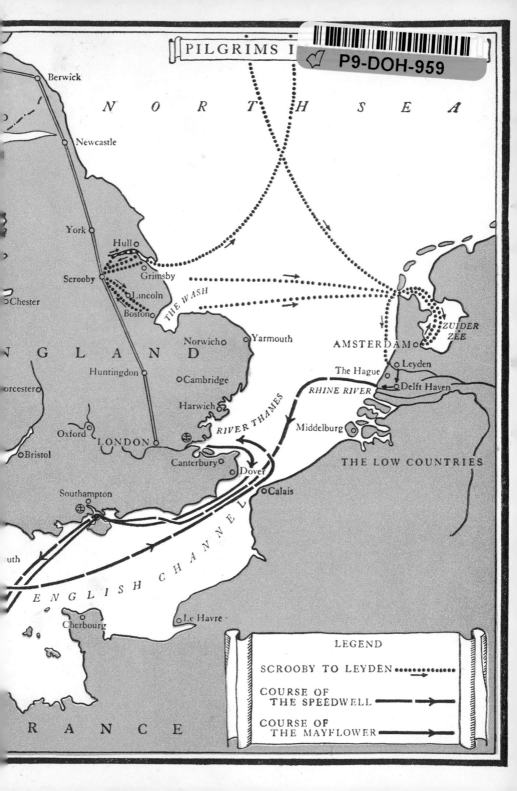

THE PILGRIM READER

By George F. Willison

THE PILGRIM READER

BEHOLD VIRGINIA:
The Fifth Crown

SAINTS AND STRANGERS
Being the Lives of the Pilgrim Fathers
& Their Families with Their Friends & Foes

HERE THEY DUG THE GOLD

The Pilgrim Reader

THE STORY OF THE PILGRIMS
AS TOLD BY THEMSELVES &
THEIR CONTEMPORARIES
FRIENDLY & UNFRIENDLY

George F. Willison

DOUBLEDAY & COMPANY, INC.

Garden City, New York, 1953

LIBRARY OF CONGRESS CATALOG CARD NUMBER 53–5045

COPYRIGHT, 1953, BY GEORGE F. WILLISON
ALL RIGHTS RESERVED
PRINTED IN THE UNITED STATES
AT
THE COUNTRY LIFE PRESS, GARDEN CITY, N.Y.
FIRST EDITION

To

Dana, Cammie, Bam, Mac,
Hellie, Tom, Mother Ferril

Saints, All

Preface

THE PILGRIM STORY has been told many times. But it never was better told, to my feeling, than by the Pilgrims themselves and by their contemporaries, both friendly and unfriendly. Their eyewitness accounts of that story as it unfolded down the years cannot be matched.

In this book it has been my hope and aim to present the unfolding scene as it appeared to the actors in it and to some of the audience, so to speak.

It is fortunate that so many of the actors and the audience wrote so well, with such a sense of the dramatic and with such a sharp eye for graphic, revealing, and often amusing detail—not only Governor William Bradford with his magnificent history of Plymouth Plantation, but Edward Winslow, Pastor John Robinson, Deacon Robert Cushman, Thomas Weston, James Sherley, Nathaniel Morton, John Pory, Isaack de Rasieres, Thomas Morton of Merry Mount, and Governor John Winthrop of Massachusetts, to name a few.

There is in their firsthand observations an immediacy of perception, a freshness of view, a human warmth, a sense of pulsing life with all its hopes and sorrows, its daily triumphs and defeats, its grand designs and homely details, that are engrossing and deeply moving.

As will appear, much of the story is carried in the form of letters, for I am of Governor Bradford's mind when he remarked that "letters are by some wise men counted ye best parte of histories," and we should be thankful to him for preserving so many dealing with Pilgrim concerns.

And for the most part, what good crisp letters they were, affording an intimate glimpse into general affairs and individual character to be found nowhere else. In them, the Pilgrims really come alive as they unguardedly reveal themselves in adding up their satisfactions or giving vent to their exasperations, on occasion hurling themselves with biting wit and devastating scorn upon some hated foe.

Mine is not a book of documents. But it is built upon the documents, major and minor, which carry the Pilgrim story from its Scrooby beginnings about 1606 down to the death of Bradford in 1657.

To this I have added a short introductory piece and an Afterword, which, in brief, brings the story of the Plymouth Colony down to 1692, when it was absorbed, much against its will, by the stronger Massachusetts Bay Colony.

Many events in the Pilgrim story were described by more than one participant or observer. I have not included the various accounts, but have chosen only that one which, in my opinion, best carries the narrative forward as a running story.

None of the chief sources is presented in full, but only in part —in such part as I judged useful for my purpose. In such parts I have omitted repetitious material and unimportant detail, indicating such omissions in the text.

The book follows, in general, a chronological order. But there is some going forward and backward in time to bring related matters together into clearer focus and not leave them loosely strewn along the pages. I have done this, for example, with Bradford's long and quite tedious accounts of the distressing state of Pilgrim finance after 1630, which I have endeavored to telescope and consolidate as much as possible.

How the material from the ancient documents should be presented raised a serious question. Should the passages be left as originally written or first printed, with all of their seventeenth-century idiosyncrasies and eccentricities of spelling, idiom, syntax, abbreviation, capitalization, punctuation, paragraphing, etc.?

Well, it seemed best to tamper with them as little as possible, making only such changes as necessity seemed to require in the interests of easier reading and readier understanding, to remove the worst road blocks in the way of the general reader. This book is addressed to him—and to her—being designed to bring together between two covers a great body of interesting and important material that lies widely scattered in many different sources, some of them not readily available.

I set myself the goal of trying to present faithfully the germane matter in the various texts, and their essential manner in all respects.

My rule of thumb has been this, and I have tried to apply it as consistently as possible, which is not easy in such a mass of verbal idiosyncrasies and eccentricities as I met, varying from writer to writer.

Passages stand in their original form unless I saw good reason to modify some almost unrecognizable spelling of a word ("adventer" for "adventure") or to put in or take out a punctuation mark. But I have not slavishly followed obvious typographical errors, or equally obvious slips of the writer's pen. When a "the" is missing and needed for easy comprehension, I have quietly inserted it without cluttering the page with "[the]."

Some of the writers appearing here wrote "then" for "than," and "hear" for "here," and "of" for "off." I have not followed them in this. Nor have I followed others, like Nathaniel Morton, who capitalized almost every other word. None of them used the apostrophe. I do.

Seventeenth-century punctuation seems to have been conceived solely to confuse. Writers and printers threw commas and parentheses and other marks around with wild abandon. I have tried to retain as much of their open-handed practice as possible. But I have not hesitated to use my own punctuating system, which I think is somewhat more clarifying on how the parts of an often very complex sentence hang together and what the whole of it means.

Nor have I hesitated to break up interminable sentences into their independent component parts—nor to break up long paragraphs. Some of Bradford's run for six pages at a stretch.

Abbreviations and contractions I have usually chosen to spell out. Inconsistently, but not without reason, I have kept the familiar "ye," while writing out the less familiar "yt," for "that."

But these are, in reality, minutiae. The structure, idiom, syntax, and phrasing of all sentences—their bones, as against their dress—stand as they stood in the originals.

At the beginning of the Bibliography is a note on the chief documents used.

My thanks go to Cornelia Goodhue for valuable editorial assistance, to the New York State Library at Albany for many thoughtful and exceptional services, and to Harcourt, Brace and Company for permission to use certain materials from my *Saints and Strangers*—the two end-paper maps, Appendix A (a roster of the Pilgrim company), and brief portions of the text.

Where used, that text has been, for the most part, revised and "improved" and tailored to fit the body of this book. But where the matter is the same, I have not rewritten it for merely verbal change.

GEORGE F. WILLISON

South Hill
November 18, 1952

Contents

THE PILGRIM READER

Foreground & Background

T HE PILGRIM STORY, now so central in our tradition, began far back—long before any of the Pilgrims were born.

It was only a part, but a vital and dramatic part, of a story that went back as far as 1517, when "that stubborn monk," Martin Luther, nailed his ninety-five theses to the door of Wittenberg Cathedral. His bold challenge of the authority of the Pope, the unquestioned heir of Saint Peter, still the King of Kings, the overlord of all the crowned heads of Europe, together with his denunciations of the "abuses" in the Roman church, marked the end of an epoch stretching over centuries.

Luther's action shook Christendom to its foundations and loosed all the forces of long-festering revolt that soon swept Europe in the great movement since known as the Reformation.

Though religious in origin, that movement was not wholly religious in character. It had profound social, political, and economic implications as well, all of them anti-authoritarian in nature. Those in power quickly sensed this and tried to stem the rising tide and drown the insistent cries for reform in all fields.

England had broken with Rome not for reasons of doctrine, but because Henry VIII wished to divorce Catherine of Aragon and marry Anne Boleyn, though this was rather the occasion than the cause of the quarrel which had been going on for centuries. It was the last battle in a long fight against papal power and pretensions.

In setting up the Church of England with himself as its Pope, Henry admitted a few reforms. But in his view the new national church should merely be a "purified" Roman church, and it soon became evident that purification would consist largely of keeping within the kingdom the immense ecclesiastical revenues that had formerly gone to Rome.

Henry did forbid the worship of "idols," and images and shrines throughout the realm were destroyed, with a particular eye on the gold, silver, and jewels that might be salvaged to help swell the royal coffers.

More important, Henry decreed that there should be a Bible in every church. And it was to be in English, not in Latin—a revolutionary departure. Now, for the first time, the plain Englishman could read the Scriptures for himself and come to his own conclusions about them, without benefit of clergy. Here was born the right to independence of judgment, to freedom of conscience, that the Pilgrims later so stubbornly demanded.

But in all else the Anglican church remained Roman in cast and character.

The church first began to assume a Protestant aspect under Henry's sickly son, Edward VI, who came to the throne at the age of nine, with the Duke of Somerset as Protector. Favoring change, the Duke sponsored the first Book of Common Prayer (1549) and the Edwardian Service Book (1552), the initial step in shaping a Protestant ritual.

But Edward soon died and was succeeded by Mary, a zealous and bigoted Catholic, daughter of Catherine of Aragon. The Pope was again recognized as the spiritual and temporal overlord of Europe. The Anglican church was suppressed. Hundreds of its members—men, women, and children—were hanged or burned at the stake. Many Protestant leaders fled to the Continent, to the Calvinist and Lutheran centers at Geneva, Basle, Frankfort, and Strasbourg, where they met with far more radical ideas than any yet espoused in England.

But "Bloody" Mary's reign was short, and in 1558 Anne Boleyn's daughter, Elizabeth, ascended the throne. Once more England broke with the Pope and outlawed the Roman rite. Elizabeth deposed many bishops with papal leanings and mitered some of the less radical Protestants who had fled the country in Mary's time.

But the Queen was not a reformer and pursued a wary course from the start, being well aware that England was still largely Catholic in sympathy and belief, as it would remain down to the defeat of the Spanish Armada in 1588. So far as Protestantism was an assertion of national independence, she favored it. But she personally preferred the Roman Mass to the simpler Protestant service.

Caught between implacably hostile forces, Elizabeth played one against the other, throwing sops to each in turn. She had the Edwardian Service Book revised to restore the "Black Rubric," as kneeling at communion was styled by the more extreme anti-Papists. Intervening in the controversy raging about clerical vestments, the hated "rags of Rome," she decreed that in conducting Sunday services ministers were to wear "a comely surplice, with sleeves." Then with a bow to the Protestants she ordered that the cope was to be worn only at communion and that priests were not to wear "hattes but in their journeinge."

As Church and State were one, Elizabeth demanded absolute uniformity of belief, and machinery to enforce uniformity existed in the Court of High Commission. Dominated by the bishops, this was the English model of the Court of the Holy Inquisition and shared the latter's faith in the stake and gallows as the surest means of spreading the gentle teachings of Christ.

Hundreds of "heretics" were jailed; some were hanged or burned, at the order of the bishops, whose authority was based not upon statutory law but upon the limitless royal prerogative. They could summon and examine anyone at all and condemn suspects upon no other evidence than their own frightened and confused replies. If they refused to answer from fear of incriminating themselves, punishment was even more certain.

The kingdom's prisons, all frightful dungeons, were filled with people helplessly awaiting the bishops' pleasure, or displeasure, with no recourse whatever at law, for the writ of habeas corpus had yet to be devised to curb such arbitrary power and its always oppressive use.

But Elizabeth and her bishops could not stifle the voices of those who were seeking a new and better order of things, a greater measure of freedom for all men, a higher and nobler conception of life based upon the intrinsic worth and dignity of the individual.

Disturbed by the state of the church which was reflected in all society, true radicals in that they wished to get at the root of things, these men dug into Scripture to find out where "disorder" first crept in. The more they examined Scripture, the less warrant they could find for much current belief and observance. The originally simple Christian faith had been corrupted by time and "human invention."

The church, they declared, should be restored to its "ancient purity"—or, as the Pilgrims later phrased it, "to its primative order, libertie, & bewtie."

The orthodox were disturbed by such views, and in 1565 Archbishop Parker denounced those holding them as "these precise men." It was a graphic label, and it stuck. Reformers were soon known as the Precisians, somewhat later as the Puritans—so named for their theological doctrine, it should be observed, and not for their moral code, which was a later growth.

The reformers had many sharp and well-grounded complaints to make about the church. They objected to the great host of "dumb" ministers who seldom or never preached. Pluralism had been forbidden, but many clerics still held scores of pulpits and church livings, appearing only to collect their stipends. Country parishes frequently went for years at a time without religious services. Altogether, the church was "a pache of popery, and a pudle of corruption."

Was not the sign of the cross, hated as part of the Roman rite, still being made over infants at baptism? Were not dispensations still being sold to those who could pay for them—ten shillings for dispensing with the publication of banns before marriage, forty shillings for permission to eat meat on fast days? Was not the church operating that elaborate fee-and-fine system known as the Indulgences, a primary cause of Luther's revolt and a noisome scandal in the Roman church?

And would any deny that the higher clergy were brazenly making "merchandise of the Church of God," bestowing scores of profitable offices upon themselves and performing none, alienating its lands, wasting its woods, and disposing of church rights and revenues as if these were their personal property?

As a result, as even Archbishop Parker's biographer had to admit, "the churchs ran greatly to decays, were kept filthy and nasty, and undecent for God's worship."

Several of Elizabeth's bishops were plain rascals and had to be deposed for looting the parishes in their charge. Others led grossly sensual lives. All lived in the greatest magnificence and luxury. A great troop of white horse and hundreds of flunkeys in scarlet livery, set off with gold chains and gold braid, accompanied the Archbishop of Canterbury on his travels.

And these were the prelates who, to clothe their worldly pride and arrogance, clung so passionately to the "rags of Rome"!

Churchmen, protested the reformers, should be distinguished "by their doctrines, not their garments; their conversation, not their dress; their purity of mind, not their adornment of person." Here was the origin of the Puritan animus against "gay apparel." Anyone bedecked in silks, satins, and laces must be as "antichristian" as a bishop.

But none of the Puritans, not even the most "forward" of them, ever denounced the "abuses" with the vehemence of a distinguished churchman, Dr. Laurence Chaderton, an inspired scholar-poet, one of those who later gave us the magnificent King James Version of the Bible, which has molded our speech and thought for centuries.

In a remarkable sermon at Cambridge in 1578, Chaderton declared, mincing no words, that the church was "a huge masse of old and stinkinge workes, of conjuring, witchcraft, sorcery, charming, blaspheming the holy name of God, swearing and forswearing, profaning of the Lord's Sabbothe, disobediance to superiours, contempt of inferiours; murther, Manslaughter, robberies, adulterye, Fornication, covenant-breaking, false witness-bearing, lieing . . ."

The church was filled with hypocrites and harbored renegades. There was everywhere an imperative need for honest and zealous pastors "to admonish, correct, suspende, and excommunicate such noysome, hurtfull, & monstruous beastes out of the house of God, without respect of persons."

But critics got no support from the "antichristian prelates," who more commandingly insisted that all conform and hold their tongues. As the pressure increased, many of the Puritans, especially those more comfortably situated in life, began to give way and resigned themselves to at least a nominal conformity.

But there were others of greater faith and courage, men—and women, too—of passion and conviction, who were not to be intimidated. If there was no place for them in the church, they would withdraw and establish one of their own. They would defy the bishops, even the Queen—though from the start they swore their absolute loyalty to Elizabeth, declaring with some truth that they were far better subjects than most of those who prosecuted and persecuted them in her name.

In 1578, shortly after Chaderton had spoken, a graduate of the university returned to Cambridge, the Reverend Robert Browne, and soon created a storm with his "forward" sermons. Opposition forced him to retire to Norwich two years later. There he was soon jailed, on complaint of the local bishop, for holding private meetings "of the vulgar sort of people . . . to the number of one hundred at a time."

Appealing to Lord Burghley, Lord Treasurer and chief minister of the realm, a distant kinsman, Browne obtained his release. Again the bishop jailed him. Again Burghley released him. Once more the bishop jailed him. Thereupon, at their first opportunity, Browne and his followers escaped to Holland, blazing a trail that the Pilgrims and many more would follow.

The exiles settled at Middelburg, where in 1582 Browne published two works of the greatest consequence, *A Treatise of Reformation without Tarying for Anie* and *A Booke which Sheweth the Life and Manner of all True Christians*. One of the most creative religious thinkers of his day, Browne exerted a profound and determining influence upon all the Pilgrim leaders.

In his works Browne first formulated the principles upon which the revolutionary Independent movement took shape, crystallizing vague ideas that had been circulating for some time, bringing reform out of the closet into the market place.

Browne rejected Calvin's thesis that the church could not be reformed until the state took action, which was a most unrealistic view when the Church and State were one.

Rather, said Browne, the kingdom of God was "not to be begun by whole parishes, but rather by the worthiest [in them], were they ever so few."

In every parish these should withdraw from the church—secede, separate, as they had warrant to do by Scripture*—and organize themselves under a mutual covenant "to forsake & denie all ungodliness and wicked fellowship, and to refuse all ungodlie communion with Wicked Persons."

It was the right of every congregation so organized to select its pastor and other officers in a democratic manner, with all adult male communicants having a vote—women, of course, were still the legal chattels of their lords and masters.

If other groups followed the same course, the several congregations should remain quite independent of one another. They might co-operate in a voluntary fellowship. But there should be no bishops, no archbishops, no central organization or authority of any kind. There was no warrant for these in the Bible.

One could search the Holy Book from cover to cover without finding anything faintly resembling the hierarchical structure of the Roman or Anglican churches, with their rectors, vicars, rural deans, chaplains, chancellors, archdeacons, prebendaries, bishops, and archbishops. All of these offices were "human inventions."

The only "lawfull" form of the church was simple indeed, said Browne, citing I Corinthians 12:28:

And God hath ordeined some in the Church: *as* first Apostles, secondly Prophets, thirdly teachers, then them that doe miracles; after

*Paul: "Come out from among them, and be ye separate, saith the Lord, and touch not the unclean thing."

them, the giftes of healing, helpers [deacons], governours [elders], diversitie of tongues.*

For more details on their duties, Browne cited I Timothy 5:17 and Romans 12:6–8. But in developing their "Holy Discipline," the Brownists relied, above all, upon the unapostolic marginal notes—"human inventions" indeed!—which appeared besides these verses in the Geneva Bible.

The Holy Discipline was well named. It was only for the holy, only for those who led unblemished lives. In Calvin's view, the "true" church embraced the entire baptized population. But Browne objected to any such sweeping inclusion of communicants "without regard to personal character." His was to be a "priesthood of believers," a church of "Saincts." Whether baptized or not, the irreligious were to be excluded.

And the lives of the Saints, as a matter of course, were to be subjected to the closest scrutiny and continuous review, for every act and word—even a passing thought—weighed in the balance. Constant criticism of one's self and others became a required and positive religious duty.

From this sprang that sometimes fruitful searching of soul and that quite as often mean-spirited prying into the most intimate affairs of one another's lives which marked the Separatist churches without exception and caused almost all of them to founder.

Within two years Browne's was shattered by bitter quarrels and recriminations. Returning to England, Browne made his peace with the bishops by blasting his own people, the Brownists, being rewarded with a rectorship in Northamptonshire, where he served out his life in the Anglican church quite as if he had never denounced it as a "Moloch" and an "infamous corruption."

But the earlier Browne had planted seeds that were to sprout and flourish, and the University of Cambridge was a principal seedbed. From it came many "forward" Puritans, some of whom

---

*The verse reads so in the Geneva or "Breeches" Bible of 1560, which the Pilgrims and all the Separatists used. It reads almost identically in the King James Version of 1611 and the Revised Version of 1881.

founded the Massachusetts Bay Colony, others of whom played leading roles in the Great Rebellion that unseated the "antichristian" bishops, overturned the Anglican church, cost Charles I his head, and erected a new Commonwealth under Oliver Cromwell.

More important to the Pilgrim story, from Cambridge came a number of Separatist martyrs—John Udall, John Greenwood, Henry Barrow, and John Penry, among others. Most of these were certainly known to the founder of the original Pilgrim congregation, William Brewster, later the congregation's beloved elder. With the exception of Barrow, Brewster had been at Cambridge with all of these. He and Penry, hanged as operator of the wandering and "seditious" Martinist press, were classmates at Peterhouse College, having matriculated on the same day.

In the spring of 1593, Greenwood and Barrow had gone to the gallows for "devising and circulating seditious books." Lord Burghley, who had Puritan leanings in spite of the scoffs of the Queen and her gibes at "his brothers in Christ," interceded for the prisoners, protesting that the blood of reformers essentially in agreement with Protestant tenets should not be shed "in a land where no Papist has been touched for religion by death."

The Archbishop of Canterbury, John Whitgift, once a reformer, peremptorily demanded their execution. Burghley gave him and the bishops "some round taxing words" and carried the matter to Elizabeth. But as none of the Privy Council supported him, Archbishop Whitgift, the Queen's venomous "little black husband," had his way with the prisoners, immediately jailing hundreds of other dissidents.

Egged on by Whitgift and his bishops, Parliament reluctantly passed the most savage law of Elizabeth's reign, aimed at Brownists and "other Sectaries and disloyal persons."

By this law—it was to run for only five years, but was successively renewed well into the reign of Charles I—anyone who absented himself from the Anglican service for more than a month, or who attempted in any way to persuade others to do so, or who attended "any unlawfull assemblies, conventicles, or meetings under colour or pretence of any Exercise of Religion," was to be imprisoned without bail until he gave surety to conform.

If the dissident did not conform within three months, he was to quit the realm, on pain of death without benefit of clergy. If he ever returned, he was to be summarily executed.

This measure was pushed through Parliament by the "malice of the bishops, . . . which hath earned them much hatred of the common people," reported Thomas Phillipes, better known as "Morice, the Decipherer," for his feat in decoding the secret messages that sent Mary Queen of Scots to death for conspiracy against the Crown.

In his letter on the "malice of the bishops," Morice also reported the hangings of Penry and "two of the principal Brownists, Barrow and Greenwood, . . . so as that Sect is in effect extinguished."

But Morice was quite mistaken here, being not so apt at deciphering the future.

This was not the end of the Brownist movement and the Separation. It was only the beginning, as the Pilgrim story with all of its trials and adventures makes plain.

So many therefore of these professors as saw ye evill of these things in these parts, and whose harts ye Lord had touched with heavenly zeale for his trueth, they shooke off this yoake of antichristian bondage, and as ye Lord's free people joyned themselves (by a covenant of the Lord) into a church estate, in ye felowship of ye gospell, to walke in all his wayes made known or to be made known unto them, according to their best endeavours, whatsoever it should cost them, the Lord assisting them.

And that it cost them something, this ensewing historie will declare.

—Of Plimoth Plantation

I

In England

. . . they shooke off this yoake of antichristian bondage and, as ye Lord's free people, joyned themselves (by
a covenant of the Lord) into a church estate . . .

—William Bradford

BRADFORD'S
HISTORY*
And first, of ye occasion and inducements thereunto, the which, that I may truly unfould, I must
begine at ye very roote & rise of ye same.
The which I shall endevor to manefest in a plaine stile, with
singuler regard unto ye simple trueth in all things, at least as near
as my slender judgmente can attaine the same.

1. Beginnings

It is well knowne unto ye godly and judicious how ever since
ye first breaking out of ye light of ye gospell in our Honourable
Nation of England . . . what warrs & oppositions ever since
Satan hath raised, maintained, and continued against the Saincts
from time to time, in one sorte or other.

Sometimes, by bloody death and cruell torments; other whiles,
imprisonments, banishments & other hard usages; as being loath

*From Governor William Bradford's *Of Plimoth Plantation*—hereafter, Bradford's History.

Written at Plymouth between 1630 and 1650, the work carries the Pilgrim
story from its beginnings down to 1647. Long lost, the manuscript was first
published in full in 1856.

Unless otherwise noted, all original passages from here to p. 103 are from
the same source.

All chapter titles and section headings are the editor's.

his kingdom should go down, the trueth prevail, and ye churches of God revert to their ancient puritie and recover their primative order, libertie, & bewtie.

But when he could not prevail by these means against the maine trueths of ye gospell but that they began to take rooting in many places, being watered with ye blooud of ye martyrs and blessed from heaven with a gracious encrease, he then began to take him to his anciente strategems, . . . to sow errors, heresies, and wonderful dissentions amongst ye professors themselves* (working upon their pride & ambition, with other corrupte passions incident to all mortall men—yea, to ye Saincts themselves in some measure), by which woefull effects followed.

As not only bitter contentions, hartburnings, & schisms with other horrible confusions, but Satan took occasion & advantage thereby to foyst in a number of vile ceremoneys, with many unprofitable canons & decrees, which have since been as snares to many poore & peaceable souls, even to this day† . . .

The one side laboured to have ye right worship of God & discipline of Christ established in ye church according to ye simplicitie of ye gospell, without the mixture of men's inventions, and to have & be ruled by ye laws of God's word dispensed in those offices & by those officers of Pastors, Teachers, & Elders, &c., according to ye Scriptures.

The other partie, though under many colours & pretences, endeavored to have ye episcopall dignitie (after ye popish manner) with their large power & jurisdiction still retained, with all their courts, cannons, & ceremonies, togeather with all such livings, revenues, & subordinate officers, with other such means as formerly upheld their antichristian greatnes and enabled them with lordly power to persecute ye poore servants of God . . .

*Used here in a special sense, the term "professors" signified, as a Pilgrim pastor later explained, all of those who professed belief in the "forward" views of the Puritan preachers and attended their services—being, in general, those seeking radical religious reform.

†This passage was probably written in 1630, at which time, as he himself tells us, Bradford began what he called his "scribled writings." Bradford is here alluding to events of a generation or two before, in the reigns of Queen Elizabeth and her immediate predecessor, "bloody" Mary.

And many the like to stop the mouthes of ye more godly, to bring them to yeeld to one ceremoney after another, and one corruption after another; by these wiles beguiling some & corrupting others till at length they began to persecute all ye zealous professors in the land . . . if they would not submitte to their ceremonies & become slaves to them & their popish trash, which have no ground in ye word of God, but are relikes of that man of sin.

And the more ye light of ye gospell grew, ye more they urged their subscriptions to these corruptions . . .

And to cast contempte the more upon ye sincere servants of God, they opprobriously & most injuriously gave unto & imposed upon them that name of Puritans . . .

And lamentable it is to see ye effects which have followed. Religion hath been disgraced; the godly greeved, afflicted, persecuted; and many exiled. Sundrie have lost their lives in prisons & other ways.

On the other hand, sin hath been countenanced; ignorance, profaness & atheisme increased; & the papists encouraged to hope againe for a daye . . .

2. The Lord's Free People

As in other places in the land, so in ye North parts, many became inlightened in ye word of God and had their ignorance & sins discovered unto them, and begane by his grace to reforme their lives and make conscience of their wayes.

The work of God was no sooner manifest in them but, presently, they were both scoffed and scorned by ye prophane multitude, and ye ministers urged with ye yoke of subscription, or els must be silenced. And ye poore people were so vexed with apparators & pursuants & ye commisarie courts* as truly their affliction was not small.

*These local courts sat under the authority of the dread Court of High Commission, dominated by the bishops and fiercely dedicated to stamping out

Which, notwithstanding, they bore sundrie years with much patience till they were occasioned (by ye continuance & encrease of these troubles and others means which ye Lord raised up in those days) to see further into things by the light of ye word of God.

How not only these base and beggarly ceremonies were unlawfull, but also that ye lordly & tiranous power of ye prelates ought not to be submitted unto* . . . And that their offices & callings, courts & cannons, &c., were unlawfull and antichristian, being such as have no warrant in ye word of God, but ye same that were used in poperie & still retained . . .

So many therefore of these proffessors [in North England] as saw ye evill of these things, and whose harts ye Lord had touched with heavenly zeale for his trueth, they shooke off this yoake of antichristian bondage and, as ye Lord's free people, joyned themselves (by a covenant of the Lord) into a church estate, in ye felowship of ye gospell, to walke in all his wayes made known or to be made known unto them, according to their best endeavours,† whatsoever it should cost them, the Lord assisting them.

And that it cost them something, this ensewing historie will declare.

"heresy," which was anything not approved by the authorities. It was as highhanded in its procedures and as arbitrary in its judgments as its contemporary engine of tyranny, the Star Chamber, from which there was no appeal. Scores had already perished at the decree of the Court of High Commission, which was nothing more than the Court of the Holy Inquisition sitting in Anglican vestments and under another name.

*This was treason at a time when Church and State were one. For holding such views, many had been hanged, burned at the stake, or locked up in one or another of the kingdom's foul prisons, all of them sinkholes of brutality, vice, and disease. As often as not, a jail sentence was a death sentence in those days.

†All Separatists took similar covenants in founding their churches, each quite independent of the others.

3. The Scrooby Congregation

These people became 3 distincte bodys, or churches, & in regard of distance of place did congregate severally, for they were of sundrie townes & villages—some in Nottinghamshire, some in Lincolnshire, and some in Yorkshire, where they border nearest togeather.

In one of these churches, besides others of note, was Mr. John Smith [Smyth], a man of able gifts & a good preacher, who afterwards was chosen their pastor. But these, afterwards falling into some errours in ye Low Countries, there for ye most part buried themselves & their names.*

But in this other church, . . . ye subjecte of our discourse, besides other worthy men, was Mr. Richard Clifton [Clyfton], a grave & reverend preacher, who by his paines & diligens had done much good and, under God, had been a means of ye conversion of many.

And also that famous and worthy man, Mr. John Robinson, who afterwards was their pastor for many years, till ye Lord tooke him away by death. Also, Mr. William Brewster, a reverent man, who afterwards was chosen an elder of ye church and lived with them till old age.

This second and smaller congregation, an offshoot of the one at Gainsborough near by, met in and around Scrooby, a tiny and inconsequential hamlet lying approximately in the center of England, almost at the tip of the narrow northern neck of Nottinghamshire. It was an isolated countryside in the fenlands, rather poor and sparsely settled—about as unlikely a place as one could imagine for raising a standard of revolt that would have such profound influence down to our own day.

*Meeting secretly at Gainsborough in Lincolnshire, just across the River Trent from Nottinghamshire, this first Separatist church in the North had been founded about 1606 by the Reverend John Smyth, one of the most interesting and engaging figures of the early Separation. All in the district worshiped under him for a time, so that Smyth was, in a real sense, the first Pilgrim pastor.

A "meane townlet," Scrooby was distinguished only by a small stone church, St. Wilfred's, which still stands, and by a great manor house, "of tymber," which stood beside the sluggish River Ryton with a moat about it. The house and the extensive manor around it belonged to the archbishopric of York, as it had for almost a thousand years. Here in the "palace," which contained some forty rooms and a private chapel, the archbishops of York held court on their rare visits to this distant part of their see.

Even more exalted visitors had stopped here from time to time —Princess Margaret Tudor, daughter of Henry VII, and even a king, Henry VIII, who came in 1541 with many great and merry gentlemen and stayed the night. Thus, for a day, Scrooby was virtually the capital of the realm.

Nothing of the old manor house remains today but a few remnants of its walls, long since incorporated in the structure of a "plain farm tenement" built upon the ruins of the palace after it had crumbled and fallen down, being demolished in 1637.

The front wall of this farmhouse bears a plaque which records that here

lived
WILLIAM BREWSTER
from 1588 to 1608, and where he organized the Pilgrim Church, of which he became the ruling elder, and with which, in 1608, he removed to Amsterdam, in 1609 to Leyden, and in 1620 to Plymouth,
where he died
April 16, 1644

4. William Brewster

Unhappily, the memorial plaque errs in several respects. Brewster did not die in 1644, but in 1643.

More important, he had lived at the manor many years before 1588. It had been his home since 1575, when he had come there as a boy of nine or ten upon the appointment of his father, also named William, as bailiff and receiver of Scrooby Manor.

It was his father's duty to manage the extensive manorial es-

tate, collect rents from tenants, and sit as a magistrate in minor
matters, for which he received, in addition to the use of the manor
house and the fruits of its grounds, a nominal salary of £3 6s. 6d.
($165) a year.*

The old manorial establishment was decaying when the Brewsters moved in. But it was still imposing, having within the moat
a number of small houses, several large stables, a granary, a black-
smithy, a bakehouse, and a brewhouse, as well as the usual ken-
nels and dovecotes.

The stables, as well as the bakehouse and brewhouse, enabled
the senior Brewster to carry on his additional duties as master of
the local station on the royal post. Under his commission he was
obligated to keep a tavern for the refreshments of the royal cour-
iers and the occasional wayfarer along the Great North Road,
which ran from London to Scotland and passed by the gates of
the manor.

As postmaster, the older Brewster received a salary of £30 8s.
4d. ($1,525) a year. Profits from the tavern and the hire of horses
ran high. And what with no rent to pay and his every need supplied by the manor's fields and gardens, the boy's father was a
man of relative wealth and consequence in the isolated district.

Here at Scrooby Manor, young Brewster spent the next five
years of his life, somehow managing to acquire some formal education. This meant no more than that he could read and write,
sing the psalms, parse a little Latin, and endure a great deal of flog-
ging, which was systematically and powerfully applied, with or
without provocation, being highly esteemed as the very essence
of learning.

At a time when not one child in ten received any schooling
whatever, even in the larger cities, the Brewsters must have been
at great pains and expense to see that their son had such an advantage in the lonely countryside. Who taught the boy is not

---

*Monetary sums throughout have been roughly equated with the real value—
i.e., purchasing power—of the pre-war 1940 dollar.

For purposes of approximation, I have translated £1 as $5.00 and multiplied
that by ten.

The approximation is rather too low than too high, it would seem. At the
time, skilled workers received 1s. a day, which on the scale used here (roughly,
a ratio of 1 to 10), would be the equivalent in 1940 dollars of a daily wage of
$2.50, or $15 for a six-day week.

known. Perhaps it was another and apparently unrelated Brewster, one of the few university men in the neighborhood, the Reverend Henry Brewster, vicar at the hamlet of Sutton-cum-Lound a few miles away.

In any case, in 1580 young Brewster, now an adolescent of fifteen, packed up and rode off down the Great North Road, astride one of his father's horses, to enter the University of Cambridge. There he came under strong Puritan influences, being "first seasoned with ye seeds of grace and vertue," and "attained some learning—viz., ye knowledg of ye Latine tongue & some insight in ye Greeke."

But after two years, without waiting to take a degree, Brewster went to London to become a "secretarie" to one of Queen Elizabeth's most successful and adroit diplomats, "that religious and godly gentleman," Sir William Davison, who treated the youth, now seventeen, "more like a sonne than a servante." Sir William found him, according to Bradford, "so discreete and faithfull as he trusted him above all others that were aboute him."

For five years Brewster lived at Queen Elizabeth's brilliant court, glimpsing all of the great figures of the day—Lord Burghley, Sir Walter Raleigh, Sir Francis Drake, Archbishop Whitgift of Canterbury, the Queen's "little black husband," and the Queen herself—though he doubtless eyed them from a respectful distance.

Then suddenly, in 1587, his master fell from grace. Made a scapegoat for the execution of Mary Queen of Scots, Davison was committed to the Tower of London, where he remained for two years, with Brewster loyally tending him and performing "manie faithfull offices in servise in ye time of his troubles."

His master in disgrace, his hopes of a career at court ruined, young Brewster, now in his early twenties, returned home in 1589, after nine years' absence. Upon his father's death the next year he became tavernkeeper, postmaster, and overseer of Scrooby Manor. Possessed of an ample income, he soon married Mary (Wentworth?) and, by the time the Scrooby congregation was formed about fifteen years later, had three children—Jonathan, aged thirteen; Patience, a girl of six; and a second daughter, Fear, a child in arms—all of whom appear in the Plymouth records.

5. Young William Bradford

But Brewster virtually had a fourth child, young William Bradford, only seventeen when the Scrooby congregation was formed, but already active in its affairs.

A sickly and rather precocious youth destined to become the strongest, ablest, and most diversely gifted of the Pilgrim Fathers, Bradford had been born to a prosperous yeoman family at Austerfield, Yorkshire, a few miles up the Great North Road from Scrooby.

Soon after Bradford's birth, his father died, and when his mother remarried a few years later, she sent her four-year-old to live with his grandfather, another William Bradford. Not long after, both his grandfather and his mother died, and the boy went to live with his paternal uncles, Robert and Thomas, "who devoted him, like his ancestors, unto the affairs of husbandry."

The unhappy orphan suffered a "soon and long" sickness, evidently psychological in origin, for it passed away as he grew older and more contented. But painful as it was, Bradford always regarded it as a blessing in disguise, for it had kept him, he used to say, "from the vanities of youth."

By the time he was twelve, he was already deeply read in the Scriptures and soon met another youth similarly preoccupied. The latter introduced him to the Puritans in the neighborhood, the first step in Bradford's "holy, prayerfull, watchful, and fruitfull Walk with God, wherein he was very exemplary."

All the youth's relatives opposed his course, saying that he would lose everything he had—his lands, his good name, even his very soul—if he continued to associate with "fantasticall schismatics." But Bradford had convinced himself that he was on the right path, "nor could the wrath of his uncles, nor the scoff of his neighbors, now turned upon him as one of the Puritans, divert him from his pious inclinations."

Fortunately, young Bradford, lonesome and bewildered, soon came under the knowing and gentle hand of William Brewster, who befriended the unhappy orphan and virtually adopted him as his son, the beginning of an intimacy that decisively shaped

the Pilgrim story and inspired Bradford to one of his most elo-
quent passages in which he thus described, many years later, his
old friend Brewster:

6. A Special Stay

Afterwards [i.e., after young Brewster left London], he wente
and lived in ye country in good esteeme amongst his freinds and
ye gentlemen of those parts, espetially the godly and religious.

He did much good in ye countrie where he lived in promoting
and furthering religion, not only by his practiss & example and
provocking and incouraging of others, but by procuring of good
preachers to ye places thereaboute and drawing on of others to
assiste & help forward in such a worke, he himselfe being most
commonly deepest in ye charge & sometimes above his abillitie.

And in this state he continued many years, doing ye best he
could and walking according to ye light he saw till ye Lord
revealed further unto him.

And in ye end, by ye tirrany of ye bishops against godly
preachers & people, in silencing the one & persecuting ye other,
he and many more of those times begane to looke further into
things, and to see into ye unlawfullnes of their callings and ye
burthen of many anti-christian corruptions, which both he and
they endeavored to cast off . . .

After they were joyned togither in communion, he was a
special stay & help unto them. They ordinarily mett at his house
on ye Lord's day (which was a manor of ye bishops), and with
great love he entertained them when they came, making provission for them to his great charge* . . .

For his personall abilities, he was qualified above many. He
was wise and discreete and well spoken, having a grave & de-

---

*With his always fine sense of the dramatic and ironic, Bradford must have
smiled as he wrote this, remembering the days when the hunted and necessarily
furtive Separatists at Scrooby held their secret and "subversive" meetings in
the archiepiscopal palace, where Brewster probably entertained them in the
tavern, the largest room in the house.

liberate utterance; of a very cheerfull spirite, very sociable & pleasante amongst his freinds; of a humble and modest mind; of a peaceable disposition; undervallewing himselfe & his owne abilities, and sometimes overvallewing others; inoffensive and innocente in his life & conversation, which gained him ye love of those without [the congregation] as well as those within.

Yet he would tell them plainly of their faults & evills, both publickly & privately, but in such a manner as usually was well taken from him.

He was tender-harted and compassionate of such as were in miserie . . . And none did more offend & displease him than such as would haughtily and proudly carry & lift up themselves, being rise from nothing, and having little else in them to commend them but a few fine clothes or a little riches more than others.

In teaching, he was very moving & stirring of affections; also, very plaine & distincte in what he taught, by which means he became ye more profitable to ye hearers.

He had a singular good gift in prayer, both publick & private, in ripping up ye hart & conscience before God, in ye humble confession of sinne and begging ye mercies of God in Christ for ye pardon of ye same.

He always thought it were better for ministers to pray oftener and devide their prayers than be longe & tedious in ye same (excepte upon sollemne & spetiall occations, as in days of humiliation & ye like) . . .

For ye governmente of ye church (which was most proper to his office), he was carefull to preserve good order in ye same and to preserve puritie both in ye doctrine & communion, and to suppress any errour or contention that might begin to rise up amongst them.

And accordingly, God gave good success to his indeavors therein all his days . . .

7. The Scrooby Pastor, Richard Clyfton

One of Brewster's earliest allies in the neighborhood was the Reverend Richard Clyfton, rector at Babworth, a village about six miles southeast of Scrooby. A "forward" minister of the Puritan school, Clyfton had been preaching there for twenty years, exerting a great influence throughout the surrounding countryside. Brewster and his family used to tramp down the road to Babworth every Sabbath to be "illuminated."

A man of fifty, a patriarchal figure "with a great white beard," Clyfton was now called to minister to the "heretics" at Scrooby. Later, much fault was found with Clyfton, the first pastor of the original Pilgrim congregation. Enemies pronounced him "a most simple and piteous teacher, . . . weak in the Scriptures, unable to convince his gainsayers, and careless to deliver his doctrine pure, sound, and plain."

But Bradford and others testified that much good had been done by his "faithfull and painfull minnestry, both in preaching and Cattechising," and that his "paines & diligens" had been the means of converting many.

And certainly none challenged his sincerity and courage at this time when, with a growing family, he abandoned his assured living in the Anglican church and threw in his lot with the poor, despised, and hounded Separatists.

8. Flight

But after these things, they could not long continue in any peaceable condition, but were hunted and persecuted on every side, so as their former afflictions were but as flea-bitings in comparison with those which now came upon them.

For some were taken & clapt up in prison. Others had their houses besett & watcht night and day & hardly escaped their hands. And ye most were faine to flie & leave their howses & habitations, and the means of their livelihood.

Yet these & many other sharper things which afterward befell them were no other than they looked for and therefore were ye better prepared to bear them by ye assistance of God's grace & spirit.

Yet seeing themselves thus molested, and that there was no hope of their continuance there, by a joynte consent they resolved to goe into ye Low Countries, where they heard was freedome of Religion for all men . . .

So after they had continued togeither aboute a year and kept their meetings every Sabbath in one place or other, exercising the worship of God amongst themselves notwithstanding all ye dilligence & malice of their adversaries, . . . they resolved to get over into Holland as they could, which was in ye year 1607 & 1608 . . .

Being thus constrained to leave their native soyle and countrie, their lands & livings, and all their freinds & famillier acquaintance, it was much and thought marvelous by many.

But to goe into a countrie they knew not (but by hearsay), where they must learne a new language and get their livings they knew not how, it being a dear place & subjecte to ye miseries of warr, it was by many thought an adventure almost desperate, a case intolerable, & a miserie worse than death—espetially seeing they were not acquainted with trades nor traffique (by which that countrie doth subsiste), but had only been used to a plaine countrie life & ye innocente trade of husbandrey . . .

Yet this was not all. For though they could not stay, yet they were not suffered to goe. But ye ports & havens were shut against them,* so as they were faine to seek secret meanes of conveance, & to bribe & fee ye mariners, & give exterordinarie rates for their passages.

And yet were they oftentimes betrayed (many of them), and both they & their goods intercepted & surprised, and thereby put to great trouble & charge . . .

*The law forbade any subject to leave the realm without permission of the Crown, so that the Separatists' attempts to reach Holland provided another ground for prosecution and persecution. The Gainsborough congregation, led by John Smyth, had already made its escape to Amsterdam.

There was a large companie of them purposed to get passage at Boston, in Lincolnshire, and for that end had hired a ship wholly to themselves & made agreement with the master to be ready at a certaine day and take them and their goods in at a conveniente place, where they accordingly would all attend in readines.

So after long waiting & large expences, though he kept not the day with them, yet he came at length & tooke them in, in ye night. But when he had them & their goods abord, he betrayed them, having beforehand complotted with ye searchers & other officers so to doe.

[These officers] tooke them and put them into open boats, & there rifled & ransaked them, searching them to their shirts for money—yea, even ye women furder than became modestie—and then carried them back into ye towne & made them a spectackle & wonder to ye multitude, which came flocking on all sides to behould them.

Being thus first by the catchpoule officers rifled & stript of their money, books, and much other goods, they were presented to ye magestrates, and messengers sent to informe ye lords of ye Counsell of them, and so they were committed to ward. Indeed, ye magestrats used them courteously and shewed them what favour they could, but could not deliver them till an order came from ye Counsell table.*

But ye issue was that after a month's imprisonment ye greatest parte were dismiste, & sent to ye place from whence they came. But seven of ye principall were still kept in prison and bound over to the Azzises.†

9. Escape

The next spring [1608] there was another attempt made by some of these and others to get over at another place. And it fell

*That is, from the all-powerful Privy Council.
†Pastor Clyfton and Ruling Elder Brewster were two of these. The seven were never arraigned and in time released.

out that they light of [chanced upon] a Dutchman at Hull, having a ship of his owne belonging to Zealand. They made agreemente with him and acquainted him with their condition, hoping
to find more faithfullnes in him than in ye former of their owne
nation.

He bad them not fear, for he would doe well enough. He was
by appointment to take them in betweene Grimsby & Hull,
where there was a large common a good way distante from any
towne.*

Now, against the prefixed time, the women & children, with
ye goods, were sent to ye place in a small barke which they had
hired for that end, and ye men were to meete them by land.†

But it so fell out that they were there a day before the ship
came and, ye sea being rough and ye women very sicke, prevailed with ye seamen to put into a creeke hard by, where they
lay on ground at low water. The next morning ye ship came,
but they were fast & could not stir till aboute noone.

In ye meantime, ye ship's master, perceiving how ye matter
was, sent his boate to be getting ye men abord, whom he saw
ready, walking aboute ye shore. But after ye first boatfull was
gott abord, the master espied a great company, both horse &
foote, with bills & guns & other weapons, for ye countrie was
raised to take them.

Ye Dutchman, seeing that, swore his countrie's oath, "sacre-
mente," and having ye wind faire, waiged his Ancor, hoysed
sayles, & away.

But ye poore men which were gott abord were in great distress
for their wives and children, which they saw thus to be taken
and left destitute of their helpe—and for themselves also, not
having a cloath to shifte them with more than they had on their

*On the east coast, just south of the mouth of the Humber.

†As transport by water was much easier and cheaper, the boat was carrying
the women, children, and baggage. The men set out on foot for the east coast,
some forty miles distant. In good time, the boat sailed down the Ryton into
the Idle, then into the Trent, and at length into the broad estuary of the
Humber, where it tacked southeast down the coast toward the appointed
rendezvous.

backs, & some scarce a penny aboute them, all they had being abord ye barke. It drew tears from their eyes. And anything they had, they would have given to have been ashore againe.

But all in vaine. There was no remedy. They must thus sadly part.

And afterward, [those on board] endured a fearfull storme at sea, being fourteen days or more before they arrived at their port, in seven whereof they neither saw son, moone, nor stars, & were driven near ye coast of Norway, the mariners themselves often despairing of life . . .

[But the Lord] in ye end brought them to their desired haven, where ye people came flocking, admiring their deliverance, the storme having been so longe & sore, in which much hurt had been done, as ye master's freinds related unto him in their congratulations.*

But to returne to the others, . . . the rest of ye men that were in greatest danger made shift to escape away before ye troope could surprise them, those only staying that best might be assistant unto ye women.

And pitifull it was to see ye heavie case of these poore women in this distresse. What weeping & crying on every side! Some for their husbands that were carried away in ye ship . . . Others not knowing what should become of them & their little ones. Others againe melted in tears seeing their poore little ones hanging aboute them, crying for feare, and quaking for cold.

Being thus apprehended, they were hurried from one place to another, and from one justice to another, till in ye end they knew not what to doe with them.

For to imprison so many women & innocent children for no other cause (many of them) but that they must goe with their husbands seemed to be unreasonable, and all would crie out at them.

*The "desired haven" of this unhappy and thoroughly frightened group was Amsterdam. Young William Bradford was one of those who spent a miserable two weeks on a voyage that ordinarily took only a day or two. Upon arrival he was arrested on suspicion that he was an escaped felon. Soon released, he apprenticed himself to a French silkmaster to learn a new trade.

And to send them home againe was as difficult, for they alledged, as ye trueth was, they had no homes to goe to, for they had either sold or otherwise disposed of their houses & livings.

To be shorte, after they had been thus turmoyled a good while and conveyed from one constable to another, they were glad to be ridd of them, in ye end, upon any termes. For all were wearied & tired with them, though in ye mean time they (poore soules) indured miserie enough . . .

And in ye end, notwithstanding all these stormes of opposstion, they all gatt over at length, some at one time & some at another, and some in one place and some in another, and mett together againe according to their desires, with no small rejoycing.

II
In Holland

So they grew in knowledge & other gifts & graces of ye
spirite of God, & lived togeather in peace & love and
holines, and many came unto them from diverse parts of
England, so as they grew a great congregation.
                                                —*William Bradford*

The refugees from Scrooby, by one route or another, con-
verged upon Amsterdam. Having stayed behind with Brewster
to help the weakest over, one of the last to reach Amsterdam
was Richard Clyfton, who arrived in August 1608.

How many crossed from Scrooby at this time is not known.
Only fifteen can be identified, and most of these were children.
There were the Clyftons with three children, aged nine to nineteen; William and Mary Brewster, also with three children, one
a babe in arms; "Teacher" John Robinson and his wife, with at
least two small children; and William Bradford, now approaching
twenty.

These are the only members of the emigrant group—indeed,
with very few exceptions, the only members of the original
Scrooby congregation—who are known by name. As that congregation had always been poor and relatively small, it may be
that the Clyfton, Brewster-Bradford, and Robinson households—
with only six adults among them—made up the larger part of
those at Scrooby who in the end, after so many setbacks, retained
both the will and the means to escape.

And of these households, only Brewster's ever reached the New
World.

1. Amsterdam

Being now come into ye Low Countries, they saw many goodly & fortified cities, strongly walled and garded with troopes of armed men. Also, they heard a strange & uncouth language and beheld ye differente manners & customs of ye people, with their strange fashions and attires, all so farr differing from that of their plaine countrie villages wherein they were bred & had so long lived, as it seemed they were come into a new world.

But these were not ye things they much looked on or long tooke up their thoughts, for they had other work in hand & another kind of warr to wage & maintaine.

For though they saw faire & bewtifull cities flowing with abundance of all sorts of welth & riches, yet it was not long before they saw ye grimme & grisly face of povertie coming upon them like an armed man, with whom they must bukle & incounter, and from whom they could not fly. But they were armed with faith & patience against him and all his encounters . . .

Now when Mr. Robinson, Mr. Brewster, & other principall members were come over (for they were of ye last & stayed to help ye weakest over before them), such things were thought on as were necessarie for their settling and best ordering of ye church affairs.

One of Europe's largest and richest cities, Amsterdam had many flourishing handicraft industries and a far-flung maritime trade. Here the newcomers had no need to fear heavy-handed bailiffs or the violence of their neighbors, for, as orthodox bigots everywhere complained, Amsterdam was "the Fair of all the Sects, where all the Pedlars of Religion have leave to vend their Toyes."

In Holland the Pilgrims enjoyed to the full the "freedom of conscience" which they so vehemently demanded for themselves— if not for others.

2. The Ancient Brethren

The Scrooby exiles had been drawn to Amsterdam by the presence there of a large English congregation, the Brethren of the Separation of the First English Church in Amsterdam, more generally known as the Ancient Brethren. With three hundred or more members, largely from London and the West of England, this congregation was the pride of the Separation. It had recently built a large new meeting house in the Bruinistengange, or Brownists Alley, as a narrow lane in the heart of the old city is still known.

Those from Scrooby also found many old friends and neighbors here—John Smyth and those who had fled from Gainsborough, some seventy or eighty strong, who had arrived about a year before. They had already quarreled with the Ancient Brethren on doctrinal grounds and established themselves as the Brethren of the Separation of the Second English Church in Amsterdam.

Doubtless because they were too few in number, Clyfton and his flock from Scrooby did not organize themselves as a separate congregation. Nor did they follow their friend Smyth. Rather, to their profound regret, they associated themselves with the Ancient Brethren. Though they never formally joined that congregation, they worshiped with it for more than a year.

The Ancient Brethren had been formed in London more than ten years earlier, in 1595, after the execution or imprisonment of many of their leaders. The pastor of the church was the Reverend Francis Johnson, originally of Yorkshire and a Cambridge graduate, who had been among those imprisoned for years.

The second-in-command, the teacher, was Henry Ainsworth, a renowned scholar in his day and a gentle soul whom the Pilgrims always greatly admired. "A very learned man," said Bradford, "ready and pregnant in the Scriptures, . . . eminent in the knowledge of tongues," who taught well "without tossing and turning his book." It was Ainsworth's *Book of Psalmes; Englished both in Prose & Metre*, which the Pilgrims used for generations.

The structure of the church of the Ancient Brethren was typical of that of all churches in this branch of the Separation. Under Francis Johnson and Ainsworth were four "grave" elders, in Bradford's phrase, and a number of "able and godly" deacons.

There was also a deaconess, an "anciente Widow," who collected alms, tended the needy, and altogether was an "ornament to her calling," especially during the services on the Sabbath, when she sat "in a conveniente place, . . . with a little birchen rod in her hand, and kept little children in great awe, from disturbing the congregation."

And truly, wrote Bradford in later years when time had obliterated the memory of many untoward things, the Ancient Brethren had good officers and contained "many worthy men."

"And if you had seene them in their bewty and order as we have done," he told the young men of Plymouth in his *First Dialogue* addressed to them, "you would have bin much affected therewith, we dare say."

Certainly that was not the opinion of Bradford and his brethren when at Amsterdam. On the contrary, they were shamed and shocked by the Ancient Brethren and their angry quarrels. Lurid scandals rocked the congregation.

One of Bradford's "grave" elders was Daniel Studley, a consummate rogue and an enterprising lecher, "fitter for the stewes than to be an elder in any Christian society."

A number had resigned from the church because of him, publicly denouncing him in round Elizabethan terms as "a beastly camel, . . . a filthie Swine, . . . a slipperie Eel, . . . a hard shellfish, . . . a hypocritical Camelion, . . . a Griffon, . . . a Night-Crow, so often and so ordinarily haunting with other men's wives at unseasonable times of the night, as namely Mistresses M., V., C., K., D., and divers others heretofore."

Another former member blazoned the congregation a "brokerage of whores," for which he was sued for slander. The Dutch magistrates dismissed the charge, which further damaged the Ancient Brethren's repute, and assessed costs against Studley, Francis Johnson, and others who had brought suit. Studley later had to be thrown out of the church as incorrigible, but at this time he was one of its most powerful and influential members.

These scandals helped to bring on bitter doctrinal disputes, for Pastor Johnson began to take higher and higher ground in his

attempts to defend Studley and other officers against the criticism
of the rank and file. It was evident that a violent explosion was
not far off.

Those from Scrooby suffered a very painful and embarrassing
time at Amsterdam, though one would never guess it from the
Pilgrim records. In his history Bradford dismissed the matter with
this laconic note:

And when they had lived at Amsterdam about a year, Mr.
Robinson . . . and some others of best discerning, seeing how
Mr. John Smith and his companie was allready fallen into contention with ye church that was there before them, . . . and
also that ye flames of contention were like to breake out in that
anciente church itselfe (as afterwards lamentably came to pass).

Which things they prudently foreseeing, thought it was best
to remove before they were any way engaged with ye same,
though they well knew it would be much to ye prejudice of
their outward estates both at present & in licklyhood in ye
future, as indeed it proved to be.

For these & some other reasons they removed to Leyden . . .

3. Exodus

Early in 1609, the leaders of the Scrooby group wrote to the
burgomasters of Leyden:*

With due submission and respect, Jan Robarthse [John Rob-
inson], Minister of the Divine Word, and some members of the
Christian Reformed religion, . . . to the number of one hundred person or thereabouts, men and women, represent that
they are desirous of coming to live in this city by the first of
May next, and to have the freedom thereof in carrying on their
trades without being a burden in the least to any one.

They therefore address themselves to your Honours, humbly

*Translations of this letter and the burgomasters' reply appear in the *Historical
Magazine*, Vol. III (1859), pp. 357-58.

praying that your Honours will be pleased to grant them free consent to betake themselves as aforesaid . . .

To which the burgomasters replied, plainly with an eye on the quarrelsome and scandalous Ancient Brethren:

The Court, in making a disposition of this present Memorial, declare that they refuse no honest persons free ingress to come and have their residence in this city, provided such persons behave themselves and submit to the laws and ordinances. And therefore, the coming of the Memorialists will be agreeable and welcome.

Thus done in their session at the Council House, the 12th day of February, 1609 . . .

In fleeing Amsterdam, the Scrooby "Saincts" lost their pastor, for Richard Clyfton chose to remain behind, a decision he lived to regret.

But the Scrooby group gained many new recruits. Many of the discontented Ancient Brethren went with them, a number rising to prominence at Leyden and subsequently at Plymouth.

Ruling Elder Studley took the exodus as a reflection on himself, a personal insult. The seceding brethren, he raged, were "ignorant idiots, noddy Nabalites, dogged Doegs, faire-faced Pharisses, shameless Shemites, malicious Machivillians," and so the jangles at Amsterdam continued.

4. Leyden

. . . [So] they removed to Leyden, a fair & bewtifull citie, and of a sweete situation, but made more famous by ye universitie wherewith it is adorned* . . .

But wanting that traffic by sea which Amsterdam injoyes, it

*Founded in 1575 to commemorate the burghers' heroic defense of their city and their faith against the Spanish, the sword of the Holy Inquisition, the University of Leyden had already become one of the best of its day, the intellectual and spiritual capital of Protestant Europe.

was not so beneficiall for their outward means of living & estates. But being now here pitchet, they fell to such trades & imployments as best they could, valewing peace & their spirituall comforte above any riches whatsoever, and at length they came to raise a competente & comfortable living, but with hard and continuall labour.

A few in the congregation had sufficient means to establish small businesses of their own, setting themselves up as merchants of cloth and other things. But most had to work from dawn till dark for miserable wages in the least skilled and worst-paid operations of the textile, metal, leather, building, and other trades.

Bradford became a fustian maker. Young Jonathan Brewster, now sixteen, was a ribbon maker. Others were variously employed as wool combers, cloth finishers, silk makers, felt makers, button makers, tailors, hatters, glovers, cobblers, leather dressers, metalworkers, carpenters, stone- and brickmasons, hod carriers, printers, blockmakers and pump makers, as the Leyden records reveal.

Some of the more enterprising became citizens of Leyden, largely for business reasons, for only citizens could belong to the powerful trade and merchant guilds which controlled all skilled work and commercial enterprises in the city. A number of future Pilgrim Fathers appear in this group—Isaac Allerton, of London, a tailor, later assistant governor at Plymouth for many years; Degory Priest, of London, a hatter; Richard Masterson, of Sandwich, a wool comber, subsequently a Pilgrim deacon; and two merchants, Thomas Rogers and John Turner.

In 1612, just turned twenty-two, Bradford became a citizen of Leyden and soon married young Dorothy May, aged sixteen, daughter of a long-prominent member of the Ancient Brethren. Buying a small house, he settled with her on the banks of the Achtergracht, or Back Canal, where a son was soon born to them, named John.

During these years there was much marrying in the congregation, both among the young and the somewhat older. Death carried away many Saints, and most widows and widowers showed an eager desire, even within a few weeks of bereavement, to exchange their single blessedness for the comforts, conveniences, and innocent pleasures of marriage.

Having spent most of his estate in aiding the congregation at Scrooby, William Brewster had a particularly hard time of it at first, as Bradford noted:

After he came into Holland, he suffered much hardship, . . . having a great charge and many children, and in regard to his former breeding & course of life not so fitt for many imployments as others were, espetially such as were toylesume & laborious. But yet he ever bore his condition with much cheerfullness and contentation.

Towards ye later parte of those 12 years spente in Holland, his outward condition was mended, and he lived well & plentifully. For he fell into a way (by reason he had ye Latine tongue) to teach many students who had a desire to lerne ye English tongue, to teach them English. And by this method they quickly attained it with great facilitie, for he drew rules to lerne it by, after ye Latine manner, and many gentlemen, both Danes & Germans, resorted to him as they had time from other studies, some of them being great men's sonnes.

He also had means to set up printing (by ye help of some freinds) and so had imploymente inoughg. And by reason of many books which would not be allowed to be printed in England, they might have had more than they could doe.

5. The Pilgrim Press

Another story that Bradford chose not to tell is that of Brewster's printing shop, now famed as the Pilgrim Press. Bradford omitted it for politic reasons that will become obvious.

Late in 1616 or early in 1617, Brewster gave up his private tutoring in English to establish a publishing business, in which many friends assisted him. His principal partner was the son of a well-to-do family of Kentish gentry, Thomas Brewer, "a Gentleman of a good house, both of land and living, which none of his [religious] profession in these parts are," so the English ambassador later remarked.

Sixteen years younger than Brewster, who was now in his early fifties, Brewer had been living in Leyden for several years, attending the university as a student of literature. Years later, after his return to Kent, Brewer was tried for encouraging others to preach "in houses, barns, and woods that the Church of England is the Whore of Babilon, and the Synagogue of Satan, &c." For this he was jailed as a "perfect Brownist," and kept in prison for fourteen years.

But at Leyden he was not a Brownist, being a Calvinist, a member of the local Scottish Church so called, though he "walked in communion with Master Robinson and also with Master Ainsworth" on occasion.

While they differed in their creeds, Brewster and Brewer were loyal partners and worked well together. Brewer provided most of the capital while Brewster acted as editor in chief and general manager of the office and print shop which they established on the Koorsteeg, or Choir Alley—now better known in its Latin form, Vicus Chorali, thanks to the Pilgrim Press.*

Enemies of the Anglican church, anxious to overthrow it and its many "abuses," both Brewer and Brewster were determined to spread "ye light" among the English. Brewster was especially eager to circulate the works of John Robinson, who was now writing volume after volume in defense of "ye trueth" against "hydra-headed errour."

But it was not easy to reach the minds of the English, imprisoned as they were in an iron ring of censorship. An inheritance from Roman Catholic days, the bishops enjoyed almost limitless powers as "guardians of faith and morals." No book could be published in the realm, or imported, without their approval—an arbitrary power exercised through a law requiring that all publications had to be registered with the Company of Stationers, a conservative London guild closely watched by the Church and the Court.

Neither the Tudors nor the Stuarts made any pretense of tol-

---

*Though the print shop opened on the Koorsteeg, it occupied an irregular extension of Brewster's house, which stood on the Stincksteeg, or Stink Alley. Obviously, for many reasons, a Choir Alley address was better than one on Stink Alley. Also, in case of trouble, a separate address might be useful. This ruse was so successful that only recently has it been discovered that the two addresses identified the two ends of Brewster's L-shaped house.

erating freedom of the press. To them it was an abomination, a diabolical instrument to upset the divine and eternal order of things. But others read the divine order differently.

Brewster and Brewer bought several fonts of type and other necessary equipment. From London they brought over a master printer, John Reynolds, to direct mechanical operations. The latter brought along as his assistant, or apprentice, a youth of "very active genius," twenty-two-year-old Edward Winslow, destined to become one of the most distinguished Pilgrim Fathers.

Family tradition has it that Winslow, born at Droitwich in the West of England, the eldest of five sons and three daughters, was a young gentleman of "qualitie" who, when making the grand tour of the Continent traditional for sons of the upper classes, fell in with the Leyden company and overnight embraced the rigors and hardships of the Separation. Perhaps, but it is evident that Winslow had been trained as a printer and had worked for Reynolds in London.

Making remarkably good speed with cumbersome equipment, the Choir Alley press issued three books within a few months. One was in Dutch; the other two were in Latin. None dealt with the controversial issues of the day, so that no exception could be taken to them if they fell under the jaundiced eye of an Anglican bishop. All were dated 1617 and bore the imprint of the house:

Lugduni Batavorum
Apud Guiljelmum Brewsterum
In vico Chorali

Of all the books published by Brewster, only these three non-controversial books bore the house imprint, for the purpose of the press was not as innocent as it seemed. The three signed works were a screen to hide its real purpose, which was, as the English ambassador at The Hague soon complained, "to print prohibited books to be vented underhand in his Majestie's kingdoms."

Just how many "licentious" works the press published is not certain, though its volume during its brief existence was considerable for the time. Students of the question differ, estimating the number from fifteen to eighteen, differing on titles beyond a certain point. All agree, however, on eight titles—the three signed works and five others, which included John Robinson's *The*

People's Plea for the Exercise of Prophecy (1618), a strong defense of the Separatist position.

For two years all went well, and Brewster had "imploymente inoughg."

6. John Robinson

Being thus settled after many difficulties, they continued many years in a comfortable condition, injoying much sweete & delightfull societie & spirituall comforte togeather in ye wayes of God, under ye able ministrie and prudente governmente of Mr. John Robinson & Mr. William Brewster, who was an assistante unto him in ye place of an Elder . . .

I know not but it may be spoken to ye honour of God, & without prejudice to any, that such was ye true pietie, ye humble zeale, & fervent love of this people . . . towards God and his waies, and ye single-hartedness & sincere affection one towards another, that they came as near ye primative patterne of ye first churches as any other church of these later times . . .

So they grew in knowledge & other gifts & graces of ye spirite of God, & lived togeather in peace & love and holines, and many came unto them from diverse parts of England, so as they grew a great congregation.

The defection of Clyfton brought to the fore "that famous & worthy man," John Robinson, the most beloved and respected of the early company, a man of stature in an age of great men. Now in his early thirties, Robinson was another of those "godlie & painfull" students of divinity from Cambridge who were raising such a stir in the world.

Upon his graduation from the university, Robinson had remained there several years as a tutor, becoming dean of Corpus Christi College in 1600. Wishing to marry, which was against the rules, he resigned four years later and with his bride went to Norwich, where he became assistant minister of St. Andrew's and was "worthily reverenced of all the city for the grace of God in him."

At the university Robinson had been deeply influenced by the "forward" views of William Perkins, as Brewster had been before him, and this influence continued at Norwich, which had remained an active reformist center since Robert Browne's day.

Increasingly tortured by doubts about Anglican doctrine and ritual, he had been at St. Andrew's less than a year when he found himself one of three hundred ministers throughout the realm deprived of office for "branding the ceremonies." He continued to preach in private halls, however, until the local bishop put a stop to that and excommunicated some of his followers—which proved to them, they told him, "what small hope there is of curing the Canker in your Church."

Always a sincere and sensitive soul, Robinson found himself in a painful position, harassed by doubts on every side. He was reluctant to go forward. He was quite unwilling to turn back. After wrestling with his soul for two years, he finally made his decision and joined those who were surreptitiously meeting in the manor house at Scrooby.

"Had not the truth been in my heart as a burning fire, shut up in my bones," he once exclaimed in recalling those days of spiritual anguish, "I had never broken the bonds of flesh and blood wherein I was so straightly tied, but had suffered the light of God to have been put out in mine own unthankful heart by other men's darkness."

Joining the Scrooby congregation as a humble private member, Robinson was overshadowed by Clyfton for a time but soon rose from the ranks, becoming second-in-command as "teacher" of the group.

It was Robinson who led the exodus from Amsterdam, and none of the early Saints had quite his hold on the affection and respect of all who knew him, as Bradford—among many others—makes plain:

Yea, such was ye mutuall love & reciprocall respecte that this worthy man had to his flocke and his flocke to him that it might be said of them, as it once was of that famous Emperour Marcus Aurelious and ye people of Rome, that it was hard to judge whether he delighted more in having such a people, or they in having such a pastor. His love was greate towards them, and his care was allways bente for their best good, both for soule and body.

For besides his singuler abilities in devine things, wherein he excelled, he was also very able to give directions in civill affaires and to foresee dangers & inconveniences, by which means he was very helpfull to their outward estates & so was every way as a commone father unto them.

And none did more offend him than those that were close and cleaving to themselves and retired from ye commone good; as also such as would be stiff & rigid in matters of outward order and invey against ye evills of others, and yet be remisse in themselves and not so carefull to express a vertuous conversation.

They, in like manner, had ever a reverente regard unto him & had him in precious estimation, as his worth & wisdom did deserve . . .

As he was a man learned and of a solled Judgment,* and of a quick and sharp witt, so was he also of a tender Conscience, and very sincere in all his wayes, a hater of hipocresie and dissimulation, and would be very plaine with his best frinds. He was very Curteous, affible, and sociable in his Conversation, and towards his owne people espetially.

He was an acute and exact disputant, very quick and Reddy . . . He was never satifyed in himself untill he had searched any Cause or argument he had to deale in thoroughly and to the bottome.

And we have heard him somtimes say to his familiars that many times, both in writing and disputation, he knew he had sufficiently answered others, but many times not himself, and was ever desirous of any light. And the more able, Learned, and holy the persons were, the more he desired to Confer and Reason with them.

He was very profittable in his minnestry and Comfortable to his people. He was much beloved of them, and as loving was

*This paragraph and the three following are from Bradford's *A Dialogue, or the Sum of a Conference betweene some Yonge-men born in New England, and sundry Ancient-men that came out of Holand and Old England*, written in 1648 and copied into the Plymouth church records.

he unto them . . . In a word, he was much esteemed and Reverenced of all that knew him and his abillities, both of frinds and strangers.

7. The Green Gate in Bell Alley

Though formally organized in the Separatist manner, the Leyden congregation never gave itself a name. After several years of great hardship, during which it met here and there where it could, the congregation went into debt to provide itself with a permanent place of worship, buying a "spacious" old house on the Kloksteeg, or Bell Alley, in the older part of the city.

Known as the Groenepoort, or Green Gate, it stood opposite to and under the shadow of the Pieterskerk, a towering cathedral, and served as a parsonage as well as a meetinghouse.

Behind the house was a garden, and beyond this an open lot, walled on three sides and opening in back on the Donckeregrafte, or Dark Canal. In this open lot, some fifty yards square, many small houses were built, one almost on top of the other, to shelter the poorer members of the congregation.

Every Sabbath the Saints assembled at the Green Gate early in the morning, at least by eight, to enjoy the first of two extended services. As they filed in, members were not allowed to sit where they pleased in cozy little family groups. The men sat on hard wooden benches on one side of the aisle, the women on the other, while the children were placed off by themselves under the stern eye and strong hand of the deacons.

This was known as "dignifying the meeting," an institution carried to Plymouth, where it survived for generations, almost to the nineteenth century.

First a prayer was offered. To pray, the Saints stood up, never going down on their knees, for that was an "idolatrous" Roman practice.

Nor did they ever use set prayers—not even the Lord's Prayer. As Robinson later declared in taxing the Dutch with this "heresy," anybody could read a prayer. It was as meaningless and puerile a performance as for a child "to read of a book or prayer (saying), Father, I prey you give me bread, or fish, or an egg."

After the opening prayer, improvised and usually lasting an hour or more, Pastor Robinson opened his huge Geneva Bible and read a passage aloud—always with comment and exposition, for mere "dumb reading" was regarded by the Saints as one of the graver sins of the Anglican church.

Next a psalm was sung, without instrumental music of any kind, for the Holy Discipline banned that—in particular, the organ, the "Divill's bag-pipes."

Nor was there musical notation of any kind to aid the singing. Tunes were sung from memory. Someone set the pitch, usually one of the deacons, and all raised their voices together, singing the song as a simple melody, for the Saints agreed with Calvin that part singing was "frivolous and unbecoming the House of God."

To compound their difficulties, they had to stumble as best they could through such tongue-tying verses as these in Ainsworth's psalmbook:

And th'earth did shake and quake and styrred bee
   grounds of the mount: & shook for wroth was hee.
Smoke mounted, in his wrath, fyre did eat
   out of his mouth; from it burned-with heat.

No wonder some of the Saints spoke contemptuously about the singing. It was so bad, they protested, that "the congregation was made a laughing stocke to strangers who, on occasion, came to see them in their publike worship." In his day Ainsworth was famed as a great scholar, and his prose was much admired. But his "Englishing" of the Psalms was so wretched that many critics insisted there must be two Henry Ainsworths.

After the psalm came the sermon, which ordinarily continued for two hours at least. It was not preached from a pulpit, but from a low dais upon which stood a simple wooden table. In black clothes and black gloves, Robinson paced up and down behind this table as he expounded his text with a quiet and moving eloquence that his audience never forgot.

The sermon done, another psalm was sung. On appropriate occasions Robinson then administered the sacraments. After the deacons had passed the collection plates, a benediction ended the Sabbath morning service, about noon.

Again, early in the afternoon, the congregation assembled for a less formal exercise known as "prophecying." After an opening prayer, Pastor Robinson or Ruling Elder Brewster chose a text, spoke to it briefly, and then opened the meeting for general discussion.

Only men could speak. Women had no voice in the church, for a prohibition against this had been laid down by St. Paul. The Saints had taken John Smyth severely to task for his "errour" in allowing "females" to speak up in meeting, even encouraging them in public "censures" of their husbands and other wayward males—an unheard-of and obviously dangerous procedure.

More than anything else, it was this "prophecying" by laymen which scandalized the orthodox and led them to sneer at all Separatist preachers as "rude mechanick fellows." But that only proved their ignorance of Scripture, said Robinson, pointing triumphantly to "Acts xiii, 14, &c."

Another general service was held during the week, every Thursday (known as Lecture Day), at which time Robinson, Brewster, or some other officer of the church discoursed on a wide range of subjects, usually more sacred than profane.

At its most flourishing the Green Gate congregation had more than three hundred members. Among them there were not more than twenty from Scrooby, yet this group dominated the congregation. Plainly, its dominance rested not upon numbers but the leadership it offered—more particularly, upon the character, devotion, and high abilities of Brewster and Robinson. That the church continued to grow in size and reputation was, in large measure, their personal triumph.

8. Crosses and Sorrows

After they had lived in this cittie some 11 or 12 years, . . . and sundrie of them were taken away by death, & others began to be well stricken in years, the grave mistress Experience having taught them many things, . . . they began to incline to this conclusion, of removal to some other place. Not out of any new-fangledness or other such like giddie humor by which men are oftentimes transported to their great hurt & danger, but for sundrie weightie & solid reasons . . .

And first, they saw & found by experience the hardness of ye place & countrie to be such as few in comparison would come to them, and fewer that would bide it out and continew with them. For many that came to them, and many more that desired to be with them, could not endure that great labour and hard fare, with other inconveniences . . .

Yea, some preferred & chose ye prisons in England rather than this libertie in Holland with these afflictions. . . .

Secondly, they saw that though ye people generally bore all these difficulties very cheerfully & with a resolute courage, being in ye best & strength of their years, yet old age began to steal on many of them, and their great & continuall labours, with other crosses and sorrows, hastened it before ye time, so as . . . they would be in danger to scatter by necessities pressing them, or sinke under their burdens, or both . . .

Thirdly, as necessitie was a taskmaster over them, so they were forced to be such not only to their servants, but in a sort to their dearest children, the which . . . produced sundrie sad and sorrowful effects.

For many of their children that were of best dispositions and gracious inclinations, having learned to bear ye yoake in their youth and willing to bear parte of their parents' burden, were oftentimes so oppressed with their hevie labours that, though their minds were free and willing, yet their bodies bowed under ye weight of ye same and became decreped in their early youth, the vigor of nature being consumed in ye very budd as it were.

But that which was more lamentable . . . was that many of their children by these occasions, and ye great licentiousness of youth in that countrie and ye manifold temptations of the place, were drawne away by evill examples into extravagante & dangerous courses, getting ye raines off their neks & departing from their parents . . .

Lastly, and which was not least, a great hope & inward zeal they had of laying some good foundation, or at least to make some way thereunto, for ye propagating & advancing ye gospell of ye kingdom of God in those remote parts of ye world . . .

The place they had thoughts on was some of those vast & unpeopled countries of America which are frutfull & fitt for habitation, being devoyd of all civill inhabitants, where there are only salvage & brutish men which range up and downe little otherwise than ye wild beasts of ye same.

This proposition being made publike and coming to ye scanning of all . . . caused many fears & doubts amongst them. Some, from their reasons & hopes conceived, laboured to stirr up & incourage the rest to undertake & prosecute ye same. Others againe, out of their fears, objected . . . that it was a great designe and subjecte to many unconceivable perills & dangers. . . .

It was furder objected that it would require greater sums of money to furnish such a vioage, and to fit them with necessaries, than their consumed estates would amount to. And yet they must, as well, looke to be seconded with supplies . . .

It was answered that all great & honourable actions are accompanied with great difficulties, and must be both enterprised and overcome with answerable courages.

It was granted ye dangers were great, but not desperate; the difficulties were many, but not invincible. For though there were many of them likely, yet they were not certaine. It might be sundrie of ye things feared might never befall. Others, by providente care & ye use of good means, might in a great measure be prevented. And all of them, through ye help of God, by fortitude and patience, might either be borne or overcome.

True it was that such attempts were not to be made and undertaken without good ground & reason; not rashly or lightly, as many have done for curiositie or hope of gaine, &c.

But their condition was not ordinarie; their ends were good & honourable; their calling, lawfull & urgente; and therefore they might expecte ye blessing of God in their proceeding.

Yea, though they should lose their lives in this action, yet might they had comforte in the same, and their endeavours would be honourable.

They lived here but as men in exile & in a poore condition, and as great miseries might possibly befall them in this place, for . . . there was nothing but beating of drums and preparing for war, the events whereof are allway uncertaine* . . .

After many other perticular things answered & alledged on both sides, it was fully concluded by ye major parte to put this designe in execution, and to prosecute it by the best means they could.

*The twelve-year truce between the Netherlands and Spain, signed early in 1609, was running out. War did break out after its expiration in 1621, and in 1648 the United Netherlands finally won its formal independence from Spain.

III
The Virginia Business

It doth often trouble me to thinke that in this bussines
we are all to learne and none to teach.

—*Robert Cushman*

Some—& none of ye meanest—had thoughts & were ernest for
Guiana* or some of those fertile places in those hott climates.
Others were for some parts of Virginia, where ye English had
allready made enterance & begining . . .

For Virginia, it was objected that if they lived among ye English which were there planted, or so near them as to be under
their government, they should be in as great danger to be troubled and persecuted for the cause of religion as if they lived in
England, and it might be worse.

And if they lived too farr off, they should neither have
succour nor defense from them.

But at length the conclusion was to live as a distincte body by
themselves under ye generall government of Virginia, and by
their friends to sue to his Majestie that he would be pleased to
grant them freedom of Religion . . .

1. A Damp in the Business

Whereupon, 2 were chosen & sent into England (at ye charge
of ye rest) to sollicite this matter, who found the Virginia Company very desirous to have them goe thither and willing to grant

*In South America, along its Caribbean shore. Some of the Saints had evidently
been reading Sir Walter Raleigh's fabulous account of its gold mines and other
riches, published in his *Discoverie of Guiana*, based on his expedition there
in 1595.

them a patent . . . And som of ye cheefe of that Company doubted not to obtaine their suit of ye King for liberty in Religion & to have it confirmed under ye King's broad seal, according to their desires.

But it proved a harder peece of worke than they tooke it for. For though many means were used to bring it aboute, yet it could not be effected . . .

Yet thus farr they prevailed in sounding his Majestie's mind, that he would connive at them & not molest them, provided they carried themselves peaceably.

But to allow or tolerate them by his publick authoritie, under his seale, they found it would not be. And this was all the cheefe of ye Virginia companie or any other of their best freinds could doe in ye case.

Yet they perswaded them to goe on, for they presumed they should not be troubled . . .

But this made a dampe in ye busines and caused some distraction, for many were afraid that if they should unsettle themselves, & put off their estates, and goe upon these hopes, it might prove dangerous and but a sandie foundation . . .

But some of ye cheefest thought otherwise, and . . . other messengers were dispatched [in 1617] to end with ye Virginia Company as well as they could, and to procure a patent with as ample and good conditions as they might by any means obtaine . . .

2. Robert Cushman and John Carver

The "other" messengers were two deacons of the Green Gate congregation, Robert Cushman and John Carver, both later prominent in the Pilgrim story.

Though less well known today, Cushman was the more important of the two, faithfully serving the Pilgrims at Plymouth for many years. Originally from Canterbury, evidently one of the seceding Ancient Brethren, Cushman had become a wool comber at Leyden. Approaching forty, having recently lost his wife and a child, he had just remarried when he was called upon to leave his bride and undertake a difficult and irksome mission that kept him almost continuously in England for many years.

His colleague was John Carver, "a pious, faithful, and very beneficiall instrument." Though now famed as the first governor at Plymouth, Carver remains a rather ill-defined figure, with many things about him unexplained.

A well-to-do merchant in his early fifties, one of the older in the congregation, Carver had been born at Doncaster, Yorkshire, ten miles up the Great North Road from Scrooby. His wife and Robinson's were sisters, being daughters of a prosperous yeoman family of Sturton-le-Steeple, a village a few miles southeast of Scrooby. The Carvers had other connections with the Scrooby group but do not appear to have been members of the original congregation.

Also, the Carvers had been living in Leyden for some time, having settled there even before the exodus from Amsterdam in 1609.

But they cannot be identified as members of the Green Gate congregation till 1616, when their names first suddenly appear in the Pilgrim records, occupying many a page thereafter. It had evidently taken the prosperous and respectable Carver some time to decide to throw in his lot with the impoverished Separatist radicals.

But having decided, he never looked back, assuming greater and greater responsibilities as he marched resolutely forward. Though the richest man in the group, Carver was nevertheless "of singular Piety and Rare for humillitie, which appeared (as otherwise) soe by his great Condesendencye."

Crossing to London, Cushman and Carver approached the Virginia Company through one of its leading members, Sir Edwin Sandys, who was already known to some at Leyden.

Curiously, the father of Sir Edwin had been one of the archbishops of York from whom the Brewsters had held Scrooby Manor. A libertarian in his religious and political views, having already had trouble with the bishops for advocating toleration and with the King for opposing his absolutist pretensions, Sandys promised his aid to those at Leyden and, as both the Pilgrim and Virginia Company records reveal, did everything in his power to help them.

3. Instances of Inducement

And here it will be requisite to inserte a letter or two that may give light on these proceedings.

A coppie of a letter from Sir Edwin Sands . . .

London
November 12, 1617*

After my hartie salutations:

The agents of your congregation, Robert Cushman & John Carver, have been in communication with diverse select gentlemen of his Majestie's Counsell for Virginia and . . . have given them that good degree of satisfaction which hath carried them [the Council] with a resolution to sett forward your desire in ye best sort that may be, for your owne & the publick good . . .

If therefore it may please God so to directe your desires as that, on your part, there fall out no just impediments, I trust by ye same direction it shall likewise appear that, on our part, all forwardnes to sett you forward shall be found . . .

And so I betake you with this designe (which I hope verily is ye worke of God) to the gracious protection and blessing of ye Highest.

Your very loving friend,
Edwin Sandys

Their answer was as followeth:

Leyden
Desem: 15, 1617

Righte Worshipful:

Our humble duties remembred . . . with all thankfull acknowledgmente of your singuler love, expressing itselfe, as oth-

---

*Unless otherwise noted, all dates are Old Style (Julian calendar), for England and the colonies continued to use the Julian calendar until 1752, long after other peoples had abandoned it.

For current New Style (Gregorian calendar), add ten days.

erwise, so more spetially in your great care and earnest endeavor of our good in this weightie bussines aboute Virginia . . .

Nothwithstanding, for your encouragmente in ye work, . . . we will not forbear to mention these instances of inducement.

1. We veryly beleeve & trust ye Lord is with us . . . and that he will graciously prosper our indeavours according to ye simplicitie of our harts therein.

2. We are well weaned from ye delicate milke of our mother countrie and enured to ye difficulties of a strange and hard land, which yet, in great part, we have by patience overcome.

3. The people are, for the body of them, as industrious & frugall, we think we may safely say, as any company in the world.

4. We are knitt togeather as a body in a most stricte & sacred bond and covenante of the Lord . . .

5. Lastly, it is not with us as with other men, whom small things can discourage or small discontentments cause to wish themselves at home againe.* We know our entertainmente in England, and in Holland . . .

These motives we have been bold to tender unto you, which you, in your wisdome, may also imparte to any other of our worshipfull freinds of ye Counsell . . .

Yours much bounden in all duty,

John Robinson

William Brewster

4. The Seven Articles

The Leyden leaders, rightly fearing the hostility of the King and the bishops, had drawn up in the hope of conciliating them

---

*This referred to the clamors of those in Virginia, many of whom wished to return home and could not, being forcibly detained. None could leave without the governor's permission, which was seldom given—and never to the "common sorte." Nor were "small things" the cause of their discontent and discouragement. Life in Virginia at this time was literally a hell. Hunger stalked the land. Disease was endemic. Nine out of ten of those sent out to labor along the James died, usually within a year of arrival. The colonists had no rights whatever, being governed by savage martial law and forced to work for the sole benefit

a confession of faith in the form of Seven Articles. Drafted with tongue in cheek, this document tried to minimize and obscure the differences between the Brownist and Anglican creeds.

Cushman and Carver passed it along to the Privy Council, which was not impressed, demanding less ambiguous information on many points. Forwarded to Leyden by Sir John Wolstenholme, this demand made those at the Green Gate very uneasy.

Remarking that it was "greevious unto us that such unjust insinuations are made against us," Robinson and Brewster wrote to Wolstenholme and enclosed two statements, asking Sir John to submit to the Privy Council whichever he thought would be most acceptable to their lordships.

The first breefe note was this:

Touching ye Ecclesiastical ministrie—namely, of pastors for teaching, elders for ruling, & deacons for distributing ye church's contribution, as allso for ye two Sacraments, baptisme and ye Lord's supper—we doe wholy and in all points agree with ye French reformed churches, according to their publick confession of faith.

The oath of Supremacie we shall willingly take if it be required of us* . . .

John Rob:
William Brewster

The second was this:

Touching ye Ecclesiastical ministrie, . . . we agree in all things with the French reformed churches, . . . though some small differences are to be found in our practices—not at all in

of the Company and its shareholders. Virginia was little better than a slave camp. Details on the early life of the Old Dominion appear in my *Behold Virginia: The Fifth Crown.*

*People swearing this oath—and it was required of all subjects—renounced papal authority in all ecclesiastical and civil matters and acknowledged in all spiritual affairs the supremacy of the Crown, acting through the Church of England. No good Roman Catholic could take this oath, nor could any convinced Separatist.

How those at Leyden could take this oath with good conscience is not clear, for they had already repudiated the Church of England.

ye substance of the things, but only in some accidentall circumstances.

1. As first, their ministers doe pray with their heads covered; ours, uncovered.

2. We chose none for Governing Elders but such as are able to teach, which abilitie they doe not require.

3. Their elders & deacons are annual, or at most for two or three years; ours, perpetual.

4. Our elders doe administer their office in admonitions & excommunications for publick scandals publickly & before ye congregation; theirs, more privately & in their consistories.

5. We doe administer baptisme only to such infants whereof ye one parent at ye least is of some church, which some of their churches doe not observe . . .

Other differences, worth mentioning, we know none in these points.

Then aboute ye oath, as in ye former.

John R.
W. B.

This letter to Wolstenholme—or "Worssenham," as Bradford wrote it—was entrusted for delivery to a friend, a London Separatist, later a member of the Leyden congregation, Sabin Staresmore, who soon wrote the Green Gate about it.

London
Feb. 14, 1617 [1618]*

Your letter to Sir John Worstenholme I delivered allmost as soone as I had it, . . . and staid with him during ye opening & reading. There were two papers inclosed. He read them to himselfe, as also ye letter. And in ye reading, he spake to me & said, Who shall make them? viz., ye ministers.

*Though written in what we should now regard as 1618, the letter was dated 1617 for the reason that the English did not begin the new year on January 1, but on March 25. Precisely, the date should be written Feb. 14, 1617/18. But to minimize apparatus, I shall hereafter date all documents and events as if the English had used January 1 as the start of the new year.

I answered his Worship that ye power of making was in ye
church, to be ordained by ye imposition of hands by ye fittest
instruments they had.* It must either be in ye church or from
ye pope, & ye pope is Antichrist.

Ho! said Sir John, what ye pope holds good, as in ye Trinitie,
that we doe well to assente to. But, said he, we will not enter
into dispute now.

And as for your letters, he would not show them at any hand
lest he should spoyle all . . .

I could have wished to know ye contents of your two inclosed, at which he stuck so much, espetially ye larger.

I asked his Worship what good news he had for me to write
tomorrow.

He told me very good news, for both the King's Majestie and
ye bishops have consented . . .

Yours,

S. S.

Unhappily, the King and the bishops had not consented to grant
them "liberty in Religion," though Sandys had managed to have
the congregation's petition brought before the King.

These [the messengers to England]† also found God going
along with them, and got Sir Edwin Sandys, a religious Gentleman then living, to stirre in it, who procured Sir Robert
Naunton, then principall Secretary of State to King James of
famous memory, to move his Majesty by a private motion to
give way to such a people (who could not so comfortably live
under the government of another State) to enjoy their liberty
of Conscience under his gracious protection in America, where
they would endeavour the advancement of his Majestie's do-

*That is, the Brownist congregations chose and put into office their own
pastors, without any laying on of hands from above. Anglican and Roman
parishes took what ministers were assigned to them by the higher church
authorities.

†The paragraphs from here to the end of this section are from Edward Winslow's *Hypocrisie Unmasked* (1646). Though written long after the event, they
have an authentic ring.

minions, and the enlargement of the Gospel by all due means.

This, his Majesty said, was a good and honest motion. And asking what profits might arise in the part we intended (for our eye was upon the most Northern parts of Virginia), 'twas answered,

"Fishing."

To which he replyed, with his ordinary asseveration,

"So God have my Soule, 'tis an honest Trade, 'twas the Apostles' owne calling," &c.

But afterwards, he told Sir Robert Naunton (who took all occasions to further it) that we should confer with the Bishops of Canterbury and London, &c.

Whereupon, we were advised to persist upon his first approbation, and not to entangle ourselves with them . . .

5. The Blackwell Disaster

At length, in the spring of 1619, agents were sent to London "to end with ye Virginia Company as well as they could," one being Robert Cushman, who soon reported—only bad news:

London
May 8, 1619

To my loving freinds, &c.,

I had thought long since to have written unto you, but could not effecte that which I aimed at . . . The maine hinderance of our proceedings in ye Virginia bussines is ye dissensions and factions, as they terme it, amongst ye Counsell & Company of Virginia, which are such as that, ever since we came up, no bussines could by them be dispatched.

The occasion of this trouble amongst them is that a while since Sir Thomas Smith [Smythe], repining at his many offices & troubls, wished ye Company of Virginia to ease him of his office in being Treasurer & Governor of ye Virginia Company.

Whereupon, ye Company tooke occasion to dismisse him and chose Sir Edwin Sandys as Treasurer & Governor of ye Company . . . But Sir Thomas Smith, when he saw some part of his honour lost, was very angrie & raised a faction to cavill & contend aboute ye election. . . . And what issue things will come to, we are not yet certaine.

It is most like Sir Edwin will carrie it away. And if he doe, things will goe well in Virginia. If otherwise, they will goe ill enough allways. We hope in some 2 or 3 Court days* things will settle.

Mean space, I thinke to goe downe into Kent & come up againe aboute 14 days or 3 weeks hence, except either by these aforesaid contentions or by ye ill tidings from Virginia, we be wholly discouraged, of which tidings I am now to speake.

Captaine Argollt is come home this weeke, . . . but his tidings are ill. He saith Mr. Blackwell's ship came not there till March, but going towards winter, they still had norwest winds which carried them to the southward beyond their course. And ye master of ye ship & some 6 of ye mariners dieing, it seemed they could not find ye bay till after long seeking & beating aboute.

Mr. Blackwell is dead, & Mr. Maggner, ye Captain. Yea, there are dead, he saith, 130 persons, one & other, in that ship.

It is said there was, in all, 180 persons in ye ship, so as they were packed togeather like herings. They had amonst them ye fluxe, and allso wante of fresh water. So as it is here rather wondered at that so many are alive than that so many are dead. The marchants here say it was Mr. Blackwell's fault to pack so many in ye ship‡ . . .

---

*The meetings of the Virginia Company were styled "courts."

†This was Captain Samuel Argall, governor in Virginia, who had just looted the colony, to the rage of the Company, and was shielded from punishment by powerful protectors.

‡This disaster, one of many such on the way to Virginia, sent a chill down the spines of those at Leyden. They were contemplating a similar voyage, and Ruling Elder Francis Blackwell and his company were fellow Separatists, well known to most of them, having been members of the Ancient Brethren.

Sinking deeper and deeper into poverty, as those at Leyden were doing, Blackwell and his group had crossed to London, where they immediately got into trouble, as the Ancient Brethren usually did. Seized in a raid on a secret

Heavie newes it is, and I will be glad to hear how farr it will discourage. I see none here discouraged much, but rather desire to larne to beware by other men's harmes, and to amend that wherein they have failed . . .

It doth often trouble me to thinke that in this bussines we are all to learne and none to teach. But better so than to depend upon such teachers as Mr. Blackwell was . . .

The ship that Mr. Blackwell went in will be here shortly. It is as Mr. Robinson once said; he thought we should hear no good of them . . .

For myselfe, I hope to see an end of this bussines ere I come, though I am sorie to be thus from you. If things had gone roundly forward, I should have been with you within these 14 days . . .

Mr. B. is not well at this time. Whether he will come back to you or goe into ye north, I yet know not . . .

Yours in all readines, &c.,

Robert Cushman

6. The Hunt for "Mr. B."

The Saints at the Green Gate were unhappy. And now, in the midst of their multiplying troubles, unexpectedly came a new one, to their great personal concern and general embarrassment.

It involved their beloved Ruling Elder, William Brewster. His print shop was in serious trouble, and it is no wonder that Cushman reported enigmatically that "Mr. B." was not well at this time. He had become the object of an international man hunt, though the Pilgrim records do not reflect a hint of this.

One of the books secretly issued by the Choir Alley press,

Separatist meeting, Blackwell "slipped his own neck out of ye collar" by betraying Sabin Staresmore and other friends of those at Leyden.

At his trial Blackwell denied his Separatist principles and thus "won ye bishops' favour (but lost ye Lord's)," saying that this was "all for the best," for he could now open the way to a better world for all the Separatists.

"But if such events follow ye bishops' blessing," growled Bradford, "happie are they who escape ye same."

Perth Assembly, had come to the attention of the Anglican bishops and the King himself, all of whom were highly incensed and calling for blood.

The book, published from a manuscript smuggled out of Scotland, was a sharp attack upon James I and his bishops for tyrannically attempting to force episcopacy upon the stiff-necked Scots, who had already established a Presbyterian kirk of their own.

Ironically, it was not a Brownist work, but this Calvinist book, that brought the Pilgrim Press to grief and strengthened the Saints' resolve to be moving again.

Copies of *Perth Assembly* had been packed in French wine vats and smuggled back into Scotland, where they were secretly circulated and widely read. The authorities picked up one in April 1619 and loudly denounced the work as an "atrocious and seditious libel." This was a most dangerous and embarrassing development, for Brewster was one of those in London negotiating with the Virginia Company.

Suspicion first fell upon an Edinburgh bookseller-printer, James Cathkin, who was seized and jailed. Taking warning, Brewster quietly disappeared, not to be seen again till the *Mayflower* was on the high seas.

Three months later Cathkin was released when the English ambassador at The Hague reported that he had just picked up a most offensive book entitled *Perth Assembly*, "written with much scorn and reproach" of James and his bishops. Sir Dudley Carleton added that, so far as he could discover, it had been published "by a certain English Brownist of Leyden, as are most of the Puritan books sent over of late days into England."

A few days later he identified the culprit as "one William Brewster, a Brownist, who hath been for some years an inhabitant and printer at Leyden."

But the knave was no longer there, having "within these three weeks removed from thence and gone to dwell in London, where he may be found out and examined."

Carleton was mistaken. Brewster had accompanied Cushman to London early in the year and had vanished after the first alarm three months before.

At the King's command, a determined search for Brewster now

began, both in England and Holland, with Brewster's brethren doing everything possible to confuse and confound the authorities—and obviously succeeding very well, as is evident from Sir Dudley Carleton's dispatches.

Brewster was back in Leyden again, the ambassador reported a few weeks later.

No, that was wrong. And it was unlikely that he would return, "having removed from thence both his family and goods"—which was false.

Sorry, but Brewster was in Leyden after all. He had been seen on the streets there.

No, he was not in Leyden. He was in Amsterdam and preparing to move to the town of Leiderdorp, "thinking there to be able to print prohibited books without discovery," the thoroughly baffled ambassador reported.

"But I shall lay in wait for him," he promised, "both there and in other places."

Disgusted with his envoy's fumbling efforts, the King commanded Carleton to demand the aid of the Dutch authorities and "deal roundly with them for the apprehension of him, the said Brewster, as they tender his Majesty's friendship."

Triumphantly, Carleton reported three weeks later that Brewster had been caught at last, at Leyden, where he had been seized while lying sick in bed. Officers had also arrested "one Brewer, of his profession, a Brownist, who was an assistant to him in his printing," and steps had been taken "to have their books and printing letters seized."

But the next day, to his great chagrin, Carleton had to admit that he was again mistaken. The bailiff, "being a dull drunken fellow," had arrested the wrong man and let Brewster slip.

If Sir Dudley had not been such a dull fellow himself, he might have suspected long since that he was nowhere near his quarry, that he was being misled in a very clever manner by false clues, for all this while Brewster appears to have been safely concealed somewhere in England, probably at Scrooby or in the neighborhood.

Brewster's partner, Thomas Brewer, was taken to London after his arrest to be examined by the King and his ministers, who finally released him.

Brewster's fonts of type and all other equipment were impounded. The door of the print shop in Choir Alley was nailed up, and this was the end of the Pilgrim Press, which in its brief and stormy life had been as active as any of its day.

The international man hunt for the fugitive Ruling Elder continued, which worried his brethren at the Green Gate and reinforced their resolve to get away to the New World quickly and as best they could.[1]

7. The Wincob Patent

But at last, after all these things, . . . they had a patent granted and confirmed [in February 1620] under ye Companie's seal . . .

By ye advice of some freinds,* this patente was not taken in ye name of any of their own, but in ye name of Mr. John Wincob (a religious gentleman then belonging to ye Countess of Lincoln), who intended to goe with them.

But God so disposed as he never went, nor they ever made us of this patente which had cost them so much labour and charge . . .

A right emblime it may be of ye uncertaine things of this world, that when men have toyled themselves for them, they vanish into smoke . . .

This patente being sente over for them to view & consider, . . . they had a sollemne meeting and a day of humiliation to seeke ye Lord for his direction.

And their pastor took this texte, 1 Sam. 23. 3, 4, *And David's men said unto him, see, we be afraid here in Judah, how much*

---

*No doubt one of these was Sir Edwin Sandys, who had reason to fear complications from the Saints' religious beliefs.

Now head of the Virginia Company, Sandys was eagerly seeking new recruits, for the colonists along the James had been dying like flies.

Just the year before, in 1619, the Company had shipped out more than twelve hundred people. During the year almost one thousand died on the ships or in the colony. Mortality during 1620, when the Pilgrims should have gone, ran even higher.

more if we come to Keilah against ye host of Phillistines? Then David asked counsell of ye Lord againe, &c.

From which texte he taught many things very aptly and befitting their present occasion and condition, strengthening them against their fears and perplexities, and incouraging them in their resolutions.

After which, they concluded both what number and what persons should prepare themselves to goe with ye first. For all that were willing to have gone could not gett ready in so shorte a time.

Neither, if all could have been ready, had there been means to have transported them altogether.

Those that staied, being ye greater number, required ye pastor to stay with them . . . The other then desired ye elder, Mr. Brewster, to goe with them, which was also condescended unto . . .

It was also promised to those that went first, by ye body of ye rest, that if ye Lord gave them life & means & opportunity, they would come to them as soon as they could . . .

It was also agreed on by mutuall consente and covenante that those that went should be an absolute church of themselves, as well as those that stayed, seeing in such a dangerous vioage and a removall to such a distance it might come to pass that they should (for ye body of them) never meete againe in this world . . .

IV
Weston's Company

Mr. Weston maks himselfe merry with our endeavors about buying a ship. But we have done nothing in this but with good reason, as I am perswaded. Nor yet that I know in anything else, save in these two: ye one, that we imployed Robert Cushman; . . . the other, that we have so much relyed, by implicite faith as it were, upon generalities.

—*John Robinson*

Aboute this time, whilst there were perplexed with ye proceedings of ye Virginia Company & ye ill news from thence aboute Mr. Blackwell & his companie, . . . some Dutchman made them faire offers aboute going with them.*

1. Thomas Weston and His Merchant Adventurers

Also, one Thomas Weston, a merchant of London, came to Leyden about ye same time, who was well acquainted with some of them and a furtherer of them in their former proseedings. Having much conferance with Mr. Robinson & other of ye cheefe of them, he perswaded them to goe on (as it seems) & not to meddle with ye Dutch or too much depend upon ye Virginia Company. For if that failed, . . . he and such mar-

---

*Just as the Wincob patent was granted, the New Netherlands Company offered those at the Green Gate generous terms if they would settle at New Amsterdam, their small trading post on the lower tip of the island of Manhattan, at the mouth of the Hudson River.

chants as were his freinds (togeather with their owne meanes) would sett them forth.*

They should make ready and neither feare wante of shipping nor money, for what they wanted should be provided . . . They were to draw such articles of agreemente and make such propositions as might ye better induce his freinds to venture . . .

Articles were drawne & agreed unto, and were showne unto him and approved by him, and afterwards by their messenger (Mr. John Carver) sent into England, who, togeather with Robert Cushman, were to receive ye moneys & make provission both for shipping & other things for ye vioage—with this charge, not to exseede their commission, but to proseed according to ye former articles . . .

So those that were to go prepared themselves with all speed and sold off their estates, and (such as were able) put their moneys into ye common stock, which was disposed by those appointed for ye making of generall provissions.

About this time, also, they heard both by Mr. Weston and others that sundrie Honourable Lords had obtained a large grante from ye King for ye more northerly parts of that countrie derived out of ye Virginia patente, and wholly secluded from their Governmente, and to be called by another name— viz., New England.† Unto which Mr. Weston and ye cheefe of them began to incline it was best for them to goe, as for other reasons, so cheefly for ye hope of present profit to be made by ye fishing that was found in that countrie.

But, as in all bussineses, ye acting parte is most difficult, espe-

*An ironmonger by trade, a bold and restless spirit, a typical merchant adventurer of the day, Thomas Weston was a man of many schemes and stratagems, having a hand in many enterprises, licit and illicit. Though better at promise than performance, as the Pilgrims soon learned, his brisk and businesslike air gave them new hope and confidence at this time.

†So named by Captain John Smith of Virginia fame, who had conducted an exploration of the New England coast in 1614, publishing his important findings in his *Description of New England* (1616).

Bradford was mistaken in saying that New England had already been granted to "sundrie Honourable Lords." The revised patent did not pass the seals until the *Mayflower* had sailed, which caused complications, as will appear.

tially where ye work of many agents must concurr, so it was found in this, for some of those . . . in England fell off & would not goe. Other marchants & freinds that had offered to adventure their moneys withdrew and pretended many excuses . . . In ye midst of these distractions, they of Leyden who had put off their estates and laid out their moneys were brought into a great streight, fearing what issue these things would come to . . .

But now another difficultie arose, for Mr. Weston and some others that were for this course, either for their better advantage or rather for ye drawing on of others, as they pretended, would have some of those conditions altered that were first agreed on at Leyden.

2. Articles of Agreement

The articles of agreement, in brief, were these:
1. The colonists and the merchant adventurers were to be partners in a joint stock enterprise for seven years, "during which time all profits & benefits that are gott by trade, traffick, trucking, working, fishing, or any other means" were to be credited to their joint account, or placed in the common store of the settlement.

Out of this common store, the settlers were "to have their meate, drink, apparell, and all provissions."

2. The colonists were to be free two days a week to work for themselves and not for the joint account.

3. At the end of seven years, "ye capitall & profits" were to be divided among the colonists and adventurers upon the basis of the number of shares owned by each.

But the houses, home lots, and gardens of the colonists were not to be so divided. They were to belong to the individual colonists who had made and built them with their own hands.

4. Anyone contributing £10 ($500) either in money or provisions was to be rated as having one share in the enterprise, and so for every £10 "adventured."

5. Anyone going to the colony, if aged sixteen or more, was to "be rated at £10," or a single share, whether he had invested anything or not.

6. Youngsters of ten to sixteen were rated at a half share.

7. Those under ten were to "have noe other share in ye division but 50 acers of unmanured land."

Weston and his associates demanded the deletion of two clauses. First, the planters were not to have at the end of seven years a clear title to their "houses & improved lands, espetially gardens & home lotts"—the adventurers were to retain a half interest in these.

Second, they struck out the clause granting the colonists "two days in a weeke for their owne private imployments, for ye more comfort of themselves and their families."

3. Quirimonies and Complaints

Ye two agents sente from Leyden, or at least one of them, . . . did consente [to Weston's demands], seeing else that all was like to be dashte & ye opportunitie lost, and that they which had put off their estates and paid in their moneys were in hazard to be undone.

They presumed to conclude with ye marchants on those terms, in some things contrary to their orders & commission, & without giving them [at Leyden] notice of ye same. Yea, it was concealed lest it should make any furder delay, which was ye cause afterward of much trouble & contention . . .

But because letters are by some wise men counted ye best parte of histories, I shall shew their greevances hereaboute by their owne letters . . .

A letter of Mr. Robinson's to John Carver:

Leyden
June 4, 1620

My dear freind & brother,*

. . . You doe thoroughly understand by our generall letters ye state of things here, which indeed is very pitifull, espetially by wante of shipping and not seeing means likely, much less

---

*Or rather, brother-in-law. Carver and Robinson had married sisters, Catherine and Bridget (White), of Sturton-le-Steeple, near Scrooby.

certaine, of having it provided.* Withal, there be great want of money & means to doe needfull things . . .

Besides, whereas diverse are to pay in some part of their moneys yet behinde, they refuse to doe it till they see shipping provided, or a course taken for it. Neither doe I thinke is there a man here would pay anything if he had againe his money in his purse.

You know right well we depended on Mr. Weston alone, and upon such means as he would procure for this commone bussines, and when we had in hand another course with ye Dutchmen, broke it off at his motion and upon ye conditions by him shortly after propounded . . .

That he should not have had either shipping ready before this time, or at least certaine means and course, and ye same knowne to us for it, or have taken order otherwise, cannot in my conscience be excused . . .

Mr. Weston makes himselfe merry with our endeavors about buying a ship. But we have done nothing in this but with good reason, as I am perswaded.

Nor yet that I know in anything else save in these two—ye one, that we imployed Robert Cushman, who is (though a good man & of spetiall abilities in his kind, yet) most unfitt to deal for other men by reason of his singularitie and too great indifferancie to any conditions, and (for to speak truly) we have had nothing from him but termes & presumptions . . .

About ye conditions, you have our reasons for our judgments of what is agreed. And this spetially should be borne in minde, that the greatest parte of ye Collonie is like to be imployed constantly not upon dressing their perticuler land & building houses, but upon fishing, trading, &c.

*What those at Leyden had wanted from the Virginia Company was not merely a patent, but free shipping. This the Company was unable to provide, being bankrupt, as it was to remain down to its dissolution a few years later, in 1624, when it "broke," never having paid its shareholders a ha'penny on the £200,000 ($10,000,000) they had invested. It is not to be wondered at, then, that Weston and his partners were inclined to go slow and insist upon amending the articles of agreement to their advantage.

So as ye land & houses will be but a trifle of advantage to ye adventurers. And yet the devission of it a great discouragemente to ye planters, who would with singuler care make it comfortable with borrowed houres from their sleep.

The same consideration of common imployments constantly by ye most is a good reason not to have ye two daies in a weeke denied ye few planters for private use . . .

Consider also how unfit that you & your likes must serve a new apprenticeship of seven years and not a day's freedome from taske.

Send me word what persons are to goe, who of usefull faculties, & how many, & perticulerly of everything . . . Time will suffer me to write no more.

Fare you & yours well allways in ye Lord, in whom I rest.

Yours to use,
John Robinson

Smarting under the criticism of his brethren for consenting to the change in "ye conditions," Cushman sharply wrote them to ask if they thought he had "no brains."

No, they replied, but they wished he would "exercise them therein"—to which Cushman acidly replied:

Brethren,

I understand by letters and passages that have come to me that there are great discontents & dislike of my proceedings amongst you.

Sorrie I am to hear it, yet contente to bear it, as not doubting but that, partly by writing and more principally by word when we shall come togeather, I shall satisfie any reasonable man . . . Take then, brethren, this as a step to give you contente.

First, for your dislike of ye alteration of one clause in ye conditions [about the final disposition of the settlers' houses and gardens], if you conceive right, there can no blame lye on me at all.

For ye articles first brought over by John Carver were never seene by any of ye adventurers here excepte Mr. Weston. Nor did any of them like them because of that clause—nor Mr. Weston himself after he had well considered it* . . .

Without ye alteration of that clause, we could neither have means to gett thither, nor supplie whereby to subsiste when we were there.

Yet notwithstanding all these reasons, which are not mine but other men's wiser than myselfe, without answer to any one of them, here cometh over many quirimonies and complaints against me lording it over my brethren, and making conditions fitter for theeves & bond slaves than honest men, and that of my owne head I did what I list . . .

Those at the Green Gate contended that, as they were risking not only their money but their lives, they were entitled to a larger share in the final dividend than the merchant adventurers. Wrote Cushman:

True, but doe they put us upon it? Doe they urge or egg us? Hath not ye motion & resolution always been in ourselves? Doe they any more than, in seeing us resolute if we had means, help us to means upon equall termes & conditions? If we will not goe, they are content to keep their moneys.

Thus, I have pointed at a way to loose those knots, which I hope you will consider seriously, and let me have no more stirre about them.

Now furder, I hear a noise of slavish conditions by me made . . .

If you mean it of ye two days in a week for perticuler, as some insinuate, you are deceived. You may have three days in a week for all of me, if you will.

And when I have spoken to ye adventurers of times of working, they have said they hope we are men of discretion & conscience and so fitt to be trusted ourselves with that . . .

As for them at Amsterdam, . . . if any practice of mine dis-

---

*Because of the clause, many adventurers had withdrawn from the enterprise, and even more were hesitant to risk their money.

courage them, let them draw back. I will undertake they shall have their money again presently paid here.

Or if the company thinke me to be ye Jonas, let them cast me off before we goe. I shall be content to stay with good will, having but ye cloaths on my back.

Only let us have quietnes and no more of these clamors. Full little did I expecte these things which are now come to pass.

Yours,

R. Cushman

Both Cushman and Weston were so discouraged with "ye fainted state of ye bussines" that both thought of giving it up. But they finally decided to give it "one more trial."

If his presence in London had not been required to keep the enterprise afloat, Cushman wrote Leyden, he would have returned to the Green Gate to answer the clamors against him:

Mean space, entreate our freinds not to be too busie in answering matters before they know them.

If I doe such things as I cannot give reasons for, it is like you have sett a fool aboute your bussines and so turne ye reproofe to yourselves, & send another, and let me come againe to my Combes . . .

And so I take my leave of you all, in all love & affection.

I hope we shall gett all here ready in 14 days.

Your pore brother,

June 11, 1620   Robert Cushman

4. Jangles among the Agents

Besides these things, there fell out a differance amongst those three that received the moneys & made ye provissions in England. For besides . . . Mr. Carver & Robert Cushman, there was one chosen in England to be joyned with them to make ye provissions for ye vioage.

His name was Mr. Martin.* He came from Bellerica in Essex, from which part came sundrie others to goe with them, as also from London & other places. And therefore it was thought meete & conveniente by them in Holland that these Strangers that were to goe with them should appointe one thus to be joyned with them—not so much for any great nead of their help, as to avoyd all susspition or jelosie of any partiallitie.

And indeed, their care for giving offence, both in this & other things afterward, turned to great inconvenience unto them, as in ye sequell will appear. But, however, it showed their equall & honest minds.

The provissions were, for ye most parte, made at Southampton, contrarie to Mr. Weston's & Robert Cushman's mind (whose counsells did most concurr in all things). A touch of which things I shall give in a letter of his [Cushman's] to Mr. Carver . . .

London
June 10, 1620

Loving freind,

I have received from you some letters full of affection & complaints. And what it is you would have of me, I know not.

For your crying out, Negligence, negligence, negligence, I marvell why so negligente a man was used in ye Bussines.

Yet know you that all that I have power to doe here shall not be one hour behind, I warrant you.

You have reference to Mr. Weston to help us with money more than his adventure. Whereas he protesteth that, but for his promise, he would not have done anything. He saith we take a heady course and is offended our provissions are made so farr off; as also that he was not made acquainted with our quantitie of things; and saith that in now being in three places so farr remote, we will, with going up & downe, and wrangling & expostulating, pass over ye summer before we will goe.

*Christopher Martin, who had been for at least three years a member of the Virginia Company, from which he and his partners had received a large grant there. Evidently a "foward" Puritan, Martin had recently clashed with the Anglican authorities on their manner of catechizing.

And to speake ye trueth, there is fallen already amongst us a flatt schisme, and we are readier to goe to dispute than to sett forth a vioage . . .

We have reckoned, it should seem, without our host. Counting upon 150 persons, there cannot be found above £1,200 [$60,000] & odd moneys of all ye ventures you can reckon, besides some cloath, stockings, & shoes, which are not counted. So we shall come shorte at least £300 or £400 [$20,000] . . .

You fear we have begun to build & shall not be able to make an end. Indeed, our courses were never established by counsell . . .

You wrote to Mr. Martin to prevente ye making of ye provissions in Kent. Which he did and sett downe his resolution how much he would have of everything, without respecte to any counsell or exception.

Surely, he that is in a societie & yet regards not counsell may better be a king than a consorte.

To be short, if there be not some other dispossition settled unto than yet is, we that should be partners of humilitie and peace shall be examples of jangling & insulting . . .

Yet your money which you there must have, we will get provided for you instantly. £500 you say will serve. For ye rest, which here & in Holland is to be used, we may goe scratch for it.

For Mr. Crabe,* of whom you write, he hath promised to goe with us. Yet I tell you, I shall not be without feare till I see him shipped, for he is much opposed. Yet I hope he will not faile.

Thinke ye best of all, and bear with patience what is wanting, and ye Lord guide us all.

Your loving friend,
Robert Cushman

*"He was a minister."—Bradford's note. As to his being "much opposed," this probably reflected the fact that, as will be seen, there were many Puritans among the adventurers, and these were opposed to sending over any Separatist minister, even John Robinson.

5. Prayers, Tears, Fasting, and Feasting

At length, after much travail and these debates, all things were got ready and provided. A small ship* was bought & fitted in Holland, which was intended as to serve to help to transport them, so to stay in ye cuntrie and attend upon fishing and such other affairs as might be for ye good & benefite of ye colonie when they came there. Another was hired at London, of burden about 9 score [180 tons], and all other things gott in readines.

So being ready to departe, they had a day of solleme humiliation, their pastor taking his texte from Ezra. 8. 21. *And there at ye river, at Ahava, I proclaimed a fast that we might humble ourselves before our God and seeke of him a right way for us, and for our children, and for all our substance.*

Upon which, he spente a good parte of ye day very profitably, and suitable to their presente occasion. The rest of the time was spente in powering out praiers to ye Lord with great fervencie, mixed with abundance of tears . . .

WINSLOW'S HYPOCRISY† For the wholsome counsell Mr. Robinson gave that part of the Church . . . at their departure from him to begin the great worke of plantation in New England, amongst other wholsome instructions and exhortations, he used these expressions, or to the same purpose.

We are now, ere long, to part asunder, and the Lord knoweth whether ever he should live to see our faces again. But whether the Lord had appointed it or not, he charged us before God and his blessed Angels to follow him no further than he followed Christ.

---

*"Of some 60 tune."—Bradford's note. This vessel, a pinnace, was the *Speedwell*, commanded by a Captain Reynolds. Weston may have been making himself "merry" about her because she was in such bad disrepair that the Saints, after buying her, had the added expense of stepping in new masts and fitting her with a new suit of sail.

†From Edward Winslow's *Hypocrisie Unmasked* (1646)—hereafter Winslow's Hypocrisy.

And if God should reveal anything to us by any other instrument of his, to be as ready to receive it as ever we were to receive anything from his ministery, for he was very confident the Lord had more truth and light yet to breake forth out of his holy Word . . .

Here, also, he put us in mind of our Church-Covenant (at least, that part of it) whereby we promise and covenant with God, and one with another, to receive whatsoever light or truth shall be made known to us from his written Word; but, withall, exhorted us to take heed what we received for truth, and well to examine and compare, and weigh it with other Scriptures, before we received it.

For, saith he, *It is not possible the Christian world should come so lately out of such Antichristian darknesse, and that the full perfection of knowledge should breake forth at once.*

Another thing he commended to us was that we should use all meanes to avoid and shake off the name of Brownist, being a meer nick-name and brand to make Religion odious, and the professors of it, to the Christian world.

And to that end, said he, I should be glad if some godly Minister would goe over with you, or come to you, before my comming. For, said he, there will be no difference between the unconformable [Puritan] ministers and you when they come to the practise of the ordinances out of the Kingdome . . .

And be not loath to take another Pastor or Teacher, saith he, for that flock that hath two shepheards is not indangered, but secured by it . . .

[They] that stayed at Leyden feasted us that were to goe at our Pastor's house, being large, where we refreshed ourselves, after our teares, with singing of Psalmes, making joyfull melody in our hearts, as well as with the voice, there being many of the congregation very expert in Musick.

And indeed, it was the sweetest melody that ever mine eares heard.

6. Sad and Mournful Parting

BRADFORD'S
HISTORY

And ye time being come when they must departe, they were accompanied by most of their brethren out of ye citie unto a towne sundrie miles off, called Delfes-Haven,* where the ship lay ready to receive them.

So they lefte that goodly & pleasante citie which had been their resting place near twelve years. But they knew they were pilgrimes & looked not much on those things, but lift[ed] up their eyes to ye heavens, their dearest cuntrie, and quieted their spirits.

When they came to ye place, they found ye ship [the *Speedwell*] and all things ready. And such of their freinds as could come with them followed after them. And sundrie also came from Amsterdam to see them shipte and take their leave of them.

That night was spent with little sleepe by ye most, but with freindly entertainmente & christian discourse, and other reall expressions of true christian love.

The next day,† the wind being faire, they wente aborde, and their freinds with them, where truly dolfull was ye sight of that sad and mournful parting, to see what sighs and sobbs and praiers did sound amongst them—what tears did gush from every eye, & pithy speeches peirst each harte—that sundry of ye Dutch strangers that stood on ye key [quay] as spectators could not refraine from tears . . .

But ye tide (which stays for no man) calling them away that were thus loath to departe, their reverend pastor, falling downe on his knees (and they all with him), with watrie cheeks com-

---

*Delft Haven, on the Maas, a little below Rotterdam, about twenty miles overland from Leyden.

†"This was about 22 of July [1620]."—Bradford's note.

mended them with most fervente praiers to the Lord and his blessing.

And then with mutuall imbrases and many tears, they tooke their leaves one of another, which proved to be ye last leave to many of them.

V

Speedwell
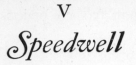

Freind, if ever we make a plantation, God works a mirakle . . .

—Robert Cushman

Of the three hundred Saints at the Green Gate, less than fifty
embarked on the *Speedwell*.

Some of the brethren had brought along their entire families,
down to babes in arms—even in embryo. The former London
tailor, Isaac Allerton, once of the Ancient Brethren and now
rapidly rising to power and influence among the Leyden Saints,
was on board with his wife Mary, who was pregnant and had the
care of three small children, aged four to eight. With William
White, wool carder, had come his wife Susanna, also pregnant,
and their only child, Resolved, a boy of five.

Others had come with their wives, but not their children, as
was the case with Bradford. He and Dorothy had decided to leave
behind, probably in Robinson's care, their young son John, aged
five, who was to see his mother never again, and his father not for
many years. The parting here must have been "truly dolfull" for
all three, especially if the frightened child cried out and clung
desperately to his mother as she kissed him for the last time and
turned away, sobbing and shaken with love and grief—a prelude
to tragedy.

There were three women on board without their husbands. One
was Mary Cushman, with her young stepson, Thomas, who years
later at Plymouth would succeed Brewster as Ruling Elder. She
was planning to meet her husband when the pinnace touched in
England, where Deacon Cushman was still swamped with troubles.

The second was Catherine Carver, who was also to join her
husband at Southampton. The Carvers were childless, but Catherine had brought along a twenty-year-old girl, Desire Minter, a

member of the congregation, as well as a young maidservant and a servant boy.

The third was Mary Brewster, now a grandmother, who had come with her two youngest children, "Wrastle" (Wrestling) and Love, boys of six and nine. Her two daughters, Patience and Fear, remained behind at Leyden with their older brother, Jonathan, now a man of twenty-seven, who came a year later, and the two girls followed. Still in hiding, the Ruling Elder hoped to slip on board to join his wife and sons when the pinnace touched in England.

Others had come without their wives and younger children, but with their older sons. Still others, like Deacon Samuel Fuller, had decided to risk the venture alone, planning to send for their families if they survived.

Altogether, so far as the records disclose, just forty-six of those at Leyden sailed on this "adventure almost desperate." And almost half of these—nineteen in all—were children.

And it had taken three years—a sharp commentary on the congregation's resources—to get even so small and weak a company to sea.

Favored with a "prosperus winde," the company soon dropped anchor at Southampton, "where they found the bigger ship, come from London, lying ready with all the rest of their company."

The larger ship, the now celebrated *Mayflower*, had on board about eighty passengers, all of them strangers to those from Leyden, constituting a separate and quite distinct group.

These "Strangers" were not Brownists or members of any other Separatist school. They belonged to the Church of England—not from any strong conviction, perhaps, but because they had been born and baptized in that faith. A few of them seem to have belonged to the rebellious Puritan wing of that church. But most of them, it seems, were as uncritically orthodox as any Anglican bishop.

The Strangers had been recruited at large in London and southeastern England by the merchant adventurers, who did not care how they prayed so long as they worked. What these Strangers were seeking in the New World, like the tens of millions who followed them across the Atlantic for three centuries, was not spiritual salvation but a larger economic opportunity, a chance to better their worldly lot, no matter what might happen to them or their souls in the hereafter.

For some time, therefore, they stoutly resisted the Saints' attempts to convert them to "ye trueth." This generated considerable friction and precipitated several serious conflicts that almost wrecked New Plimoth, for the smaller Leyden group was in control and determined that the majority should accept the Holy Discipline, whether they wished to or not.

Here at Southampton the Saints and Strangers met for the first time.

1. Quarrels with Weston

After a joyfull wellcome and mutual congratulations, with other frendly entertainements, they fell to parley about their bussines, how to dispatch it with ye best expedition, as allso with their agents about ye alterations of ye conditions.

Mr. Carver pleaded he was imployed here at Southampton and knew not well what ye other had done at London. Mr. Cushman answered he had done nothing but what he was urged to, partly by ye grounds of equity and more especially by necessitie. Otherwise, all had been dasht, and many undone . . .

Mr. Weston likewise came up from London to see them dispatcht and to have ye conditions confirmed. But they refused and answered him that he knew right well that these were not according to ye first agreemente. Neither could they yeeld to them without ye consente of the rest that were behind. And indeed, they had spetiall charge . . . from the cheefe of those that were behind, not to doe it.

At which he was much offended and tould them they must then looke to stand on their owne leggs. So he returned in displeasure, and this was ye first ground of discontente between them.

And whereas there wanted well near £100 [$5,000] to clear things at their going away, he would not take order to disburse a pennie, but let them shift as they could. So they were forst to sell off some of their provissions to stop this gap, which was

some three or four score firkins of butter,* which commoditie
they might best spare, having provided too large a quantitie of
that kind.

Then they write a letter to ye marchants & adventurers aboute
ye diferances concerning ye conditions, . . . subscribed with
many names of ye cheefest of ye company.

Southampton
Aug. 3, 1620

Beloved frends,

Sory we are that there should be occasion of writing at all unto
you, partly because we ever expected to see ye most of you here,
but espetially because there should any differance at all be conceived betweene us.

But seeing it falleth out that we cannot confer togeather, we
thinke it meete (though briefly) to show you ye just cause &
reason of our differing from those articles last made by Robert
Cushman, without our commission or knowledge. And though
he might propound good ends to himselfe, yet it no way justifies
his doing it . . .

We never gave Robert Cushman commission to make any one
article for us, but only sent him to receive moneys upon articles
before agreed on, and to further ye provisions till John Carver
came to assiste him in it.

Yet since you conceive yourselves wronged, we thought meet
to add a branch to ye end of our 9th article as will allmost heale
that wound of itselfe, which you conceive it to be.

And that it may appeare to all men that we are not lovers of
ourselves only, but desire also ye good & inriching of our freinds
who have adventured your moneys with our persons, we have
added our last article to ye rest, promising you againe by letters
in ye behalfe of the whole company that if large profits should
not arise within ye 7 years, that we will continue togeather
longer with you if ye Lord give a blessing.

---

*A firkin of butter weighs 56 pounds, so that fourscore totaled more than two
tons—or 4,480 pounds.

This, we hope, is sufficiente to satisfie any in this case, espetialy freinds . . .

We are in shuch a strait at presente as we are forced to sell
away £60 worth of our provissions to cleare ye haven, & withall
put ourselves upon great extremities, scarce having any butter,
no oyle, not a sole to mend a shoe, nor every man a sword to
his side, wanting many muskets, much armoure, &c.

And yet we are willing to expose ourselves to shuch eminente
dangers as are like to ensue, & trust to ye good providence of God,
rather than his name & truth should be evill spoken of for us.

Thus saluting all of you in love and beseeching ye Lord to give
a blessing to our endeavore and keepe all our harts in ye bonds
of peace & love, we take leave & rest,

Yours, &c.

It was subscribed with many names of ye cheefest of ye
company.

2. Robinson's Advice

At their parting, Mr. Robinson wrote a letter to ye whole
company, . . . in which ye tender love & godly care of a true
pastor appears:

Lovinge Christian friends,

I doe hartily & in ye Lord salute you all as being they with
whom I am presente in my best affection and most ernest long-
ings after you, though I be constrained for a while to be bodily
absente from you.

I say constrained, God knowing how willingly & much rather
than otherwise I would have borne my part with you in this
first brunt, were I not by strong necessitie held back for ye
present. Make accounte of me in ye meanwhile as of a man devided in myselfe with great paine, and as (natural bonds set
aside) having my better parte with you.

And though I doubt not but that in your godly wisdoms you
both foresee & resolve upon that which concerneth your present

state & condition, both severally & joyntly, yet have I thought it but my duty to add some furder spurr of provocation unto them who run allready—if not because you need it, yet because I owe it in love & dutie.

And first, as we are daily to renew our repentance with our God, . . . so doth ye Lord call us in a singuler manner upon occasions of shuch difficultie & danger . . . to a both more narrow search & carefull reformation of your ways in his sight, lest he, calling to remembrance our sins forgotten or unrepented of, take advantage against us & in judgmente leave us for ye same to be swallowed up in one danger or other . . .

Now next, after this heavenly peace with God & our own consciences, we are carefully to provide for peace with all men what in us lieth, espetially with our associates. And for that, watchfullness must be had that we neither at all in ourselves doe give nor easily take offense being given by others . . .

But besides these, there are diverse motives provoking you, above others, to great care & conscience this way.

As first, you are, many of you, strangers as to ye persons, so to ye infirmities one of another, and so stand in need of more watchfullness this way lest when shuch things fall out in men & women as you suspected not, you be inordinately affected with them. Which doth require at your hands much wisdome & charitie for ye covering & preventing of incident offenses that way . . .

Lastly, whereas you are become a body politick, using amongst yourselves civill governmente, and are not furnished with any persons of spetiall eminencie above ye rest to be chosen by you into office of government, let your wisdome & godlines appear not only in chusing shuch persons as doe entirely love and will promote ye common good, but also in yeelding unto them all due honour & obedience in their lawfull administration.

Fare you well in him whom you trust, and in whom I rest.

An unfained well-wisher of your hapie
success in this hopefull voyage,
John Robinson

All things being now ready, & every bussines dispatched, the company was called together, and this letter read among them, which had good acceptation with all, and after-fruit with many.

Then they ordered & distributed their companie for either ship as they conceived for ye best, and chose a Governor & two or three assistants to order ye people by ye way and see to ye disposing of their provisions, and shuch like affairs* . . .

3. Leaky as a Sieve

Which being done, they sett sayle from thence aboute ye 5th of August . . .

Being thus put to sea, they had not gone farr but Mr. Reynolds, ye master of ye lesser ship, complained that he found his ship so leakie as he durst not put further to sea till she was mended. So ye master of ye bigger ship (called Mr. Jonas†) being consulted with, they both resolved to put into Dartmouth & have her there searched & mended, which accordingly was done, to their great charge & losse of time and a faire winde . . .

While the *Speedwell* lay at Dartmouth being mended, the harassed and now thoroughly discouraged Robert Cushman wrote to one of his Leyden brethren, a silkworker, Edward Southworth, then in London with his wife.

Dartmouth
Aug. 17 [1620]

Loving friend,

My most kind remembrance to you & your wife, . . . whom in this world I never looke to see againe.

*The agent representing the Strangers, Christopher Martin, was placed in charge of the passengers on the *Mayflower*. His assistant, Cushman, was to "order" the smaller company of Saints on the *Speedwell*.

†Captain Christopher Jones, skipper and part owner of the *Mayflower*, well acquainted with the tempestuous North Atlantic.

For besides ye eminente dangers of this viage, which are no less than deadly, an infirmitie of body hath ceased [seized] me, which will not in all likelyhoode leave me till death.

What to call it I know not. But it is a bundle of lead, as it were, crushing my harte more & more these 14 days, as that, allthough I doe ye actions of a living man, yet I am but as dead. But ye will of God be done.

Our pinnace will not cease leaking. Else, I think we had been halfe way to Virginia. Our viage hither hath been as full of crosses as ourselves have been of crookedness.

We put in here to trim her & I thinke, as others also, if we had stayed at sea but three or four hours more, she would have sunke right downe. And though she was twice trimmed at Hampton, yet now she is open and leakie as a seive.

There was a board a man might have pulled off with his fingers, two foote longe, where ye water came in as at a mole hole.

We lay at Hampton seven days in fair weather waiting for her, and now we lye here waiting for her in as faire a wind as can blowe. And so have done these four days, and are like to lye four more, and by that time ye wind will happily turn [to an unfavorable quarter] as it did at Hampton.

Our victualls will be halfe eaten up, I thinke, before we goe from the coast of England. And if our viage last longe, we shall not have a month's victualls when we come to ye countrie.

Near £700 [$35,000] hath been bestowed at Hampton. Upon what, I know not. Mr. Martin saith he neither can nor will give any accounte of it. And if he be called upon for accounts, he crieth out of unthankfullnes for his paines & care, that we are susspitious of him, and flings away & will end nothing.

Also, he so insulteth over our poore people [the Saints], with shuch scorne & contempte, as if they were not good enough to wipe his shoes.

It would break your hart to see his dealing and ye mourning of our people. They complaine to me, & alass! I can doe nothing for them. If I speake to him, he flies in my face as mutinous and saith no complaints shall be heard or received but by himselfe, and saith they are forward & a waspish discontented people, & I doe ill to hear them.

There are others that would lose all they have put in, or make satisfaction for what they have had, if they might depart. But he will not hear them, nor suffer them to goe ashore lest they should run away.

The sailors also are so offended at his ignorante boldness in meddling & controling in things he knows not what belongs to, as that some threaten to misscheefe him. Others say they will leave ye ship & goe their way.

But at ye best, this cometh of it, that he makes himselfe a scorne & laughing stock unto them.

As for Mr. Weston, except grace doe greatly sway with him, he will hate us ten times more than ever he loved us, for not confirming ye conditions . . . Better ye viage to have been broken off then than to have brought such miserie to ourselves, dishonour to God, & detrimente to our loving freinds as now is like to doe . . .

And Mr. Martin—he said he never received no moneys on those conditions, that he was not beholden to ye marchants for a penny, that they were bloudsuckers, & I know not what.

Simple man! He indeed never made any conditions with the marchants, nor ever spake with them.

But did all that money flie to Hampton, or was it his owne? Who will goe & lay out money so rashly & lavishly as he did, and never know how he comes by it, or on what conditions? . . .

He hath but £50 in, & if he should give up his accounts, he would not have a penny left him, as I am persuaded . . .

Freind, if ever we make a plantation, God works a mirakle, especially considering how scant we shall be of victualls and, most of all, ununited amongst ourselves & devoyd of good tutors & regimente. Violence will break all.

Where is ye meek & humble spirit of Moyses? & of Nehemiah who reedified ye walls of Jerusalem & ye state of Israell? Is not ye sound of Rehoboam's braggs daily heard amongst us? . . .

If I should write to you of all the things which promiscuously forerun our ruin, I should overcharge my weak head and greeve your tender hart.

Only this, I pray you prepare for evill tidings of us every day . . . I see not in reason how we shall escape even ye gasping of hunger starved persons. But God can doe much, & his will be done . . .

Poore William Ring & myselfe doe strive who shall be meate first for ye fishes, but we looke for a glorious resurrection . . .

I had a desire to make a breefe relation of our estate to some freind. I doubt not but your wisdom will teach you seasonably to utter things as hereafter you shall be called to it.

That which I have written is true, & many things more which I have forborne . . .

Pass over my weake manner, for my head is weake, & my body feeble.

Ye Lord make me strong in him, & keepe both you & yours.

Your loving freind,
Robert Cushman

As at Southampton, the *Speedwell* was again searched from stem to stern. Some leaks were found and mended.

And now it was conceived by the workmen & all that she was sufficiente, & they might proceede without either fear or danger.

So with good hopes from thence, they put to sea againe, conceiving they should goe comfortably on, not looking for any more lets of this kind.

But it fell out otherwise, for after they were gone to sea again above 100 leagues [300 miles] beyond Land's End, holding company togeather all this while, the master of ye small ship complained his ship was so leake as he must bear up or sinke at sea, for they could scarce free her with much pumping.

So they came to consultation againe, and resolved both ships to bear up back againe & put into Plymouth, which accordingly was done.

But no speciall leak could be found, and it was judged to be

ye generall weaknes of ye ship and that she would not prove
sufficiente for the voiage.

Upon which, it was resolved to dismisse her & parte of ye
companie, and proceede with ye other ship. The which, though
it was greevous & caused great discouragemente, was put into
execution . . .

Those that went back were, for the most parte, such as were
willing so to doe, either out of some discontente or fear they
conceived of ye ill success of ye vioage, seeing so many crosses
befall, & the time of year so farr spente.* But others, in regarde
of their owne weaknes and charge of many yonge children,
were thought least usefull and most unfitt to bear ye brunte of
this hard adventure . . .

Amongst those that returned was Mr. Cushman & his familie,
whose hart & courage was gone from them before, as it seems
. . . And though it discover some infirmities in him (as who
under temptation is free), yet after this he continued to be a
spetiall instrumente for their good, and to doe ye offices of a
loving freind & faithfull brother unto them . . .

So after they had tooke out such provission as ye other ship
could well stow and concluded both what number and what
persons to send back, they made another sad parting, ye one ship
going back to London . . .

And thus, like Gedion's armie, this small number was divided,
as if ye Lord . . . thought these few too many for ye great
worke he had to doe.

*Their bad luck with the ill-named *Speedwell* cost the Pilgrims dearly—in
money and the loss of six precious weeks, which meant that they would arrive
in the wilderness just as winter was setting in and that snow would be flying
before they could provide adequate shelter.

VI

A Weighty Voyage

Being thus arrived in a good harbor and brought safe to land, they fell upon their knees & blessed ye God of heaven who had brought them over ye vast and furious ocean and delivered them from all ye periles & miseries thereof, againe to sett their feete upon ye firme and stable earth, their proper element.

—*William Bradford*

September 6. These troubles being blowne over, and now all being compacte in one shipe, they put to sea againe with a prosperus winde, which continued diverce days togeather, which was some incouragmente unto them.

Yet, according to ye usuall maner, many were afflicted with sea-sicknes . . .

1. The *Mayflower* Company

Though a large vessel for her day, displacing 180 tons, the *Mayflower* was crowded to the gunwales, having 102 passengers on board with all of their necessary gear and supplies for establishing a new beachhead in America along the wild North Atlantic shore.

Apple-cheeked, broad of beam, double-decked, with high superstructures fore and aft, square-rigged except perhaps for a lateen sail on the mizzen, the *Mayflower* was indeed a "fine ship," as Cushman had described her.

She was also a "sweet ship," having been engaged for some years in the Mediterranean wine trade, though she no doubt bore about her some trace of the fish, turpentine, tar, and other smelly products she had once carried from Norway.

No notion is more firmly implanted in the American mind than that those on the *Mayflower* were a friendly and homogeneous group, all from Scrooby by way of Amsterdam and Leyden, closely knit by personal and family ties and by the hardships they had suffered together because of their religious faith.

As a matter of fact, only three were from Scrooby—William and Mary Brewster, and William Bradford. Of those on board, little more than a third came from the Green Gate at Leyden.

The others, the great majority, were Strangers, divided into several groups—freemen, hired hands, and indentured servants.

The last, who numbered eighteen, were not servants in our sense of the word. With one or two exceptions, they were not housemaids, cooks, butlers, valets, or other flunkies to wait upon the personal needs of the Pilgrims.

On the contrary, they had been brought along by those who could afford the investment to do the heaviest kind of labor. It was their bounden duty to fell trees, hew timbers, build houses, clear and plow fields, tend crops, gather the harvest, and do whatever their masters commanded. During their period of indenture, which ran from four to seven years, they were fed and otherwise cared for by their masters. But they received no wages, being virtually slaves, and were often bought and sold as such.

Curiously, it is among the Strangers, not the Saints, that one finds the three Pilgrims now best known, thanks to Longfellow's verses—Myles Standish, John Alden, and Priscilla Mullins.

A girl of eighteen, Priscilla may have been a Separatist, for Cushman was early in touch with her father, William Mullins—or "Molines," as he wrote it—"a man pious and well-deserving, endowed also with a considerable outward Estate." Family tradition has it that he was a Huguenot and came from France to join the expedition. The fact is that he had long been a prosperous merchant at Dorking, Surrey, about thirty miles southwest of London. It is probable that his name, like so many among the English, was of Norman origin.

Priscilla's husband-to-be, John Alden, had been signed on at Southampton as a cooper to tend the company's precious barrels of beer, "strong water," and plain water. A "hopfull yonge man" of twenty, from Harwich, Essex, Alden was "much desired." Tall, blond, and of exceptional physical strength, Alden was offered a contract obligating him to remain in the colony for a year, after which he was free to stay or go. "But he stayed," said Bradford, "and maryed here," in time having eleven children.

Myles Standish was an older man, a professional soldier of thirty-six or thereabouts, another hard-bitten graduate of "that universitie of the warrs," the Netherlands, which had given Virginia so many governors and commanders.

Though now perhaps the best known of the Pilgrims, at least by name, Standish remains something of an enigma. A veil of mystery still enshrouds "Captaine Shrimpe," as an enemy dubbed him because he was short and squat, with red hair and a florid complexion that flamed to crimson when he flew into a rage—which was often.

Though the facts are uncertain, he appears to have been born at Chorley, Lancashire, about 1584, which made him Bradford's senior by six years or more. Early left an orphan, according to tradition, he went off to the wars in the Netherlands before he was twenty, shipping with the troops sent by Queen Elizabeth to help the Dutch against Spain.

When English troops were withdrawn after the truce in 1609, Lieutenant Standish presumably returned home with them. But he had meantime, somewhere, met John Robinson, for the two were acquainted, as will appear. But Standish's life is almost a blank page up to the day he boarded the *Mayflower*. At some time down the years he had married, and he had his wife with him. Nothing is known about her except that her first name was Rose and that she died soon after the landing at Plymouth.*

The Saints and their families were a minority on board. There were forty of them in all. The freemen among the Strangers, together with their families, numbered thirty-nine. But the Strangers also included eighteen indentured servants and five hired hands.

Regarded in another light, the composition of the company is even more surprising and even quite startling. This pioneer band —and no pioneers ever faced a more hazardous or arduous task— consisted of fifty men, twenty women, and a simply preposterous

*For the passengers on the *Mayflower* and later Pilgrim ships, see Appendix.

number of children—thirty-two in all, or almost a third of the company. And three more were born on the ship.

2. More Troubles

After they had injoyed faire winds and weather for a season, they were incountered many times with cross winds, and met with many feirce stormes, with which ye ship was shrewdly shaken and her upper works made very leakie. And one of the main beams in ye midd ship was bowed & cracked, which put them in some fear that ye ship could not be able to perform ye vioage.

So some of ye cheefe of ye company, perceiving ye mariners to fear ye sufficiencie of ye ship, as appeared by their mutterings, they entered into serious consultation with ye master & other officers of ye ship, to consider ye danger in time and rather to returne than to cast themselves into a desperate inevitable perill.

And truly there was great distraction & differance of opinion amongst ye mariners themselves . . .

But in examening of all opinions, the master & others affirmed they knew the ship to be stronge & firme under water. And for the buckling of ye maine beam, there was a great iron scrue ye passengers brought out of Holland, which would raise ye beam into place. The which being done, the carpenter & master affirmed that with a post put under it, set firme in ye lower deck & otherways bound, he would make it sufficiente.

As for ye decks & upper workes, they would calke them as well as they could. And though, with ye working of ye ship, they would not long keepe staunch, yet otherwise there would be no great danger if they did not overpress her with sail.*

*As mountainous seas swept over the ship, icy water dripped down upon the terrified passengers huddled uncomfortably in the narrow quarters below, chilling them to the bone.

With no heat, with no sanitation facilities except a foul-smelling bucket, with only an occasional hot dish and no fresh food, those on the *Mayflower* lived on a tiresome and upsetting diet of "salt horse," hardtack, beer, dried fish, and cheese, which brought on scurvy and other diseases. Any ocean voyage

So they committed themselves to ye will of God & resolved to proceed. In sundrie of these stormes the winds were so feirce, & ye seas so high, as they could not bear a knot of saile, but were forced to hull for diverce days togither.

And in one of them, as they lay at hull in a mighty storme, a lustie yonge man (called John Howland), coming upon some occasion above ye gratings, was, with a seel [roll] of ye ship, throwne into ye sea.

But it pleased God that he caught hold of ye top-saile halyards, which hunge overboard & ran out at length. Though he was sundrie fathoms under water, . . . yet he held his hold . . . till he was hauled up by ye same rope to ye brim of ye water and then, with a boat hooke & other means, got into ye ship againe, & his life saved.

And though he was something ill with it, yet he lived many years after and became a profitable member both in church & commonwealthe.*

In all this viage, there died but one of the passengers, which was William Butten, servant to Samuell Fuller . . .

3. Landfall

After long beating at sea, they fell with that land which is called Cape Cod. The which being made & certainly knowne to be it, they were not a little joyfull.

After some deliberation had amongst themselves & with ye master of ye ship, they tacked aboute and resolved to stand for ye southward (ye winde & weather being faire), to finde some place about Hudson's river for their habitation.

But after they had sailed that course aboute halfe ye day, they fell amongst deangerous shoulds [shoals] and roring breakers,

---

three centuries ago was, even at best, a frightful ordeal, and the *Mayflower* had her share of troubles.

*John Howland, aged twenty-eight, was one of five servants in the Carvers' household. A "plaine-hearted Christian," he later became an assistant governor at Plymouth.

and they were so farr intangled therewith as they conceived themselves in great danger.

And ye wind shrinking upon them withall, they resolved to beare up againe for ye Cape and thought themselves happy to gett out of those dangers before night overtooke them, as by God's providence they did.

And ye nexte day, they gott into ye Cape-harbor, where they ridd in safetie.*

Being thus arrived in a good harbor and brought safe to land, they fell upon their knees & blessed ye God of heaven who had brought them over ye vast & furious ocean and delivered them from all ye perils & miseries thereof, againe to set their feete on ye firme and stable earth, their proper elemente.

And no marvell if they were thus joyefull, seeing wise Seneca was so affected with sailing a few miles on ye coast of his owne Italy as he affirmed that he had rather remaine twentie years on his way by land than pass by sea to any place in a short time, so tedious & dreadful was ye same unto him.

But here I cannot but stay and make a pause, and stand half amazed at this poore people's presente condition—and so I thinke will the reader, too, when he well considers ye same.

Being thus passed ye vast ocean and a sea of troubles, . . . they had now no freinds to wellcome them, nor inns to entertaine or refresh their weather-beaten bodies—no houses, or much less townes, to repaire to, to seeke for succoure . . .

And for ye season, it was winter. And they that know ye winters in that cuntrie know them to be sharp & violent, & subjecte to cruell & feirce stormes, deangerous to travel to known places—much more to search an unknown coast.

Besides, what could they see but a hidious & desolate wildernes, full of wild beasts & willd men? And what multituds there might be of them, they knew not . . .

For summer being done, all things stood upon them with a

*It was the eleventh of November (Old Style) when they dropped anchor at the tip of Cape Cod, in what is now Provincetown Harbor. The tired and weather-beaten passengers were now sixty-six days out of Plymouth, ninety-eight out of Southampton, almost four months out of Delft Haven.

wetherbeaten face. And ye whole cuntrie, full of woods &
thickets, represented a wild & savage heiw. If they looked behind
them, there was ye mighty ocean which they had passed and was
now as a maine bar & gulf to separate them from all ye civill
parts of ye world.

If it be said they had a ship to succour them, it is trew. But
what heard they dayly from ye master & company? but that,
with speede, they should looke out a place with their shallop . . .
at some near distance, for ye season was shuch as he would not
stirr from thence till a safe harbour was discovered by them,
where they might be and he might goe without danger . . .

Yea, it was muttered by some that if they gott not a place in
time, they would turne them & their goods ashore & leave them.

Let it also be considered what weake hopes of supply &
succour they left behinde them . . .

It is true, indeed, ye affections & love of their brethren at
Leyden was cordiall & entire towards them. But they had little
power to help them, or themselves. And how ye case stood between them & ye marchants at their coming away hath already
been declared.

What could now sustaine them by ye spirite of God & his
grace? May not, & ought not, the children of these fathers rightly
say:

*Our faithers were Englishmen which came over this great
ocean, and were ready to perish in the wildernes.* But they cried
unto ye Lord, and he heard their voyce and looked on their
adversitie, &c.*

*Let them therefore praise ye Lord because he is good, & his
mercies endure forever†* . . .

4. Whither Bound?

Ostensibly, the Pilgrims had been bound for Virginia—more
particularly, for "some place about Hudson's river," in Bradford's

*"Deu: 26. 5, 7."—Bradford's note.
†"107 Psa. v. 1, 2, 4, 5, 8."—Bradford's note.

phrase—or in Winslow's, "our eye was upon the most Northern parts of Virginia."

They had a patent for a "particular plantation" somewhere in Virginia, it is true. But the lands under the jurisdiction and at the disposal of the Virginia Company under its 1609 charter did not reach anywhere near the Hudson, extending north two hundred miles from Point Comfort, approximately to the point where Philadelphia now stands.

It is true, also, that after making a landfall near the tip of Cape Cod the ship stood off "for ye southward," as if bound elsewhere. But having sailed not many miles down the coast, the *Mayflower* was brought sharply around and circled back into Cape Cod Bay, where she was now riding quietly at anchor.

"The deangerous shoulds and roring breakers" encountered at the elbow of the Cape do not explain this turning back or the fact that, with wind and weather fair, they made no effort to go on. If they had really wished to proceed, they could easily have avoided the shoal waters at Pollock Rip by standing a few miles out to sea, as those at the helm well knew—if not Captain Jones, then First Mate John Clarke, who had brought ships along this northern route to Virginia several times, having passed this way just the year before.

Years later, when writing his history, Bradford declared that Captain Jones had refused to go on. And a half century later, Bradford's nephew and secretary, Nathaniel Morton, asserted that he had received "late and certaine intelligence"—which he never offered—that the skipper of the *Mayflower* had been bribed by the Dutch to keep the Pilgrims away from their trading posts along the Hudson.

In their records, for politic reasons, the Pilgrims strove to make the inference clear that the sudden turn of events had forced them almost overnight to change their plans about going to Virginia. But from the sequence of events it would appear that they had changed their plans some time before and never intended to go beyond New England.

For one thing, New England offered this overwhelming advantage—there was no established government there, and no Anglican Church already upon the ground, as in Virginia, so that the Saints could order their civil and religious affairs as they liked, with no fear of immediate interference.

While they were still in Leyden and having difficulties with the First (London) Virginia Company, which was bankrupt and unable to offer them means of transportation, Thomas Weston had talked with them about New England and the profits to be had from the fisheries there.

New England and its waters had been granted to the Second (Plymouth) Virginia Company. This Company, even before the founding of Jamestown, had established a settlement at Sagadahoc, near the mouth of the Kennebec, in what is now Maine. This settlement was soon abandoned, its high hopes "frozen to death," which so discouraged the Company that it did nothing for some years.

But now, under the leadership of Sir Ferdinando Gorges, a powerful noble of Somersetshire, long interested in exploration and colonization, the Company was eager to have another try at developing its large grant which had not yet paid a penny in dividends.

Weston and the Leyden leaders had been in touch with Sir Ferdinando and his partners about New England, "unto which," as Bradford reports, "Mr. Weston and ye cheefe of them begane to incline it was best for them to goe."

But at the moment Gorges' Company could not issue them a patent. The Company was in process of reorganization, having surrendered its charter in the hope of obtaining a new and enlarged one from the King, which it succeeded in obtaining, being reincorporated as the Council for New England.

The new charter, however, had not yet passed the seals when the Pilgrims were ready to sail, which added a new complication. They could not sail without a patent. Fortunately, they had one. Rather than wait for a new one, they decided to use that for clearance and put to sea, ostensibly headed for Virginia.

But it seems clear from subsequent events that there was an understanding between Sir Ferdinando Gorges and his partners on the one hand and the merchant adventurers and the Leyden leaders on the other that the emigrants would settle in New England, both sides agreeing that legal formalities could be straightened out later without any difficulty, as proved to be the case.

Before sailing, the Pilgrim leaders had talked with Captain John Smith, whose popular fame rests upon his two short years in Virginia—years of unmitigated disaster, for which he was more responsible than most.* His fame should rather rest upon the fact that he spent the remainder of his life trying to promote the colonization of New England.

It was Smith who gave New England its name when exploring its coast south from Maine in 1614, publishing his findings two years later in *A Description of New England*. The work contained a remarkably accurate map of the region, which the Pilgrims had studied and now had with them.

Before their departure, Smith had proposed that they take him along as a guide and adviser. But the Pilgrims declined, remarking that it was cheaper to buy his book than hire him. With the result, said Smith tartly, "that their humorous ignorances caused them for more than a year to endure a wonderful deal of miserie with infinite patience, . . . thinking to finde things better than I advised them."

It was perhaps just as well for Smith that he had not come along. Always restive under any control, Smith was never one to take orders. And if here he had proved to be even half as headstrong, quarrelsome, and insubordinate as he had at Jamestown, the stiff-necked Saints would have quickly put him in his place—if need be, in irons.

And if he had resisted, Captain Smith, for all his fabulous exploits, would have met more than his match in Captain Standish, brought along to command the Pilgrim forces and never one to brook interference. Both men were quick-tempered and hot in anger, and they would certainly have clashed if Smith had reached for the reins, as he was always disposed to do.

One final point on where the Pilgrims really planned to settle. When word at length reached London of the Pilgrims' whereabouts, so far from their announced destination, Weston and his partners evinced no slightest surprise.

Nor did the Pilgrims ever offer them an explanation.

---

*For a detailed account of Smith's career and almost incredible follies at Jamestown, see my *Behold Virginia: The Fifth Crown*.

In this one matter at least, the merchant adventurers and the Pilgrims seem to have understood one another well enough. Apparently they had agreed beforehand that the less said about it, the better, to avoid any complications with the King, the Privy Council, and the Virginia Company.

Even before the *Mayflower* dropped anchor after her long voyage, those on board knew of their leaders' decision to remain here in New England. There was no talk of proceeding further, which produced a new crisis.

5. Mutiny on the *Mayflower*

After months of rocking along in the overcrowded ship, tired of their stale narrow quarters, all of the passengers were eager to go ashore, if only for an hour or two, to stretch their legs and refresh themselves on the "firme and stable earth, their proper elemente."

But no one was allowed to go immediately. Some very serious business had to be settled first. Things had taken an alarming turn as the ship came into the harbor.

BRADFORD'S
HISTORY
[Immediate action was necessary], occasioned by ye discontented & mutinous speeches that some of the strangers amongst them had let fall from them in ye ship—That when they came ashore, they would use their owne libertie; for none had power to command them, the patente they had being for Virginia, and not for New-england, which belonged to another Government, with which ye Virginia Company had nothing to doe.

Unfortunately, that is all that Bradford or anyone tells us about this grave crisis, out of which came one of our great American documents. We do not even know who the rebels were, except that they were "strangers." Bradford knew their names, of course. But in his otherwise detailed chronicle, he is strangely reticent here, perhaps to spare embarrassment to some of those from London who later saw "ye light" and became Saints.[1]

Whoever the rebels were, mutiny was brewing and could not

be tolerated. If there was any talk of hanging the malcontents from the yards, there is no mention of it in the records. Perhaps there was none, for the company obviously needed every man it could muster for the tremendous task ahead.

Still, something had to be done. Mutiny could not simply be ignored.

To meet the explosive situation, the Saints in command decided to rely once again upon the Word. They sat down to draft as formal and formidable document as they knew how. It was properly spattered with a few "by these presents" and other odd bits of legal jargon, probably the handiwork of Brewster, who had been a minor magistrate at Scrooby and was the only university man on board.

Obviously modeled upon the church covenants long in use among the Separatists, the document was soon finished. All on board were summoned to a meeting, probably in the skipper's cabin on the poop deck, where Brewster or perhaps Carver slowly and impressively read aloud what has since become, after two centuries of neglect, a world-famous pronouncement—one of the foundation stones of our American experiment.

6. The Mayflower Compact

BRADFORD'S HISTORY   "In ye name of God, Amen. We whose names are underwritten, the loyall subjects of our dread soveraigne Lord, King James, . . . having undertaken for ye glorie of God, and advancemente of ye Christain faith, and honour of our king & countrie, a voyage to plant ye first colonie in ye Northerne parts of Virginia, doe by these presents solemnly & mutually in ye presence of God, and one of another, covenant & combine ourselves togeather into a civill body politick for our better ordering & preservation & furtherance of ye ends aforesaid; and by vertue hereof to enacte, constitute, and frame such just & equall lawes, ordinances, acts, constitutions, & offices, from time to time, as shall be thought most meete & convenient for ye generall good of ye Colonie, unto which we promise all due submission and obedience.

"In witnes whereof, we have hereunder subscribed our names at Cap-Codd, ye 11 of November, . . . Ano: Dom. 1620² . . ."

[This covenant was] ye first foundation of their governmente in this place, occasioned partly by ye discontented & mutinous speeches that some of the strangers amongst them had let fall, . . . and partly that shuch an acte done (this their condition considered) might be as firme as any patent—and in some respects, more sure . . .

After this, they chose—or rather, confirmed—Mr. John Carver (a man godly & well approved amongst them) their Governour for that year.

This was by popular election, presumably with all the freemen voting, Saints and Strangers alike. Annual elections of all major officers, from the governor down, continued at Plymouth till the day in 1692 when the Old Colony, to its great grief and dismay, was swallowed up by Massachusetts.

Here on the deck of the *Mayflower*, at this first general assembly of the Pilgrims, was born that great democratic institution, the New England town meeting, first established at Plymouth and thence transplanted elsewhere.

This eventful day on the strife-torn *Mayflower* is memorable for another thing. John Carver's real title to fame is not so much that he was the Pilgrims' first governor, but rather that he was the first colonial governor in the New World, and perhaps the first in history, to be chosen by the colonists themselves in a free election.

From the start, therefore, the Pilgrims enjoyed a surprising degree of independence and self-government, free from outside interference. They ordered their affairs as they saw fit, and not as dictated by others. They may have foreseen that this would be the case if they settled in New England.

In any case, they were far better off in this respect than if they had gone to Virginia, where, from its founding down to the Revolution, the governors and all chief officers were appointed in London, first by the Company, later by the Crown—and what a sorry lot of greedy incompetents they were, for the most part, thinking of little but pelf and self.

By their bold initiative, the Pilgrims spared themselves all the mismanagement and other evils of absentee control. Their elected leaders made mistakes, of course. But they were alert and responsive to the needs of their people and gave them good government and honest, straightforward administration. For the most part, they dispensed justice and favors with an even hand, never sacrificing the many to a privileged few.

Though the Pilgrims did not believe in equalitarian democracy, they were moving in that direction, for equalitarian democracy was implicit in their doctrine and the rites of the Separatist meetinghouse. They first gave it political expression in the Mayflower Compact, which promised "just & equall lawes."

VII

Discoveries

And sure it was God's good providence we found this
corne, for else we know not how we should have done.
—*Mourt's Relation*

BRADFORD'S HISTORY   Being thus arrived at Cap-Cod ye 11 of November, and necessitie calling them to looke out a place for habitation (as well as the master's & mariners' importunitie), they having brought a large shallop [or longboat] with them out of England, stowed in quarters in ye ship, they now gott her out & sett their carpenters to worke to trimme her up. But being much brused & shattered in ye ship with foule weather, they saw she would be longe in mending . . .

MOURT'S RELATION*   The same day, as soon as we could, we set ashore fifteen or sixteen men well-armed, with some to fetch wood, for we had none left—as also to see what the land was and what inhabitants they could meet with . . .

At night our people returned, but found not any person nor habitation, and laded their boat with juniper, which smelled very sweet & strong and of which we burned the most part of the time we lay there . . .

There was the greatest store of fowle that ever we saw. And every day we saw whales playing hard by us. Of which, in that

*Written by Bradford and Winslow, but signed by a "G. Mourt"—probably a printer's error for George Morton, from the vicinity of Scrooby and a member of the Leyden congregation, later a Pilgrim Father. This detailed chronicle of the Pilgrims' doings during their first year in the New World was entitled *A Relation, or Journall, of the Beginnings and Proceedings of the English Plantation settled at Plimoth, in New England* (London, 1622)—hereafter, Mourt's Relation.

place, if we had instruments & meanes to take them, we might have had a very rich return—which, to our great greefe, we wanted.

Our Master & his Mate* and others experienced in fishing professed we might have made £3,000 or £4,000 worth of oil. They preferred it above Greenland whale-fishing and purpose the next winter to fish for whale here.

For cod we assayed, but found none. There is good store, no doubt, in their season. Neither gott we any fish all the time we lay here but some little ones on the shore . . .

Munday, the 13th of November, . . . our people went on shore to refresh themselves, and our women to wash [i.e., do the laundry], as there was great need . . .

The Bay is so round and circling that, before we could come to anchor, we went round all the points of the compass. We could not come near the shore by three quarters of an English mile because of shallow water, which was a great prejudice to us. For our people, going on shore, were forced to wade a bow-shot or two in going aland, which caused many to get cold and coughs, for it was many times freezing cold weather . . .

We found great mussels, and very fat and full of sea pearl. But we could not eat them, for they made us all sicke that did eat, as well saylors as passengers. They caused us to cast and scour . . .

1. The First Discovery

Mourt's Relation   But whilst we lay thus, still hoping for our shallop to be ready within five or six dayes at the furthest, . . . some of our people, impatient of delay, desired for our better furtherance to travel by land into the country (which was not without appearance of danger . . .), to see

*The name of the first mate was John Clarke, an experienced hand on this side of the Atlantic, having been many times to Virginia, where in a strange incident he was captured by the Spanish in 1611 and held a prisoner for five years. The Pilgrims had good cause to remember and memorialize the *Mayflower's* able and kindly first mate.

whether it might be fitt for us to seat in or no. And the rather because, as we sailed into the harbour, there seemed to be a river opening itselfe into ye maine land.

The willingness of the persons was liked. But the thing itselfe, in regard of the danger, was rather permitted than approved.

And so, with cautious directions and instructions, sixteen men were set out, with every man his musket, sword, and corselet, under ye command of Captaine Miles Standish, unto whom were adjoined, for counsel and advice, William Bradford, Stephen Hopkins, and Edward Tilley.*

Wednesday, the 15th of November, they were set ashore. And when they had ordered themselves in the order of a single file and marched about the space of a mile by the sea [along the beach], they espied five or six people, with a dog, coming towards them. They were salvages, who, when they saw them, ran into the woods and whistled their dog after them.

> The Pilgrims struck into the woods after the Indians, "to discover if there might be more of them lying in ambush."
>
> Luckily for these innocents, no ambush had been laid. Otherwise, the stronger and abler part of the company might have been wiped out here, with fatal consequences also for those on the *Mayflower*.
>
> Plunging through the woods after the Indians, "falling into such thickets as were ready to tear their cloaths & armore in peeces," the explorers were "most distressed for wante of drinke," having brought with them no water or beer, only a small bottle of *aqua vitae*—perhaps brandy, or more probably good Holland gin.
>
> The next morning, after a watchful night, they finally came upon "springs of fresh water," now known as the Pilgrim Spring,

*This is the first mention of Standish in the Pilgrim records. Stephen Hopkins was the only Stranger given any important post at this time, presumably because he knew something about the ways of the wilderness from his days in Bermuda and Virginia more than ten years before.

The third adviser, Edward Tilley, was one of the Green Gate Saints, probably another of the seceding Ancient Brethren. Originally from London, Tilley had been a clothworker at Leyden. For what reason he was chosen is not clear. Perhaps he had been in the New World before. If so, he and Hopkins were the only two on board who knew from experience what hazards and hardships they were facing.

which was "ye first New-england water they drunke of and was, in their great thirste, as pleasante unto them as wine or beer had been in for-times."

Heading south along the bay shore into what is now the township of Truro, at the wrist of the Cape, they had a look at the river which they had noted from the *Mayflower* as they came in around the tip of the Cape.* There seemed to be a likely harbor at its mouth. But whether it was a river or only a tidal inlet, they had no time to discover, for they had been commanded to be out only two days.

In marching along, they had come upon "certaine heaps of sand," which piqued their curiosity.

MOURT'S
RELATION
One whereof was covered with old mats and had a wooden thing like a mortar whelmed [arched] on the top of it, and an earthen pot laid in a little hole at the end thereof. We, musing what it might be, digged and found a bow and, as we thought, arrows. But they were rotten . . .

But because we deemed them graves, we put in the bow again and made it up as it was, and left the rest untouched, because we thought it would be odious unto them to ransack their sepulchres . . .

Also, we found a great kettle, which had been some ship's kettle brought out from Europe.

There was also a heap of sand made like the former, but it was newly done, . . . which we digged up. And in it we found a little old basket full of fair Indian corne.

And we digged further and found a fine, great, new basket full of very fair corne of this year, with some 36 goodly ears of corne, some yellow and some red, and others mixed with blue, which was a very goodly sight . . .

We were in suspense what to do with it and the kettle. And at length, after much consultation, we concluded to take the kettle and as much of the corne as we could carrie away with

*The Pamet River, as it is still known, so named by the Pilgrims for the Pamet Indians who inhabited these parts.

us.* And when our shallop came, if we could find any of the people and come to parley with them, we would give them the kettle againe and satisfie them for their corne.

So we took all the ears and put a good deal of loose corn in the kettle for two men to bring away on a staff. Besides, they that could put any into their pockets filled the same. The rest we buried, for we were so laden with armour that we could carry no more . . .

So we returned, leaving further discovery to our shallop . . . And thus we came both wearie & welcome home, and delivered our corne into the store to be kept for seed, for we knew not how to come by any and therefore were very glad, purposing as soon as we could meet with any inhabitants of that place, to make them large satisfaction.

This was our First Discovery.

While the shallop was repairing, our people did make things as fitting as they could . . . in seeking out wood, & helving of tooles, and sawing of timber to build a new shallop.

But the discommodiousness of the harbour did much hinder us, for we could neither go to, nor come from, the shore but at high water, which was much to our hindrance & hurte.

For oftentimes they waded to the middle of the thigh, and oft to the knees, to go to and come from land. Some did it necessarily, and some for their pleasure. But it brought to the most, if not all, coughs and colds (the weather proving suddenly cold & stormie), which afterwards turned to the scurvie, whereof many died.

2. Return to Cornhill

MOURT'S RELATION   When our shallop was fitt [about ten days later], . . . there was appointed twenty-four men of our owne, all armed, to goe and make a more full discovery of the river before mentioned.

When we were set forth, it proved rough weather and cross

*While digging up and appropriating the corn, the Pilgrims posted sentinels "in a round ring," being well aware that the Indians might object to this larceny.

winds, so as we were constrained, some in the shallop and others in the long boat, to row to the nearest shore . . . and then to wade out above the knees.

The wind was so strong as the shallop could not keep the water, but was forced to harbour there that night. But we marched six or seven miles further and appointed the shallop to come to us as soon as they could.

It blowed and did snow all that day and night, and froze withall. Some of our people that are dead took the original of their death here.

The next day, . . . we sailed to the river we formerly discovered, which we named Cold Harbour. To which, when we came, we found it not navigable for ships. Yet we thought it might be a good harbour for boats, for it flows there twelve feet at high water . . .

[After another cold night ashore] we marched to the place where we had the corne formerly, which place we called Cornhill,* and digged & found the rest, of which we were very glad.

We also digged in a place a little further off and found a bottle of oil. We went to another place, which we had seen before, and digged, & found more corne . . .

Whilst some of us were digging up this, some others found another heap of corne, which they digged up also.

So we had, in all, about ten bushels, which will serve us sufficiently for seed.

And sure it was God's good providence that we found this corne, for else we know not how we should have done. For we knew not how we should find or meet with any of the Indians, excepte it be to do us a mischiefe.

Also, we had never in all lickelihood seen a grain of it if we had not made our first journey, for the ground was now covered with snow & so hard frozen that we were fain with our curtle-axes [cutlasses] and short swords to hew and carve the ground a foot deep, and then to wrest it up with levers, for we had forgot to bring other tools . . .

*As the high sand knob along the bay shore at Truro is still known.

Thus much of our Second Discovery.

Having discovered [Cornhill], it was controversial amongst us what to do touching our abode and settling there. Some thought it best, for many reasons, to abide there.

As first, that there was a conveniente harbour for boats, though not for ships.

Secondly, good corne ground ready to our hands as we saw by experience in the goodly corne it yielded . . .

Thirdly, Cape Cod was like to be a place of good fishing . . .

Fourthly, the place was likely to be healthful, secure, and defensible.

But the last and especial reason was that now the heart of winter and unseasonable weather was come upon us, so that we could not goe upon coasting and discovery without danger of losing men and boat, upon which would follow the overthrow of all, especially considering what variable winds and sudden storms do there arise.

Also, cold and wet lodging had so tainted our people (for scarce any of us was free from vehement colds) that if they should continue long in that estate, it would indanger the lives of many and breed diseases and infection amongst us.

Again, we had yet some beer, butter, flesh, and other such victualls, which would quickly be all gone, and then we should have nothing to comforte us in the great labour and toil we were like to undergo at the first . . .

Others again urged greatly the going to Anguum or Angoum,* a place twenty leagues off to the northwards, which they had heard to be an excellent harbour for ships, better ground, and better fishing.

Secondly, for anything we knew, there might be, hard by us, a far better seat . . .

Thirdly, the water was but in ponds, and it was thought there would be none in summer, or very little.

Fourthly, the water there must be fetched up a steep hill.

But to omit many Reasons and Replies, . . . it was in the end

*Or rather, Agawam, later Ipswich, Massachusetts.

concluded to make some discovery within the Bay—but in no case, so far as Angoum.*

Besides, Robert Coppin, our pilot,† made relation of a great navigable river and good harbour in the other headland of the Bay, . . . in which he had once been. And because that one of the wild men with whom they had some trucking stole a harping iron [harpoon] from them, they called it Thievish Harbour.

And beyond that place, they were enjoined not to goe.

3. "Men, Indeans!"

MOURT'S
RELATION

Whereupon a company was chosen to goe out upon a Third Discovery . . .

So ten of our men were appointed, who were of themselves willing to undertake it—to wit: Captain Standish, Master Carver, William Bradford, Edward Winslow, John Tilley, Edward Tilley, John Howland; and three of London, Richard Warren, Stephen Hopkins, and Edward Dotey; and two of our seaman, John Allerton and Thomas English.

Of the ship's company, there went two of the Master's mates, Master Clarke and Master Coppin, the master gunner, and three saylors . . .

Wednesday, the 6th of December,‡ we sett out, being very cold & hard weather.

We were a long while after we launched from the ship before we could get clear of a sandy point . . . In which time, two were very sicke, and Edward Tilley had like to have sounded [swooned] away. The gunner was also sicke unto death . . .

---

*"About this time, Mrs. Susanna White was delivered of a son, who was named Peregrine; he was the first of the English that was born in New England . . ." —Marginal note in Nathaniel Morton's *New England's Memoriall*.
  Previously, at sea, Mrs. Stephen Hopkins had given birth to a son, appositely named Oceanus.
†One of the mates on the *Mayflower*.
‡The Pilgrims had made their landfall almost four weeks before. The wintry weather was getting sharper every day, with snow already flying, but the question of where to settle was still undecided.

At length, we got clear of the sandy point and got up our sayles. And within an hour or two, we got under the weather shore and then had smoother water & better sayling. But it was very cold, for the water froze on our clothes and made them, many times, like coats of iron.

We sayled six or seven leagues by the shore, but saw neither creek nor river. At length, we mett with a tongue of land, being flat, off from the shore with a sandy point.* We bore up to gain this point . . .

As we drew near the shore, we espied some ten or twelve Indians very busy about a black thing. What it was we could not tell . . . We landed a league or two from them and had much ado to put ashore anywhere, it lay so full of flat sands.

When we came to shore, we made us a barricado, and got firewood, and set out our sentinels, and betook us to our lodging, such as it was. We saw the smoke of the fire which the salvages made that night aboute four or five miles from us.

In the morning, we divided our company. Some eight in the shallop, and the rest on shore, went to discover this place . . . We saw two becks of fresh water, which were the first running streams that we saw in the country—but one might stride over them.

We found also a great fish, called a grampus, dead on the sands.† They in the shallop found two of them also, in the bottom of the Bay, dead in like sort . . . They would have yielded a great deale of oil if there had been time and means to have taken it . . .

We then directed our course along the sea sands to the place where we first saw the Indians. When we were there, we saw it was also a grampus which they were cutting up . . .

All this while, we saw no people. We went ranging up and downe till the sun began to draw low, and then hasted out of ye

*What is now Billingsgate Point in the township of Wellfleet.

†This was the Pilgrims' first acquaintance with the grampus, or blackfish—also known as the social or howling whale (*Globicephalus melas*), a creature about fifteen feet long, which for generations played such a large part in the economy of the Pilgrims' descendants along Cape Cod.

woods that we might come to our shallop—which, when we were out of the woods, we espied a great way off . . .

So being both wearie & faint, for we had eaten nothing all that day, we fell to make our randevous* and get firewood, which always cost us a great deal of labour.

By the time we had done and our shallop come to us, it was within night. And we fed upon such victuals as we had and betook us to our rest after we had set our watch.

About midnight, we heard a great & hideous crie, and our sentinels called, "Arm! Arm!"

So we bestirred ourselves and shot off a couple of muskets, and the noyse ceased. We concluded that it was a company of wolves or foxes, for one [of the sailors] told us he had heard such a noyse in Newfoundland.

About five in the morning, we began to be stirring. And two or three, which doubted whether their pieces would go off or no, made trial of them and shot them off—but thought nothing at all.

After prayer, we prepared ourselves for breakfast and for a journey. And it being now the twilight in the morning, it was thought meet to carry the things down to the shallop.

Some said it was not best to carry the armour down. Others said they would be the readier. Two or three said they would not carry theirs till they wente themselves—but mistrusting nothing at all.

As it fell out, the water not being high enough [to float and bring in the shallop], they laid the things down on the shore and came up to breakfast.

Anon, all on ye suddaine, we heard a great & strange crie, which we knew to be the same voyces [heard in the night], though they varied their notes.

One of our companie, being abroad, came running in and

*". . . So they made them a barricado (as usually they did every night) with loggs, stakes, & thike pine bowes, ye height of a man, leaving it open to leeward, partly to shelter them from ye cold & wind (making their fire in ye middle & lying arounde it), and partly to defend themselves from any sudden assaults of ye savages, if they should surround them."—Bradford's History.

cried, "They are men! Indeans! Indeans!"—and withal, their arrowes came flying amongst us.

Our men ran out with all speed to recover their armes as, by the good providence of God, they did . . .

The crie of our enemies was dreadfull, espetially when our men ran out to recover their arms. Their note was after this manner:

"Woach! Woach! Ha! Ha! Hach! Woach!"

Our men were no sooner come to their arms but the enemy were readie to assault them. There was a lustie man, and no whit less valiante, who was thought to be their Captaine and stood behind a tree within half a musket-shot of us and there let his arrowes fly among us . . .

He stood three shots of a musket. At length, one took full aime at him [making the bark and splinters of the tree fly about his ears], after which he gave an extraordinarie cry, and away they went all!

We followed them about a quarter of a mile, . . . shouted all together two several times, and shot off a couple of muskets. This we did that they might see we were not affrade of them, nor any way discouraged.

We took up eighteen of their arrowes . . . Many more no doubt were shot . . . Yet, by the especial providence of God, none of them either hit or hurte us, though many came close by us and on every side of us. And some coats which hung up in our barricado were shot through and through.

So, after we had given God thanks for our deliverance, we tooke our shallop and went on our journey, and called this place the First Encounter.*

*This "huggery" occurred at Nauset, so named for the local Indians, a formidable tribe. Part of the township of Eastham, just above the elbow of the Cape, is still known as Nauset.

4. Thievish Harbor

BRADFORD'S
HISTORY

From hence they departed & coasted all along, but discerned no place likely for a harbor & therefore hasted to a place that their pilot did assure them was a good harbor, which he had been in, and that they might fetch it before nightfall.

Of which they were glad, for it begane to be foule weather.

After some hours sailing, it began to snow & raine. And about ye middle of ye afternoone, ye wind increased & ye sea became very rough, and they broke their rudder, & it was as much as 2 men could doe to steer her with a cupple of oares.

But their pilot bad them be of good cheere, for he saw ye harbor.

But ye storme increasing & night drawing on, they bore what sail they could to get in while they could see. But herwith they broke their mast in 3 peeces, & their sail fell overboard in a very grown sea, so as they had like to be cast away.

Yet by God's mercie, they recovered themselves &, having ye flood [tide] with them, struck into ye harbore.

But ye pilot was deceived in ye place and said, ye Lord be mercifull unto them, for his eyes never saw that place before. And he and the master mate [John Clarke] would have run her ashore, in a cove full of breakers, before ye winde.

But a lusty seaman which steered, bad those which rowed, if they were men, about with her, or else they were all cast away, the which they did with speed.

So he bad them be of good cheer & row lustily, for there was a faire sound before them, & he doubted not but they would find one place or other where they might ride in saftie.

And though it was very darke and rained sore, yet they gott under ye lee of a smalle island . . . But they knew not this to be an island till morning and were divided in their minds.

Some would keepe to ye boate for fear they might be amongst

ye Indeans. Others were so weake and cold they could not endure, but got ashore & with much adoe got fire (all things being so wett). And ye rest were glad to come to them. For after midnight, ye wind shifted to the north-west, & it froze hard.

But though this had been a day & night of much trouble & danger unto them, yet . . . ye next day was a faire sunshiny day, and they found themselves to be on an island* secure from ye Indeans, where they might drie their stuffe, fix their peeces, & rest themselves, and gave God thanks for his mercies in their manifould deliverances.

And this being the last day of ye weeke, they prepared there to keepe ye Sabbath.†

On Munday [December 11, 1620‡], they sounded ye harbor and found it fitt for shipping, and marched into ye land & found diverse cornfields & little running brooks, a place (as they supposed) fitt for situation.

At least, it was ye best they could find, and ye season & their present necessitie made them glad to accepte of it.

So they returned to their ship againe with this news to ye rest of their people, which did much comforte their harts.

> All needed comfort, especially Bradford, who returned to the ship to learn that his young wife Dorothy, only twenty-three, had drowned in his absence. The circumstances of her death are not known, though legend has it that she accidentally fell from the ship while it was riding quietly at anchor.[1]

*Which they named Clark's Island, as it is still known, thus honoring the *Mayflower's* intrepid first mate, who led the storm-tossed Pilgrim party ashore here, being the first to step foot on this island in Plymouth Harbor.

†Not even the imperative necessity of finding a place to settle with the least possible delay could move the Saints to break the Sabbath, though some of the Strangers in the party may have been a bit restive and impatient about the delay.

‡The date is Old Style. For current New Style, as remarked before, add ten days. Thus Forefathers' Day, commemorating the first landing at Plymouth, is now, after much confusion, celebrated on December 21 each year.

It was on this "Munday," presumably, that the Pilgrims landed on Plymouth Rock, though there is nothing about that in the records. The story about the Rock, in fact, goes back only to 1769, when the First Comers had been in their graves for a century or more. The Rock's almost universal fame as a great national patriotic institution is of still more recent growth.

VIII

Hard and Difficult Beginnings

But that which was most sadd & lamentable was that in
2 or 3 months' time, halfe of their company dyed . . .
—*William Bradford*

After a delay of three days, during which the reports of the Third Discovery were argued pro and con, the *Mayflower* weighed anchor and headed for Thievish Harbor—or Plymouth, as Captain John Smith had named it when exploring the coast six years before.

But with the wind in the wrong quarter, the ship had to turn back. The next day, with a fair wind, she made another try. And just before the wind shifted, Captain Jones slipped his vessel between the long sandy spits almost enclosing the harbor and hauled around to the north, dropping anchor off Clark's Island in what was later known as the Cow Yard, for a great cow whale once caught and killed there.

And now it was Saturday again, to be spent in making preparations for the Sabbath.

Plymouth Harbor impressed the Pilgrims. Large and well sheltered, ringed with woods and alive with waterfowl, it was "in the fashion of a sickle, or a fishhook." Altogether, it seemed a "most hopefull place."

On Monday a party went ashore for more exploration, marching up the bay side seven or eight miles, passing what had been cornfields, but seeing not an Indian nor an Indian house. The area seemed to be deserted, which puzzled them, as it did for some time.

The soil, in general, was good—"excellent black mould, and fat in some places." They found many kinds of trees and wild fruits, herbs, and berries, as well as sand and gravel and fine clay—"no better in the world, excellente for pots and will wash like soap; and great store of stone, though somewhat soft; and the best water that ever we dranke . . ."

Again the next day a party went ashore "to discover further," proceeding even farther northward up the shore to discover a "very pleasante river," which they named for the kindly skipper of the *Mayflower*.

Here along the Jones River, in what is now the village of Kingston, many wished to settle. But others objected that it was too heavily wooded, too exposed to Indian attack, and too far from their fishing, their "principall profit."

The objectors, led by Bradford, crossed to Clark's Island to have another look at that, arguing that it would be at least secure from the Indians. But it was found to have many other disabilities, and the explorers returned to the *Mayflower* that night without being any nearer a solution of their most pressing problem.

1. Their Randevous

MOURT'S
RELATION

So in the morning, after we had called on God for direction, we came to this resolution—to goe presently ashore againe, and to take a better view of two places we thought most fitting for us, for we could not now take time for further search or consideration, our victuals being much spente, especially our Beere, and it now being the 20th of December [almost six weeks since their landfall].

After our landing and viewing of the places so well as we could, we came to a conclusion, by the most voyces, to seat on ye mainland, on the first place, on high ground where there is a great deale of Land cleared, and hath been planted with Corne three or four years agoe. And there is a very sweete brook runnes under a hill side, . . . where we may harbour our shallops and boates exceeding well, and in this brooke much good fishe in their seasons; on the further side of the river also, much Corne ground cleared.

In one field is a great hill on which we poynt to make a plat-

forme & plant our Ordinance, which will command all round
about.

So there we made our randevous and a place for some of our
people, aboute twentie, resolving in the morning to come all
ashore and to build houses.

But the next morning, . . . it was stormie & wet, that we
could not goe ashore . . . All that night it blew and rained extremely, . . . and it was such foul weather that we were forced
to let fall our anchor and ride with three anchors ahead.

Friday, the 22nd [of December]. The storme still continued
so that we could not get a-land, nor they come to us aboard.
This morning, goodwife Allerton was delivered of a son, but
dead borne.

Saturday, the 23th. So many of us as could wente ashore, felled
and carried timber to provide ourselves stuff for building.

Sunday, the 24th. Our people on shore heard a crie of some
salvages, as they thought, which caused an alarme and to stand
on their guard, expecting an assault. But all was quiet.

Munday, the 25th day. We wente on shore—some to fell timber, some to saw, some to rive, and some to carry, so no man
rested all that day . . . That nighte we had a sore storme of
wind & raine.

This day, December 25, was Christmas, of course. But that made
no difference—at least not to the Saints, who did not celebrate it
as a holiday (holy day) or recognize it in any way.

In their eyes, Christmas was a "human invention," another
Roman "corruption," a devilish survival of heathen days.

Their views on this had been set forth at some length by John
Robinson, who informed the Dutch in his *Just and Necessarie
Apologie* that they could never be "true" Christians until they
stopped celebrating Christmas—and Easter, too, for that matter.
There was no warrant for either in Scripture.

For obvious reasons, Christ had never celebrated Easter.

As for Christmas, Robinson confessed that he did not know
just when Christ had been born. But he was certain of one thing
—"December 25th cannot be the time."

And why celebrate the Saviour's birth, he said, and not the circumcision?

The Strangers in the company were not interested in such esoteric matters. They missed the traditional festivities and good cheer of the Yuletide, made more lugubrious by the fact that the Pilgrims had run out of beer just the day before and were now reduced to drinking water.

But Christmas night, on board the *Mayflower*, there was a little good cheer. Not sharing the Saints' scruples about the occasion, Captain Jones broke out a barrel of the ship's beer and invited all, Saints and Strangers alike, to drink with him—which all did, to their content.

And so on board we had diverse times, now and then, some Beere; but on shore, none at all.

Tuesday, the 26th. It was foule weather, that we could not goe ashore.

2. Laying Out New Plimoth

MOURT'S RELATION

Wednesday, the 27th. We wente to work againe [on Plymouth's first building, the Common House, construction of which began on Christmas Day].

Thursday, the 28th of December. So many of us as could wente to work on the hill where we purposed to build a Platforme for our ordnance, . . . and might be easier impaled, having two rows of houses and a faire street.

So, in the afternoone, we went to measure out the grounds [on the north bank of Town Brook, from the beach up to the foot of the hill].

And first, we tooke notice of how manie families there were, willing all single men that had no wives to joyne some family, as they thought fitt, that so we might build fewer houses. Which was done, and we reduced them to nineteen families.

To greater families, we allotted larger plots—to every person, halfe a Pole in breadth & three in length* . . . We thought this proportion was large enough, at ye first, for houses & gardens, to impale them around, considering the weaknes of our people, many of them growing ill with colds . . .

So lots were cast where every man should lie. Which was done, and staked out . . .

Friday & Saturday. We fitted ourselves for our labour. But our people on shore were much troubled and discouraged with raine and wet, those dayes being very stormie and cold . . .

Monday, the 1st of January [1621]. We went betimes to work. We were much hindered in lying so far off from the land, and faine to go as the tide served, so that we lost much time. For our ship drew so much water that she lay almost a mile and a halfe off . . .

Wednesday, the 3rd of January. Some of our people, being abroad to get and gather thatch, saw greate fires of the Indians and were at their cornfields; yet saw none of ye salvages, nor had seen any of them since we came to this Bay.†

Thursday, the 4th of January. Captaine Miles Standish, with four or five more, went to see if they could meet with any of the salvages in that place where the fires were made. They went to some of their houses, but not lately inhabited. Yet they could not meet with any.

As they came home, they shot at an eagle & killed her, which was excellente meat, . . . hardly to be discerned from mutton.

Friday, the 5th of January. One of the sailors found alive upon the shore a herring, which the Master had to his supper. Which put us in hope of fish, but as yet we had got but one cod. We wanted small hooks.

Saturday, the 6th of January. Master Martin was very sicke

---

*A pole equals a rod—that is, 5.5 yards, or 16.5 feet—so that the individual lots were approximately eight feet wide and fifty feet deep.

These lots were only for present use, not permanent possession, for the articles of agreement stipulated that there was to be no "dividente" of land till the end of seven years.

†This puzzled and worried the Pilgrims. What were the Indians up to? Why were they keeping out of sight? For their own diabolical reasons, it was suspected.

and, to our judgmente, no hope of life. So Master Carver was sent for to come aboard, to speake with him about his Accounts* . . .

Tuesday, the 9th January, was a reasonable faire day, and we went to labour that day in the building of our towne, in two rows of houses for more safetie. . . We agreed that everie man should build his owne house, thinking by that course men would make more haste than working in common.

The Common House, in which for the first we made our randevous, being nearly finished, wanted only covering, it being about twentie feet square. Some would make mortar, and some gather thatch, so that, in foure days, halfe of it was thatched.

The Common House stood just above the beach at the foot of the street—New England's first "Main Street"—long known merely as The Street, now famed as Leyden Street, the finest in old Plymouth. It was a very short street, rising sharply from the beach to the foot of a high knob soon named Fort Hill, now the renowned and beautiful Burial Hill.

The largest structure in early Plymouth, the Common House was of wattle-and-daub construction, having a high steep roof thatched with "sedges."

Up the street on both sides were the building lots of the several "households," each determined by lot. There was here no wild scramble for the best plots, no greedy and violent land-grabbing.

In the beginning the planters probably improvised shelter as best they could, perhaps in the form of conical huts made of branches and turf such as charcoal burners in England used. Later, as opportunity served, the Pilgrims began building a few "small cottages," also of wattle-and-daub construction, with steep thatched roofs.

The Pilgrims did not build log cabins for the good reason that they did not know how. Apparently so native to America, the log cabin is actually a "furriner," being first brought to our shores by the Swedes and Finns some years later, in the 1640s, when they came to settle along the Delaware.

*The "waspish" Christopher Martin, treasurer of the *Mayflower* group, soon died. His accounts were found to be in great disorder, as Cushman had warned they would be, which enkindled more disputes and distractions.

Soon after the completion of the Common House, the Pilgrims began building against it a shed, or lean-to, in which to store their tools and provisions. "But at noon it rained so that we could not worke."

Day after day, week in and week out, for months together, the same dismal note sounds in the Pilgrim records—". . . aboute noone, it began to raine . . . at night, it did freeze & snow . . . still the cold weather continued . . . very wet and rainy, with the greatest gusts of wind ever we saw . . . stormie & cold . . . frost and foule weather hindered us much; this time of the yeare seldom could we worke half the weeke."

Nevertheless, work went slowly forward, and New Plimoth began to take shape along the high north bank of Town Brook. Just behind the houses, the bank pitched sharply down to the rich bottom lands along the brook, where the Pilgrims laid out their "meersteads" and gardens.

Across the street, stretching west and north to the edge of the clearing, lay open fields soon planted with corn.

3. New Discomforts

MOURT'S RELATION   Thursday, the 11th [of January]. William Bradford being at worke, for it was a faire day, was vehemently taken with a grief & paine, and so shot to his huckle-bone it was doubted [feared] that he would have instantly dyed. He got cold in the former Discoveries, espetially ye last, and felt some paine in his ancles betimes. But he grew a little better towards night and in time, through God's mercie in the use of means, recovered.

Friday, the 13th. [12th?] We went to worke. But about noon it began so to raine that it forced us to give over worke.

This day, two of our people put us in great sorrow and care.

There were four sent to gather and cut thatch in the morning. And two of them, John Goodman and Peter Browne, having cut thatch all the forenoon, went to a further place & willed the other two to bind up that which was cut and to follow them.

So they did, being about a mile and a half from our Plantation.

But when the two came after, they could not find them nor hear anything of them at all, though they hallooed & shouted as loud as they could. So they returned to the company and told them of it.

Whereupon, Master Carver and three or four more went to seeke them, but could hear nothing of them. So they, returning, sent more. But that night they could hear nothing at all of them.

The next day, they armed out ten or twelve men, verilie thinking the Indians had surprised them, but could neither see nor hear anything at all. So they returned with much discomfort to us all.

> Late that night, famished and frostbitten, the two missing men stumbled into the plantation, having been off hunting deer with a sickle and having marvelous adventures with "lyons."[1]

Those on shore were much comforted at their return. But they on shipboard [not yet knowing of their return] were greeved, as deeming them lost.

But the next day [Sunday], being the 14th of January, in the morning, about six of the clock, the wind being very greate, they on shipboard spied their great new randevous on fire, which was to them a new discomforte, fearing because of the supposed losse of the men that ye salvages had fired it.

Neither could they presently goe to them for want of water [it was low tide]. But after three quarters of an hour, they went, as they had purposed . . . , to keepe the Sabbath on shore, because now there [on shore] was the greater number of people.

At their landing, they heard good tidings of the returne of the two men, and that the house was fired occasionally [accidentally] by a spark that flew into the thatch, which instantly burnt it all up. But the roof stood, and little hurt . . .

The house was as full of beds as they could lie, one by another. And their muskets were charged. But, blessed be God, there was no harme done . . .

The most loss was Master Carver's and William Bradford's,

who then lay sick in bed and if they had not risen with good speed, had been blown up with powder . . .

Friday, the 9th [of February]. Still the cold weather continued that we could do little worke. That afternoon, our little house for our sicke people was set on fire by a spark that kindled in the roof. But no harme was done . . .

Though the fires directly injured no one, they did nothing to improve the health of those who had to rise from their sickbeds and run out into the cold for their lives. These mishaps struck the Pilgrims a hard and cruel blow from which many of them never recovered.

4. The General Sickness

BRADFORD'S HISTORY   In these hard & difficulte beginings they found some discontents & murmurings arise amongst some, and mutinous speeches & carriages in others. But they were soone quelled & overcome by ye wisdome, patience, and just & equall carriage of things by ye Governor and better part, which clave faithfully togeather in ye maine.

But that which was most sadd & lamentable was that in 2 or 3 months' time, halfe of their company dyed, espetially in Jan: & February, being ye depth of winter, and wanting houses & other comforts, being infected with ye scurvie & other diseases, which this long vioage & their inacomodate condition had brought upon them.

BRADFORD'S POCKET BOOK*   Dec. 4. Dies Edward Thompson, servant of Mr. White, the first that dies since their arrival.

Dec. 6. Dies Jasper, a boy of Mr. Carver's.

Dec. 7. Dorothy, wife to Mr. William Bradford.

*Bradford's Pocket Book is now lost, but some of its entries were copied or paraphrased by the Reverend Thomas Prince, of the Old South Church, Boston, who incorporated them in his *Chronological History of New England in the Form of Annals* (1736)—hereafter, Prince's Annals.

Dec. 8. James Chilton . . .

Dec. 21. Dies Richard Britterige, the first who dies in this [Plymouth] harbour . . .

Dec. 24. Lord's Day, . . . dies Solomon Martin, the sixth and last who dies this month . . .

Jan. 21. Dies Rose, the wife of Capt. Standish . . . N.B. This month, 8 of our number die.

Feb. 21. Die Mr. William White, Mr. William Mullins, with 2 more. And the 25th, dies Mary, the wife of Mr. Issac Allerton. N.B. This month, 17 of our number die . . .

Mar. 21. Dies Elizabeth, the wife of Mr. Edward Winslow.

The first Offence since our arrival is of John Billington, . . . and is this month convented before the whole company for his contempt of the Captain's lawfull command* with opprobrious speeches, for which he is adjudged to have his neck and heels tied together. But upon humbling himself and craving pardon, and it being the first offence, he is forgiven.

N.B. This month, 13 of our number die . . .

BRADFORD'S HISTORY

So as there dyed sometimes 2 or 3 a day . . . [and] of 100 & odd persons, scarce 50 remained. And of these, in ye time of most distres, there was but 6 or 7 sound persons who, to their great comendations be it spoken, spared no pains, night nor day, but with abundance of toyle and hazard of their own health, fetched them woode, made them fires, drest their meat, made their beds, washed their lothsome cloaths, cloathed & uncloathed them—in a word, did all ye homly & necessarie offices for them which dainty & quesie stomacks cannot endure to hear named.

And all this willingly & cheerfully, without any grudging in ye least, shewing herein their true love unto their freinds & bretheren—a rare example & worthy to be remembered.

Two of these 7 were M. William Brewster, their reverend Elder, & Myles Standish, their Captain & military commander,

*Standish had called him to stand his turn as watch, a duty required of all and especially important at this time when the Pilgrim company lay almost prostrate.

unto whom myselfe & many others were much beholden in our
low & sicke condition . . .

And what I have said of these, I may say of many others who
dyed in this generall visitation, & others yet living, that whilst
they had health—yea, or any strength continuing—they were not
wanting to any that had need of them. And I doubt not but
their recompence is with ye Lord.

5. Pattern of Mortality

In this first awful winter at Plymouth, which was a compara-
tively mild one as New England winters go, whole families
perished—four in fact, numbering twelve persons in all. One was
that of the unpopular Christopher Martin, treasurer of the company.

By early spring, when the worst was over, only three married
couples remained unbroken. The Brewsters were one of these and
the Stephen Hopkins another. Some women lost their husbands.
More men lost their wives. The death of both parents left many
children orphaned, including Priscilla Mullins, John Alden's future bride, who was taken in by the Brewsters.

The "generall visitation" took its highest toll among the wives,
only five of eighteen surviving. More than half of the heads of
households perished. Mortality also ran high among the single
men, hired hands, and servants. Of twenty-nine, nineteen died.

Only the very young escaped to bring down the general aver-
age. Of seven daughters, none died; and of thirteen sons, only
three. This may have been quite by chance. But it rather suggests
that parents in general, and mothers in particular, sacrificed themselves for their children.

Only one household came through the epidemic unscathed,
without any loss at all, which mystified the Saints. For it was "one
of ye prophanest families among us," rasped Bradford, "and I
know not by what freinds shufled into the company"—that of
John Billington, Stranger from London, who later distinguished
himself as the only Pilgrim Father to be hanged.

The epidemic also took a heavy toll among the *Mayflower*

crew, carrying off half the sailors, three of the mates, the master gunner, the bosun, and the cook. Many of these, the Pilgrims felt, deserved their fate, especially the bosun, a "prowd yonge man," who used to "curse & scofe at ye passengers."

When Bradford was ill and pleaded for some beer, the bosun and his cronies mocked at him and his suffering, swearing that "if he were their owne father, he should have none."

Hearing of this, Captain Jones intervened and promised "beer for them that had need of it, though he drunke water homeward bound."

And now the bosun himself fell sick, and the Saints softened even his hard heart by caring for him in his illness after his "boone companions in drinking & joyllity" had abandoned him. As a consequence, the villain repented. Confessing that he had "abused them in word & deed," he publicly acknowledged his sins—but too late!

"O!" he cried from his deathbed. "You, I now see, shew your love like Christians indeed one to another. But we let one another lye & dye like doggs."

The sick were violently physicked in the manner of the day by Giles Heale, the ship's doctor, and by Deacon Samuel Fuller, the Pilgrims' "physition-chirurgeon," who possessed a smattering of the lore that then passed for medical science. But their bleedings and other remedies apparently did not do much good. The Pilgrims thought so little of Giles Heale that they never once mentioned his name, and it was not until 1889 that scholars discovered his presence on the *Mayflower* and his subsequent profitable practice in London.

With most of the planters and the crew of the *Mayflower* either dead or seriously ailing, even a feeble attack upon Plymouth could have proved fatal. Tradition has it that the Pilgrims, in their anxiety, secretly buried their dead at night on Cole's Hill, above Plymouth Rock, leveling off the graves and planting them with corn to conceal their great and growing losses.

For all this while, with the company daily growing weaker, "ye Indeans came skulking about them."

IX
Welcome!

Thus their peace & aquaintance was pretty well established with the natives aboute them . . .
—*William Bradford*

What worried and puzzled the Pilgrims was that they had not
yet caught sight of an Indian. Where were they? What were they
doing?

It was obvious that there were Indians in the neighborhood.
Smoke from their fires had often been seen rising in the distance.

Also, it was evident from the cleared fields along Town Brook
that Plymouth had recently been the center of a large Indian
community. What had happened to these people?

There was a mystery here which made the Pilgrims quite
uneasy. It all looked very suspicious.

Then one day late in January, six weeks after putting into the
harbor, Captain Jones spied two Indians intently watching the
ship from Clark's Island near by. Seeing themselves observed, they
quickly vanished, which did nothing to quiet the Pilgrims' fears
and suspicions.

They were sure that unseen eyes were watching them from the
dark rim of the forest. This was a deeply disturbing thought and
not unfounded.

1. Military Orders

MOURT'S
RELATION
Friday, the 16th day [of February], was a faire
day. But ye northerly winde continued, which continued the frost.

This day, after noone, one of our people, being a-fowling
and having taken a stand by the creek side in the reeds, about a

mile and a halfe from our Plantation, there came by him twelve Indians, marching towards our Plantation. And in the woods, he heard the noyse of many more.

He lay close till they were passed. And then, with what speed he could, he went home and gave the alarm.

So the people abroad in ye woods returned & armed themselves, but saw none of them. Only toward the evening, they made a great fire, aboute the place where they were first discovered.

Captaine Miles Standish and Francis Cooke,* being at worke in the woods, coming home, left their tools behinde them. But before they returned, their tools were taken away by the salvages.

This coming of ye salvages gave us occasion to keep more strict watch, and to make our peeces & furniture [muskets and equipment] more readie, which with the moisture & raine were out of temper.

Saturday, the 17th day, in the morning, we called a meeting for the establishing of Military Orders amongst ourselves. And we chose Miles Standish our Captaine and gave him authoritie of command in affayrs.†

And as we were in consultation hereabouts, two salvages presented themselves upon the top of a hill over against our plantation‡ . . . and made signes unto us to come unto them.

We likewise made signs unto them to come to us. Whereupon, we armed ourselves and stood ready, and sent two over the brook towards them—to wit, Captaine Standish and Stephen Hopkins, who went towards them. Only one of them had a mus-

---

*A man in his middle forties, one of the Leyden Saints, probably one of the original congregation at Scrooby, for he came from a hamlet near by—Blyth, Nottinghamshire. He had come with his son John, a lad of eight, later a deacon at Plymouth. Cooke's wife, Hester (Mayhieu), a converted Walloon, came three years later on the *Anne*, with three children, aged five to eight.

†From this time to his death thirty-five years later, Standish commanded the small but formidable Pilgrim army. In all councils of state his voice carried almost as much weight as that of Ruling Elder Brewster and the annually elected governor.

‡Known as Strawberry Hill, rising opposite Fort Hill, on the south side of Town Brook.

ket, which they laid down on the ground in their sight, in signe of peace and to parley with them.

But the salvages would not tarry their coming. A noise of a great many more was heard behind the hill, but no more came in sight. This caused us to plant our great ordnance in places most conveniente.

Wednesday, the 21st of February, the Master came on shore, with many of his saylors, and brought with him one of the great peeces, called a Minion, and helped us to draw it up the hill, with another peece that lay on shore, and mounted them, and a Saker and two Bases.*

He brought with him a very fat goose to eate with us. And we had a fat crane and a mallard & a dried neat's tongue, so we were kindly and freindlie together . . .

Wednesday, the 7th of March. The wind was full east, cold but faire . . . This day some garden seeds were sown.

2. Samoset

No doubt owing to the General Sickness, almost a month passed before another meeting was called to plan the defense of Plymouth. With most of the rank and file ailing, Standish and other leaders may have thought that there was little point in setting up a force if it was to be "all chiefs, and no Indians."

MOURT'S
RELATION
Friday, the 16th [of March] . . . This morning, we determined to conclude the Military Orders which we had begun to consider of before, but were interrupted by the salvages . . .

And whilst we were busied hereabout, we were interrupted again, for there presented himself a salvage, which caused an alarm.

---

* All of these were cannon weighing from twelve hundred to fifteen hundred pounds. The largest, the sacre, fired a 3.5-inch ball and had an extreme range of one thousand feet. When fired, these cannon were quite as likely to explode and kill the gun crew as hit a target at fifty paces. Still, after they were mounted on Fort Hill, their reverberating booms impressed the simple savages and even the Pilgrims themselves, giving them a new assurance.

He very boldly came all alone and along the houses, straight to the randevous, where we intercepted him, not suffering him to goe in, as undoubtedly he would out of his boldness.

He saluted us in English and bad us "Wellcome!" For he had learned some broken English* among the Englishmen that came to fish [New England waters], . . . and knew by name the most of the Captaines, Commanders, and Masters that usually came there.

He was a man free in speeche, so farr as he could expresse his mind, and of seemely carriage.

We questioned him of many things. He was the first salvage we could meete withall. He said he was not of these parts, but of Morattigon,† and one of the Sagamores or Lords thereof . . . He discoursed of the whole countrie and of every province, and of their Sagamores & their number of men and strength.

The wind beginning to rise a little, we cast a horseman's coate about him, for he was starke naked, only a leather aboute his waist with a fringe about a span longe, or little more. He had a bow and two arrowes, the one headed and the other unheaded. He was a tall straight man, the hair of his head blacke—long behind, only short before—none on his face at all.

He asked for some beere. But we gave him strong water, and bisket, and butter and cheese, & pudding, and a peece of mallard, all of which he liked well.

He told us the place where we now live is called Patuxet, and that aboute four years ago all the inhabitants died of an extraordinarie plague, and there is neither man, woman, nor child remaining.‡ So as there is none to hinder our possession, or lay claime to it.

All the afternoone we spente in communication with him.

*". . . which they could well understand, but marvelled at it."—Bradford's history.

†Or Pemaquid, now part of Bristol, Maine. Samoset had sailed down the coast to these parts with an English captain, Thomas Dermer, who had touched at Plymouth just six months before the Pilgrims arrived.

‡The Pilgrims accepted this tragedy philosophically, saying that the Lord in His mercy had not forgotten "His owne" in thus "opening up a way for them." For once they agreed with King James when he said that the "wonderful

We would gladly have been ridd of him at night, but he was not willing to goe . . .

Then we thought to carry him on shipboard, wherewith he was well contente, and went into the shallop. But the wind was high, and the water scante, that it could not returne back.

We lodged him that night at Stephen Hopkins' house, & watched him.

The next day, . . . Saturday, in the morning, we dismissed the salvage, and gave him a knife, a bracelet, and a ring. He promised within a night or two to come again and to bring with him some of the Massasoyts, our neighbors, with such beavers' skins as they had, to trucke with us . . .

[On the following day] came again the salvage, and brought with him five other tall, proper men . . . These left, according to our charge given him before, their bows & arrows a quarter of a mile from our towne . . .

They had, every man, a deere skin on him. And the principal of them had a wildcat's skin, or such like, on the one arm. They had, most of them, long hosen up to their groins, close made; and above their groins, to their waist, another leather. They were altogether like the Irish trousers.

They are of complexion like our English Gypsies. No hair, or very little, on their faces; on their heads, long hair to their shoulders, only cut before, some trussed up before with a feather, broadwise like a fan; others, with a fox's tail hanging out . . .

Some of them had their faces painted black, from ye forehead to the chin, four or five fingers broad; others, after other fashions, as they liked . . .

We gave them entertainmente as we thought was fitting for them. They did eate liberally of our English victuals. They made

---

plague" was proof that God was "determined that these large and goodly territories . . . shall be enjoyed" by the English.

The plague—probably smallpox—had been brought by the English and other Europeans who came every year to fish the Maine coast.

Whoever was responsible, it was fortunate for the Pilgrims that in their enfeebled state they did not have to contest possession of the ground with the Patuxet, until so recently a large and formidable tribe.

semblance unto us of friendship and amity. They sang and danced after their manner, like Antics . . .

They brought three or four [beaver] skins. But we would not trucke at all that day [as it was the Sabbath], but wished them to bring more and we would trucke for all, which they promised within a night or two . . . And they brought us all our tooles againe, which were taken in the woods in our men's absence.

So, because of the day, we dismissed them so soon as we could.

But Samoset, our first acquaintance, either was sicke or fayned himselfe so, and would not goe with them and stayed with us till Wednesday morning. Then we sente him to them to know the reason they came not, according to their words. And we gave him a hat, a pair of stockings & shoes, a shirt, and a peece of cloth to be aboute his waist . . .

Monday and Tuesday proved faire days. We digged our grounds and sowed our garden seedes.

Wednesday, a fine warme day. We sente away Samoset . . .

This day, with much adoe, we got our Carpenter that had been sicke of the scurvie to fit our shallop, to fetch all from aboard* . . .

That day, we had againe a meeting to conclude the Lawes and Orders for ourselves, and to confirme those Military Orders that were formerly propounded & twice broken off by the salvages' coming. But so they were ye third time.

For after we had been an hour together, on the top of the hill over against us† two or three salvages presented themselves & made semblance of daring us, as we thought.

So Captaine Standish with another, with their muskets, wente over to them, with two of the Master's mates that followed them without armes, having two muskets with them.

---

*On this day, March 21, 1621, three months after entering the harbor, the last of the Pilgrims—probably women and children, for the most part—left the *Mayflower* to live henceforth on shore. Evidently there were now sufficient houses to receive them. Also, Captain Jones was getting his vessel ready for the voyage home.

†Again, Strawberry Hill.

They whetted and rubbed their arrows & strings, and made show of defiance. But when our men drew near them, they ran away. Thus we were againe interrupted by them.

Thursday, the 22nd of March, was a very faire warm day.

Aboute noone, we met againe about our public business. But we had scarce been an hour together when Samoset came againe; and Squanto, the only [surviving] native of Patuxet, . . . [who] could speake a little English, with three others. They brought with them some fewe skins to trucke and some red herrings, newly taken & dried, but not salted.

And signified unto us that their greate Sagamore, Masasoyt, was hard by, with Quadequina, his brother, and all their men.

3. Massasoit, the Big Chief

Though his name was Ousamequin, or Yellow Feather, the sagamore was better known then, as now, by his title of Massasoit, or Big Chief, for he was overlord of all these parts, including Cape Cod and the islands to the south. He was the sachem of the Wampanoag, the strongest people hereabouts, who had their chief seat some forty miles to the southwest, at Sowams,* on the north shore of Narragansett Bay.

MOURT'S
RELATION
They [Samoset and Squanto] could not well expresse in English what they would. But after an houre, the King came to the top of a hill over against us and had in his train sixtie men, that we could well beholde them; and they, us.

We were not willing to send our Governor to them, and they unwilling to come to us. So Squanto went againe to him, who brought word that we should send one to parlee with him.

Which we did, which was Edward Winslow,† to know his mind, and to signifie the mind & will of our Governor, which was to have trading and peace with him.

*Now Barrington, Rhode Island.
†This was the first of many diplomatic missions that Winslow successfully carried out as the Pilgrims' shrewd and adroit ambassador at large.

We sent to the King a pair of Knives, and a copper chair, with a Jewell in it. To Quadequina, we sent likewise a knife and a Jewell to hang in his eare; and withall a Pot of strong water, a good quantitie of bisket, & some butter, which were all willingly accepted.

Our messenger make a speeche unto him, that King James saluted him with words of love and peace, and did accept of him as his friend and ally, and that our Governor desired to see him and trucke with him, and to confirme a peace with him, as his next neighbour.

He liked well of the speech and heard it attentively, though the interpreters did not well expresse it.

After he had eaten and drunk himselfe, and given the rest to his company, he looked upon our messenger's sword & armour, . . . with intimation of his desire to buy it. But on the other side, our messenger showed his unwillingness to part with it.

In the ende, he lefte him [Winslow] in the custodie of Quadequina, his brother, and came over the brooke—and some twentie men following him, leaving all their bows & arrowes behind them. (We kept six or seven as hostages for our messenger.)

Captaine Standish and Master Williamson* met the King at the brooke, with halfe a dozen musketeers. They saluted him; and he, them. So on going over, the one on the one side, and the other on the other, conducted him to a house then in building, where we placed a green rug and three or four cushions.

Then instantly came our Governour, with drum and trumpet after him, & some few musketeers.

After salutations, our Governour kissing his hand, the King kissed him, and soe they sat downe . . .

In his person, he is a very lustie man, in his best yeares, an able body, grave of countenance & spare in speeche. In his attire, little or nothing differing from his followers, only in a great chaine of white bone-beads aboute his neck. And at it, behinde his neck, hangs a little bag of tobacco, which he dranck & gave us to drink.†

*A mate on the *Mayflower*.
†The Pilgrims never smoked tobacco; they "dranck" it in earthen pipes.

His face was painted a sad red, like murrey [mulberry] . . .
All his followers likewise were in their faces, in parte or in
whole, painted—some blacke, some red, some yellow, and some
white; some with crosses, and other antick workes. Some had
skins on them, and some naked—all strong, tall—all men in appearance . . .

The Governor called for some strong water & drank to him.
And he drank a great draughte that made him sweate all the
while after. He called for a little fresh meate, which the King
did eate willingly, and did give his followers.

They then treated of peace, which was

1. That neither he nor any of his should injure or doe hurt
to any of our people.

2. And if any of his did hurte to any of ours, he should send
the offender that we might punish him.

3. That if any of our tools were taken away when our people were at work, he should cause them to be restored. And if
ours did any harme to any of his, we would do the like to them.

4. If any did unjustly war against him, we would aid him. If
any did war against us, he should aid us.

5. He should send to his neighbour confederates to certifie
them of this, that they might not wrong us, but might be likewise comprised in ye conditions of peace.

6. That when their men came to us, they should leave their
bows & arrows behind them, as we should do our peeces when
we came to them.

7. Lastly, that doing thus, King James would esteeme of him
as a freind and ally.

All of which the King seemed to like very well, and it was
applauded of his followers* . . .

---

*This simple, straightforward mutual-assistance pact, without any diplomatic
double talk, was a master stroke. The peace it established was not violated and
never seriously strained during Massasoit's lifetime. It continued for more than
a half century, down to King Philip's War in 1675–76. Without it, the small
Pilgrim company could scarcely have survived.

The good sense and fair play of the Pilgrims here stand in sharp contrast
to the shortsighted policies of Captain John Smith and other leaders in Virginia,
who spent most of their time in fruitlessly chasing the Indians "up & downe"

So, after all was done, the Governour conducted him to the brooke. And there they embraced each other, and he departed, we diligently keeping our hostages.

We expected our messenger's coming. But anon, word was brought us that Quadequina was coming, . . . who presently came, and a troop with him. So likewise we entertained him & conveyed him to the place prepared, . . . and he did kindlie like of our entertainement. So we conveyed him likewise, as we did the King . . .

But divers of their people stayed still . . . Two of his people would have stayed all night, but we would not suffer it . . .

Samoset and Squanto, they stayed all night with us. And the King and all his men lay all night in ye woods, not above halfe an English mile from us—and all their wives and women with them.

They said that, within eight or nine days, they would come & set corne on the other side of the brooke and dwell there all summer, which is hard by us.

That night, we kepte good watch. But there was no appearance of danger.

4. Last Sight of the *Mayflower*

MOURT'S
RELATION

The next morning, divers of their people came over to us, hoping to get some victuals, as we imagined. Some of them told us the King would have some of us come see him.

Captaine Standish and Isaac Allerton wente venturously, who

for their corn, neglecting to plant any of their own, hoping to live off pillage, and starving every winter as a consequence. The running war that resulted bled the colony white, though Powhatan was as generous as Massasoit and even more forbearing. The calculated provocations of the whites led to the almost fatal massacre of 1622 and to another almost as serious in 1644, both diabolically devised by one of the great Indian chiefs, Powhatan's younger brother, Opechancano, who contrived the last, which was effected with complete surprise, when he was almost a hundred years old.

were welcomed of him after their manner. He gave them three or foure groundnuts, and some tobacco . . .

Squanto wente at noon to fish for eels. At night he came home with as many as he could well lift in one hand, which our people were glad of. They were fatt & sweet. He trod them out with his feet, and so caught them with his hands, without any other instrumente.

This day [March 23], we proceeded on with our commone business, from which we had been so often hindered by the salvages' coming, and concluded both of Military Orders and of some Lawes & Orders as we thought behoofefull for our presente estate and condition.

And did likewise choose our Governour for this year, which was Master John Carver, a man well approved amongst us* . . .

BRADFORD'S
HISTORY

They now begane to dispatch ye ship away which had brought them over, which lay till aboute this time, or ye beginning of Aprill.

The reason on their parte why she stayed so long was ye necessitie and danger that lay upon them, for it was well towards ye ende of Desember before she could land anything here, or they able to receive anything ashore.

Afterwards, ye 14 of January, the house which they had made for a generall randevoze, by casualty, fell afire, and some were faine to retire aboard for shelter.

Then the sicknes begane to fall sore amongst them, and ye weather so bad as they could not make much sooner dispatch.

Againe, the Governor & cheefe of them, seeing so many dye and fall downe sick dayly, thought it no wisdom to send away the ship, their condition considered and ye danger they stood in from ye Indeans, till they could procure some shelter, and therefore thought it better to draw some more charge upon themselves & freinds than hazard all.

The master and sea-men likewise, though before they hasted

*As was English practice at the time, the Pilgrim new year began on March 25, not January 1, so that Carver was re-elected two days before his term expired.

ye passengers ashore to be gone, now many of their men being dead, . . . and many lay sick & weake, ye master durst not put to sea till he saw his men begine to recover, and ye hart of winter over.

Weighing anchor on April 5, the *Mayflower* tacked out of the harbor, breaking the Pilgrims' last tie with the Old World, leaving them alone in the wilderness with no hope of escape. No doubt they gathered on the beach to wave a last sad farewell as they wondered uneasily whether they had the strength to carry on by themselves.

Bringing his vessel home, Captain Jones soon died, probably another victim of that first awful winter at Plymouth. When last seen not long after the death of her owner and master, the *Mayflower* was lying in her home port of Rotherhithe, Surrey. She was then in such very bad trim that she was valued at less than £140 with all of her fittings and "one suit of worne sails," perhaps those that had carried her to Plymouth four years before.

5. The King at Home

BRADFORD'S HISTORY

Having in some sorte ordered their bussines at home, it was thought meete to send some abroad to see their new friend, Massasoit, and to bestow upon him some gratuitie to bind him ye faster unto them; as also, that hereby they might view ye countrie, and see in what manner he lived, what strength he had aboute him, and how ye ways were to his place, if at any time they should have occasion.

So ye 2 of July, they sente Mr. Edward Winslow & Mr. Hopkins, with ye foresaid Squanto for their guide,* who gave him a suite of cloaths and a horseman's coate [of red cotton, with lace], with some other small things, which were kindly accepted . . .

They found his place [Sowams] to be 40 miles from hence,

*Samoset had returned home to his people in Maine.

ye soyle good, & ye people not many, being dead & abundantly wasted in ye late great mortalitie which fell in all these parts, . . . wherein thousands of them dyed, they not being able to burie one another. Their sculls and bones were found in many places, lying still above ground where their houses & dwellings had been—a very sad spectacle to behould . . .

In their message the Pilgrims assured Massasoit that he and his people were always "welcome" at Plymouth. But as rations were low there, they wished he would "hinder the multitude from oppressing us with themselves." But if any had beaver skins, they should come, of course. Also, Massasoit was asked to inform the Pamet Indians that those at Plymouth were eager "to make satisfaction to the full" for the corn they had dug up and appropriated when they first arrived on Cape Cod.

MOURT'S
RELATION
For answer to our message, he told us we were welcome, and he would gladly continue that peace and friendship which was betweene him and us. And for his men, they should no more pester us as they had done. Also, that he would send to Pamet, and would help us with corne for seed, according to our request.

This being done, his men gathered near to him, to whom he turned himselfe and made a great speech, they sometimes interposing and, as it were, confirming & applauding him in what he said. The meaning whereof was, as farr as we could learne, thus:

Was not he, Massasoit, Commander of the countrie aboute them? Was not such a towne his, and the people of it? And should they not bring their skins unto us?

To which they answered: these were his, and would be at peace with us, and bring their skins to us.

After this manner, he named at least thirtie places. And their answer was as aforesaid to every one, so that as it was delightfull, it was tedious unto us.

This being ended, he lighted tobacco for us and fell to discoursing of England and the King, His Majestie, marvelling that he would live without a wife . . .

Late it grew, but victuals he offered none, for indeed he had not any, being come so newly home. So we desired to rest.

He laid us on the bed with himself and his wife, they at one end and we at the other, it being only planks laid a foot from the ground and a thin mat upon them. Two more of his chief men, for want of room, pressed by and upon us, so that we were worse wearie of our lodging than of our journey . . .

The next day, being Thursday, many of their Sachems or pettie governors came to see us, and many of their men also . . .

Aboute one of the clocke, Massasoit brought two fishes that he had shot. They were like bream, but three times so big and better meate. These being boiled, there were at last fortie looked for share in them. This meal only we had in two nights and a day. And had not one of us bought a partridge, we had taken our journey fasting.

Very importunate he was to have us stay with him longer. But we desired to keep the Sabbath at home and feared we should be light-headed for want of sleep, for what with bad lodging, the savages' barbarous singing (for they use to sing themselves asleep), lice & fleas within doors, and muskeetoes without, we could hardly sleep all the time of our being there. We much feared that if we should stay any longer, we should not be able to recover home for wante of strength.

So that, on Friday morning [July 6], before sun-rising, we took our leave and departed, Massasoit being both grieved and ashamed that he could no better entertain us. And retaining Tisquantum to send from place to place to procure trucke for us, he appoynted another, called Tokamahamon [or Hobomok], in his place.

> Like Squanto, Hobomok came to live at Plymouth. He was a "proper lustie man, and a man of accounte for his vallour & parts amongst ye Indeans, and continued very faithfull and constant to ye English till he dyed." A member of Massasoit's war council, he had rank among the Wampanoag as a "pinese," which signified that he was one of their "cheefest champions."
>
> At Plymouth, Hobomok served almost as Massasoit's resident

minister or ambassador, keeping his master well informed of all that went on there, performing many useful missions both for the Pilgrims and the Big Chief, several times mediating their differences.

6. Adventures on Cape Cod

BRADFORD'S
HISTORY

[Soon after the visit to Sowams], one John Billington lost himselfe in ye woods & wandered up & downe some 5 days, living on berries & what he could find.*

At length, he lighted on an Indean plantation 20 miles south of this place, called Manamet [Manomet]. They conveyed him furder off, to Nawsett [Nauset], amongst those people that had before set upon ye English when they were coasting . . .

But ye Governor caused him to be enquired for among ye Indeans, and at length Massasoit sent word where he was. And ye Governor sent a shallop for him & had him delivered.

> On this expedition the Pilgrims were well received and plentifully feasted all along Cape Cod, even by the Nauset, who with no seeming provocation had so sharply attacked them at the First Encounter. But when they had talked with the Nauset, they saw the "huggery" in another light, saying that it was "no marvell" they were attacked.
>
> For one thing, they had built their barricado right "in the midst of them," having failed "through snow or otherwise" to observe their village a short way off.

*Young John was only seven, but apparently he had already become quite a woodsman. Earlier, his brother Francis, a boy of nine, had discovered in his prowling a large lake some three miles back of Plymouth—Billington Sea, as it is still known.

Still earlier, the two boys had almost blown up the *Mayflower* while she was anchored at the tip of the Cape, making squibs and shooting off muskets in their father's cabin, with an open keg of gunpowder only a few feet away.

In the light of his subsequent behavior, it is almost certain that their father was among those talking mutiny as the ship came in, and he had already clashed violently with Captain Standish.

However "prophane," the Billingtons seem to have been a fearless and venturesome lot, though conspicuously wanting in discretion and judgment.

Second, the Nauset told them a bitter tale of treachery. Seven years before, in 1614, when Captain John Smith had sailed for home after his New England explorations, he had left behind one of his ships under a Captain Thomas Hunt. The latter had been ordered to follow as soon as he had loaded up his ship with corn, beaver pelts, and other articles from the Indians.

Circling Cape Cod Bay, Hunt put in at a number of points, pretending trade. Suddenly he seized and bound the Indians he had lured on board, about thirty in all, including seven of the Nauset, and sailed away to Spain to sell the "poor silly salvages for rials of eight" in the Málaga slave market.

The Pilgrims were shocked and commiserate.

MOURT'S RELATION We told them we were sorrie that any Englishman should give them that offence, that Hunt was a bad man, and that all the English that heard of it condemned him for the same.

But for us, we would not offer them any such injurie, though it would gain us all the skins in the countrie.

BRADFORD'S HISTORY Those people [along Cape Cod] also came [to Plymouth] and made their peace, and they gave full satisfaction to those whose corne they had found & taken when they were at Cap-Codd.

Thus, their peace & acquaintance was pretty well established with the natives aboute them.

X

Special Providences and Thanksgiving

Our harvest being gotten in, our Governor sentc four men out fowling that so we might, after a more special manner, rejoyce together after we had gathered the fruit of our labours.

—*Edward Winslow*

BRADFORD'S HISTORY   Squanto continued with them and was their interpreter, and was a spetiall instrumente sent of God for their good, beyond their expectation. He directed them how to set their corne, where to take fish and to procure other comodities, and was also their pilott to bring them to unknowne places for their profitt, and never left them till he dyed . . .

1. Squanto

Nothing could have been more providential than that the Pilgrims should have been befriended and adopted by Squanto, or Tisquantum, the last of the Patuxet.

In their pilgrimages from England to Holland, and from Holland to the American shore, the Saints had seen something of the world. But Squanto had seen far more of it than any of them, being much more widely traveled, having been a pilgrim himself —against his will, on at least one occasion.

In 1605, falling in with an exploring party led by Captain George Waymouth, Squanto had been persuaded to accompany them to England, where his talk of the New World had had much to do, as Sir Ferdinando Gorges reported, with inspiring the English to renewed interest in colonization—an interest which led to the founding of the North (Plymouth) and South (London) Virginia companies, the cornerstones of what became the far-flung British empire in America.

Squanto remained in England almost ten years, until 1614, when he returned with Captain John Smith's expedition to explore the New England coast. Unhappily for him—but happily, too, as it turned out—Squanto was one of those "silly savages" who were kidnaped here at Patuxet and along Cape Cod by that "bad man," Captain Thomas Hunt, who carried them to Spain and there sold them as slaves at £20 ($1,000) a man.

Most of the enslaved Indians passed to an unknown fate, perhaps spending their lives as curious blackamoors in the harems of Fez or Algiers. But Squanto and a few more were taken in hand by friars at Málaga, "to be instructed in the Christian faith."

In time Squanto managed to get away to England, where he lived for several years with a rich merchant, John Slanie, treasurer of the Newfoundland Company. Through him he met Captain Thomas Dermer, one of Gorges' men, who was preparing an expedition for further exploration of New England.

Squanto sailed with him in 1619. In Maine waters Samoset came on board, and the ship worked her way slowly down the coast, dropping anchor here at Plymouth just six months before the Pilgrims arrived—Squanto to find that plague had wiped out all his people and that he only survived because of "bad Mr. Hunt," a strange providence.

Quitting the ship, Squanto went to live with Massasoit's people. But he seems not to have been very happy there. and from the day he met the Pilgrims, he never left them.

2. New Life

BRADFORD'S HISTORY

The spring now approaching, it pleased God the mortalitie began to cease amongst them. And ye sick and lame recovered apace, which put, as it were, new life into them, though they had borne their sadd affliction with as much patience & contentednes as I think any people could doe.

But it was ye Lord which upheld them and had beforehand prepared them, many having long borne ye yoake—yea, from their youth . . .

Afterwards, they (as many as were able) began to plant their corne, in which service Squanto stood them in great stead, showing them both ye manner how to set it and, after, how to dress & tend it. Also, he told them excepte they got fish & set with it (in these old grounds), it would come to nothing.

And he showed them in ye middle of Aprill they should have store enough [of fish] come up ye brooke, . . . and taught them how to take it, and where to get other provisions necessarie for them, all which they found true by triall & experience.*

Some English seed they sewed, as wheat & peas. But it came not to good, eather by ye badnes of ye seed, or latenes of ye season, or both, or some other defecte.

3. William Bradford, Governor

BRADFORD'S HISTORY   In this month of Aprill, whilst they were bussie about their seed, their Governor (Mr. John Carver) came out of ye field very sick, it being a hott day. He complained greatly of his head and lay downe, and within a few howers his sences failed, so as he never spake more till he dyed, which was within a few days after.

Whose death was much lamented and caused great heavines amongst them, as there was cause. He was buried in ye best manner they could, with some vollies of shott by all that bore armes.

---

*Squanto taught them how to build weirs in Town Brook to catch the spring run of herring—or rather, alewives. These alewives were not only a welcome addition to the Pilgrims' scanty larder but were used under Squanto's direction to fertilize the fields. On every corn hill, so tradition has it, three alewives were placed spokewise, with their heads together, and guard was kept day and night to keep off the wolves.

And his wife, being a weak woman, dyed within 5 or 6 weeks after him.

Shortly after, William Bradford was chosen governor in his stead. And being not yet recovered of his illnes, in which he had been near ye point of death, Isaac Allerton was chosen to be an Assistante unto him, who by renewed election every year continued sundry years togeather.

The choice of Bradford, who had just turned thirty-one, is an important milestone in Pilgrim history in several respects. For one thing, it signalized the fact that a new generation of leaders had been coming forward and was about to take command.

Up to this time, affairs had been conducted largely by Elder Brewster, Pastor Robinson, Deacon Carver, and Deacon Cushman. All of them were older men, and now this group was scattered—Carver was dead, Cushman was in London, Robinson was in Leyden, and only Brewster was here in Plymouth.

These men still commanded the highest respect, and they spoke with unchallenged authority. But they spoke more and more in the role of elder statesmen.

Actual conduct of affairs, day-to-day direction of operations, even questions of high policy, became increasingly the responsibility of an able and diversely talented group of younger men—of Bradford, practical and astute, a good organizer and efficient administrator, a tireless and devoted leader having at once a grasp of detail and great foresight; of Assistant Governor Allerton, now in his middle thirties, a shrewd and sharp trader, who took over Plymouth's business dealings; of Captain Myles Standish, also in his middle thirties, the small but formidable commander-in-chief of the small but formidable Pilgrim army.

Though not yet an elective officer, young Edward Winslow, now twenty-six, was rapidly coming to the fore. Later a governor, he was now chiefly employed as an envoy on more delicate diplomatic missions. Suave and plausible—"a cunning, smooth-tongued fellow," said a critic—Winslow had a fine sense of tact and the good sense to use it, rare qualities among his brethren, who were generally inclined to be blunt and unbending in even the smallest matters.

The rise of this younger group brought a new vigor to Pilgrim affairs, an unaccustomed note of bold and sharp decision. There was less backing and filling and long-winded debate, no more costly procrastination in taking action. Rather, as will appear, decisions were often too hastily made on the spur of the moment. Still, whether for better or worse, it represented a change.

Even more important, there appeared among the new leaders a subtle shift of concern from purely spiritual to more secular matters. Not that the Holy Discipline was neglected—God forbid! But when action was to be taken, there was a growing disposition to consider not only what was religiously "lawfull," but what was practically expedient and immediately profitable.

This shift reflected another fact, one generally overlooked but of the greatest consequence. Unlike all of the older leaders, not one of the younger group was an officer of the Church.

This was a fortuitous and unpremeditated development, it would seem. But it was no less important for that, and to it can be attributed the blessing that, at Plymouth, the civil authority always retained supreme control both *de jure* and *de facto*, never abdicating to the Church and allowing the professional religious to usurp its functions.

In the Old Colony, from first to last, ministers ministered, performing their own proper services, but they never ruled. Unlike the Puritan communities later established to the north around Boston Bay, Plymouth was never priest-ridden—or pastor-ridden. Here there were no John Cottons and no Mathers to dictate public policy and to lay down the law both for Church and State.

In the short-lived Pilgrim empire the "voice of God" thundering from the pulpit never drowned out the voice of the people speaking through their annually elected representatives and civil magistrates. Plymouth early laid down the rule that only communicants in good standing could vote, thus limiting the franchise to the faithful. But Plymouth was never a theocracy in the sense that the Massachusetts Bay Colony was for generations.

The Saints and their descendants stuck to first principles, acting upon their belief that the Church consisted primarily of the great body of communicants and not of those who happened for the moment to be ministering. They were often very hard on their pastors, taking them severely to task for many things, showing

great independence of them and their opinions, being quite unwilling to accept a new set of autocratic bishops under another
name.

As will be seen, pastors always had a rather rough time of it
at Plymouth.

4. The First Marriage

BRADFORD'S
HISTORY
    May 12 [1621] was ye first mariage in this
place, which, according to ye laudable custome of
ye Low-Cuntries, . . . was thought most requi-
site to be performed by the magistrate as being a civill thing
upon which many questions aboute inheritances doe depend,
with other things most proper to their cognizans and most con-
sonante to ye scriptures, Ruth 4., and nowhere in ye gospell to
be layed on ye ministers as part of their office . . .

And this practiss hath continued amongst not only them, but
hath been followed by all ye famous churches in these parts to
this time—Ano. 1646.

It continued even longer, down to the middle of the next
century. It was not until 1760 that marriages were recorded in
the Plymouth church registers.

There was much shock and sharp talk among the orthodox in
1708 when Hannah Sturtevant, Winslow's great-granddaughter,
was married with benefit of clergy in the first ceremony of the
kind at Plymouth.

With Governor Bradford officiating, the first marriage at
Plymouth joined Edward Winslow, who had lost his wife two
months before, and Mrs. Susanna White, a widow of three
months, who brought him two children and bore him more, including Josiah, a later governor.

The celebrated John Alden-Priscilla Mullins romance may have
begun at this time. Though the date is not known, they were
probably married later this year or early in 1622, and in due
course had nine children. The poet Longfellow, who brought
them their posthumous fame, was one of their descendants.

5. The Skins of the Modest Women of the Massachusetts

MOURT'S
RELATION
It seemed good to the companie in general that though the Massachusetts [Indians] had often threatened us, as we were informed, yet we should goe amongst them—partly to see the country, partly to make peace with them, and partly to procure their trucke.

For these ends, the Governor chose ten men fitt for the purpose, and sent Tisquantum and two other salvages to bring us to speech with the people and interpret for us. We set out aboute midnight [September 18, 1621], the tide then serving for us . . .

[At one place] we sent two salvages to looke for the inhabitants, and to informe them of our ends in coming, that they might not be fearfull of us. Within a mile of this place, they found the women of the place together, with their corne in heaps, whither we supposed them to be fled for feare of us . . .

With much feare they entertayned us at firste. But seeing our gentle carriage towards them, they tooke hart and entertayned us in the best manner they could, boiling cod and such other things as they had for us.

At length, with much sending for, came one of their men shaking and trembling with feare. But when he saw we intended them no hurte but came to trucke, he promised us his skins also . . .

Here Tisquantum would have us rifle the savage women and take their skins & all such things as might be serviceable for us.

"For," said he, "they are a bad people and have often threatened you."

But our answer was:

"Were they never so bad, we would not wronge them or give them any just occasion against us. For their words, we little weighed them. But if they once attempted anything against us, then we would deal far worse than he desired."

Having well spente the day, we returned to the shallop, almost all of the women accompanying us to trucke, who sold their coats from their backs and tied boughs about them—but with great shamefastness, for indeed they are more modest than some of our English women are. We promised them to come againe to them; and they us, to keep their skins . . .

They returned in saftie, and brought home a good quantity of beaver, and made reporte of ye place, wishing they had been there seated. But it seems ye Lord, who assigns to all men ye bounds of their habitations, had appoynted it for another use.*

6. Harvest

MOURT'S RELATION†   You will understand that in this little time that a few of us have been here, we have builte seven dwelling houses, and four for the use of the Plantation, and have made preparation for divers others.

We set last spring some twentie acres of Indian corne and sowed some six acres of barley and peas. And according to ye manner of the Indians, we manured our ground with herrings, or rather shads [or rather, alewives], which we have in great abundance and take with great ease at our doors.

Our corne did prove well and—God be praised!—we had a good increase of Indian corne, and our barley indifferent good. But our peas not worth the gathering, for we feared they were too late sown. They came up very well and blossomed, but the sun parched them in the blossom.

BRADFORD'S HISTORY   They began to gather in ye small harvest they had, and to fitt up their houses and dwellings against winter, being all well recovered in health & strength, and had all things in good plenty. For as some were

*This last wistful paragraph is from Bradford's history. The Pilgrims early became aware that there were better sites for settlement than Plymouth with its narrow grounds and shallow harbor.

†The following appears in the *Relation* as a letter from Winslow, addressed to a "loving and old freind" in England and dated December 11, 1621, exactly a year after the first landing here at Plymouth.

thus imployed in affairs abroad, others were exercised in fishing aboute codd & bass & other fish, of which they tooke good store, of which every family had their portion.

All ye summer there was no wante. And now began to come in store of foule, as winter approached . . . And besides water-foule, there was great store of wild Turkies, of which they tooke many, besides venison, &c. Besides, they had aboute a peck of meal to a person or now, since harvest, Indean corne to that proportion, which made many afterwards write so largely of their plenty here to their friends in England, which were not fained but true reports.

7. Thanksgiving

MOURT'S RELATION*   Our harvest being gotten in, our Governor sente four men out fowling that so we might, after a more special manner, rejoyce together after we had gathered the fruit of our labours. These four, in one day, killed as much fowl as, with a little help besides, served the company almost a week, at which time, amongst other recreations, we exercised our armes, many of the Indians coming amongst us.

And amongst the rest, their greatest King, Massasoit, with some ninety men, whom, for three days, we entertained and feasted.

And they went out and killed five deer, which they brought to the Plantation, and bestowed on our Governor and upon the Captaine and others.

And although it be not always so plentifull as it was at this time with us, yet, by the goodness of God, we are so farr from wante that we often wish you partakers of our plentie.

To feed ninety hungry braves—not only once, but for three days—faced the Pilgrims with a problem of grave concern, and they must have been seriously worried as they looked in their

*Again from Winslow's published letter to a friend in England.

cupboards. While the shelves were not bare, they held relatively little, far from enough to carry them over to the next harvest, contrary to Winslow's easy talk about their "plentie."

Happily, Massasoit and his men solved the problem by undertaking to feed themselves in large part, providing all with venison and other things.

At this first Thanksgiving feast in New England, which occurred late in October or early in November, the Pilgrims and their guests ate their fill of venison, roast duck, roast goose, clams and other shellfish, succulent eels, white and corn bread, leeks and watercress and other "sallet herbes," topped with wild plums and dried berries as dessert—all washed down with wine, both white and red, "very sweete & strong," made from the wild grape.

Though there is no mention of it in the records, the banqueters may also have enjoyed some of the wild "Turkies" whose swiftness of foot as they fled through the woods constantly amazed the Pilgrims. Neighboring bogs were filled with cranberries, but it is doubtful if the Pilgrims had yet found a happy use for them. Nor was the table graced with a later and even happier invention —pumpkin pie.

This celebration was so successful, so satisfying to body and soul alike, that the Pilgrims held another the next year, repeating it more or less regularly for generations.

In time it became traditional in New England to enjoy the harvest feast with Pilgrim trimmings, a tradition carried to other parts of the country as restless Yankees moved westward.

But it remained a regional or local holiday until 1863 when, during the Civil War, President Lincoln proclaimed our first national Thanksgiving and, disregarding the centuries-old Pilgrim tradition of holding it somewhat earlier, usually in October, set apart the last Thursday in November for the purpose.

XI

Fortune

And consider that ye life of the bussines depends on ye
lading of this ship.

—Thomas Weston

BRADFORD'S HISTORY   In November, aboute that time twelfe month
that they themselves came, there came in a small
ship to them unexpected or unlooked for,* in
which came Mr. Cushman (so much spoken of before), with
35 persons to remaine & live in ye plantation, which did not a
litle rejoyce them.

1. *Fortune*

BRADFORD'S HISTORY   And they, when they came ashore and found
all well, and saw plentie of vitails in every house,
were no less glad.

For most of them were lusty younge men, and many of them
wild enough, who little considered whither or aboute what
wente, till they came into ye harbor at Cap-Codd and there
saw nothing but a naked and barren place. They then begane
to thinke what should become of them if the people here were
dead, or cut off by ye Indeans.

They begane to consulte (upon some speeches that some of
ye seamen had cast out) to take ye sails from ye yard, lest ye
ship should gett away and leave them there.

But ye master, hearing of it, gave them good words and told
them if anything but well had befallen ye people here, he hoped

*"She came ye 9th to ye Cap"—precisely a year to the day after the *Mayflower's*
landfall at the tip of Cape Cod.

he had vitails enough to carry them to Virginia. And whilst he had a bit, they should have their parte, which gave them good satisfaction.

So they were landed. But there was not so much as bisket-cake or any other victails for them.* Neither had they any bedding but some sorrie things they had in their cabins, nor pot nor pan to dress any meate in, nor overmany cloaths, for many of them had brusht away their coats & cloaks at Plimoth as they came.

But there was sent over some burching-lane suits in ye ship, out of which they were supplied.

The plantation was glad of this addition of strength, but could have wished many of them had been of better condition, and all of them better furnished with provisions.

But that could not now be helpte.

The vessel was the *Fortune* of London, of fifty-five tons, under the command of Captain Thomas Barton.

She had on board twelve more of those at Leyden. One of the first to come ashore was Deacon Robert Cushman, who had evidently given up his fear of becoming "meate for ye fishes." He had brought along his son Thomas, a boy of fourteen, later a leader of the church at Plymouth.

Another from Leyden was Jonathan Brewster, now almost thirty and a widower at the moment, having lost his wife and child four years before.

This group of Saints also included Moses Symonson [Simmons] and Philippe de la Noyc [Delano], both French-speaking Walloons who had joined the Green Gate congregation. Nor were they the only Walloon Saints at Plymouth.

As on the *Mayflower*, most of those on the *Fortune*—two thirds, to be exact—were Strangers, recruited at large by the merchant adventurers. One of these was a youth of twenty-one, a carriage maker of London, Thomas Prence, later a governor. Another was "Goodwife" Martha Ford, recently widowed, who was "delivered of a sonne the first night she landed," it was noted at the time, "& both are doing very well."†

---

*"Nay, they [at Plymouth] were faine to spare ye ship some to carry her home." —Bradford's note.

†For the passengers on the *Fortune*, see Appendix.

2. News from Leyden

Leyden
June 30, 1621

ROBINSON'S
WORKS*

Much-beloved Brethren:

Neither the distance of place nor distinction of body can at all either dissolve or weaken that bond of true Christian affection in which the Lord by his Spirit hath tied us together.

My continual prayers are to the Lord for you. My most earnest desire is unto you from whom I will no longer keep (if God will) than means can be procured to bring with me the wives and children of divers of you and the rest of your brethren, whom I could not leave behind me without great injury both to you and them, and offence to God and all men.

The death of so many of our dear friends and brethren, oh! how grievous hath it been to you to bear, and to us to take knowledge of . . .

And how many, even of us, God hath taken away here and in England since your departure, you may elsewhere take knowledge of . . .

Brethren, I hope I need not exhort you to obedience unto those whom God hath set over you in church and commonwealth . . .

God forbid! I should need exhort you to peace which is the bond of perfection, and by which all good is tied together, and without which it is scattered . . .

And the God of peace and grace and all goodness be with you in all the fruits thereof, plenteously, upon your heads now and for ever. All your brethren here remember you with great love . . .

Yours ever in the Lord,
John Robinson

*From Robert Ashton's *Works of John Robinson* (1851)—hereafter, Robinson's Works.

3. Complaints from London

BRADFORD'S
HISTORY In this ship Mr. Weston sent a large letter to Mr. Carver, ye late Governor, now deseased, full of complaints & expostulations aboute former passages at Hampton and ye keeping ye ship so long in ye country, and returning her [the *Mayflower*] without lading, &c. . . .
Part of Mr. Weston's letter:

London
July 6, 1621

I durst never acquainte ye adventurers with ye alteration of ye conditions first agreed on betweene us, which I have since been very glad of. For I am well assured that had they knowne as much as I doe, they would not have adventured a halfe-penny of what was necessary for this ship.

That you sent no lading [cargo] in the ship is wonderful, and worthily distasted.

I know your weaknes was the cause of it. And I beleeve more weaknes of judgmente than weaknes of hands.

A quarter of ye time you spente in discoursing, arguing, & consulting, would have done much more. But that is past, &c.

If you mean, bona fide, to performe the conditions agreed upon, doe us ye favor to coppy them out faire and subscribe them with ye principall of your names.

And likewise give us accounte as perticulerly as you can how our moneys were laid out, and then I shall be able to give them some satisfaction whom I am now forsed with good words to shift off.

And consider that ye life of the bussines depends upon ye lading of this ship, which, if you doe to any purpose, . . . *I promise you I will never quit ye bussines, though all the other adventurers should.*

We have procured you a Charter, the best we could, which is better than your former, and with less limitations.*

For anything that is els worth writing, Mr. Cushman can informe you.

I pray write instantly for Mr. Robinson to come to you.

And so praying God to blesse you with all graces necessary both for this life & that to come, I rest,

Your very loving frend,

Tho. Weston

4. Dangers of Self-Love

At the insistence of the adventurers, who were supported in this by the Leyden leaders, Cushman had expressly come to persuade the Pilgrims to sign the altered articles of agreement, which they now reluctantly agreed to do.

They did this partly to quiet some of their own people who were arguing that, in the absence of any signed agreement, the original understanding with the merchant adventurers no longer held. And there was no reason, therefore, why they should be bound by the stipulation that all property and profits should be held in common for the joint account of the planters and adventurers for a period of seven years.

These men were clamoring to have the lands divided up on a permanent basis so that each might have his own "perticuler" to do with as he pleased. These land-hungry planters chose to forget that if this were done, the adventurers would quite abandon the enterprise and leave Plymouth without hope of obtaining aid or supply from any quarter.

Aware of this danger, Cushman undertook to impress upon all the necessity of honoring the joint stock arrangement as a matter not only of moral obligation but of practical expediency as well.

---

*As soon as the *Mayflower* returned and the merchant adventurers learned of the Pilgrims' exact whereabouts, they surrendered the patent obtained from the Virginia Company and obtained a new one from the Council for New England. Signed by Sir Ferdinando Gorges and his partners, this later patent was issued in the name of John Pierce, clothworker of London, and of his associates in the company of the merchant adventurers. These were to hold the patent in trust for the settlers until a final settlement was made under the articles of agreement.

The entire company—with the newcomers, now numbering about ninety in all—crowded into the Common House to hear the Deacon preach on "The Sin and Danger of Self-Love," taking as his text I Cor. 10:24: *Let no man seek his own: But every man another's wealth.*

CUSHMAN'S SERMON* The occasion of these words of the Apostle Paul was because of the abuses which were in the Church of Corinth. Which abuses arose chiefly through swelling pride, self-love, and conceitedness . . .

The parts of this text are two: 1, a *Dehortation;* 2, an *Exhortation.* The Dehortation, *Let no man seek his own.* The Exhortation, *But every man another's wealth.*

In handling of which, I will, first, open the words; secondly, gather the doctrine; thirdly, illustrate the doctrine by Scriptures, experience, and reasons; fourthly, apply the same, to every one his portion . . .

But that I may not walk in generalities, the particular ways by which men seek their own are these:

First, such as are covetous seek their own by seeking riches, wealth, money, as Felix, pretending love unto Paul, sent for him often. But it was in hope of money . . . Their hearts are set upon the pelf in this world. And for love of it, all things are let slip . . .

The second way by which men seek their own is when they

---

*This sermon, under the title of *The Danger of Self-Love, and the Sweetnesse of True Friendship,* was published in London in 1622, with an "Epistle Dedicatory to his loving Friends, the Adventurers for New England, together with all Well-Willers and Well-Wishers thereunto."

Cushman's is the only Pilgrim sermon we have, and it is scarcely typical. For one thing, there is not a word about Separatist doctrine and the superior ways of the Saints. There was good reason for this omission. The sermon was preached to Saints and Strangers alike, so that any sectarianism was out of place. Besides, Cushman's theme was an impassioned plea for the closest possible unity.

As is evident here and from his letters, the good deacon was at once a wise, sensible, humane, cultivated, and highly literate man, with an eye for the human scene and a sharp pen and wit, though this former wool comber does refer to himself in the "Epistle Dedicatory" as a "poor weakling, . . . a frail man [who] professeth to know nothing as he ought to know it."

seek ease, or pleasure, as the Scribes and Pharisees, who would not touch the burden with one of their fingers . . .

The third way is when men seek their own bellies, as some did in the apostle's time, which went about with new doctrines and devices, knowing that the people have itching ears and would easily entertain and willingly feed such novelists, which brought in dissensions, schisms, and contentions . . . They were shadows in God's service. But when feasting came, then they were substances. Then, they were in their element . . .

The fourth way by which men seek their own is by seeking outward honor, fame, and respect with men, . . . and it is wonderful to see how some men are *desirous of vaine glory* . . . And let a man mark some men's talk, stories, discourses, &c., and he shall see their whole drift is to extol and set out themselves, and get praise and commendation of men.

Now the contrary was seen in Paul. He saith, *He needed no letters of commendation.* And again, *He is not affected with men's praise.*

And here is indeed the difference between an humble-minded christian and a proud self-lover. An humble man often hath praise, as David, Hezekiah, and Josiah. But he seeks it not. He desires it not. He is content to go without it . . .

But a proud self-lover, he seeks it still, get it or not get it. And if he get it, he is fully satisfied. If he get it not, he hangs his head like a bullrush and hath no comfort.

The fifth way by which men seek their own is by *seeking to have their wills* . . . And truly, some men are so prince-like, or rather papal, that their very will and word is become a law. And if they have said it, it must be so. Else, there is no rest or quietness to be had. Let never so many reason be brought to the contrary, it is but fighting with the wind.

They are like the obstinate Jews, who, when against God's law and reason, they asked a king, though Samuel showed them it would turn in the end to their smart, yet still held the conclusion and said, nay, *But we will have a King.*

Thus men are caught by their own words and insnared by

the straitness of their own hearts, and it is death to them not to have their wills. And howsoever sometimes (like Jezebel) they are cut short of their purposes, yet self-willed men will strut like Absalom . . . and threaten like profane Esau, Gen. 27. 41 . . .

Now brethren, I pray you, remember yourselves and know that you are not in a retired monastical course, but have given your name and promises one to another, and covenanted here to cleave together in the service of God and the king.

What then must you do? May you live as retired hermits and look after nobody?

Nay, you must still seek the wealth of one another and enquire as David, how liveth such a man? How is he clad? How is he fed? He is my brother, my associate. We ventured our lives together here and had a hard brunt of it, and we are in league together.

Is his labor harder than mine? Surely, I will ease him.

Hath he no bed to lie on? Why, I have two; I'll lend him one.

Hath he no apparel? Why, I have two suits; I'll give him one of them.

Eats he coarse fare, bread, and water, and I have better? Why, surely, we will part stakes. He is as good a man as I, and we are bound each to other, so that his wants must be my wants, his sorrows my sorrows, his sickness my sickness, and his welfare my welfare, for I am as he is.

And such a sweet sympathy were excellent, comfortable—yea, heavenly—and is the only maker and conservator of churches and commonwealths. And where this is wanting, ruin comes on quickly, as it did in Corinth . . .

It wonderfully encourageth men in their duties when they see the burthen equally borne. But when some withdraw themselves and retire to their own particular ease, pleasure, or profit, what heart can men have to go on in their business? . . . Great matters have been brought to pass where men have cheerfully, as with one heart, hand, and shoulder, gone about it, both in wars, buildings, and plantations. But where every man seeks himself, all cometh to nothing . . .

The country is yet raw, the land untilled, the cities not builded, the cattle not settled. We are encompassed about with a helpless and idle people, the natives of the country, which cannot in any comely or comfortable manner help themselves, much less us.

We also have been very chargeable to many of our loving friends which helped us hither, and now again supplied us, so that before we think of gathering riches, we must, even in conscience, think of requiting their charge, love, and labor. And cursed be that profit or gain which aimeth not at this! . . .

Never measure thy course by the most, but by the best—yea, and principally by God's word . . .

And let there be no prodigal person to come forth and say, give me the portion of lands and goods that appertaineth to me, and let me shift for myself. It is yet too soon to put men to their shifts. Israel was seven years in Canaan before the land was divided unto tribes, much longer before it was divided unto families.

And why wouldst thou have thy particular portion but because thou thinkest to live better than thy neighbor, and scornest to live so meanly as he?

But who, I pray thee, brought this particularizing first into the world?

Did not Satan, who was not content to keep that equal state with his fellows, but would set his throne above the stars? Did not he also entice man to despise his general felicity and happiness, and go try particular knowledge of good and evil?

And nothing in this world doth more resemble heavenly happiness than for men to live as one, being of one heart and of one soul. Neither anything more resembles hellish horror than for every man to shift for himself.

For if it be a good mind and practice thus to affect particulars, *mine* and *thine*, then it should be best also for God to provide one heaven for thee, and another for thy neighbor . . .

And as you are a body together, so hang not together by skins and gymocks. But labor to be jointed together and knit by flesh and sinews. Away with envy at the good of others, and rejoice in his good, and sorrow for his evil . . . And if you profess friendship, be friends in adversity, for then a friend is known and tried, and not before.

Lay away all thought of former things, and forget them, and think upon the things that are. Look not gapingly one upon another, pleading your goodness, your birth, the life you lived, the means you had and might have had.*

Here you are by God's providence under difficulties. Be thankful to God it is no worse, and take it in good part that which is, and lift not up yourself because of former privileges. When Job was brought to a dung-hill, he sat down upon it . . .

Consider, therefore, what you are now, and whose you are.

Say not, I could have lived thus and thus. But say, thus and thus I must live.

For God and natural necessity requireth, if your difficulties be great, you have need to cleave the faster together, and comfort and cheer up one another, laboring to make each other's burden lighter.

There is no grief so tedious as a churlish companion, and nothing makes sorrows easy more than cheerful associates.

Bear ye, therefore, one another's burthen, and be not a burthen one to another. Avoid all factions, frowardness, singularity, and withdrawings. And cleave fast to the Lord and one to another continuously. So shall you be a notable precedent to these poor heathens, whose eyes are upon you . . .

So also shall you be an encouragement to many of your christian friends in your native country, to come to you, when they hear of your peace, the love and kindness that are amongst you.

But above all, it shall go well with your souls when that God of peace and unity shall come to visit you with death, as he hath done many of your associates, you being found of him not in murmurings, discontents, and jars, but in brotherly love. And

---

*What persons Cushman was here shooting at, I don't know. But some at Plymouth must have been putting on airs and pleading special privileges, for Cushman points up the subject again.

peace may be translated from this wandering wilderness unto that joyful and heavenly Canaan.

Amen.

In his "Epistle Dedicatory," signed at Plymouth and dated December 12, 1621, Cushman wrote:

It pertaineth not to my purpose to speak anything either in praise or dispraise of the country . . . And thus much I will say for the satisfaction of such as have any thought of going hither to inhabit:

That for men which have a large heart and look after great riches, ease, pleasures, dainties, and jollity in this world, . . . I would not advise them to come there, for as yet the country will afford no such matters.

But if there be any who are content to lay out their estates, spend their time, labors, and endeavors for the benefit of them that shall come after and in desire to further the gospel among those poor heathens, quietly contenting themselves with such hardships and difficulties as, by God's Providence, shall fall upon them, being yet young and in their strength, such men I would advise and encourage to go, for their ends cannot fail them . . .

And who so rightly considereth what manner of entrance, abiding, and proceedings we have had amongst these poor heathens since we came, will easily think that God has some great work to do towards them.

They were wont to be the most cruel and treacherous people in all these parts, even like lions. But to us, they have been like lambs, so kind, so submissive and trusty, as a man may truly say, many christians are not so kind nor sincere . . . And we, for our parts, through God's Grace, have with that equity, justice, and compassion carried ourselves towards them as that they have received much favor, help, and aid from us, but never the least injury or wrong by us* . . .

Our care hath been to maintain peace amongst them, . . . and when any of them are in want, as often they are in the

---

*"They offer us to dwell where we will."—Cushman's note.

winter when their corn is done, we supply them to our power
and have them in our houses eating and drinking and warming
themselves. Which thing (though it be something a trouble to
us), yet because they should see and take knowledge of our
labors, orders, and diligence both for this life and a better, we
are content to bear it.

And we find in many of them, especially of the younger sort,
such a tractable disposition both to religion and humanity as
that, if we had the means to apparel them and wholly to retain
them with us (as their desire is), they would doubtless in time
prove serviceable to God and man.

And if ever God send us means, we will bring up hundreds
of their children, both to labor and learning . . .

And you, my loving friends, the adventurers to this plantation, as your care has been first to settle religion here before
either profit or popularity, so, I pray you, go on to do it much
more. And be careful to send godly men, though they want some
of that worldly policy which this world hath in her own generation. So, though you lose, the Lord shall gain.

I rejoice greatly in your free and ready minds to your powers
—yea, and beyond your powers—to further this work, that you
thus honor God with your riches. And I trust you shall be repaid
again double and treble in this world, yea, and the memory of
this action will never die . . .

Be not therefore discouraged, for no labor is lost, nor money
spent, which is bestowed for God.

Your ends were good. Your success is good. And your profit
is coming, even in this life—and in the life to come, much
more . . .

5. Bradford's Defense of His Brethren

BRADFORD'S   This ship was speedily dispatch away, being
HISTORY   laden with good clapboard as full as she could
              stowe, and 2 hoggsheads of beaver and otter skins
which they had got with a few trifling commodities brought

with them at first, being altogeather unprovided for trade. Neither was there any amongst them that ever saw a beaver skin till they came here and were informed by Squanto.

The fraight was estimated to be worth near £500 [$25,000].*

Mr. Cushman returned backe also with this ship, for so Mr. Weston & ye rest had appoynted him, for their better information.

And he doubted not, nor themselves neither, but they should have a speedy supply, considering allso how by Mr. Cushman's perswation, and letters received from Leyden wherein they willed them so to doe, they yeelded to ye aforesaid conditions and subscribed them with their hands.

But it proved otherwise, for Mr. Weston, who had made that large promise in his letter, . . . that if all ye rest should fall off, yet he would never quit the bussines but stick to them if they yeelded to ye conditions and sente some lading in ye ship, and of this Mr. Cushman was confident . . .

But all proved but wind, for he was ye first and only man that forsooke them—and that before he so much as heard of ye returne of this ship, or knew what was done (so vaine is ye confidence in man). But more of this in its place.

A letter in answer to [Weston's] written to Mr. Carver was sent to him from ye Governor . . .

Sir:

Your large letter writen to Mr. Carver . . . I have received ye 10 of November, wherein (after ye apologie made for yourselfe) you lay many heavie imputations upon him and us all.

Touching him, he is departed this life, and now is at rest in ye Lord from all those troubles and incoumbrances with which we are yet to strive.

---

*This represented almost half of the money advanced by the merchant adventurers. Another such cargo and the Pilgrims would be free of debt. For the moment things looked very bright indeed.

Though landlubbers all, the Pilgrims had come to be fishermen. But fishing was "a thing always fatal to them," as Bradford later remarked. It was well for them that Squanto put them in the fur trade.

He needs not my appologie, for his care and pains was so great for ye commone good, both ours and yours, as that therewith (it is thought) he oppressed himselfe and shortened his days, of whose loss we cannot sufficiently complaine.

At great charges in this adventure I confess you have beene, and many losses may sustain. But ye loss of his and many other honest and industrious men's lives cannot be vallewed at any prise.

Of ye one, there may be hope of recovery. But ye other no recompence can make good . . .

You greatly blame us for keeping ye ship so long in ye countrie and then to send her away emptie. She lay 5 weeks at Cap-Codd whilst with many a weary step (after a long journey) and the indurance of many a hard brunte, we sought out in the foule winter a place of habitation.

Then we went in so tedious a time to make provision to shelter us and our goods, aboute which labour many of our armes & leggs can tell us to this day we were not necligent.

But it pleased God to visit us then with death dayly, and with so generall a disease that the living were scarce able to burie the dead . . .

And now to be so greatly blamed for not fraighting ye ship doth indeed goe near us and much discourage us. But you say you know we will pretend weaknes.

And doe you think we had not cause?

Yes, you tell us you beleeve it, but it was more weaknes of judgmente than of hands. Our weaknes herein is great, we confess. Therefore, we will bear this check patiently, amongst ye rest, till God send us wiser men.

But they which told you we spent so much time in discoursing & consulting, &c., their harts can tell their toungs they lie.

They cared not, so they might salve their owne sores, how they wounded others.

Indeed, it is our callamitie that we are (beyond expectation) yoked with some ill-conditioned people who will never doe good, but corrupte & abuse others, &c.

The rest of ye letter declared how they had subscribed those conditions according to his desire and sente him ye former accounts very perticulerly—also, how ye ship was laden, and in what condition their affairs stood, that ye coming of these people [without provisions] would bring famine upon them unavoydably if they had not supply in time (as Mr. Cushman could more fully informe him & ye rest of ye adventurers)—also, that seeing he was now satisfied in all his demands, that offences would be forgotten, and he remember his promise, &c. . . .

6. Winslow's Useful Advice

Smarting under Weston's sharp and sarcastic criticisms, the Pilgrims worked hard and fast in freighting the *Fortune*.

She was carrying, among other things, some manuscripts by Bradford, Winslow, and perhaps others, which related the adventures and excitements, as well as the trials and the tragedies, of the *Mayflower* voyage and the Pilgrims' first year at Plymouth. These were the manuscripts—or at least part of them—that soon came to publication as a *Relation, or Journall*, by "G: Mourt."

These papers included a letter already referred to, which was incorporated in *Mourt's Relation*—that of Edward Winslow, addressed to a "loving and old freind" in England. In this letter, obviously designed to attract new settlers, Winslow drew an over-pretty picture of the "great abundance" at Plymouth and offered "certaine usefull directions for such as intend a Vioage into those Parts":

MOURT'S RELATION   We have found the Indians very faithfull in their Covenant of Peace with us, very loving and ready to pleasure us . . . And we, for our parts, walk as peaceably and safely in the woods as in the highways of England. We entertain them familiarly in our houses; and they, as friendly, bestowing their venison on us.

They are a people without any religion or knowledge of God,[1] yet very trusty, quick of apprehension, ripe-witted, just.

The men and women go naked—only a skin about their middles.

For the temper of the air here, it agreeth well with that in England. If there be any difference at all, this is somewhat hotter in summer.

Some think it to be colder in winter, but I cannot out of experience so say.

The air is very clear and not foggy, as hath been reported. I never in my life remember a more seasonable year than we have here enjoyed. And if we once have but kine, horses, and sheep, I make no question but men might live as contented here as in any part of the world.

Of fish and fowle, we have great abundance. Fresh cod, in the summer, is but coarse meate with us. Our bay is full of lobsters all the summer, and affordeth other fish.

In September, we can take a hogshead of eels in a night with small labour, and can dig them out of their beds.

All the winter, we have mussels and clams at our doors. Oysters we have none near, but we can have them brought by the Indians when we will.

All the spring time, the earth sendeth forth naturally very good sallet herbs. Here are grapes, white and red, and very sweete & strong; strawberries, gooseberries, raspas [raspberries], &c; plums of three sortes, white, black, and red, being almost as good as a damson; abundance of roses, red, white, and damask, single but very sweet indeed.

The country wanteth only industrious men to employ . . .

These things I thought good to let you understand, being the truth of things, as near as I could experimentally take knowledge of, that you might in our behalfe give God thanks, who had dealt so favourably with us . . .

Now because I expect your coming unto us, with others of our friends whose company we much desire, I thought good to advertise you of a few things needful.

Be careful to have [on your ship] a very good Bread-room to put your biscuits in.

Let your casks for beer and water be ironbound for the first tyre [tier], if not more.

Let your meal be so hard trodd in your caske that you shall need an adze or hatchet to worke it out with.

Trust not too much on us for corne at this time, for, by reason of this last company that came, we shall have little enough till harvest.

Be carefull to come by [have access to] some of your meal to consume [eat] by the way. It will much refresh you . . .

Bring juice of lemons, and take it fasting. It is of good use.*

For hott waters, Anniseed Water is the best. But use it sparingly.

If you bring anything for comfort in the country, butter or sallet oil, or both, are very good.

Bring paper and linseed oil for your windows—with cotton yarn for your lamps . . .

Build your cabins as open as you can, and bring good store of clothes and bedding with you.

Bring every man a musket, or fowling piece. Let your piece be long in the barrel, and fear not the weight of it, for most of our shooting is from stands [sticks used as supports] . . .

Let your shot be most for big fowls. And bring store of powder and shott.

I forbear further to write for the present, hoping to see you by the next returne. So I take my leave, commending you to the Lord for a safe conduct unto us.

Resting in him,
Your loving friend,
E. W.

7. Pirates

The *Fortune*, with her treasure in furs and thirteen persons on board, bounded along without incident until she was near the English coast, where she was seized by a French privateer and taken to the Ile de Dieu, off the coast of Poitou, commanded by

*For scurvy and "ship's fever."

Monsieur le Marquis de Cera. The piratical marquis took everything of value on board, to the great loss of the Pilgrims and the
adventurers, and to the extreme anxiety and discomfort of Cushman and all on board, who protested in an official complaint,
making these charges:

COLONIAL
PAPERS*
That Monsieur de Cera kept Thomas Barton,
master of the ship, seven days close prisoner in
his castle, and the rest of the company under guard.
And commanded his soldiers to pillage them, who left them not
so much as a kettle to boil their meat in, nor a can to drink in.

That Monsieur de Cera took away the goods of the adventurers in beaver skins and other commodities to the value of £400
[$20,000] at least.

That he took away of the owners a new sheet cable, an
anchor, two murderers [small cannon] with their chambers,
eight calivers [hand guns] with bandileers, a flag, ensign, powder, shot, ropes, lines, and other instruments to the value of £50.

That he suffered his company to pillage the company.

That he took away all their apparel, not leaving some of them
a hat to their heads, nor a shoe to their feet, to the damage of £50
at least . . .

And having detained them thirteen days—and fed them with
lights, livers, and entrails, because he suffered his soldiers to eat
all their good victuals—at length he sent them aboard a little lean
flesh, a hogshead of small wine, some little bread and vinegar,
to victual them home.

But, withall, prepounded to them to testifie under their hands
that he had taken from them but two hogsheads of fox skins.†
Else, he said, they should not have their liberty.

The loss of the cargo on the ship struck both the Pilgrims and
the adventurers a stunning blow. In her way, the *Fortune* was as
ill-named as the *Speedwell*. The Pilgrims had much bad luck with
their ships.

*This document is ⅀112, in *S. P. Colonial*, Vol. V.
†The piratical marquis evidently did not know the difference between a beaver
and a fox skin.

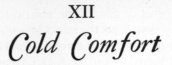

XII

. . . I fear you must stand on your leggs, and trust (as
they say) to God and yourselves.
                                        —*Thomas Weston*

BRADFORD'S
HISTORY
After ye departure of this ship, . . . the Governor and his Assistante, having disposed these late comers into severall families as they best could, tooke an exacte accounte of all their provissions in the store and proportioned ye same to ye number of persons, and found that it would not hold out above 6 months at halfe allowance—and hardly that!

And they could not well give less this winter time, till fish came in againe.

So they were presently put to half allowance, one as well as another, which began to be hard. But they bore it patiently under hope of supply.

Soon . . . , ye great people of ye Narigansets,* in a braving manner, sente a messenger unto them with a bundle of arrows, tyed aboute with a great sneak-skine, which their interpretours told them was a threatening, & a challenge.

Upon which, ye Governor, with ye advice of others, sente them a round answer, that if they had rather have warre than peace, they might begin when they would. They had done them no wrong. Neither did they fear them, . . .

And by another messenger sente ye sneake-skine back with bullits in it. But they would not receive it, and sente it back againe . . .

*This tribe lived on the western shore of Narragansett Bay and was "reported to be many thousands strong," wrote Winslow.

1. The Pale

BRADFORD'S
HISTORY But this made them ye more carefully to looke to themselves, so as they agreed to inclose their dwellings with a good strong pale [palisade, or stockade], and make flankers in convenient places, with gates to shutt, which were every night locked and a watch kept. And when need required, there was also warding in ye daytime.

And ye company was, by ye Captaine's and ye Governor's advise, devided into 4 squadrons. And every one had their quarter apoynted them, unto which they were to repaire upon any suddane alarme.

And if there should be any crie of fire, a company was appointed for a gard, with muskets, whilst others quenchet ye same, to prevent Indean treachery.

This was accomplished very cheerfully, and ye towne impayled round by ye beginning of March [1622], in which every family had a pretty garden plot secured.

Eleven feet high and almost a mile in circumference, the palisade was built of long poles driven into the ground and laced together at the top with tough wild vines. The "palizado" ran up from the beach along the north bank of Town Brook, around Fort Hill, and back down to the beach along the far side of the clearing.

2. First Christmas Ashore

BRADFORD'S
HISTORY On ye day called Christmas-day [with all laboring on the stockade], ye Governor called them out to worke (as was used). But ye most of this new company [from the *Fortune*] excused themselves, and said it wente against their conscience to work on that day.

So ye Governor told them that if they made it a matter of

conscience, he would spare them, till they were better informed.

So he led away ye rest and left them. But when they came home at noone from their worke, he found them in ye streete at play, openly—some pitching ye barr, & some at stoole-ball, and shuch like sports.

So he went to them and tooke away their implements, and told them that it was against his conscience that they should play & others worke.

If they made ye keeping of it a matter of devotion, let them keepe to their houses.

But there should be no gameing or revelling in ye street.

Since which time, nothing has been attempted that way—at least, openly.

In writing this last sentence some years later, Bradford might have added that it was a good thing that nothing of the sort had been attempted, openly or covertly.

The Pilgrims' attitude toward Christmas persisted at Plymouth until the nineteenth century. As late as 1820, anyone who celebrated the Yuletide in any way was frowned upon as a dread " 'Piscopal."

3. Squanto Plays His Own Game

BRADFORD'S HISTORY   At ye spring of ye year [1622], they had appointed ye Massachusets to come againe and trade with them, and begane now to prepare for that vioag about ye later end of March.

But upon some rumors heard, Hobomok, their Indean, tould them of some jealocies [suspicions] he had. He feared they were joyned with ye Narighansets and might betray them if they were not carefull.

He intimated also some jealocie of Squanto by what he gathered from some private whisperings betweene him and other Indeans.

But they resolved to proseede and sente their shallop with 10 of their cheefe men aboute ye beginning of Aprill, and both Squanto & Hobomok with them, in regarde to ye jealocie betweene them.

But they had not been gone longe but an Indean belonging to Squanto's family came running, in seeming great fear, and tould them that many of ye Narihgansets, . . . and he thought also Massasoit, were coming against them, and that he gott away to tell them, not without danger.

And being examined by ye Governour, he made as if they were at hand, and would still be looking back as if they were at his heels.

At which the Governor caused them to take armes & stand on their garde. And supposing ye boat to be still within hearing (by reason it was calme) caused a warning peece or 2 [cannon] to be shote off, the which they heard and came in.

But no Indeans appeared. Watch was kepte all night, but nothing was seene.

Hobomok was confidente for Massasoit, and thought all was false. Yet ye Governor caused him to send his wife privately [to Sowams] to see what she could observe (pretending other occasions). But there was nothing found, and all was quiet.

After this, they proseeded on their vioge to ye Massachusetts and had good trade, and returned in saftie, blessed be God.

But by these former passages and other things of like nature, they began to see that Squanto sought his owne ends, and plaid his owne game, by putting ye Indeans in fear, and drawing gifts from them to enrich himselfe, making them beleeve he could stir up warr against whom he would, & make peace for whom he would.

Yea, he made them beleeve they kept ye plague buried in ye ground and could send it amongst whom they would, which did much terrifie the Indeans, and make them depend more on him and seeke more to him than to Massasoit, which procured him envie and had like to have cost him his life.

GOOD
NEWES*

Here let me not omitte one notable though wicked practice of this Tisquantum, who (to the end he might possess his countrymen with the greater feare of us, and so consequentlie of him) told them we had the plague buried in our storehouse, which, at our pleasure, we could send forth to what place or people we would and destroy them therewith, though we stirred not from home.

Being . . . sente for by the Governor to this place where Hobomok was and some other of us, the ground being broke in the midst of the house whereunder certaine barrels of powder were buried (though unknown to him), Hobomok asked him what it meant?

To whom he readilie answered, That was the place wherein the plague was buried, whereof he formerly told him and others.

After this, Hobomok asked one of our people whether such a thing were? And whether we had such command of it?

Who answered, No, but the God of the English had it in store and could send it at his pleasure, to the destruction of his and our enemies.

The English were as credulous as the Indians. And Squanto had not been so far wrong. Gunpowder was a "plague" to the Indians.

4. Massasoit Scowls

GOOD
NEWES

[Returning from Massachusetts Bay], we found Massasoit at the Plantation, . . . being much offended and inraged against Tisquantum, whom the Governor pacified as much as he could for the presente.

But not long after his departure, he sent a messenger to the Governor, intreating him to give way to the death of Tisquantum, who had so much abused him.

But the Governor answered, although he had deserved to die both in respect of him and us, yet for our sakes he desired he

*Good Newes from New England (1624), by Edward Winslow—hereafter, Good Newes.

would spare him—and the rather because without him he knew not well how to understand Massasoit or any other of the Indians.

With this answer the messenger returned, but came again not long after, accompanied with divers others, [bringing the chief's demand for Squanto] as being one of his subjects, whom by our first Articles of Peace we could not retaine.

Yet because he would not willingly do it without the Governor's approbation, [the messengers] offered him many beavers' skins for his consent thereto, saying that, according to their manner, their sachem had sent his own knife and they therewith to cut off his head and hands, and bring them to him.

To which the Governor answered, it was not the manner of the English to sell men's lives at a price . . . and therefore refused their beavers as a gift.

But he sent for Tisquantum, who, though he knew their intent, yet offered not to fly, but came and accused Hobomok as the author and worker of his overthrow, yielding himself to the Governor to be sente or not, according as he thought meet.

But at the instant when our Governor was ready to deliver him into the hands of his executioners, a boat was seen at sea to cross before our town and fall behind a headland not far off.

Whereupon, having heard many rumours of the French and not knowing whether there were any combination between the salvages and them, the governor told the Indians he would first know what boat that was, ere he would deliver him into their custody.

But being mad with rage, and impatient at delay, they departed in great heate.

5. Bad News from the Eastward

BRADFORD'S HISTORY The boat proved a shallop which came from a ship which Mr. Weston & another had set out a-fishing at a place called Damarins-cove,* 40 leagues to ye eastward of them . . . This boat brought 7 pas-

*Damariscove Island, off the Maine coast.

sengers, and some letters. But no vitails, nor any hope of any. Some part of which letters I shall set downe:

London
Jan: 12, 1622

Mr. Carver:

In my last letters by ye *Fortune*, in whom Mr. Cushman wente and who, I hope, is with you, for we daly expect ye ship back again. She departed hence . . . not over well provided with necessaries, by reason of ye parsemonie of ye adventurers.

I had solisited them to send a supply of men and provisions before she came. They all answer they will do great matters when they hear good news—nothing before. So faithfull, constant, & carefull of your good are your olde & honest freinds that if they hear not from you, they are like to send no supplie, &c.

I am now to relate ye occasion of sending this ship [the *Sparrow*], hoping if you give credit to my words, you will have a more favorable opinion of it than some here, who taxed me with minding my owne ends, which is in part true, &c.

Mr. Beauchamp and myselfe bought this little ship and have set her out—partly, if it may be, to uphold* ye plantation, as well as doe others good as ourselves; and partly, to gett back what we are formerly out, though we are otherwise censured, &c.

This is ye occasion we have sent this ship and these [seven] passengers on our owne account, whom we desire you will frendly entertaine & supply with such necessaries as you can spare, and they wante, &c.

And among other things, we pray you to lend or sell them some seed corne. And if you have ye salt remaining of ye last year, that you will let them have it for their present use, and we will either pay you for it, or give you more when we have our salt-pan to worke, which we desire may be set up in one of ye little islands in your bay . . .

Some of ye adventurers have sent you herewith some direc-

*"I know not which way."—Bradford's note.

tions for your furtherance in ye commone bussines, who are like
those St. James speaks of, that bid their brother eat and warme
himself, but give him nothing. So they bid you make salt, and
uphold the plantation. But send you no means wherewithall to
doe it . . .

I find ye generall so backward and your freinds at Leyden so
cold that I fear you must stand on your leggs, and trust (as they
say) to God and yourselves.

Your loving freind,
Tho: Weston

Sundry other things I pass over, being tedious & impertinent.

All this was but cold comfort to fill their hungrie bellies and
a slender performance of his late promiss. And as little did it
either fill or warme them as those ye Apostle James spake of, by
him before mentioned.

And well might it make them remember what ye psalmist
saith, Psa. 118. 8. *It is better to trust in the Lord than have confidence in man*. And Psa. 146. *Put not your trust in princes*
(much less in ye marchants), *nor in ye sonne of man, for there
is no help in them* . . .

And as they were now fayled of supply by him and others in
this their greatest neede and wante, which was caused by him
and ye rest who put so great a company of men upon them as
ye former company were, without any food, and came at such
a time as they must live almost a whole year before any could
be raised . . . , so, upon ye pointe, they never had any supply
of vitales more afterwards (but what the Lord gave them otherwise), for all ye company sent at any time was allways too short
for those people that came with it . . .

Yet they tooke compassion on those 7 men [from the *Sparrow*] . . . and gave them as good as any of their owne, . . .
who might have starved if ye plantation had not succoured them.

6. Aid beyond Expectation

BRADFORD'S HISTORY   Amidst these streights, and ye desertion of those from whom they had hoped for supplies, and when famine began now to pinch them sore, they not knowing what to doe, the Lord (who never fails his) presents them with an occasion, beyond all expectation.

This boat which came from the eastward brought them a letter from a stranger, of whose name they had never heard before, being a captaine of a ship come there a-fishing . . .

To all his good freinds at Plimoth, these, &c.
Freinds, cuntrimen, & neighbours:
I salute you, and wish you all health and hapines in ye Lord. I make bould with these few lines to trouble you because, unless I were unhumane, I can doe no less.

Bad news doth spread itselfe too far. Yet I will so farr informe you that myselfe, with many good freinds in ye south colonie of Virginia, have received such a blow that 400 persons large will not make good our losses.*

Therefore, I doe intreat you (allthough not knowing you) that ye old rule which I learned when I went to schoole may be sufficient—that is, Hapie is he whom other men's harmes doth make to beware.

And now againe and againe, wishing all those that willingly

---

*This was an oblique reference to the fearful massacre that had occurred in Virginia just a few months before—on Good Friday, March 22, 1622—when the great Opechancano, Powhatan's younger brother and successor, and his braves took the settlers along the James quite by surprise and, almost at one stroke, slaughtered 347 men, women, and children.

Apparently friendly, they had been sitting that morning in the planters' houses when suddenly, at the stroke of eight, they struck, seizing the planters' own weapons to destroy them and their families, killing one out of four in the colony, razing all chief settlements except Jamestown, which escaped by a providential last-minute warning.

As many Indians frequented Plymouth and Massasoit was still angry at Bradford's refusal to surrender Squanto to have his head and hands chopped off, the Pilgrims took the warning to heart.

would serve ye Lord all health and happines in this world and everlasting peace in ye world to come. And so I rest.

Yours,
John Hudlston*

By this boat ye Governor returned a thankfull answer, as was meete, and sent a boate of their own with them, . . . in which Mr. Winslow was sente to procure what provissions he could of ye ships, who was kindly received by ye foresaid gentill-man, who not only spared what he could, but writ to others to doe ye like.†

By which means he gott some good quantitie and returned in saftie, by which ye plantation had a duble benefitte—first, a present refreshing by ye food brought; and secondly, they knew ye way to those parts for their benefitte hereafter.

But what was gott, & this small boat brought, being devided among so many, came but to a little.

Yet, by God's blessing, it upheld them till harvest.

It arose but to a quarter of a pound of bread a day to each person, and ye Governor caused it to be dayly given them.

*Or rather, John Huddleston, who had been to Virginia many times, being one of the captains regularly employed by the Virginia Company. He had come to fish New England waters to help relieve the famine of those who had survived the massacre along the James.

From the phrases used in expressing his religious attitudes, Huddleston would appear to have been an extreme Puritan or even a Separatist, as his further kindness also seems to indicate.

Huddleston was a close friend of Sir Edwin Sandys, leader of the Virginia Company, who had been so sympathetic in trying to forward the plans of the Green Gate Congregation. It was perhaps through Sandys that Huddleston came to take a friendly interest in the settlement at Plymouth. Except for the remarkable kindness and generosity of this "stranger," the Pilgrims would have perished, as they themselves confessed.

†Good Newes—"[Huddleston and the other captains] would not take bills for the same, but did what they could freely, wishing their store had been such as they might in greater measure have expressed their owne love and supplied our necessities, for which they sorrowed, provoking one another to the utmost of their abilities . . .

"Having dispatched there, I returned home with all speede convenient, where I found the state of the colonie much weaker than when I lefte it, for till now we were never without some bread—the wante whereof much abated the strength and flesh of some, and swelled others."

Otherwise, had it been in their owne custody, they would have eate it up & then starved.

But thus, with what els they could get, they made pretie shift till corne was ripe.

7. The Fort

GOOD
NEWES
In the time of these straits, . . . the Indians began againe to cast many insulting speeches, glorying in our weakness and giving out how easy it would be, ere long, to cut us off.

Now also Massasoit seemed to frown on us, and neither came or sent to us as formerly.

These things occasioned further thoughts of fortification . . .

BRADFORD'S
HISTORY
This sommer, they builte a fort with good timber, both strong & comly, which was of good defence, made with a flat roofe & batllments, on which their ordnance were mounted, and where they kepte constante watch, espetially in time of danger. It served them allso for a meeting house and was fitted accordingly for that use.*

It was a great worke for them in this weaknes and time of wants. But ye deanger of ye time required it. And both ye continuall rumors of ye fears from ye Indeans here, espetially ye Narigansets, and also ye hearing of that great massacre in Virginia, made all hands willing to despatch ye same.

8. Plymouth's Second Harvest

BRADFORD'S
HISTORY
Now ye wellcome time of harvest approached, in which all had their hungrie bellies filled.
But it arose but to a little in comparison to a full year's supplie—partly, by reason they were not yet well

---

*It served them not only as a fort and meetinghouse but as a statehouse and jail for many years.

acquainted with ye manner of Indean corne (and they had no other); allso, their many other imployments, but cheefly their weaknes for wante of food to tend it as they should have done.

Also, much was stolne both by night & day before it became scarce eatable, & much more afterward.

And though many were well whipt (when they were taken) for a few ears of corne, yet hunger made others (whom conscience did not restraine) to venture.

So it well appeared that famine must still insue ye next year allso, if not some way prevented, or supplie should faile, to which they durst not trust.

Markets there were none to goe to, but only ye Indeans, and they [at Plymouth] had no trading commodities.

9. A Pirate as Providence

BRADFORD'S HISTORY

Behold now, another providence of God: a ship comes into ye harbor, one Captain Jons being cheefe therein . . .

This ship had store of English beads (which were then good trade) and some knives, but would sell none but at dear rates, and also a good quantitie togeather.

Yet they were glad of ye occasion and faine to buy at any rate. They were faine to give after the rate of cento per cento, if not more, and pay away coat beaver at 3s [$7.50] per pound, which a few years after yeelded 20s [$50].

But by this means they were fitted againe to trade for beaver & other things, and intended to buy what corne they could . . .

GOOD NEWES

And had not the Allmighty, in his all-ordering Providence, directed him to us, it would have gone worse with us than ever it had been, or ever after was, for, . . . in want of supply, we were worne out of all manner of trucking stuffe, not having any meanes lefte to help ourselves by trade.

This ship was the *Discovery*. Homeward bound from Virginia, she had been unsuccessful in a fur-trading expedition. This explains why she had on board, providentially, such a store of knives, beads, and trinkets for the Indian trade. As events proved, the Pilgrims would have starved if she had been carrying a more general cargo.

In gouging the Pilgrims and charging them piratical rates for his "stuffe," the skipper of the ship was acting in character, it seems, for he was an old hand at piracy.

In 1617, he had been in trouble with the powerful East India Company for plundering some of its ships in the Far East. Nor had he reformed. In 1625, three years after his chance visit to Plymouth, Captain Jones put into Jamestown with a Spanish vessel in tow, saying that he had taken her as a prize in the Caribbean.

This was bad enough. But it also appeared that he had been plundering English ships as well. The Virginia authorities ordered an investigation. But Captain Jones soon died, which ended the inquiry.

Merely on the basis of name, it was confidently asserted for centuries that this "Captain Jons," christened Thomas, was the same Captain Jones who had been master of the *Mayflower*—that the latter had visited Plymouth again and ended his career flying the Jolly Roger.

This could not be disproved, for no one knew the Christian name or the subsequent career of the kindly skipper of the *Mayflower* until 1902, when a scholar, turning over the musty records of the British Admiralty, discovered that his name was Christopher, not Thomas, and that he had gone to his grave months before the *Discovery* dropped anchor at Plymouth.

Though he died soon after his return from carrying over the first Pilgrim company, probably another victim of that first awful winter at Plymouth, the story still runs that Captain Christopher Jones was the piratical master of the *Discovery*, an intermittent flyer of the Skull and Crossbones.

10. John Pory

BRADFORD'S
HISTORY
There was in this ship a gentle-man by name of Mr. John Poory [Pory]. He had been secretarie in Virginia and was now going home passenger in this ship. After his departure, he writ a letter to ye Governor, in ye postscripte whereof he hath these lines:

[P.S.] To yourselfe and Mr. Brewster I must acknowledge my-selfe many ways indebted, whose books I would have you thinke very well bestowed on him who esteemeth them shuch juells.

My haste would not suffer me to remember (much less to begg) Mr. Ainsworth's elaborate worke upon ye 5 books of Moyses.*

Both his & Mr. Robinson's doe highly comend the authors as being most conversante in ye scriptures of all others.

And what good (who knows) it may please God to worke by them through my hands (though most unworthy), who finds shuch high contente in them.

God have you all in his keeping.

Your unfained and firme freind,

John Pory

Aug. 28, 1622

These things I here inserte for honour sake of ye author's memorie, which this gentleman doth thus ingeniously acknowl-edge. And himselfe, after his returne, did this poore plantation much credite amongst those of no mean ranck.

An indefatigable "gossip," one of the best and most amusing letter writers of his day, Pory had had an interesting career. He

---

Annotations upon the Fourth Book of Moses, called Numbers, by Henry Ainsworth, their old friend of Amsterdam days, "teacher" of the Ancient Brethren, whose *Book of Psalmes* the Pilgrims were using. After the split in the Ancient Brethren, the Ainsworthians obtained possession of the meetinghouse in the Bruinistengange (Brownists Alley) and were still meeting there, as they continued to do for almost eighty years. Ainsworth's church outlived Robin-son's by a half century.

had shown much promise as a young man, becoming a protégé of
the great Richard Hakluyt, who guided his studies in "cosmog-
raphie and foreign histories." Having published a work on Africa, which was well received, Pory then served five or six years
in the House of Commons before crossing to the Continent,
where he spent some time, traveling widely as far east as Turkey.

In the process Pory became something of a problem to his host
of friends, many being among the most exalted in the realm, for
even in those days of gargantuan appetites he was celebrated as
a trencherman and a tosspot. He was forever getting into scrapes,
and his friends were called upon time and again to recue him from
a debtor's prison or worse.

Once, when he was "in pawn" in Italy, one of his friends wrote
others to ask them to contribute to his relief, saying that poor
John Pory was sadly in need of meat and money, "for drink he
will find out for himself, if it be above ground, or no deeper than
the cellar."

Returning to England, Pory was penniless as usual. In 1618,
through the influence of friends, he was offered the post of sec-
retary-recorder in Virginia, to succeed John Rolfe, who was in
disfavor for suspected complicity in the depredations of Governor Samuel Argall, who had ruthlessly looted the colony.

Pory was interested. But when he asked the officers of the Virginia Company what allowance he would get for his voyage and
what salary or fees he might expect to receive at Jamestown, they
were "as dry as Pumystones, which is the reason I mean not to
adventure my carcase in so dangerous a business for nothing."

When the new governor, Sir George Yeardley, promised to
make his new post worth at least £200 ($10,000) a year,* Pory
accepted, provided Yeardley would lend him £50 to outfit himself for the voyage.

Soon after his arrival in Virginia, Pory had the honor of being
chosen Speaker of the first representative assembly to meet on
our shores—on July 30, 1619, a day to be remembered—when
Governor Yeardley, the members of the Council, and the duly
elected Burgesses, together constituting the General Assembly,

---

*Bradford was not receiving a penny as governor. It was not until 1633 that
the governor was paid anything, and then his salary was set at £20 ($1,000) a
year.

met in the church at Jamestown, sitting in the "Quire" in want of a better place, and there adopted the Great Charter and began some measure of self-government.*

But Pory was now in disfavor and on his way home, having been rather curtly dismissed from his post. He had been caught in "duble-dealing," working behind the back of Sir Edwin Sandys, the head of the Virginia Company. He was also charged with being the "carver" of his own fortune by charging the planters intolerable fees for registering deeds and performing other routine duties.

It would be interesting and amusing to know what this aging roué, now in his fifties, talked about with Bradford and Brewster. The latter may have tried to reform him, as Pory's postscript implies. If he was seriously interested in discussing Ainsworth, Robinson, the Holy Discipline, and other works of the Separation, it was the only time in his life that he showed any concern for such matters.

Perhaps he was just pulling someone's leg, at which he was a master hand, and was genially repaying his hosts for their hospitality by telling them what they wished to hear, that these Separatist works, through his hands, "though most unworthy," might do "good (who knows)."

One of Pory's close friends and frequent correspondents was Sir Dudley Carleton, the English ambassador at The Hague, who had led the man hunt for that "seditious" printer, the elusive "Mr. B." Pory must have known something about this, and probably he and Brewster enjoyed a good laugh together at Sir Dudley's discomfiture.

In any case, this man of the world and the Saints got on very well together and, as Bradford noted, he always spoke well of them. Shortly after his return home, he wrote a letter in praise of them to the Earl of Southampton, head of the Virginia Company.

*This occurred almost a year and a half before the Pilgrims held their first assembly on the deck of the *Mayflower* and adopted the Mayflower Compact.

11. Plymouth in 1622

PORY'S
LETTER*
By whome this new Plimouth . . . is now pres-
entlie inhabited, your Lordshipp and the honorable
Companie do know better than myselfe . . .

[After the Pilgrims' first wanderings on Cape Cod], it pleased Almightie God (who had better provided for them than their owne hearts could imagine) to plant then upon the seate of an old towne, which divers [years] before had been abandoned by the Indians. So they both quietlie and justlie sate downe without either dispossessing anie of the natives, or being resisted by them, and without shedding so much as one drop of blood.

Which felicitie of theirs is confirmed unto them even by the voyces of the salvages themselves, . . . so that the right of those Planters to it is altogether unquestionable—a favour which, since the first discoverie of America, God hath not vouchsafed, so far as ever I could learne, upon anie Christian nations within that Continent . . .

And to describe to your Lordshipp the excellencie of the place: first, the harbour is not only pleasant for aire and prospect, but most sure for shipping, both small and greate, being land-locked on all sides.

The towne is seated on the ascent of a hill, which, besides the pleasure of variable objects entertaining the unsatisfied eye, such is the wholesomenes of the place (as the Governor told me) that for the space of one whole yeare, of the two wherein they had beene there, dyed not one man, woman, or child.

This healthfulnes is accompanied with much plentie, both of fish and fowle, everie day in the year,† as I know no place in the world that can match it.

In March, the eels come forth out of places where they lie bedded all winter, into the fresh streames and thence into the

---

*From Champlin Burrage's *John Pory's Lost Description of Plymouth* (1918).
†This was mightily extravagant, as the hungry Pilgrims could have told him.

sea, and in their passages are taken in pots. In September, they
runne out of the sea into the fresh streames to bed themselves
in the ground all winter, and are taken againe in pots as they
returne homewards.

In winter, the inhabitants digge them up,* being bedded in
gravell not above two or three foote deep. And all the rest of
the yeare, they may take them in pots in the salt water of the
bay.

They are passing sweete, fat, and wholesome, having no taste
at all of mudd, and are as greate as ever I saw anie.

In Aprill & May come up another kinde of fish—which they
call herring, or old wives—in infinite skulls [schools] into a small
river running under the towne [Town Brook], . . . the water
of the sayd river being in manie places not above halfe a foote
deepe. Yea, when a heape of stones is reared up against them a
foote high above the water, they leape and tumble over, and will
not be beaten backe with cudgels . . .

The inhabitants during the sayd two moneths take them up
everie day in hogsheads. And with those they eate not, they
manure the ground, burying 2 or 3 in each hill of corne.† And
[they] may, when they are able, if they see cause, lade whole
ships with them . . .

Into another river some two miles to the north-east of
Plymouth, all the moneth of May the great smelts passe up to
spawne in troupes innumerable, which, with a scoupe, or a
boule, or a peece of bark, a man may cast up upon the banke.

About midway come into the harbour the manie skulls of
basse and blew fish, which they take with skaines [seines]—some
fishes of a foote and a halfe, some of two foote, and some of 3
foote long; and with hookes, those of 4 and 5 foote long. They
enter also at flowing water [high tide] up into the small creeks,
at the mouths whereof the inhabitants, spreading their nets, have
caught 500 and 700 at a time. These continue good May, June,
Julie, and August.

*As Squanto had taught them.
†Again, as Squanto had taught them.

Now, as concerning the blew fish, in delicacie it excelleth all kinds of fish that ever I tasted—I except not the salmon of the Thames in his prime season, nor anie other fish.*

We called it by a compound name of blacke, white, blew, sweete, fat—the skinne and skale, blew; the flesh next under the scale, for an inch, deepe blacke and as sweete as the marrow of an oxe; the residue of the flesh underneath, purelie white, fat, and of a taste requiring noe addition of sauce.

By which allureing qualities it may seeme dangerouslie tending to a sarfeit. But we found by experience that, having satisfied and, in a manner, glutted ourselves therewith, it proved wholesome unto us and most easie of digestion.

In the same bay, lobsters are in season during the 4 moneths—so large, so full of meate, and so plentifull in number as no man will beleeve that hath not seene. For a knife of 3 halfe pence, I bought 10 lobsters that would well have dined 40 labouring men. And the least boy in the shippe, with an houre's labour, was able to feed the whole companie with them for two dayes . . .

Muskles and slammes [mussels and clams] they have all the yeare long, . . . being the meanest of God's blessings here and such as these people fat their hogs with at a low water, [which] if ours upon an extremitie did enjoy in the South Colonie, they would never complain of famine or want, although they wanted bread . . .

From the begining of September till the end of March, the bay, in a manner, is covered with all sorts of water fowle in such sort of swarmes and multitudes as is rather admirable than credible.†

The reasons of their continuall plentie for those 7 moneths in the yeare may be the continuall tranquillitie of the place, being guarded on all sides from the furie of stormes; as also, the abun-

*From such a gourmand and gourmet, who had sampled dishes all over Europe in the highest, gayest, and most sybaritic circles, this was high praise indeed for *Pomatomus saltatrix*, New England's "blew" fish.

†Pory was here again rather stretching himself, as he evidently knew, it appears, from his ring on the word "credible."

dance of food they finde at low water, the bottome of the bay then appearing as a greene meadow . . . And therefore this bay is such a pond for fowle as, in any man's knowledge of our nation that hath seene it, all America hath not the like . . .

Touching their fruite, I will not speake of their meaner sort— as of raspes [raspberries], cherries, gooseberries, strawberries, delicate plumbes, and others. But they have commonly, through the country, 5 severall sorts of grapes, some whereof I have tasted, being fairer and larger than anie I ever saw in the South Colonie, but of a muskadell taste, which, being transplanted, would prosper better in the south* . . .

In this land (as in other parts of this maine) they have plentie of deere and of turkies, as large and as fat as in anie other place. So much for the wholsemnes and plentie of the countrie.

Now, as concerning the qualities of the people, how happie were it for our people in the Southern Colonie if they were as free from wickednes and vice as these are in this place!

And their industrie as well appeareth by their building—as by a substantiall pallisado about their [towne], of 2,700 foote in compasse, stronger than I have seen anie in Virginia.

And lastlie, by a blockhouse, which they have erected in the highest place of the towne to mount their ordinance upon, from whence they may commaund all the harbour.

As touching their correspondencie with the Indians, they are freinds with all their neighbours . . . One thing which made them to be much respected was the revenge which they attempted in the night upon Combotant [Corbitant], . . . because they were (though falselie) informed that he had slaine Tisquanto, Sir Ferdinando Gorges' Indian, who lived as their servant under their protection, interpreting the injurie done to him as done to themselves.

Besides, when Tisquanto was earnestlie required to be sent home by the greate king, they chose rather to hazard a falling

---

*For more than ten years, to the neglect of essentials, Virginia had been vainly trying to establish a wine industry.

out with him than to breake their faith and promise with
Tisquanto, who had been sure to have gone to the pot if they
had delivered him up.

Which fayth and courage of theirs hath made other distracted
Indians to retire themselves into their protection, of whose la-
bour and service they have made good use, but especiallie of
Tisquanto's . . .

I have one great designe—namelie, to finde out what Sea that
is which the Frenchmen put downe in their cards [charts] to
west in 40 degrees over against the bottome of the sayd bay,
whether or no an inlett of the South Sea.

From the start, driven by the delusions and directions of the
managers of the enterprise at home, Virginia had been distracted
by hopes of finding gold, pearl, and the South Sea. Almost a half
century after Pory wrote of Plymouth, Virginians were still
hopefully seeking the South Sea, convinced that it lay only a few
hundred miles to the westward.

As a result of such distracting objectives, dictated by those at
home who knew nothing about the country, the colonists along
the James had never yet planted enough corn, relying upon uncertain supplies from London. That frightful winter of 1609–10,
when nine out of ten died and the surviving "anatomies" could
scarcely crawl from their beds, was well named the Starving
Time.

But all of Virginia's years up to this time had been one long
starving time, filled with agony, death, and frustration, as the
Virginia Company piled distraction upon distraction, ordering
the colonists to get on with wineworks, ironworks, silkworks,
and saltworks.

After fifteen years, Virginia had achieved no more security
and permanence than Plymouth in little more than a year and a
half.

Though they never gave thanks for them, among the greatest
blessings the Pilgrims enjoyed were these: that from the first they
were forced to be on their own, not relying upon aid from any
quarter; that they had to dig in if they were to sustain themselves;
that they were not distracted by directives from home, by the

vagaries of absentee management, so that they could direct their energies as seemed best to them.

Though the Pilgrims bitterly complained of it, Weston's desertion of them was really a godsend, for it left them free to manage their affairs and govern themselves as they saw fit.

And their judgments in this were good, as time proved.

XIII

Intruders

As for Mr. Weston's company, I thinke them so base in condition (or ye most parte) as, in all apearance, not fitt for an honest man's company.

—*John Pierce*

GOOD
NEWES
In the end of June or beginning of July [1622] came into our harbour two ships of Master Weston's—the one called the *Charity;* the other, the *Swan*—having in them some fifty or sixty men sente over at his charge to plant for him.

These we received in our town, affording them whatsoever courtesy our mean condition could afford. There, the *Charity,* being the bigger ship, left them, having many passengers which she was to land in Virginia.

In the meane time, the body of them refreshed themselves at Plymouth whilst some, most fit, sought out a place for them. The little store of corne we had was exceedinglie wasted by the unjuste and dishonest walking of these strangers, who though they would sometimes seem to helpe us in our labour aboute our corne, yet spared not, day and night, to steal the same—it being then eatable and pleasant to taste, though green and unprofitable.

And though they received much kindness, set light both by it and us, not sparing to requite the love we shewed them with secret backbitings, revilings, &c.

1. Weston's Desertion

London
Aprill 10, 1622

Mr. Bradford, these, &c:
     The *Fortune* is arrived, of whose good news touching your estate & proceedings I am very glad to hear.

And howsoever she was robbed on ye way by ye Frenchmen, yet I hope your loss will not be great, for ye conceite of so great a returne doth much animate ye adventurers, so that I hope some matter of importance will be done by them, &c.

As for myselfe, I have sold my adventure & debts unto them, so as I am quit of you, & you of me, for that matter.

Now, though I have nothing to pretend as an adventurer amongst you, yet I will advise you a little for your good, if you can apprehend it.

I perceive & know as well as another ye dispositions of your adventurers, whom ye hope of gaine hath drawne on to this they have done. And yet I fear that hope will not draw them much furder.

Besides, *most of them are against ye sending of them of Leyden, for whose cause this bussines was first begun.* And some of ye most religious (as Mr. Greene by name) excepts against them.

So that my advice is (you may follow it if you please), that you forthwith break off your joynte stock, which you have warente to doe both in law & conscience, for ye most parte of ye adventurers have given way to it by a former letter . . .

But I shall leave you to your discretion.

I desired diverce of ye adventurers, as Mr. Peirce, Mr. Greene, & others, if they had anything to send you, either vitails or letters, to send them by these ships.

And marvelling they sent not so much as a letter, I asked our passengers what letters they had. And with some difficultie, one of them told me he had one, which was delivered him with great charge of secrecie. And for more securitie, [he had been instructed] to buy a paire of new shoes & sow it betweene ye soles for fear of intercepting.

I, taking ye letter, wondering what misterie might be in it, broke it open and found this treacherous letter subscribed by ye hands of Mr. Pickering & Mr. Greene, which letter, had it come to your hands without answer, might have caused ye hurt, if not ye ruine, of us all.

For assuredly, if you had followed their instructions and shewed us that unkindness which they advise you unto, to hold us in distruste as enimies, &c., it might have been an occasion to have set us togeather by ye eares, to ye distruction of us all . . .

2. Beware! Beware!

Though angry and feeling much abused, Weston forwarded the intercepted letter in which several of the adventurers charged that Weston would allow no letters to go on his ships. These adventurers warned the Pilgrims against the company he had sent out, led by his younger brother Andrew. The latter was "a heady yong man, & violente," they said, "and set against you there & ye company here, plotting with Mr. Weston their owne ends, which tend to your & our undoing." This was confirmed by another secret and more reliable source.

BRADFORD'S   For after the receit of ye former letters, the
HISTORY   Governor received one from Mr. Cushman, who
went home in ye ship [*Fortune*] and was allways intimate with Mr. Weston (as former passages declare). And it was much marvelled that nothing was heard from him all this while.

But it should seeme it was ye difficulty of sending, for this letter was directed as ye letter of a wife to her husband, who was here, and brought by him to ye Governor.

It was as followeth:

Beloved Sir:

I hartily salute you, with trust of your health and many thanks for your love.

By God's providence, we got well home ye 17 of Feb., being robbed by ye Frenchmen by ye way and carried by them into France, and were kepte there 15 days and lost all that we had that was worth the taking. But thanks to God, we escaped with our lives & ship.

I see not that it worketh any discouragment here. I purpose, by God's grace, to see you shortly. I hope in June nexte, or before.

In ye mean space, know these things and, I pray you, be advertised a little.

Mr. Weston hath quite broken off from our company through some discontents that arose betwext him and some of our adventurers, & hath sold all his adventures, & hath now sent 3 small ships for his perticuler plantation . . . And he, with ye rest, purposeth to come himselfe—for what end, I know not.

The people which they carry are no men for us. Wherefore, I pray you, entertaine them not. Neither exchainge man for man with them, excepte it be some of your worst . . .

If they offer to buy anything of you, let it be such as you can spare, and let them give ye worth of it. If they borrow anything of you, let them leave a good pawne . . .

I fear these people will hardly deale so well with ye savages as they should. I pray you, therefore, signifie to Squanto that they are a distincte body from us, and we have nothing to doe with them. Neither must [we] be blamed for their falts, much less can warrente their fidelitie . . .

Our friends at Leyden are well and will come to you, as many as can, this time . . .

And ye Lord God of sea & land bring us comfortably togeather againe, if it may stand with his glorie.

Yours,
Robert Cushman

On the other side of ye leafe in ye same letter, came these few lines from Mr. John Pierce, in whose name the patente was taken . . .

Worthy Sir:

I desire you to take into consideration that which is written on ye other side, and not any way to damnifie your owne collony . . .

But as for Mr. Weston's company, I thinke them so base in condition (for ye most parte) as in all appearance not fitt for an honest man's company. I wish they prove otherwise.

My purpose is not to enlarge myselfe, but cease in these few lines, and so rest,

Your loving freind,
John Pierce

3. An Unwelcome Rival

GOOD
NEWES
At length, their coasters [Weston's explorers and surveyors] returned, having found in their judgmente a place fit for plantation within the Bay of Massachusetts, at a place called by the Indeans, Wichagucusett.*

To which place, the body of them wente with all conveniente speed, leaving still with us such as were sicke and lame—by the Governor's permission, though on their parts undeserved—whom our surgeon [Deacon Fuller] recovered gratis for them, and they fetched home as occasion warranted.

They had not been longe from us ere the Indians filled our ears with clamours against them for stealing their corne, and other abuses conceived by them.

At which we greeved the more . . . But we knew no means to redress those abuses save reproofe, and advising them to better walking, as occasion served . . .

In the end of September or beginning of October [1622]

*Or rather, Wessagusset, now part of the city of Weymouth.

Master Weston's bigger ship, called the *Charity*, returned for England and left their colonie sufficiently victualed . . . The lesser, called the *Swan*, remained with his colony for further help . . .

BRADFORD'S HISTORY   Shortly after harvest, Mr. Weston's people, who were now seated at ye Massachusetts and by disorder (as it seems) had made havock of their provissions, began now to perceive that want would come upon them. And hearing that they here had bought trading comodities & intended to trade for corne, they writ to ye Governor and desired they might joyne with them, and they would imploy their small ship [the *Swan*] in ye servise, and furder requested either to lend or sell them so much of their trading comodities as their part might come to, and they would undertake to make paymente when Mr. Weston or their supply came.

The Governor condescended upon equall terms of agreemente, thinking to goe aboute ye Cape to ye southward with ye ship, where some store of corne might be got.

4. Loss of Squanto

BRADFORD'S HISTORY   All things being provided, Captain Standish was appointed to goe with them [in the Pilgrim shallop], and Squanto for a guide & interpreter . . .

But ye winds put them in againe. And putting out ye second time, [Standish] fell sick of a feavor.

So ye Governour wente himselfe. But they could not get aboute ye shoals of Cap-Cod for flats & breakers. Neither could Squanto direct them any better, nor ye master [of the *Swan*] durst venture any further, so they put into Manamoyack Bay,* and got what they could there.

In this place Squanto fell sicke of an Indean feavor, bleeding

*Or rather, Monomoy, at the elbow of the Cape, on its ocean side, in what is now the township of Chatham. It was here that the *Mayflower* had encountered the "deangerous shoulds and roring breakers" that presumably forced her to reverse her course.

much at ye nose (which ye Indeans take for a simptome of death), and within a few days dyed there, desiring ye Governor to pray for him, that he might goe to ye Englishmen's God in heaven, and bequeathed sundrie of his things to sundry of his English freinds as remembrances of his love, of whom they had a great losse . . .

GOOD NEWES

Which crossed their southward trading . . . From thence they departed, and the wind being faire for the Massachusetts, went thither, and the rather because the savages upon our motion had planted much corne for us.

When they came thither, they found a great sickness to be amongst the Indians—not unlike the plague, if not the same. They renewed their complaints to our Governor against that other Plantation seated by them, for their injurious walking.

And indeed, the trade both for furs and corne was overthrown in that place, they [at Wessagusset] giving as much for a quart of corne as we used to doe for a beaver's skin, so that little good could be done there.*

From thence, they returned into the bottom of the Bay of Cape Cod, to a place called Nauset, where the sachem used the Governor very kindly, and where they bought eight or ten hogs-heads of corne and beans.

Also at a place callede Mattachiest,† where they had like kind entertainment, and corne also.

During the time of their trade in these places, there were so greate and violent storms as the ship was much endangered. And our shallop was cast away, so that they had now no means to carry the corne aboard that they had bought . . .

Hereupon, the Governor caused the corne to be made in a round stack, and bought mats and cut sedge to cover it, and gave charge to the Indians not to meddle with it, promising him that dwelt next to it a reward if he would keepe vermin also from it.

Which he undertook, and the sachem promised to make good

*It was this spoiling of the beaver and corn trade that the Pilgrims particularly resented, for upon that trade their very lives depended.
†In the present township of Yarmouth, Cape Cod.

. . . So he took leave of them, being resolved to leave the ship and take his journey home by land with our owne company, sending word to the ship that they should take their first opportunity to go for Plymouth . . .

And having procured a guide, it being no less than fifty miles to our Plantation, he set forward, receiving all respect that could be from the Indians in his journey, and came safely home, though weary and surbated [footsore].

Whither, some three days after, the ship also came. The corne being divided which they had got, Master Weston's company wente to their owne plantation, it being further agreed that they should returne with all conveniente speed, and bring their carpenter, that they might fetch the rest of the corne and save their shallop.

> The corn on the Cape was fetched home by Captain Standish while Bradford went to several inland villages to buy more, being used "very kindlie" in all.

> The corn and beans bought with the trinkets from the *Discovery* kept the Pilgrims from starving. But with ninety mouths to feed, the supply came to really very little, and hunger stalked the town.

5. Havoc at Wessagusset

BRADFORD'S HISTORY   After these things, in Feb: [1623], a messenger came from John Sanders, who was left cheefe over Mr. Weston's men in ye bay of Massachusetts, who brought a letter shewing the great wants they were fallen into, and he would have borrowed a hogshead of corne of ye Indeans, but they would lend him none. He desired advice whether he might take it from them by force to succore his men till he came from ye eastward, whither he was going [in the hope of meeting with English fishing ships in Maine waters and there obtain supplies].

It may be thought strange that these people should fall into these extremities in so short a time, being left competently provided when ye ship [the *Charity*] left them and had an addition by that moyetie of corn that was got by trade. Besides, much they gott of ye Indians where they lived, by one means & other.

It must needs be their great disorder, for they spent excessively whilst they had or could get it—and it may be wasted part among ye Indeans (for he that was their cheef was taxed by some amongst them for keeping Indean women, how truly I know not).

And after they began to come into wants, many sold away their cloathes and bed coverings. Others (so base were they) became servants to ye Indeans and would cutt them woode & fetch them water for a capfull of corne.

Others fell to plaine stealing both night & day from ye Indeans, of which they greevously complained . . . Yea, in the end they were faine to hange one of their men whom they could not reclaime from stealing, to give ye Indeans contente.[1]

In ye end, they came to that misery that some starved & dyed with cold & hunger. One, in gathering shell-fish, was so weake as he stuck in ye mudd, and was found dead in ye place.

At last, most of them lefte their dwellings & scattered up & downe in ye woods & by ye water side, where they could find ground nuts & clams, here 6 and there ten.

By which carriages, they became contemned & scorned of ye Indeans, and they begane to insulte over them in a most insolente manner. Insomuch, many times, as they lay thus scattered abroad and had set on a pot with ground nuts or shell-fish, when it was ready, the Indeans would come and eate it up.

And when night came, whereas some of them had a sorie blanket or such like to lappe themselves in, the Indeans would take it and let ye other lye all nighte in the cold, so as their condition was very lamentable . . .

Yea, so base were some of their own company as they wente & told ye Indeans that their governor was purposed to come and take their corne by force, which, with other things, made them to enter into a conspiracie against ye English, of which more
. . .

6. The Pilgrims Urge Caution

Governor Sanders' threat to seize the Indians' corn deeply disturbed the Pilgrims. One of the Massachusetts Indians had been entrusted with delivering Sanders' letter to Bradford.

GOOD
NEWES
The Governor upon receipte thereof asked the messenger what store of corne they had, as if he had intended to buy of them [the Massachusetts tribe].

Who answered, very little more than that they reserved for seede, having already spared all they could.

Forthwith, the Governor and his Assistante sent for many of us to advise with them herein . . . No way approving of this intended course, the Governor answered his letter and caused many of us to set our hands thereto, the contents whereof were to this purpose.

We altogether disliked their intendment as being against the law of God and Nature, shewing how it would cross the worthy ends and proceedings of the King's Majesty and his honourable Council for this place, . . . and also the propagation of the knowledge and law of God, and the glad tidings of Salvation, which we and they were bound to seek . . .

For our own parts, our case was almost the same as theirs, having but a small quantity of corn left, . . . enforced to live on groundnuts, clams, mussels, and such other things as the country naturally afforded—and which did and would maintain strength, and were easy to be gotten.

All which things they had in great abundance—yea, oysters also, which we wanted—and therefore necessity could not be said to constrain them thereunto.

Moreover, that they should consider, if they proceeded therein, all they could so get would maintain them but a small time. And then they must, perforce, seek their food abroad, which, having made the Indians their enemies, would be very difficult for them . . .

Also, that they should consider their own weakness, being most swelled and diseased in their bodies, and therefore the more unlikely to make their party good against them.

And that they should not expect any help from us in that or any the like unlawful actions.

Lastly, that howsoever some of them might escape, yet the Principal Agents should expect no better than the gaol house whensoever any special officer should be sent over by His Majesty or his Council for New England, which we expected, and who would undoubtedly call them to account for same.

These were the contents of our answer, which was directed to their whole colony . . .

XIV

Massacre at Wessagusset

Wituwamat and the other man the rest killed, and took
the youth, whom the Captaine caused to be hanged.

—Good Newes

The news of Sanders' proposed treachery at Wessagusset, disclosed by some of his own people, had spread like wildfire
through the forests, to remind the Indians of many sad experiences with white marauders.

Knowing of the correspondence between Wessagusset and
Plymouth, they suspected the Pilgrims of being involved. To the
Indians it doubtless appeared—and it was a reasonable surmise—
that the planters at Wessagusset and Plymouth were partners.
Had they not been foraging together on the *Swan* just a few
weeks before?

1. Standish at Manomet

GOOD NEWES In the beginning of March [1623], having refreshed
himselfe, [Standish] took a shallop and went to Manomet* to fetch home that which the Governor had
formerly bought, hoping also to get more corne from them. But
he was deceived in his expectation, not finding that entertainmente he found elsewhere, and the Governor had here received†
. . .

---

*In the present township of Sandwich, Cape Cod.

†Standish never got along very well with the Indians, being too testy and too
touchy about the dignity of himself and his office. Just a few weeks previously, in fetching home the corn from Nauset and Cummaquid, he had had
trouble at both places, raising a rumpus about trifles and issuing loud ultima-

Captain Standish (being now far from the boat and not above two or three of our men with him, and as many with the shallop) was not long at Canacum the Sachem's house, but in came two of the Massachusetts men.

The chief of them was called Wituwamat, a notable insulting villain, one who had formerly imbrued his hands in the blood of English and French, and had oft boasted of his own valour and derided their weakness—especially because, as he said, they died crying, making sour faces, more like children than men.

This villain took a dagger from about his neck, which he had gotten of Master Weston's people, and presented it to the sachem —and after, made a long speech in an audacious manner, framing it in such sort as the Captain, though he be the best linguist amongst us, could not gather anything from it. The end of it was afterward discovered to be as followeth:*

The Massachusetts had formally concluded to ruinate Master Weston's colony and thought themselves, being about thirty or forty men, strong enough to execute the same.

Yet they durst not attempt it till such time as they had gathered more strength to themselves to make their party good against us at Plymouth, concluding that if we remained (though they had no other arguments to use against us), we would never leave the death of our countrymen unrevenged. And therefore their safety could not be without the overthrow of both plantations.

To this end, they had formerly solicited this sachem, as also the other called Iyanough, at Mattachiest, and many others to assist them, and now againe came to prosecute the same.

And since there was so fair an opportunity offered by the Captain's presence, they thought it best to make sure of him and his company.

After his message was delivered, his entertainmente much

tums. It is clear from the records that the Indians vastly preferred the gentler and unmilitary ways of Bradford and Winslow, who always had easier relations and far better success with them.

*For reasons that will become apparent, this ex post facto account of what was said must be taken with more than a grain of salt—a dose of them.

exceeded the Captain's, insomuch as he scorned at their behavior and told them of it.

After which, they would have persuaded him, because the weather was cold, to have sent to the boat for the rest of his company. But he would not, desiring according to promise that the corn might be carried down, and he would content the women for their labour, which they did . . . The wind serving the nexte day, they returned home.

2. Winslow: Medicine Man

GOOD NEWES During the time the Captaine was at Manomet, news came to Plymouth that Massasoit was like to die, and that at the same time there was a Dutch ship [from New Amsterdam] driven so high on the shore by stresse of weather, right before his dwelling, that till the tides increased, she could not get off.

Now, it being a commendable manner of the Indians when any, especially of note, are dangerously sick, for all that professe friendship to them to visit them in their extremity, either in their persons or else to send some acceptable persons to them.

Therefore, it was thought meet, being a good and warrantable action, that as we had ever professed friendship, so we should now maintaine the same by observing this their laudable custom—and the rather, because we desired to have some conference with the Dutch, not knowing when we should have so fit an opportunity.

To that end, myself [Winslow] having formerly been there and understanding in some measure the Dutch tongue, the Governor again laid this service upon myself and fitted me with some cordialls to administer to him, having one Master John Hamden* (a Gentleman of London, who then wintered with us and desired much to see the country) for my consort, and Hobomok for our guide.

*The identity of this "Hamden" is a mystery.

So we set forward . . . The next day, about one of the clock, we came to a ferry in Corbitant's countrie* . . . There they told us that Massasoit was dead and that day buried, and that the Dutch would be gone before we could get thither, having hove off their ship already.

This news struck us blank—but especially Hobomok, who desired we might returne with all speed. I told him:

"I would first think of it, considering now that, he being dead, Corbitant was the most like to succeed him and that we were not above three miles from Mattapuyst, his dwelling place. Although he were but a hollow-hearted friend towards us, I thought no time so fit as this to enter into more friendly terms with him . . .

"And though it were somewhat dangerous in respecte of our personal safetie, . . . yet esteeming it the best means, leaving the event to God in his mercy, I resolved to put it in practice if Master Hamden and Hobomok durst attempt it with me."

Whom I found willing to that, or any other course, that might tend to the general good. So we went towards Mattapuyst.

In the way, Hobomok, manifesting a troubled spirit, brake forth into these speeches:

"*Neen womasu Sagimus! Neen womasu Sagimus!* &c. My loving Sachem! My loving Sachem! Many have I known, but never any like thee."

And turning to me, he said:

"Whilst I lived, I should never see his like amongst the Indians . . .

"He was no liar. He was not bloody and cruel like other Indians. In anger and passion, he was soon reclaimed, easy to be reconciled towards such as had offended him, ruled by reason

---

*Corbitant was a neighboring sachem who had his chief seat at Nemasket, now Middleborough, about fifteen miles west of Plymouth. The Pilgrims had had trouble with him on one occasion when he threatened Squanto's life, saying that if Squanto were killed the English would lose their tongue.

Corbitant took to his heels when Standish marched on Nemasket and besieged the sachem's house, shooting and wounding several of his people. Being a "notable politician," Corbitant used Massasoit to make his peace, "but was shie to come neare them a longe while after."

in such measure as he would scorne the advice of mean men, and that he governed his men better with few strokes than others with many; truly loving, where he loved."

Yea, he feared we had not a faithful friend left among the Indians, showing how he ofttimes restrained their malice, &c., continuing a long speech with such signs of lamentation and unfeigned sorrow as it would have made the hardest heart relent.

At length, we came to Mattapuyst . . . But Corbitant the Sachem was not at home, but at Pokanoket [Sowams], which was five or six miles off . . .

Here we inquired againe concerning Massasoit. They thought him dead, but knew no certainty.

Whereupon, I hired one to go with all expedition to Pokanoket, that we might know the certainty thereof and, withal, to acquaint Corbitant with our being there.

About half an hour before sun-setting, the messenger returned and told us that he was not yet dead—though there was no hope we should find him living.

Upon this, we . . . set forward with all speed, though it was late within night ere we got thither.

About two of the clock that afternoon, the Dutchmen departed, so that in that respect our journey was frustrate.

When we came thither, we found the house so full of men as we could scarce get in, though they used their best diligence to make way for us.

They were in the midst of their charms for him, making such a hellish noise as it distempered us that were well, and therefore unlike to ease him that was sicke.

About him were six or eight women, who chafed his arms, legs, and thighs to keep heat in them.

When they had made an end of their charming, one told him that his friends the English were come to see him. Having understanding left, but his sight was wholly gone, he asked, "Who was come?"

They told him, "Winsnow"—for they cannot pronounce the letter "l" but ordinarily [use] "n" in place thereof.

He desired to speak with me.

When I came to him, and they told him of it, he put forth his hand to me, which I tooke. Then he said twice, though very inwardly:

"Keen Winsnow"—which is to say, "Art thou Winslow?"
I answered, *"Ahhe"*—that is, "Yes."
Then he doubled these words:
"Matta neen wonckanet namen"—that is to say, "O Winslow, I shall never see thee again!"

Then I called Hobomok and desired him to tell Massasoit that the Governor, hearing of his sickness, was sorry for the same.

And though, by reason of many businesses, he could not come himself, yet he sent me with such things for him as he thought most likely to do him good in this his extremity. And whereof, if he pleased to take, I would presently give him, which he desired.

And having a confection of many comfortable conserves, &c., on the point of my knife I gave him some, which I could scarce get through his teeth. When it was dissolved in his mouth, he swallowed the juice of it, whereat those that were about him much rejoiced, saying he had not swallowed anything in two days before.

Then I desired to see his mouth, which was exceedingly furred, and his tongue swelled in such a manner as it was not possible for him to eat such meat as they had, his passage being stopped up.

Then I washed his mouth and scraped his tongue, and got abundance of corruption out of the same. After which, I gave him more of the confection, which he swallowed with more readiness.*

Then he desiring to drink, I dissolved some of it in water and gave him thereof. Within half an hour, this wrought a great alteration in him in the eyes of all that beheld him. Presently after,

---

*It would be interesting to know what these "comfortable conserves" were. They were probably jellies and preserves made from wild fruits and berries—strawberries, blueberries, plums, cherries, and others.

his sight began to come to him, which gave him and us good encouragement.

In the meantime, I inquired how he slept and when he went to the stool?

They said he slept not in two days before, and had not had a stool in five.

Then I gave him more [of the conserves] and told him of a mishap we had by the way in breaking a bottle of drinke which the Governor also sent him. Saying if he would send any of his men to Patuxet [Plymouth], I would send for more of the same —also, for chickens to make him broth, and for other things which I knew were good for him—and would stay for the re-turne of the messengers if he desired.

This he took marvellous kindly and appointed some who were ready to go by two of the clock in the morning, against which time I made ready a letter declaring therein our good success, the state of his body, &c., desiring to send me such things as I sent for and such physic as the Surgeon [Deacon-Doctor Sam-uel Fuller] durst administer to him.

He requested me that, the day following, I would take my piece and kill some fowl and make him some English pottage, such as he had eaten at Plymouth, which I promised.

After, his stomach coming to him [i.e., his appetite return-ing], I must needs make him some without fowl before I went abroad, which somewhat troubled me, being unaccustomed and unacquainted in such businesses, especially having nothing to make it comfortable [tasty], my consort being as ignorante as myself.

But being we must do somewhat, I caused a woman to bruise some corn and take the flour from it. And we set the grut [groats], or broken corn, in a pipkin, for they have earthen pots of all sizes.

When the day broke, we wente out . . . to seek herbs, but could not find any but strawberry leaves, of which I gathered a handful and put in the same.

And because I had nothing to relish it, I wente forth againe and pulled up a saxafras root,* and sliced a piece thereof and boiled it till it [the broth] had a good relish, and then took it out againe.

The broth being boiled, I strained it through my handkerchief and gave him at least a pint, which he drank and liked it very well. After this, his sight mended more and more.

Also, he had three moderate stools and took some rest, insomuch as we, with admiration, blessed God for giving his blessing to such raw and ignorant means, making no doubt of his recovery, himself and all of them acknowledging us the instruments of his preservation.†

The morning he caused me to spend in going from one to another amongst those that were sicke in the town, requesting me to wash their mouths also, and give to each of them some of the same I gave him, saying they were good folk.

This pains I took with willingness, though it were much offensive to me, not being accustomed to such poisonous savours.

After dinner, he desired me to get him a goose or a duck, and make him some pottage therewith with as much speed as I could.

So I took a man with me, and made a shot at a couple of ducks some six score paces off [more than 100 yards], and killed one, at which he wondered. So we returned therewith and dressed it, making more broth therewith, which he much desired.

Never did I see man, so low brought, recover in that measure in so short a time.

The fowl being extraordinary fat, I told Hobomok I must take off the top thereof [skim off the fat], saying it would make him very sicke againe if he did eat it.

He acquainted Massasoit therewith, who would not be persuaded to it, though I pressed it very much, showing the strength

---

*Sassafras was then deemed a sovereign cure for almost all human ills.

†What would have happened, one wonders, if Massasoit had died under Winslow's ministrations? Would the Indians, in fury, have fallen upon the amateur doctor-chef and then upon Plymouth? As is evident from his story, Winslow must have had some very anxious moments as a "medicine man."

thereof and the weakness of his stomach, which could not pos-sibly bear it.

Notwithstanding, he made a gross meal of it, and ate as much as would well have satisfied a man in health.

About an hour after, he began to be very sicke and, straining very much, cast up the broth againe and, in overstraining himself, began to bleed at the nose and so continued the space of four hours.

Then they all wished he had been ruled, concluding now he would die, which we much feared also.

They asked me what I thought of him?

I answered, "His case was desperate; yet, it might be, it would save his life. For if it ceased in time, he would forthwith sleep and take rest, which was the principal thing he wanted."

Not long after, his blood stayed, and he slepte at least six or eight hours.

When he awaked, I washed his face, and bathed and suppled his beard and nose with a linen cloth.

But, on a sudden, he chopt [accidentally dipped] his nose in the water and drew up some therein, and sent it forth with such violence as he began to bleed afresh.

Then they thought there was no hope.

But we perceived it was but the tenderness of his nostril, and I therefore told them I thought it would stay presently, as indeed it did.

The messengers were now returned. But finding his stomach come to him, he would not have the chickens killed, but kept for breed.

Neither durst we give him any physic, which was then sent, because his body was so much altered since our instructions.

Neither saw we any need, not doubting now of his recovery if he were carefull, . . . he being now able to sit upright of himselfe . . .

Upon his recovery, he brake forth in these speeches:

"Now I see the English are my friends and love me. And

whilst I live, I will never forget this kindness they have showed me."

And he never did. With tact, courage, and improvised skill, but thanks largely to the grace of God, Winslow had adroitly accomplished another difficult and important mission. During the forty remaining years of his life, Massasoit never once violated the peace treaty signed at Plymouth and cemented here so magically with "comfortable conserves."

3. Corbitant and the Seventh Commandment

GOOD NEWES   Being fitted for our returne, we tooke our leave of him . . . That night, through the earnest request of Corbitant, who till now remained at Sowams, or Pokanoket, we lodged with him at Mattapuyst.

By the way, I had much conference with him—so likewise at his house—he being a notable politician, yet full of merry jests and squibs, and never better pleased than when the like are returned upon him . . .

He demanded how we, being but two, durst come so far into the countrie. I answered:

"Where was true love, there was no feare, and that my heart was so uprighte towards them that, for mine own part, I was fearless to come among them."

"But," said he, "if your love be such, and it bring forth such fruits, how cometh it to pass that when we come to Patuxet, you stand upon your guard, with the mouths of your pieces presented towards us?"

Whereunto I answered:

"It was the most honourable and respectful entertainmente we could give them, it being an order amongst us so to receive our best respected friends . . . "

But, shaking his head, he answered that he liked not such salutations.

Further, observing us to crave a blessing on our meals before we did eat, and after to give thanks for the same, he asked us what was the meaning of that ordinary custom?

Hereupon I took occasion to tell them of God's works of Creation and Preservation, of his Laws and Ordinances, especially of the Ten Commandments, all which they hearkened unto with great attention and liked well of.

Only the Seventh Commandment they excepted against, thinking there were many inconveniences in it, that a man should be tied to one woman, about which we reasoned a good time . . .

Here we remained only that night, but never had better entertainmente amongst any of them.

4. Hobomok's Story

GOOD NEWES The day following,* in our journey, Hobomok told me of a private conference he had with Massasoit, who charged him perfectly to acquainte me therewith . . .

At our coming away, he called Hobomok to him and privately (nonc hearing save two or three of his *Pineses*, who are of his Council) revealed the plot of the Massachusetts against Master Weston's colony—and so against us—saying that the people of Nauset, Pamet, Succanesett, Mattachiest, Agowaywam [all on Cape Cod], and the Isle of Capawack [Martha's Vineyard] were joined with them . . .

Therefore (as we respected the lives of our countriemen and our owne after-safety) he advised us to kill the men of Massachusetts who were the authors of this intended mischiefe.

And whereas we were wont to say we would not strike a stroke till they first began, if, said he, upon this intelligence, they [at Plymouth] made this answer, tell them that when their countrymen at Wessagusset are killed, they not being able to defend themselves, then it will be too late to recover their lives.

*That is, on the second day from Sowams—a point to remember as the plot thickens, getting very thick indeed.

Nay, through the multitude of adversaries, they shall with great difficulty preserve their own.

And therefore he counselled without delay to take away the principals, and then the plot would cease. With this, he charged him thoroughly to acquainte me by the way, that I might informe the Governor at my first coming home . . .

Which having done, [Hobomok] used many arguments himselfe to move us thereunto.

That night, we lodged at Nemasket.

And the day following, about the midway betweene it and home, we met two Indians, who told us Captaine Standish was that day gone to the Massachusetts.

Hobomok's story was as remarkable as the alleged circumstances under which it was told.

If Massasoit had such an urgent warning to give the Pilgrims, why did he not impart it to Winslow, who had been at his elbow for days in doing his puzzled best to save his life?

Why did he speak "privately" to Hobomok about a matter of such vital concern to Plymouth?

Why did Hobomok wait until the second day along the trail to inform Winslow of Massasoit's advice to proceed "without delay"?

Why, if the Cape Indians were involved in the conspiracy, had not Massasoit offered to call them to heel?

They were his subjects. If they were now in league with the Massachusetts, then they were in revolt, which would have been startling news indeed. But there is no slightest shred of evidence to suggest this.

Having heard the warning, why did not Winslow hasten to Plymouth with all speed instead of stopping the night at Nemasket?

And why was it that, loitering along the next day, Winslow learned from two Indians coming from Plymouth that Captain Standish "was that day gone to the Massachusetts"?

Plymouth, it appears, had already decided to take action against Wessagusset and the Indians there. Always somewhat ashamed of that action, the Pilgrims made Hobomok's tale the inspiration and justification of what they did. But this story has a fatal fault —it would seem from the records that they decided to take Massasoit's alleged advice even before they heard it, third hand, from Winslow's lips.

The Pilgrims had good reasons of their own for moving against Wessagusset and the "intruders" there, troublesome rivals in the corn and beaver trade.

5. Snares and Traps

GOOD
NEWES

But contrarie winds againe drove him [Standish] back, so that we found him at home . . .

The Governour, . . . not being [empowered] to undertake warr without the consent of the bodie of the Companie, made knowne [Winslow's account of Hobomok's story] in public court, offering it to the consideration of the companie, it being high time to come to resolution, how sudden soever it seemed to them . . .

This bussines was no less troublesome than grievous. And the more because it is so ordinary in these times for men to measure things by the events thereof. And especially for that we knew no means to deliver our countrymen and preserve ourselves than by returning their malicious and cruel purposes upon their own heads and causing them to fall into the same pit they digged for others—though it much grieved us to shed the blood of those whose good we ever intended and aimed at as a principal in all our proceedings.

But in the end, we came to this public conclusion, that because it was a matter of such weight as every man was not of a sufficiency to judge nor fitness to know, . . . therefore the Governor, his Assistant, and the Captaine should take such to themselves as they thought most meet, and conclude thereof.*

Which done, we came to this conclusion, that Captain Stan-

---

*The names and the number of those chosen to consult with Bradford, Allerton, and Standish are not known. Winslow was one, however, and Stephen Hopkins was probably another.

dish should take so many men as he thought sufficiente to make his party good against all the Indians in the Massachusetts Bay.

And because, as all men know that have had to do in that kind, it is impossible to deal with them upon open defiance, but to take them in such traps as they lay for others, therefore he should pretend to trade as at other times.

But first, [he should] go to the English [at Wessagusset] and acquainte them with the plot* and the end of his coming . . .

Upon this, Captaine Standish made choice of eight men and would not take more because he would prevent jealousy [suspicion] . . .

Now was our fort made fit for service, and some ordnance mounted. And though it may seem a longe work, it being ten months since it was begun, yet we must note that where so great a work is begun with such small means, a little time cannot bring it to perfection.

Besides, those works which tend to the preservation of men the Enemy of Mankind will hinder what in him lieth, sometimes blinding the judgment and causing reasonable men to reason against their own safety—as, amongst us, divers, seeing the worke prove tedious, would have dissuaded us from proceeding, flattering themselves with peace and security, and accounting it rather a work of superfluity and vainglory than simple necessity.

But God (whose providence hath waked and, as I may say, watched over us whilst we slept), having determined to preserve us from these intended treacheries, undoubtedly ordained this as a special means to advantage us and discourage our enemies, and therefore so stirred up the hearts of the governors and other forward instruments as the work was just made serviceable against this needfull and dangerous time, though we ignorante of the same.

The day before Standish's "trading" party sailed, one Phineas Pratt stumbled into Plymouth "with a small pack on his back,"

---

*Not the Pilgrims' plot, but the alleged Indian conspiracy against them. Those at Wessagusset were quite surprised to learn that they were in danger.

having fled from Wessagusset, saying that the people there, "by what he observed, would be all knokt in ye head shortly."

A Massachusetts brave, it seems, had been sent after him to kill him along the way. But Pratt arrived safely, though not knowing a foot of the way, while the Indian, so the Pilgrims said, got lost in his native woods, missed both Pratt and Plymouth, and ended up at Manomet, twenty miles to the south.

Returning, this strangely unknowledgeable brave found Plymouth and stopped there, "still pretending friendship." But Bradford had him arrested, putting him in irons under guard in the new fort. No charge was made against the prisoner, who was merely told that he would have to be "content to remaine till the returne of Captain Standish from the Massachusetts." The Pilgrims did not intend to have their "designes" frustrated by allowing him to return to Wessagusset and sound the alarm there.

6. Massacre

GOOD NEWES The Captain, being now come to the Massachusetts, went firste to the ship [the *Swan*], but found neither man nor so much as a dog therein.

Upon the discharge of a musket, the master and some others of the plantation showed themselves, who were on shore gathering ground nuts and getting other food.

After salutation, Captain Standish asked them how they durst so leave the ship and live in such security? Who answered, like men senseless of their own misery:

They feared not the Indians, but lived [with them] and suffered them to lodge with them, not having sword or gun or needing the same.

To which the Captain answered: If there were no cause, he was the gladder.

But upon further inquiry, understanding that those whom John Sanders had . . . left in his stead to govern the rest were at the plantation, thither he went—and, to be brief, made known the Indians' purpose and the end of his own coming . . .

These men, comparing other circumstances with that they now heard, answered they could expect no better. And it was God's mercy that they were not killed before his coming, desiring therefore that he would neglect no opportunity to proceed.

Hereupon he urged them to secrecy, yet withal to send special command to one third of their company that were farthest off to come home, and there enjoined them, on paine of death, to keep [within] the town, himself allowing them a pint of Indian corn to a man for day, though that store he had was spared out of our seed.

The weather proving very wet and stormy, it was the longer before he could do anything.

In the meantime, an Indian came to him and brought some furs . . . And though the Captain carried things as smoothly as he possibly could, yet at his return he [the Indian] reported he saw by his eyes that he [Standish] was angry in his heart, and therefore [the Indians] began to suspect themselves discovered.

This caused one Pecksuot, who was a *Pinese*, being a man of notable spirit, to come to Hobomok, who was then with them, and told him he understood that the Captain was come to kill himself [Pecksuot] and the rest of the savages there.

"Tell him," he said, "we know it, but fear him not. Neither shall we shun him, but let him begin when he dare. He shall not take us unawares."

Many times after, divers of them, severally or a few together, came to the plantation to him, where they would whet and sharpen the points of their knives before his face, and use many other insulting gestures and speeches.

Amongst the rest, Wituwamat bragged of the excellency of his knife. On the end of the handle there was pictured a woman's face.

"But," said he, "I have another at home wherewith I have killed both French and English. And that hath a man's face on it and, by and bye, these two must marry . . ."

Also, Pecksuot, being a man of greater stature than the Captain, told him though he were a great captain, yet he was but a little man. And said he:

"Though I be no sachem, yet I am a man of great strength and courage."

These things the Captain observed, yet bore with patience for the present.

On the next day, seeing he could not get many of them together at once, and this Pecksuot and Wituwamat being both together, with another man and a youth of some eighteen years of age, which was a brother to Wituwamat* . . . , and having about as many of his own company in the room with them, [Standish] gave the word to his men.

And the door being fast shut, [Standish] began himself with Pecksuot and, snatching his own knife from his neck, though with much struggling, killed him therewith, the point whereof he had made as sharp as a needle and ground the back also to an edge.

Wituwamat and the other man the rest killed, and took the youth, whom the Captain caused to be hanged.

But it is incredible how many wounds these two *Pineses* received before they died, not making any fearful noise, but catching at their weapons and striving to the last.

Hobomok stood by all this time as a spectator and meddled not, observing how our men demeaned themselves in this action. All being here ended, smiling, he brake forth into these speeches to the Captain:

"Yesterday, Pecksuot, bragging of his own strength and stature, said, 'Though you were a great captain, yet you were but a little man.' But today, I see you are big enough to lay him on the ground."

But to proceed. There being some women [present] at the time, Captain Standish left them in the custody of Master Weston's people at the town and sent word to another company that

---

*These four Indians had been invited to enjoy a feast with Standish and his party, according to a charge later made by one of the Pilgrims' bitter enemies, Thomas Morton of Merry Mount.

had intelligence of things to kill those Indian men that were amongst them.

These killed two more. Himself [Standish] also, with some of his own men, went to another place, where they killed another. But through the negligence of one man, an Indian escaped, who discovered and crossed their proceedings . . .

Captain Standish took the one half of his men, and one or two of Master Weston's, and Hobomok, still seeking to make spoile of them and theirs. At length, they espied a file of Indians, which made towards them amain. And there being a small advantage in the ground by reason of a hill near them, both companies strove for it.

Captain Standish got it. Whereupon they retreated and took each man his tree, letting fly their arrows amain, especially at himself and Hobomok.

Whereupon Hobomok cast off his coat and being a known *Pinese*, theirs being now killed, chased them so fast as our people were not able to hold way with him . . .

Our men could have but one certain mark—and then but the arm and half face of a notable villain as he drew at Captain Standish, who, together with another, both discharged at once at him and brake his arm. Whereupon, they fled into a swamp.

When they were in the thicket, they parleyed, but to small purpose, getting nothing but foul language. So our Captain dared the sachem to come out and fight like a man, showing how base and womanlike he was in tonguing it as he did. But he refused and fled.

So the Captain returned to the plantation, where he released the women, and would not take their beaver coats from them, nor suffer the least discourtesy to be offered them.

Now were Master Weston's people resolved to leave their plantation and go for Monhegan, hoping to get passage and return to [England] with the fishing ships.

The Captain told them that, for his owne part, he durst there live with fewer men than they were.

Yet since they were otherways minded, according to his order from the governors and people of Plymouth, he would help them with corn competente for their provision by the way, which he did* . . .

And seeing them set saile and clear of the Massachusetts Bay, he tooke leave and returned to Plymouth, whither he came in safety, blessed be God!, and brought the head of Wituwamat with him, . . . the head being brought to the Fort and set up [on a spike, where the bleaching skull remained for years] . . .

Concerning those other people [the tribes along Cape Cod] that intended to join with the Massachusetts against us—though we never went against any of them, yet this sudden and unexpected execution, together with the just judgment of God upon their guilty consciences, so terrified and amazed them as, in like manner, they forsook their houses, running to and fro like men distracted, living in swamps and other desert places, and so brought manifold diseases amongst themselves.

Whereof many are dead—as Canacum, the sachem of Manomet; Aspinet, the sachem of Nauset; Iyanough, the sachem of Mattachiest . . .

I fear I have been too tedious both in this and other things. Yet when I considered how necessary a thing it is that the truth, and the grounds of this action especially, should be made known, and . . . the reports undoubtedly will be various, I could not but enlarge myself where I thought to be most brief.

Neither durst I be too brief lest I should eclipse and rob God of that honour, glory, and praise which belongeth to him for preserving us from falling when we were at the pit's brim, and yet feared nor knew not that we were in danger.

*That Wessagusset would have to be abandoned after the attack doubtless entered the Pilgrims' calculations, as revealed by Standish's instructions to give them corn and see them gone. The Pilgrims were as eager to get rid of white "intruders" as insulting redskins.

7. Concerning Those Poor Indians

But one of the Saints, and the greatest of them, failed to detect God's hand in any of this. When news of it reached Leyden, John Robinson wrote in part:

Des: 19, 1623

BRADFORD'S
HISTORY
Concerning ye killing of those poor Indians, which we heard at first by reporte and since by more certaine relation, oh! how happy a thing had it been if you had converted some before you killed any.

Besides, where bloud is once begun to be shed, it is seldome stanched off a long time after.

You will say they deserved it. I grant it. But upon what provocations and invitements by those heathenish Christians?

Besides, you, being no magistrates over them, were to consider not what they deserved, but what you by necessitie were constrained to inflicte.

Necessitie of this, espetially of killing so many (and many more, it seems, they would if they could), I see not. . . . And indeed I am afraid lest, by these occasions, others should be drawne to affecte a kind of ruffling course in the world . . .

Upon this occasion, let me be bould to exhorte you seriously to consider of ye disposition of your Captaine, whom I love and am perswaded ye Lord in great mercie, and for much good, hath sent you him, if you use him aright. He is a man humble and meek amongst you, and towards all in ordinarie course. But now if this be meerly from a humane spirit, there is cause to fear that by occasion, espetially of provocation, there may be wanting that tendernes of ye life of man (made after God's image) which is meete.

It is a thing more glorious in men's eyes than pleasing in God's, or conveniente for Christians, to be a terrour to poore barbarous people . . .

XV

Gaunt Hunger

. . . at some times, in some seasons, at noone, I have seen
men stagger by reason of faintness, for wante of food
. . .

—*Edward Winslow*

BRADFORD'S
HISTORY

Shortly after, Mr. Weston came over with some
of ye fishermen under another name, and ye disguise of a blacke-smith, where he heard of ye ruine
and dissolution of his colony.

He got a boat, and with a man or 2 came to see how things
were.

But by ye way, for wante of skill, in a storme, he cast away
his shallop . . . & hardly escaped with his life, and afterwards
fell into the hands of ye Indians who pillaged him of all he saved
from the sea, & stripped him of all his cloaths to his shirt.

1. Weston Again

BRADFORD'S
HISTORY

At last, he . . . borrowed a suite of cloaths and
got means to come to Plimoth.
A strange alteration there was in him to such as
had seen & known him in his former flourishing condition.

So uncertaine are ye mutable things of this unstable world.
And yet men set their harts upon them, though they dayly see
ye vanity thereof.

After many passages and much discourse (former things boyl-
ing in his mind, but bit in, as was discerned), he desired to bor-

row some beaver of them, and tould them he had hope of a ship
& good supply to come to him, and then they should have anything for it they stood in need of.

They gave little credit to his supplie, but pitied his case and
remembered former curtesies.

They tould him he saw their wants, and they knew not when
they should have any supply. Also, how ye case stood betweene
them & their adventurers he well knew.

They had not much beaver. And if they should let him have
it, it were enough to make a mutinie among ye people, seeing
there was no other means to procure them food which they so
much wanted, & cloaths allso.

Yet they tould him they would help him, considering his
necessitie, but must doe it secretly for ye former reasons.

So they let him have 100 beaver skins, which waighed 170 odd
pounds. Thus they helpt him when all ye world failed him. And
with this means he went againe to ye ships, and stayed his small
ship & some of his men, & bought provissions and fitted himselfe—
and it was ye only foundation of his after course.

But he requited them ill, for he proved after a bitter enimie
unto them upon all occasions, and never repayed them anything
for it, . . . but reproches and evill words.

Yes, he divolged it to some that were none of their freinds,
. . . [saying] that he could set them all togeather by ye ears
because they had done more than they could answer for in letting him have this beaver . . .

2. New Land Dispensation

BRADFORD'S
HISTORY

All this while no supply was heard of. Neither
knew they when they might expecte any.

So they begane to thinke how they might raise
as much corne as they could and obtaine a better crop than they
had done, that they might not still thus languish in miserie.

At length, after much debate of things, the Governor (with

ye advise of ye cheefest amongst them) gave way that they should set corne every man for his own perticuler, and in that regard trust to themselves.

In all other things, to goe in ye generall way, as before.

And so they assigned to every family a parcell of land, according to the proportion of their number for that end,* only for present use (but made no devission for inheritance), and ranged all boys & youths under some familie.

This had very good success, for it made all hands very industrious, so as much more corne was planted than otherwise would have been by any means ye Governor or any other could use, and saved him a great deall of trouble and gave farr better contente.

The women now wente willingly into ye field and took their little ones with them to set corne, which before would allege weaknes and inabilitie—whom to have compelled would have been thought great tiranie and oppression.

3. All Victuals Spent

GOOD
NEWES

In the midst of Aprill, we began to set, the weather being then seasonable, which much incouraged us, giving us good hope of after plenty . . .

But it pleased God, for our further chastisement, to send a great drought. Insomuch, as in six weekes, there scarce fell any rain, so that the stalk of that [which] was first set began to send forth the ear before it was come to half growth, and that which was later [planted] not like to yield us any at all—both blade and stalk hanging the head and changing colour in such a manner as we judged it utterly dead.

Our beans also ran not up, according to their wonted manner, but stood at a stay—many being parched away, as though they had been scorched before the fire.

Now were our hopes overthrown, and we discouraged, and our joye turned into mourning . . .

*In general, a household was allotted an acre for each of its members.

BRADFORD'S   After their corne was planted, all their victails
HISTORY   were spente, and they were only to rest on God's
              providence—at night, not many times knowing
where to have a bitt of anything ye next day.

And so, as one well observed, they had need to pray that God
would give them their dayly bread above all people in ye world.

Yet they bore these wants with great patience & allacritie of
spirite, and that for so long a time as for ye most part of 2 years—
which makes me remember what Peter Martire writes in magni-
fying ye Spaniards.

"They," saith he, "led a miserable life for 5 days togeather,
with ye parched graine of maize only, and that not to saturitie"
—and then concluds "that shuch pains, shuch labours, and shuch
hunger, he thought none living who is not a Spaniard could
have endured."

But alass! these [at Plymouth], when they had maize (that is,
Indean corne), they thought it as good as a feast, and wanted not
only for 5 days togeather, but sometimes 2 or 3 months togeather.
And neither had bread nor any kind of corne . . .

They having but one boat left and she not over well fitted,
they were devided into several companies, 6 or 7 to a gang or company, and so wente out with a net they had bought, to take bass
& such like fish, by course, each company knowing their turne.

No sooner was ye boate discharged of what she brought but
ye next company tooke her and wente out with her.

Neither did they returne till they had caught something,
though it were 5 or 6 days before. For they knew there was
nothing at home, and to goe home emptie would be a great discouragemente to ye rest. Yea, they strove who should doe best.

If she stayed longe or got little, then all went to seeking shell-
fish, which at low water they digged out of ye sands. And this
was their living in ye sommer time till God sente them better.
And in winter they were helped with ground nuts and foule.

Also, in ye sommer, they gott now & then a dear, for one or
2 of ye fittest was apoynted to range ye woods for that end, &
what was gott that way was devided amongst them.

4. Further Crosses and Frustrations

BRADFORD'S
HISTORY

At length, they received some letters from ye adventurers, too long and tedious here to record, by which they heard of their furder crosses and frustrations, beginning in this manner:

[London
December 21, 1622]

Loving freinds,

As your sorrows & afflictions have bin great, so our crosses & interceptions in our proceedings here have not been small.

For after we had with much trouble & charge sente ye *Paragon* away to sea and thought all ye paine past, within 14 days after she came againe hither, being dangerously leaked and brused with tempestious stormes, so as she was faine to be had in ye docke and a £100 [$5,000] bestowed upon her—all ye passengers lying upon our charge for 6 or 7 weeks, and much discontent and distemper was occasioned thereby, so as some dangerous evente [mutiny] had like to insewed.

But we trust all shall be well and worke for ye best and your benefite if yet with patience you can wait, and have but strength to hold in life . . .

This ship [the ill-named *Paragon*] was bought by Mr. John Peirce and set out at his owne charge upon hope of great matters. These passengers & ye goods the company sent in her, he tooke in for freight, for which they agreed with him to be delivered here.

This was he in whose name their first patente was taken, by reason of acquaintance and some alliance that some of their friends had with him. But his name was used only in trust.

But when he saw they were here hopefully thus seated and by ye success God gave them, had obtained ye favour of ye Counsell of New England, he goes and sues to them for another patent of much larger extent (in their names), which was easily obtained.

But he meant to keep it to himselfe and allow them what he pleased, to hold of him as tenants and sue to his courts as cheefe Lord . . .

But ye Lord marvelously crost him. For after his first returne and ye charge above mentioned, when she was againe fitted, he pesters himselfe and takes in more passengers—and those not very good to help to bear his losses—and sets out ye 2nd time.

But what ye event was will appear from another letter from one of ye cheefe of ye company, dated ye 9 of April, 1623, writ to ye Governor here . . .

Loving freind,

When I wrote my last letter, I hoped to have received one from you well nigh by this time.

But when I wrote in Dec., I little thought to have seen Mr. John Peirce till he had brought some good tidings from you.

But it pleased God, he brought us wofull tidings of his returne when he was half-way over, by extraime tempest, wherein ye goodnes & mercie of God appeared in saving their lives, being 109 souls . . .

Now, with great trouble & loss, we have got Mr. John Peirce to assigne over ye grand patent to ye companie, which he had taken in his owne name, and made quite void our former grante.

I am sorrie to write how many here thinke that the hand of God was justly against him, . . . in regard he, whom you and we so confidently trusted (but only to use his name for ye company) should aspire to be lord over us all, and so make you & us tenants at his will and pleasure . . .

I desire to judge charitably of him. But his unwillingness to part with his royall Lordship, and ye high rate he set it at, which was £500 [$25,000] which cost him but £50, makes many speake and judge hardly of him.

The company is out, for goods in his ship, with charge aboute ye passengers, £640 [$32,000] . . -

These were their owne words and judgmente of this man's
dealing & proceedings . . .

And yet, though there was never got other recompense than
the resignation of this patente and ye shares he had in adventure
for all ye former great sums, he was never quiet, but sued them
in most of ye cheefe courts in England, and when he was still
cast, brought it to ye Parlemente.

But he is now dead, and I will leave him to ye Lord.

5. Rain-making

BRADFORD'S   I may not omit how, notwithstanding all their
HISTORY   great paines & industrie and ye great hopes of a
                       large cropp, the Lord seemed to blast & take away
the same, and to threaten further & more sore famine unto them
by a great drought, . . . insomuch as ye corne begane to wither
away, though it was set with fishe, the moysture whereof helped
it much.

Yet, at length, it begane to languish sore, and some of ye drier
grounds were parched like withered hay . . .

Upon which, they sett apart a solemne day of humilliation to
seek ye Lord by humble & fervente prayer in this great distresse . . .

GOOD   To that end, a day was appoynted by public author-
NEWES   ity and set aparte from all other employments, hoping
                       that the same God which had stirred us up hereunto,
would be moved hereby in mercie to look downe upon us and
grant the request of our dejected souls if our continuance there
might, any way, stand with his glory, and our good.

But, O the mercie of our God, who was as readie to hear, as
we to ask.

For though in the morning, when we assembled together,
the heavens were as clear, and the drought as like to continue,
as ever it was, yet, our exercise continuing some eight or nine
hours, before our departure the weather was overcast.

The clouds gathered together on all sides and on the nexte morning distilled such soft, sweete, and moderate showers of raine, continuing some fourteen days, and mixed with such seasonable weather, as it was hard to say whether our withered corne or drooping affections were most quickened or revived.

Such was the bounty and goodness of our God.

Of this, the Indians, by means of Hobomok, took notice, who, being in the towne, and this exercise in the midst of the week, said it was but three days since Sunday and therefore demanded of a boy what was the reason thereof.

Which, when he knew and saw what effects followed thereupon, he and all of them admired the goodness of God towards us that wrought so great a change in so short a time, showing the difference between their conjuration and our invocation in the name of God for rain—theirs being mixed with such storms and tempests as sometimes, instead of doing them good, it layeth the corn flat on the ground to their prejudice, but ours in so gentle and seasonable a manner as they never observed the like . . .

Wherein others may see that which we are bound to acknowledge—viz., that if ever any people in these later ages were upheld by the providence of God after a more special measure than others, then we were, and therefore are the more bound to celebrate the memory of his goodness with everlasting thankfullnes.

For in those forenamed straits, such was our state as, in the morning, we had often our food to seeke for the day, and yet performed the duties of our callings—I mean, the other daily labours to provide for after-time.

And though at some times, in some seasons, at noone, I have seen men stagger by reason of faintness, for wante of food, yet, ere night, by the good providence and blessing of God, we have enjoyed such plentie as though the windows of heaven had been opened unto us.

XVI

Anne *and* Little James

And though we have not sent you all we would (because
our cash is small), yet it is that we could, &c.
—Merchant Adventurers

BRADFORD'S   About ye latter end of June [1623] came in
HISTORY   a ship with Captaine Francis West, who had a
                commission to be admirall of New England, to
restraine interlopers and such fishing ships as came to fish & trade
without a licence from ye Counsell for New England, for which
they should pay a round sume of money.

But he could do no good of them, for they were too stronge
for him, and he found ye fishermen to be stuberne fellows.

And their owners, upon complainte to ye Parlemente, procured an order that fishing should be free.

He told ye Governor they spoke with a ship at sea . . . that
was coming for this plantation, in which were sundrie passengers.
And he marvelled she was not arrived, fearing some miscariage,
for they lost her in a storme, . . . which relation filled them full
of feare, yet mixed with hope.

The master of [West's] ship had some 2 hogsheads of peas
to sell. But seeing their wants, held them at £9 sterling [$450]
a hoggshead, & under £8 he would not take, and yet would have
beaver at an under-rate.

But they told him they had lived so long without and would
doe still, rather than give so unreasonably.

So they wente from hence to Virginia.

1. New Members

BRADFORD'S
HISTORY About 14 days after came in this ship called ye *Anne*, whereof Mr. William Peirce* was master. And aboute a weeke or 10 days after came in ye pinnace [the *Little James*], which in foule weather they lost at sea, a fine new vessel of about 44 tune, which ye company had builte to stay in ye cuntrie.

They brought about 60 persons for ye generall, some of them being very usefull persons and became good members of ye body. And some were ye wives and children of such as were here already. And some were so bad as they were faine to be at charge to send them home againe ye next year.

Also, besides these, there came a company that did not belong to ye generall body, but came on their perticuler and were to have lands assigned them and be for themselves, yet to be subjects to ye generall government, which caused some diferance and disturbance amongst them, as will after appear† . . .

Doubling Plymouth's population, ninety-three passengers arrived on the ships, and thirty-five of these—or more than a third—were children. As on previous ships, Strangers constituted the larger part of the company. There were only thirty-two Saints from Leyden—five men, nine women, and eighteen children.

The Brewsters were united again with the arrival of their daughters, Patience, a woman of twenty-three, and Fear, now a girl of seventeen. Fear soon married Assistant Governor Allerton, who had three children by his first marriage. Within the year Patience became the wife of a future governor, young Thomas Prence, formerly a carriage maker of London, who had come a Stranger on the *Fortune* and had since become a Saint.

There was also on board another member of the original

---

*Known as "the ferryman of the North Atlantic," later a settler in the Massachusetts Bay colony.
†For the names of the passengers, see Appendix.

Scrooby congregation, the last ever to reach Plymouth—George Morton ("G. Mourt"), a prosperous merchant and "pious gracious servante of God." He had with him his wife, five children, and his wife's sister.

The last was Mrs. Alice (Carpenter) Southworth, widow of Edward Southworth, silk maker, by whom she had had two sons, Constant and Thomas. As both were under ten, she had left them behind, sending for them five years later, and in time both became men of note in the colony.

Alice had evidently come at the invitation of Bradford, for they were almost immediately married, eventually having three children.

George Morton died not long after landing, and the Bradfords took in his wife and virtually adopted their five children, the last of whom was Ephraim, only a few weeks old, having been born at sea, later an "ornamente" of the church, serving as deacon for many years.

The oldest of the Morton children was Nathaniel, a boy of seven. Tutored by Bradford, he later became his uncle's secretary and agent, also serving down the years in many capacities —as town clerk, secretary of the colony, and secretary of the Plymouth church. As secretary of the church, he laboriously copied into its records some few passages and many more paraphrases of Bradford's *Of Plimoth Plantation*, using his uncle's manuscripts as part of the source material for his own *New England's Memoriall* (1669). Granted many tracts of land for his services, Morton died one of the richest men in the colony.

The Saints from Leyden on these ships also included Deacon Fuller's wife, his third, and the family of John Jenney, brewery worker, originally of Norwich, who more than ten years later, in 1636, was licensed to build Plymouth's first mill "for grinding and beating of corne," using the water power of Town Brook.

There were more French-speaking Walloons in this company —among others, Mrs. Hester (Mayhieu) Cooke, who had come with three small children to join her husband, one of the *Mayflower* veterans, and Godbert Godbertson, later anglicized as Cuthbert Cuthbertson, who had with him his wife Sarah (Allerton) and three children by their several marriages, this being his second and her third.

Among the Strangers came the wife and five children of "grave" Richard Warren of the *Mayflower* group, once a merchant of London. There was Francis Sprague, who later added to the amenities of New Plimoth by opening up a tavern.

Captain Standish had wooed and won another bride, by mail, and she now came for the wedding, one Barbara by name. That is all that is known about her except that she bore the captain five children and died about 1650. Family tradition has it that Standish's "beloved" Barbara was the sister of his first wife, Rose, who had died in the General Sickness.

With the coming of these ships, immigration stopped until 1629. Plymouth would remain a town of not more than two hundred people for another six years.

2. Daunted and Dismayed

BRADFORD'S
HISTORY

These passengers, when they saw their low & poore condition ashore, were much daunted and dismayed, and according to their diverse humors were diversely affected.

Some wished themselves in England againe. Others fell a-weeping, fancying their own miserie in what they saw now in others; some, pitying the distress they saw their freinds had long been in and still were under.

In a word, all were full of sadness.

Only, some of their old freinds rejoysed to see them, and that it was no worse with them. For they could not expecte it should be better and now hoped they should injoye better days togeather.

And, truly, it was no marvell they should be thus affected, for they were in a very low condition. Many were ragged in aparell, & some little better than halfe naked, though some that were well stored before, were well enough in this regard.

But for food, they were all alike, save some that had got a few peas of ye ship that was last here.

The best dish they could presente their freinds with was a

lobster, or a peece of fish, without bread, or anything else but a cupp of fair spring water.

And ye long continuance of this diet, and their labours abroad, had something abated ye freshnes of their former complexion. But God gave them health and strength, in good measure, and shewed them by experience ye truth of that word, Deut. 8. 3. *That man liveth not by bread only* . . .

[Under the circumstances], the old planters were affraid that their corne, when it was ripe, should be imparted to ye new-comers, whose provissions, . . . they feared, would fall short before ye year wente aboute (as indeed it did). They came to ye Governor and besought him that, as it was before agreed that they should set corne for their perticuler, and accordingly had taken extraordinary pains thereaboute, they might freely injoye the same. And they would not have a bite of ye victails now come, but waite till harvest for their owne.

And let ye new-comers injoye what they had brought. They would have none of it, excepte they could purchase any of it of them by bargaine or exchainge.

Their request was granted them, for it gave both sides good contente.

For ye new-commers were as much afraid that ye hungrie planters would eat up ye provissions brought, and they should fall into ye like condition . . .

3. News from London

BRADFORD'S   I shall here againe take libertie to inserte a few
HISTORY   things out of such letters as came in this ship, desir-
             ing rather to manefest things in their words and
apprehensions than in my owne, as much as may be, without
tediousness:

Beloved freinds,

I kindly salute you all, with trust of your healths & welfare, being right sorie that no supplie hath been made to you all this while. For defence whereof, I must referr you to our generall letters.

Neither, indeed, have we now sent you many things which we should & would, for wante of money.

But persons, more than inough (though not all we should), for people come flying in upon us, but moneys come creeping in to us.

Some few of your freinds have come . . . So they come dropping to you. And by degrees, I hope ere long you shall enjoye them all.

And because people press so hard on us to goe, and often such as are none of the fittest, I pray you write ernestly to ye Treasurer and directe what persons should be sente.

It greeveth me to see so weake a company sent you. And yet, had I not been here, they had been weaker.

You must still call upon the company here to see that honest men be sente you, and threaten to send back if any other come, &c.*

We are not any way so much in danger as by corrupte and noughty persons . . . Neither is there need we should take any lewd men, for we may have honest men enew, &c.

Your assured freind,

R. C.†

The following was from ye generall [i.e., the merchant adventurers' company] . . . . This letter was subscribed with 13 of their names:

Loving freinds,

We most hartily salute you in all love and harty affection, being yet in hope that the same God which hath hithertoo preserved you in a marvelous manner doth yet continue your lives and health, to his owne praise and all our comforts . . .

---

*Like the Virginia Company, the merchant adventurers doubtless found that they did not have much choice in the matter. In recruiting "strangers," they had to take what people were willing to go. They apparently exercised more discretion, however, for at Plymouth there were never the loud complaints about "idle varlets & deboched hands" that constantly echoed along the James.

†Robert Cushman.

We would not have you discontente because we have not sent you more of your old freinds—and in spetiall, him [John Robinson] on whom you most depend.

Farr be it from us to neglecte you, or contemne him. But as ye intente was at first, so ye evente at last will show it, that we will deal fairly and squarly answer your expectations to the full.

There are also come unto you some honest men to plant upon their perticulers beside you, a thing which if we should not give way unto, we should wrong both them and you—them, by putting them on things more inconveniente; and you, for that being honest men, they will be a strengthening to ye place and good neighbours unto you.

Two things we would advise you of, which we have likwise signified them here—first, ye trade for skins to be retained for the generall till ye devidente; 2ndly, that their settling by you be with such distance of place as is neither inconvenient for ye lying of your lands, nor hurtfull to your speedy & easie assembling togeather.

We have sente you diverse fishermen, with salte, &c. Diverse other provisions we have sente you, as will appear in your bill of lading.

And though we have not sent all we would (because our cash is small), yet it is that we could, &c. . . .

And so ye Lord be with you & send us joyfull news from you, and inable us with one shoulder so to accomplish & perfecte his worke so as much glorie may come to Him that confoundeth ye mighty by the weak, and maketh small thinges great.

To whose greatnes, be all glorie for ever & ever.

4. John Oldham's Particular Company

BRADFORD'S HISTORY

Also, . . . there came a company that did not belong to ye generall body, but came on their perticuler, and were to have lands assigned them and be for themselves, yet to be subjecte to ye generall Government, which caused some differance and disturbance amongst them, as will after appeare . . .

These were ye conditions agreed on betweene ye colony and them:

First, that ye Governor, in ye name and with ye consente of ye company, doth in all love and frendship receive and imbrace them, and is to allote them competente places for habitations within ye towne, and promiseth to shew them all such other curtesies as shall be reasonable for them to desire, or us to performe.

2. That they, on their parts, be subjecte to all such laws & orders as are already made, or hereafter shall be, for ye publick good.

3. That they be freed and exempte from ye generall imployments of the said company (which their presente condition of communitie requireth), excepte commune defense & such other imployments as tend to ye perpetuall good of ye collony.

4thly. Towards ye maintenance of Government & publick officers of ye said collony, every male above ye age of 16 years shall pay a bushell of Indean wheat, or ye worth of it, into ye commone store.

5thly. That (according to ye agreemente ye marchants made with them before they came) they are to be wholly debarred from all trade with the Indeans for all sorts of furrs and such like commodities, till ye time of ye communalitie be ended . . .

Those that came on their perticuler looked for greater matters than they found, or could attaine unto, aboute building great houses and such pleasant situations for them as themselves had fancied—as if they would be great men, & rich, all of a sudaine.

But they proved castles in ye aire.

The leader of this group, the only one of its kind sent to Plymouth, was John Oldham, "a man of parts, but high-spirited and extremely passionate." His party consisted of ten persons, one of whom was Roger Conant, salter of London, a man in his early thirties and "a pious, sober, and prudente gentleman," later to make a name for himself in New England.

5. Sir Ferdinando's Devious Hand

BRADFORD'S
HISTORY

About ye middle of September [1623] arrived Captaine Robert Gorges* in ye Bay of the Massachusetts, with sundrie passengers and families, intending there to begine a plantation, and pitched upon ye place Mr. Weston's people had forsaken [at Wessagusset].

He had a commission from ye Counsell of New-England to be generall governor of ye cuntrie, and they appoynted for his counsell & assistance Captaine Francis West, ye aforesaid admiral, Christopher Levite [Levett], Esquire, and ye Governor of Plimouth for ye time being, &c.

Allso, they gave him authoritie to chuse such others as he should find fit. Allso, they gave (by their commission) full power to him & his assistants . . . to doe and execute what to them should seem good in all cases Capitall, Criminal, and Civill, &c., with diverce other instructions.†

He gave them notice of his arrivall by letter. But before they could visite him, he went to ye eastward with ye ship he came in. But a storme arising (and they wanting a good pilot to harbor them in those parts), they bore up for this harbor. He and his men were here kindly entertained. He stayed here 14 days‡ . . .

[Captain Gorges] tooke his leave and went to ye Massachusetts by land, being very thankfull for his kind entertainement.

*Son of Sir Ferdinando Gorges, head of the Council for New England.

†Engineered by Sir Ferdinando Gorges, this was the intervention that Plymouth had long feared, putting an end to the Pilgrims' virtual independence in Church and State. Their affairs would now be directed and controlled by non-Saints, a horrible prospect.

‡Thomas Weston put into Plymouth at this time in the *Swan*, and the new governor general took him severely to task for his "abuses." Saved from punishment on Bradford's plea for him, Weston soon went to Virginia, becoming a member of the House of Burgesses there in 1628. Moving to Maryland, he was elected to the Assembly in 1642, soon returning to England, where he died a few years later at Bristol. Though "a staff of reed" to Plymouth, Weston appears to have been a man of parts.

His ship stayed here and fitted herselfe to goe for Virginia, having some passengers there to deliver.

And with her returned sundrie of those from hence which came over on their perticuler—some, out of discontente and dislike of ye cuntrie; others, by reason of a fire that broke out and burnt ye houses they lived in, and all their provisions, so as they were necessitated thereunto.

This fire was occasioned by some of ye seamen that were roystering in a house where it first begane, makeing a great fire in very cold weather, which broke out of ye chimney into ye thatch, and burnte downe 3 or 4 houses and consumed all ye goods & provissions in them.

The house in which it begane was right against their storehouse, which they had much adoe to save, in which were their common store & all their provissions—ye which, if it had been lost, ye plantation had been overthrowne.

But through God's mercie it was saved by ye great dilligence of ye people & care of ye Governor & some aboute him.

Some would have had ye goods throwne out. But if they had, there would have been much stolne by the rude company that belonged to these 2 ships [Gorges' and Weston's], who were allmost all ashore.

But a trusty company was plased within, as well as those that with wet-cloaths & other means kept ye fire without, that if necessitie required, they might have them out with all speed. For they suspected some malicious dealling, if not plaine treacherie.

And whether it was only suspition or no, God knows.

But this is certaine—that when ye tumulte was greatest, there was a voyce heard (but from whom, it was not knowne) that bid them looke well aboute them, for all were not freinds that were near them.

And shortly after, when the vemencie of ye fire was over, smoke was seen to arise within a shed that was joyned to ye end of ye storehouse, which was watled up with bowes [boughs], in ye withered leaves whereof ye fire was kindled—

where some, running to quench, found a longe firebrand of an ell longe lying under ye wall on ye inside, which could not possibly come there by cassualtie [accident] but must be laid there by some hand, in ye judgmente of all that saw it.

But God kept them from this deanger, whatever was intended . . .

The Governor [Gorges] and some that depended upon him returned for England, having scarcely saluted ye cuntrie in his governmente, not finding the state of things here to answer his qualitie & condition.

The people dispersed themselves. Some went for England; others, for Virginia. Some few remained and were helped with supplies from hence.

The Governour had brought over a [hated Anglican] minister with him, one Mr. [William] Morrell, who, about a year after ye Governour returned, tooke shipping from thence.

He had I know not what power and authority of superintendencie over other churches granted him, and sundrie instructions for that end.

But he never shewed it or made any use of it (it should seeme he saw it was in vaine).*

This was, in effecte, ye end of a 2nd plantation at that place [Wessagusset].

There was allso this year some scatering beginings made in other places, as at Paskataway, by Mr. David Thomson; at Monhigan and some other places, by sundrie others.†

*Wisely refraining from going to Plymouth to stir up a hornets' nest there by asserting his "superintendencie," the Reverend William Morrell spent his time writing a long Latin poem on New England, which he then translated for publication, on the "Ayre, Earth, Water, Fish and Fowles of that Country," being particularly impressed by its great "ghusts of wind."

†David Thompson, an enterprising Scotsman, established himself at the mouth of the Piscataqua River, in what is now Portsmouth, New Hampshire, but soon moved to an island in Boston Harbor—Thompson's Island, as it is still known.

6. Winslow to England

BRADFORD'S
HISTORY

This ship was in a shorte time laden with clap-bord by ye helpe of many hands. Also, they sente in her all ye beaver and other furrs they had.
And Mr. Winslow was sente over with her to informe of all things and procure such things as were thought needfull for their presente condition.

Winslow was carrying the manuscript of his *Good Newes from New-England* and a long letter* to the adventurers, signed by Bradford as governor and Allerton as assistant governor, to this effect:

Plimoth
Sept. 8, 1623

Beloved and kind freinds:

We have received your letters both by the *Anne* and the *James* . . . and by them, a large and liberall supply, for which, together with your loving and honest letters, we give you harty thanks . . .

If God had seen it good, we should have been right glad if it had come sooner, both for our good and your profite. For we have been in a langwishing state and also faine to put away our furrs at a small vallew to helpe us to some necessaries, . . . so as we have little or nothing to send you, for which we are not a little sorie . . .

We put away as much at one time or another of bevar as, if they had been saved together and sold at the best hand, would have yealded £300 or £400 [$20,000].

And these are nothing to those we have lost for wante of means to gather them when the time was, which, I fear, will scarce ever be againe, seeing the Dutch on one side, and the French on the other, and the fishermen and other plantations

*This letter, unexpectedly found in the British Admiralty papers in 1903, appears in the *American Historical Review*, Vol. 8.

between, both have & doe furnish the salvages not with toyes and trifles, but with good and substantial commodities, as kettles, hatchets, and clothes of all sorts—yea, the French doe store them with biskay [Biscay] shallops fitted both with sails and ores, . . . as also with peices, powder, and shott, for fowling and other purposes . . .

We have writ to the Counsell for another patente for Cape Ann—to wit, for the westerside of it, which we know to be as good a harbor as any in this land and is thought to be a good fishing place* . . .

It is for certain that great profite is here raised by fishing . . . And if we could once fall into the right course about it and be able to manage it, it would make good all . . .

It would be a principall stay and a comfortable help to the Colonie if they had some cattle . . .

First, it would much encourage them and be, in time, a greater ease both for tillage of ground and carriage of burden.

2ndly, it will make vitails both more plentifull and comfortable . . .

Especially, goats are very useful for the first and very fit for this place, for they will here thrive very well . . . For kine and other cattle, it will be best, when any come, that it be in the spring†. . . .

Touching our governmente, you are mistaken if you think we admite weomen and children to have to doe in the same, for they are excluded, as both reason and nature teacheth they should be.

Neither doe we admite any but such as are above the age of 21 years, and they also but only in some weighty matters when we thinke good . . .

Now, whereas you think we have been too credulous in receiving insinuations against you and too rash in complaining and censuring of you, as also that to pertickular men letters have been written not with that discretion and deliberation which was meet

---

*Now Gloucester, Massachusetts, long a famed fishing center.
†Plymouth, as yet, had no cows, goats, sheep, or other livestock—and no horses either.

—we answer, what others have written, we know not . . . Only what we have written, we best know and can answer.

And first, we wishte you would either roundly supply us, or else wholly forsake us, that we might know what to doe.

This you call a short and peremptorie resolution. Be it as it will, we were necessarily occasioned by our wants (and the discontents of many) thereunto.

Yet it was never our purpose, or once came into our minds, to enter upon any course before we knew what you would doe upon an equall treaty of things according to our former (as we conceived) bonds betweene us . . .

If necessity or passion have caried others furder, your wisdome (I doute not) will bear it.

As for Capten Standish, we leave him to answere for himselfe [for the action at Wessagusset?]. But this we must say, he is as helpfull an Instrument as any we have, and as carefull of the general good, and doth not well approve himselfe [i.e., he is modest] . . .

Thus againe giving you hartie thanks for your loving affections and large hands extended unto us, we rest,

Your loving freinds to use,
William Bradford, Governor
Isaac Allerton, Assistante

7. Plenty and to Spare

BRADFORD'S HISTORY

By this time, harvest was come. And instead of famine, now God gave them plentie, and ye face of things was changed to ye rejoycing of ye harts of many, for which they blessed God.

And ye effect of their particuler planting was well seene, for all had, one way & another, pretty well to bring ye year aboute. And some of ye abler sorte and more industrious had to spare and sell to others, so as any generall wante or famine hath not been amongst them since . . .

Within less than three years, a truly remarkable feat, the Pilgrims had become self-sustaining and were now securely established on the rough New England coast. In view of their small number and meager resources, it was really a stupendous accomplishment, achieved by hard work, sensible planning, and general devotion to duty by Saints and Strangers alike.

At a cost of £200,000 ($10,000,000) and 9,000 lives—nine out of ten of those shipped to the colony—sixteen-year-old Virginia was not yet self-sustaining or secure. Disaster after disaster there —before the grisly Starving Time and after—had failed to teach the Virginians that they had to put their hand to the plow and keep it there, that they must become self-supporting, that they were fools to depend upon any but themselves for their food and their very lives.

Through sheer tenacity and unbending purpose, guided by their sharp wits and good judgment, the Pilgrims had quickly conquered the wilderness about them. And the victory was their own, for as Bradford once observed, they had never had any substantial aid from any quarter.

XVII
Sixes and Sevens

I am sorry there is no more discretion used by some in their letters hither. Some say you are starved in body & soule; others, that you eate piggs & doggs that dye alone . . .

—*Robert Cushman*

BRADFORD'S HISTORY   The time for new elections of their officers for this year [1624] having come, and ye number of their people increased, and their troubles and occasions therewith, the Governor desired them to chainge ye persons as well as renew ye election; and also, to adde more Assistants to ye Governor for help & counsell, and ye better carrying on of affairs, showing that it was necessarie it should be so.

If it was any honour or benefite, it was fitte others should be made pertakers of it.

If it was a burthen (as doubtles it was), it was but equall others should help to bear it, and that this was ye end of annuall elections.

The issue was that, as before there was but one Assistante, they now chose 5, giving the Governor a duble voyce.* And afterward [in 1633] they increased them to seven . . .

---

*Plymouth would not hear of Governor Bradford's desire to retire, returning him to his post and keeping him continuously in office till his death more than thirty years later, almost always as governor.

Under the new enlarged administration, Allerton remained the first and principal assistant governor. The names of the other four are unknown. But there is reason to believe that they were Standish, Winslow, Stephen Hopkins, and Richard Warren, all of the *Mayflower* group.

1. Shipwreck

BRADFORD'S
HISTORY It rests now that I speake a word about ye pinnace [*Little James*] spoken of before, which was sent by ye adventurers to be imployed in ye cuntrie.

She was a fine vessell and bravely set out, with her flages, & streamers, pendents, & wastcloaths, &c. And I fear ye adventurers did overpride themselves in her, for she had ill success.

However, they erred grossly in two respects about her.

First, though she had a sufficiente maister, yet she was rudely manned. And all her men were upon shares, and none was to have any wages but the master.

Secondly, whereas they mainly lookt at trade, they had sent nothing of value to trade with.

When the men came here and mette with ill counsell from Mr. Weston & his crue, with others of ye same stampe, neither ye master nor Governour could scarce rule them. They exclaimed that they were abused & deceived, for they were tould they should goe for a man of warr and take I know not whom, French & Spaniards, &c. They would neither trade nor fish excepte they had wages.

In fine, they would obey no command of ye maisters, so it was apprehended they would either run away with ye vessell, or get away with ye ships.

So as Mr. Peirce & other of their freinds perswaded the Governor to change their condition and give them wages, which was accordingly done.

And she was sente about ye Cape to ye Narigansetts to trade. But they made a poore vioage of it . . .

Allso, in her returne home, at ye very entrance of their owne harbore, she had like to have been cast away in a storme and was forced to cut her mainmast by ye bord to save herselfe from driving on ye flats that lye without, called Brown's Ilands—the force of ye wind being so great as made her anchors give way, and she drove right upon them. But her mast & tackling being gone, they held her till ye wind shifted . . .

They, having with some truble & charge new-masted and rigged their pinass, in ye beginning of March [1624] they sent her well vitailed to the eastward on fishing.

She arrived safely at a place near Damariscove and was there well harbored in a place where ships used to ride, there being also some ships allready arrived out of England.

But shortly after, there arose such a violent & extraordinarie storme as ye seas broak over such places in ye harbor as was never seene before, and drove her against great roks, which beat such a hole in her bulke as a horse and cart might have gone in— and after, drove her into deep-water, where she lay sunke.

The master was drowned. The rest of ye men, all save one, saved their lives, with much adoe. All her provision, salt, and what else was in her, was lost.

And here I must leave her to lye till afterward.

2. Despair at Leyden

BRADFORD'S   Shortly after, Mr. Winslow came over [re-
HISTORY   turning from his visit to London] and brought a
pretty good supply, and the ship [the *Charity*] came on fishing, a thing fatall to this plantation.

He brought 3 heifers & a bull, the first beginning of any cattle of that kind in ye land, with some cloathing & other necessaries . . . —but withall, ye reporte of a strong faction amongst the adventurers against them, and especially against ye coming of ye rest from Leyden; and with what difficulty this supply was procured . . .

Some letters from them shall better declare these things, being as followeth . . .

Leyden
Des: 19, 1623

My loving & much beloved freind [Bradford],

. . . Of your love and care for us here, we never doubted. So we are glad to take knowledge of it in that fulness we doe. Our love & care to and for you is mutuall, though our hopes of coming unto you be small and weaker than ever . . .

The adventurers, it seems, have neither money nor any great mind of us, for ye most parte. They deney it to be any part of ye covenants betwixte us that they should transporte us. Neither doe I looke for any further help from them till means come from you.

We here are strangers, in effecte, to ye whole course, and so both we and you [who were the principals] intended in this bussines are scarce accessaries, &c.

My wife, with me, re-salute you & yours.

Unto him who is ye same to his in all places, and nere to them who are farr from one another, I comend you and all with you, resting,

Yours truly loving,
John Robinson

His to Mr. Brewster:

Leyden
Des: 20, 1623

Loving and dear freind and brother:

That which I most desired of God in regard of you—namely, ye continuance of your life and health, and the safe coming of these sent unto you—that I most gladly hear of and praise God for the same.

And I hope Mrs. Brewster's weake and decayed state of body will have some repairing by the coming of her daughters, and the provisions in this and former ships . . . Which makes us with more patience bear our languishing state and ye deferring of our desired transportation—which I call desired, rather than hoped for . . .

For first, there is no hope at all that I know or can conceive of, of any new stock to be raised for that end. So that all must depend upon returns from you, in which are so many uncertainties as that nothing with any certaintie can thence be concluded.

Besides, howsoever, for ye presente, the adventurers alledge nothing but want of money, which is an invincible difficulty. Yet if that were taken away by you, others without doubt will be found.

For the better clearing of this, we must dispose ye adventurers into 3 parts, and of them some 5 or 6 (as I conceive) are absolutely bent for us, above any others.

Other 5 or 6 are our bitter professed adversaries. The rest, being the body, I conceive to be honestly minded & loveingly also towards us, yet such as have others (namely, ye forward preachers)* nearer unto them than us, and whose course, so farr as there is any difference, they would rather advance than ours . . .

And I perswade myselfe that, for me, they of all others are unwilling I should be transported, espetially such of them as have an eye that way themselves, as thinking if I come there, their market will be marred . . .

A notable experimente of this they gave in your messenger's [Winslow's] presence, constraining ye company to promise that none of the money now gathered should be expended or imployed to ye help of any of us towards you . . .

Whether any larned man† will come unto you or not, I know not. If any doe, you must consult *Consiliu capere in arena.*

Be you most hartily saluted, & your wife with you, both from me & mine. Your God & ours, and ye God of all his, bring us together if it be his will, and keep us in the meanwhile and allways to his glory, and make us servisable to his Majestie, and faithfull to the end.

Amen.

Your very loving brother,

John Robinson

*That is, Puritan rather than Separatist preachers.
†A minister, that is.

3. Troubles in London

[London]
Jan: 25, 1624

BRADFORD'S
HISTORY

Most worthy & loving freinds,
Your kind & loving letters I have received and
render you many thanks, &c.

It hath pleased God to stirre up ye harts of our adventurers to
raise a new stock for ye setting forth of this ship, called ye
Charitie, with men & necessaries, both for ye plantation and ye
fishing, though accomplished with great difficulty, in regard we
have some amongst us which undoubtedly aime more at their
owne private ends, and ye thwarting & opposing of some here
and other worthy instruments* of God's glory elsewhere, than
at ye generall good and furtherance of this noble & laudable
action . . .

But why should I trouble you or myselfe with these restless
opposers of all goodnes? . . . On Thursday, ye 8 of Jan., we
had a meeting aboute the artickls betweene you & us, where
they would rejecte that which we, in our late letters, prest you
to grant (an addition to ye time of our joynt stock) . . .

[They] offered to sell their adventures, and some were willing
to buy. But I, doubting [fearing] they would raise more scandale
and false reports and so diverse wayes doe us more hurt by going
off in such a furie than they could or can by continuing adventurers amongst us, would not suffer them.

But on ye 12 of Jan., we had another meeting. But in the
interime, diverse of us had talked with most of them, privately,
and had great combats & reasoning, pro & con.

But at night, when we met to read ye generall letter, we had
ye loveingest and frendlyest meeting that ever I knew,† and our
greatest enemies offerd to lend us £50. So I sent for a potle of

---

*"He means Mr. Robinson."—Bradford's note.
†"But this lasted not long . . ."—Bradford's note.

wine (I wish you could doe ye like), which we drank freindly together.

Thus God can turne ye harts of men when it pleaseth him, &c.

Thus, loving freinds, I hartily salute you all in ye Lord, hoping ever to rest,

Yours to my power,
James Sherley*

Another letter [this from Cushman to Bradford]:

Jan. 24, 1624

Beloved Sir, &c:

We have now sente you, we hope, men & means to settle these 3 things—viz., fishing, salt-making, and boat-making. If you can bring them to some perfection, your wants may be supplyed. I pray you to bend yourselfe what you can to settle these bussinesses . . .

This ship carpenter is thought to be the fittest man for you in the land and will no doubte doe you much good. Let him build you 2 catches [ketches], a lighter, and some 6 or 7 shallops as soone as you can.

The salt-man is a skillfull & industrious man. Put some to him that may quickly apprehende ye misterie of it . . .

We have tooke a patente for Cape Anne, &c. . . .

The preacher we have sent is (we hope) an honest plaine man, though none of ye most eminente and rare. About chusing him into office, use your owne liberty & discretion.

He knows he is no officer amongst you, though perhaps custome & universalitie may make him forget himselfe. Mr. Winslow & myselfe gave way to his going to give contente to some here, and we see no hurt in it, but only his great charge of children . . .

---

*James Sherley had succeeded Thomas Weston as treasurer and chief officer of the merchant adventurers' group, which remained a voluntary association, never being officially incorporated. Sherley was a goldsmith who lived on Crooked Lane, not far from his shop at the sign of the Golden Horseshoe on London Bridge.

I am sorry there is no more discretion used by some in their letters hither.* Some say you are starved in body & soule—others, that ye things here spoken of, ye goodnes of ye cuntry, are gross and palpable lyes—that there is scarce a foule to be seene, or a fish to be taken, and many such like.

I would such discontented men were here againe, for it is a miserie when ye whole state of a plantation shall be thus exposed to ye passionate humours of some discontented men . . . Mean space, it is all our crosses, and we must bear them.

I am sorie we have not sent you more and other things. But in truth, we have rune into so much charge to victaile ye ship, provide salte & other fishing implements, &c., as we could not provide other comfortable things, as butter, suger, &c.

I hope the returne of this ship and the *James* will put us in cash againe. The Lord make you full of courage in this troublesome bussines, which must now be stuck unto till God gives us rest from our labours. Fare well in all harty affection.

Your assured freind,
R. C.

4. Religious and Other Complaints

BRADFORD S HISTORY   With ye former letter written by Mr. Sherley, there were sente sundrie objections, concerning which he thus writeth:

"These are the cheefe objections which they that are now returned make against you and the countrie. I pray you consider them and answer them by the first conveniencie . . ."

I shall here set them downe with ye answers then made unto them and sent over at ye returne of this ship, which did so confound ye objectors as some confessed their falte, and others deneyed what they had said and eate their words . . .

1. obj. was diversitie aboute Religion.

Ans: We know no such matter, for here was never any

*"This was John Oldham & his like."—Bradford's note.

controversie or opposition, either publicke or private (to our knowledg), since we came.*

2. ob: Neglecte of familie duties on ye Lord's Day.

Ans: We allow no such thing, but blame it in ourselves and others.

3. ob: Wante of both the sacrements.

Ans: The more is our greefe that our pastor is kept from us, by whom we might injoye them† . . .

4. ob: Children not catechised, nor taught to read.

Ans: Neither is true, for diverse take pains with their owne as they can. Indeede, we have no commone schoole for want of a fitt person, or hithertoo means to maintaine one, though we desire now to begine.‡

5. ob: Many of ye perticuler members of ye plantation will not work for ye generall.

Ans: This allso is not wholy true. For though some doe it not willingly, & others not honestly, yet all doe it. And he that doth worst gets his owne foode & something besides . . .

6. ob: The water is not wholsome.

Ans: If they mean not so wholsome as ye good beer and wine in London (which they so dearly love), we will not dispute with them. But els, for water, it is as good as any in ye world (for ought we knowe) . . .

7. ob: The ground is barren and doth bear no grasse.

Ans: It is here (as in all places) some better & some worse . . . The cattle find grasse, for they are as fatt as need be. We wish we had but one for every hundred that here is grasse to keep . . .

8. ob: The fish will not take salt to keepe sweete.

*And Bradford might have added that it was a good thing no opposition had dared show its face, for the Saints demanded as strict uniformity as their hated enemies, the "anti-Christian" Anglican bishops. Bradford's reply was disingenuous, for many of the Strangers had not yet joined the Pilgrim church. They would have preferred the Anglican rite if they might have exercised it.

†As the Pilgrims had no pastor and Ruling Elder Brewster was not authorized to administer the sacraments, those at Plymouth could not enjoy the Lord's Supper and no children could be baptized.

‡The first school was not established till more than a half century later.

Ans: This is as true as that which was written: that there is scarce a foule to be seene, or a fish to be taken—things likely to be true in a cuntrie where so many sayle of ships come yearly a-fishing. They might as well say, there can no ale or beer in London be kept from sowering.

9. ob: Many of them are theevish, and steal one from another.

Ans: Would that London had been free from that crime. Then we should not have been trobled with these here. It is well knowne sundrie have smarted well for it. And so are ye rest like to doe if they be taken.

10. ob: The countrie is annoyed with foxes and woulfes.

Ans: So are many other good cuntries, too . . .

11. ob: The Dutch are planted near Hudson's Bay [River] and are likely to overthrow the trade.

Ans: They will come and plante in these parts also, if we and others doe not, but goe home and leave it to them. We rather commend them, than condemne them, for it.

12. ob: The people are much annoyed with muskeetoes.

Ans: They are too delicate and unfitte to begine new plantations and collonies, that cannot enduer the biting of a muskeeto.

We would wish such to keepe at home till at least they be muskeeto-proofe . . .

5. More Losses and Crosses

BRADFORD'S HISTORY — The ship [the *Charity*] which brought this supply was speedily discharged, and with her master & company sent to Cape Anne (of which place they had gott a patente, as before is shewed), on fishing. And because ye season was so farr spente, some of ye planters were sent to help to build their stage, to their owne hinderance.

But partly by ye lateness of ye year, and more espetialy by ye baseness of ye master, one Baker, they made a poore viage of it. He proved a very drunken beast and did nothing (in a manner) but drink & guzzle, and consume away ye time & his victails. And most of his company followed his example . . .

So as ye loss was great, and would have been more to them but that they kept one a-trading there, who in those times got some store of skins, which was some help unto them.

The ship-carpenter that was sent them was an honest and very industrious man, and followed his labour very diligently and made all that were imployed with him doe ye like. He quickly builte them 2 very good & strong shallops (which, after, did them greate service), and a great and strong lighter, and had hewne timber for 2 catches [ketches].

But that was lost, for he fell into a feaver in ye hote season of ye year. And though he had the best means ye place could afford, yet he dyed, of whom they had a very great loss and were very sorie for his death.

But he whom they sent to make salte was an ignorante, foolish, self-willed fellow. He bore them in hand he could doe great matters in making salt-works.

So he was sente to seeke out fitt ground for his purpose. And after some serch, he tould ye Governor that he had found a sufficiente place, . . . but he must have 8 or ten men to be constantly imployed. He was wished to be sure that ye ground was good and other things answerable. Otherwise, he would bring upon them a great charge by imploying himselfe and so many men.

But he was, after some triall, so confidente as he caused them to send carpenters to rear a frame for a large house to receive ye salte & such other uses.

But in the end, all proved vaine. Then he layed the fault to ye ground, in which he was deceived. But if he might have the lighter to carry clay, he was sure then he could doe it.

Now, though ye Governour & some others foresaw that this would come to little, yet they had so many malignant spirits amongst them that would have laid it upon them, in their letters of complainte to ye adventurers, as to be their fault that would not suffer him to goe on to bring his work to perfection, . . .

so as they were faine to let him goe on till all men saw his vanity.

For he could not doe anything but boyle salt in pans, & yet would make them that were joyned with him beleeve there was so great a misterie in it as was not easie to be attained, and made them doe many unnecessary things to blind their eyes, till they discerned his subtletie.

The next year, he was sente to Cape Anne, and ye pans were set up there where the fishing was.

But before summer was out, he burnte the house, and the fire was so vehemente as it spoyled the pans, at least some of them, and this was the end of that chargable bussines.

6. An Acre of Ground

BRADFORD'S HISTORY And before I come to other things, I must speake a word of their planting this year [1624], they having found ye benifite of their last year's harvest and setting corne for their particuler, having thereby with a great deale of patience overcome hunger & famine.

Which maks me remember a saing of Seneca's, *Epis:* 123. *That a great parte of libertie is a well governed belly, and to be patiente in all wants.*

They begane now highly to prize corne as more precious than silver. And those that had some to spare begane to trade one with another for small things, by ye quarte, potle, & peck, &c. For money they had none. And if any had, corne was preferred before it.

That they might therefore encrease their tillage to better advantage, they made suite to the Governor to have some portion of land given to them for continuance—and not by yearly lotte, for by that means that which ye more industrious had brought into good culture (by much pains) one year, came to leave it ye nexte, and often another might injoye it, so as the dressing of their lands were the more sleighted over, & to less profite.

Which being well considered, their request was granted. And

to every person was given only one acrre of land, to them & theirs, as nere ye towne as might be, and they had no more till ye 7 years were expired. The reason was, that they might be kept close together for more saftie and defence, and ye better improvement of ye generall imployments.

Which condition of theirs did make me often thinke of what I had read in Plinie of ye Romans' first beginnings in Romulus' time. *How every man contented himselfe with 2 acres of land, and had no more assigned them. And chap. 3. It was thought a great reward to receive at ye hands of ye people of Rome a pinte of corne. And long after, the greatest presente given to a Captaine that had gotte a victory over their enemies was as much ground as he could till in one day. And he was not counted a good but a dangerous man that would not contente himselfe with 7 acres of land. As also, how they pound their corne in morters,* as these people [at Plymouth] were forcte to doe many years before they could get a mill.

XVIII
Plymouth's First Pastor

I purposed before I came to undergoe hardnes. Therefore I shall, I hope, cheerfully bear ye conditions of ye
place, though very mean. And they have changed my
wages ten times allready.

—John Lyford

BRADFORD'S HISTORY The 3rd eminente person (which ye letters before mention) was ye minister which they sente
over—by name, John Lyford, of whom & whose
doing I must be more large, though I shall abridge things as much
as I can.

A graduate of Oxford, now in his late forties, Lyford had spent
many years ministering to small parishes in England and Ireland.
With him had come his wife and five children.

1. As If Made All of Love

BRADFORD'S HISTORY When this man came ashore, he saluted them
with that reverence & humilitie as is seldome to be
seen—and indeed, made them ashamed, he so
bowed and cringed unto them—and would have kissed their
hands if they would have suffered him.

Yea, he wept & shed many tears, blessing God that had brought
him to see their faces, and admiring ye things they had done in
their wants, &c.—as if he had been made all of love, and ye
humblest person in ye world.

And all ye while (if we may judge by his after carriages) he was but like him mentioned in Psa: 10. 10., that croucheth & boweth, that heaps of poore may fall by his might.

Or like to that dissembling Ishmaell,* who, when he had slaine Gedelia, went out weeping and mette them that were coming to offer incense in ye house of ye Lord, saying, come to Gedelia, when he ment to slay them.

They gave him the best entertainment they could (in all simplisitie) and a larger allowance of food out of ye store than any other had. And as the Governor had used in all waightie affairs to consulte with their Elder, Mr. Brewster, together with his assistants, so now he called Mr. Lyford also to counsell with them in their waightiest bussineses.

After some short time, he desired to joyne himselfe a member to ye church here, and was accordingly received.

He made a large confession of his faith, and an acknowledgement of his former disorderly walking, and his being intangled with many corruptions which had been a burthen to his conscience,† and blessed God for this opportunitie of freedom & libertie to injoye ye ordinances of God in puritie among his people, with many more such like expressions.

I must here speake a word also of Mr. John Oldham, who was a co-partner with him in his after courses.

He had beene a cheefe sticler in ye former faction among ye perticulers, and an intelligencer to those in England. But now . . . he desired former things might be forgotten, and that they would looke upon him as one that desired to close with them in all things . . .

Upon this, they shewed all readynes to imbrace his love, and carry towards him in all frendlynes, and called him to counsell with them in all cheefe affairs, as ye other, without any distrust at all.

*"Jer. 41. 6."—Bradford's note.
†His "former disorderly walking" and "corruptions," as used here, meant only that he had been a member of the Church of England and had practiced the Anglican rite.

Thus all things seemed to goe very comfortably and smoothly amongst them, at which they did much rejoyce.

2. Private Meetings and Whisperings

BRADFORD'S HISTORY

But this lasted not long, for both Oldham and he grew very perverse and shewed a spirite of great malignancie, drawing as many into faction as they could.

Were they never so vile or profane, they did nourish & back them in all their doings, so long as they would but cleave to them and speak against ye church here.

So as there was nothing but private meetings and whisperings amongst them, they feeding themselves & others with what they would bring to pass in England by the faction of their freinds there—which brought others, as well as themselves, into a fool's paradise.

Yet they could not carry so closely but much of both their doings & sayings were discovered. Yet outwardly, they still set a faire face on things.

At length, when ye ship [the *Charity*] was ready to goe, it was observed Lyford was long in writing, & sente many letters, and could not forbear to communicate to his intimates such things as made them laugh in their sleeves . . .

The Governor and some other of his friends, knowing how things stood in England, and what hurt these things might do, tooke a shallop and wente out with the ship a league or 2 to sea, and called for all of Lyford's & Oldham's letters . . .

He found above 20 of Lyford's letters, many of them large, and full of slanders & false accusations, tending not only to their prejudice, but to their ruine & utter subversion.

Most of the letters they let pass, only tooke copies of them. But some of ye most materiall they sent true copies of them, and kept ye originalls, lest he should deney them, and that they might produce his owne hand against him . . .

This ship went out towards evening, and in the night ye Governor returned.

They were somewhat blanke at it. But after some weeks, when they heard nothing, they then were as briske as ever, thinking nothing had been knowne, . . . and that the Governor went but to dispatch his own letters.

The reason why the Governor & the rest concealed these things the longer was to let things ripen, that they might ye better discover their intents and see who were their adherents.

And ye rather because, amongst ye rest, they found a letter of one of their confederates, in which was written that Mr. Oldham & Mr. Lyford intended a reformation in church and commonewealth. And as soone as the ship was gone, they intended to joyne togeather and have the sacrements, &c.

3. Tumults

BRADFORD'S HISTORY   For Oldham, few of his letters were found (for he was so bad a scribe as his hand was scarce legible). Yet he was as deepe in ye mischeefe as the other. And thinking they were now strong enough, they begane to pick quarrells at everything.

Oldham, being called to watch (according to order), refused to come, fell out with ye Capten [Standish], called him raskell, and beggerly raskell—and resisted him, drew his knife at him, though he offered him no wrong, nor gave him no ille termes, but with all fairness required him to do his duty.

The Governor, hearing ye tumulte, sent to quiet it. But he ramped more like a furious beast than a man, and cald them all treatours, and rebells, and other such foule language as I am ashamed to remember.

But after he was clapt up awhile, he came to himselfe, and with some slight punishmente was let goe . . .

But to cut things short, at length it grew to this issue, that Lyford with his complices, without ever speaking one word either to ye Governor, Church, or Elder, withdrew themselves and set up a publick meeting aparte on ye Lord's day* . . .

It was now thought high time, to prevente further mischeefe, to calle them to accounte.

4. Judgment Day

BRADFORD'S
HISTORY

So ye Governor called a courte [which met in the Fort] and summoned the whole company to appeare, and then charged Lyford & Oldham with such things as they were guilty of, . . . that they were plotting against them and disturbing their peace, both in respecte of their civill & church state—which was most injurious, for both they and all ye world knew they came hither to injoye ye libertie of their conscience and ye free use of God's ordinances . . .

But they were stiffe & stood resolutely upon ye deneyall of most things, and required proofe . . . Lyford denyed that he had anything to doe with them in England, or knew of their courses . . . Then his letters were produced & some of them read, at which he was struck mute.

But Oldham begane to rage furiously because they had intercepted and opened his letters, threatening them in very high language. And in a most audacious and mutinous manner stood up & called upon ye people, saying:

"My masters, where is your harts? Now shew your courage! You have oft complained to me of so & so. Now is ye time if you will doe anything! I will stand by you, &c."

Thinking that everyone (knowing his humor) that had soothed and flattered him, or otherwise in their discontent had uttered anything unto him, would now side with him in open rebellion.

But he was deceived, for not a man opened his mouth. But all were silent, being strucken with the injustice of ye thing.

*As the Saints themselves had done at Scrooby, without leave and in defiance of the authorities. But, like all doctrinaires, they ignored the inconsistency. They alone had the "trueth." All else was "Sathan's worke."

Then ye Governor turned his speech to Mr. Lyford, and asked him if he thought they had done evill to open his letters. But he was silent & would not say a word, well knowing what they might reply.

Then ye Governor shewed the people he did it as a magistrate, and was bound to it by his place, to prevent ye mischeefe & ruine that this conspiracie and plots of theirs would bring on this poor colony.

But he, besides his evill dealing here, had delte treacherously with his freinds that trusted him, & stole their letters & opened them, and sent coppies of them, with disgracefull annotations, to his freinds in England.

And then ye Governor produced them and his other letters under his owne hand (which he could not deney), and caused them to be read before all ye people, at which all his friends were blanke and had not a word to say* . . .

After the reading of his letters before the whole company, he was demanded what he could say to these things. But all ye answer was, that Billington and some others had informed him of many things and made sundrie complaints, which they now deneyed . . .

And so they wente on from poynte to poynte and wisht him, or any of his freinds & confederates, not to spare them in any-thing. If he or they had any proofe or witness of any corrupte or evill dealing of theirs, his or their evidence must needs be there present, for there was the whole company and sundery strangers.

He said he had been abused by others in their informations (as he now well saw), and so had abused them. And this was all the answer they could have, for none would take his parte in anything . . .

Then they delte with him aboute his dissembling with them aboute ye church, and that he professed to concur with them in

*With his always fine sense of the dramatic, Bradford must have enjoyed this scene in which he was the *demiourgos*.

all things, . . . and yet now he contested against them and drew a company aparte, & sequestered himselfe, and would go minister the sacrements (by his Episcopall calling) without ever speaking a word unto them, either as magistrates or bretheren.

In conclusion, he was fully convicted and burst into tears, and "confest he feared he was a reprobate, his sinns were so great that he doubted God would pardon them; he was unsavorie salte, &c, and that he had so wronged them as he could never make them amends, confessing all he had written against them was false & nought, both for matter and manner."

And all this he did with as much fullness as words & tears could express.

After their triall & conviction, the court censured them to be expeld from the place—Oldham presently, though his wife & family had liberty to stay all winter or longer, till he could make provission to remove them comfortably.*

Lyford had liberty to stay 6 months. It was, indeede, with some eye to his release, if he carried himselfe well in the meantime, and that his repentance proved sound.

Lyford acknowledged his censure was farr less than he deserved. Afterwards, he confest his sin publickly in ye church, with tears more largely than before . . .

And Samuell Fuller (a deacon amongst them), and some other tender-harted men amongst them, were so taken with his signes of sorrow & repentance as they professed they would fall upon their knees to have his censure released . . .

*Expulsion was a severe punishment on the wild frontier. Oldham went north some thirty miles and established a settlement at Nantasket, now the town of Hull, on the lower shore of Boston Bay. With him went a number of discontented Pilgrims, including Roger Conant, founder of Salem in the Massachusetts Bay Colony, and William Hilton and his family, who founded Dover, New Hampshire, and were prominent in the early history of that area.

The rumpus at Plymouth had been caused in part by the birth of a child to the young William Hiltons. As they were Anglicans, the infant could not be baptized here. Anxious about this, they appealed to Lyford, who arranged a private baptism, "signing the babe with a sign of the Cross on the forehead." The Saints hated the sign of the cross as another Roman "corruption," having as little use for it as for Christmas.

So they began againe to conceive good thoughts of him upon this his repentance, and admitted him to teach amongst them as before.

5. Second Fall from Grace

BRADFORD'S
HISTORY

But that which made them all stand amazed in the end, and may doe all others that shall come to hear ye same (for a rarer president can scarce be showne), was that after a month or two, notwithstanding all his former confessions, convictions, and publick acknowledgements, both in ye face of ye church and whole company, with so many tears & sadd censures of himselfe before God & men, he should goe againe to justifie what he had done.

For secretly he wrote a 2nd letter to ye adventurers in England, in which he justified all his former writings (save in some things which tended to their damage) . . .

Lyford sent his last letter in great secrecie. But ye party intrusted with it gave it to ye Governor . . .

Aug: 22.
Ano: 1624

Worthy Sirs:

Though the filth of mine owne doings may justly be cast in my face, . . . yet that ye truth may not hereby be injured, yourselves any longer deluded, nor injurious dealing carried out still with bold out-facings, I have adventured once more to write unto you.

First, I doe freely confess I delte very indiscreetly in some of my perticuler letters which I wrote to private friends . . .

And had it not been for ye respecte I have unto you, and some other matters of private regard, I had returned againe at this time by ye pinnace for England. For here I purpose not to abide unless I receive better incouragemente from you than from the church (as they call themselves) here I doe receive.

I purposed before I came to undergoe hardnes. Therefore I shall, I hope, cheerfully bear ye conditions of ye place, though very mean. And they have changed my wages ten times allready.

I suppose my letters, or at least coppies of them, are come to your hands . . . I pray you take notice of this, that I have written nothing but what is certainly true, and I could make so appear plainly to any indifferente men, whatsoever colours be cast to darken ye truth—and some there are very audacious this way.

Besides, many other matters are farr out of order here. My mind was not to enlarge myselfe any further, but in respecte of diverse poore souls here, ye care of whom belongs in parte to you, being here destitute of the means of salvation.

For howsoever ye church are provided for to their contente, who are ye smallest number in ye collony and doe so appropriate ye ministrie to themselves, holding this principle, that ye Lord hath not appointed any ordinary ministrie for ye conversion of those that are without, so that some of ye poor souls have with tears complained of this to me, and I was taxed for preaching to all in generall.

Though, in truth, they have had no ministrie here since they came but such as may be performed by any of you, . . . whatsoever great pretences they make.

But herein they equivocate, as in many other things they doe . . . I rest, &c.,

Remaining yours ever,
John Lyford, Exille

They made a breefe answer to some things in this letter . . . And first, [he] complains that we have changed his wages ten times.

We never agreed with him for any wages, nor made any bargen at all with him—neither know of any that you have made.

You sent him over to teach amongst us, and desired he might be kindly used. And more than this, we know not . . .

It will appear . . . that he hath ever had a larger allowance of food out of ye store for him and his than any, and clothing as his neede required, a dwelling in one of our best houses, and a man wholly at his owne command to tend his private affairs. What cause he hath therefor to complaine, judge ye . . .

Againe, he saith he was taxed for preaching to all in generall.

This is a meere untruth, for this dissembler knows that every Lord's day some are appointed to visit suspected places, & if any be found idling and neglecte ye hearing of ye word (through idleness or profaneness), they are punished for ye same. Now, to procure all to come to hear, and then to blame him for preaching to all, were to play ye mad man.

Next, he saith they have had no ministrie there since they came, whatsoever pretences they make, &c.

We answer, the more is our wrong that our pastor is kept from us, and then reproach us for it . . .

Yet have we not been wholly destitute of ye means of salvation, as this man would make ye world beleeve. For our reverend Elder [Brewster] hath laboured diligently in dispencing the word of God unto us . . . And be it spoken without ostentation, he is not inferriour to Mr. Lyford (& some of his betters) either in gifts or larning, though he would never be perswaded to take higher office upon him.

6. Hand of God

BRADFORD'S
HISTORY His [Lyford's] time being now expired, his censure was to take place, . . . as he had dubled his evill, as is before noted.

But first, behold ye hand of God concerning him, wherein that of ye Psalmist is verified. Psa: 7. 15. He hath made a pitte & digged it, and is fallen into the pitte he made.

For when he was delte with aboute his second letter, his wife was so affected with his doings as she could no longer conceal her greefe and sorrow of mind, but opens ye same to one of their deacons & some other of her freinds . . .

Which was to this purpose, that she feared some great judgment of God would fall upon them, and upon her, for her husband's cause.

Now that they were to remove, she feared to fall into ye Indeans' hands and be defiled by them, as he had defiled other women; or some such like judgmente as God had threatened David, 2. Sam. 12. 11. I will raise up evill against ye, and will take thy wives & give them, &c.

And upon it showed how he had wronged her—as first, he had a bastard by another before they were married . . . He not only stiffly denied it but, to satisfie her, tooke a solemne oath there was no such matter. Upon which, she gave consente and married with him.

But afterward, it was found true, and ye bastard brought home to them. She then charged him with his oath, but he prayed pardon, and said he should else not have had her.

And afterward, she could keep no maids but he would be medling with them. And some times she hath taken them in ye manner, as they lay at their bed's feete, with such other circumstances as I am ashamed to relate.

The woman, being a grave matron & of good cariage all ye while she was here, spoake these things out of ye sorrow of her harte, sparingly, and yet with some further intimations.

And that which did most seeme to affecte her (as they conceived) was to see his former cariage in his repentance, not only here with ye church but formerly about those things, shedding tears and using great & sadd expressions, and yet eftsoones falls into the like things . . .

From hence, Lyford went to Nantasket, in ye Bay of ye Massachusetts, with some other of his freinds with him, where Oldham allso lived. From thence, he removed to Namkeke [Naumkeag], since called Salem. But after there came some people over, whether for hope of greater profite or what ends else I know not, he left his freinds that followed him, and went from thence to Virginia, where he shortly after dyed, and so I leave him to ye Lord.

His wife afterwards returned againe to this cuntrie, and thus much of this matter.

7. Thumps and Reconciliation

BRADFORD'S   The winter [of 1624–25] was passed over in
HISTORY   their ordinarie affairs without any spetial matter
worth noting, except that many who before stood
something off from ye church, now seeing Lyford's unrighteous
dealing and malignitie against ye church, now tendered themselves to ye church and were joyned to ye same, professing that
it was not out of their dislike of anything that they had stood off
so long, but a desire to fitte themselves better for such a state,
and they saw now ye Lord cald for their help.

And so these troubles produced a quite contrary effecte in
sundrie here than those adversaries hoped for. Which was looked
at as a great worke of God—to draw on men by unlikely means
and that in reason which might rather have set them further off
. . .

At ye spring of ye year, about ye time of their Election Court,
Oldham came againe amongst them. And though it was a part
of his censure for his former mutiny and miscarriage not to returne without leave first obtained, yet in his daring spirite he
presumed without any leave at all, being also set on & hardened
by ye ill counsell of others.

And not only so, but suffered his unruly passion to run beyond ye limits of all reason and modestie, insomuch that some
strangers which came with him were ashamed of his outrage and
rebuked him.

But all reproofes were but as oyle to ye fire, and made ye
flame of his choler greater. He called them all to nought in this
his mad furie, and a hundred rebells and traytors, and I know
not what.*

But in conclusion, they committed him [to the fort] till he

*As a friend once observed, Oldham could be "a mad jack in his mood."

was tamer, and then appointed a gard of musketeers which he was to pass through. And every one was ordered to give him a thump on ye brich, with ye butt end of his musket, and then he was conveyed to ye water side, where a boat was ready to carry him away. Then they bid him goe & mende his manners . . .

But that I may here make an end with him . . . After the removall of his familie from hence, he fell into some straits (as some others did). And aboute a year or more afterwards, toward winter, he intended a vioage for Virginia. But it pleased God that ye barke that carried him and many other passengers were in that danger as they dispaired of life. So as many of them fell to prayer, so also did they begine to examine their consciences and confess such sins as did most burthen them.

And Mr. Oldham did make a large and free confession of ye wrongs and hurt he had done to ye people and church here . . .

It pleased God to spare their lives, though they lost their vioage.

And in time afterwards, Oldham carried himselfe fairly towards them, and acknowledged ye hand of God to be with them, and seemed to have an honourable respecte for them; and so farr made his peace with them as he, in after time, had libertie to goe and come, and converse with them, at his pleasure.

He went after this to Virginia and had there a great sickness, but recovered and came back againe to his familie in ye Bay and there lived till some store of people came over.*

At length, going a-trading in a small vessell among ye Indeans and being weakly manned, upon some quarell they knockt him on ye head with a hatched, so as he fell downe dead & never spake word more . . . And this his death was one ground of the Pequente [Pequot] warr which followed.

*Oldham helped found Watertown, a community of far more liberal views than Plymouth, and was its leading citizen for years, being instrumental in establishing there the first Board of Selectmen to be elected in New England, in 1634.

XIX
Heavy Tidings

And if either prayers, tears, or means would have saved his life, he had not gone hence . . .
—*Roger Smith*

BRADFORD'S HISTORY This storme [the Lyford-Oldham affair] being thus blowne over, yet sundrie sad effects followed ye same.

For the Company of Adventurers broake in peeces. And ye greatest parte wholly deserted ye colony in regarde of any further supply, or care of their subsistence.

And not only so, but some of Lyford's & Oldham's freinds and their adherents set out a ship on fishing, on their owne account.

And getting ye starte of ye ships that came to the plantation, they tooke away their stage & other necessary provisions that they had made for fishing at Cap-Anne ye year before [in 1624], at their great charge, and would not restore ye same excepte they would fight for it.*

But ye Governor sent some of ye planters to help ye fishermen to build a new one, and so let them keepe it.

This ship also brought them some small supply of little value. But they made so pore a bussines of their fishing (neither could

---

*And who had seized their stage, or wharf, but a company led by Oldham and Lyford! They had moved across the bay from Nantasket.

Roger Conant was superintendent of the new settlement, with Lyford as pastor and Oldham as overseer of trade.

Captain Standish demanded the surrender of the stage "very peremptorily." Those on the wharf rolled up hogsheads as a barricade and laughed at him, saying that the Pilgrims' patent to the ground was worthless—as it was.

There would certainly have been bloodshed, another Wessagusset, if it had not been for the intervention of Roger Conant and Captain William Peirce, whose ship was standing by.

these men make them any returne for ye supply sente) so as, after this year, they never looked more after them.

The Pilgrims, in short, abandoned Cape Ann and all their claims and possessions there. So, too, did the "interlopers." Led by Conant, they soon moved back down the coast about fifteen miles and founded Naumkeag, which became Salem a few years later.

1. Demands from the Adventurers

BRADFORD'S HISTORY   Some of them sent (in ye name of ye rest) certaine reasons of their breaking off from ye plantation—and some tenders, upon certaine conditions, of reuniting againe . . .

Then they add, . . . that we may goe on in trade with better contente & credite, our desires are as followeth:

First, that as we are partners in trade, so we may be in government there, as the patente doth give us power, &c.

2. That the French discipline may be practised in the plantation, as well in the circumstances thereof as in the substance, whereby ye scandallous name of ye Brownists and other church differences may be taken away.

3. Lastly, that Mr. Robinson and his company may not goe over to the plantation unless he and they will reconcile themselves to our church by a recantation under their hands, &c.

Their answer, in part, to these things was then as followeth:

Whereas you tax us for dissembling with his majestie & ye adventurers aboute ye French discipline, you doe us wrong, for we both hold & practice ye discipline of ye French & other reformed churches, . . . in effecte and substance.

But whereas you would tye us to the French discipline in every circumstance, you derogate from ye liberties we have in Christ Jesus.

The Apostle Paule would have none to follow him in anything but wherein he follows Christ.

Much less ought any Christian or church in ye world doe it.

The French may erre, we may erre, and other churches may erre, and doubtless doe in many circumstances . . .

And it is too great arrogancie for any man, or church, to thinke that he or they have so sounded ye word of God to ye bottome as precislie to sett down ye Church's discipline without error in substance or circumstance, as that no other without blame may digress or differ in anything from ye same* . . .

2. Friendly Letters from Leyden

[London
December 18, 1624]

BRADFORD'S
LETTER BOOK

To our beloved freinds,
Salutations . . .

Though the thing we feared be come upon us, and ye evill we strove against has overtaken us, yet we cannot forgett you, nor our freindship and fellowship which togeather we have had some years . . .

The former course for the generalitie here is wholly dissolved from what it was. And whereas you & we were formerly sharers and partners in all viages & deallings, this way is no more.

But you and we are left to bethinke ourselves what course to take in ye future that your lives, & our monies, be not lost.

The reasons and causes of this alteration have been these:

First and mainly, ye many losses and crosses at sea, and abuses of seamen, which have caused us to rune into so much charge, debts, & ingagements as our states & means were not able to goe on without impoverishing ourselves . . .

Secondly, as here hath been a faction and siding amongst us now more than 2 years, so now there is an utter breach & sequestration amongst us, and in two parts of us a full desertion and

*This was a sage observation. In striving to impose the Holy Discipline upon the Strangers, the Saints might well have thought of their own "too great arrogancie" in laying down the law.

But most of us, unfortunately, can see only one "trueth" at a time. Whatever we can't see or understand is "heresy," or worse.

forsaking of you, without any intente or purpose of medling more with you.

And though we are persuaded the maine cause of this their doing is wante of money (for neede whereof men use to make many excuses). Yet other things are by many pretended, and not without some colour urged, which are these:

1st, a distaste of you there, for that you are (as they affirme) Brownists, condemning all other churches and persons but yourselves, and those in your way; and that you are contentious, cruel, and hard-hearted among your neighbors, and towards such as in all points, both civill and religious, jump not with you.

And that you are negligente, careless, wastefull, and unthrifty, and suffer all generall goods and affairs to go at sixes and sevens, and spend your time in idleness and talking and confering, and care not what be wasted, worne, and torn out when all things come so easily and so cheap unto you.

2ly. A distaste and personal contempt of us for taking your parts and striving to defend you, insomuch as it is hard to say whether you or we are least loved of them.

Now what use either you or we may make of these things, it remains to be considered—and the more, for that we know the hand of God to be presente in all these things, and he no doubt would admonish us of something . . . And as we ourselves stand ready to imbrace all occasions that may tend to ye furtherance of so hopefull a work, rather admiring of what is than grudging for what is not, so it must rest in you to make all good againe.

And if in nothing else you can be approved, yet let your honestie & conscience be still approved & lose not one jot of your innocencie amidst your crosses & afflictions* . . .

Now we thinke it but reason that all such things as there appertaine to the generall be kept & preserved togeather, and rather

---

*In talking of "honestie & conscience," these adventurers were referring specifically to the Pilgrims' hoped-for "conscience of making restitution and paying those debts and charges which hath befallen to bring you there and send those things which you have had." They then entered a long moral and theological plea for the continuance of the joint stock though the company had "broake all in peeces."

increased dayly, than any way be dispersed or imbeseled away for any private ends or intents whatsoever.

And after your necessities are served, you gather togeather such commodities as ye cuntrie yeelds & send them over to pay debts & clear ingagements here, which are not less than £1,400 [$70,000]. And we hope you will doe your best to free our ingagements . . .

Let us all indeavour to keep a faire & honest course, and see what time will bring forth, and how God in his providence will worke for us . . .

And lastly, be you all intreated to walke circumspectly and carry yourselves so uprightly in all your ways as that no man may make just exceptions against you . . .

We have sent you some cattle, cloath, hose, shoes, leather, &c., but in another nature than formerly, as it stood us in hand to doe.

We have committed them to ye charge & custody of Mr. Allerton and Mr. Winslow as our factors, at whose discretion they are to be sould and commodities to be taken for them, as is fitting . . .

Goe on, good freinds, comfortably. Pluck up your harts cheerfully and quit yourselves like men in all your difficulties, that notwithstanding all displeasure and threats of men, yet ye work may goe on . . . and not be neglected, which is so much for ye glorie of God, and the furthrance of our countrie-men, as that a man might with more comforte spend his life in it than live ye life of Mathusala in wasting ye plentie of a tilled land or eating ye fruite of a growne tree.

Thus with harty salutations to you all, and harty prayers for you all, we lovingly take our leave this 18th of December, 1624.

Your assured freinds, to our power
James Sherley (sick)*
William Collier
Thomas Fletcher
Robert Holland

*As Sherley was sick, the above letter had been penned by Robert Cushman at Sherley's dictation. The second signer, William Collier, a brewer of London, later came to Plymouth with his family to become a Pilgrim Father.

Mr. Cushman to Governor Bradford:

[London]
December 22, 1624

Sir,

My hearty love remembered unto you, and unto your wife, with trust of your healths and contentments amidst so many difficulties.

Mr. Sherley, who lieth even at the pointe of death, entreated me even with tears to write to excuse him and signifie how it was with him. He remembers his hearty and, as he thinks, his last salutations to you and all the rest who love our common course.

If God does againe raise him up, he will be more for you (I am persuaded) than ever he was. His unfeigned love towards us hath been such as I cannot indeed expresse . . .

His patience and contentment in being oppressed hath been much. He hath sometimes lent £800 [$40,000] at one time for other men to adventure in this business—all to draw them on—and hath indeed by his free-heartedness been the only glue of the company.

And if God take him now away, I scarce think much more would be done save to inquire at the dividend what is to be had.

He saith he hath received the tokens you sent, and thanks you for them. He hath sente you a cheese, &c. Also, he hath sent a heifer to the plantation, to begin a stock for the poor. There is also a bull and three or four jades to be sold unto you, with many other things for apparel and other uses . . .

And I hope, though the first project cease, yet it shall be never the worse for you, neither will any man be discouraged, but wait on God, using the good means you can . . .

For myselfe, as I have laboured by all means to hold things here together, so I have patiently suffered this alteration, and do yet hope it shall be good for you all if you be not too rash and hasty, which, if any be, let them take heed that they reap not the fruit of their owne vanities . . .

I hope the failings of your friends here will make you the

more friendly one to another, that so all our hopes may not be dashed. Labour to settle things both for your civil and religious courses as firm and as full as you can.

Lastly, I must intreat you still to have a care of my son as of your own, and I shall rest bound unto you. I pray you let him sometime practise writing. I hope by the next ships to come unto you.

In the mean space and ever, the Lord be all your direction and turn all our crosses and troubles to his glory and our comforts, and give you to walk so wisely and holily as none may justly say but that they have always found you honestly minded, though never so poor.

Salute all our friends. And supply, I pray you, what is failing in my letters.

3. Losses, and Pirates Again

BRADFORD'S HISTORY [The adventurers] sente over also 2 ships on fishing, on their owne accounte. The one was ye pinass [the *Little James*] that was cast away ye last year here in ye countrie, and recovered by ye planters . . .

The other was a great ship [the *Charity* again], which was well fitted with an experienced master & company of fishermen to make a viage & to goe to Bilbo or Sabastians with her fish.*

The lesser, her order was to load with cor-fish [salt fish, especially cod] and bring home the beaver that should be received for ye good sold to ye plantation.

These goods . . . were at deare rates. For they put 40 in ye hundred upon them for profite and adventure outward bound. And because of ye venture of ye paiment homeward, they would have 30 in ye 100 more, which was in all 70 per cent—a thing thought unreasonable by some, and too great an oppression upon ye poore people as their case stood . . .

*That is, to Bilbao or San Sebastián, Spain.

This bigger ship made a great viage of good drie fish, the which, if they had gone to a [Spanish] market, would have yeelded them (as such fish was sold that season) £1,800, which would have enriched them.

But because there was a bruite of warr with France, ye master neglected (through timerousness) his order and put first into Plimoth [England] & after into Portsmouth, and so lost the opportunitie and came by the loss.

The lesser ship had as ill success, though she was as hopful for ye marchants' profite. For they had filled her with goodly cor-fish taken upon ye banke, as full as she could swim. And besides, she had some 800 pounds weaight of beaver, besides other furrs to a good value from ye plantation.

The master, seeing so much goods come, put it abord ye bigger ship for more safetie. But Mr. Winslow, their factor in this busines, was bound in a bond of £500 to send it to London in ye small ship . . .

So it went in ye small ship, and he sent bills of lading in both.

The master was so carefull, being both so well laden, as they went joyfully home togeather. For he towed ye lesser ship at his sterne all ye way over-bound. And they had such fayr weather as he never cast her off till they were shot deep into ye English Chanell, almost within sight of Plimoth.

And yet, there, she was unhaply taken by a Turks' man-of-warr and carried into Saly, where ye master and men were made slaves, and many of ye beaver skins were sold for 4d a peece.*

Thus was all their hops dasht, and the joyfull news they meant to carry home turned to heavie tidings.

Some thought this a hand of God for [the adventurers'] too great exaction of ye poore plantation.

But God's judgments are unseerchable; neither dare I be bould therewith.

---

*Captured by Barbary pirates prowling the English coast, the pinnace was carried away to Salé, Morocco. Nothing more was ever heard of the *Little James,* which first came in with pennons gaily flying and then pursued such an erratic course. Not all pirates did the Pilgrims a good turn. Their paths crossed surprisingly often, and would again.

But, however, it shows ye uncertainty of all human things, and what little cause there is of joying in them or trusting to them.

4. Standish to London

BRADFORD'S
HISTORY   In the bigger of these ships was sent over Captaine Standish from ye plantation, with letters & instructions both to their freinds of ye company which still clave to them, and also to ye Honourable Counsell of New England.

To ye company, to desire that, seeing they meant only to let them have goods upon sale, they might have them upon easier termes, for they should never be able to bear such high interest, or to allow so much per cent.

Also, that what they would doe in that way, that it might be disburst in money or such goods as were fitte and needful for them, & bought at best hand.

And to acquainte them with ye contents of his letters to ye Counsell, . . . which was to this purpose—to desire their favour & help that such of ye adventurers as had thus forsaken & deserted them might be brought to some order, and not to keepe them bound and themselves be free. But that they might either stand to their former covenants, or else come to some faire end, by dividente or composition . . .

Governor Bradford to Mr. Cushman:*

New Plimoth
June 9, 1625

BRADFORD'S
LETTER BOOK   Loving and kind freind,
I most heartily thank you and would be right glad to see you here, with many other of our old and dear freinds, that we might strengthen and comforte one another after our many troubles, travels, and hardships.

I long greatly for freinds of Leyden, but I fear I shall now
*Standish was carrying this letter.

scarce ever see them, save in heaven. But the will of the Lord be done.

We have rid ourselves of the company of many of those who have been troublesome unto us, though I fear we are not yet rid of the troubles themselves.

I hear Oldham comes himselfe into England. The which, if he do, beware of him, for he is very malicious and much threatens you, thinking he has some advantage by some words you have spoken.

Touching his factious doings and our proceedings with him, I refer you for it and many other things to Captain Standish, whom we have thought most meet, for sundry reasons,* to send at this time.

I pray you be as helpfull to him as you can—espetially in making our provissions, for therein he hath the least skill . . . Special care is to be had in procuring us good trucking stuff, for without it we can do nothing. The reason why heretofore we have got so little is because we never had any that was good till Mr. Winslow brought some over.

Our people will never agree in any way again to unite with the Company, who have cast them off with such reproach and contempt, and also returned their bills and all their debts upon their heads.

But as for those our loving freinds who have and still do stick to us, and are deeply engaged for us and most carefull of our goods, for our parts we will ever be ready to do anything that shall be thought equall and meet.

But I think it will be best to press a clearance with the Company, either by coming to a dividend or some other indifferent course or composition. For the longer we hang and continue in this confused and lingering condition, the worse it will be.

For notwithstanding any persuasion to the contrary, many

---

*As remarked before, Standish never joined the Pilgrim church. One reason for his choice here may have been precisely because he was not one of the Saints, who were at the moment in such high disfavor among all but a few of the adventurers.

protest they will never build houses, fence grounds, or plant fruits for those who not only forsake them, but use them as enemies, lading them with reproach and contumely.

Nay, they will rather ruin that which is done than they should possess it.

Whereas, if they knew what they should trust to, the place would quickly grow and flourish with plenty, for they never felt the sweetness of the country till this year—and not only we, but all planters in the land begin to do it . . .

Your son and all of us are in good health (blessed be God); he received the things you sent him. I hope God will make him a good man.* My wife remembers her love unto you and thanks you for her spice.

Billington still rails against you and threatens to arrest you, I know not wherefore. He is a knave, and so will live and die . . .

But time cuts me off . . .

And so with renewed salutations and best love remembered unto you, I commend you and all our affairs to the guidance of the Most High, and so rest,

Your assured loving friend,
William Bradford

BRADFORD'S
LETTER BOOK
To the right Honourable his Majestie's Council for New England, these be, &c:
June 28, A.D. 1625

Right Honourable,

The assurance we have of your noble dispositions to relieve the oppressions of the innocent doth cause us to fly unto you, as to a sanctuary, in this our just cause . . .

We are many people, consisting of all sorts, as well women and children as men, and are now left and forsaken of our adventurers, who will neither supply us with necessaries for our subsistence, nor suffer others that would be willing. Neither can

---

*God did, for young Thomas Cushman grew up to be Brewster's successor as Ruling Elder, being "very studious & sollicitous for the peace & prosperity of the church, & to prevent & heale all breeches."

we be at liberty to deal with others, or provide for ourselves. But they keep us tied to them, and yet they will loose from us.

They have not only cast us off, but entered into a particular course of trade and have, by violence and force, taken at their pleasure our possession at Cape Ann, traducing us with unjust and dishonest clamours abroad, disturbing our peace at home, and some of them threatening that if ever we grow to any good estate, they will then nip us in the head . . .

Our humble suit therefore to your good Lordships and Honours is that, seeing they have so unjustly forsaken us, you would vouchsafe to convene them before you and take such order as we may be free from them, and they come to a division with us, that we and ours may be delivered from their evil intents against us . . . The prosecution of this we have committed to our agent, Captain Myles Standish, who attends your honourable pleasures . . .

In all humbleness we committ ourselves to your honourable direction and protection, and rest with the knowledge, consent, and request of the whole plantation, ever at commandment.

William Bradford, Governor

BRADFORD'S
HISTORY
But [Standish] came in a very bad time, for ye state was full of trouble, and ye plague very hote in London, so as no business could be done. Yet he spake with some of ye Honourd Counsell, who promised all helpfullness to ye plantation which lay in them.

And sundrie of their freinds ye adventurers were so weakened with their losses ye last year, by ye losse of ye ship taken by the Turks, and ye losse of their fish, . . . so as, though their wills were good, yet their power was little. And there dyed such multitudes weekly of ye plague as all trade was dead, and little money stirring.

Yet, with much adoe, he tooke up £150 (& spent a good deal of it in expences) at 50 per cent, of which he bestowed in trading goods & such other most needfull comodities as he knew requisite for their use . . .

In ye mean time, it pleased ye Lord to give ye planters peace and health and contented minds, and so to blesse their labours as they had corne sufficient (and some to spare to others), with other foode. Neither ever had they any supply of foode but what they first brought with them.

After harvest this year [1625], they sente out a boat's load of corne 40 or 50 leagues to ye eastward, up a river called Kenibeck*—it being one of those 2 shallops which their carpenter had built them ye year before, for bigger vessell had they none.

They had laid a little deck over her midships to keepe ye corne drie. But ye men were faine to stand out all weathers without shelter, and that time of ye year begins to grow tempestious.

But God preserved them and gave them good success, for they brought home 700 pounds of beaver, besides some other furrs, having little or nothing else [to trade] but this corne, which themselves had raised out of ye earth.

This viage was made by Mr. Winslow & some of ye old standards, for seamen they had none.

5. John Robinson Dies

BRADFORD'S
HISTORY
About ye beginning of April [1626], they heard of Captain Standish's arrival [in Maine waters, on an English fishing vessel], and sent a boat to fetch him home and ye things he had brought.

Welcome he was, but ye news he brought was sadd in many regards.

Not only in regarde of the former losses before related, which their freinds had suffered—by which some, in a manner, were undone; others, much disabled from doing any further help; and some, dead of ye plague.

But also, that Mr. Robinson, their pastor, was dead—which struck them with much sorrow & sadness, as they had cause.

*The Kennebec, in Maine. The Pilgrims were reaching out more and more in the fur trade, hoping in this way to pay their debts and buy supplies.

His and their adversaries had been long & continually plotting how they might hinder his coming hither, but ye Lord had appointed him a better place.

Concerning whose death & the manner thereof, it will appeare by these few lines writ to ye Governor & Mr. Brewster:

Leyden
Aprill 28, 1625*

Loving & kind frinds, &c.

I know not whether this will ever come to your hands, or miscarrie, as other my letters have done. Yet in regard of ye Lord's dealing with us here, I have a great desire to write unto you, knowing your desire to beare a parte with us, both in our joyes & sorrows, as we doe with you.

These therefore are to give you to understand that it hath pleased the Lord to take out of this vaell of tears your and our loving & faithfull pastor, and my dear & Reverend brother, Mr. John Robinson, who was sick some 8 days.

He begane to be sick on Saturday, in ye morning. Yet ye next day, being the Lord's day, he taught us twise. And so ye weeke after, grew weaker . . .

The phisick he tooke wrought kindly in man's judgmente. But he grew weaker every day, feeling little or no paine, and sensible to ye very last.

He fell sicke ye 22 of Feb., and departed this life ye 1st of March. He had a continuall inwarde ague, but free from infection, so that all his freinds came freely to him.

And if either prayers, tears, or means would have saved his life, he had not gone hence . . .

We wanting him & all church governors, yet we still by ye mercie of God continue & hold close togeather in peace and

---

*This letter had been a year in transit. Robinson, as will appear, had been in his grave more than thirteen months before the Saints at Plymouth learned of their grievous loss. Nothing in all their troubled career quite so stunned them. They had lived from year to year in the hope that their beloved pastor would somehow find means of coming to comfort and content them as he had for more than ten years at Leyden. And now, when not yet fifty, he had been struck down in his prime.

quietnes, and so hope we shall doe, though we be very weake.

Wishing (if such were ye will of God) that you & we were againe united togeather in one, either there or here, but seeing it is ye will of ye Lord thus to dispose of things, we must labour with patience to rest contented till it please ye Lord otherwise to dispose.

For news, is here not much. Only as in England we have lost our old king, James, who departed this life aboute a month agoe, so here they have lost ye old prince, Grave Mourise [Graf Maurice] . . .

Thus with my love remembered, I take leave & rest,

Your assured loving freind,
Roger White*

BRADFORD'S
LETTER BOOK

To our most dear and entirely beloved brethren, Mr. William Bradford and Mr. William Brewster . . .

Leyden
Nov. 30, 1625

Most dear christian friends and brethren,

As it is no small grief unto you, so it is no less unto us that we are constrained to live thus disunited each from other, especially considering our affections each unto other for the mutuall edifying and comfort of both in these evill days wherein we live . . .

But our dearly beloved brethren, concerning your kind and respective [respectful?] letter, . . . we cannot answer your desire and expectation by reason it hath pleased the Lord to take to himselfe out of this miserable world our dearly beloved pastor.

Yet, for ourselves, we are minded, as formerly, to come unto you when, and as, the Lord affordeth means, though we see little hope thereof at present, as being unable of ourselves.

And that our friends will help us, we see little hope.

And now, brethren, what shall we say further unto you? Our

*White was the brother of the pastor's wife, Bridget Robinson—and so, too, of Catherine Carver.

desires and prayers to God is (if such were his good will and pleasure) we might be reunited for the edifying and mutual comfort of both, which, when he sees fit, he will accomplish.

In the mean time, we committ you unto him and to the word of his grace . . .

And thus entreating you to remember us in your prayers, as we also doe you, we for this time commend you and all your affairs to the direction and protection of the Almighty, and rest,

Your assured loving friends,

And brethren in the Lord,

Francis Jessop

Thomas Nash

Thomas Blossom

Roger White

Richard Masterson*

6. Cushman's Death

BRADFORD'S
HISTORY
[Standish] further brought them notice of ye death of their anciente freind, Mr. Cushman, whom ye Lord tooke away allso this year, & aboute this time, who was as their right hand with their freinds ye adventurers, and for diverce years had done & agitated all their bussines with them to their great advantage.

He had written to ye Governor but some few months before of ye sore sickness of Mr. James Sherley, who was a cheefe freind to ye plantation and lay at ye pointe of death, declaring his love & helpfullnes in all things, and much bemoaned the loss they should have of him if God should now take him away, as being ye stay & life of ye whole bussines.

*Of the five signers, two became Pilgrim Fathers. Thomas Blossom, "a holy man & experienced sainct," had embarked on the *Speedwell* and was one of those who turned back with Cushman in 1620. He came in 1629 with his wife and two children, immediately became a deacon, and died in the smallpox epidemic of 1633. Richard Masterson, "a second Stephen," also came in 1629 with his wife and two children, immediately became a deacon, and likewise perished in the smallpox epidemic of 1633.

As allso, his owne purpose this year to come over and spend his days with them.

But he that thus writ of another's sickness knew not that his owne death was so near.

It shows allso that a man's ways are not in his owne power, but in his hands who hath ye issues of life and death. Man may purpose, but God doth dispose.

Their other freinds in Leyden wrote many letters to them full of sad laments for their heavie loss. And though their wills were good to come to them, yet they saw no probabilitie of means how it might be effected . . . And many, being aged, begane to drop away by death.

All which things . . . being well weighed and laid togither, it could not but strike them with great perplexitie. And to looke humanly on ye state of things as they presented themselves at this time, it is a marvell it did not wholly discourage them and sinck them.

But they gathered up their spirits. And ye Lord so helped them, whose worke they had in hand, as now when they were at lowest, they begane to rise againe.[1]

XX

Wampum

And so this, with their other provisions, cut off the trade
quite from ye fisher-men and, in great part, from other
of ye stragling planters.

—William Bradford

BRADFORD'S
HISTORY
    Having now no fishing bussines or other things
to intend but only their trading & planting, they
sett themselves to follow the same with the best
industrie they could.

The planters, finding their corne—what they could spare from
their necessities—to be a commoditie (for they sold it at 6s a
bushell), used great diligence in planting ye same.

And ye Governor and such as were designated to manage the
trade (for it was retained for ye generall good, and none were
to trade in perticuler), they followed it to the best advantage
they could.

1. Joint Trading Ventures

BRADFORD'S
HISTORY
    And wanting trading goods, they understood
that a plantation which was at Monhegan . . .
was to breake up, and diverse usefull goods were
there to be sold.

The Governor and Mr. Winslow tooke a boat and some
hands, and wente thither.

But Mr. David Thompson who lived at Piscataqua, understanding their purpose, tooke opportunitie to goe with them,
which was some hinderance to them both.

For they [at Monhegan], perceiving their joynte desire to buy, held their goods at higher rates—and not only so, but would not sell a parcell of their trading goods excepte they sold all.

So, lest they should further prejudice one another, they agreed to buy all & devide equally between them.

They bought allso a parcell of goats which they distributed at home as they saw neede & occasion, and tooke corne for them from ye people—which gave them good content.

Their moyety of ye goods came to above £400 starling.

There was also that spring [1626] a French ship cast away at Sagadahoc, in which were many Biscaie [Biscay] ruggs & other commodities, . . . which were allso bought in partnership, and made their parte arise to above £500 [$25,000].

This, they made shifte to pay for, for ye most part, with ye beaver & commodities they had gott ye winter before, & what they had gathered up that summer . . .

With these goods and their corne after harvest, they gott good store of trade, so as they were enabled to pay their ingagements against ye time & to get some cloathing for ye people . . .

But now they begane to be envied, and others wente and filled ye Indeans with corne, and beat downe ye prise, giving them twise as much as they had done and under-traded them in other commodities allso . . .

And finding they ran a great hazard to goe so long viages in a small open boat, espetialy ye winter season, they begane to thinke how they might gett a small pinass—as for ye reason afforesaid, so also because others had raised ye prise with ye Indeans above ye halfe of what they had formerly given, so as in such a boat they could not carry a quantity sufficient to answer their ends.

They had no ship carpenter among them, neither knew how to get one at present. But they having an ingenious man that was a house carpenter, who had also wrought with ye ship carpenter (that was dead) when he built their boats, at their request he put forth himselfe to make a triall that way of his skill . . .

[He] tooke one of ye biggest of their shallops and sawed her in ye midle, and so lengthened her some 5 or 6 foote, and strengthened her with timbers and so builte her up, and laid a deck on her, and so made her a conveniente and wholsome vessell, very fitt & comfortable for their use, which did them service 7 years after . . .

2. Composition with the Adventurers

BRADFORD'S HISTORY   This year [1626], they sent Mr. Allerton* into England and gave him order to make a composition with ye adventurers upon as good terms as he could, . . . but yet injoyned him not to conclude absolutely till they knew ye termes and had well considered of them—but to drive it to as good an issew as he could, and referr ye conclusion to them.

Also, they gave him a commission, under their hands & seals, to take up some money—provided it exceeded not such a summe specified, and gave him order how to lay out ye same for ye use of ye plantation . . .

At ye usuall season for ye coming of ships [in the spring of 1627], Mr. Allerton returned and brought some usefull goods with him, according to ye order given him, for upon his commission he tooke up £200 [$10,000], which he now gott at 30 per cent.† . . .

He declared unto them allso how, with much adoe and no small trouble, he had made a composition with ye adventurers by the help of sundrie of their faithfull freinds there, who had allso tooke much pains thereabout.

The agreement, or bargen, he had brought a draft of, with a

*Bradford's principal assistant since 1621, Allerton now became the Pilgrims' business agent. Always enterprising and now a man of forty, he had just recently married Fear, the younger of the Brewsters' daughters, a girl of twenty, bringing her three children by his first marriage, the oldest being in his early teens.

†Allerton had been authorized to borrow only £100, at low interest. He paid no attention to his instructions, and if any of his brethren had been blessed with second sight, they might have seen trouble ahead.

list of their names thereto annexed, drawne by the best counsell
of law they could get to make it firme . . .

This "bargen" was signed by forty-two of the adventurers.
Under its terms, they agreed to surrender all of their rights in the
colony and to free the planters absolutely from debts to them for
a sum of £1,800 ($90,000), to be paid at the rate of £200 ($10,000)
a year, for nine years.

The adventurers had already spent some £7,000 on the colony,
so that the "bargen" represented a substantial loss to them.

Still, the settlement was a reasonable one, according to Captain
John Smith, experienced in these matters, for he pointed out that
the Virginia Company had spent £200,000 ($10,000,000) without
a sixpence in return.

But however small the £1,800 "bargen" may have seemed to the
adventurers, it worried the Pilgrims.

After all, they were at once so few and so poor. Plymouth had
not grown since 1624, when it numbered about 180 persons,
young and old. It had only thirty-two houses and was wholly
dependent upon a meager corn crop and an uncertain fur trade.
The "bargen" represented £100 ($5,000) for every man, woman,
and child in the colony.

It was a great risk, as it proved to be, but they decided to
accept it.

This agreemente was very well liked of & approved by all ye
plantation, and consented unto, though they knew not well how
to raise ye payment and discharge their other ingagements, and
supply the yearly wants of ye plantation, seeing they were
forced for their necessities to take up money or goods at so high
interests.

3. First Land Dividend

BRADFORD'S
HISTORY

Yet they undertooke it. And 7 or 8 of ye cheefe
of ye place became joyntly bound for ye paimente of this £1,800 (in behalfe of ye rest) at ye
severall days, in which they ran a great adventure, as their present

state stood, having many other heavie burthens allready upon them, and all things in an uncertaine condition amongst them . . .

Now, though they had some untowarde persons mixed amongst them from the first, which came out of England, and more afterwards by some of ye adventurers as freindship or other affections led them—though sundrie were gone; some for Virginia, and some to other places—yet diverse were still mingled amongst them, about whom ye Governor & counsell, with other of their cheefe freinds, had serious consideration how to settle things in regard of this new bargen or purchase in respecte of ye distribution of things, both for ye presente and future.

For ye present, excepte peace and union were preserved, they should be able to doe nothing, and in danger to overthrow all, now that other tyes & bonds were taken away.

Therefore, they resolved, for sundrie reasons, to take all amongst them that were either heads of families, or single yonge men that were of abillity and free and able to governe themselves with meete discretion, . . . into this partnership or purchass.

First, they considered that they had need of men & strength, both for defence and carrying on of bussinesses.

2ly, most of them had borne their parts in former miseries & wants with them and therefore, in some sort, but equall to partake in a better condition if ye Lord be pleased to give it.

But cheefly, they saw not how peace would be preserved without so doing, but danger & great disturbance might grow to their great hurte & prejudice otherwise.

Yet they resolved to keep such a mean in the distribution of lands and other courses as should not hinder their growth in others coming to them.

So they called the company togeather and conferred with them, and came to this conclusion: that ye trade should be managed as before, to help pay the debts; and all such persons as were above named should be reputed and inrolled for purchasers—single free men to have a single share, and every father of a familie to be allowed to purchase so many shares as he had persons in his family* . . .

As for servants, they had none but what either their masters should give them out of theirs, or their deservings should obtaine from ye company afterwards.

Thus, all were to be cast into single shares according to the order abovesaid, and so every one was to pay his part, according to his proportion, towards ye purchase & all other debts . . .

This gave all good contente.

4. Distribution by Lot

BRADFORD'S HISTORY   And first, accordingly, the few cattle which they had were devided, which arose to this proportion—a cowe to 6 persons or shares, & 2 goats to ye same, which were first equalized for age & goodness, and then lotted for—single persons consorting with others as they thought good, & smaller familys likewise. And swine, though more in number, yet by ye same rule.

Then they agreed that every person or share should have 20 acres of land devided unto them, besides ye single acres they had allready.

And they appoynted [to lay out the land] were to begin first on ye one side of ye towne, & how farr to goe, and then on ye other side in like manner, and so to devide it by lot. And they appointed sundrie by name to doe it, and tyed them to certaine rules to proceed by—as that they should only lay out settable or tillable land, at least such of it as should abut on ye water side (as ye most they were to lay out did), and pass by ye rest as refuse and commune. And what they judged fitt should be so taken.

And they were first to agree of ye goodness & fitness of it before the lott was drawne, and so it might as well prove some

*There were, in all, twenty-seven Purchasers.

of their own as another man's. And this course they were to hold throughout.

But yet seeking to keepe ye people togither as much as might be, they allso agreed upon this order by mutuall consent before any lots were cast—that whose lots soever should fall next ye towne, or most conveniente for nearness, they should take to them a neighbor or two whom they best liked, and should suffer them to plant corne with them for 4 years. And afterwards, they might use as much of theirs for as long a time, if they would.

Allso, every share or 20 acres was to be laid out 5 acres in breadth by the water side, and 4 acres in length, excepting nooks & corners, which were to be measured as they would bear to best advantage.

But no meadows were to be laid out at all, nor were not for many years after, because they were but strait of meadow grounds. And if they had been now given out, it would have hindered all addition to them afterwards. But every season, all were appoynted where they should mow, according to ye proportion of cattle they had.

This distribution gave generally good contente and settled men's minds.

Also, they gave ye Governor and 4 or 5 of ye speciall men amongst them ye houses they lived in.* Ye rest were valued & equalised at an indifferent rate, and so every man kept his owne. And he that had a better allowed something to him that had a worse, as ye valuation wente.

5. The Undertakers

BRADFORD'S
HISTORY

They now sent (with ye returne of ye ships) Mr. Allerton againe into England, giving him full power under their hands & seals to conclude the former bargaine with ye adventurers, and sent their bonds for ye paimente of the money.

*Brewster, Standish, Winslow, and Allerton, it would seem.

Allso, they sent what beaver they could spare to pay some of their ingagements & to defray his charges, for those deepe interests still kepte them low.

Also, he had order to procure a patente for a fitt trading place in ye river of Kennebec . . .

Before they sente Mr. Allerton away for England, ye Governor and some of their cheefe freinds had serious consideration not only how they might discharge those great ingagements which lay so heavily upon them, but also how they might (if possibilie they could) devise means to help some of their freinds and brethren of Leyden over unto them, who desired so much to come to them, and they desired as much their company.

To effecte which, they resolved to run a high course and of great adventure, not knowing otherwise how to bring it aboute.

Which was to hire ye trade of ye company for certaine years, and in that time to undertake to pay that £1,800 and all ye rest of ye debts that then lay upon ye plantation, which was about £600 more, and so to set them free and returne the trade to ye generallitie at ye end of ye terme.

Upon which resolution, they called ye company togeither and made it clearly appear unto all what their debts were, and upon what terms they would undertake to pay them all in such a time, and sett them clear.

But their other ends [of bringing over more Saints from Leyden] they were faine to keepe secrete, having only privately acquaynted some of their trusty freinds therewith, who were glad of ye same, but doubted how they would be able to performe it.

So, after some agitation of the thing with ye company, it was yeelded unto and the agreemente made . . .

> Bradford, Allerton, and Standish were granted a monopoly to the colony's trade. They could invite any they chose to become partners—or "undertakers"—with them. As partners, they chose Brewster, Winslow, John Alden, John Howland, and young Thomas Prence, aged twenty-seven, later to be governor. Arriving a Stranger on the *Fortune*, Prence was now a zealous Saint

and Brewster's son-in-law, having married his older daughter, Patience.

Under the agreement, only the Undertakers were to use the colony's trading posts and larger boats. They could dispose as they wished of all furs, knives, beads, and other "trucking stuffe" in the common store. Every year each Purchaser was to pay them three bushels of corn, or six pounds of tobacco, "at ye undertakers' choyse."

In return, the Undertakers would pay off all of the colony's debts and supply Plymouth with £50 of shoes and hose a year, to be sold for corn at 6s. ($15) a bushel.

This arrangement was to continue for six years, at which time all rights and privileges were to revert to the "generallitie"—or rather, to the Purchasers.

It was a hopeful and ingenious scheme. But like most of the Pilgrims' hopeful schemes, it later caused bitter quarrels and years of confusion and distraction.

6. Aptucxet and the Dutch

BRADFORD'S HISTORY

That they might ye better take all convenient opportunities to follow their trade, both to maintaine themselves and to disingage them of those great sums which they stood charged with and bound for, they resolved to build a small pinass at Manomet, a place 20 miles from ye plantation, standing on ye sea to ye southward of them.

Unto which, by another creeke on this side, they could carry their goods within 4 or 5 miles and then transport them overland to their vessel and so avoyd the compassing of Cap-Codd and those deangerous shoulds, and so make any viage to the southward in much shorter time, and with farr less danger.

Also, for ye saftie of their vessell & goods, they builte a house there and kept some servants, who also planted corne and raised some swine, and were allwayes ready to goe out with ye barke when there was occasion.*

*This trading post was at Aptucxet, on Buzzards Bay, at the mouth of the Manomet River. The headwaters of the Manomet reached within a few miles

All which tooke good effecte and turned to their profite . . .

This year allso [1627], they had letters and messengers from ye Dutch plantation, sent by ye Governor there [Peter Minuit], written both in Dutch & French . . .

Their letters were as followeth, it being their manner to be full of complementall titles:

Eedele, Eerenfeste, Wyse, Vorrsinnige Heeren, den Goveernour ende Raeden in Nieu-Pliemuen residerende, onse seer Goede vrinden:

Den directeur ende Raed van Nieu-Nederlande wensen vwe Edn:, eerenfesten ende wijse voorsinnige geluck salichitt† . . .

We have often before this wished for an opportunitie, or an occasion, to congratulate you and your prosperous and praise-worthy undertakings, and Government of your colony there. And the more in that we, also, have made a good beginning to pitch ye foundation of a collonie here . . .

Therefore, we could not forbear to salute you with these few lines, with presentation of our good will and servise unto you in all frendly-kindness & neighbourhood.

And if it so falls out that any goods that come to our hands from our native countrie may be serviceable unto you, we shall take ourselves bound to help and accommodate you therewith, either for beaver, or any other wares or marchandize that you should be pleased to deale for.

And if in case we have no commodity at present that may give you contente, if you please to sell us any beaver, or otter, or such

---

of those of the Scusset, which flowed in the opposite direction into Cape Cod Bay. The Pilgrims early made use of these streams and the short easy portage between them, traveling a route now followed by the Cape Cod Canal.

It was by way of Aptucxet that the Pilgrims established relations with the Dutch along the Hudson.

Upon the foundations of the original structure here, in what is now the village of Bourne, a replica of the old trading post has been constructed.

†That is: "Noble, worshipful, wise, and prudent Lords, the Governor and Councillors residing in New Plymouth, our very dear friends: The Director and Council of New Netherland wish to your Lordships, worshipful, wise, and prudent . . ." A little of this went a long way in Bradford's opinion, and he added, "The rest I shall render in English, leaving out the repitition of superfluous titles."

like comodities for ready money, and let us understand thereof
by this bearer in writing (whom we have appoynted to stay 3 or
4 days for your answer), we shall depute one to deale with you
at such place as you shall appointe.

In ye mean time, we pray the Lord to take you, our honoured
good friends and neighbours, into his holy protection.

By the appointment of ye Governor and Counsell, &c.

Isaak de Rasier, Secretaris

From ye Manhatas, in ye fort Amsterdam,
March 9, 1627

To this they returned answer as followeth:

New-Plim:
March 19

To the Honoured, &c.,

The Governor & Counsell of New-Plim: wisheth, &c. We
have received your letters, &c., wherein appeareth your good
wills & frendship towards us, but is expressed with over-high
titles, more than belongs to us or is meete for us to receive.

But for your good will and congratulations of our prosperitie
in these small beginnings of our poore colonie, we are much
bound to you and with many thanks doe acknowledg ye same,
taking it both for a great honour done unto us and for a certaine
testimonie of your love and good neighbourhood.

Now these are further to give your Worshipps to understand
that it is to us no small joye to hear that his majestie [King
Charles] hath not only been pleased to confirme ye anciente
amitie, alliance, and frendship [between their two countries],
. . . but hath himselfe strengthened the same with a new union,
the better to resist ye pride of that commone enemy, ye Spaniard,
from whose cruelty the Lord keep us both, and our native
countries.

Now forasmuch as this is sufficiente to unite us togeather in
love and good neighbourhood in all our dealings, yet many of
us are further obliged by the good and curteous entreaty which

we have found in your countrie, having lived there many years with freedome and good contente. As also, many of our freinds doe to this day.

For which, we and our children after us are bound to be thankfull to your Nation and shall never forgett ye same, but shall hartily desire your good & prosperity as our owne forever.

Likewise, for your freindly tender & offer to accommodate and help us with any commodities or marchandise you have or shall come to you, either for beaver, otters, or other wares, it is very acceptable.

And we doubt not but in a short time we may have profitable commerce & trade togeather.

But for this year, we are fully supplyed with all necessaries, both for cloathing and other things. But hereafter, it is like we shall deale with you, if your rates be reasonable.

And therefore, when you please to send to us againe, we desire to know how you will take beaver by ye pounde, & otters by ye skine, and how you will deale per cent for other comodities, and what you can furnishe us with.

As likwise, what other commodities from us may be acceptable unto you, as tobacco, fish, corne, and other things, and what prises you will give, &c.

Thus hoping that you will pardon & excuse us for our rude and imperfecte writing in your language, and take it in good part because, for want of use, we cannot so well express what we understand, nor hapily understand everything so fully as we should.

And so we humbly pray the Lord for his mercie's sake that he will take both us and you into his keeping & gratious protection.

By ye Governor and Counsell of New Plimoth,

Your Worshipps' very good freinds & neighbours, &c.

7. Wampum

BRADFORD'S
HISTORY

This year the Dutch sent againe unto them from their plantation both kind letters and also diverse commodities as suger, linen cloth, Holland finer & course stuffe, &c.

They came up with their barke to Manomet [Aptucxet], to their house there, in which came their Secretarie Rasier,* who was accompanied with a noyse of trumpeters and some other attendants, and desired that they would send a boat for him, for he could not travill so farr overland.

So they sent a boat . . . and brought him to ye plantation, with ye cheefe of his company.

And after some few days' entertainmente, he returned to his bark, and some of them wente with him and bought sundry of his goods.

After which beginning thus made, they sente often times to ye same place and had entercourse togeather for diverce years. And amongst other commodities, they vended much tobaco for linen cloath, stuffs, &c., which was a good benefite to ye people, till the Virginians found out their plantation.

But that which turned most to their profit in time was an entrance into the trade of Wampampeake,† for they now bought aboute £50 of it of them; and they told them how vendable it was at their forte Orania [Fort Orange],‡ and did perswade them they would find it so at Kenebeck.

And so it came to pass, in time, though at first it stuck, & it was 2 years before they could put off this small quantity, till ye inland people knew of it. And afterwards, they could scarce ever gett enough for them for many years togeather.

---

*Isaack de Rasieres, who was "their upper commis, or chief merchant, and second to the Governor, a man of fair and genteel behavior," said Bradford.
†The Indian *wampumpeag* ("white strings of money")—more briefly, wampum.
‡Now Albany, New York.

And so this, with their other provissions, cutt off the trade quite from ye fisher-men and, in great part, from other of ye stragling planters.

And strange it was to see the great alteration it made in a few years amonge ye Indeans themselves. For all the Indeans of these parts & ye Massachusetts had none or very little of it but ye sachems & some spetiall persons, that wore a little of it for ornamente. Only it was made & kepte amonge ye Nariganssets & Pequents, which grew rich & potent by it* . . .

Neither did the English of this plantation or any other in ye land till now they had knowledge of it from ye Dutch, so much as know what it was, much less that it was a comoditie of that worth & valew.

But after it grue thus to be a comoditie in these parts, these [neighboring] Indeans fell into it allso, and to learne how to make it, for ye Narigansets doe geather ye shells of which they make it on their shores.

And it hath continued a current commoditie aboute this 20 years [until 1647], though it may prove a drugg in time . . .

White and purple beads made of periwinkle and quahaug shells, wampum was sold in strings a fathom (six feet) long. As their first supply, the Pilgrims bought 1,200 feet of this money, buying 200 fathoms at approximately $1.00 a foot. Becoming the common medium of exchange, wampum freed them from clumsy barter arrangements based upon corn. Besides, with the Indians' new-found fancy for this "money," wampum gave the Plymouth Undertakers a virtual monopoly in the New England fur trade for a few years.

*The Narragansett and Pequot lived west of Narragansett Bay, in what became Rhode Island and Connecticut.

8. Plymouth in 1627: a Dutch View

After his visit, De Rasieres wrote his impressions of Plymouth in a letter to an Amsterdam friend.

DE RASIERES' LETTER*   From Aptucxet the English can come in six hours, through the woods, passing several little rivulets of fresh water, to New Plymouth . . . They muster about fifty families.

At the south side of the town there flows down a small river of fresh water [Town Brook], very rapid, but shallow, . . . where, in April and the beginning of May, there come so many shad which want to ascend that river that it is quite surprising.

This river the English have shut in with planks, and in the middle with a little door, which slides up and down, and at the sides with trellice work . . .

At the mouth they have constructed it with planks, like an eel pot with wings, where in the middle there is also a sliding door, and with trellice work at the sides,† so that between the two there is a square pool into which the fish aforesaid come swimming in such shoals . . . that at one tide there are ten thousand to twelve thousand fish in it . . .

They draw out the fish with baskets, each according to the land he cultivates, and carry them to it, depositing in each hill three or four fishes, and in these they plant their maize, which grows as luxuriantly therein as though it were the best manure in the world.

And if they do not lay these fishes therein, the maize will not grow, so that such is the nature of the soil.

New Plymouth lies on the slope of a hill stretching east towards the seacoast, with a broad street, about a cannon shot of

*This letter, as given in part here, is from the translation appearing in *Narratives of New Netherland* (1909), edited by J. Franklin Jameson.
†No doubt as Squanto had taught them.

eight hundred feet long, leading down the hill, with a highway crossing in the middle* . . .

The houses are constructed of hewn planks, with gardens also enclosed behind and at the sides with hewn planks, so that their houses and court yards are arranged in very good order, with a stockade against sudden attack.

And at the end of the streets there are three wooden gates. In the centre, on the cross street, stands the Governor's house, before which is a square stockade, upon which four patereros [cannon] are mounted so as to enfilade the streets.

Upon the hill they have a large square house with a flat roof, made of thick sawn planks, stayed with oak beams, upon the top of which they have six cannon, which shoot iron balls of four and five pounds and command the surrounding country.

The lower part they use for a church, where they preach Sundays and the usual holidays.

They assemble by beat of drum, each with his musket or fire-lock, in front of the Captain's door. They have their cloaks on and place themselves in order, three abreast, and are led by a sergeant without beat of drum.

Behind, come the Governor in a long robe. Beside him, on the right hand, comes the preacher, with his cloak on;† and on the left hand, the Captain, with his side-arms and cloak on, and with a small cane in his hand.

And so they march in good order, and each sets his arms down near him. Thus, they are constantly on their guard, night and day . . .

They have made stringent laws and ordinances upon the subject of fornication and adultery, which laws they maintain and enforce very strictly indeed, even among the tribes which live amongst them . . .

*The highway (now Main Street) meandered off into the cornfields to the north and twisted its way down to Town Brook and across it to the cornfields on the south.

†De Rasieres was in error here. Except for Lyford, who had long since departed, the Pilgrims had not had a pastor since they arrived seven years before. He probably mistook Ruling Elder Brewster for the preacher.

Their farms are not so good as ours because they are more stony and, consequently, not so suitable for the plough.

They apportion their land according as each has means to contribute to the 18,000 guilders which they have promised to pay those who sent them out. Whereby, they have their freedom without rendering an account to anyone.

Only, if the King should choose to send a Governor-General, they would be obliged to acknowledge him as sovereign over-lord.

The maize seed which they do not require for their own use is delivered over to the Governor, at three guilders the bushel, who, in his turn, sends it in sloops to the north for the trade in skins among the savages. They reckon one bushel of maize against one pound of beaver's skin . . .

They have better means of living than ourselves because they have fish so abundant before their doors . . .

The tribes in their neighborhood . . . are better conducted than ours because the English give them the example of better ordinances and a better life; and who also, to a certain degree, give them laws in consequence of the respect they, from the very first, have established amongst them.

XXI

A Double Blessing

And now, good Sir, I hope that you & ye rest of God's people . . . will say that here was a right foundation layed, and that these 2 blessed servants of ye Lord came in at ye dore, and not at ye windowe.

Deacon Charles Gott

BRADFORD'S
HISTORY
    After Allerton's arrival in England, he acquainted them with his commission and full power to conclude ye bargan & purchase. Upon the view whereof and ye delivery of ye bonds for ye paymente of ye money yearly, it was fully concluded, and a deede fairly ingrossed in partchmente was delivered him, under their hands & seals, confirming the same.

Morover, he delte with them aboute other things according to his instructions, as to admitt some of these their good freinds into this purchase if they pleased, and to deal with them for moneys at better rates, &c.

Touching which, I shall here inserte a letter of Mr. Sherley's . . . writ to ye Governor, as followeth:

London
Nov. 17, 1628

Sir:

I have received yours of ye 26 of May, . . . with ye barrell of otter skins, . . . for which I got a bill of store and so tooke them and sould them togeather at £78 12s. [$3,930] . . .

It is true (as you write) that your ingagments are great. Not only the purchass, but you are yet necessitated to take up ye stock you work upon.

And that not at 6 or 8 per cent as it is here let out, but at 30, 40—yea—& some at 50 per cent, which, were not your gaines great and God's blessing on your honest indeavors more than ordinarie, it could not be that you should longe subsiste . . .

Your honest & discreete agent, Mr. Allerton, hath . . . tould me you were contented to accepte of me & some few others to joyne with you in ye purchass, as partners.

For which I kindly thank you and all ye rest, and doe willingly accepte of it. And though absente, I shall willingly be at such charge as you & ye rest shall think meete.

And this year, I am contented to forbear my former £50 and the 2 years' increase [interest] for ye venture . . . I have perswaded Mr. Andrews and Mr. Beachamp* to doe ye like, so as you are eased of ye high rate you were at ye other 2 yeares . . . I say, we leave it freely to yourselves to allow us what you please, and as God shall blesse . . .

I also see by your letter you desire I should be your agente or factor here. I have ever found you so faithfull, honest, and upright men as I have ever resolved with myselfe (God assisting me) to doe you all ye good lyeth in my power.

And therefore, if you please to make choyce of so weak a man, both for abillities and body, to performe your busines, I promise (ye Lord enabling me) to doe ye best I can according to those abillities he hath given me.

And wherein I faile, blame yourselves that you made no better choyce . . .

Thus commending you & yours, . . . I ever rest,

Your faithfull loving freind,

James Sherley

*These two friendly adventurers were Richard Andrews, a haberdasher, and John Beauchamp, salter, both of London.

1. Allerton's Private Trade

BRADFORD'S
HISTORY

Mr. Allerton, having setled all things thus in a good and hopfull way, he made haste to returne in ye first of ye spring with their supply for trade . . .

He brought a resonable supply of goods for ye plantation, and without those great interests as before is noted. And brought an accounte of ye beaver sould, and how ye money was disposed for goods, & ye payments of other debtes—having paid all debts abroad to others save to Mr. Sherley, Mr. Beachamp, & Mr. Andrews, from whom likewise he brought an accounte, which, to them all, amounted not to above £400, for which he had passed bonds.

Allso, he had payed the first paymente for ye purchass . . . So as they now had no more foreine debtes but ye abovesaid £400, . . . and ye rest of ye yearly purchass monie.

Some other debtes they had in ye cuntrie. But they were without interest, & they had wherewith to discharge them when they were due.

To this pass, the Lord had brought things for them.*

Allso, he brought them further notice that their freinds & some others, that would joyne with them in their trade & purchass, did intend to send over to Leyden for a competente number of them, to be here the next year without fayle, if ye Lord pleased to blesse their journey.

He also brought them a patente for Kenebeck. But it was so straite & ill-bounded as they were faine to renew & inlarge it the next year . . .

This year Mr. Allerton brought over a yonge man for a min-

---

*Though they still owed £2,000 ($100,000), they had reduced their "foreine" debt by £400 ($20,000) within this single year. The Pilgrims were jubilant and optimistic, always a bad omen with them.

ister to ye people here. Wheather upon his owne head, or at ye motion of some freinds there, I well know not.

But it was without ye church's sending, for they had been so bitten by Mr. Lyford as they desired to know ye person well whom they should invite amongst them.

His name was Mr. Rogers. But they perceived, upon some trial, that he was crazed in his braine, so they were faine to be at further charge to send him back ye next year . . .

After his returne, he grue quite distracted. And Mr. Allerton was much blamed that he would bring such a man over, they having charge enough otherwise.

Mr. Allerton, in ye years before, had brought over some small quantitie of goods upon his owne perticuler, and sould them for his owne private benefite, which was more than any man had yet hitherto attempted.

But because he had otherwise done good service, and also he sould them among ye people, by which their wants were supplied, and he aledged it was the love of Mr. Sherley and some other freinds that would needs trust him with some goods, conceiving it might doe him some good and none hurte, it was not much lookt at, but passed over.

But this year [1628] he brought over a greater quantitie. And they were so intermixte with ye goods of ye generall, as they knew not which was theirs & which was his, being pact up together. So as they well saw that if any casualty had befalne at sea, he might have laid ye whole on them if he would, for there was no distinction.

Also, what was most vendible, and would yeeld presente pay, usually that was his.

And he now begane allso to sell abroad to others of foreine places, which, considering their commone course, they began to dislike.

Yet, because love thinkes no evill, nor is susspitious, they tooke his faire word for excuse, and resolved to send him againe this year for England, considering how well he had done ye former bussines, and what good acceptation he had with their freinds there; as also, seeing sundry of their freinds from Leyden were sente for, which would or might be much furthured by his means.

Againe, seeing the patente for Kenebeck must be inlarged . . . And it was conceived, in a manner, ye same charge would serve to inlarge this at home,* and he that had begane ye former ye last year would be ye fittest to effecte this.

So they gave him instructions and sente him for England this year againe [1629]. And in his instructions bound him to bring over no goods on their accounte but £50 in hose & shoes, and some linen cloth (as they were bound by covenante when they tooke ye trade).

Also, some trading goods to such a value—and in no case to exseed his instructions, nor runne them into any further charge, he well knowing how their case stood.

Also, that he should so provide that their trading goods came over betimes. And whatsoever was sent on their accounte should be pact up by itselfe, marked with their marke, and no other goods to be mixed with theirs.

For so he prayed them to give him such instructions as they saw good, and he would follow them to prevente any jellocie or farther offence . . .

And thus they conceived they had well provided for all things.

2. More Saints from Leyden

BRADFORD'S HISTORY   Mr. Allerton, safly arriving in England and delivering his letters to their freinds there and acquainting them with his instructions, found good acceptation with them.

And they were very forward & willing to joyne with them in ye partnership of trade, & in ye charge to send over ye Ley-

*That is, the Plymouth patent, which was faulty. The Pilgrims were very anxious to obtain a new royal patent with enlarged and clearly defined bounds.

den people, a company whereof were allready come out of Holland and prepared to come over . . .

[London]
May 25, 1629

BRADFORD'S
LETTER BOOK

To my worthy and well-beloved friend, Mr. William Bradford, &c. Most loving and most respected Sir,

Having but two days past parted from my dear and only daughter, by reason whereof nature forceth me to be full of grief and heaviness, . . . be entreated, therefore, to accept these few lines . . .

Here are now many of your and our freinds from Leyden coming over, who, though for ye most parte but a weak company, yet herein is a good parte of that end obtained which was aimed at, and which hath been so strongly opposed by some of our former adventurers.

But God hath his working in these things which man cannot frustrate.

With them, we have allso sent some servants in ye ship called the•*Talbut,* that went hence lately, but these come in ye *May-flower* . . .

Mr. Beachamp & myselfe, with Mr. Andrews & Mr. Hatherly, are, with your love and liking, joyned partners with you*
. . .

We have disbursed the charges of setting them out and transporting them over. And what allowance or agreemente you and your assistants please to make with us, we will accept of
. . .

I doubt not but beaver will continue a good price still, at 15

*That is, they became partners of the eight Plymouth Undertakers responsible for paying all of the colony's debts. As most of the debts were owed to the London partners, this seems a curious arrangement, undertaking to pay what was owed them. Perhaps they hoped the Plymouth partners might do more than pay their debts, and make a profit. If so, it was a bad dream.
Like the others, the fourth London partner, Timothy Hatherly, feltmaker of London, had long been interested in the colony. In 1623, in fact, he had come to Plymouth on the *Anne,* intending to stay. But losing his house and goods in a large fire at that time, he almost immediately returned home.

or 16 shillings per pound. It is daily more and more worn here
. . .

Your loving friend to command,

James Sherley

BRADFORD'S   [Those bound for Plymouth] had passage with
HISTORY   ye ships that came to Salem, that brought over
              many godly persons to begine ye plantations &
churches of Christ there & in ye Bay of Massachusetts . . .

Their charge, as Mr. Allerton brought it in afterwards on
account, came to above £550 [$27,500], besides their fetching
hither from Salem & ye Bay, where they and their goods were
landed—viz., their transportation from Holland to England, &
their charges lying there, and passages hither, with clothing
provided for them . . .

And besides all this charge, their freinds & brethren here
were to provide corne & other provissions till they could reap
a crop, which was long before . . . And this charge of maintaining them all this while was little less than ye former summe.*

These things I note perticulerly for sundry regards.

First, to shew a rare example therein of brotherly love and
Christian care in performing their promises and covenants, too
—& in a sorte, beyonde their power—that they should venture
so desperately to ingage themselves to accomplish this thing,
and bear it so cheerfully. For they never demanded, much less
had, any repaymente of all these great summes thus disbursed.

2ly, it must needs be that there was more than of man in these
acheevements that should thus readily stirre up ye harts of such
able frinds [in London] to joyne in partnership with them in
such a case and cleave so faithfullie to them as these did in so
great adventures—and the more so, because the most of them
never saw their faces to this day . . .

It must needs be, therefore, the spetiall worke and hand of
God.

3ly, that these poore people here in a wilderness should, not-

*Making the cost approximately £1,000 ($50,000) in all.

withstanding, be inabled in time to repay all these ingagements, and many more unjustly brought upon them through the unfaithfullnes of some . . .

In ye mean time, I cannot but admire his ways and workes towards his servants, and humbly desire to blesse his holy name for his great mercies hitherto.

3. Salem

The year before, in the summer of 1628, the vanguard of the great Puritan migration to "ye Massachusetts" had disembarked at Salem, or Naumkeag as it was then still known, led by Captain John Endecott.

Always high-handed, Endecott soon clashed with the Old Planters of the town, who had come from Cape Ann and established themselves there under the Pilgrims' one-time friends, Roger Conant and that "dissembling Ishmael," the Reverend John Lyford. After many sharp fights, the Puritans routed the Old Planters and, self-righteously and with unconscious irony, renamed the town Salem—from the Hebrew *shalom*, peace.

Lyford departed for Virginia, where he soon died. Conant led most of the Old Planters across the North River to found Beverly —"Beggarly," the newcomers dubbed it.

Endecott's company had come in sick and weak. Scurvy and infectious fevers had broken out on the *Abigail*, as on the *Mayflower* eight years before. Disease was brought ashore and carried away half of the Puritan vanguard, and many of Conant's company as well.

Hearing that Plymouth had someone with "skill in such diseases," Endecott appealed to the Pilgrims for help, and they sent him their "physition & chirurgeon," Deacon-Doctor Samuel Fuller.

His was a momentous visit, for Fuller ministered not only to the ailing bodies of his patients, but to their troubled souls as well.

These Puritans had long been critical of the Anglican church and its ways. But they hesitated to separate, as those at Scrooby had done. They went on practicing a nominal conformity, partly because of ideological objections to "schisme," but even more because they were trimmers, not having the courage of their convictions.

For the most part, they stood higher on the social scale than the Pilgrims, and therefore had more to lose by forthrightly rebelling against "antichristian tiranie." They hesitated to jeopardize their bread and butter, their fine houses, and even their creature comforts, not to speak of the danger of being jailed and losing their very lives. They were deterred from speaking out by the heavy hands of the bishops and the civil authorities, as events proved.

For with that fear removed when they found themselves beyond the reach of bailiffs and the bishops' "catchpoule" officers, they were open to persuasion, and the Plymouth deacon, Samuel Fuller, had little difficulty in bringing them over to the Separation and having them embrace the Holy Discipline.

Even before the *Talbot* and the second *Mayflower* put in at Salem, bearing far more Puritans than Pilgrims, Governor Endecott had written Governor Bradford about his and his people's gropings toward the "true" way in religion.

Naumkeag
May 11, 1629

BRADFORD'S
LETTER BOOK

Right worthy Sir,

It is a thing not usual that servants to one master and of one household should be strangers. I assure you I desire it not. Nay, to speake more plainly, I cannot be so to you.

God's people are all marked with one and ye same marke, and sealed with one and ye same seale, and have—for ye maine —one & ye same harte, guided by one & ye same spirite of truth.

And where this is, there can be no discorde. Nay, here must needs be sweete harmonie . . .

I acknowledge myselfe much bound to you for your kind love and care in sending Mr. Fuller among us, and rejoyce much that I am by him satisfied touching your judgments of ye outward forme of God's worshipe.

It is, as farr as I can yet gather, no other than is warrented by ye evidence of truth, and ye same which I have proffessed and maintained ever since ye Lord in mercie revealed himselfe unto me, being farr from ye commone reporte that hath been spread of you touching that perticuler . . .

Your assured loving friend,

Jo: Endecott

Now, shortly after the writing of this letter, came [those on the *Talbot* and *Mayflower*] and quickly grew into church order, and set themselves roundly to walk in all the ways of God, as will appear by this letter following:

Salem

July 30, 1629

Most worthy and much respected friend, Mr. Bradford,

I, with my wife, remember our service unto you and yours, thanking you most humbly for your great kindness when we were at Plymouth with you.

Sir, I make bold to trouble you with a few lines to certifie you how it hath pleased God to deale with us since you heard from us—how, notwithstanding all opposition that hath been here and elsewhere, it hath pleased God to lay a foundation, the which, I hope, is agreeable to his Word in everything.

The 20th of July, it pleased ye Lord to move ye hart of our Governor to set it aparte for a solemne day of humilliation for ye choyce of a pastor & teacher—the former parte of ye day being spente in praier & teaching; the latter parte, aboute ye election, which was after this manner.

The persons thought on (who had been ministers in England) were demanded concerning their callings.

They acknowledged there was a two-fold calling—the one, an inward calling, when ye Lord moved ye harte of a man to take that calling upon him and fitted him with gifts for ye same; the second, the outward calling, was from ye people, when a company of beleevers are joyned togither in covenante, to walke togither in all ye ways of God, and every member (being men) are to have a free voyce in ye choyce of their officers, &c.

So these two servants of God clearing all things by their answers (and being thus fitted), we saw no reason but that we might freely give our voyces for their election after this trial . . .

So the most voyce was for Mr. Skelton to be pastor, and Mr. Higginson to be teacher.

And they accepting the choyce, Mr. Higginson, with three or four more of the gravest members of ye church, layed their hands on Mr. Skelton, using prayers therewith. This being done, then there was imposition of hands on Mr. Higginson . . .

Now, good Sir, I hope that you & ye rest of God's people . . . will say that here was a right foundation layed, and that these 2 blessed servants of ye Lord came in at ye dore, and not at ye windowe . . .

So I rest,

At your service in what I may, till death,
[Deacon] Charles Gott

MORTON'S
MEMORIAL
After some conference, . . . they pitched upon the 6th of August for their entering into a solemn Covenant with God and one another, and also for the ordaining of their ministers, of which they gave notice to the church at Plimoth (that being the only church that was in the Country before them) . . . And, accordingly, it was desired of Mr. Higginson to draw up a Confession of Faith and Covenant, in Scripture-language . . .

When the sixth of August came, it was kept as a day of fasting and prayer, in which, after the sermons and prayers of the two ministers, in the end of the day the foresaid Confession of Faith and Covenant being solemnly read, they proceeded to the ordaining of Mr. Skelton pastor and Mr. Higginson teacher of the church there.

Mr. Bradford, the Governour of Plimouth, and some others with him, coming by sea, were hindered by cross winds, that they could not be there at the beginning of the day. But they came into the assembly afterward and gave them the right hand of fellowship, wishing all prosperity and blessed success unto such good beginnings . . .

BRADFORD'S HISTORY So the long stay & keeping back [of the Leyden Saints] was recompensed by ye Lord to their freinds here with a duble blessing, in that they not only injoyed them now beyond their late expectation (when all their hops seemed to be cutt off), but, with them, many more godly freinds & Christian brethren as ye beginning of a larger harvest unto ye Lord, in ye increase of his churches & people in these parts—to ye admiration of many, and allmost wonder of ye world, that of so small beginnings so great things should insue . . .

But it was ye Lord's doing, & ought to be marvellous in our eyes.

4. Plymouth's First Settled Pastor

BRADFORD'S HISTORY There was one Mr. Ralfe Smith & his wife & familie that came over into ye Bay of ye Massachusetts and sojourned, at presente, with some stragling people that lived at Nantasket [Hull].

Here, being a boat of this place putting in there on some occasion, he ernestly desired that they would give him & his, passage for Plimoth, and some such things as they could well carrie, having before heard that there was liklyhood he might procure house-room for some time till he should resolve to settle there if he might, or elsewhere as God should dispose. For he was werie of being in that uncouth place, & in a poore house that would neither keep him nor his goods drie.

So, seeing him to be a grave man & understanding he had been a minister, though they had no order for any such thing, yet they presumed and brought him.

He was here accordingly kindly entertained & housed, &

had ye rest of his goods & servants sente for, and exercised his gifts amongst them.

And afterwards, he was chosen into ye ministrie and so remained for sundrie years.

Smith had arrived at Salem earlier in 1629, coming on the *Talbot* with the Reverends Skelton and Higginson, who had since been chosen the principal officers of the church there, leaving Smith without employment.

In addition, the more conservative Massachusetts Bay adventurers had learned that he was an avowed Separatist and objected to his presence in the town.

"Passage was granted to him before we understood his difference of judgment in some things from our ministrie," the adventurers wrote Captain Endecott. "And though we have a very good opinion of his honesty, we give you this order, that unless he will be conformable to our government, *you suffer him not to remain within the limits of your grant*."

Forced from Salem, Smith crossed the bay to Nantasket, where the Pilgrims ran upon him and thus, quite by chance, acquired their first settled minister.

Another of those "painefull" students of divinity from Cambridge, Smith had absurd pretensions as a scholar and at first greatly enjoyed his "studdie in new Plimmouth in new Ingland," strewing the scripts of his sermons with unintelligible Greek and Latin phrases mixed together with abandon.

Though the Pilgrims soon found him to be a man of "very weake partes," they put up with him for seven years, which must have been especially painful to those who remembered John Robinson at Leyden.

5. The Last of the Pilgrims

London
March 8, 1630

BRADFORD'S   Most worthy Sir and my continual loving
LETTER BOOK   friend, Mr. Bradford,

Your letter of the 21st of May from Plymouth, and of the 6th of September from Salem, I have received, whereby I understand of your health and welfare, and of all your friends, for which great mercies and blessings the Lord make us thankfull . . .

I see further the agreemente you have made with ye generallitie, in which I cannot understand but you have done very well both for them & you, and also for your freinds at Leyden . . .

Nay, had you not taken this course, I doe not see how you should accomplish ye end you first aimed at, and some others indevored these years past.

We know it must keep us from ye profite which otherwise, by ye blessing of God and your indeavors, might be gained. For most of those that came in May, & these now sente, though I hope honest & good people, yet not like to be helpfull to raise profite but rather—nay, certaine—must some while be chargable to you & us; at which it is lickly, had not this wise & discreete course been taken, many of your generallitie would have grudged . . .

Your unfained & ever loving freind,

James Sherley

P.S. Mr. Bradford, give me leave to put you in mind of one thing.

Here are many of your Leyden people now come over [on the *Handmaid*]. And though I have ever had good thoughts of them, yet believe not everyone what they shall report of Mr. Allerton.

He hath been a trusty honest friend to you all, either there or here. And if any do (as I know, some of them are apt to) speak ill of him, believe them not.

Indeed, they have been unreasonably chargable, yet grudge and are not contented.

Verily, their indiscreet carriage here hath so abated my affection towards them, as were Mrs. Robinson well over, I would not disburse one penny for the rest.

This offence was given by some of them, which redounded to the prejudice of the whole. And indeed our friends, which sent this latter company, were to blame.

For they now sent all the weakest and poorest, without any of note and better discretion and government amongst them, contrary to our minds and advice. For they thought if these were got over, the others might come when they would.

But partly this distaste, but especially the great charge which both these companies came to, coming so near together, put a bar in the way. For though this company were the fewer in number, yet their charge came to a £100 more.

And notwithstanding this indiscretion, yet they were such as feared God, and were to us both welcome and usefull, for the most part.

They were also kept at our charge eighteen months, and all new appareled and other charges defrayed.

The *Handmaid*, the last of the Pilgrim ships, was carrying some sixty passengers, chiefly from Leyden. None can be identified.

On board were two Puritan "gentlemen" bound for the Bay Colony. Having sampled the rigors of Boston, one of them returned to Plymouth and settled there to become one of the last of the Pilgrim Fathers, Samuel Eddy, a tailor, son of an Anglican vicar.

Arrangements had been made to have Bridget Robinson come with three of her children—Isaac, Mercy, and Fear. But at the last minute, for some reason, the pastor's widow drew back and never had another opportunity for passage.

The only Robinson to reach the New World was young Isaac, who came several years later, when he was twenty-two, and made a name for himself in a curiously ironic way. He, too, became a "separatist," like his father before him.

Separating from the Pilgrim church, rejecting the Holy Discipline, he became a Quaker. Charged with "sundrie scandels and falsehoods," disenfranchised and dismissed from all offices, Robinson repaired to Succanesett (Falmouth), on the south shore of Cape Cod, where he kept a tavern for many years.

As the aged died and the younger forgot the past, old ties with Leyden grew weaker and weaker. Troubles beset the congregation remaining at the Green Gate. Many brethren complained of the "lack of appropriate exercises since his [Robinson's] death, so that they cannot be edified in the way they might were they members of some other church provided with a pastor."

Some of the discontented joined the local Scottish Church, so called, which was an English-speaking unit of the Calvinist Dutch Church. Others returned to England. Still others moved back to Amsterdam to join the Separatists there.

In 1637, the small and impoverished congregation at Leyden lost its meetinghouse, the Groenepoort, where all had once been so happy under John Robinson, particularly in those days before the exodus when the congregation had been numerous and strong.

Bridget Robinson died in 1643, breaking a last link with the old days. And in 1655, two years before Bradford's death, what remained of the Green Gate congregation was absorbed by the local Scottish Church, which long outlived its former rival, continuing to hold services down to 1807.

6. Deacon Fuller: Salver of Bodies and Souls

MORTON'S
MEMORIAL
This year [1630] it pleased God in his rich grace to transport over into ye Bay of Massachusetts divers honourable Personages and many worthy Christians, whereby the Lord began in a manifest manner and way to make known the great thoughts which he had of planting the Gospel in this remote and barbarous wilderness, and honouring his own way of instituted worship, causing such and so many to adhere thereunto and fall upon the practice thereof.

Among the rest, a chief one amongst them was that famous Patern of Piety and Justice, Mr. John Winthrop, the first governour of that jurisdiction, accompanied with divers other precious Sons of Sion, which might be compared to the most fine gold . . .

They came over with a fleet of ten ships, three of them arriving first at Salem, in which several of the chiefest of them came, who repaired, sundry of them, in some short time into the Bay of the Massachusetts.

The other seven ships arrived at Charlestown, where it pleased the Lord to exercise them with much sickness. And being destitute of housing and shelter, and lying up and down in booths, some of them languished and died . . .

A letter to myselfe from Samuel Fuller . . .

BRADFORD'S
LETTER BOOK   Massachusetts
                                               June 28, 1630

Sir,

The gentlemen here lately come over (as I suppose you understand of their arrival by Jonathan Brewster) are resolved to sit down at the head of the Charles River, and they of Matapan [Dorchester] purpose to go and plant with them.

I have been at Matapan at the request of Mr. [the Reverend John] Warham, and let some twenty of these people bleed.

I had conference with them till I was weary. Mr. Warham holds that the invisible church may consist of mixed people—godly and openly ungodly. Upon which point we had all our conference, to which, I trust, the Lord will give a blessing . . .

The Governour* is a godly, wise, and humble gentleman, and very discreete, and of a fine and good temper.

We have some privy enemies in the Bay, but (blessed be God) more freinds. The Governour hath had conference with me, both in private and before sundry others. Opposers there is not wanting, and Satan is busy. But if the Lord be on our side, who can be against us?

The Governour hath told me he hoped we will not be wanting in helping them, so that I think you will be sent for.

Here is a gentleman, one Mr. Cottington [William Coddington], a Boston man, who told me that Mr. Cotton's charge at

*This was the celebrated John Winthrop, who superceded Endecott as the chief in command of the Bay colony.

Hampton was,* that they should take advice of them at Plymouth and should do nothing to offend them . . .
Other things I would have writ of, but time prevents me . . .
Yours in the Lord Christ,
Samuel Fuller

[More news of "heavenly progress" in Massachusetts]

Salem
July 26, 1630
To our loving brethren and christian friends . . .
Beloved, &c.,
Being at Salem the 25th of July, being the Sabbath, after the evening exercise, Mr. Johnson having received a letter from Governour Winthrop manifesting the hand of God to be upon them and against them at Charlestown, in visiting them with sickness and taking divers from amongst them—not sparing the righteous, but partaking with the wicked in those bodily judgments—it was therefore, by his desire, taken into the godly consideration of the best here, what was to be done to pacify the Lord's wrath.

And they would do nothing without our advice—I mean those members of our church there known unto them: viz., Mr. Fuller, Mr. Allerton, and myself [Winslow]—requiring our voices, as their own, when it was concluded that the Lord was to be sought in righteousness.

And so, to that end, the sixth day (being Friday) of this present week is set apart that they may humble themselves before God and seek him in his ordinances.

And that then, also, such godly persons as are amongst them and known each to other, publickly at the end of the exercise,

---

*Vicar of St. Botolph's at Boston, Lincolnshire, the Reverend John Cotton, "his head a living Index to the Sacred Volume," came to Massachusetts three years later, in 1633, and was chosen "teacher" of the First Church of Boston. A powerful and shifty theocrat, he reigned as the virtual Pope of the Bay colony for many years.

His oldest son, another John, later ministered at Plymouth, from 1669 to 1697, when he was disgraced and thrown out for his "Notorious Breaches of the Seventh Commandment."

make known their godly desire and practice the same: viz., solemnly to enter into covenant with the Lord to walk in his ways . . .

And as they desired to advise with us, so do they earnestly entreat that the church at Plymouth would set apart the same day, for the same ends, beseeching God as to withdraw his hand of correction, so to establish and direct them in his ways.

And though the time be very short, yet since the causes are so urgent, we pray you to be provoked to this godly work, wherein God will be honoured, and they and we undoubtedly have sweet comfort in doing so . . .

> Your brethren in the faith of Christ,
> and fellowship of the gospel,
> Samuel Fuller
> Edward Winslow

To his loving friend, Mr. William Bradford . . .

> Charlestown
> August 2, 1630

Sir,

There is come hither a ship, . . . which brings this news out of England . . .

Bishop Laud is Chancellor of Oxford, and five sundry ministers are to appear before the High Commission, among whom, Mr. Cotton, of Boston, is one.*

The sad news here is that many are sick, and many are dead. The Lord, in his mercy, look upon them!

Some are here entered into a church covenant. The first were four: namely, the Governour Mr. John Winthrop, Mr. [Isaac] Johnson, Mr. [Thomas] Dudley, and Mr. [the Reverend John] Wilson.†

---

*When the Court of High Commission moved against him two years later, the Reverend John Cotton took to his heels and fled in disguise to London, where he concealed himself until he escaped to the Bay colony in July 1633, slipping through the watch that had been set for him at all ports.

†"That blessed Servant of Christ," Isaac Johnson, the richest man in the colony, soon died, as did his wife, Lady Arbella, daughter of the Earl of Lincoln. Dudley, a man of arrogant manners and narrow religious views, was deputy

Since that, five more are joined unto them and others, it is like, will add themselves to them daily. The Lord increase them both in number and holiness, for his mercy's sake.

I here lose time, and long to be at home. I can do them no good, for I want drugs and fitting things to work with. I purpose to be at home this week (if God permit), and Mr. Johnson and Captain Endecott will come with me . . .

Here are divers honest christians that are desirous to see us— some, out of the love which they bear us and the good persuasion they have of us; others, to see whether we be so evill as they have heard of us.

We have a name of love and holiness to God and his saints. The Lord make us answerable, and that it be more than a name— or else, it will do us no good . . .

Your loving brother-in-law,
Samuel Fuller

Thus, out of smalle beginings, greater things have been prodused by his hand that made all things of nothing, and gives being to all things that are.

And as one small candle may light a thousand, so ye light here kindlcd hath shonc to many—yea, in some sorte, to our whole nation.

Let ye glorious name of Jehova have all ye praise.

In 1630 alone, 1,000 people came to settle in the Bay colony. This was more than three times as many as had come to Plymouth in ten years, With their slender resources, the Pilgrims could not hope to keep pace with the large and well-financed Puritan migration, which continued at an increasing rate.

7. The Pilgrim Saddle on the Bay Horse

In a sense, the Pilgrims' great adventure was over. Heroically, they had blazed a new path, not only in the world but in the realm

---

governor. A graduate of Eton and Cambridge, a fiery bigot, Wilson became the first pastor of the First Church of Boston, which he organized at this time. Such were the new Saints.

of the spirit. But now came others with superior strength and influence to crowd ahead of them and take the lead.

The Pilgrim empire still had sixty years of independent life before it would be swallowed up by "ye Massachusetts." But the Old Colony, as it now came to be known, was more and more overshadowed by the relative giant to the north, as Bradford later noted in his one essay at verse:*

Almost ten years we lived here alone,
In other places there were few or none;
For Salem was the next of any fame,
That began to augment New England's name.
But after, multitudes began to flow,
More than well knew themselves where to bestow,
Boston then began her roots to spread
And quickly soon she grew to be the head
Not only of the Massachusetts Bay,
But all trade and commerce fell in her way.

Warming to his subject, Bradford really got down to earth:

New plantations were in each place begun
And with inhabitants were filled soon . . .
All sorts of roots and herbs in gardens grow,
Parsnips, melons, cucumbers, radishes,
Skirets, beets, coleworts, and fair cabbages . . .
Many good wholesome berries here you'll find,
Fit for man's use, almost of every kind . . .
Nuts and grapes of several sorts are here,
If you will take the pains them to seek for.

Cattle of every kind do fill the land;
Many now are kill'd, and their hides tann'd . . .
Here store of cows, which milk and butter yield,

---

*Penned some years later, in 1654, these lyrics were entitled "Some Observations of God's Mercifull Dealing with us in this Wildernesse, and His Gracious Protection over us These Many Years, Blessed be His Name." Bradford prized them above all his other writings, even his masterful history, recommending to his heirs these "usefull verses . . . to be improved as you shall see meet."

Wisely, they did nothing about them, but they were later published in the Mass. Hist. Soc. Collections, Series I, Vol. 3.

And also oxen, for to till the field . . .
Horses here likewise now do multiply,
They prosper well, and yet their price is high.
Here are swine, good store; and some, goats do keep,
But now most begin to get store of sheep . . .

But that which did 'bove all the rest excel,
God in his word with us here did dwell;
Well ordered churches in each place there were,
And a learn'd ministry was planted here . . .
Oh, how great comfort was it now to see
The churches to enjoy free liberty! . . .

Though the coming of the first great Puritan company in 1630 deprived the Pilgrims of their ascendancy in New England, yet this was their hour of greatest triumph, for the Pilgrim saddle was on the Bay Horse, as the phrase went. They had brought the powerful Puritans into the fold, making Saints of them, though the latter were still pretending that they had not separated from the Church of England, but only from its corruptions and "abuses."

Still, whatever they said, it had come to pass, as John Robinson had predicted long ago, "there will be no difference between uncomformable Ministers and you when they come to the practice of the Ordinances out of the Kingdome."

At home the Puritans had known nothing like the Brownist meetinghouse with its essentially democratic concepts, which the Pilgrims now gave them. Nor had they known anything resembling that parallel, distinctive, and also essentially democratic institution, the New England town meeting, established by the Pilgrims ten years before.

The two institutions were interlocked, springing from the same source—the Brownist covenant to walk together in the ways of God, with "every member (being men) . . . to have a free voyce in ye choyce of their officers, &c."

Indeed, in a real sense, the two were one. The annual town meeting for discussing and deciding all joint affairs was only the church sitting on secular business.

In the beginning and for many years after, both sat in the meetinghouse and consisted of the same people—that is, communicants in good standing, for no others could vote at Plymouth or in the Bay. But this undemocratic restriction gradually had to give way, undermined in large part by the democratic equalitarianism implicit in the doctrine of those who imposed the restriction.

It is no accident that our more liberal and less dogmatic churches came out of the "Congregationall way," in which there was no room for authoritarianism, though some of the Massachusetts theocrats desperately tried to impose such an order, with some success for a time.

These, then, were the gifts—the Brownist meetinghouse and the New England town meeting—that the Pilgrims gave the Puritans. Their influence, radiating far and wide from Massachusetts, contributed as much as—and perhaps more than—any other single influence in creating an American *mythos* and *ethos*, shaping the ideas, ideals, manners, customs, ways of life, and moral values of millions of Americans down to our own day.

XXII

Merry Mount

And after they had gott some goods into their hands, and gott much by trading with ye Indeans, they spent it as vainly, in quaffing & drinking both wine & strong waters, in great exsess—and, as some reported, £10 worth in a morning.

—*William Bradford*

BRADFORD'S HISTORY — Aboute some 3 or 4 years before this time [or more precisely, in 1625], there came over one Captaine Wollaston (a man of pretie parts), and with him 3 or 4 more of some eminencie, who brought with them a great many servants, with provissions & other implements for to begine a plantation. And pitched themselves in a place within the Masssachusetts, which they called, after their Captain's name, Mount Wollaston.*

Amongst whom was one Mr. Morton, who, it would seeme, had some small adventure (of his owne or other men's) amongst them, but had little respecte amongst them and was sleighted by ye meanest servants.

Having continued there some time [about three years] and not finding things to answer their expectations, nor profite to arise as they looked for, Captaine Wollaston takes a great part of ye sarvants and transports them to Virginia, where he puts them off at good rates, selling their time to other men, and writes back to one Mr. Rassdall, one of his cheefe partners—and accounted their marchant—to bring another parte of them to Vir-

---

*About twenty-five miles north of Plymouth in what is now the city of Quincy, just beyond Weston's old settlement at Wessagusset.

ginia likewise, intending to put them off there as he had done
ye rest.*

And he [Wollaston], with ye consente of ye said Rassdall,
appoynted one Fitcher to be his Livetenante and governe ye
remaines of ye plantation till he, or Rassdall, returned to take
further order thereaboute.

1. Dancing and Frisking Together

BRADFORD'S
HISTORY

But this Morton aforesaid, having more craft
than honestie (who had been a kind of petie-
fogger of Furnefell's Inne), in ye others' absence watches an oppertunitie (commons being but hard amongst
them), and gott some strong drink & other junkats, & made them
a feast.

And after they were merie, he begane to tell them he would
give them good counsell.

You see, saith he, that many of your fellows are carried to
Virginia. And if you stay till this Rassdall returns, you will also
be carried away and sould for slaves with ye rest.

Therefore, I would advise you to thruste out this Levetenant
Fitcher. And I, having a parte in this plantation, will receive you
as my partners and consociates.

So may you be free from service. And we will converse, trade,
plante, & live togeather as equalls, & supporte & protecte one
another—or to like effect.

This counsell was easily received.† So they tooke oppertunitie

*It was common practice to sell or hire out bond servants for the period of
their indenture. Even Thomas Weston, that hard-bitten trader, spoke out
against this heartless traffic in bond slaves. In New England, servants were "sold
upp and Downe like horses," he protested, and for that reason he "held it not
lawfull to carie any."

†As well it might, for Morton was not only freeing his own servants from
bondage but protecting others from being sold like cattle to the tobacco
planters in Virginia, where work was hard, food scarce, and mortality high. His
motives were not entirely humanitarian—as whose are? He hoped to profit
from this arrangement, as he did.

and thrust Levetenante Fitcher out-a-dores, and would suffer him to come no more amongst them. But forct him to seeke bread to eate, and other releefe from his neighbours, till he could get passage for England.

After this, they fell to great licenciousness and led a dissolute life, powering out themselves into all profaneness. And Morton became lord of misrule, and maintained (as it were) a schoole of Athisme.

And after they had gott some goods into their hands, and gott much by trading with ye Indeans, they spent it as vainly in quaffing & drinking both wine & strong waters, in great exsess— and, as some reported, £10 [$500] worth in a morning.

They also set up a May-pole, drinking and dancing aboute it many days togeather, inviting the Indean women for their consorts, dancing and frisking togither (like so many fairies, or furies rather),* and worse practices—as if they had anew revived & celebrated the feasts of ye Roman Goddess Flora, or ye beastly practices of ye madd Bacchinalians.

Morton likewise, to shew his poetrie, composed sundry rimes & verses, some tending to lasciviousnes and others to ye detraction & scandall of some persons, which he affixed to this idle or idoll May-pole.

They changed allso the name of their place. And instead of calling it Mount Wollaston, they called it Merie-mount, as if this joylity would have lasted ever.

2. Thomas Morton

So began a unique settlement, one of the gayest that ever graced our shores—Thomas Morton's celebrated Merry Mount, as it came to be known, though it was not originally so named. Being such close neighbors, the prim Saints and "lascivious" Morton were soon at swords' points. One or the other of them had to go.

*On the Pilgrims' calendar of sins, nothing bore a more scarlet marking than "dauncing."

Hating Merry Mount and all of its ways, angry and alarmed by their rival's quick success in the fur trade, the Pilgrims did their best to disparage and discredit Morton.

Far from being a nobody, "a kind of petie-fogger of Furnefell's Inne," as Bradford tried to make out, Morton was an aristocrat, descended from a long line of distinguished soldiers entitled to bear a coat of arms. On that account he was disposed to look down his nose at the humble Pilgrims.

Probably a graduate of Oxford, trained in the law, Morton had practiced his profession as a member of Clifford's Inn. But the law was the least of his interests. He had read widely in Greek and Latin, quoted frequently from the ancient poets, dabbled in verse himself, and had been one of those who sang, drank, and rollicked with the great Ben Jonson and his cronies at the immortal Mermaid Tavern.

Nor did he maintain a "schoole of Athisme." So far as he was interested in religion at all, Morton appears to have been an Anglican of conventional views, knowing little and caring less about the Saints' Holy Discipline.

Always something of a scapegrace, Morton had married an elderly widow for her money in 1620. When her sons called upon him for an accounting of her estate, Morton disappeared, coming to New England for a visit, according to his later story. If so, he probably came in 1622 and helped found Wessagusset, perhaps returning to England the same year.

In any case, he came again in 1625 as one of Captain Wollaston's aides, arriving on the *Unity* "with 30 servants and provisions of all sorts for a plantation."

Morton left a lively picture of the plantation after he took charge there.

MORTON'S
NEW CANAAN* The inhabitants, having translated the name of their habitation to Ma-re Mount, and being resolved to have the new name confirmed for a memorial to after ages, did devise amongst themselves to have it performed in a solemne manner, with Revels and merriment after the old English custome.

*From Morton's *New English Canaan* (1637)—hereafter Morton's New Canaan.

They prepared to sett up a Maypole upon the festival day, . . . and therefore brewed a barrell of excellente beere, and provided a case of bottles, to be spent with all good cheare, for all commers of that day.

And because they would have it in a compleat forme, they had prepared a song fitting to the time and present occasion.

And upon Mayday, they brought the Maypole to the place appointed, with drumes, gunnes, pistols, and other fitting instruments for that purpose, and there erected it with the help of the Salvages that came thither of purpose to see the manner of our Revels.

A goodly pine tree of 80 foote long was reared up, with a peare [pair] of Buckshorns nayled on somewhat neare unto the top of it, where it stood as a faire sea marke for directions how to finde out the way to mine Hoste of Ma-re Mount.*

And because it should more fully appeare to what end it was placed there, they had a poem in readiness made, which was fixed to the Maypole to shew the new name confirmed upon that plantation, which, . . . being enigmattically composed, pusselled the Separatists most pittifully to expound it . . .

The Poem

Rise, Oedipus, and if thou canst, unfould
What meanes Caribdis underneath the mould
When Scilla sollitary on the ground
(Sitting in forme of Niobe) was found† . . .

---

*While Morton, fond of bad puns and always ready to tease the "precise Separatists," called it Ma-re Mount, or Mount by the Sea, the Pilgrims were not mistaken in thinking of it as "Merie Mount."

†The poem continued at some length in this vein. What it all meant, if anything, is a secret that died with its author. Confessing that it was somewhat obscure, Morton attributed some of the Saints' rage against him to the fact that they could not understand it. They were, he said, always bothering their heads about "things that were immaterial." But racking their brains on the matter, Bradford and others were quite sure that it tended "to ye detraction & scandall" of the Saints. And certainly, there was no mistaking the meaning of the second poem Morton penned and nailed to the Maypole.

The setting up of this Maypole was a lamentable spectacle to the precise Separatists that lived at New Plimmouth. They termed it an Idoll. Yea, they called it the Calfe of Horeb, and stood at defiance with the place, naming it Mount Dagon, threatening to make it a woefull mount and not a merry mount . . .

There was likewise a merry song made, which (to make their Revells more fashionable) was sung with a Chorus, every man bearing his part, which they performed in a daunce, hand in hand about the Maypole, whiles one of the Company sung and filled out the good liquor, like Gammedes and Jupiter.

The Songe

Cor.

> Drinke and be merry, merry, merry, boyes;
> Let all your delight be in Hymen's joyes;
> Iô to Hymen, now the day is come,
> About the mery Maypole take a Roome.

> Make green garlons, bring bottles out,
> And fill sweet Nectar freely about.
> Uncover thy head and fear no harme,
> For here's good liquor to keepe it warme.

> Then drinke and be merry, &c.
> Iô to Hymen, &c.

> Nectar is a thing assigned
> By the Deitie's owne minde
> To cure the hart opprest with greife,
> And of good liquors is the cheife.

> Then drinke, &c.
> Iô to Hymen, &c.

> * * *

> Give to the Nymphe that's free from scorne
> No Irish stuff nor Scotch over-worne.

Lasses in beaver coats, come away,
Ye shall be welcome to us night and day

To drinke and be merry, &c.
Iô to Hymen, &c.

This harmless mirth, made by younge men that lived in hope
to have wifes brought over to them, that would save them a
laboure to make a voyage to fetch any over, was much distasted
by the precise Seperatists, . . . troubling their braines more
than reason would require about things that are indifferent.

3. Trade in Firearms

BRADFORD'S
HISTORY

Now to maintaine this riotous prodigallitie
and profuse excess, Morton, thinking himselfe
lawless, and hearing what gaine ye French &
fisher-men made by trading of peeces, powder, & shotte to ye
Indeans, he, as head of this consortship, begane ye practise of
ye same in these parts.

And first, he taught them how to use them, to charge & discharge, and what proportion of powder to give ye peece according to ye size or bigness of ye same, and what shotte to use for
foule and what for deare.

And having thus instructed them, he imployed some of them
to hunte & fowle for him, so as they became farr more active
in that imployment than any of ye English by reason of their
swiftness of foote & nimblnes of body, being also quick-sighted,
and by continuall exercise well knowing ye hants of all sorts of
game.

So when they saw ye execution that a peece could doe, and
ye benefite that might come by ye same, they became madd, as
it were, after them and would not stick to give any prise they
could attaine to for them, accounting their bowes & arrowes but
bables in comparison of them.

And here I may take occasion to bewaile ye mischefe that this wicked man began in these parts,* and which . . . [from] base covetousnes prevailing in men that should know better, has now at length gott ye upper hand and made this thing commone, notwithstanding any laws to ye contrary.

So ye Indeans are full of peeces, all over, both fouling peeces, muskets, pistols, &c., . . . wherewith they are ordinarily better fitted & furnished than ye English themselves . . .

O, the horiblnes of this vilanie! . . . Oh! that princes & parlements would take some timely order to prevent this mischeefe, and at length to suppress it, by some exemplerie punishmente upon some of these gaine-thirstie murderers (for they deserve no better title) before their collonies in these parts be overthrowne by these barbarous savages, thus armed with their owne weapons by these evill instruments and traytors to their neighbours and cuntrie. But I have forgott myselfe and have been too long in this disgression. But now to returne.

This Morton, having thus taught them ye use of peeces, he sould them all he could spare. And he and his consorts detirmined to send for many out of England and had, by some ships, sente for above a score.

The which being knowne, and his neighbours meeting ye Indeans in ye woods armed with guns of this sort, it was terrour unto them who lived straglingly and were of no strength in any place. And other places (though more remote) saw this mischeefe would quickly spread over all, if not prevented.

Besides, they saw they should keep no servants, for Morton would entertaine any. And all ye scume of ye countrie, or any discontents, would flock to him from all places if this nest was not broken. And they should stand in more fear of their lives & goods (in short time) from this wicked & deboste crue than from ye salvages themselves.

So sundrie of ye cheefe of ye stragling plantations, meeting

---

*Morton did not begin the "mischefe." Six years before, in 1622, the arms traffic with the Indians was so brisk that it had been forbidden under a proclamation by King James, who had since died.

togither, agreed by mutuall consente to sollissite those of Plimoth (who were then of more strength than all of them) to joyne with them to prevente ye further growth of this mischefe and suppress Morton & his consorts before they grewe to further head and strength* . . .

Those of Plimoth, being thus sought to by their messengers & letters, and waying both their reasons and commone danger, were willing to afford them their help, though themselves had least cause of fear or hurte.

So, to be short, they first resolved joyntly to write to him, and in a freindly & neighborly way to admonish him to forbear those courses, & sent a messenger with their letters to bring his answer.

But he was so highe as he scorned all advise, and asked who had to doe with him? He had and would trade peeces with ye Indeans in dispite of all, with many other scurillous termes full of disdaine.

They sente to him a second time, and bad him be better advised and more temperate in his termes, for ye countrie could not beare ye injurie he did. It was against their commone saftie and against ye king's proclamation.

He answered in high terms as before, and that ye king's proclamation was no law, demanding what penaltie was upon it?

It was answered, more than he could bear—his majestie's displeasure.

But he insolently persisted and said ye king was dead, and his displeasure with him, & many ye like things. And threatened, withall, that if any came to molest him, let them looke to themselves, for he would prepare for them.

*For many good reasons, as will appear, the Pilgrims tried to make out that the "stragling" planters initiated the move against Morton. But the Pilgrims' modesty in this deceived no one, least of all Morton's friend and patron, Sir Ferdinando Gorges.

The "stragling" planters included a number of Pilgrim Fathers who had been expelled or had left Plymouth in disgust—John Oldham of Nantasket, the Roger Conant-John Lyford group at Naumkeag (Salem), and William Hilton, who had left at the time of the Lyford-Oldham troubles and founded Cocheco, later Dover (New Hampshire), on the Piscataqua River, about ten miles above its mouth.

4. Battle of Merry Mount: Pilgrims' Version

BRADFORD'S
HISTORY

Upon which they saw there was no way but to take him by force. And having so farr proceeded, now to give over would make him farr more hautie & insolente.

So they mutually resolved to proceed, and obtained from ye Governor of Plimoth to send Captaine Standish and some other aid with him,* to take Morton by force.

The which accordingly was done. But they found him to stand stiffly in his defence, having made fast his doors, armed his consorts, set diverse dishes of powder & bullets ready on ye table. And if they had not been overarmed with drinke, more hurte might have been done.

They summoned him to yeeld. But he kept his house, and they could gett nothing but scoffes & scorns from him. But at length, fearing they would do some violence to ye house, he and some of his crue came out—but not to yeeld, but to shoote.

But they were so steeled with drinke as their peeces were too heavie for them. Himselfe with a carbine (overcharged & allmost halfe fild with powder and shotte, as was after found) had thought to have shot Captaine Standish. But he stept to him, & put by his peece, & tooke him.

Neither was there any hurte done to any of either side, save that one was so drunke that he ran his owne nose upon ye pointe of a sword that one held before him . . . But he lost but a little of his hott blood.

Morton was brought away to Plimoth, where he was kepte till a ship went from ye Ile of Sholst† for England, with which he was sente to ye Counsell of New England, and letters written to give them information of his course & carriage.

And also, one was sent at their common charge [John Old-

*Standish took eight Pilgrims with him.
†The Isles of Shoals, in northern waters, off the mouth of the Piscataqua.

ham, the Pilgrims' "malicious" enemy of a few years back] to informe their Honours, & to prosecute against him.

But he fooled off ye messenger after he was gone from hence. And though he wente for England, yet nothing was done to him—not so much as rebukte, for ought was heard . . .

5. This Outrageous Riot: Morton's Version

MORTON'S
NEW CANAAN
[After the frisking about the Maypole, those at Plymouth] sought occasion against my honest host of Ma-re Mount to overthrow his ondertakings, and to destroy his plantation, quite and cleane . . .

The Separatists, envying the prosperity and hope of the plantation at Ma-re Mount (which they perceaved beganne to come forward, and to be in a good way for gaine in the Beaver trade) conspired together against mine Host especially (who was the owner of that Plantation), and made up a party against him, and mustered up what aid they could, accounting of him as of a great Monster.

Many threatening speeches were given out both against his person and his habitation, which they divulged should be consumed with fire.

And taking advantage of the time when his company (which seemed little to regard their threats) were gone up into the inlands to trade with the Salvages for Beaver,* they set upon my honest host at a place called Wessaguscus [Wessagusset] where, by accident, they found him . . .

And they chardged him (because they would seeme to have some reasonable cause against him to sett a glosse upon their mallice) with criminal things . . .

In briefe, mine host must indure to be their prisoner untill they could contrive it so that they might send him for England (as they said), there to suffer according to the merit of the fact

---

*Altogether, Morton had only seven men at Mare Mount, it appears. Four of these were inland at the moment.

which they intended to father upon him, supposing (belike) it would prove a hainous crime.

Much rejoycing was made that they had gotten their capitall enemy (as they concluded him) . . . The conspirators sported themselves at my honest host that meant them no hurt, and were so jocund that they feasted their bodies, and fell to tippling, as if they had obtained a great prize . . .

Mine host fained greefe and could not be persuaded either to eate or drinke, because he knew emptiness would be a meanes to make him as watchful as the Geese kept in the Roman Cappitall. Whereon, the contrary part, the conspirators would be so drowsy that he might have an opportunity to give them a slip . . .

Six persons of the conspiracy were set to watch him, . . . but he kept waking. In the dead of night (one lying on the bed for further surety), up gets mine Host and got to the second dore that he was to passe, which, notwithstanding the lock, he got open and shut it after him with such violence that it affrighted some of the conspirators.

The word, which was given with an alarme, was:

O, he's gon! He's gon! What shall wee doe? He's gon!

The rest (halfe asleepe) start up in a maze and, like rams, ran their heades one at another, full butt in the darke.

Their grande leader, Captaine Shrimpe,* tooke on most furiously and tore his clothes for anger, to see the empty nest and their bird gone. The rest were eager to have torne their haire from their heads, but it was so short that it would give them no hold† . . .

In the meane time, mine Host was got home to Ma-re Mount through the woods. . . . And there he prepared powther, three pounds dried, for his present imployement, and four good gunnes for him and the two assistants left at his howse, with bullets of

---

*Short and squat, Captain Standish had red hair and a florid complexion, which flamed to crimson when he got mad—which was often—so that "Captaine Shrimpe" struck home.

†The Pilgrims, like the common people in England, wore their hair close-cropped, being "Roundheads," as Oliver Cromwell's men would soon be dubbed by the "Cavaliers," who affected long flowing locks.

several sizes, three hundred or thereabouts, to be used if the conspirators should pursue him thither . . .

Now Captaine Shrimpe, the first Captaine in the Land (as he supposed), must doe some new act to repaire this losse, and . . . takes eight persons more to him. And (like the nine Worthies of New Canaan), they imbarque with preparation against Ma-re Mount where this Monster of a man, as their phrase was, had his denne.

The whole number, had the rest not bin from home, being but seven, would have given Captaine Shrimpe (a quondam Drummer) such a wellcome as would have made him wish for a Drumme as bigg as Diogenes' tubb, that he might have crept into it out of sight . . .

The nine worthies, comming before the Denne of this supposed Monster (this seven-headed hydra, as they termed him), began, like Don Quixote against the Windmill, to beate a parly and to offer quarter if mine Host would yeeld, for they were resolved to send him for England and bad him lay down his arms.

But he (who was the Sonne of a Souldier), having taken up armes in his just defence, replyed that he would not lay by those armes because they were so needefull at sea if he should be sent over.

Yet, to save the effusion of so much worthy bloud as would have issued out of the vaynes of these 9 worthies of New Canaan if mine Host should have played upon them out of his port holes (for they came within danger like a flocke of wild geese, as if they had bin tayled one to another as colts to be sold at a faier), mine Host was content to yeelde upon quarter, and did capitulate with them in what manner it should be for more certainty, because he knew what Captaine Shrimpe was.

He expressed that no violence should be offered to his person, none to his goods, nor any of his household; but that he should have his armes and what else was requisite for the voyage. Which was agreed upon . . .

But mine Host no sooner set open the dore and issued out,

but instantly Captaine Shrimpe and the rest of the worthies stepped to him, layd hold of his armes, and had him downe. And so eagerly was every man bent against him (not regarding any agreemente made with such a carnall man), that they fell upon him as if they would have eaten him. Some of them were so violent that they would have a slice with scabbert, and all for haste . . .

Captaine Shrimpe and the rest of the nine worthies made themselves (by this outragious riot) master of mine Hoste of Ma-re Mount and disposed of what he had at his plantation . . .

[They] carried him to their towne of Plimmouth, where . . . they would have dispatched him, as Captaine Shrimpe in a rage professed that he would doe with his pistoll, as mine Host should set his foote into the boat.

Howsoever, the cheife Elder's voyce in that place was more powerful than any of the rest, who concluded to send mine Host, without any other thing to be done to him . . .

And when the wind served, they tooke mine Host into their shallop, hoysed Saile, and carried him to the northern parts, where they left him upon a Island [late in 1628], . . . without gunne, powther, or shot, or dogge, or so much as a knife to get anythinge to feede upon, or any other cloathes to shelter him with in winter than a thinne suit which he had on at that time . . .

Upon this island he stayed a moneth at least, and was releeved by salvages that . . . would bringe bottles of strong liquor to him, and united themselves into a league of brotherhood with mine Host—so full of humanity are these infidels before those Christians.

From this place sailed mine Host [in a fishing vessel] that landed him safe in England, at Plimmouth. And he stayed in England untill the ordinary time for shipping to set forth for these parts, . . . noe man being able to tax him with anythinge.

6. To His Old Nest Again

Elated at their easy triumph in liquidating Merry Mount, persuaded that the "habitation of the wicked should no more appear
in Israel," the Pilgrims were never more surprised than when
the "lord of misrule" put in at Plymouth the next year, "in the
very faces of them, to their terrible amazement to see him at liberty," observed Morton, obviously enjoying the scene.

BRADFORD'S   Mr. Allerton gave them great and just offense
HISTORY   . . . in bringing over this year [1629], for base
                  gaine, that unworthy man and instruments of mis-
cheefe, Morton, who was sent home but ye year before for his
misdemenors.

He not only brought him over, but into ye towne—as it were,
to nose them—and lodged him at his owne house. And for a
while, he used him as a scribe to do his bussines, till he was
caused to pack him away.

So he wente to his old nest in ye Massachusetts . . .

Their many complaints against Morton, the Pilgrims learned,
had been ignored in England. He was "not so much as rebukte,
for ought was heard," so that they were not surprised when word
presently came that Morton was at it again—firearms, firewater,
Indian maids, Maypole, and all.

In calling him to account, the Pilgrims had not made any pretense to legal jurisdiction over Merry Mount. Their faulty patent,
they realized, could not be stretched so far. Morton's presence
was undesirable, however, and they were resolved in one way
or another to purge the land of him.

Things now stood on another footing. The new Massachusetts Bay patent embraced Merry Mount, so that Governor John
Endecott spoke with authority in summoning Morton and other
"stragling" planters to Salem, where they were to swear obedience to the new colony and give surety for their good behavior.
Deacon-Doctor Fuller had already visited Salem to make Saints
of the newcomers there.

MORTON'S
NEW CANAAN

In the mean time, . . . there was a great swelling fellow of Littleworth* crept over to Salem, . . . and tooke unto him a councell. And a worthy one, no doubt, for the Cowkeeper of Salem [Endecott, again] was a prime man in those imployments . . .

This man, thinking none so worthy as himselfe, took upon him infinitely. He made warrants in his owne name (without relation to his Majestie's authority in that place) † and summoned a generall appearance at the worshipfull towne of Salem.

There, in open assembly, was tendered certaine Articles devised betweene him and their new pastor, Master Eager [Samuel Skelton], who had renounced his old calling to the ministry receaved in England by warrant of God's word, and taken a new one there by their fantasticall way imposed . . .

To these Articles every planter, old and new, must signe or be expelled from any manner of aboade within the compass of the land contained within that grant . . .

The tenor of the Articles were these: *That in all causes, as well Ecclesiasticall as Politicall, we should follow the rule of God's word.*

This made a shew of good intent, and all the assembly (only mine Host replyed) did subscribe. He would not, unlesse they would add this Caution: *So as nothing be done contrary or repugnant to the Lawes of the Kingdome of England.*

These words, he knew from former experience, were necessary, . . . for the construction of the Word would be made by them of the Separation, to serve their owne turnes . . .

It was then agreed upon that there should be one generall trade used within that patent‡ . . .

All were united, but mine Host refused.

Two truckmasters were chosen; wages, prefixed . . . But be-

---

*So Morton always referred to Governor Endecott.

†It was Endecott who later publicly cut the red cross of St. George out of the royal standard, saying that it smacked of popery, for which he was censured and disqualified from office for a year.

‡The Massachusetts Bay Company had prescribed that there was to be a joint-stock monopoly to exploit the fur trade. There was to be no "free trade."

fore the end of 6 months, the partners in this stock (handled by the Truckmasters) would have an accompt . . .

The accompt being made betweene Captaine Littleworth and the two Truckmasters, it was found that, instead of increasing the proffit, they had decreased it. For the principall stock, by this imployment, was fretted so, that there was a great hole to be seene in the very middle of it . . .

But mine Host, that sturred not his foote at all for the matter, did not only save his stock from such a canker, but gained sixe and seaven for one.

In the meane time, he derided the Contributors for being catch'd in that snare . . .

7. Another Portrait of Deacon-Doctor Fuller

At Salem, Morton had evidently met the Pilgrims' "phyisition & chirurgeon," who had been called there to tend the sick. And Morton was at his savagely malicious best on him.

MORTON'S
NEW CANAAN
The church at Plimmouth, having due regard to the weale publike and Brethren that were come over, and knowing that they would be busily imployed to make provision for the cure of Soules, and therefore might neglect the body for that time, did hold themselves to be in duty bound to make search for a fitting man that might be able (if so neede requir'd) to take the charge upon him in that place of imployment, and therefore called a Councell of the whole Synagoge.

Amongst which company, they chose out a man that long time had bin nurst up in the tender bosome of the Church, one that had speciall gifts.

He could wright and reade. Nay, more, he had tane the oath of abjuration,* which is a speciall stepp—yea, and a maine degree unto preferment . . . They stile him Doctor, and forth they send him to gaine imployment and opinion.

*That is, he had renounced the Anglican church.

What luck is it that I cannot hit on his name?

But I will give you him by periphrasis, that you may know him when you meete him next.

He was born at Wrington, in the County of Somerset, where he was bred a butcher.* He weares a longe beard and a Garment like the Greeke that begged in Paul's Church [old St. Paul's, London].

This new-made Doctor comes to Salem to gratulate, where he findes some are newly come from sea and ill at ease. He takes the patient and the urinall, eyes the state there, findes the *Crasis Syptomes* and the *attomi natantes,* and tells the patient that his disease was winde, which he had tane by gapeing feasting overboard at Sea [that is, the patient had been seasick], but he would quickly ease him of that griefe and quite expell the winde.

And this he did performe with the gifts he had. And then he handled the patient so handsomly that he eased him of all the winde he had, in an instant [in short, the patient died].

And yet I hope this man may be forgiven if he [the patient] were made a fitting plant for Heaven.†

How he went to worke with his gifts is a question. Yet he did a great cure for Captaine Littleworth. He cured him of a disease called a wife.

And yet I hope this man may be forgiven if she were made a fitting plant for Heaven.

By this meanes he was allowed 4d [$4.00] a moneth, and the Chirgeon's chest, and made Phisition Generall of Salem, where he exercised his gifts so well that of full 42 that there he tooke to cure, there is not one has more cause to complaine, or can say black's his eye . . .

But then I hope this man may be forgiven if they were all made fitting plants for Heaven.

But in mine opinion, he deserves to be set upon a palfrey and led up and downe in triumph through New Canaan, . . . that men might know where to find a Quacksalver.

---

*Fuller was born at Redenhall, Norfolk, and had been a say maker at Leyden.
†This alludes to Fuller's success in making Saints of those at Salem.

8. To the Bilboes

MORTON'S
NEW CANAAN And here comes their Joshua,* too, among them . . . These are the men that come prepared to ridd the land of all pollution . . . These men have brought a very snare indeed. And now mine Host must suffer. The Book of Common Prayer which he used, to be despised. And he must not be spared.

Now they are come, his doom beforehand was concluded on. They have a warrant now† . . .

A Court is called of purpose for mine host . . . There they all, with one assent, put him to silence, crying out:

Hear the Governour! Hear the Governour!

Who gave this sentence against mine Host at first sight; that he should be first put in the Bilbowes; his goods should all be confiscated; his plantation should be burned downe to the ground, because the habitation of the wicked should no more appear in Israel; and his person banished from those territories; and this put in execution with all speede.

*Joshua Temperwell, as Morton called Governor John Winthrop. Morton disliked him, but he treated him, if not with respect, at least with some restraint.

†Winthrop had arrived with a warrant of some kind, to be used as needed, based upon some vague reports or suspicions that Morton might have committed some crime.

It was quite invalid. It could not legally run into New England any more than into Ireland or Scotland.

If the tables had been reversed and the warrant had come for one of the Puritans, Winthrop would have been the first to scrap it. These warrants from home, always resented by the colonies, contributed to the irritation that exploded in the American Revolution.

In this case, though the warrant was used as a pretext against Morton, it was not entered in the records, obviously because of the fear that it might be used as a precedent.

9. *New English Canaan*

BRADFORD'S
HISTORY So, . . . it was not long but by his miscarriage he gave them just occation to lay hands on him. And he was by them againe sent prisoner into England, where he lay a good while in Exeter Jaole.

For besides his miscarriage here, he was vemently suspected for ye murder of a man that had adventured moneys with him when he came first into New-England, and a warrante was sente from ye Lord Cheefe Justice to apprehend him. By vertue whereof, he was by the Governor of ye Massachusetts sent into England.

And for his misdemenors amongst them, they demolisht his house, that it might no longer be a roost for such uncleane birds to nestle in.

Yet he got free againe and writ an infamouse & scurrillous booke against many godly & cheefe men of ye cuntrie, full of lyes & slanders, and fraight with profane callumnies against their names and persons, and ye ways of God.

After the captain of another ship declined to transport him, Morton was sent back on the Pilgrim ship, the *Handmaid*, and almost starved en route, having been given few provisions by his captors.

Whether he spent any time in the Exeter jail, as Bradford reports, is not clear. It would seem not, for he soon went to work for Sir Ferdinando Gorges at the happy task, for him, of trying to void the Plymouth and Bay charters, enjoying himself almost as much in this as in scarifying the Saints in *New English Canaan*, which was dedicated to the Lords of the Commission for Regulating Plantations and designed to incite Archbishop Laud and his minions to take action against the "heretics" in New England. And it almost succeeded in its purpose.

An amusing and witty satire, Morton's book is certainly not to be taken too literally. But it often strikes close to the heart, unfolding aspects of early New England nowhere else revealed. To dismiss the work as worthless because Morton was "immoral," as so many sobersides have done, is simply to be stupid.

Whatever his morals, Mine Host of Ma-re Mount was a shrewd observer and commanded as sharp a pen as Bradford's.

In his portraits of the Saints, there is as much truth—and as little—as in theirs of him. There is nothing to choose between them. Both are caricatures.

As the Saints read Morton, they squirmed with rage, impotent at the moment. But they would have their revenge on him—in time.

XXIII

Allerton: First Yankee Trader

Oh, the greefe & trouble that man, Mr. Allerton, hath
brought upon you and us! . . . And to thinke on it
draws many a sigh from my harte, and teares from my
eyes . . .

—*James Sherley*

BRADFORD'S   The Leyden people being come over, and sun-
HISTORY   dry of ye generallitie seeing & hearing how great
ye charge was like to be, they begane to murmure
and repine at it, notwithstanding ye burden lay on other men's
shoulders, espetially at ye paying of ye 3 bushells of corne a year,
according to ye former agreement when ye trade was lett [to
the Undertakers] for ye 6 years aforesaid.

But to give them contente herein allso, it was promised that,
if they could doe it in ye time without it, they would never
demand it.

And indeed, it was never paid [so that Plymouth's entire debt
fell upon the eight Undertakers—Bradford, Allerton, Standish,
Brewster, Winslow, John Alden, John Howland, and Thomas
Prence—to their constant worry and subsequent great loss]

1. Patent Business

BRADFORD'S   Concerning Mr. Allerton's proceedings about ye
HISTORY   inlarging & confirming their patent, both that at
home & Kenebeck, will best appear by another
letter of Mr. Sherley's . . .

March 19, 1630

Most worthy & loving freinds, &c.

Some of your letters I received in July, & some since by Mr. Peirce. But till our maine busines, ye patent, was granted, I could not settle my mind nor pen to writing.

Mr. Allerton was so turmoyled about it as, verily, I would not, nor could not, have undergone it if I might have had £1,000.

But ye Lord so blessed his labours (even beyond expectation in these evill days) as he obtained ye love & favor of great men in repute & place. He got granted from ye Earl of Warwick & Sir Ferdinando Gorges all that Mr. Winslow desired in his letters to me—& more also, which I leave to him to relate.

Then he sued to ye King to confirme their grante and to make you a corporation, and so to inable you to make & execute lawes in such a large & ample manner as ye Massachusetts plantation hath it, which ye King graciously granted, referring it to ye Lord Keeper to give order to ye solisiter to draw it up, if there were presidente for it.

So ye Lord Keeper furthered it all he could, and allso ye solissiter.

But as Festus said to Paul: With no small sum of money obtained I this freedom, for by ye way many riddles must be resolved and many locks must be opened with ye silver—ney, ye golden—key.*

Then it was to come to ye Lord Treasurer, to have his warrente for freeing ye customs for a certaine time. But he would not doe it . . .

But there is no fear nor doubte but it will be granted, for [Allerton] hath ye cheefe of them to freind. Yet it will be marvelously needfull for him to returne by ye first ship that comes from hence.

For if you have this confirmed, then were you compleate, and might bear such sway & goverment as were fitt for ye ranke &

*Sherley had reason to suspect that the Bay was trying to block the grant of a royal charter to Plymouth. See his letter in Mass. Hist. Soc. Collections, Vol. 3, pp. 71–72.

place that God hath called you unto, and stop ye mouths of base and scurrulous fellowes that are ready to question & threaten you in every action you doe.

And besides, if you have ye customs free for 7 years inward, & 21 outward, ye charge of ye patent will soon be recovered. And there is no fear of not obtaining it.

But such things must work by degrees. Men cannot hasten it as they would.

Wherefore, we (I write in behalfe of all our partners here) desire you to be earnest with Mr. Allerton to come, and his wife to spare him this one year more, to finish this great & waighty bussines, which we conceive will be much for your good . . .

For I am persuaded Sir Ferdinando (how loving and freindly soever he seems to be) knows he can—nay, purposeth—to overthrow, at his pleasure, all the patents he grants.*

But this being obtained, he will be frustrate of his intente. And unless a Parliament should call them in (which is not likely), you need not fear . . .

By which it appears what progress was made herein, & in part what charge it was, and how left unfinished, and some reasons for ye same.

But in truth, as was afterwards apprehended, the maine reason was Mr. Allerton's policie, to have an opportunitie to be sent over againe, for other regards—and for that end, procured them thus to write.

For it might then well enough have been finished [but for] that clause aboute ye custumes, which was Mr. Allerton's & Mr. Sherley's device,† and not at all thought on by ye colony here, nor much regarded.

Yet it might have been done without it, having passed the

---

*The scheming Gorges had long dreamed of acquiring all of New England as a vast feudal estate with himself as overlord.

†Freedom from customs for the period sought would have been a valuable privilege. As the Bay enjoyed it under its charter, Allerton and Sherley were seeking a like privilege for Plymouth, which would seem to have been prudent under the circumstances.

King's hand. Nay, it was conceived it might then have been done with it, if he had pleased.

But covetousnes never brings ought home, as ye proverbe is. For this opportunitye being lost, it was never accomplished, but a great deale of money vainly & lavishly cast away aboute it, as doth appear upon their accounts . . .

2. A Pilgrim Father Hanged

BRADFORD'S   This year [1630] John Billington ye elder (one
HISTORY   that came over with ye first) was arrained and
both by grand & petie jurie found guilty of willfull murder by plaine & notorious evidence, and was for the same accordingly executed.

This, as it was ye first execution amongst them, so was it a matter of great sadnes unto them.

They used all due means about his triall, and tooke ye advice of Mr. Winthrop and other ye ablest gentlemen in ye Bay of ye Massachusetts that were then newly come over, who concured with them that he ought to dye, and ye land be purged from blood.

He and some of his had often been punished for miscarriages before, being one of ye profanest families amongst them. They came from London, and I know not by what freinds shufled into their company.

His fact was that he waylaid a yong man, one John Newcomin, about a former quarell and shote him with a gune, whereof he dyed.

The manner of execution is not stated. It was the practice of the day for murderers to be hanged, drawn, and quartered. Perhaps his old friends merely hanged poor John Billington, which would have been distasteful enough. The unpleasant duty may have been put upon Standish as captain of the guard.

Public executions were also the practice of the day, and Billington's last rites may have been witnessed by his wife Ellen, who later remarried, and by their older son, Francis, a boy of eighteen, who married a few years later and left a large family.

Their younger son, John, who as a boy of six had wandered off into the woods soon after the landing and somehow made his way down to Cape Cod many miles distant, was spared his father's final disgrace, having died of gangrene a few years previously.

Billington's was the first capital offense, and there would not be another for eight years. Early Plymouth was remarkably free of violence, even in minor forms.

3. Mr. Allerton's Singular Way

BRADFORD'S HISTORY
Having procured a patente for Kenebeck, they now erected a house up above in ye river, in ye most convenientest place for trade as they conceived,* and furnished the same with commodities for that end, both winter & sommer—not only with corne, but also with such other commodities as ye fishermen had traded with them, as coats, shirts, ruggs & blankets, biskett, peas, &c.

And what they could not have out of England, they bought of the fishing ships and so carried on their business as well as they could . . .

Concerning the rest of Mr. Allerton's instructions, in which they strictly injoined him not to exceed that £50 in goods before mentioned, nor to bring any but trading commodities, he followed them not at all, but did quite the contrarie—bringing over many other sorts of retaile goods, selling what he could by the way, on his owne accounte, and delivering the rest, which he said to be theirs, into ye store.

And for trading goods, he brought but little in comparison, excusing the matter [by saying that] they had laid out much about ye Leyden people, & patent, &c . . .

And as for passing his bounds & instructions, he laid it on Mr. Sherley . . .

*At Cushenoc, in what is now Augusta, Maine. John Howland was the first agent in charge.

But next year, they should have what trading goods they would send for, if things were now well settled, &c.

And thus they were put off. Indeed, Mr. Sherley writ things tending this way . . .

By this it appears that there was a kind of concurrance be- tweene Mr. Allerton and them in these things, and that they gave more regard to his way & course in these things than to ye advise from hence, which made him bold to presume above his instructions, and to run on in ye course he did, to their greater hurt afterwards.

These things did much trouble them here, but they well knew not how to help it, being loath to make any breach or conten- tion hereaboute.

Another secret cause was herewith concurrente. Mr. Allerton had married ye daughter of their Reverend Elder, Mr. Brewster (a man beloved & honoured amongst them, and who tooke great paines in teaching & dispencing ye word of God unto them), whom they were loath to greeve or any way offend, so as they bore with much in that respecte . . .

Besides, though private gaine, I doe perswade myselfe, was some cause to lead Mr. Allerton aside in these beginnings, yet I thinke—or at least, charitie carries me to hope—that he intended to deal faithfully with them, in ye maine, and had such an opinion of his owne abilitie, and some experience of ye benefite that he had made in this singuler way, as he conceived he might both raise himselfe an estate and allso be a means to bring in such profite to Mr. Sherley (and it may be ye rest), as might be lickly to bring in their moneys againe with advantage—and it may be, sooner than from the generall way . . .

I say charitie makes me thus conceive, though things fell out otherwise, and they missed of their aimes, and ye generall suf- fered abundantly thereby . . .

And their ingagements of this year were great indeed, when they came to know them (which was not wholly till 2 years after).

And that which made them ye more, Mr. Allerton had taken up large summes at Bristol at 50 per cent againe—which he excused, that he was forcte to it because, otherwise, he could at ye spring of ye year get no goods transported . . .

4. Disastrous Bargain in Salt

BRADFORD'S
HISTORY

This paying of 50 per cent and the difficulty (as was beleeved) of having their goods transported in ye fishing ships at ye first of ye year, which was ye cheefe season for trade, put them upon another projecte.

Mr. Allerton, after ye fishing season was over, lit of a bargan of salte at a good fishing place and bought it, which came to aboute £113. And shortly after, he might have had £30 cleare profite for it, without any more trouble aboute it.

But Mr. Winslow coming that way from Kenebeck, & some other of their partners in ye barke, they mett with Mr. Allerton. And falling into discourse with him, they stayed him from selling ye salte and resolved, if it might please ye rest, to keep it for themselves and to hire a ship in ye west cuntrie [of England] to come on fishing for them, on shares, according to ye custome.

And seeing she might have her salte here ready, and a stage ready builte & fitted where the salte lay safely landed & housed, instead of bringing salte, they might stowe her full of trading goods, as bread, peas, cloth, &c. And so they might have a full supply of goods without paying fraight and in due season, which might turne greatly to their advantage.

Coming home, this was propounded and considered on, and approved by all but ye Governor, who had no mind to it, seeing they had allways lost by fishing.

But ye rest were so ernest, as thinking that they might gaine well by ye fishing in this way. And if they should save—yea, or lose—something by it, ye other benefite would be advantage inough.

So, seeing their ernestness, he gave way, and it was referred to their freinds in England to allow or disallow of it.

5. A Very Profane Young Man

BRADFORD'S HISTORY [There was] another bussines contrived by Mr. Allerton and them there, without any knowledge of ye partners here . . . I shall relate it in a further part of Mr. Sherley's letter . . .

Bristoll
March 19, 1630

I am to aquainte you that we have thought good to joyne with one Edward Ashley (a man I thinke that some of you know). But it is only of that place whereof he hath a patente, in Mr. Beachamp's name . . .

And now, if you please to be partners with us in this, we are willing you shall. Mr. Allerton had no power from you to make this new contract. Neither was he willing to doe anything therein without your consente & approbation . . .

Now, in case you are not willing in this perticuler to joyne with us, fearing ye charge & doubting ye success, yet thus much we intreate of you—to afford him all the help you can, either by men, commodities, or boats. Yet not but that we will pay you for anything he hath . . .

And now, loving friends & partners, if you joyne in Ashley's patent & bussines, though we have laid out ye money and taken up much to stock this bussines & the other, yet I thinke it conscionable and reasonable that you should bear your shares and proportion of ye stock, if not by present money, yet by securing us for so much as it shall come to . . .

I know you are so honest & conscionable men as you will consider hereof and returne such an answer as may give good satisfaction. There is none of us that would venture as we have done, were it not to strengthen & settle you more than our owne perticuler profite . . .

This bussines aboute Ashley did not a little trouble them. For though he had wit & abillitie enough to manage ye bussines, yet some of them knew him to be a very profane yonge man, and he had for some time lived amongst ye Indeans as a savage, & wente naked amongst them, and used their manners (in which time, he got their language).

So they feared he might still run into evill courses (though he promised better), and God would not prosper his ways.

As soone as he was landed at ye place intended, called Penobscot,* some 4 score leagues from this place, he writ (& afterwards came) for to desire to be supplyed with wampampeake, corne against the winter, and other things.

They considered these were their cheefe commodities and would be continually needed by him, and it would much prejudice their owne trade at Kenebeck if they did not joyne with him in ye ordering of things. And on ye other hand, if they refused to joyne with him and afford any supply unto him, they should greatly offend their above-named freinds [Sherley and the London partners] . . .

Besides, they considered that if they joyned not in ye bussines, they knew Mr. Allerton would be with them in it & so would swime, as it were, betweene both—to ye prejudice of both, but of themselves espetially. For they had reason to thinke this bussiness was cheefly of his contriving, and Ashley was a man fitte for his turne and dealings.

So they, to prevent a worse mischeefe, resolved to joyne in ye business and gave him supplies in what they could, & overlooked his proceedings as well as they could.

The which they did ye better by joyning an honest yonge man that came from Leyden with him as his fellow (in some sort), and not merely as a servante. Which yonge man being discreete, and one whom they could trust, they so instructed as kept Ashley, in some good measure, within bounds† . . .

*This new trading post was built at the mouth of the Penobscot River, at Pentagoet—now Castine, Maine.

†The "discreete" young Saint was Thomas Willet, in his early twenties, who had recently arrived on the second *Mayflower*. Years later, in 1664, when a

Ashley, being well supplyed, had quickly gathered a good parcell of beaver. And like a crafty pate, he sent it all home and would not pay for ye goods he had had of ye plantation here, but lett them still stand on ye score, and tooke up still more.

Now, though they well knewe his aime, yet they let him goe on, and writ of it into England. But partly by ye beaver they received & sold (of which they were sencible), and partly by Mr. Allerton's extolling of him, [Sherley and his friends] cast more how to supplie him than ye plantation, and something to upbraid them with it.

They [at Plymouth] were forced to buy him a barke allso, and to furnish her with a master & men to transporte his corne & provisions, of which he put off much . . .

6. Winslow to London

BRADFORD'S HISTORY   Upon ye consideration of ye bussines about ye patent & in what state it was left, and Mr. Sherley's ernest pressing to have Mr. Allerton come over againe to finish it & perfect the accounts, &c., it was concluded to send him over againe, though it was with some fear & jeolocie.

Yet he gave them fair words and promises of well performing all their bussineses according to their directions, and to mend his former errors.

So he was accordingly sent with full instructions for all things, with large letters to Mr. Sherley & ye rest, both aboute Ashley's bussines and their owne supply of trading comodities. And how much it did concerne them to be furnished therewith. And what they had suffered for wante thereof. And of what little use other goods were in comparison thereof.

And so likewise aboute this ship to be hired [in England] and fraught with trading goods, which might both supply them &

---

joint English-colonial expedition marched against the Dutch along the Hudson and captured New Netherland, Willet became the first English mayor of New York City, as New Amsterdam was renamed, serving for three years, until 1667, when he returned to Plymouth.

Ashley, and ye benefite thereof—which was left to their con-
sideretion, to hire & set her out, or not—but in no case, to send
any excepte she was thus fraighte with trading goods . . .

They looked ernestly for a timely supply this spring [1631]
by the fishing ship which they expected, and had been at charge
to keepe a stage for her. But none came; nor any supply heard
of for them.

At length, they heard some supply was sent to Ashley by a
fishing ship, at which they something marveled—and the more,
that they had no letters from Mr. Allerton or Mr. Sherley. So
they went on with their bussines as well as they could.

At length, they heard of Mr. Peirce's* arrival in ye Bay of ye
Massachusetts, who brought passengers & goods thither. They
presently sent a shallop, conceiving they should have something
by him.

But he told them he had none, and that a ship was sett out
on fishing [the *Friendship*]. But after 11 weeks beating at sea,
she mett with such foull weather as she was forcte back againe
for England and, ye season being over, gave off ye vioage.

Neither did he hear of much goods in her for ye plantation,
. . . for he had heard something from Mr. Allerton tending that
way.

But Mr. Allerton had bought another ship [the *White Angel*]
and was to come in her, and was to fish for bass to the eastward,
and to bring goods, &c.

These things did much trouble them, and half astonish them.
Mr. Winslow, having been to the eastward, brought newes of
the like things, with some more perticulers, and that it was like
Mr. Allerton would be late before he came.

At length, they, having an oppertunitie, resolved to send Mr.
Winslow with what beaver they had ready into England to see
how ye squares wente, being very jeolouse [suspicious] of these
things & Mr. Allerton's courses, and writ such letters and gave
him such instructions as they thought meet—and if he found
things not well, to discharge Mr. Allerton from being any longer

*Captain William Peirce, master of the *Lyon*.

agent for them or to deal any more in ye bussines, and to see how ye accounts stood, &c.

7. Timothy Hatherly

BRADFORD'S HISTORY   About the middle of summer [1631] arrives Mr. Hatherly in ye Bay of ye Massachusetts (being one of ye partners), and came in ye same ship that was set out on fishing, called ye *Friendship*.*

They presently sent to him, making no question but that now they had goods come, and should know how all things stood . . .

But he told them there was not much for them in this ship— only 2 packs of Bastable [Barnstable] ruggs and 2 hoggsheads of meatheglin,† drawne out in wooden flackets. But when these flackets came to be received, there was left but 6 gallons of ye 2 hogsheads, it being drunke up under ye name of leakage, and so lost.

But the ship was filled with goods for sundrie gentlemen & others that were come to plant in ye Massachusetts, for which they paid fraight by ye tun. And this was all the satisfaction they could have at presente.

So they bought this small parcell of goods, & returned with this nues and a letter as obscure, which made them much to marvell thereat:

> [London]
> March 25, 1631

Gentle-men, partners, and loving freinds, &c.

Breefly this: we have this year set forth a fishing ship and a trading ship, which latter we have bought, and so have disbursed a great deale of money, as may and will appeare by ye accounts.

And because this ship (called ye *White Angell*) is to acte 2

---

*Having "lost" her fishing voyage, the ship was put to use carrying cargo for the Puritans at the Bay. The *Friendship* belied her name, as will be seen, causing years of conflict and acrimonious debate.

†Metheglin, or mead, is a heady intoxicant made of fermented honey. Xenophon's army had attested to its potency some 2,000 years before.

parts (as I may say), fishing for bass and trading—and that while Mr. Allerton was imployed aboute ye trading, the fishing might suffer by carelessnes or neglecte of ye sailors—we have entreated your and our loving freind, Mr. Hatherley, to goe over with him, knowing he will be a comforte to Mr. Allerton, a joye to you, . . . a great stay to ye bussines, and so a great contente to us, that if it should please God ye one should faile (as God forbid), yet ye other would keepe both reconings and things uprighte.

For we are now out great sumes of money . . . When we were out but £400 or £500 [$25,000] apiece, we looked not much after it, but left it to you & your agente (who, without flaterie, deserveth infinite thanks & comendations, both of you & us, for his pains, &c.).

But now, we are out double—nay, triple—apiece, &c., which makes us both write and send over our freind, Mr. Hatherley . . .

The maine end of sending him is to see ye state and accounte of all ye bussines, of all which we pray you informe him fully, though ye ship & bussines wait for it and him.

For we should take it very unkindly that we should intreat him to take such a journey and that, when it pleaseth God he returnes, he could not give us contente & satisfaction in this perticuler, through defaulte of any of you . . .

I would not have you take anything unkindly. I have not writ out of jeolocie of any unjuste dealing.

Be you all kindly saluted in ye Lord, so I rest,

Yours in what I may,

James Sherley

It need not be thought strange that these things should amaze and trouble them . . .

At length, Mr. Hatherley & Mr. Allerton came unto them (after they had delivered their goods). And finding them strucken with some sadness aboute these things, Mr. Allerton told them that ye ship *White Angel* did not belong to them, nor their accounte. Neither need they have anything to doe with her, excepte they would.

And Mr. Hatherley confirmed ye same . . . And as for ye fishing ship [the *Friendship*], he told them they need not be much troubled . . . For this later viage it would arise to profite by ye fraight of ye goods, and ye sale of some katle which he shipped and had allready sold, . . . so as they should not have this put on their accounte at all, excepte they would . . .

After these things, Mr. Allerton wente with his ship aboute his bass fishing. And Mr. Hatherley, after he tooke knowledge how things stood at ye plantation (of all which, they informed him fully), he then desired a boate of them to goe and visite ye trading houses, both Kenebeck and Ashley's at Penobscote, for so they in England had injoyned them.

They accordingly furnished him with a boate & men for ye viage, and aquainted him plainly & thorowly with all things, by which he had good contente and saw plainly that Mr. Allerton plaid his owne game . . .

Ashley likewise was taken in a trap (before Mr. Hatherley's return), for trading powder & shotte with ye Indeans, and was seized upon by some in authoritie . . . It was also manifest against him that he had committed uncleannes with Indean women (things that they feared at his first imployment, which made them take this strict course with him in ye beginning). So, to be shorte, . . . he was sent home prisoner . . .

Mr. Allerton followed his affaires & returned [to England, taking Hatherly] with his *White Angell*, being no more imployed by ye plantation.

But these bussinesses were not ended till many years after—nor well understood of a longe time, but folded up in obscuritie, & kepte in ye clouds, to ye great loss & vexation of ye plantation, who in ye ende were (for peace sake) forced to bear ye unjust burthen of them, to their allmost undoing.

They sent their letters also by Mr. Hatherley to ye partners there, to show them how Mr. Hatherley & Mr. Allerton had discharged them of ye *Friendship's* accounte, and that both affirmed that the *White Angell* did not belong at all to them—and therefore desired that their accounte might not be charged therewith.

Also, they writ to Mr. Winslow, their agente, that he, in like manner, should (in their names) protest against it if any such thing should be intended, for they would never yeeld to ye same.

As allso, to signifie to them that they renounsed Mr. Allerton wholly for being their agente, or to have anything to doe in any of their bussines.

8. *Friendship* and *White Angel*

BRADFORD'S HISTORY

Ashley being thus by ye hand of God taken away, and Mr. Allerton discharged of his imploymente for them, their bussines began againe to run in one chanell, and themselves better able to guide the same, Penobscot being wholly now at their disposing . . .

Mr. Winslow, whom they had sent over, sent them over some supply as soone as he could . . . But by no means either he or ye letters they writ could take off Mr. Sherley & ye rest from putting ye *Friendship* and *White Angel* on ye general accounte, which caused continuall contention betweene them.

I shall inserte a letter of Mr. Winslow's about these things, being as followeth:

[London
November 16, 1631]

Sir:

It fell out by God's providence that I received and brought your letters per Mr. Allerton from Bristoll to London, and doe much feare what will be ye event of things . . .

Mr. Sherley, Mr. Beachamp, & Mr. Andrews, they renounce all perticulers, protesting but for us they would not have adventured one pennie into those parts. Mr. Hatherley stands inclinable to either.

And whereas you write that he and Mr. Allerton have taken ye *White Angel* upon them for their partners here, they professe they never gave any such order, nor will make it good. If themselves [Hatherly and Allerton] will cleare ye accounte & doe it, all shall be well . . .

And concerning ye commission so long since given to Mr. Allerton, the truth is, the thing we feared is come upon us, for Mr. Sherley & ye rest have it and will not deliver it, that being ye ground of our agent's credit to procure shuch great sums.

But I looke for bitter words, hard thoughts, and sower looks from sundrie . . . I would I had more thankfull imploymente. But I hope a good conscience shall make if comfortable, &c.

The commission abovesaid was given by them under their hand and seale when Mr. Allerton was first imployed by them, and re-demanded of him in ye year '29, when they begane to suspecte his course.

He told them it was amongst his papers, but he would seeke it out & give it them before he wente. But he being ready to goe, it was demanded againe.

He said he could not find it, but it was amongst his papers which he must take with him, and he would send it by ye boat from ye eastward. But there it could not be had neither, but he would seeke it up at sea.

But whether Mr. Sherley had it before or after, it is not certaine. But having it, he would not let it goe, but keeps it to this day.

Wherefore, even amongst freinds, men had need be carefull whom they trust, and not lett things of this nature lye long unrecalled.

Some parts of Mr. Sherley's letters aboute these things . . .

[London
November 19, 1631]

Sir:

Yours I have received by our loving freinds, Mr. Allerton & Mr. Hatherley, who blessed be God, after a long & dangerous passage with ye ship *Angell*, are safely come to Bristoll. Mr. Hatherley is come up. But Mr. Allerton I have not yet seen.

We thanke you and are very glad you have disswaded him from his Spanish viage,* and that he did not goe on in these designes he intended. For we did utterly dislike of that course, as allso of ye fishing that ye *Freindship* should have performed.

For we wished him to sell ye salte and were unwilling to have him undertake so much bussines, partly for ye ill success we formerly had in those affairs, and partly being loath to disburse so much money.

But he perswaded us this must be one way that must repay us, for ye plantation would be long in doing of it.

Nay, to my rememberance, he doubted [feared] you could not be able with ye trade there to maintaine your charge & pay us . . .

For ye fishing ship, we are sorie it proves so heavie, and will be willing to bear our parts. What Mr. Hatherley & Mr. Allerton have done, no doubt but themselves will make good.† We gave them no order to make any composition, to separate you and us, in this or any other.

And I thinke you have no cause to forsake us, for we put you upon no new thing but what your agent perswaded us to, & you by your letters desired.

If he exceede your order, I hope you will not blame us, much less cast us off, when our moneys be layed out, &c.

But I fear neither you nor we have been well delte withal. For sure, as you write, half £4,000—nay, a quarter—in fitting commodities and in seasonable time, would have furnished you better than you were . . .

---

*Allerton's scheme was to buy the *White Angel*, make a trading voyage, load her up with fish, sail to Oporto, Portugal, and there sell fish, ship, ordnance, and all—at a great profit, he hoped.

†"They [at Plymouth] were too short in resting on Mr. Hatherley's honest word for his order to discharge them from ye *Freindship's* accounte . . . And he was as shorte in resting on a verball order from them . . . But they were both now taught how to deale in ye world, espetially with marchants, in such cases . . ."—Bradford's note.

The coming of ye *White Angel* on your accounte could not be more strange to you than ye buying of her was to us.

For you gave him commission* that, what he did, you would stand to. We gave him none and yet, for his credite and your sakes, payed what bills he charged on us, &c.

For that I writ she was to acte two parts, fishing & trade, beleeve me I never so much as thought of any perticuler trade, nor will side with any that doth if I conceive it may wrong you. For I ever was against it, using these words: They will eate up and destroy ye generall.

Other things I omit as tedious . . . In another letter, . . . he hath these words:

[November 24, 1631]

For ye *White Angel*, against which you write so ernestly and say we thrust her upon you contrary to ye intente of ye buyer, herein we say you forgett yourselves and doe us wrong.

We will not take it uppon us to devine what ye thoughts or intents of ye buyer was.

But what he spack, we heard, and that we will affirme and make good against any that oppose it—which is, unless she were bought and shuch a course taken, Ashley could not be supplyed.

And againe, if he were not supplyed, we could not be satisfied what we were out for you.

And further, you were not able to doe it. And he gave some reasons which we spare to relate, unless by your unreasonable refusall you will force us, and so hasten that fire which is a-kindling too fast allready, &c.

Out of another of his, bearing date Jan., 2, 1632.

We purpose to keep ye *Friendship* and ye *White Angel* for ye last year's viages on the generall accounte, hoping together

---

*"This commission is abused. He never had any for shuch end, as they well knew. Neither had they any [commission] to pay this money, nor would have paid a penny, if they had not been pleased for some other respects."—Bradford's note.

they will rather produce profite than loss, and breed less confusion in our accounts and less disturbance in our affections . . .

We have now let him ye ship* at £30 per month by charterpartie, and bound him in a bond of £1,000 to performe covenants and bring her to London (if God please).

And what he brings in her for you shall be marked with your marke, and bills of laden taken . . .

He hath brought in 3 bookes of accounts . . . The totall sume, as he hath put it, is £7,103 17s 1d . . .

We blesse God who put both you & us in mind to send each to other, for, verily, had he run on in that desperate & chargable course one year more, we had not been able to support him.

Nay, both he and we must have lyen in ye ditch, and sunck under ye burthen, &c. . . .

9. Allerton's Accounts

BRADFORD'S HISTORY   Concerning Mr. Allerton's accounts, they were so large and intrecate as they could not well understand them, much less examine & correcte them, without a great deale of time & help—and his owne presence, which was now hard to gett amongst themselves. And it was 2 or 3 years before they could bring them to any good pass, but never made them perfecte . . .

In all which, he made them debtor to him above £300, and demanded paimente of it.

But when things came to scanning, he was found above £2,000 [$100,000] debtor to them, . . . besides I know not how much that could never be cleared, and interest moneys which ate them up, which he never accounted.

Also, they were faine to allow such large bills of charges as were intolerable. The charges of ye patent came to above £500,

---

*That is, Sherley and the London Undertakers, without consulting their partners at Plymouth, had let Allerton hire the *White Angel*.

and yet nothing done in it but what was done at first without any confirmation—£30 given at a clap, and £50 spent in a journey.

No marvell, therefore, if Mr. Sherley said in his letter, if their bussines had been better managed, they might have been ye richest plantation of any English at ye time.

Yes, he scrued up his poore old father-in-law's [Brewster's] accounte to above £200 and brought it on ye generall accounte. And to befreind him, made most of it to arise out of those goods taken up by him at Bristoll, at 50 per cent, because he knew they would never let it lye on ye old man, when, alass! he, poore man [Brewster], never dreamte of any such thing—but thought that many of them had been freely bestowed on him & his children by Mr. Allerton.

Neither, in truth, did they come near that valew in worth, but that sume was blowne up by interest & high prices, which ye company did, for ye most parte, bear . . .

This year also, Mr. Sherley sent over an account, which was, in a manner, but a cash accounte [of] what Mr. Allerton had had of them and disbursed, . . . besides an account of beaver sold, . . . and a large supply which Mr. Winslow had sent, . . . and all ye disbursements aboute ye *Friendship* & *White Angel*, and what concerned their accounts from first to last—or anything else he could charge ye partners with.

So they were made debtor in ye foote of that accounte £4,770 19s. 2d.,* besides £1,000 still due for ye purchase yet unpayed, notwithstanding all ye beaver and returnes that both Ashley & they had made, which were not small.

In these accounts of Mr. Sherley's, some things were obscure, and some things twice charged, as a 100 of Bastable ruggs which came in ye *Friendship* & cost £75, charged before by Mr. Aller-

*"So as a while before, whereas their great care was how to pay the purchase and those other few debts which were upon them, now it was with them, as it was some time with Saule's father, who left careing for ye Asses and sorrowed for his sonn. I. Sam. 10. 2. So that which before they looked at as a heavie burthen, they now esteemed but a small thing and a light matter in comparison of what was now upon them . . ."—Bradford's note.

Their debts, which two years before totaled £2,000 ($100,000), now totaled almost £6,000 ($300,000).

ton, and now by [Sherley] againe—with other perticulers of like nature doubtfull, to be twice or thrice charged.

As also, a sume of £600, which Mr. Allerton denyed, and they could never understand for what it was.

They sent a note of these & such like things afterward to Mr. Sherley, by Mr. Winslow, but (I know not how it came to pass) could never have them explained.

Into these deepe sumes had Mr. Allerton run them in two years, for in ye latter end of ye year 1628, all their debts [excluding the purchase] did not amounte to much above £400, as was then noted—and now came to so many thousands . . .

And thus were they kept hoodwinckte till now they were so deeply ingaged . . .

10. Base Fellows

BRADFORD'S HISTORY   And to mend ye matter, Mr. Allerton doth, in a sorte, now deserte them. Having brought them into ye briers, he leaves them to gett out as they can.

But God crost him mightily. For he having hired ye ship [the *White Angel*] at £30 a month, he set forth againe with a most wicked and drunken crue. And for covetousnes' sake, did so overlade her—not only filling her hold, but so stuffed her betweene decks—as she was walte and could not bear sayle.

And they had like to have been cast away at sea and were forced to put for Milford Haven and new-stow her, . . . which lost them time and made them come late into ye countrie, lose their season, and make a worse viage than ye year before.

But being come into ye countrie, he sells trading commodities to any that will buy, to ye great prejudice of ye plantation here.*

But that which is worse—what he could not sell, he trustes and sets up a company of base fellows and maks them traders to run

---

*The Pilgrims had nothing good to say of Allerton's "free enterprising" ways. Nor, as the next sentence reveals, did they approve of his credit system.

into every hole, & into ye river of Kenebeck, to gleane away ye trade from ye house there, aboute ye patente and privilege whereof he had dasht away so much money . . .

Yea, not only this, but he furnishes a company and joyns with some consorts . . . and sets up a trading house beyond Penobscot,* to cut off ye trade from thence also.

After, in time, when he came to Plimoth, ye church called him to accounte for these and other grosse miscarriages.

He confessed his faulte and promised better walking, and that he would wind himselfe out of these courses as soone as he could, &c.

11. Josiah Winslow: Accountant

BRADFORD'S HISTORY   This year also, Mr. Sherley would needs send them over a new accountante. He had made mention of such a thing ye year before. But they writ him word that their charge was great allready, and they neede not increase it, as this would. But if they were well delte with, and had their goods well sent over, they could keep their accounts here themselves.

Yet he now sente one, which they did not refuse, being a yonger brother of Mr. Winslow's, whom they had been at charge to instructe at London before he came. He came over in the *White Angel* with Mr. Allerton, and there begane his first imploymente.

For though Mr. Sherley had so farr befriended Mr. Allerton as to cause Mr. Winslow to ship ye supply sente to ye partners here in this ship, and give him £4 a tun, whereas others carried

*Far up the Maine coast, this trading post at Machias was soon attacked by the French, who regarded it as a trespass on their domain. The French killed two of Allerton's men, destroyed the post, and took all the goods—"ye loss being most, if not all, Mr. Allerton's," wrote Bradford, "for though some of them should have been his partners, yet he trusted them for their partes . . . The rest of those he trusted, being loose and drunken fellows, did for ye most parte but couzzen & cheate him, . . . so that howsoever he did his freinds some hurte hereby for ye presente, yet he gat little good, and wente by ye loss by God's just hand."

for £3—and he made them pay their fraight ready downe, before ye ship wente out of ye harbore, whereas others payed upon certificate of ye goods being delivered, and their fraight came to upwards of 6 score pounds [£120]—yet they had much adoe to have their goods delivered.

For some of them were changed, as bread & peas. They were forced to take worse for better. Neither could they ever get all.

And if Josias Winslow had not been there, it had been worse, for he had ye invoyce and order to send them to ye trading posts.

12. Robbery at Pentagoet

BRADFORD'S
HISTORY

This year [1632] their house at Penobscott was robbed by ye French. And all their goods of any worth they carried away, to ye value of £400 or £500 . . .

It was in this manner. The master of ye house [Thomas Willet], and parte of ye company with him, were come in their vessell to ye westward to fetch a supply of goods which was brought over for them.

In ye meantime, comes a small French ship into ye harbore (and amongst ye company was a false Scot). They pretended they were nuly come from ye sea, and knew not where they were, and that their vesell was very leake, and desired they might haul her ashore and stop their leaks. And many French complements they used, and congees they made.

And in ye ende, seeing but 3 or 4 simple men that were servants, and by this Scotchman understanding that ye master & ye rest of ye company were gone from home, they fell of commending their gunes and muskets that lay upon racks by ye wall side, and tooke them downe to looke on them, asking if they were charged.

And when they were possesst of them, one presents a peece ready charged against ye servants—and another, a pistoll—and bid them not sturr, but quietly deliver them their goods, and carried some of ye men aborde, & made ye others help to carry away ye goods.

And when they had tooke what they pleased, they sett them at libertie and wente their way, with this mock—bidding them tell their master, when he came, that some of ye Ile of Rey gentlemen had been there.*

13. *White Angel* Again

BRADFORD'S HISTORY   Mr. Allerton, returning for England, little regarded his bond of £1,000 to performe covenants. For whereas he was bound by ye same to bring ye ship to London and pay £30 per month for her hire, he did neither of both.

For he carried her to Bristoll againe, from whence he intended to sett out againe, and so did ye 3rd time, into these parts. And though she had been 10 months upon ye former viage, at £30 per month, yet he never payed peney for hire.

It should seeme he knew well enough how to deale with Mr. Sherley . . .

And now, though he broke his bonds, kepte no covenante, paid no hire, nor was ever like to keep covenants, yet he now goes and sells him all, both ship & all her accounts, from first to last (and, in effecte, he might as well have given him ye same) . . .

This will better appere by Mr. Sherley's letter:

[London]
Des: 6, 1632

Sir:

These few lines are further to give you to understand, that seeing you & we, that never differed yet but aboute ye *White*

---

*This mock had reference to the failure of the English in attempting to take the Ile de Rhé a few years before.

Angel, which somewhat troubleth us, as I perceive it doth you.

And now Mr. Allerton being here, we have had some confferance with him about her, and find him very willing to give you & us all contente that possiblie he can, though he burthen himselfe.

He is contente to take ye *White Angel* wholly on himselfe, notwithstanding he mett with pirates nere ye coast of Ierland, which tooke away his best sayles & other provisions from her.

So as verily, if we should now sell her, she would yeeld but a small price, besides her ordnance. And to set her forth againe with fresh money, we would not, she being now at Bristoll.

Wherefore, we thought it best, both for you & us, Mr. Allerton being willing to take her, to accepte of his bond for £2,000 to give you a true & perfecte accounte, and to take ye whole charge of ye *White Angel* wholly to himselfe, from ye first to ye last.

The accounte he is to make and perfecte within 12 months of ye date of this letter, and then to pay you, at 6 and 6 months after, whatsoever shall be due unto you and us upon the foote of that accounte.

And verily, notwithstanding all ye disasters he hath had, I am perswaded he hath enough to pay all men here and there.

Only, they must have patience till he can gather in what is due to him there.

I doe not write this slightly, but upon some ground of what I have seen (and perhaps you know not of) under ye hands & seals of some, &c.

I rest,

Your assured freind,
James Sherley

But here's not a word of ye breach of former bonds & covenants, or paimente of ye ship's hire. This is passed by as if no such thing had been . . .

And for this that Mr. Sherley seems to intimate (as a secrete)

of his abilitie under ye hands & seals of some, it was but a trick,
having gathered up an accounte of what was owing from such
base fellows as he had made traders for him, and other debts
. . .

And not only this, but he doth as good as provide a sanctuary
for him.

For he gives him one year's time to prepare his accounte and
then to give up ye same to them here, and then another year
for him to make paymente of what should be due upon that
accounte. And in ye meantime, writes ernestly to them not to
interupte or hinder him from his bussines, or stay him aboute
clearing accounts, &c.

So as he, in ye meantime, gathers up all monies due for
fraighte, and any other debtes belonging either to her or ye
Friendship's accounts, as his owne perticuler—and after, sells
ship & ordnans, fish & what he had raised . . .

And who had, or what became of ye money, he best knows.

In ye meantime, their hands were bound, and could doe nothing but looke on till he had made all away into other men's
hands (save a few cattle, & a little land, & some small matters
he had here at Plimoth) and so in ye end removed, as he had
allready his person, so all his from hence . . .

Mr. Hatherly came over againe this year, but upon his owne
occasions, and begane to make preparation to plant & dwell in
ye countrie* . . . And in some reconings betweene Mr. Allerton and him, and some debts that Mr. Allerton otherwise owed
him upon dealings between them in perticuler, he drue up an
accounte of above £2,000, and would faine have ingaged ye
partners here with it, because Mr. Allerton had been their agent.

But they tould him they had been fool'd longe enough with
such things, . . . and tould him he must looke to make good
his ingagement for ye *Freindship*, which caused some trouble
betweene Mr. Allerton and him.

*Hatherly had arrived on the *Anne* in 1623, intending to settle. But in a large
fire at that time he had lost both his house and his goods, and almost immediately returned to London. Now coming again, he helped found the town of
Scituate and served the colony as an assistant governor for many years.

Mr. William Peirce did ye like—Mr. Allerton being wound into his debte also upon particuler dealings—as if they had been bound to make good all men's debts.

But they easily shooke off these things.

14. Oh, That Man!

MORTON'S
MEMORIAL
This year [1633] Mr. Edward Winslow was chosen Governour of the jurisdiction of New Plimoth. And Mr. William Bradford, Captain Miles Standish, Mr. John Howland, Mr. John Alden, Mr. John Dove [Doane], Mr. Stephen Hopkins, & Mr. William Gilson were chosen to be his Assistants in Government.*

BRADFORD'S
HISTORY
By the first returne this year, they had letters from Mr. Sherley of Mr. Allerton's further ill success, . . . with many sadd complaints, but little hope of anythinge to be gott of Mr. Allerton, or how their accounts might be either eased or any way rectified by them there. But now saw planily that the burthen of all would be cast on their backs.

The spetiall passages of his letters I shall here inserte . . .

*For the first time in twelve years, as Governor Winthrop noted, Bradford "by importunity gat off," though he continued in office as the chief assistant, being the second-in-command.

It would appear that Bradford had been strenuously trying to get off for some time, but could persuade no one to take his place. Consequently, the General Court now decreed that if one were elected governor and refused to serve, he should be fined £20, unless he had served the previous year. Under the same rules, duly elected assistants who refused to serve were to be fined £10.

Also, to make the governorship more attractive, a salary was now attached to the office—£20 ($1,000) a year. Assistants received per diem while on official duty.

At this time, too, the number of assistants was increased from five to seven. With the exception of Allerton, the names of those who had previously served are unknown. But of the seven now chosen, it is probable that Standish, Howland, Alden, and Stephen Hopkins had served as assistants before.

For the first time, too, the colony began to keep records. The first entry discloses that in 1633 there were sixty-eight freemen in a population of four hundred or more, for only communicants in good standing could be freemen.

[London]
June 24, 1633

Loving freinds,

My last was sent in ye *Mary & John*, with Mr. William Collier, &c.* I then certified you of ye great, & uncomfortable, and unseasonable loss you & we had in ye loss of Mr. Peirce's ship, ye *Lyon*.†

But ye Lord's holy name be blessed, who gives & taks as it pleaseth him. His will be done. Amen . . .

I hope Mr. Allerton is nere upon sayle with you by this. But he had many disasters here before he could gett away. Yet ye last was a heavie one. His ship, going out of ye harbor at Bristoll, by stormie weather was so farr driven on ye shore as it cost him above £100 before she could be gott off againe.

Verily, his case was so lamentable as I could not but afford him some helpe therein‡ . . . Besides, your goods were in her. And if he had not been supported, he must have broke off his viage, and so loss could not have been avoyed on all sides.

When he first bought her, I thinke he had made a saving match if he had then sunck her and never set her forth. I hope he sees ye Lord's hand is against him and will leave off these viages. I thinke we did well in parting with her . . . And now though we shall not gett much by way of satisfaction, yet we shall lose no more.

And now, as before I have written, I pray you finish all ye accounts and reconings with him there. For here he hath noth-

---

*A brewer and one of the London Undertakers, William Collier came with his wife and four children at this time to settle in the colony, quickly rising to prominence, being an assistant governor for many years.

†To add to their mounting losses, the *Lyon*, hired by the London partners and sailing under the command of Captain William Peirce, was cast away and lost near Virginia, having on board 800 pounds of beaver, some otter pelts, and copies of Allerton's accounts.

"It is time to looke aboute us before ye wrath of ye Lord breake forth to utter destriction," wrote Peirce in reporting the shipwreck to Plymouth. "Dear freinds, you may know that all your beaver and ye books of your accounts are swallowed up in ye sea."

‡Sherley's additional advance to Allerton was no doubt placed upon the Pilgrim account, a handy catchall for such things.

ing but many debts that he stands ingaged to many men for
. . .

Oh, the greefe & trouble that man, Mr. Allerton, hath brought
upon you and us!

I cannot forgett it. And to thinke on it draws many a sigh
from my harte, and teares from my eyes . . .

By Mr. Allerton's faire propositions and large promises, I
have overrun myselfe. Verily, at this time greefe hinders me
to write, and tears will not suffer me to see. Wherefore, as you
love those that ever loved you and that plantation, thinke upon
me.

Oh, what shall I say of that man who hath abused your trust
and wronged our loves!

But now to complaine is too late. Neither can I complaine
of your backwardnes, for I am perswaded it lyes as heavie on
your harts as it doth on our purses or credites.

And had ye Lord sent Mr. Peirce safe home, we had eased
both you and us of some of those debts.

The Lord, I hope, will give us patience to bear these crosses
and that great God, whose care & providence is everywhere,
. . . direct, guide, prosper, & blesse you so as that you may be
able (as I perswade myselfe you are willing) to discharge &
take off this great & heavie burthen which now lyes upon me
for your sakes and, I hope, in ye ende for ye good of you and
many thousands more.

For had not you & we joyned & continued togeather, New
England might yet have been scarce knowne . . .

So, with my continued praiers for you all, I rest,

Your assured loving friend,
James Sherley

. . . And though Mr. Sherley became more sinsible of his
owne condition by these losses, and thereby more sadly &
plainly to complaine of Mr. Allerton, yet no course was taken
to help them here, but all left unto themselves—not so much
as to examene & rectifie ye accounts, by which (it is like) some
hundreds of pounds might have been taken off.

But very probable it is, the more they saw was taken off, ye less might come unto themselves . . .

15. Exile

BRADFORD'S
HISTORY
A few observations from ye former letters, and then I shall set downe the simple truth of ye things thus in controversie betweene them—at least, so farr as by any good evidence it could be made to appeare—and so labour to be breefe in so tedious and intricate a bussines, which hunge in expostulation betweene them many years before ye same was settled . . .

First, it seemes to appere clearly that Ashley's bussines, and ye buying of ye ship, and ye courses framed thereupon, were first contrived and proposed by Mr. Allerton.

As also, that the pleas and pretences which he made of ye inabilitie of ye plantation to repaye their moneys, &c., and ye hops he gave them of doing it with profite, was more beleeved & rested on by them (at least, some of them) than anything ye plantation did or said.

2. It is like, though Mr. Allerton might thinke not to wrong ye plantation in ye maine, yet his owne gaine and private ends led him aside in these things.

For it came to be knowne, and I have it in a letter under Mr. Sherley's hand, that in ye first 2 or 3 years of his imploymente, he had cleared up £400 [$20,000] and put it into a brew-house of Mr. Collier's in London, at first under Mr. Sherley's name . . .

Againe, Mr. Sherley and he had perticuler dealings in some things. For he bought up ye beaver that sea-men & other passengers brought over to Bristoll and at other places, and charged ye bills to London, which Mr. Sherley payed.

And they got some time £50 apiece in a bargen, . . . which might make Mr. Sherley harken unto him in many things . . .

3ly. It may be perceived that, seeing they had done so much

for ye plantation, both in former adventures and late disbursements, and allso that Mr. Allerton was the first occasioner of bringing them upon these new designes—which, at first, seemed faire & profitable unto them, and unto which they agreed; but, now, seeing them turne to losse and decline to greater intanglements—they thought it more meete for ye plantation to bear them than themselves, who had borne much in other things allready.

And so tooke advantage of such comission & power as Mr. Allerton had formerly had as their agente to devolve these things upon them.

4ly. With pitie and compassion (touching Mr. Allerton) I may say with ye apostle to Timothy, I. Tim. 6. 9. *They that will be rich fall into many temtations and snares, &c., and pearce themselves through with many sorrows, &c., for the love of money is ye roote of all evill,* v. 10.

God give him to see ye evill in his failings, that he may find mercie by repentance for ye wrongs he hath done to any and this pore plantation, in spetiall . . .

Allerton abandoned Plymouth after the death in 1633 of his second wife, Fear Brewster, who had borne him a son, Isaac Allerton, Jr. Removing to the Bay, to Marblehead, Allerton lived with his elder daughter, Remember, who had recently married the local pastor, Moses Maverick.

On the eve of his departure, Allerton was by far the richest man in the colony, which certainly came as no surprise to his bilked brethren. In 1633, he had paid a tax of £3 10s. ($175). Winslow's was the next highest, at £2 5s., while Bradford's followed at £1 16s. ($90).

Among the twelve others to be assessed £1 or more were William Brewster, Jonathan Brewster, Thomas Prence (a Brewster-in-law), Deacon John Doane, John Alden, Stephen Hopkins, and Hopkins' former servant, Edward Dotey, who had served his indenture and risen in the world. In gathering chattels, he had outstripped most of those who had come as freemen, even Captain Standish, who was rated at a mere 18s. ($45).

After Allerton's disgrace and semi-voluntary exile, for he was not formally expelled, his elder son, Bartholomew, a man in his thirties, returned to England, becoming a minister there. His younger son, Isaac, a boy of six or seven, was left behind at Plymouth, in the care of the Brewsters.*

Allerton also appears to have left behind his younger daughter, Mary, who, two years later, married Deacon Robert Cushman's son, Bradford's ward, Thomas Cushman, in time Brewster's successor as Ruling Elder. Mary lived to become the last surviving member of the *Mayflower* company, outliving the old colony itself by seven years, dying in 1699, when well in her eighties.

At Marblehead, "the greatest Towne for fishing in New England," Allerton kept eight vessels busy fishing and trading up and down the coast. But after several years, the Pilgrims complained of his presence there.

He "hath too great familiarity with our common adversaries," wrote Winslow to the Bay authorities. "The truth is he loveth neither you nor us."

Allerton is next seen at New Amsterdam in 1643. Two years later, he was established as a merchant in Connecticut, at the young and growing town of New Haven, then seven years old. Here Allerton seemed to prosper with his speculations and, having married again, built a "grand house on the creek, with four porches."

Dying in 1659 at the age of seventy-three, having been separated from his old friends for almost thirty years, Allerton was honored with burial in the town square, leaving an estate of £120 ($6,000), which was considerable for the day.

This, too, was a mirage. His many debts overtopped his estate, and many claimants were left unpaid, sadly meditating on the ways of "marchants."

If Bradford had been alive, he would doubtless have found a fitting obituary for this first of the sharp Yankee traders.

---

*Young Isaac, in time, was the first Plymouth graduate from Harvard College. Later, renouncing the Saints and their Holy Discipline, he went to Anglican Virginia and became a large planter and a gay grandee, one of the Lords of the Potomac.

XXIV

Pushed Around

But whereas you say God, in his providence, cast you upon the lands, we told you before, and (upon this occasion) must not tell you still, that our mind is otherwise—and that you cast rather a partiall, if not a covetous, eye upon that which is your neighbors', and not yours . . .

—William Bradford

BRADFORD'S HISTORY   Though ye partners were thus plunged into great ingagments & oppressed with unjust debts, yet ye Lord prospered their trading, that they made yearly large returnes and had soone wound themselves out of all, if yet they had otherwise been well delt with.

1. Perils of Prosperity

BRADFORD'S HISTORY   Also, ye people of ye plantation begane [1632] to grow in their outward estates by reason of ye flowing of many people into ye cuntrie, espetially into ye Bay of ye Massachusetts. By which means, corne & cattle rose to a great price, by which many were much inriched, and commodities grue plentifull.

And yet, in other regards, this benefite turned to their hurte, and this accession of strength to their weaknes.

For now, as their stocks increased, and ye increase vendible, there was no longer any holding them togeather. But now they must of necessitie goe to their great lots; they could not otherwise keep their katle; and having oxen growne, they must have land for plowing & tillage.

And no man now thought he could live except he had catle and a great deale of ground to keep them, all striving to increase their stocks. By which means, they were scattered all over the bay, quickly.

And ye towne, in which they lived compactly till now, was left very thin and, in a short time, allmost desolate.

And if this had been all, it had been less, though too much.

But ye church must also be devided, and those that had lived so long togeather in Christian & comfortable fellowship must now part and suffer many divissions.

First, those that lived on their lots on ye other side of ye bay (called Duxberie), they could not long bring their wives & children to ye publick worship & church meetings here but with such burthen, as, growing to some competente number, they sued to be dismissed and become a body of themselves. And so they were dismiste (about this time), though very unwillingly.*

But to touch this sadd matter and handle things together that fell out afterward.

To prevent any further scattering and weakening of ye same, it was thought best to give out some good farms to spetiall persons that would promise to live at Plimoth, and likely to be helpfull to ye church and commonewelth, and so tye ye lands to Plimoth as farmes for the same. And there they might keepe their cattle & tillage by some servants, and retaine their dwellings here.

*Among others removing to Duxbury, the first of Mother Plymouth's daughters, were Philip Delano, several of the younger Brewsters, John and Priscilla Alden with five small children, and Captain Standish with his growing family. Standish's farm lay at the foot of what has long been known as Captain's Hill, now topped with a stone tower in his memory.

With Standish went Squanto's old rival, Hobomok, who, disregarding the "enticements, scoffs, and scorns" of his own people, lived with the Standishes till he died in 1642, always faithful to the Pilgrims and eager to be a Saint, still "seeking after their God, . . . leaving some good hopes in their hearts that his soul went to rest."

And so some spetiall lands were granted at a place generall, called **Green Harbor** [soon renamed Marshfield], where no allotments had been made in ye former divission—a place very well meadowed and fitt to keep and rear cattle good store.

But alass! this remedy proved worse than ye disease. For within a few years, those that had thus gott footing there rent themselves away, partly by force, and partly by wearing ye rest with importunitie and pleas of necessitie, so as they must either suffer them to goe, or live in continuall opposition and contention.*

And others still, as they conceived themselves straitened, or to want accomodation, broke away under one pretence or other, thinking their owne conceived necessitie and the example of others a warrante sufficiente for them.

And this, I fear, will be ye ruine of New-England, at least of ye churches there, & will provock ye Lord's displeasure against them.[1]

2. Smallpox Epidemic

BRADFORD'S HISTORY

It pleased ye Lord to visite them this year [1633] with an infectuous fevoure, of which many fell sicke and upwards of 20 persons dyed —men and women, besides children—and sundry of them of their anciente freinds which had lived in Holland, as [Deacon] Thomas Blossom, [Deacon] Richard Masterson, with sundry others.

*Edward Winslow was one of the "spetiall persons" who broke away to live at Marshfield, just north of Duxbury. And one who had been a London adventurer, William Thomas, "a well-approved and well-grounded Christian, well read in the Holy Scriptures and other approved authors," was another. Winslow built up a large estate there, which he named Careswell for his home in England.

Two centuries later, Daniel Webster had a house on what had been part of the Winslow estate and died there, being buried in the old Winslow Burying Ground, close to the grave of Winslow's erring stepson, Peregrine White. A stubborn "separatist," Peregrine refused to join the church till he was almost eighty, being "in the former part of his life extravagant, yet he was much reformed in his last years, and died hopefully."

And in ye end (after he had much helped others), Samuell Fuller, who was their surgeon & phisition, and had been a great help and comforte unto them, as in his facultie, so otherwise, being a deacon of ye church, a man godly and forward to doe good, being much missed after his death.

And he and ye rest of their brethren were much lamanted by them, and caused much sadnes & mourning amongst themselves, which caused them to humble themselves & seeke ye Lord. And towards winter, it pleased ye Lord ye sicknes ceased.*

This disease allso swept away many of ye Indeans from all ye places near adjoyning.

And ye spring before, espetially all ye month of May, there was such a quantitie of a great sorte of flies, like (for bignes) to wasps or bumble-bees, which came out of holes in ye ground and replenished all ye woods, and eate ye green-things, and made such a constante yelling noyes as made all ye woods ring of them, and ready to deafe ye hearers. They have not, by ye English, been heard or seen before or since.†

But ye Indeans told them that sicknes would follow. And so it did, in June, July, and August, and ye cheefe heat of sommer.

3. Opening Up Connecticut

BRADFORD'S
HISTORY

Having had formerly converse and familiarity with ye Dutch, they, seeing them seated here in a barren quarter, told them of a river called by them ye Fresh River, but now is known by ye name of Conightecute River, which they often commended unto them for a fine place, both for plantations and trade, and wished them to make use of it.

---

*The church lost all three of its deacons—Fuller, Blossom, and Masterson. The epidemic also carried away both of Brewster's daughters—Fear, Allerton's wife, and Patience, mother of five and wife of Thomas Prence, soon to serve his first of many terms as governor. Brewster's wife, the brave and patient Mary, had died five or six years before.

†The seventeen-year locust.

But, their hands being full otherwise, they let it pass.

But afterwards, there coming a company of banishte Indeans into these parts that were driven out from thence by ye potencie of ye Pequents [Pequot], which usurped upon them and drove them from thence, they often sollisted them to goe thither and they should have much trade, espetially if they would keep a house there.

And having now good store of commodities and allso need to looke out where they could advantage themselves to help them out of their great ingagements, they now begane to send that way to discover ye same and trade with ye natives.

They found it to be a fine place, but had not store of trade. But ye Indeans excused ye same in regard of ye season, and the fear ye Indeans were in of their enemies.

So they tried diverce times, not without profite, but saw ye most certainty would be by keeping a house there to receive ye trade when it came downe out of ye inland.*

These Indeans, not seeing them very forward to build there, solisited them of ye Massachusetts in like sorte (for their end was to be restored to their countrie againe).

But they in ye Bay, being but lately come, were not fitte for ye same.

But some of their cheefe made a motion to joyne with the partners here† to trade joyntly with them in that river. The which they were willing to imbrace, and so they should have built & put in equall stock together.

---

*Winslow led one of these expeditions to the Connecticut, and the Pilgrims were shocked to learn, by way of a messenger from Massasoit, that he had perished, listening with fear and sorrow as the messenger reported just how and when he had been killed.

Shortly, Winslow appeared with Massasoit, who was asked "why he sent such word, &c. He answered, that it was their manner to do so, that they might be more welcome when they came home . . ."

†That is, the eight Undertakers. It is not clear from the records whether Allerton, now in exile, was still one of these. But as the Undertakers had only debts for which they were severally and jointly bound, it is unlikely that the partners released Allerton from his bond, perhaps hoping—a forlorn hope—that he would reform.

A time of meeting [in July, 1633] was appointed at ye Massachusetts, and some of ye cheefe [Winslow and Bradford] were appointed to treat with them and wente accordingly.

But they [of the Bay] cast many fears of danger & loss and the like, which were perceived to be the maine obstacles, though they alledged they were not provided of trading goods.

But those here offered at presente to put in sufficiente for both, provided they would become ingaged for ye halfe and prepare against ye next yeare.

They confessed more could not be offered, but thanked them, and told them they had no mind to it.

They then answered they hoped it would be no offence to them if they saw it meete. They said there was no reason they should. And thus this treaty broake off.

And those here tooke conveniente time to make a beginning there, and were ye first English that both discovered that place and built in ye same, though they were little better than thrust out of it afterward.

But ye Dutch begane now to repente. And hearing of their purpose & preparation, indeavored to prevente them, & gott in a little before them and made a slight fort,* and planted 2 peeces of ordnance, threatening to stop their passage.

But they having made a small frame of a house ready and having a great new barke, they stowed their frame in her hold, & bords to cover & finishe it, having nayles & all other provisions fitting for their use.

This they did ye rather that they might have a presente defence against ye Indeans, who were much offended that they brought home & restored ye right Sachem of ye place (called Natawanute). So as they were to incounter with a duble danger in this attempte, both ye Dutch and ye Indeans.

When they came up the river,† the Dutch demanded what they intended, and whither they would goe.

*Called the House of Hope, or Fort Good Hope, where Hartford now stands.
†Under Lieutenant William Holmes, second-in-command of the Pilgrim army, being Captain Standish's chief aide.

They answered, up ye river to trade (now, their order was to goe and seat above them).

They bid them strike & stay, or els they would shoote them, & stood by their ordnance, ready fitted.

They answered, they had commission from ye Governor of Plimoth to goe up ye river to such a place. And if they did shoote, they must obey their order and proceede. They would not molest them, but would go on.

So they passed along. And though the Dutch threatened them hard, yet they shot not.

Coming to their place,* they clapt up their house quickly, and landed their provissions, and left ye companie appoynted, and sent the barke home. Afterwards, palisadoed their house about, and fortified themselves better . . .

They did ye Dutch no wrong, for they tooke not a foote of any land they bought, but went to ye place above them and bought that tract of land which belonged to these Indeans which they carried with them and their freinds, with whom ye Dutch had nothing to doe . . .

The Dutch sent word home to ye Manhatas [New Amsterdam] what was done. And in process of time, they sent a band of aboute 70 men in warrlike manner, with collours displayed, to assaulte them. But seeing them strengthened, & that it would cost blood, they came to parley and returned in peace.

And this was their enterance there who deserved to have held it, and not by frends to have been thrust out as, in a sorte, they were.

4. Killing on the Kennebec

BRADFORD'S   This year [1634] Mr. Thomas Prence was
HISTORY   chosen governor . . .
               I am now to enter upon one of ye saddest
things that befell them since they came . . .

*Some ten miles above the Dutch, at Matianuck, where the Farmington River, as it was named, joins the Connecticut in what is now Windsor.

Now, it so fell out that one Hocking, belonging to ye plantation of Pascataway,* wente with a barke and commodities to
trade in that river [the Kennebec] and would needs press into
their limits.

And not only so, but would needs goe up ye river above their
houses (towards ye falls of ye river), and intercept the trade
that should come downe to them.†

He that was cheefe of ye place forbad them, and prayed him
that he would not offer them that injurie, nor goe aboute to
infring their liberties which had cost them so dear . . . But all
in vaine. He could gett nothing of him but ill words.

So he [Howland] considered that now was ye season for
trade to come downe, and if he should suffer him to lye & take
it from them, all their former charge would be lost, and they
had better throw up all.

So, consulting with his men (who were willing thereto), he
resolved to put him from his anchors, and let him drive downe
ye river with ye streame. But commanded ye men that none
should shoote a shote upon any occasion, except he commanded
them.

He spoake to him againe, but all in vaine. Then he sent a
cuple in a canow to cutt his cable, which one of them performed.

But Hocking takes up a peece which he had layed ready, and
as ye barke sheared by ye canow, he shote him close under her
side, in ye head (I take it), so he fell downe dead instantly.

One of his fellows (that loved him well) could not hold, but

---

*Or rather, Piscataqua, along the river of that name (in New Hampshire), a
plantation formerly owned by a self-exiled Pilgrim Father, William Hilton,
the baptism of whose child with the hated "signe of the Cross" had set off the
explosion that hurled Lyford and Oldham from Plymouth. Hilton's interests
along the Piscataqua had since been acquired by several lords and other powerful personages in England, who were not to be trifled with.

†The Pilgrims were outraged by this, though they had just served the Dutch
a like turn on the Connecticut.

The trading post at Cushenoc, the Pilgrims' most prosperous one, was at this
time the charge of Assistant Governor John Howland. There was another
assistant governor present, John Alden, who had brought a barque from Plymouth with supplies.

with a musket shot Hocking, who fell downe dead and never speake word.

This was ye truth of ye thing.

The rest of [Hocking's] men carried home the vessel, and ye sad tidings of these things.

Now, ye Lord Saye & ye Lord Brooke, with some other great persons, had a hand in this plantation. They writ home to them, as much as they could to exasperate them in ye matter, leaving out all ye circomstances, as if he had been kild without any offence on his parte, . . . at which their Lordships were much offended, till they were truly informed of ye matter.

The bruite of this was quickly carried all aboute (and that in ye worst manner), and came into ye Bay to their neighbors there.

The Hocking affair "was much condemned of all men," John Winthrop wrote Plymouth, "and besides, had brought us all, and the gospel, under a common reproach of cutting one another's throats for beaver."

Even worse, it might provide high-handed King Charles with the occasion for sending over a royal governor to take charge of all New England and rule it with a despotic hand.

This was not an imaginary danger, but a real and present threat. Early in 1634, the King had created a Commission for Regulating Plantations. Headed by the choleric William Laud, Archbishop of Canterbury, an avowed and determined foe of all "heretics," the Commission had power to legislate in both civil and religious affairs, regulate trade, examine property titles, review charters—and revoke them if any contained liberties or privileges deemed harmful to the Crown.

The Saints, both at Plymouth and in the Bay, had good reason to be alarmed. Their meetinghouses would be suppressed, and the Anglican rite instituted by law, as in Virginia. They would cease to govern themselves, as they had been doing in large measure. Their charters might be voided, as they were open to challenge and attack.

With Charles drifting along the high road of absolutism, this was a serious moment for the "schismatiques" in New England.

5. John Alden Jailed

BRADFORD'S
HISTORY
Their owne barke coming home and bringing a true relation of ye matter, sundry were sadly affected with ye thing, as they had cause. It was not long before they had occasion to send their vessell into ye Bay of ye Massachusetts. But they [at the Bay] were so prepossest with this matter, and affected with ye same, as they committed Mr. Alden to prison, who was in ye bark and had been at Kenebeck, but was no actore in ye bussines, but wente to carry them supply. They dismist ye barke aboute her bussiness, but kept him for some time.

This was thought strange here,* and they sente Capten Standish to give them true information (togeather with their letters), and ye best satisfaction they could, and to procure Mr. Alden's release.

I shall recite a letter or 2 which will show the passages of these things, as followeth:†

New-towne
May 22, 1634

Good Sir:
I have received your letters by Captaine Standish . . . I have upon ye same letters sett Mr. Alden at liberty, and his sureties.

And yet, lest I should seeme to neglecte ye opinion of our Court & ye frequente speeches of others with us, I have bound

---

*Massachusetts had no jurisdiction over the Kennebec, or those at Plymouth, or the men at Piscataqua either. The Bay authorities were being very officious here, as they were often disposed to be in dealing with their neighbors. But they were worried, feeling their own interests might suffer if nothing were done about the Hocking case.

†These letters were addressed to Bradford, though he was only an assistant governor this year. But the Bay evidently regarded him as being still the chief executive, as no doubt he was in fact, spending his time training the new governor, the young and inexperienced Thomas Prence, for future service—and Prence could not have had a better mentor.

Captaine Standish to appeare ye 3 of June at our nexte Court to make affidavid for ye coppie of ye patente, and to manifest the circumstances of Hocking's provocations . . .

If any unkindness hath been taken from what we have done, let it be further & better considered, I pray you. And I hope ye more you thinke of it, the lesse blame you will impute to us
. . .

[Governor] Tho: Dudley

Another of his . . .

June 4, 1634

Sir:

I am right sorrie for ye news that Captaine Standish & other of your neighbors and my beloved freinds will bring now to Plimoth, wherein I suffer with you by reason of my opinion, which differeth from others [the majority of the General Court had declined to close the case] . . .

The late letters I received from England wrought in me diverse fears* of some trials which are shortly like to fall upon us. And this unhappie contention betweene you and us, and between you & Pascattaway, will hasten them if God, with an extraordinarie hand, doe not help us.

To reconcile this for the presente will be very difficulte. But time cooleth distempers, and a commone danger to us both, approaching, will necessitate our uniting againe.

I pray you therefore, Sir, set your wisdom & patience a-worke, and exhorte others to ye same, that things may not proceed from bad to worse . . .

Your truly loving freind in our Lord Jesus,
Tho: Dudley

By these things it appears what troubls rose hereupon, and how hard they were to be reconciled. For though they here were hartily sorrie for what was fallen out, yet they conceived

---

*"There was cause enough for these feares, which arose by ye underworking of some enemies to ye churches here . . ."—Bradford's note, in which he is alluding to the Commission for Regulating Plantations.

that they were unjustly injuried, and provoked to what was done, and that their neighbors (having no jurisdiction over them) did more than was meet thus to imprison one of theirs, and bind them to their courte.

But yet being assured of their Christian love, and perswaded what was done was out of godly zeale that religion might not suffer, nor sinne anyway covered or borne with, espetially ye guilte of blood, of which all should be very conscientious in any whomsoever, they did indeavore to appease & satisfie them ye best they could . . . This did mollifie their minds and bring things to a good & comfortable issue in ye end.

For they had this advice by Mr. Winthrop & others concurring with him that, from their court [at Plymouth], they should write to the neighbor plantations, & espetially that of ye lords at Pascataway and theirs of ye Massachusetts, to appointe some to give them a meeting at some fitt place, to consulte & determine in this matter, so as ye parties, meeting, might have full power to order & bind, &c. And that nothing be done to ye infringing, or prejudice, of ye liberties of any place.

And for ye clearing of conscience, ye law of God is that ye priest's lips must be consulted with. And therefore, it was desired that ye ministers of every plantation might be presente to give their advice in pointe of conscience.

Though this course seemed dangerous to some, yet they were so well assured of ye justice of their cause and ye equitie of their freinds as they put themselves upon it & appointed a time, of which they gave notice to ye severall places a month beforehand . . .

The place of meeting was at Boston. But when ye day & time came, none appeared but some of ye magistrates and ministers of ye Massachusetts, and their owne.*

Seeing none of Pascataway or other places came (having been thus desired, & conveniente time given them for that end), Mr.

---

*Plymouth was represented by Bradford, Winslow, and Pastor Ralph Smith. The Bay's delegates were Winthrop and the Reverends John Cotton and John Wilson.

Winthrop & ye rest said they could doe no more than they had done thus to requeste them. Ye blame must rest on them.

So they fell into a fair debating of things themselves. And after all things had been fully opened & discussed, & ye opinion of each one demanded, both magistrates and ministers, though they all could have wished these things had never been, yet they could not but lay ye blame & guilt on Hocking's owne head.

And withall, gave them* such grave & godly exhortations and advice as they thought meet, both for ye presente & future, which they allso imbraced with love & thankfullnes, promising to indeavor to follow ye same.

And thus was this matter ended, and their love and concord renewed. And also, Mr. Winthrop & Mr. Dudley writ in their behalfes to ye Lord Say & other gentlemen that were interested in that plantation, very effectually, with which, together with their owne letters and Mr. Winslow's furder declaration of things unto them, they rested well satisfied.

6. Repent, You Cruel Separatists, Repent!

Working with Sir Ferdinando Gorges, Thomas Morton of Merry Mount was delighted with the turn of events at home. In great glee he wrote an old planter, William Jeffery, who handed the letter on to John Winthrop. The latter carefully preserved it for future use, if God would only put Morton into his hands.

MORTON'S
LETTER†

[London]
May 1, 1634

My very good gossip,

. . . You shall hereby understand that, although, when I was first sent to England to make complaint against Ananias and the

---

*That is, the Plymouth delegates—and how Bradford, Winslow, and Smith must have squirmed to be thus lectured by the novice Saints of the Bay. According to Winthrop, "they acknowledged that they did hold themselves under guilt of the breach of the Sixth Commandment."

†The letter appears in Winthrop's Journal for 1644.

brethren, I effected the business but superficially (through brevity of time), I have at this time taken more deliberation and brought the matter to a better pass.

And it is thus brought about that the King hath taken the business into his own hands. The Massachusetts Patent, by order of the Council, was brought in view . . . [and] declared, for manifest abuses there discovered, to be void.*

The King hath reassumed the whole business into his own hands, appointed a committee of the Board, and given order for a General Governor of the whole territory to be sent over.

The commission is passed the Privy Seal. I did see it† . . .

And now I stay to return with the governor [Sir Ferdinando Gorges], by whom all complainants shall have relief.

So that now Jonas, being set ashore, may safely cry: Repent, you cruel Separatists, repent. There are as yet but forty days.

If Jove vouchsafe to thunder, the charter and kingdom of the Separatists will fall asunder.

Repent, you cruel schismastics, repent!

These things have happened, and I shall see (notwithstanding their boasting and false alarms in the Massachusetts, with feigned cause of thanksgiving) their merciless cruelty rewarded according to the merit of the fact, with condign punishment for coming into those parts like Sampson's foxes with fire-brands at their tails.

The King and Council are really possessed of [outraged at] their preposterous loyalty and irregular proceedings, and are incensed against them.

*The Bay authorities soon received a command to surrender their charter, which they had prudently brought with them to the New World, so that it was out of reach of those at home. On one pretext or another, they did nothing about the command. Four years later, they received another even more peremptory demand, which they likewise ignored.

Plymouth was quite as uneasy, not even having the protection of a proper royal charter.

A year after he wrote his letter, the Council for New England named Morton as solicitor "to prosecute suit at law for the repealing of the patent belonging to the Massachusetts Company."

†The Royal Commission for Regulating Plantations had passed the seals on April 28, two days before Morton wrote, so that he may well have seen it.

And although they be so opposite to the catholic axioms, yet they will be compelled to perform them—or at leastwise, suffer them to be put in practice to their sorrow . . .

And as for Ratcliffe,* he was comforted by their Lordships with the cropping of Mr. Winthrop's ears, which shows what opinion is held amongst them of King Winthrop, with all his inventions and his Amsterdam fantastical ordinances, his preachings, marriages, and other abusive ceremonies, which do exemplify his detestation of the Church of England, and the contempt of his Majesty's authority and wholesome laws, which are and will be established in those parts, *invita Minerva* . . .

Resting your loving friend,
Thomas Morton

7. Petition to the Commission

BRADFORD'S
HISTORY

Mr. Winslow was sente by them this year [late in 1634] into England, partly to informe and satisfie ye Lord Say & others in ye former matter, as also to make answer and their just defence for ye same if anything should by any be prosecuted against them at Counselltable, or elsewhere. But this matter tooke end without any further trouble.

And partly, to signifie unto ye partners in England that the terme of their trade with ye company here was out,† and therefore he was sente to finish ye accounts with them and to bring them notice how much debtor they should remaine on that account, and that they might know what further course would be best to hold . . .

---

*For "most foul, scandalous invectives against our churches and government," as Winthrop described them, Philip Ratcliffe had had his ears cut off and ordered out of Massachusetts, returning to England to make complaint there.
†That is, the contract under which the Undertakers agreed to pay all the colony's debts in return for the exclusive right to profit from the colony's trade for six years.

Mr. Winslow was very wellcome to them in England, and ye more in regard of ye large returne he brought with him, which came all safe to their hands and was well sold. And he was borne in hand (at least he so apprehended) that all accounts should be cleared before his returne and all former differences thereaboute well settled.

And so he writ over to them here that he hoped to cleare ye accounts and bring them over with him, and that the accounte of ye *White Angel* would be taken off and all things fairly ended.

But it came to pass that, being occasioned to answer some complaints made against the country at Counsell board, . . . he prefered this petition following to their Honours that were deputed Commissioners for ye Plantations:

To ye right honorable ye Lord Commissioners for ye Plantations in America.

The humble petition of Edw: Winslow, on ye behalfe of ye plantations in New-England,

Humbly shewth unto your Lordships that whereas your petitioners have planted themselves in New-England under his Majestie's most gratious protection, now so it is, right Honourables, that ye French & Dutch doe indeavor to devide ye land betweene them.

For which purpose, ye French have, on ye east side, entered and seized upon one of our houses . . . And ye Dutch, on ye west, have also made entrie upon Conigtecute River, within ye limits of his Majestie's letters patent, where they have raised a forte and threaten to expell your petitioners thence . . .

In tender consideration hereof, your petitioners humbly pray that your Lordships will either procure their peace with those foraine states, or else to give spetiall warrante unto your petitioners and ye English Collonies to right and defend themselves against all foraigne enimies . . .

This petition found good acceptation with most of them,* and Mr Winslow was heard sundry times by them and appointed further to attend for an answer from their Lordshipps . . .

But this crossed both Sir Ferdinando Gorges' & Captain Mason's designe, and ye archbishop of Counterberies by them. For Sir Ferdinando Gorges (by ye archbishop's favore) was to have been sent over generall governor into ye countrie, and was now upon dispatch and conclusion of ye bussines.

And ye archbishop's purpose & intente was, by his means & some he should send with him (to be furnished with Episcopal power), to disturbe ye peace of ye churches here, and to over-throwe their proceedings and further growth, which was ye thing he aimed at.

But it so fell out (by God's providence) that though, in ye end, he crost this petition from taking any further effecte in this kind, yet by this as a cheefe means the plot and whole bussines of his & Sir Ferdinando's fell to ye ground and came to nothing.

8. Arrest of Winslow

BRADFORD'S HISTORY　　When Mr. Winslow should have had his suit granted (as indeed upon ye pointe it was), . . . the archbishop put a stop to it. And Mr. Winslow, thinking to gett it freed, wente to ye board againe. But ye archbishop, Sir Ferdinando, and Captine Mason had, as it seems, procured Morton [of Merry Mount] to complaine.

To whose complaints Mr. Winslow made answer to ye good satisfaction of ye borde, who checked Morton and rebuked him sharply, & allso blamed Sir Ferdinando Gorges & Mason for countenancing him.

But ye archbishop had a further end & use of his presence, for he now begane to question Mr. Winslow of many things—as of

*Winthrop and others thought this petition very ill advised, as tending to limit their freedom of action by establishing a precedent that nothing could be done without the explicit authorization of the suspect Commission for Regulating Plantations.

teaching in ye church publickly, of which Morton accused him, and gave evidence that he had seen and heard him doe it.

To which Mr. Winslow answered, that some time (wanting a minister) he did exercise his gifte to helpe ye edification of his brethren when they wanted better means, which was not often.

Then aboute marriage, the which he also confessed that, having been called to place of magistracie, he had sometimes married some.

And further told their Lordships that marriage was a civille thinge, & he found nowhere in ye word of God that it was tyed to ministrie. Again, they were necessitated so to doe, having for a long time togeather at first no minister.

Besides, it was no new thing, for he had been married himselfe in Holland by ye magistrates in their Statt-house.

But in ye end (to be short), for these things ye archbishop, by vemente importunity, gott ye bord at last to consente to his comittemente. So he was comited to ye Fleet* and lay there 17 weeks, or thereaboute, before he could gitt to be released.

And this was ye end of this petition, and this bussines . . .

But ye charge fell heavie on them here, not only in Mr. Winslow's expences (which could not be small), but by ye hinderance of their bussines, both there and here . . .

Whatsoever Mr. Sherley's mind was before (or Mr. Winslow's apprehension of ye same), he now declared himselfe plainly that he would neither take ye *White Angell* from ye accounte, nor give any further accounte till he had received more into his hands . . .

9. Loss of Pentagoet

BRADFORD'S
HISTORY This year [1635] they sustained another great loss from ye French.

Monsier de Aulnay† coming into ye harbore of

---

*A notoriously corrupt and filthy prison in London.

†D'Aunay was one of the two bitter contestants for the proprietorship of Acadia. Two years earlier, his rival La Tour had sacked and destroyed Aller-

Penobscote, and having before gott some of ye cheefe that belonged to ye house abord his vessel by subtly coming upon them in their shallop, he gott them to pilote him in.

And after getting ye rest into his power, he tooke possession of ye house in ye name of ye king of France.

And partly by threatening & otherwise, made Mr. Willett (their agente there) to approve of ye sale of ye goods there unto him, of which he sett ye price himselfe, in effecte . . .

For ye house & fortification, &c., he would not allow nor accounte anything, saying that they which build on another man's ground, doe forfit ye same.*

So thus turning them out of all (with a great deale of complemente and many fine words), he let them have their shallop and some victuals to bring them home.

Coming home and relating these passages, they here were much troubled at it. And having had this house robbed by ye French once before and lost then above £500, and now to lose house & all, did much move them.

So as they resolved to consulte with their freinds in ye Bay. And if they approved of it (there being now many ships there), they intended to hire a ship of force and seeke to beate out ye French and recover it againe. Their course was well approved on, if themselves could bear ye charge.

So they hired a fair ship of above 300 tun, well fitted with ordnance, and agreed with ye master (one Girling) to this effect.

That he and his company should deliver them ye house (after

---

ton's post farther up the coast, at Machias, killing two of his men and taking "all their goods to a good valew." This did nothing to improve Allerton's abilities to repay his partners, even if he had been so minded.

*The French had long laid claim to this part of the coast. In 1603, three years before the original Virginia grant, a huge tract styled L'Acadie, extending roughly from the Hudson River to the Gulf of St. Lawrence, had been granted to some of his subjects by the French King. As early as 1604, a fort had been built near the mouth of the St. Croix, now part of the Maine-Canadian boundary. Subsequently, other forts had been built—one not far above the Penobscot, on the island of Mount Desert, near the present Bar Harbor. Sailing north from Virginia in 1613, Captain Samuel Argall had sacked and burned a number of these. The French had cause to be on their guard.

they had driven out or surprised ye French) and give them peaceable possession thereof, and of all such trading commodities as should there be found; and give ye French fair quarter & usage if they would yeeld. In consideration whereof, he was to have 700 pounds of beaver to be delivered him there, when he had done ye thing.

But if he did not accomplish it, he was to lose his labour and have nothing.

With him, they also sent their owne barke and about 20 men under Captain Standish to aide him (if need were) and to order things if the house was regained—and then to pay him ye beaver, which they kept abord their owne barke.

So they, with their bark, piloted him thither and brought him safe into ye harbore. But he was so rash & heady as he would take no advice . . . Neither would he have patience to bring his ship where she might doe execution, but begane to shoot at a distance, like a madd man, and did them no hurte at all.

The which, when those of ye plantation saw, they were much greeved, and went to him & told him he would doe no good if he did not lay his ship better to pass (for she might lye within pistoll shott of ye house).

At last, when he saw his own folly, he was perswaded and layed her well, and bestowed a few shott to good purpose.

But now, when he was in a way to doe some good, his powder was gone . . .

He advised with ye Captaine how he might be supplyed with powder . . . So [Standish] told him he would goe to ye next plantation and doe his indeavor to procure him some. But understanding by intelligence that he intended to seize on ye barke & surprise ye beaver, he sent him the powder and brought ye barke & beaver home.

But Girling never assaulted ye place more (seeing himselfe disapoyented), but went his way. And this was ye end of this bussines.

Upon ye ill success of this bussines, the Governor and Assistants here by their letters certified their freinds in ye Bay how, by his ship, they had been abused and disapoynted, and that the French partly had and were now likly to fortifie themselves more strongly, and likly to become ill neighbors to ye English . . .

[When the Bay authorities suggested a meeting], they presently deputed 2 of theirs* to treate with them, giving them full power to conclude according to the instructions they gave them, being to this purpose—that if they would afford such assistance as, togeather with their owne, was like to effecte the thing, and allso bear a considerable parte of ye charge, they would goe on.

If not, they (having lost so much allready) should not be able, but must desiste, and wait further opportunity as God should give to help themselves.

But this came to nothing, for when it came to ye issue, they would be at no charge† . . .

This thing did not only thus breake off. But some of their merchants, shortly after, sent to trade with them, and furnished them both with provissions, & powder & shott . . .

So as it is no marvell that they still grow, & incroach more & more upon ye English, and fill ye Indeans with gunes & munishtion, to ye great danger of ye English, who lye open & unfortified, living upon husbandrie—and ye other, closed up in their forts, well fortified, and live upon trade in good securitie . . .

10. Hurricane

BRADFORD'S
HISTORY
This year [1635], ye 14 or 15 of August (being Saturday), was such a mighty storme of wind & raine as none living in these parts, either English or Indeans, ever saw, being like (for ye time it continued) to those Hauricanes and Tuffons that writers make mention of in ye Indeas.

*Assistant Governors Standish and Thomas Prence.
†Plymouth always found it difficult to elicit anything more substantial than moral support from the Bay.

It began in ye morning a little before day and grue not by degrees, but came with violence in ye beginning, to ye great amasmente of many.

It blew downe sundry houses & uncovered others. Diverse vessells were lost at sea, and many more in extreme danger. It caused ye sea to swell (to ye southward of this place) above 20 foote, right up & downe, and made many of ye Indeans to clime into trees for their saftie.

It tooke off ye borded roofe of a house which belonged to the plantation at Manomet and floted it to another place, the posts still standing in ye ground. And if it had continued long without shifting of ye wind, it is like it would have drowned some parte of ye cuntrie.

It blew downe many hundred thousands of trees, turning up the stronger by the roots and breaking ye higher pine trees off in the middle. And ye tall yonge oaks & walnut trees, of good bigness, were wound like a withe—very strang & fearfull to behould.

It begane in ye southeast and parted toward ye south & east, and veered sundry ways. But ye greatest force of it here was from ye former quarters.

It continued not (in ye extremitie) above 5 or 6 hours, but ye violence begane to abate. The signes and marks of it will remaine this 100 years in these parts where it was sorest.

The moone suffered a great eclips the 2nd night after.

11. Ousted from Connecticut

BRADFORD'S HISTORY — Some of their neighbors in the Bay, hearing of ye fame of Conightecute River, had a hankering mind after it. And understanding that ye Indeans were swepte away with ye late great mortalitie, the fear of whom was an obstacle unto them before, ... they begane now to prosecute it with great eagernes.

The greatest differances fell out betweene those of Dorchester plantation* and them here. For they set their minde on that place which they [the Pilgrims] had not only purchased of ye Indians, but where they had builte, . . . whose doings and proceedings were conceived to be very injurious—to attempte not only to intrude themselves into ye rights & possessions of others, but, in effect, to thrust them out of all . . .

I shall here inserte a few lines that was writ by their own agente from thence.

Matianuck
July 6, 1635

Sir, &c.,

Ye Massachusetts men are coming almost dayly, some by water & some by land, who are not yet determined where to settle, though some have a great mind to ye place we are upon . . .

So as what they will doe, I cannot yet resolve you . . .

I shall doe what I can to withstand them. I hope they will hear reason—as that we were here first, and entered with much difficulty and danger, both in regard of ye Dutch & Indeans, and bought ye land (to your great charge, allready disbursed). And have since held here a chargeable possession, and kept ye Dutch from further incroaching, which would else long before this day have possessed all, and kept out all others, &c.

I hope these & such like arguments will stoppe them.

It was your will we should use their persons & messengers kindly, & so we have done and doe dayly, to your great charge.

For ye first company had well nie starved, had it not been for this house, for want of victuals, I being forced to supply 12 men for 9 days togeather. And those which came last, I entertained the best we could, helping both them (& ye others) with canows & guides.

*Led by their pastor, the Reverend John Wareham, the Saints from Dorchester, near Boston, showed scant courtesy and respect for the brethren at Plymouth. Two years before, it will be recalled, the Bay had declined Plymouth's proposal for joint occupation of Connecticut.

The Pilgrims' post at Matianuck (Windsor), commanded by Jonathan Brewster, now in his forties, had proved to be a profitable one.

They gott me to goe with them to ye Dutch [at Fort Good Hope] to see if I could procure some of them to have a quiet settling near them. But they did peremtorily withstand them . . .

And what trouble & charge I shall be further at, I know not. For they are coming dayly, and I expecte these back from below, whither they have gone to view ye countrie.

All which trouble & charge we undergoe for their occasion, may give us just cause (in ye judgmente of all wise & understanding men) to hold and keep that we are settled upon.

Thus, with my duty remembered, &c., I rest,

Yours to be commanded,

Jonathan Brewster

. . . After their thorough view of ye place, they began to pitch themselves upon their land, & near their house, which occasioned much expostulation betweene them, some of which are such as follow:

[Letter from Plymouth to Boston]
Brethren,

Having lately sent 2 of our body unto you to agitate & bring to an issue some matters in difference betweene us, about some lands at Conightecut, . . . upon which God by his providence cast us and, as we conceive, in a faire way of providence tendered it to us, as a meete place to receive our body now upon removall.

We shall not need to answer all ye passages of your large letter, &c.

But whereas you say God, in his providence, cast you upon the lands, we told you before, and (upon this occasion) must now tell you still, that our mind is otherwise—and that you cast rather a partiall, if not a covetous, eye upon that which is your neighbors', and not yours. And in so doing, your way could not be faire unto it.

Looke, that you abuse not God's providence in such allegations.

Theirs:

Now allbeite we at first judged ye place so free that we might, with God's good leave, take & use it without just offense to any man,* it being the Lord's waste, and for ye present altogeather voyd of inhabitants, that indeede minded ye imploymente thereof to ye right ends for which land was created, Gen. I. 28, . . . therefore did we make some weake beginnings in that good worke, in ye place afforesaid.

Their answer was to this effecte. That if it was ye Lord's waste, it was themselves that found it so—& not they—and have since bought it of ye right owners, and maintained a chargeable possession upon it all this while, as themselves could not but know.

And because of present ingagements and other hinderances which lay at presente upon him, must it therefore be lawfull for them to goe and take it from them?

It was well known that they are upon a barren place where they were by necessitie cast. And neither they, nor theirs, could longe continue upon ye same.

And why should they (because they were more ready & more able at presente) goe and deprive them of that which they had with charge & hazard provided, & intended to remove to as soon as they could & were able?† . . .

But lest I should be teadious, I will forbear other things and come to the conclusion that was made in ye end.

To make any forcible resistance was farr from their thoughts

---

*Except to the Indians, perhaps. The common attitude toward the Indians' lands was given classic expression here in Connecticut a few years later, in 1640, at a town meeting in Milford: "Voted, that the earth is the Lord's and the fulnes thereof. Voted, that the earth is given to the Saints. Voted, that we are the Saints."

†Late in 1635, John Winthrop, Jr., returned from England with a commission from Lord Saye, Lord Brooke, and others to start settlement of Connecticut, with himself as governor. Winthrop brought men, munitions, and £2,000 to build a fort at the mouth of the Connecticut River—at Saybrook, as it was named and is still known.

The Pilgrims, having no such strength and no commission, were at a grave disadvantage in this dispute.

(they had enough of that about Kenebeck), and to live in continuall contention with their freinds & brethren would be uncomfortable and too heavie a burden to bear.

Therefore, for peace sake (though they conceived they suffered much in this thing), they thought it better to let them have it upon as good termes as they could gett.

So they fell to treaty. The first thing that . . . they [of Plymouth] would have them grant was that they had a right to it. Or ells, they would never treat aboute it. The which being acknowledged & yeelded unto them, this was ye conclusion they came to in ye end, after much adoe.

That they should retaine their house and have the 16th parte of all they had bought of ye Indeans.

And ye other should have all ye rest of ye land . . . Also, they were to pay, according to proportion, what had been disbursed to ye Indeans for ye purchas.

Thus was ye controversie ended, but the unkindnes not soone forgotten . . .

This year 2 shallops going to Conightecute with goods from ye Massachusetts of such as removed thither to plante, were in an easterly storme cast away in coming into this harbore in ye night. The boatsmen were lost, and ye goods strowed up & downe at high-water marke. But ye Governor caused them to be gathered up and drawn togeather . . . Afterwards, another boate of theirs (going thither likwise) was cast away near unto Manoanscusett [Scusset], and such goods as came ashore were preserved for them.

Such crosses they mette with in their beginnings, which some imputed as a correction from God for their intrusion (to ye wrong of others) into that place.

But I dare not be bold with God's judgments in this kind.*

*But it is clear the Pilgrims felt that "it deserved them right."

12. Pequot War

This bitter quarrel was scarcely over when the Bay, with a straight face and not so much as a blush, approached Plymouth with an insistent request, a virtual demand, for aid in a war to be waged—of all places!—in Connecticut.

It was ironic, too, that hostilities had been precipitated by the scalping of two men whom the Pilgrims had small reason to love —John Oldham, who had tried to raise the flag of rebellion at the time of the Lyford troubles, and one Captain Stone, a well-born ruffian from Virginia, who had once tried to make off with a Pilgrim ship and, on another occasion, drew his knife on Winslow and tried to stab him.

Without notifying the Pilgrims or anybody, not even the exposed settlers along the Connecticut, the Bay dispatched a small force against the Indians in 1636 "to take revenge and require satisfaction for those wrongs."

Led by Captain John Endecott, the force ravaged Block Island, where Oldham and his men had been killed. Endecott then crossed to the mainland to deal with the powerful Pequot about the killing of Captain Stone and his party.

When his demands for the surrender of the guilty and for great quantities of wampum were not promptly met, Endecott fell upon the Pequot, killed a score or more, cut down their crops, seized their supplies, burned their villages, and destroyed whatever he could—and then departed for Boston, leaving those along the Connecticut at the mercy of the enraged Indians, who swept up and down the valley, killing many, even boldly assaulting the new fort at Saybrook.

When asked for aid to repair the increasingly desperate situation in Connecticut, the Pilgrims replied that they were "cordially willing." But they took this opportunity to ask many searching questions of their own.

Had the Bay forgotten its refusal to aid Plymouth in recovering from the French its trading post on the Penobscot? That Boston merchants were now trading there was notorious, as was the fact that they were surreptitiously doing business along the Kennebec.

Why, without consulting anybody, had Massachusetts provoked the Pequot? For Endecott's action had been just that, "and no more."* Now neighbors were being called upon to rescue the Bay from its own bungling.

If the Pilgrims now lent a hand, what assurance had they of receiving help when they needed it?

And what about the virtual confiscation of their lands in this same Connecticut which they were now being asked to defend?

The Pilgrims' questions were so sharp and bitter that they were not shown to the Massachusetts General Court, but only considered by the Council, and this disingenuous reply, a masterpiece of its kind, came from Winthrop to Bradford:

Boston
[May 20, 1637]

BRADFORD'S   Sir:
HISTORY   . . . Whereas you make this warr to be our
                  people's, and not to concerne yourselves otherwise
than by consequence, we do in parte consente to you therein. Yet we suppose that, in case of perill, you will not stand upon such terms, as we hope we should not doe towards you.

And withall, we conceive that you looke at ye Pequents and all other Indeans as a commone enimie, who, . . . if he prevaile, will surely pursue his advantage, to ye rooting out of our whole nation . . .

Whereas you desire we should be ingaged to aide you upon all like occasions, we are perswaded you doe not doubte of it. . . . And whereas it is objected to us that we refused to aide you against ye French, we conceive ye case was not alike. Yet, we cannot wholly excuse our failing in that matter.

Whereas you objecte that we began ye warr without your privitie & managed it contrary to your advise, the truth is that, our first intentions being only against Block Iland, and ye enter-

_____

*This charge angered John Winthrop, who noted that he "took it ill (as there was reason)."

price seeming of small difficultie, we did not so much as consider taking of advice, or looking out for aide abroad . . .

For our people's trading at Kenebeck, we assure you (to our knowledge) it hath not been by any allowance from us . . .

And whereas you objecte to us that we hold trade & correspondancie with ye French, your enemies, we answer you are misinformed. For, besides some letters which have passed betweene our late Governor and them, to which we were privie, we have neither sente not incouraged ours to trade with them. Only one vessel or two, for better conveneance of our letters, had license from our Governor to sayle thither* . . .

Now, for ye joyning with us in this warr, which indeed concerns us no otherwise than it may yourselves—viz., the releeving of our freinds & Christian brethren who are now first in danger— though you may thinke us able to make it good without you (as, if ye Lord please to be with us, we may), yet 3 things we offer to your consideration . . .

First, that if we should sinck under this burden, your opportunitie of seasonable help would be lost . . .

The second thing is this—that it concerns us much to hasten this warr to an end before ye end of this sommer. Otherwise, ye newes of it will discourage both your & our freinds from coming to us next year . . .

The third thing is this—that if ye Lord shall please to blesse our endeavours so as we end ye warr, or put it in a hopefull way, without you, it may breed such ill thoughts in our people towards you as will be hard to entertaine such opinions of your good will towards us as were fitt to be nurished among such neighbors & brethren, as we are.

And what ill consequences may follow on both sides, wise men may fear, & would rather prevente than hope to redress.

So with my harty salutations to yourselfe and all your counsell, and other good freinds with you, I rest,

Yours most assured in ye Lord,

Jo: Winthrop

*"But by this means they did furnish them, & have still continued to doe."— Bradford's note.

The Court here [at Plymouth] agreed forthwith to send 50 men at their owne charge. And with as much speed as possiblie they could, gott them armed and made them ready under sufficiente leaders, and provided a barke to carrie them provisions & tend upon them for all occasions.

But when they were ready to march (with a supply from ye Bay), they had word to stay, for ye enimy was as good as vanquished, and there would be no neede.

Creeping upon a sleeping Pequot village before dawn, a combined force from Massachusetts and Connecticut, aided by some Narrangansett, fired the stockade around the village and then attacked, killing all they met, in a frightful slaughter that forever broke the power of the Pequot, once the proud masters of the New England forests.

BRADFORD'S HISTORY Those that scaped ye fire were slaine with ye sword—some, hewed to pieces; others run through with their rapiers. So as they were quickly dispatched, and very few escaped. It was conceived they thus destroyed about 400 at this time.*

It was a fearfull sight to see them thus frying in ye fyer, and ye streams of blood quenching ye same, and horrible was ye stinck & sente thereof.

But ye victory seemed a sweete sacrifice, and they gave the prayse thereof to God . . .

WINTHROP'S JOURNAL [July 13, 1637] . . . the women and children were divided, and sent some to Connecticut, and some to Massachusetts . . . We had now slain and taken, in all, about seven hundred. We sent fifteen of the boys and two women to Bermuda, by Mr. Peirce [to be sold as slaves]. But he, missing it, carried them to Providence Isle†
. . .

[August 5] Mr. Hooker and Mr. Stone came, with Mr.

*Half of these were women and children, and the aged.
†Off the coast of Nicaragua, settled largely by Puritans, who were dispossessed by the Spanish in 1641.

Wilson, from Connecticut, by Providence . . . They brought news also of divers other Pequods which had been slain by other Indians, and their heads brought to the English.

So that now there had been slain or taken between eight and nine hundred . . .

The captives, whether sent abroad or kept at home, were enslaved. Four years later, in 1641, the Bay formally recognized the institution of slavery in its *Code of Fundamentals, or Body of Liberties,* anticipating Virginia by many years in legally instituting the "peculiar institution," being the first of the English colonies to do so.

There were Indian and Negro slaves in the Plymouth colony as early as 1646, when the authorities threatened to sell Indians or exchange them for Negroes as punishment for offenses.

Later, during King Philip's War, the Plymouth pastor was presented with an Indian slave, and he begged another to send to his brother-in-law, Increase Mather. In 1706, Cotton Mather noted in his diary, "Received a singular blessing in the gift of a likely slave, which was a smile of heaven on this family."

But it was another man of the Bay, Chief Justice Samuel Sewall —peace to his gallant soul—who was one of the first to lift his voice against human slavery, publishing in 1700 *The Selling of Joseph, A Memorial,* which frightened and outraged the more conservative.

But slaves continued to be sold in the Boston market as late as 1788, when the traffic was forbidden. But New England shipmasters continued their operations in the infamous Triangular Trade— rum to Africa, slaves to the West Indies and our South, molasses to New England, to be turned into more rum, more slaves, more molasses, *ad infinitum* and *ad nauseam.*

XXV
Church Affairs

But that which is more, that about these times the Lord was pleased, of his great goodness, richly to accomodate and adorn the colony of Plimouth (as well as other colonies in New England) with a considerable number of godly and able Gospel-Preachers . . .

—Nathaniel Morton

CHURCH
RECORDS
In anno 1629, a considerable number of the brethren which were left in Holland were transported over to us . . . Also, about that time, several Godly persons . . . and others also came to us out of England, so that we becaime, through the goodnes of God, pretty numerous and were in the best estate respecting the Church that we had been in New England, although, for minnestry, it was low for us.

For as was before noted, they had chosen Mr. Ralph Smith to be their Pastour. Yet he proved but a [poor] healp to them, . . . being of very weake partes . . . Only, they had a great healp by their Reverend Mr. Brewster, who was well accomplished with gifts . . . They also had some good healp by . . . Mr. Roger Williams.

1. Roger Williams

BRADFORD'S
HISTORY
Mr. Roger William (a man godly & zealous, having many precious parts, but very unsettled in judgmente) came over first to ye Massachusetts, but upon some discontente, lefte that place and came hither,

where he was freindly entertained, and exercised his gifts amongst them.

And after some time, he was admitted a member of ye church, and his teaching well approved, for ye benefits whereof I still blesse God and am thankful to him, even for his sharpest admonitions & reproofs, so farr as they agreed with truth.

A graduate of Cambridge and not yet thirty, Williams had already made a name for himself before he arrived at Boston early in 1631 with his wife and two small children. At Boston, Williams immediately caused offense by refusing to join the church there, declining to take communion with Governor Winthrop and his brethren on the ground that they were an "unseparated people."

To remove the stain on their conscience, the least they could do, he said, was to "make public declaration of their repentance for having taken communion with the churches of England while they lived there."

Besides, the magistrates at Boston were quite wrong in taking it upon themselves to punish breaches of the Sabbath and similar sins. That was none of their business, being properly a matter of Church, not of State.

Removing to Salem within a few months, Williams was quickly chosen as "teacher" of the church there, succeeding Francis Higginson, who had recently died. "King" Winthrop, always inclined to take high ground, wrote to protest this, expressing his amazement that they "would choose him without advising with the Council, and withal desiring them that they would forbear to proceed till they had conferred about it."

The Salem church ignored this. But a few months later, as pressure from Boston continued, Williams resigned and came to Plymouth to enjoy the Holy Discipline with a "separating" people who had had, always, the courage of their convictions, becoming their "teacher," serving with Pastor Ralph Smith.

WINTHROP'S JOURNAL* [October 25, 1632] the governor [Winthrop], with Mr. Wilson, pastor of Boston, and the two captains, &c., went aboard the *Lyon*, and from

*As published, first in 1825-26, Winthrop's journal bears the misleading and much too ambitious title of *The History of New England from 1630 to 1649*—

thence Mr. [Captain] Peirce carried them in his shallop to Wessagusset. The next morning, Mr. Peirce returned to his ship, and the governor and his company went on foot to Plymouth and came thither within the evening.

The governor of Plymouth, Mr. William Bradford (a very discreet and grave man), with Mr. Brewster, the elder, and some others, came forth and met them without the town, and conducted them to the governor's house, where they were very kindly entertained and feasted every day at several houses.

On the Lord's day, there was a sacrament, which they did partake in.

And in the afternoon, Mr. Roger Williams (according to their custom) propounded a question, to which the pastor, Mr. Smith, spake briefly. Then Mr. Williams prophesied. And after, the governor of Plymouth spake to the question; after him, the elder; then some two or three more of the congregation. Then the elder desired the governor of Massachusetts and Mr. Wilson to speak to it, which they did.

When this was ended, the deacon, Mr. Fuller, put the congregation in mind of their duty of contribution, whereupon the governor and all the rest went down to the deacon's seat, and put into the box, and then returned . . .

About five in the morning [three days later], the governor and his company came out of Plymouth, the governor of Plymouth, with the paster and elder, &c., accompanying them near a half mile out of town in the dark. The Lieut. Holmes, with two others and the governor's mare,* came along with them to the great swamp, about ten miles . . .

Thence they came to a place called Hue's Cross. The gover-

hereafter, Winthrop's Journal. It deals largely with events in the Bay colony.

At the time of this entry, Winthrop was a man of forty-four, almost exactly Bradford's age, being a year or so older. Of a wealthy family with large estates, Winthrop enjoyed an income of £600 or £700 ($35,000) a year. Bradford died the richest man in the Old Colony, leaving an estate of £900, little more than Winthrop's annual income, which is some measure of the difference between the two colonies in the matter of substance.

*This may have been the first horse at Plymouth, as there is no previous mention of one.

nor, being displeased at the name in respect that such things might hereafter give the Papists occasion to say that their religion was first planted in these parts, changed the name and called it Hue's Folly, . . . and the next day came safe to Boston.

2. "Prophecying"

The exercise of "prophecying," which had been particularly noted by Winthrop, that newly converted Saint, was held regularly every Sabbath afternoon.

Part of general Separatist practice, it had its roots in the need to explain and expound texts of Holy Writ to largely unschooled congregations, as was that at Plymouth. Even if members could read, they had few books for the most part, though Brewster, Bradford, Standish, and others had surprisingly large libraries.

More than anything else, it was this "prophecying," not only by pastors, teachers, and elders, but also by lay members, that shocked the orthodox and led them to ridicule the Separatists' services.

In his day, Thomas Morton had observed the ways of the Saints at Plymouth, Salem, and elsewhere, and let fly at them wittily and maliciously, yet with some foundation of fact, in striving to stir up Archbishop Laud to put a stop to such "fantasticall" proceedings.

MORTON'S
NEW CANAAN

The Church of the Separatists is governed by Pastors, Elders, and Deacons. And there is not any of these, though he be but a Cow-keeper, but is allowed to exercise his gifts in the publick assembly on the Lord's day, so as he does not make use of any notes for the helpe of his memory. For such things, they say, smell of lampe oyle, and there must be no such unsavory perfume admitted to come into the congregation* . . .

Now, forasmuch as by the practise of their Church every

---

*The Reverend John Cotton, teacher at Boston, was accounted a liberal in his day because he allowed that it might be "lawfull" for a preacher to make notes or even write out and memorize his sermon.

Elder or Deacon may preach, it is not amisse to discover their practise in that perticuler . . .

A Grocer—One steps up, like the Minister of Justice—with the balance only, not the sword, for feare of affrighting his auditory. He poynts at a text and handles it as evenly as he can, and teaches the auditory that the thing he has to deliver must be well weighed, for it is a very pretious thing—yes, much more pretious than gold or pearle . . .

A Taylor—Another (of a more cutting disposition) steps in his stead. And he takes a text, which he divides into many parts—to speake truly, as many as he list. The fag end of it he pares away as a superfluous remnant. He puts his auditory in comfort that he will make a garment for them and teach them how they shall put it on, and incourages them to be in love with it, for it is of such a fashion as doth best become a Christian man . . .

A Tapster—A third, he supplies the room and, in the exercise of his gifts, begins with a text that is drawne out of a fountaine that has in it no dreggs of popery. This shall prove unto you, says he, the Cup of Repentance. It is not like unto the Cup of the Whore of Babilon, which will make men drunk with the dreggs thereof. It is filled up to the brim with comfortable joyes . . .

A Cobler—Another (a very learned man indeed) goes another way to worke with his auditory, and exhorts them to walke upright in the way of their calling and not (like carnall men) tread awry. And if they should fayle in the performance of that duty, yet they should seeke for amendement while it was time, and tells them it would be too late to seek for help when the shop windowes were shutt up . . .

A very Patrick—But stay: here is one stept up in haste and, being not minded to hold his auditory in expectation of any long discourse, he takes a text and (for brevitie's sake) divides it into one part, and then runnes so fast afore with the matter that his auditory cannot follow him. Doubtless, his father was some Irish footman. By his speede, it seemes so . . .

This is the meanes (O, the meanes) that they pursue, this that comes without premeditation. This is the Superlative. And he that does not approve of this, they say is a very reprobate . . .

Many unwarrantable tenets they have likewise, . . . one whereof, being in publike practise maintained, is more notorious than the rest. I will therefore beginne with that . . .

That it is the Magistrates' office absolutely, and not the Ministers', to joyne the people in lawfull matrimony. And for this, they vouch the history of Ruth, saying Boas was married to Ruth in presence of the Elders of the people. Herein, they mistake the scope of the text.

2. That it is a relique of popery to make use of a ring in marriage, and that it is a diabolicall circle for the Divell to daunce in.*

3. That the purification used for women after delivery is not to be used.

4. That no child shall be baptized whose parents are not receaved into their Church first.†

5. That no person shall be admitted to the Sacrament of the Lord's Supper that is without [the church].

6. That the Booke of Common Prayer is an idoll; and all that use it, Idolators.‡

---

*As early as 1603, at the Hampton Court Conference attended by the bishops and representatives of the reformist Anglican clergy, the use of the ring had been questioned by a Puritan spokesman, Dr. John Reynolds, one of the great scholar-poets of the King James Version of the Bible.

†Non-communicants could not have their children baptized in early New England, though Plymouth later modified the rule to allow baptism if one of the child's parents was a member of the church in good standing. In 1670, more than four out of five free male adults in Massachusetts were without a vote because they were non-communicants, so the historian Palfrey concluded after a close study of the records.

In 1671, the Plymouth General Court decreed that only those should have the vote who were of "sober and peaceable conversation, orthodox in the fundamentals of religion." This had long been Pilgrim theory and practice.

‡Morton may have heard such words at Plymouth, and even in the Bay, where the "professors" both by training and instinct were usually rather more circumspect.

One of the great Separatist martyrs, Henry Barrow, was revered at Plymouth. Brewster and others had his lively books on their shelves—books in which Barrow repeatedly denounced the Book of Common Prayer as "a detestable idol, . . . old rotten stuffe, . . . abstracted out of the Pope's blasphemous mass-

7. That every man is bound to beleeve a professor upon his bare affirmation only, above a Protestant upon oath [which is to say that a Saint's mere word outweighed a non-Saint's sacred oath].

8. That no person hath any right to God's creatures but God's children only, who are themselves, and that all others are but usurpers of the creatures* . . .

12. And lastly, they differ from us in the manner of praying, for they winke [close their eyes] when they pray because they thinke themselves so perfect in the highe way to heaven that they can find it blindfold . . .

3. Strange Opinions and Stranger Practice

Little went into the collection box at Plymouth, it appears, for Roger Williams was paid so little that he was forced, he said, to scratch out a bare subsistence by laboring "night and day, at home and abroad, on the Land and water, at the How [hoe], at the Oare, for bread."

And yet in spite of this and his religious duties, Williams found time, which was of the greatest general advantage later, to go among the Indians. He frequently visited Massasoit and other chieftains, for God had been pleased to give him, he said, "a pain-full patient spirit, to lodge with them in their filthy smoky holes, and (even while I lived at Plymouth and Salem) to gaine their tongue."

But God had also been pleased "to put a windmill in his head," said others.

BRADFORD'S HISTORY   He, this year [1633], begane to fall into some strang oppinions, and from oppinion to practise, which caused some controversie betweene ye

---

booke, . . . an abominable & loathsome sacrifice in the sight of God, even as a dead dog."

*This was a sore point with "mine Host of Ma-re Mount." He is here implying that the Saints asserted a divine right to the beaver trade, as they frequently did to the Indian lands.

church & him, and in ye end some discontente on his parte, by occasion whereof he left them somewhat abruptly.

Yet afterwards, he sued for his dismission to ye church at Salem, which was granted, with some caution to them concerning him and what care they ought to have of him.

But he soone fell into more things there, both to their and ye government's troble and disturbance. I shall not need to name perticulers—they are too well known now to all . . .

But he is to be pitied and prayed for, and so I shall leave ye matter and desire ye Lord to shew him his errors and reduse him into ye way of truth, and give him a setled judgment and constancie in ye same.

For I hope that he belongs to ye Lord, and that he will show him mercie . . .

MORTON'S MEMORIAL   In the year 1634, Mr. Roger Williams removed from Plimouth to Salem. He had lived about three years at Plimouth, where he was well accepted as an assistant in the Ministry to Mr. Ralph Smith, then Pastor of the Church there. But he by degrees venting of divers of his own singular opinions and seeking to impose them on others, he not finding such a concurrence as he expected, he desired his dismission to the Church of Salem.

Which, though some were unwilling to, yet through the prudent counsel of Mr. Brewster (the Ruling Elder there), fearing that his continuance amongst them might cause divisions, and there being then many able men in the Bay, they would better deal with him than themselves could, and foreseeing (what he professed he feared concerning Mr. Williams, which afterwards came to pass) that he would run the same course to rigid separation and anabaptistry which John Smith, the Sebaptist at Amsterdam, had done,* the Church at Plimoth consented to his dismission.

*The Se-Baptist, or the Self-Baptizer, was, of course, their old friend from Gainsborough, John Smyth, under whom Brewster and his company of Separatists at Scrooby had first worshiped.

  The Anabaptists held that baptism was an act of faith and therefore rejected infant baptism, for no newborn infant had a faith. All therefore had to be "re-baptized," which is what Anabaptist signifies.

And such as did adhere to him were also dismissed and removed with him, or not long after him, to Salem.

He came to Salem in the time of Mr. Skelton's weakness, who lived not long after Mr. Williams was come. Whereupon, after some time, the church there called him to office. But he having in one year's time filled that place with principles of rigid separation and tending to anabaptistry, the prudent magistrates of the Massachusetts jurisdiction sent to the church of Salem, desiring them to forbear calling him to office.

Which they not hearkening to, was a cause of much disturbance. For Mr. Williams had begun and, then being in office, he proceeded more vigorously to vent many dangerous opinions.

As amongst many others, these were some: *That it is not lawfull for an unregenerate man to pray, nor take an oath—and in special, not the Oath of Fidelity to the Civil Government. Nor was it lawfull for a godly man to have communion either in family prayer, or in an oath, with such as they judged unregenerate.* And therefore, he himself refused the Oath of Fidelity and taught others so to do.

Also, *That it was not lawfull so much as to hear the godly ministers of England when any occasionally went thither,* & therefore he admonished any church-members that had done so, as for hainous sin.

Also, he spake dangerous words against the patent, which was the foundation of the government of the Massachusetts Colony.*

Also he affirmed, *That . . . there should be a general and unlimited toleration of all religions, and for any man to be punished for any matters of his conscience was persecution.*

---

*Williams wrote and circulated a tract denying the validity of the settlers' patents and charters. The land belonged to the Indians, he declared, and neither the King nor the Council for New England could rightfully dispose of any part of it. This was obviously true, but very disturbing doctrine. This, as much as anything, prompted sharp action against him.

"Why lay such stress upon your patent from King James? 'Tis but parchment," Williams wrote Governor Bradford a few years later. "James has no more right to give away or sell Massasoit's lands, and cut and carve his country, than Massasoit has to sell King James' kingdom or send Indians to colonize Warwickshire."

And further, he procured the church of Salem's consent unto letters of admonition which were written and sent by him, in their name, to the churches at Boston, Charlestown, Newtown (now Cambridge), &c., accusing the magistrates that were members of the respective churches of sundry hainous offenses which he laid unto their charge.

And though divers did acknowledge their error and gave satisfaction, yet Mr. Williams himself, notwithstanding all the pains that was taken with him by Mr. [the Reverend John] Cotton, Mr. [the Reverend Thomas] Hooker, and many others to bring him to a sight of his errors and miscarriage, and notwithstanding all the Court's gentle proceedings with him, he not only persisted but grew more violent in his way.

Insomuch as he, staying at home in his own house, sent a letter which was delivered and read in the publick church assembly, the scope of which was to give them notice, *That if the Church of Salem would not separate not only from the Churches of Old-England, but the Churches of New-England too, he would separate from them.*

The more prudent and sober part of the church, being amazed at his way, could not yeeld unto him. Whereupon, he never came to the church assembly more . . .

And not only so, but he withdrew all private religious communion from any that would hold communion with the church there, insomuch as he would not pray, nor give thanks at meals, with his own wife, nor any of his family, because they went to the church assemblies.

Divers of the weaker sort of church-members that had been thoroughly leavened with his opinions, of which number were divers women that were zealous in their way, did by degrees fall off to him, insomuch as he kept a meeting in his own house, unto which a numerous company did resort, both on the Sabbath day and at other times, in way of separation from and opposition to the church assembly there.

Which the prudent magistrates understanding, and seeing things grow more and more towards a general division and disturbance, after all other means used in vain, they passed a sentence of banishment against him out of the Massachusetts Colony, as against a disturber of the peace, both of the Church and Common-wealth.

In October 1635, the Massachusetts General Court ordered Williams to leave the colony within six weeks, later relenting a bit and allowing him to remain till spring. When Williams went on "venting his singular opinions," the angry Bay authorities issued a warrant for his arrest, having arranged to ship him back to England.

Learning of this, Williams abandoned his family and fled into the wilderness, being "sorely tossed for fourteen weeks in a bitter winter season, not knowing what bread or bed did mean."

Making his way into Massasoit's territory, he settled at Seekonk, a few miles north of Sowams, where he was joined by a few friends from Salem. Here they "began to build and plant," but Williams halted work when a letter came from Plymouth.

"I received a letter from my ancient friend, Mr. Winslow, then Governor of Plymouth, professing his own and others' love and respect for me, yet lovingly advising me, since I was fallen into the edge of their bounds, and they were loath to displease. the Bay, to remove but to the other side of the water. And then, said he, I had the country before me and might be as free as themselves, and we should be loving neighbors together."

MORTON'S
MEMORIAL
After which, Mr. Williams sat down in a place called Providence,* out of the Massachusetts jurisdiction, and was followed by many of the members of the Church of Salem, who did zealously adhere to him, and who cried out of the persecution that was against him. Some others also resorted to him from other parts.

*Moving across Narragansett Bay from Seekonk with his handful of followers, Williams named his settlement Providence in remembrance of "God's merciful providence to me in my distress," expressing a hope that it would always be "a shelter for persons distressed for conscience." True to his principles, he bought the land from Canonicus, sachem of the powerful Narragansett, making the latter a lifelong friend and thus exerting great influence among the Indians to the benefit of all the colonies.

Providence was a remarkably democratic community from the start. Williams

They had not been long there together, but from rigid separation they fell into Anabaptistry, renouncing the baptism they had received in their infancy and taking up another baptism, and so began a church in that way.

But Mr. Williams stopped not long there. For after some time, he told the people that had followed him, and joyned with him in a new baptism, that *he was out of the way himselfe, and had misled them, for he did not finde there was any upon earth that could administer Baptism.** And therefore, their last baptism was a nullity, as well as their first. And therefore, they must lay down all and wait for the coming of new Apostles.*

And so they dissolved themselves and turned *Seekers,* keeping that one principle, *That every one should have liberty to worship God according to the light of their own consciences,* but otherwise not owning any Churches or Ordinances of God anywhere upon earth.

Thus much was thought meet to be inserted here concerning the great and lamentable apostacy of Mr. Williams, that it may be a warning to all others to take heed of a gradual declining from and forsaking the Churches of Christ and Ordinances of God in them, lest they be left of God to run such a course as he hath done . . .

> Though the Plymouth Saints scowled at Williams' doctrine, some remained personally friendly, as Williams remarked, gratefully noting that "it pleased the Father of mercies to touch many hearts with relenting, amongst whom that great and precious soul, Mr. Winslow, melted and kindly visited me at Providence, and put a piece of gold into the hands of my wife, for our supply."

gave it a minimum of restrictive government, a maximum of civil liberties, and absolute religious freedom for all. There was here no division at all between "saincts" and "strangers." All were welcome; all had equal rights. For some time, it was the people's custom there to address one another as "Neighbor," a reflection of the friendly and democratic spirit of the town.

*As all had been baptized as infants and as infant baptism was "unlawfull," there was no properly baptized person to administer the rite—nor had there been any for centuries. Far back, the chain to the Apostles had been broken, and there was no way to close the gap.

4. Mr. Norton

BRADFORD'S
HISTORY Amongst ye other bussinesses that Mr. Winslow had to doe in England [in 1635], he had order from ye church to provide & bring over some able & fitt man to be their minister.*

And accordingly, he had procured a godly and a worthy man, one Mr. Glover. But it pleased God, when he was prepared for the viage, he fell sick of a feaver and dyed.

Afterwards, when he was ready to come away, he became acquainted with Mr. Norton, who was willing to come over, but would not ingage himselfe to this place otherwise than he should see occasion when he came here, and if he liked better elsewhere, to repay ye charge laid out for him (which came to aboute £70) and be at his liberty.†

He stayed aboute a year with them after he came over and was well liked of them, & much desired of them. But he was invited to Ipswich, where were many rich & able men, and sundry of his acquaintance. So he wente to them & was their minister . . .

Hungry for good sermons, having heard none for so long, not since leaving Leyden sixteen years before, the Saints forgave Norton half his charge in return "for ye pains he tooke amongst them."

Norton went on to become one of the most powerful theocrats in the Bay. Leaving Ipswich, he came to Boston, after John Cotton's death, to succeed him as "teacher" of the First Church there,

---

*The Pilgrims still had the Reverend Ralph Smith, whom they had chanced to pick up at Nantasket six years before, but they were not much "edified" by him.

†In his late twenties, a graduate of Cambridge, having been at Peterhouse College, where Brewster had studied before him, John Norton wrote "pure elegant Latin," it was said. The Pilgrims found more interest in the discovery that he was a "hard student" and "much in prayer; he would spend whole *days* in prayer." A strict disciplinarian and a narrow zealot, Norton was disposed to see sin and Satan in practically everything.

sharing the pulpit with Pastor John Wilson, another violent bigot.

Together, they led the witch hunts, the Quaker persecutions and executions, that disgraced and shamed the Bay colony. Though disappointed at the moment, Plymouth was well spared the "pure, sublime, scholastical" Norton.

Zealous for order, very critical
For what was truly congregational.

5. Teacher John Reyner

CHURCH RECORDS This yeer [1636] Mr. Ralph Smith layed downe his place of minnestry, partly by his owne willingnes, as thinking it too heavy a burden, and partly att the desire and by the perswasion of others.*

And the Church sought out for some other, haveing bin often disappointed in their hopes and desires heretofore.

And it pleased the Lord to send them an able and Godly man, Mr. John Reyner,† of a meek and humble sperite, sound in the truth, and every way unreprovable in his life and conversation. Who, after some time of tryall, they chose for their Teacher, the fruits of whose labours they injoyed many yeers, with much comfort, in peace and agreement . . .

*Smith felt that he had been much abused, as did most Plymouth pastors. Within six years, he complained, the brethren had shifted him from house to house at least a dozen times. Smith had married Deacon Richard Masterson's widow, who seems to have had some property at Leyden, and Smith now wrote her friends there urging them to sell her house and forward the proceeds as rapidly as possible, for he and his family were starving.

"It hath pleased God to tire us by great losses of fire, water, and theeves (often) in this wilderness, so that it's a mercie I yet live & have bread and water to drinke," he groaned. "I am sore weakened & unable to labor as formerlie."

But he had one thing to be thankful for—"I have got freedome . . . of that intollerable charg pressing mee nigh 7 years, but with all my small means went."

†Another graduate of Cambridge, originally from Yorkshire, a man of some independent means.

He was an able, faithfull, laboriouse preacher of the Gospell, and a wise orderer of the affairs of the Church. He was singularly indowed with a Gift and propence upon his speritt to train up children in a Cattikettical way in the grounds of Christian religion . . .

In a word, this worthy leader was richly accomplished with such Gifts and quallifications as were befitting his place, being wise, faithfull, Grave, sober, a lover of Good men, not Greedy of the matters of the world, Armed with much faith, patience, and meeknes, mixed with Currage for the cause of God.

6. Monsters and Witches

MORTON'S MEMORIAL This year [1637] there was a hideous monster born at Boston in New England, of one Mrs. Mary Dyer, a co-partner with the said Mrs. Hutchinson in the aforesaid heresies. The said monster (as it was related to me), it was without a head, but horns like a beast; scales, or a rough skin, like a fish called the thornback. It had leggs and claws like a fowl, and in other respects as a woman childe; the Lord declaring his detestation of their monstruous errors (as was then thought by some) by this prodigious birth.

This is typical of the gross delusions and superstitions of the day, even among the better schooled. But steeped as they were in the supernatural as expounded from the pulpit and often by themselves, the most learned were likely to be the least skeptical. Pointing to Scripture, they found "signes of God" everywhere—in the clouds, in lightning, in unseasonable weather, blights, snakes, caterpillars.

John Winthrop solemnly recorded in his journal for 1638 the graphic and quite incredible details about the monster, as related to him by the hysterical midwife, who presently fled, "and indeed it was time for her to be gone, for it was known that she used to give young women oil of mandrakes and other stuff to cause conception, and she grew into great suspicion to be a witch."

The monster, so Winthrop reported, had a face, but no head. Among other remarkable things, its ears stood upon the shoulders and, in back, between the shoulders, were two mouths. When Bradford heard of this, he was fascinated and wrote Winthrop to be fully informed.

Shortly after giving birth to the "prodigious" monster, Mary Dyer—"a very proper and fair woman," Winthrop granted—went to Rhode Island with her husband William, a milliner, who became the secretary of the colony there. Joining the Quakers, Mary Dyer returned to Boston to proselytize. Having been warned to keep her "pernicious and dangerous doctrine elsewhere," she was tried and sentenced to die, being hanged on Boston Common in 1660.

Curiously, and most significantly, there were no "prodigious" births in the Old Colony. Nor did the Pilgrims ever hang a Quaker—or a witch. Perhaps it was because they were not "learned." They did not sacrifice common sense and humanity to metaphysical ideas.

In any case, whatever the reasons, there were only two trials for witchcraft in the entire history of the Old Colony. In both instances, the hysterical women who claimed to be bewitched were sharply censured and fined for malicious gossip, which ended the witchcraft delusion in the Pilgrim empire.

But Massachusetts—and the Saints in Connecticut too—went on hanging witches down to those dark days at Salem Village in 1692, when a wave of hysteria swept the colony—given propulsion, if not actually set in motion, by the divines.

WINTHROP'S
JOURNAL   [June 4, 1648] At this court, one Margaret Jones of Charlestown was indicted and found guilty of witchcraft, and hanged for it.

The evidence against her was:

1. that she was found to have such a malignant touch as many persons (men, women, and children) whom she stroked or touched with any affection or displeasure, or, etc., were taken with deafness, or vomiting, or other violent pains or sickness;

2. she practising physic, and her medicines being such things

as (by her own confession) were harmless, as aniseed, liquors, etc., yet had extraordinary effects;

3. she would use to tell such as would not make use of her physic that they would never be healed and, accordingly, their diseases and hurts continued, with relapse against the ordinary course and beyond the apprehension of all physicions and surgeons;

4. some things which she foretold came to pass accordingly; other things she could tell of (as secret speeches, etc.), which she had no ordinary means to come to the knowledge of;

5. she had (upon search) an apparent teat in her secret parts as fresh as if it had been newly sucked, and after it had been scanned upon a forced search, that was withered and another began on the opposite side;

6. in the prison, in the clear daylight, there was seen in her arms, she sitting on the floor and her clothes up, etc., a little child, which ran from her into another room, and the officer following it, it was vanished.

The like child was seen in two other places to which she had relation. And one maid that saw it, fell sick upon it, and was cured by the same Margaret, who used means to be employed to that end.

Her behavior at her trial was very intemperate, lying notoriously, and railing upon the jury and witnesses, etc. And in the like distemper, she died.

The same day and hour she was executed, there was a very great tempest at Connecticut, which blew down many trees, etc.

If the tempest was the wrath of God, it was visited upon the wrong people.

7. A Pestilent Seducer: Samuel Gorton

MORTON'S MEMORIAL   Not long before these troubles [with Mrs. Hutchinson and Mrs. Dyer], there arrived at Boston one Samuel Gorton, who from thence came to Plimouth. And upon his first coming thither, gave some hopes that he would have proved a useful instrument.

But soon after, by little and little, he discovered himself to be a proud and pestilent seducer, and deeply leavened with blasphemous and Familistical opinions . . .

He was a subtile deceiver, courteous in his carriage to all at some times (for his own ends), but soon moved with passion, . . . belching out errours in Familistical allegories (if I may so call them): as (to speak with holy reverence) they rendered the Lord Christ no other than an "Imagination"; shunning not blasphemously to say "That Christ was but a shadow and resemblance of what is done in every Christian, . . . That Faith and Christ are all one."

They call the holy Word and sermons of salvation, "Tales"; the Lord's Supper, "an Abomination and a Spell"; baptism, "Vanity and Abomination"; the Ministers of the Word, "Necromancers"; and by other opprobrious terms villifie and traduce them . . .

[He] hath not shunned to say and affirm that all the felicity we are like to have, we must expect in this life, and no more; and therefore advised one with whom he had some speech to "make much of herself, for she must expect no more but what she should enjoy in this life," or words to the same effect . . .

Much more might be spoken and mentioned of this stuff, which they have not been ashamed to divulge. But a little is enough* . . .

And observing such fictions to be spread by some of his spirit

*A London clothier and an ardent spirit, Gorton had come to the New World in search of "libertie of conscience." Not finding it at Boston, he tried Plymouth.

The sect of the Familists, to which Gorton belonged, rejected formalism and exalted the spirit of divine love, and there is much that is modern and enlightened in their views. But it must be admitted that Gorton was, as described, "a most prodigious Minter of exhorbitant Novelties."

Signing himself "Professor of the Mysteries, and De Primo," Gorton later summed up his views in *An Incorruptible Key*, "composed of the CX Psalme, wherewith you may open the Rest of the Holy Scriptures" and discover—among many other things—the truth about "Fall and Resurrection, Sin and Righteousness, Ascension and Descension, Height and Depth, First and Last, Beginning and Ending, Flesh and Spirit, Wisdome and Foolishnesse, Strength and Weakness, Mortality and Immortality, Jew and Gentile, Light and Dark-

already in the country, he takes his opportunity to sow such seed at Plymouth, whereby some were seduced—in special, one John Weeks and his wife, who, in some short time, became very Atheists, looking for no more happiness than this world affords—not only in practice, such, but also in opinion.

But the said Gorton, falling into some controversie with one Mr. Ralph Smith, was summoned to the Court* . . .

WINSLOW'S   The time being come and the Court set, Gorton
HYPOCRISY   was called. But the Governor [Bradford], being
              wearied with speech to other causes, requested one
of his Assistants who was present at his commitment and privy to the whole cause, to declare the same.

This Assistant no sooner stood up to shew the country the cause of his bonds in the great affront he had given the government, but Gorton, stretching out his hand towards his face, said with a loud voice,

"If Satan will accuse the brethren, let him come downe from Jehoshuah's right hand and stand here."

And that done, in a seditious manner he turned himselfe to the people and said, with his arms spread abroad,

"Yee see, good people, how yee are abused! Stand for your liberty, and let them not be parties and judges"—with many other opprobrious speeches of that kinde.

---

nesse, Unity and Multiplication, Fruitfullness and Barrenness, Curse and Blessing, Man and Woman, Kingdom and Priesthood, All-Sufficiency and Deficiency, God and Man."

Like Roger Williams, Gorton challenged the magistrates' authority, but for a different reason. No colonial charter was valid unless it had been reviewed by the King and given his sanction—as none in New England had. Nor could the magistrates forbid what the law in England allowed, having no authority to lay down edicts of their own devising.

Still, for all his singularities, Gorton should be remembered as a stout fighter for real "freedom of religion," free of all the hedges and fences that the Saints placed about it.

*The Gortons had been living with Ralph Smith, the deposed pastor, and the trouble began, according to Gorton, because Mrs. Smith preferred his prayers to her husband's. Ordered out of the house for "unworthie and offensive speeches," Gorton refused to move, saying he had as much right there as Smith. Also, the Gortons' maid had been caught smiling in church and threatened with banishment.

Hereupon, divers Elders of churches being present, desiring leave of the Governour to speake, complained of his seditious carriage and requested the Court not to suffer these abuses, but to inflict condigne punishment.

And yet notwithstanding, all we did to him was to take the forfeiture of his foresaid bonds for his good behavior. Nay, being but low and poore in his estate, we tooke not above £8 or £10 [$500], lest it might lie too heavy upon his wife and children* . . .

MORTON'S
MEMORIAL
In some short time after, he departed to Road Island and in like manner, or worse, demeaned himself there, so as they were forced to sentence him to suffer corporal punishment by whipping. And they banished him likewise off the Island.

And from thence, he, with divers of his accomplices, went to Providence, and there he and they carried so in outrage and riotously, as they were in danger to have caused bloodshed . . .

> While there, Gorton achieved something which no one had ever accomplished before. He exhausted Roger Williams' patience, which Winthrop and the "presumptuous" Bay authorities had failed to do in spite of every effort they could summon, as Winthrop once confessed to Williams.
>
> The Saints had not seen or heard the last of Gorton.

8. The "Larned Mr. Channcy"

CHURCH
RECORDS
After Mr. Reyner had bin in place [for two years], it was desired that Mr. Charles Chauncey,† a Reverend man, should be invited, whoe, being a very Godly and learned man, they intended upon tryall to

---

*Winslow failed to add that he had also been ordered to leave the colony within fourteen days, in the dead of winter. Also, according to the Plymouth records, Gorton was fined £20. In his *Hypocrisie Unmasked*, which was aimed at Gorton, Winslow was endeavoring to show how well he had been treated at Plymouth.

†Another Cambridge graduate, a man in his middle forties, Chauncy had taught Greek and Hebrew at the university for a time. Taking a country

choose him Pastour of the Church here for the more comfortable performance of the minnestry with Mr. John Reyner, the Teacher of the same . . .

BRADFORD'S HISTORY   But there fell out some differance aboute baptizing, he [Chauncy] holding it ought to be by dipping and putting ye whole body under water, and that sprinkling was unlawfull.

The church yeelded that immersion, or dipping, was lawfull—but in this cold countrie, not so conveniente.

But they could not, nor durst not, yeeld to him in this—that sprinkling (which all ye churches of Christ doe, for ye most parte, use at this day) was unlawfull & a human invention, as ye same was prest.*

But they were willing to yeeld to him as far as they could, & to ye utmost, and were contented to suffer him to practise as he was perswaded.

And when he came to minister that ordnance, he might so doe it to any that did desire it in that way, provided he could peaceably suffer Mr. Reyner and such as desired to have theirs otherwise baptized by him, by sprinkling or powering on of water upon them, so as there might be no disturbance in ye church thereaboute.

But he said he could not yeeld thereunto.

Upon which, the church procured some other ministers to

---

parish, he was cited in 1629 for denouncing the Anglican church as "full of Idolatrie, atheism, popery, Arminianism, and heresy." William Laud, then bishop of London, ordered him "to make a submission in Latin," which he did.

Six years later, he was again in trouble for objecting to having a rail erected around the communion table. Commanded to recant by the Court of High Commission, he did, which was "greatly dishonorable," his son admitted, and "made him often uneasy to his dying day."

When trouble threatened again—this time for refusing to read the Book of Sports—he took to his heels and made his way to Plymouth, arriving in 1638.

*As John Robinson had been a "sprinkler," the Saints could not possibly admit that this practice was "unlawfull."

Nor could they agree with Chauncy's contention that it was quite wrong to celebrate the Lord's Supper at the Sabbath morning service. Obviously, said he, the proper time to serve supper is in the evening.

dispute ye pointe with him publickly—as Mr. Ralfe Partridge, of Duxberie, who did it sundrie times, very ablie and sufficiently— as allso, some other ministers within this governmente.

But he was not satisfied.

So ye church sent to many other churches to crave their help and advise in this matter and, with his will & consente, sent them his arguments written under his owne hand.

They sente them to ye church at Boston in ye Bay of Massachusetts, to be communicated with other churches there. Also, they sent the same to ye churches of Conightecutt and New-Haven, with sundrie others, and received very able & sufficient answers, as they conceived, from them and their larned ministers, who all concluded against him.

But himselfe was not satisfied therewith. Their answers are too large here to relate.

They conceived ye church had done what was meete in ye thing. So Mr. Chansey, having been ye most parte of 3 years here, removed himselfe to Scituate, where he [was] a minister to ye church there.

WINTHROP'S JOURNAL Mr. Chancey of Scituate persevered in his opinion of dipping in baptism and practised accordingly—first, upon two of his own, which being in very cold weather, one of them swooned away.*

Another, having a child about three years old, feared it would be frightened (as others had been—and one caught hold of Mr. Chancey and had near pulled him into the water), she brought her child to Boston, with letters testimonial from Mr. Chancey, and had it baptized there [by "sprinkling"].

9. Able Gospel-Preachers

MORTON'S MEMORIAL In reference unto the three years last specified [1638-41], although I have no special Providence to take notice of, . . . save the continuance of

*Which proved at least one of the Pilgrims' points against "dipping."

God's mercy and goodness in the annual election of godly and able magistrates in the jurisdiction of Plimouth.

Yet notwithstanding, we are to take notice of the continued peace and plenty with which, not only these three years (restrictively considered), but also for many years together both before and after them, New England was so marvellously gratiated.

But that which is more, that about these times the Lord was pleased, of his great goodness, richly to accommodate and adorn the colony of Plimouth (as well as other colonies in New England) with a considerable number of godly and able Gospel-Preachers, who then being dispersed and disposed of to the several churches and congregations thereof, gave Light in a glorious and resplendent manner . . .

[Those at Duxbury] being united into one Intire body, they procured Reverend Mr. Ralph Partrich [Partridge] to be their Pastour. And Mr. William Leverich alsoe was with them att the same time and preached the word of God amongst them. But he stayed not longe amongst them ere he removed to Sandwich [on Cape Cod] and was teacher of the Church there a considerable time . . .

The Church of Marshfield . . . was begun and afterwards carried on by the healp and assistance (under God) of Mr. Edward Winslow, who att the first procured severall Welsh Gentlemen of good note thither, with Mr. Blinman, a Godly able minnester, who unanimously joyned together in holy fellowship —or att least, were in a likely way thereunto.

But some desentions fell amongst them, which cause a parting not longe after, and soe the hopes of a Godly societie, as to them, was frustrated. Not long after, those that went from Plymouth . . . keeping up a communion, it pleased the Lord to send unto them a faithfull and able preacher of the Gospell, Mr. Edward Buckley, who was chosen theire Pastour and officiated in that place very profittably divers years . . .

About that time or a little before that the Church at Duxburrow became a distinct body . . . , the towne of Scittuate began, and severall of the Church of Plymouth repaired thither and seated themselves there, att which time Mr. Timothy Hatherly came out of England with his family and seated himself there alsoe. And severall other Godly ones of other places, especially divers out of Kent, repaired thither.

These all joyned together and became a comfortable and exemplary Church of God, and the Lord sent unto them that preciouse servant of his, Mr. John Laythorp [Lothrop], who came to them out of great persecution. And he became theire Pastour, to which office he was indowed with a competent measure of Gifts and eminently indowed with a great measure of brokenes of hart and humillitie of sperrit. He was much honored of the most, as he well deserved.

After some time, a considerable parte of the Church went from Scittuate to Barnstable, and theire pastour forenamed with them, where they lived divers years in Gospell order and were very exemplary for the life of Grace and power of Godlynes . . .

XXVI

End of a Tedious Business

Fear not to make a faire & reasonable offer. Beleeve me, I
will never take any advantage to plead it against you . . .
— *James Sherley*

BRADFORD'S
HISTORY
In ye former year [1635], because they perceived by Mr. Winslow's later letters that no accounts would be sente, they resolved to keep ye
beaver and send no more till they had them [the accounts], or
came to some further agreemente.

At least, they would forbear till Mr. Winslow came over, that
by more full conferance with him they might better understand
what was meete to be done.

But when he came, though he brought no accounts, yet he
perswaded them to send ye beaver, & was confident upon ye
receite of that beaver & his letters, they should have accounts ye
nexte year.

And though they thought his grounds but weake that gave
him this hope & made him so confidente, yet, by his importunitie,
they yeelded and sente ye same . . .

1. New Complaints from Abroad and Confusion at Home

BRADFORD'S
HISTORY
And now this year [1636], by another ship,
sente another round parcell . . . And shortly
after (ye same year) was sent by another ship
(Mr. Langrume, master) in beaver 719 pounds' waight, and of
otter skins 199, of which Mr. Sherley writes thus:

[London]
Sept. 14, 1636

Your letters I have received, with 8 hoggsheads of beaver
. . . Blessed be God for ye safe coming of it. I have also seen
& accepted 3 bills of exchange,* &c.

But I must now acquainte you how the Lord's heavie hand is
upon this kingdom in many places, but cheefly in this cittie, with
his judgmente of ye plague, . . . so as here is no trading, carriers
from most places put downe, nor no receiving of money, though
long due . . .

I am perswaded if I should offer to sell ye beaver at 8s per
pound, it would not yeeld money . . .

Before I accepted ye bills, I acquainted Mr. Beachamp & Mr.
Andrews with them, & how there could be no money made nor
received, and that it would be a great discredite to you—which
never yet had any [bills of exchange] turned back—and a shame
to us, having 1,800 pounds of beaver lying by us, and more
owing than ye bills come to, &c.

But all was nothing. Neither of them both will put to a finger
to help . . .

Here is the miserablest time that, I thinke, hath been known
in many ages . . . Ye Lord in mercie looke upon us . . .

Your loving freind,
James Sherley

This was all ye answer they had from Mr. Sherley, by which
Mr. Winslow saw his hops failed him. So they now resolved to
send no more beaver in that way . . .

But now came over letters from Mr. Andrews & Mr. Beachamp full of complaints, that they marveled that nothing was
sent over by which any of their monies should be payed in.

For it did appear by ye accounte sente in anno 1631 that they
were, each of them, out aboute £1,100 [$55,000] apiece, and all
this while had not received one penie towards ye same, . . .

*A Dutch ship had put into Plymouth, and the Undertakers had bought from
it trading commodities worth £500, paying for them by drawing bills of exchange on Sherley.

and blamed them here very much that all was sent to Mr. Sherley, & none to them.

They marvelled much at this, for they conceived that much of their monies had been paid in, & that yearly each of them had received a proportionable quantity out of ye large returnes sent home.

For they had sente home, since that accounte was received in anno 1631 (in which all & more than all their debts, with that year's supply, was charged upon them), these sums following* . . .

All these sumes were safly received & well sold, . . . the coat beaver usually at 20s per pound, and some at 24s; the skins at 15s & sometimes 16s . . .

It was conceived that ye former parcells of beaver came to little less than £10,000 sterling, and ye otter skins would pay all ye charge . . .

When ye former accounte was passed, all their debts (those of *White Angelle* & *Frendship* included) came but to £4,770.

And they could not estimate that all ye supplies since sent them, & bills payed for them, could come to above £2,000.

So as they conceived their debts had been payed, with advantage or interest.

But it may be objected, how comes it that they could not as well exactly sett downe their receits as their returnes, but thus estimate it.

I answer, 2 things were ye cause of it.

The first & principall was that ye new accountante [Josiah Winslow], which they in England would needs presse upon them, did wholly faile them & could never give them any accounte. But trusting to his memorie & loose papers, let things run into such confusion that neither he, nor any with him, could bring things to rights.

But being often called upon to perfecte his accounts, he desired to have such a time, and such a time, of leasure, and he

*Between November 1631 and late June 1636, as Bradford here listed the shipments, the total came to 12,530 pounds of beaver and 1,156 otter pelts.

would doe it. In ye interim, he fell into a great sicknes. And in conclusion, it fell out he could make no accounte at all . . .

They writ back to Mr. Andrews & Mr. Beachamp and told them they marveled they should write they had sent nothing home since ye last accounts, for they had sente a great deale . . . What they had sente was to them all, and to themselves as well as Mr. Sherley.

And if they did not looke after it, it was their owne falts . . .

They had now letters againe [in 1637] out of England from Mr. Andrews & Mr. Beachamp, that Mr. Sherley neither had nor would pay them any money, or give them any accounte . . .

Mr. Sherley's letters were to this purpose: that as they had left him in ye paiment of ye former bills, so he told them he would leave them in this . . .

And he was as good as his word, for they could never gett peney from him, nor bring him to any accounte, though Mr. Beachamp sued him in ye Chancerie.

But they, all of them, turned their complaints against them here, where there was least cause, and who had suffered most unjustly—first, from Mr. Allerton & them in being charged with so much of that which they never had, nor drunke for; and now, in paying all—& more than all (as they conceived)—and yet still thus more demanded, and that with many heavie charges.

They now discharged Mr. Sherley from his agencie and forbad him to buy or send over any more goods for them, and prest him to come to some end about these things.

2. More Rumblings, Shakings, and Signs of God

MORTON'S MEMORIAL   This year [1638] Mr. Thomas Prence was chosen Governour. Mr. William Bradford, Mr. Edward Winslow, Captain Miles Standish, Mr. John Alden, Mr. John Jenney, Mr. John Atwood, and Mr. John Brown were chosen Assistants in Government.

This year three men were executed for robbing and murther-

ing an Indian near Providence, which, besides the evidence that
came against them, they did in substance confess against themselves, and were condemned by legal tryal.

Some have thought it a great severity to hang three English
for one Indian. But the more considerate will easily satisfie themselves for the legality of it . . .

BRADFORD'S
HISTORY

This year, about ye 1 or 2 of June, was a great
& fearfull earthquake. It was in this place heard
before it was felt. It came with a rumbling noyse,
or low murmure, like unto remote thunder. It came from ye
norward & passed southward.

As ye noyse approached nearer, the earth begane to shake and
came at length with that violence as caused platters, dishes, &
such like things as stoode upon shelves to clatter & fall downe.
Yea, persons were afraid of ye houses themselves.

It so fell out that, at ye same time, diverse of ye cheefe of
this towne were mett together at one house conferring with
some of their freinds that were upon their removall from ye
place (as if ye Lord would hereby show ye signes of his displeasure in their shaking a-peeces, & removalls one from another).

However, it was very terrible for ye time. And as ye men
were set talking in ye house, some women & others were without ye dores, and ye earth shooke with that violence as they
could not stand without catching hold of ye posts and pales that
stood next them. But ye violence lasted not long.

And about halfe an hower, or less, came another noyse &
shaking, but neither so loud nor strong as ye former, but quickly
passed over, and so it ceased.

It was not only on ye seacoast. But ye Indeans felt it within
land, and some ships that were upon ye coast were shaken by it.

So powerfull is ye mighty hand of ye Lord as to make both
the earth & sea to shake, and the mountains to tremble before
him, when he pleases. And who can stay his hand?

It was observed that ye sommers were not so hotte & seasonable for ye ripening of corne & other fruits as formerly—but

more cold & moyst, & subjecte to erly & untimely frosts, by which, many times, much Indean corne came not to maturitie.

But whether this was any cause, I leave it to naturallists to judge.

MORTON'S
MEMORIAL* . . . Let us take notice that Writers have rendred the cause of Earthquakes to be, *That when it happeneth that Air and windy Spirits and Exhalations are shut up in the Caverns of the Earth, or have such passage as is too narrow for them, they then striving to break their prisons shake the Earth and make it tremble.*

They speak likewise of the several kindes of them: as first, When the whole force of the Wind driveth to one place, there being no contrary motion to let or hinder it. Many Hills and Buildings have been rushed down by this kinde of Earthquake, especially when the Wind causing it was strong. For if it be a feeble Wind, it only looseneth or unfasteneth Foundations. If less feeble, then, without further harm the Earth only shakes, like one sick of an Ague.

Secondly, The second kinde is a swelling of the Earth, the which, when the Wind is broken out of its prison, the Earth returns to its place again.

Thirdly, . . .

These particulars are treated of at large by approved Authors, and here only hinted, to the intent that we may take notice of the special Providence of God to New England in this behalf, that we have not as yet felt the misery of the worst of the kindes of Earthquakes forenamed, nor swallowed up in them.

But those we have been sensible of, have been rather gentle Warnings unto us to shake us out of our earthly-mindedness, spiritual security, and other sins, lest the Lord do come against us with Judgements of this kinde in the sorest and worst sort of them, or otherwise by removing the present blessing of Godly government from us.

*Morton, who was soon to be the colony's secretary, recorded this passage some years later, after an earthquake in 1662. No doubt his more informed brethren shared his views. This might be known as the indigestion theory of earthquakes.

3. Inflation

BRADFORD'S
HISTORY They received this year [1638] more letters from England, full of renewed complaints. . .

It pleased God, in these times, so to blesse ye cuntry with such access & confluance of people into it as it was thereby much inriched, and cattle of all kinds stood at a high rate for diverce years together.

Kine were sold at £20, and some at £25 apiece—yea, sometimes at £28 [$1,400]; a cow calfe, usually at £10; a milch goate, at £3 & some at £4; and female kids, at 30s and often at 40s apiece.

By which means, ye anciente planters, which had any stock, begane to growe in their estates. Corne also wente at a round rate—viz., 6s a bushell.

So as other trading begane to be neglected, and the old partners (having now forbidden Mr. Sherley to send them any more goods) broke off their trade at Kenebeck and, as things stood, would follow it no longer.

But some of them (with others they joyned with), being loath it should be lost by discontinuance, agreed with ye company for it and gave them aboute ye 6th parte of their gaines for it.*

With ye first fruits of which they builte a house for a prison . . .

It is curious that the Pilgrims chose to use their gains to build a prison and not a meetinghouse. They were still holding services in the old oak bastion on Fort Hill, as they would continue to do for more than ten years.

But the prison structure and the institution itself, as later re-

---

*Bradford was one of these who leased the trading post at Cushenoc. Trade there was declining and in 1661 the Kennebec patent was sold for £400 to four Boston men. One of these was John Winslow, Edward's second brother, who had abandoned Plymouth some time before, having married Mary Chilton of the *Mayflower* group—the girl who, by some accounts, was the first of the Pilgrims to set foot on Plymouth Rock. These Winslows had ten children.

marked by a historian of the town, a native son, gave Plymouth an air of "permanency" that it had lacked before.

4. Invitation to London Declined

MORTON'S
MEMORIAL
This year [1639] Mr. William Bradford was chosen Governour of Plimouth [and with the exception of 1644, when Winslow was chosen, continued to serve down to his death almost twenty years later, in 1657] . . .

This year Harvard College was erected at Cambridge, in New England* . . .

BRADFORD'S
HISTORY
In these two years [1639–40] they had sundry letters out of England to send one over to end the bussines and accounte with Mr. Sherley, who now professed he could not make up his accounts without ye help of some from hence, espetially Mr. Winslow's.

They had serious thought of it, and ye most parte of ye partners here thought it best to send.

But they had formerly written such bitter and threatening letters as Mr. Winslow was neither willing to goe, nor that any other of ye partners should.

For he was perswaded if any of them wente, they should be arrested, and an action of such a summe layed upon them as

---

*Four years earlier, in 1635, Plymouth had acquired its first school—a small private school taught by Bridget, widow of Deacon-Doctor Fuller. It was not until 1663 that the General Court concerned itself with education, recommending that a schoolmaster be hired in every Old Colony town. Nothing happened until seven years later, when the Cape Cod fishery was leased to provide a meager annual subsidy of not more than £5 ($250) for each school. Though not free, these schools were open to all, at low tuition.

Plymouth's opened in 1671 but soon closed because of quarrels about the curriculum. After almost twenty years, another schoolmaster was hired in 1699, and it was about time, to judge from the Town Fathers' decree in setting rates:

"Every scollar that Coms to wrigh or syfer or to lern latten, shall paye 3 pence pr. weke; if to Read onlie, then to pay 3 half pence per weke."

By public subscription, Plymouth built its first schoolhouse six years later, in 1705. By law, schoolmasters were to be paid each year "at least £12 [$600] in current merchantable pay, to be raised by rate on all the inhabitants of the towne."

they should not procure baele, but must lye in prison, and then they would bring them to what they liste.

Or otherwise, they might be brought into trouble by ye archbishop's means, as ye times then stood . . .

Winslow did not wish to go to jail again at Archbishop Laud's orders, as he had a few years back, and the times were dangerous.

England was teetering on the edge of revolution as Charles I more and more arbitrarily pushed Stuart pretensions to absolutism framed by his father, King James. Neither of them had any use for Parliament—least of all for the time-honored rights and privileges of the House of Commons. Both were inflexibly set against any reform, either in Church or State. Leaders of the opposition were jailed without warrant and without cause, merely at the royal caprice.

There had been no meeting of Parliament for ten years now, not since early 1629, when the King had commanded it to adjourn. By established constitutional procedure, it was Parliament that voted money and levied taxes. Refusing to summon Parliament for that or any other purpose, Charles had been living on forced loans, ship money and other exactions, heavy fines for real or alleged offenses, outrageous seizures of property, and the sale of public offices and monopolistic rights.

At the same time, urged on by the King, who was suspected of leaning toward Romanism through the influence of his French wife, Archbishop Laud had been tyrannically enforcing the strictest conformity in religious matters, taking higher and higher ground, striking out at the Puritans and other dissenters on every hand. The only reason he had not yet used the Commission for Regulating Plantations to enforce conformity in New England was that he and his royal master were too occupied with problems at home.

Besides, their experience in trying to impose Anglican episcopacy upon the stiff-necked Presbyterian Scots had given them pause. For the purpose, they had drawn up a new prayer book with decidedly Romish trimmings, having already ordered the Scottish clergy to don white surplices and cast away their black Genevan gowns.

The first service under the new dispensation was held at St.

Giles', Edinburgh, on July 23, 1637, a Sunday, with many high dignitaries attending. The Dean of St. Giles' had scarcely opened the service when a devout parishioner, one Jenny Geddes, stood up and tossed a stool at his head, narrowly missing the miter of the Bishop of Edinburgh. There was a tremendous commotion and a great crash of glass as sticks and stones came flying through the windows, thrown by the angry crowd outside.

The hostilities that began here on this "Stony Sabbath" soon spread and set in motion a chain of events that ultimately dragged both Laud and Charles to the block.

But in 1639 they were still riding high, and Winslow had good reason to fear their heavy hand. When the Pilgrims consulted with John Winthrop about sending someone, he advised against it.

5. Break in the Stock Market

BRADFORD'S HISTORY   Yet that their equall & honest minds might appeare to all men, they made them this tender:
       To referr ye case to some gentlemen and marchants in ye Bay of ye Massachusetts, such as they should chuse and were well knowne unto themselves . . .

But this did not please them, but they were offended at it—without any great reason, for ought I know . . . So this came to nothing.

And afterward, Mr. Sherley writ that if Mr. Winslow would meet him in France, ye Low Countries, or Scotland, let ye place be knowne and he come to him there.

But in regard of ye troubles that now begane to arise in our owne nation, and other reasons, this did not come to any effecte.

That which made them so desirous to bring things to an end was, partly, to stop ye clamours and aspertions raised & cast upon them hereaboute,* though they conceived themselves to sustaine

---

*Saying that he planned to give a large part of the money collected for the relief of the poor in the Bay colony, Richard Andrews had assigned his interests to John Winthrop, so that Winthrop and other Massachusetts Saints now joined the chorus of those baying at the Plymouth Undertakers to pay their "debts."

the greatest wrong and had most cause of complainte; and partly, because they feared ye fall of cattle, in which most parte of their estates lay.

And this was not a vaine feare, for they fell indeede before they came to a conclusion.

And that so suddenly as a cowe that but a month before was worth £20 and would have so passed in any paymente, fell now to £5 and would yeeld no more. And a goate, that wente at £3 or 50s, would now yeeld but 8s or 10s at most.

All men feared a fall of cattle. But it was thought it would come by degrees, and not from ye highest pitch at once to ye lowest, as it did, which was greatly to ye damage of many and ye undoing of some.

Another reason was: they, many of them, grew aged (and indeed, a rare thing it was that so many partners should live all together so many years as these did) and saw many changes were like to befall. So as they were loath to leave these intanglments upon their children and posteritie, who might be driven to remove places as they had done—yea, themselves might doe it yet before they dyed.

WINTHROP'S
JOURNAL
[June 2, 1641] The parliament of England, setting upon a general reformation both of Church and State, the Earl of Strafford being beheaded, and the archbishop (our great enemy) and many others of the great officers and judges, bishops and others, imprisoned and called to account, this caused all men to stay in England in expectation of a new world.*

*Finally at the end of his rope, Charles had been forced to summon Parliament, which, in April 1640, met for the first time in eleven years. But since it insisted upon the redress of grievances before it granted any money, it was quickly dissolved.

Charles again took to his old oppressive course. But with the Scots in the field against him in the second Bishops' War, he had to give way a few months later, summoning what became renowned as the Long Parliament.

The Long Parliament moved quickly to change the entire complexion of things. It impeached the King's chief minister, Thomas Wentworth, Earl of Strafford. It threw Archbishop Laud into the Tower of London. It abolished the dread Court of High Commission, the Star Chamber, all other extra-legal courts, and extra parliamentary taxation. It released those imprisoned for politi-

So as few coming to us, all foreign commodities grew scarce, and our own of no price.

Corn would buy nothing. A cow which cost last year £20 might now be bought for £4 or £5, etc. And many gone out of the country, so as no man could pay his debts. Nor the merchants make return into England for their commodities, which occasioned many there to speak evil of us . . .

They thought fit also to send some chosen men into England to congratulate the happy success there, and to satisfy our creditors of the true cause why we could not make so current payment now as in former years we had done, and to be ready to make use of any opportunity God should offer for the good of the country here.

As also, to give any advice, as it should be required, for the settling the right form of church disciple there . . . The men chosen were Mr. Hugh Peter, pastor of the church in Salem; Mr. Thomas Welde, pastor of the church in Roxbury, and Mr. William Hibbins, of Boston* . . .

6. Sherley's Compromise Proposal

BRADFORD'S HISTORY   Mr. Sherley, being wearie of this controversie and desirous of an end (as well as themselves), writ to Mr. John Atwood and Mr. William Collier, 2 of ye inhabitants of this place and of his spetiall aquaintance,† and

cal and religious reasons. It suppressed that bugbear of the Puritans and all the Saints, the Book of Sports, which allowed youngsters to play, and oldsters to game and gambol on the Sabbath, and even to frisk about the Maypole on occasion.

*A number of prominent men returned to England at this time, especially from Massachusetts and Connecticut, and many of them rose to prominence in the parliamentary cause and later under Cromwell.[1]

†As noted before, William Collier, brewer of London and one of the adventurers, had come with his family to settle in the colony in 1633. He was an assistant governor at this time, as he had been before and would be almost continuously down to 1665. His daughter Sarah had married Love Brewster. Another daughter, Mary, was the second wife of Assistant Governor Thomas Prence. Still another daughter, Elizabeth, had married Bradford's stepson,

'desired them to be a means to bring this bussines to an end . . .
And he writ to themselves allso to that end . . .

Clapham
May 18, 1641

Sir,

My love remembered, &c. . . .

If you desire an end, as you seeme to doe, there is (as I conceive) but 2 wayes: that is, to parfecte all accounts, from ye first to ye last, &c. . . . I fear you can never make a perfecte accounte on all your petty viages, out & home, too & againe, &c.

So then ye second way must be by bidding, or compounding. And this way, first or last, we must fall upon, &c.

If we must warr at law for it, do not you expecte from me, neither will I from you, but to cleave ye hair. And then, I dare say, ye lawyers will be most gainers, &c.

Thus let us set to ye worke—one way or other—and end, that I may not allways suffer in my name & estate. And you are not free.

Nay, ye gospell suffers by your delaying and causeth ye professors of it to be hardly spoken of, that you, being many & now able, should combine & joyne togeather to oppress & burden me, &c.

Fear not to make a faire & reasonable offer. Beleeve me, I will never take any advantage to plead it against you, or to wrong you . . . Let each give way a little that we may meete, &c. . . .

Now, blessed be God, ye times be much changed here. I hope to see many of you returne to your native countrie againe and have such freedome & libertie as ye word of God prescribes.

Our bishops were never so near a downfall as now. God hath

Constant Southworth, also frequently an assistant governor in later years. Collier was the richest man in the colony.

Wealthy and also of London, John Atwood was "a godly man, singularly endowed with the grace of Patience," an endowment that would stand him in good stead in this tedious business.

miraculously confounded them and turned all their popish &
Machavillian plots & projects on their owne heads, &c. . . .
Be you and all yours kindly saluted, &c. So I ever rest,

Your loving friend,

James Sherley

Just six days before Sherley had penned this letter, in a dramatic
scene that he may have witnessed, the Earl of Strafford, cowardly
abandoned by the King after years of faithful service, was led to
his execution on Tower Hill. He had written Laud to ask for his
final benediction.

As the Earl was led past the Tower of London, the former
Archbishop came to the window of his cell and blessed him from
afar, and then fainted, probably foreseeing that he would travel
this road to the headsman's axe, as he did four years later.

Strafford's execution and the imprisonment of "Thorough"
Laud shook the kingdom to its foundations. Formal hostilities in
the Great Rebellion had not yet begun. But they would soon, in
the summer of the next year, when Charles rode into Notting-
ham, not far from Scrooby, and raised the royal standard, calling
upon all loyal subjects to rally round and suppress all heretics and
malcontents.

7. Ghost of the *White Angel* Laid at Last

BRADFORD'S
HISTORY
Being thus by [Sherley's] letter and allso by Mr.
Atwood's & Mr. Collier's mediation urged to bring
these things to an end (and ye continuall clamors
from ye rest), and by none more urged than by their owne
desires, they tooke this course (because many scandals had been
raised upon them).

They appoynted these 2 men before mentioned to meet on a
certaine day and called some other freinds on both sides—and
Mr. Freeman, brother-in-law of Mr. Beachamp.*

---

*Edmund Freeman had arrived in 1635, settling in the Bay colony. Two years
later, he came to Plymouth and soon moved on to found Sandwich, on Cape
Cod, sharing his partners' desire "to worship God and make some money."

And having drawne up a collection of all ye remains of ye stock in whatsoever it was, as housing, boats, bark, and all implements belonging to ye same, . . . with ye remaines of all commodities, as beads, knives, hatchetts, cloth, or anything else, . . . with all debts, as well those that were desperate as others more hopefull, . . . they found ye sume in all to arise (as ye things were valued) to aboute £1,400 [$70,000].

And they, all of them, tooke a voluntary but a sollem oath in ye presence one of another and of all their freinds . . . that this was all that any of them knew of or could remember. And Josias Winslow did ye like for his parte.

But ye truth is, they wronged themselves much in ye valuation. For they reckoned some cattle as they were taken of Mr. Allerton—as for instance, a cowe in ye hands of one cost £25, and so she was valued in this accounte.

But when she came to be passed in parte of paymente after ye agreemente, she would be accepted but at £4 15s.

Also, being tender of their oaths, they brought in all they knew owing to the stock. But they had not make ye like diligente search what ye stocke might owe to any, so as many scattering debts fell upon [them] afterwards, more than now they knew of.

Upon this, they drew certaine articles of agreemente betweene Mr. Atwood, on Mr. Sherley's behalfe, and themselves.

In payment of all their debts, including charges for the voyages of the *Friendship* and *White Angel*, "made or pretended," the Plymouth Undertakers agreed to pay Sherley, Andrews, and Beauchamp the sum of £1,200 ($60,000), to be paid £400 down and the remainder at the rate of £200 a year, for four years.

Sherley and Andrews accepted this arrangement and sent their releases. But Beauchamp demanded £400 more. His London partners advised those at Plymouth not to pay him. Beauchamp's account should not be accepted, declared Andrews, except "on oath in chancerie." The aging Sherley wrote in one of his last letters that they should pay him no more than £100—and he was cheating them at that.

But as always, the Plymouth partners paid. In 1645, to satisfy

Beauchamp's claims, they pledged their estates as security. And when the mess brought on by Allerton was finally settled a few years later, Bradford had to sell a large farm, Standish and Alden 300 acres, while Winslow and Prence had to sell their houses.

XXVII

Moral Matters

And thus, by one means or other, in 20 years' time it is a question whether ye greater part be not growne ye worser.

—*William Bradford*

MORTON'S
MEMORIAL
About these times [the early 1640s] the Lord was pleased, of his great goodness, richly to accommodate and adorn the colony of Plimouth (as well as other colonies in New England) with a considerable number of godly and able Gospel-Preachers, who then being dispersed and disposed of to the several churches and congregations thereof, gave Light in a glorious and resplendent manner as burning and shining Lights.

Which mercy and transcendent favour, had not Sin and Satan's envy interposed, might have rendered them greatly happy and prosperous, it being observed that where Gospel-dispensation flourisheth, there Prosperity in other respects may usually be expected.

1. Sin and Satan's Envy

BRADFORD'S
HISTORY
Marvilous it may be to see and consider how some kind of wickednes did grow & breake forth here in a land where the same was so much witnessed against, and so narrowly looked unto, & severely punished when it was knowne—as in no place more, or so much, that I have known or heard of—insomuch as they have been

somewhat censured, even by moderate and good men, for their severitie in punishments.

And yet all this could not suppress ye breaking out of sundrie notorious sins—as this year [1642], besides others, gives us too many sad presidents and instances—espetially drunkennes and unclainnes.

Not only incontinencie betweene persons unmarried, for which many, both men & women, have been punished sharply enough, but some married persons allso.*

But that which is worse, even sodomie and bugerie (things fearful to name) have broak forth in this land, oftener than once.

I say it may be justly marveled at and cause us to fear & tremble at the consideration of our corrupte natures, which are so hardly bridled, subdued, & mortified—nay, cannot by any other means but ye powerfull worke & grace of God's spirite.

But (besides this) one reason may be, that ye Divell may carrie a greater spite against the churches of Christ, and ye gospell here, by how much ye more they indeavour to preserve holynes and puritie amongst themselves, and strictly punisheth the contrary when it ariseth either in church or commonewealth, that he might cast a blemishe & staine upon them in ye eyes of ye world who use to be rash in judgmente.

I would rather thinke thus than that Satane hath more power

*Under the Plymouth code, adultery was a capital offense. But in all the history of the colony it was never punished as such, though it was in Massachusetts and Connecticut.

The penalty in the Old Colony was severe enough, however. Convicted of seducing an Indian, "Goodwife" Mendame of Duxbury was sentenced "to be whipt at a cart's tayle through the town's streets, and to weare a badge with the capital letters AD cut in cloth upon her left sleeve, . . . and if shee shall be found without it abroad, then to be burned in the face with a hott iron."

The Pilgrims believed that a child was born exactly nine months after conception, and woe to any young married couple that had offspring more than a day or two before that time. As a consequence, many an innocent young wife was placed in the stocks, with her anguished husband beside her, for having a child "before ye natural time of women after marriage." Later, the Pilgrims learned something of the facts of life and adopted the "seven months' rule," but not before hundreds of innocents had suffered public shame and disgrace.

in these heathen lands, as some have thought, than in more Christian nations—espetially, over God's servants in them.

2. Another reason may be, that it may be in this case, as it is with waters when their streames are stopped or dammed up, when they gett passage they flow with more violence, and make more noys and disturbance, than when they are suffered to run quietly in their owne channels.

So wickednes being here more strictly stopped by strict laws, and ye same more nearly looked unto, so as it cannot run in a commone road of liberty as it would and is inclined, it searches everywhere and at last breaks out where it getts vente.

3. A third reason may be, here (as I am verily perswaded) is not more evills in this kind, nor nothing near so many by proportion, as in other places. But they are here more discovered and seen, and made publick by due serch, inquisition, and due punishment.

For ye churches looke narrowly to their members, and ye magistrates [watch] over all more strictly than in other places.

Besides, here the people are but few in comparison of other places, which are full & populous, [where people] lye hid, as it were, in a wood or thickett. And many horrible evills by that means are never seen nor knowne.

Whereas here they are, as it were, brought into ye light and set in ye plaine feeld—or rather, on a hill, made conspcious to ye view of all.

2. Inquiries from Boston

BRADFORD'S
HISTORY

But to proceed. There came a letter from ye Governor in ye Bay to them here touching matters of ye forementioned nature . . .

Boston
[March 28, 1642]

Sir:

Having an opportunity to signifie ye desires of our Generall Court in two things of spetiall importance, I willingly take this

occasion to imparte them to you, that you may imparte them
to ye rest of your magistrates, and also to your Elders, for counsell, and give us your advise in them.

The first is concerning heinous offences in point of uncleannes. The perticuler cases, with ye circomstances, and ye questions thereupon, you have here inclosed.

The 2nd thing is concerning ye Ilanders at Aquidnett, seeing the cheefest of them are gone from us in offences either to
churches or commonewealth, or both* . . .

Neither is it only in a faction that they are devided from us.
But in very deed they rend themselves from all ye true churches
of Christ and, many of them, from all ye powers of magestracie.

We have had some experience hereof by some of their un-
derworkers, or emissaries, who have lately come amongst us
and have made publick defiance against magistracie, ministrie,
churches, & church covenants, &c., as antichristian—secretly,
also sowing ye seeds of Familisme and Anabaptistrie, to ye infection of some and danger to others.

So that we are not willing to joyne with them in any league
or confederacie at all,† but rather that you would consider &
advise with us how we may avoyd them and keep ours from
being infected by them.

Another thing I should mention to you. For ye maintenance
of ye trade for beaver, if there be not a company to order it in

---

*These were Anne Hutchinson and her Familist followers. Five years before,
in 1637, Mrs. Hutchinson had been expelled from Massachusetts "for ignorance
of Christ" on eighty-two counts!—"some heretical, some blasphemous, some
erroneous, and all incongruous," according to Cotton Mather.

Going to Narragansett Bay and settling on the island of Aquidneck—or
Rhode Island, as it came to be called—they wrote Plymouth to inquire if they
could remain there, thinking that the island might lie within the Plymouth
grant.

The Pilgrims raised no objections, "considering they were their countrymen
and fellow subjects that were thus distressed and destitute of habitation, although they held their errors in as great dislike as those from whence they
came."

†This refers to discussions that eventuated in a New England confederacy the
next year. Ever since the end of the Pequot War, in 1637, Connecticut and
New Haven, feeling themselves dangerously exposed on the wild western
frontier, had been urging a closer union among the Saints.

every jurisdiction among ye English, which companies should agree in generall of their ways in trade, I suppose that trade will be overthrowne, and ye Indeans will abuse us . . .

Thus not further to trouble you, I rest, with my loving rememebrance to yourselfe, &c.,

Your loving friend,
Richard Bellingham

The note inclosed follows on ye other side.*
[To Bellingham's letter, Bradford replied:]

Worthy & beloved Sir:

Your letter (with ye questions inclosed) I have communicated with our Assistants, and we have referred ye answer of them to such Reverend Elders as are amongst us, some of whose answers thereto we have sent here inclosed . . .

For ourselves (you know our breedings & abillities), we rather desire light from yourselves & others whom God hath better inabled, than to presume to give our judgments in cases so difficulte and of so high a nature.†

Yet under correction and submissison to better judgments, we propose this one thing to your prudent considerations.

As it seems to us in ye case even of willfull murder, that though a man did smite or wound another with a full purpose or desire to kill him (which is murder in a high degree before God), yet if he did not dye, the magistrate was not to take away ye other's life.‡

So by proportion in other grosse & foule sins, though high attempts & near approaches to ye same be made, and such as in

---

*But the note describing the "heinous offences" is not on the other side, or elsewhere in the manuscript. If put in, it was taken out by someone before 1728, when the manuscript came into the possession of the Reverend Thomas Prince, who noted that folio page 243, on which it might have been written, was missing. The cases involved sodomy and the rape of two small girls, as set forth in Winthrop's Journal for 1641.

†Bradford was being unnecessarily humble and almost apologetic here. When it came to good sense and good judgment and a feel for common humanity, the Pilgrims, whatever their breeding and formal accomplishments, were always far "better inabled" than the men of the Bay.

‡"Exod: 21. 22. Deu: 19. 11. Num: 35. 16, 18."—Bradford's note.

the sight & account of God may be as ill as ye accomplishmente of ye foulest acts of that sin, yet we doute whether it may be safe for ye magistrate to proceed to death. We thinke, upon ye former grounds, rather he may not.

As for instance in ye case of adulterie (if it be admitted that it is to be punished with death, which to some of us is not cleare), if ye body be not actually defiled, then death is not to be inflicted. So in sodomic & beastialitie, if there be not pene-tration.

Yet we confesse foulnes of circomstances and frequencie in ye same doth make us remaine in ye darke and desire further light from you, or any, as God shall give.

As for ye 2nd thing, concerning ye Ilanders, we have no con-versing with them, nor desire to have, furder than necessitie or humanity may require.

And as for trade, we have as farr as we could ever therein held an orderly course, & have been sorry to see ye spoyle thereof by others, and fear it will be hardly recovered.

But in these or any other things which may concerne ye com-mone good, we shall be willing to advise & concure with you in what we may.

Thus, with my love remembered to yourselfe and ye reste of our worthy friends, your Assistants, I take leave & rest,

Your loving friend,

W. B.

Plim: 17, 3 month, 1642.*

3. Mosaic Law

BRADFORD'S
HISTORY
Now follows ye ministers' answers. And first, Mr. Reyner's.

Qest: What sodmiticall acts are to be punished

---

*The Pilgrims began to adopt the Bay's affectation of dropping the "pagan" names of the months, indicating them by numbers instead. Thus, the date of Bradford's letter is May 17, 1642, for the English began the new year in March, as noted before.

with death, and what very facte (ipso facto) is worthy of death, or if ye fact itselfe be not capitall, what circomstances concurring may make it capitall? . . .

2. Quest: How farr a magistrate may extracte a confession from a delinquente to accuse himselfe of a capitall crime, seeing *Nemo tenetur prodere seipsum?** . . .

Q. 3. In what cases of capitall crimes one witnes, with other circomstances, shall be sufficiente to convince? Or is there no conviction without 2 witnesses?

In brief depositions, Teacher John Reyner of Plymouth and Pastor Ralph Partridge of Duxbury substantially agreed on all three points.

First, sodomy, rape, and other unnatural sins were capital crimes to be punished with death, as prescribed by the Mosaic Law.

Second, the use of torture and other means to extract a confession "is contrary to ye nature of vindictive justice, . . . and it will therefore . . . be ye provocking and forcing of wrath, compared to ye wringing of ye nose, Pro. 30. 33., which is as well forbidden ye fathers of ye countrie as of ye family, Ephe. 6. 4., as produsing many sad & dangerous effects."

Third, in trying a man for his life, one witness was not sufficient to convict him. There could be "no safe proceedings unto judgmente without two witnesses, as Numb. 35. 30., Deut; 19. 15 . . ."

But from Scituate, from the "larned Mr. Channcy," came a stupendous document, an exhaustive treatise on "carnall copulation" in its every phase and form, running on page after page, each bristling with numerous citations on every point.

BRADFORD'S HISTORY . . . The answer unto [the first question] I will lay downe . . . in these following conclusions: 1. That ye judicials of Moyses, . . . grounded on ye law of nature, or ye decalogue, are immutable and perpetuall. See ye authors following [ten lines of them] . . . And more might be added. I forbear, for brevitie's sake, to set downe their very words . . .

*No one is required to incriminate himself.

2. That all sinnes mentioned in the question were punished
with death by ye judiciall law of Moyses, as adultry, Levit. 20.
10., Deut. 22. 22., Esech. 16. 38., John 8. 5., . . . So incest is
to be punished with death, Levit. 20. 11, 22. Beastiality likwise,
Lev. 20. 15, Exod. 22. 19. Rapes in like manner, Deut. 22. 25.
Sodomie in like sort, Levit. 18. 22 & 20, 13. And all presumptuous sins, Numb. 15. 30, 31., . . . as discovering of nakednes,
Levit. 18. 20., which is retegere pudenda, as parts per euphe-
mismum (saith Junius), or detegere ad cubandum (saith Willett) . . . That also is considerable, Deut. 25. 11, 12 . . .
Againe, some sinnes of this nature are simple, others compound,
. . . but when there is a mixture of diverce kinds of lust, . . .
this is capitall, double & triple. Againe . . . But I must hasten
to ye other questions.

2. Question ye second, upon ye pointe of examination, how
farr a magistrate may extracte a confession from a delinquente
to accuse himselfe in a capitall crime . . .

If it be mente of extracting by requiring an oath (ex officio,
as some call it) & that in capitall crimes, I fear it is not safe, nor
warranted by God's word . . .

But now, if ye question be mente of inflicting bodyly torments to extracte a confession from a mallefactor, I conceive
that in matters of highest consequence such as doe concerne ye
saftie or ruine of states or countries, magistrates may proceede
so farr to bodily torments as racks, hote-irons, &c. . . .

Question 3. In what cases of capitall crimes, one witness with
other circumstances shall be sufficiente to convicte, or is there
no conviction without 2 witnesses?

Deut. 19. 25. God hath given an express rule that in no case
one witness shall arise in judgmente, espetially not in capitall
cases. God would not put our lives into ye power of any one
tongue . . . But if a man witness against himselfe, his owne
testomony is sufficiente, as in ye case of ye Amalakite, 2. Sam.
1. 16 . . .

Lastly, I see no cause why in waighty matters, in defecte of
witnesses & other proofes, we may not have recourse to a lot,

as in ye case of Achan, Josu. 7. 16., which is a clearer way in such doubtfull cases (it being solemnly & religiously performed) than any other that I know* . . . But all this under correction . . .

Charles Channcy

4. A Very Sad Spectacle

BRADFORD'S
HISTORY
After ye time of ye writing of these things befell a very sadd accidente of the like foule nature in this governmente, this very year [1642], which I shall now relate.

There was a youth whose name was Thomas Granger. He was a servant to an honest man of Duxbery,† being about 16 or 17 years of age. (His father & mother lived at the same time at Scituate.)

He was this year detected of buggery (and indicted for ye same) with a mare, a cowe, two goats, five sheep, 2 calves, and a turkey.

Horrible it is to mention, but ye truth of ye historie requires it.

He was at first discovered by one that accidentally saw his lewd practise towards the mare (I forbear perticulers).

Being upon it examined and committed, in ye end he not only confest ye fact with that beast at that time, but sundrie times before, and at severall times with all ye rest of ye forenamed in his indictment.

And this, his free confession, was not only in private to ye magistrates (though at first he strived to deney it), but to sun-

*The Saints' objection to cards and all games of chance was less the "moral" one that these might lead to "idle courses," but rather, as Cotton Mather explained, that "lots, being mentioned in the sacred oracles of Scripture as used only in weighty cases and as an acknowledgment of God sitting in judgment, . . . cannot be made the tools and parts of our common sports without, at least, such an *appearance of evil* as is forbidden in the word of God."

"Seven come eleven," is one prayer no proper Saint ever offered lightly.

†Love Brewster, the Ruling Elder's second son. now in his thirties.

drie, both ministers & others—and afterwards, upon his indict-
mente, to ye whole court & jury, and confirmed at his execution.

And whereas some of ye sheep could not so well be knowne
by his description of them, others with them were brought before him, and he declared which were they, and which were
not.

And accordingly, he was cast by ye jury and condemned,
and after executed, about ye 8 of September, 1642.

A very sade spectackle it was. For first the mare, and then
ye cowe, and ye rest of ye lesser cattle, were kild before his
face, according to ye law, Levit: 20. 15. And then he himselfe
was executed.

The cattle were all cast into a great & large pitte that was
digged of purpose for them, and no use made of any part of
them . . .

5. Doubts about New Canaan

BRADFORD'S HISTORY But it may be demanded how it came to pass
that so many wicked persons and profane people
should so quickly come over into this land & mixe
themselves amongst them, seeing it was religious men that begane ye work, and they came for religion's sake?

I confess this may be marvelled at—at least, in time to come,
when the reasons thereof should not be knowne, and ye more
because here was so many hardships and wants mett withall. I
shall therefore indeavor to give some answer hereunto.

And first, according to that in ye gospell, it is ever to be remembered that where ye Lord begins to sow good seed, there
ye envious man [Satan] will endeavore to sow tares.

2. Men being come over into a wildernes in which much labour & servise was to be done aboute building & planting, &c.,
when they could not have such as they would, were glad to take
such as they could. And so, many untoward servants . . .
were thus brought over, both men & women kind, who, when

their times were expired, became families of themselves, which gave increase hereunto.

3. Another and a maine reason hereof was that men, finding so many godly disposed persons willing to come into these parts, some begane to make a trade of it, to transport passengers & their goods, and hired ships for that end. And then, to make up their fraight and advance their profite, cared not who ye per-sons were, so they had money to pay them.

And by these means, the cuntrie became pestered with many unworthy persons, who, being come over, crept into one place or other.

4. Againe, the Lord's blessing, usually following his people, as well in outward as spirituall things (though afflictions be mixed withall), doe make many to adhere to ye people of God, as many followed Christ for ye loaves' sake, John 6. 26. And a mixed multitude came into ye wildernes with ye people of God out of Egypt of old, Exod. 12. 38.

So allso, there were sente, by their freinds, some under hope that they would be made better; others, that they might be eased of such burthens, and they kept from shame at home that would necessarily follow their dissolute courses.

And thus, by one means or other, in 20 years' time it is a question whether ye greater part be not growne ye worser.

Bradford's contention that sin was introduced and mainly prac-ticed by the "mixt multitude" is not borne out by the records. But whatever the source, the aging governor was more and more dis-couraged.

A few years later, thumbing through the pages of his manu-script history, he came upon his transcription of a letter from Sherley, written more than twenty years before, early in 1624.

In that letter Sherley had described how the merchant adven-turers had almost broken up in angry quarrels. But that night, after much work on his part, he brought them together again and they had the lovingest and friendliest meeting that ever was, he said, "so I sent for a potle of wine (I would you could doe ye like)" . . .

Turning over the leaf of the manuscript, Bradford disconsolately remarked:

It is worthy to be observed how ye Lord doth change times & things.

For what is now more plentifull than wine? And that of ye best, coming from Malago, ye Cannaries, and other places, sundry ships lading in a year.

So as there is now more cause to complaine of ye excess and abuse of wine (through men's corruption), even to drunkennes, than of any defecte or wante of ye same.

Witnes this year 1646.

The good Lord lay not ye sins & unthankfullnes of men to their charge, in this perticuler.

6. Death of Brewster

BRADFORD'S HISTORY   I am to begine this year [1643] with that which was a matter of great saddnes and mourning unto them all.

Aboute ye 18 of Aprill dyed their Reverend Elder, and my dear & loving friend, Mr. William Brewster, a man that had done and suffered much for ye Lord Jesus and ye gospell's sake, and had bore his parte in weal and woe with this poore persecuted church above 36 years, in England, Holland, and in this wildernes, and done ye Lord & them faithfull service in his place & calling.

And notwithstanding ye many troubls and sorrows he passed through, the Lord upheld him to a great age. He was near fourskore years of age (if not all out) when he dyed.

He had this blessing added by ye Lord to all ye rest, to dye in his bed, in peace, amongst ye midst of his freinds, who mourned & wepte over him, and ministered what help & comforte they could unto him, and he againe recomforted them whilst he could.

His sicknes was not long. And till ye last day thereof, he did not wholly keepe his bed. His speech continued till somewhat more than halfe a day [before he died], & then failed him. And aboute 9 or 10 a clock that evening, he dyed without any pangs at all.

A few howers before, he drew his breath short. And some few minutes before his last, he drew his breath long, as a man fallen into a sound sleepe, without any pangs or gaspings, and so sweetly departed this life unto a better.

I would now demand of any, what was he ye worse for any former sufferings?

What doe I say, worse?

Nay, sure he was ye better, and they now added to his honour.

What though he wanted ye riches and pleasures of ye world in this life, and pompous monuments at his funerall?

Yet ye memoriall of ye just shall be blessed when ye name of ye wicked shall rott (with their marble monuments). Pro: 10. 7.

I should say something of his life, if to say a little were not worse than to be silent. But I cannot wholly forbear* . . .

After they were joyned togither in communion [at Scrooby], he was a spetiall stay & help unto them . . . He was cheefe of those that were taken at Boston, and suffered ye greatest loss, and of ye seven that were kept longst in prison, and, after, bound over to ye assises.

After he came into Holland, he suffered much hardship . . . But yet he ever bore his condition with much cherfullnes and contentation. Towards ye later parte of these 12 years spente in Holland, his outward condition was mended, and he lived well & plentifully . . .

---

*Here Bradford begins his long, beautiful, and very moving tribute to the gentle and knowing man who had virtually adopted him as a son so many years before. Parts of this tribute have already appeared at relevant points in the forward pages of this book—for instance, Brewster's career at Cambridge, at the Court, at Scrooby, and in Holland. The rest, with the repetition of a few paragraphs, is given here.

But now removing into this countrie, all these things were laid aside againe, and a new course of living must be framed unto. In which, he was no way unwilling to take his parte and to bear his burthen with ye rest, living many times without bread or corne many months togeather, having many times nothing but fish—and often wanting that also—and drunk nothing but water for many years togeather—yea, till within 5 or 6 years of his death.

And yet he lived (by ye blessing of God) in health till very old age. And besides that, he would labour with his hands in ye fields as long as he was able.

Yet when the church had no other minister, he taught twise every Saboth—and that both powerfully and profitably, to ye great contentment of ye hearers and their comfortable edification.

Yea, many were brought to God by his ministrie. He did more in this behalfe in a year than many doe . . . in all their lives.

For his personall abilities, he was qualified above many. He was wise and discreete and well spoken, having a grave & deliberate utterance, of a very cherfull spirite, very sociable & pleasante amongst his friends, of a humble and modest mind, of a peaceable disposition, under-vallewing himself & his owne abilities and sometimes over-valewing others', inoffencive and innocente in his life & conversation, which gained him ye love of those without, as well as those within.

Yet he would tell them plainely of their faults & evils, both publickly & privatly, but in such a manner as usually was well taken from him.

He was tender harted and compassionate of such as were in miserie . . . And none did more offend & displease him than such as would hautily and proudly carry & lift up themselves, being rise from nothing, and having little else in them to commend them but a few fine cloaths, or a little riches more than others.

In teaching, he was very moving & stirring of affections—also, very plaine & distincte in what he taught—by which means he became ye more profitable to ye hearers. He had a singuler good gift in prayer, both publick & private, in ripping up ye hart & conscience before God . . .

For ye governmente of ye church (which was most proper to his office), he was carefull to preserve good order in ye same and to preserve puritie, both in ye doctrine & communion of ye same, and to suppress any errour or contention that might begine to rise up amongst them.

And accordingly, God gave him good success to his indeavors herein all his days, and he saw ye fruite of his labors in that be-halfe. But I must break off, having only thus touched a few, as it were, heads of things.*

7. Not by Bread Alone

bradford's history I cannot but here take occasion not only to mention, but greatly to admire, ye marvelous providence of God that, notwithstanding ye many changes and hardships that these people wente through, and ye many enemies they had, and the difficulties they mette withal, that so many of them should live to very old age!

It was not only this reverend man's condition (for one swallow maks no summer, as they say), but many more of them did ye like, some dying aboute and before this time, and many still living who attained to 60 years of age, and to 65, diverse to 70 and above, and some near 80, as he did.

It must needs be more than ordinarie, and above naturall reason, that so it should be. For it is found in experience that change of aire, famine or unholsome foode, much drinking of water, sorrows & troubls, &c.—all of them are enemies to health, causes of many diseases, consumers of naturall vigoure and ye bodies of men, and shorteners of life.

*Here Bradford was not only paying tribute to his old friend and mentor. He was also drawing what, in his conception, was the portrait of a perfect Saint—one that all should emulate.

And yet of all these things they had a large parte, and suffered deeply in ye same.

They wente from England to Holland, where they found both worse air and dyet than that they came from. From thence (induring a long imprisonmente, as it were, in ye ships at sea), into New-England. And how it hath been with them here, hath allready beene showne. And what crosses, troubls, fears, wants, and sorrowes they had been lyable unto, is easie to conjecture.

So, as in some sorte, they may say with ye Apostle, 2. Cor: 11. 26, 27., they were *in journeyings often, in perils of water, in perills of robbers, in perills of their owne nation, in perils among ye heathen, in perills in ye wildernes, in perills in ye sea, in perills among false brethren, in wearines & painfullnes, in watching often, in hunger and thirst, in fasting often, in cold and nakednes.*

What was it then that upheld them?

It was God's vissitation that preserved their spirits . . . God, it seems, would have all men behold and observe such mercies and works of his providence as these towards his people, that they, in like cases, might be incouraged to depend upon God in their trials, & also blesse his name when they see his goodnes towards others.

Man lives not by bread only, Deut: 8. 3.

It is not by good & dainty fare, by peace & rest, and hart's ease, in injoying ye contentments and good things of this world only, that preserves health and prolongs life.

God, in such examples, would have ye world see & behold that he can doe without them. And if ye world will shut their eyes and take no notice thereof, yet he would have his people to see and consider it.

Daniell could be better liking with pulse* than others were with ye king's dainties.

Jacob, though he went from one nation to another people, and passed through famine, fear, & many afflictions, yet he lived till old age and dyed sweetly, & rested in ye Lord, as infinite

*Pulse is a mess, or porridge, of beans, peas, or other legumes.

others of God's servants have done, and still shall doe (through God's goodnes), notwithstanding all ye malice of their enemies.

When ye branch of ye wicked shall be cut off before his day, Job: 15. 32., *and ye bloody and deceitfull men shall not live out halfe their days.* Psa: 55. 23.

8. Another Ghost Appears

Not long after Brewster's death, who should suddenly appear in Plymouth but that "lord of misrule," Thomas Morton of Merry Mount, "starved out of England" by the wars there. The Pilgrims could not have been more surprised if Satan himself had come to mock them and deride them in their grief and many troubles.

The authorities did not know quite what to do with this "serpent," for Morton still had powerful friends at home. His patron, Sir Ferdinando Gorges, was one of the King's Men and Morton also made out that he had powerful Puritan friends as well and had come out as their agent.

Plymouth wrote John Winthrop about the problem, which concerned him too.

[Plymouth
September 11, 1643]

WINSLOW'S LETTER*

Concerning Morton, our Governor gave way that he should winter here, but begone as soon as winter breaks up. Captain Standish takes great offence thereat, especially as he is so near him at Duxbury and goeth sometimes a-fowling in his ground.

He cannot procure the least respect amongst our people, liveth meanly at 4s [$10] per week, and content to drink water so he may diet at that price.

But admit he hath protection, yet it were worth the while to deal with him till we see it. The truth is, I much question his pretended employment, for he hath here only showed the frame

*This letter appears in Series IV Mass. Hist. Soc. Collections, Vol. 6, p. 175.

of a Common-weale and some old sealed commissions, but no inside known.

As for Mr. Rigby, . . . he hath good hap to light on two of the arrantest known knaves that ever trod on New English shore to be his agents, east and west, as Cleaves and Morton* . . .

And for my part (who, if my heart deceive me not, can pass all the evil instrumentality he brought on me), would not have this serpent stay amongst us, who, out of doubt, in time will get strength to him if he be suffered, who promiseth large portions of land about New Haven, Narragansett, &c., to all that will go with him.

But he hath promise of but one person, who is old, weak, and decrepid, a very atheist and fit companion for him.

But, indeed, Morton is the odium of our people . . .

After a winter at Plymouth, during which Standish often threatened to shoot him, Morton is next reported late in June 1644, when Captain John Endecott informed Winthrop of the rumor that Morton had gone by sea to Gloucester, "hoping from thence to get a passage to the Eastward," down into Maine where, so report had it, there was a strong party of King's Men.

"I sent a warrant to Gloucester to apprehend him, if he be there," wrote Endecott. "It is most likelie that the Jesuites, or some that way disposed, have sent him over to doe us mischiefe, to raise up our enemies round about us, both English & Indean."

The Massachusetts authorities were itching to lay hands on Morton. But if he passed by way of Gloucester, he escaped them, for he is next seen in Rhode Island, as reported a month later by one of the magistrates there, William Coddington, a rather recent exile from Massachusetts, where he had vainly tried to block the expulsion of Anne Hutchinson and her followers for eighty-two "ignorances of Christ."

"For Morton," Coddington wrote Winthrop early in August, "he was insinuating who was for the King at his first coming to

*George Cleaves was another of Gorges' men. Alexander Rigby, for whom Cleaves and Morton claimed to be working, was a wealthy Puritan and a member of the Long Parliament. Rigby had interests in Maine and evidently toward the west also.

Portsmouth, and would report to such as he judged to be of his mind, he was glad to meet with so many Cavaliers . . . and he had lands to dispose of in each province, and from Cape Ann to Cape Cod was one* . . . and that he had wrong in the Bay to the value of £200, and made bitter compliants thereof.

"But Morton would let it rest till the Governor† came over to right him, and did insinuate he knew whose roast his spits and jacks turned."

A month later, somehow, perhaps while trying to slip through Massachusetts into Maine, Morton fell into the clutches of the Bay authorities and was hauled to Boston.

WINTHROP'S JOURNAL [September 9, 1644.] At the court of assistants, Thomas Morton was called forth presently, after the lecture, that the country might be satisfied of the justice of our proceeding against him.

There was laid to his charge his complaint against us at the Council Board, which he denied. Then we produced the copy of the bill exhibited by Sir Christopher Gardner, &c., wherein we were charged with treason, rebellion, etc., wherein he was named as party or witness. He denied that he had any hand in the information, only as a witness.

To convince him to be the principal party, it was showed:

1. That Gardner had no occasion to complain against us, for he was kindly used and dismissed in peace . . .

2. Morton had set forth a book against us,‡ and had threat-

*This would have embraced almost all of the Plymouth and Massachusetts patents.

†The Governor General, Sir Ferdinando Gorges.

‡Luckily for him, the authorities apparently did not have a copy of *New English Canaan* to present against him. John Endecott, notoriously violent and vindictive, was in the chair, being governor that year. And how he would have exploded at hearing publicly read those passages in which Morton had styled him "a great swelling fellow, of Littleworth, . . . the Cow-Keeper at Salem."

It was Endecott who, in 1635, had cut the red cross of St. George out of the royal ensign, saying that it smacked of popery. Not wishing to be quite so explicit, the Bay authorities found his act to be "rash and without discretion, taking upon him more authority than he had, and not seeking advice of the Court, etc.; uncharitable, in that he, judging the cross, etc., to be sin, did content himself to have reformed it at Salem, not taking care that others might be brought out of it also; laying a blemish also upon the rest of the magis-

ened us, and had procured a *quo warranto* against us, which he
did not deny.

3. His letter was produced, written soon after to Mr. Jeffrey,
his old acquaintance and intimate friend . . .

> This was the letter, written in 1634, in which—to the refrain
> of "Repent, you cruel Separatists, repent!"—Morton had an-
> nounced that the Massachusetts patent had been voided and that
> the King was sending over a governor general, with Morton as
> aide, to bring the Separatists to conformity in all things, even to
> worshiping in accordance with "catholic axioms."
>
> With no specific indictment against him, Morton petitioned
> for his release two months later. But the General Court thought
> "fit that further evidence be sent for into England, . . . and he
> to lie in prison in the meantime, unless he find sufficient bail."
>
> Languishing in jail six months later, Morton addressed another
> petition to the General Court.

MORTON'S
PETITION*

To the Honored Court at Boston Assembled:
The humble petition of Thomas Morton, prisoner.
Your petitioner craveth the favour of this honored Court to cast back your eyes and behold what your poore
petitioner hath suffered in these parts.

First, the petitioner's house was burnt, and his goods taken
away.

Secondly, his body clapt into Irons and sent home in a desperate ship, unvittled, as if he had been a man worthy of death
. . .

Now the petitioner craves this further, that you would be
pleased to consider what is laid against him—taking it for granted
to be true, which is not proved—whether such a poore worme

---

trates, as if they would suffer idolatry, etc.; and giving occasion to the state
of England to think ill of us—for which they adjudged him worthy admonition,
and to be disabled for one year from bearing any public office . . ."

As Morton had written in *New English Canaan*, the Saints could match the
Jesuits for "policie."

*The petition, from the Massachusetts archives, appears in the introduction by
Charles Francis Adams, Jr., to his edition of *New English Canaan* (1883).

as I had not some cause to crawle out of this condition above mentioned.

Thirdly, the petitioner craves this favoure of you, as to view his actions lately towards New England, whether they have not been serviceable to some gentlemen in the country. But I will not praise myselfe.

Fourthly, the petitioner coming into these parts which he loveth on godly gentlemen's imployments and your worshipps having a former jelosy of him, and a late untrue intelligence of him, your petitioner has been imprisoned manie moneths and laid in Irons to the decaying of his Limbs.

Let your petitioner finde soe much favoure as to see that you can passe by former offence. Which finding, the petitioner hopes he shall stand on his watch to doe service as God shall enable him.

Thomas Morton

[Endorsements]

The house of Deputies desire the honored magistrates to return them a reason wherefore the petitioner came not to his triall the last quarter Courte, according to graunte (as they conceave) of a former petition presented to the Courte by him.

Robert Bridges

The reason why he came not to his tryall was the not cominge of evidence out of England against him, which we expect by the next ship.

Thomas Dudley, Governer

The house of Deputies have made choyce of Major Gibbons* and Captain Jennison to treate with the honored magistrates about this petition of Morton.

Robert Bridges

---

*Curiously, Major Edward Gibbons had been one of Morton's men at Merry Mount. But he had long since left "joylity" behind him, being now a respectable Saint, a member of the General Court, commander of the Boston military forces, and a prosperous merchant in the Virginia and West Indies trade, where his dealings were not above suspicion.

WINTHROP'S JOURNAL   Having been kept in prison about a year in expectation of further evidence out of England, he was again called before the Court. And after some debate what to do with him, he was fined £100 [$5,000] and set at liberty.

He was a charge to the country, for he had nothing, and we thought not fit to inflict corporal punishment upon him, being old and crazy, but thought better to fine him and give him his liberty—as if it had been to procure his fine but, indeed, to leave him opportunity to go out of the jurisdiction, as he did soon after [never having been arraigned or brought to trial].

And he went to Agamenticus [York, Maine], and living there poor and despised, he died within two years later.

XXVIII
Union and Dispersion

O, that these ancient members had not dyed or been
dissipated (if it had been the will of God) . . .
—*William Bradford*

BRADFORD'S
HISTORY
By reason of ye plottings of the Narigansets
(ever since the Pequent warr), the Indians were
drawne into a generall conspiracie against ye English in all parts, as was in part discovered ye yeare before and
now [in 1643] made more plaine and evidente by many discoveries and free conffessions of sundrie Indeans, . . . with such
other concuring circomstances as gave them sufficiently to understand the trueth thereof and to thinke of means how to prevente ye same, and secure themselves.

1. United Colonies of New England

BRADFORD'S
HISTORY
Which made them enter this more near union
& confederation following:

Articles of Confederation betweene ye Plantations under ye Govermente of Massachusetts, ye Plantations
under ye Governmente of New Plimoth, ye Plantations
under ye Governmente of Conightecute, and ye Government
of New Haven,* with ye Plantations in combination therewith.

*The New Haven colony, later absorbed by Connecticut, had been founded
in 1638, after the Pequot War.

Whereas we all came into these parts of America with one and ye same end and aime—namely, to advance the kingdome of our Lord Jesus Christ & to injoye ye liberties of ye Gospell in puritie with peace;

And whereas in our settling (by a wise providence of God) we are further dispersed upon ye seacoasts and rivers than was at first intended, so that we cannot, according to our desires, with conveniencie communicate in one governmente & jurisdiction;

And whereas we live encompassed with people of severall nations and strange languages [the French and Dutch], which hereafter may prove injurious to us and our posteritie;

And forasmuch as ye natives have formerly committed sundrie insolencies and outrages upon severall plantations of ye English, and have of late combined themselves against us;

And seeing by reason of those distractions in England, and by which they know we are hindered from that humble way of seeking advice or reaping those comfortable fruits of protection which at other times we might well expecte;

We therefore doe conceive it our bounden duty, without delay, to enter into a presente consociation amongst ourselves, for mutuall help & strength in all our future concernments.

1. Wherefore, it is fully agreed and concluded by & betweene ye parties or jurisdictions above named . . . that they all be and henceforth be called by ye name of the United Colonies of New England.

The said United Colonies . . . doe joyntly & severally hereby enter into a firme & perpetuall league of frendship & amitie, for offence and defence, mutuall advice and succor upon all just occasions, both for preserving & propagating ye truth of ye Gospell, and for their owne mutual saftie and wellfare* . . .

---

*In view of great current problems—in particular, the various plans to confederate Western Europe—the articles of confederation, the first designed to promote closer union on our shores, have pointed relevance and interest. Their main operative clauses appear in the notes.[1]

At a meeting of ye commissioners for ye confederation held at Boston, ye 7th of Sept., it appearing that the Generall Court of New Plimoth and ye severall townships thereof have read & considered & approved these articles of confederation, as appeareth by commission . . . to Mr. Edward Winslow and Mr. William Collier to ratifie and confirme ye same on their behalfes, we therefore, ye Commissioners for ye Massachusetts, Conightecutt, & New Haven doe also for our several governments subscribe unto them.

The United Colonies was an exclusive organization. It did not embrace all of New England. It was restricted to Saints.

When Roger Williams inquired about the confederacy, he was informed that his colony was not eligible, that he should join it to one or another of his neighbors.

Knowing that the Saints, especially those in the Bay, had an eye on the territories around Narragansett Bay, Williams went to London at this time and obtained a charter for the "Providence Plantations," which included those on Aquidneck, or Rhode Island, as it was now renamed.

The settlements in New Hampshire and Maine were likewise excluded. Sir Ferdinando Gorges held Maine as a vast feudal estate, with himself as overlord. As he was one of the King's Men, his settlements were obviously ineligible.

In the articles of confederation there was not one mention of allegiance to England. The four colonies proceeded as if they were independent sovereign states, not beholden to King or Parliament. Charles I was still nominally the sovereign. But at just this time Massachusetts took occasion to strike out of the magistrates' oath of office this central clause, "You shall bear true faith and allegiance to our sovereign Lord, King Charles," on the ground that he had violated the privileges of Parliament, opened war upon it, and thereby lost much of his kingdom and many of his subjects. But there was no swearing of true faith and allegiance to Parliament, either.

By reason of its greater weight in population and wealth, Massachusetts dominated the United Colonies from the start. The Bay had already pronounced it treason for anyone to attempt in any way "to disturb our peace, directly or indirectly, by drawing a party under pretence that he is for the King of England," and now led the confederacy in breaking off all trade and other relations with Virginia, Bermuda, and the Barbados because these colonies favored the royalist cause.

In one of its first acts, again with the Bay taking the lead, the confederacy recommended that all league members take strong measures "against excesse and disorder in apparell, drink, and all other loose and sinfull miscarriages not fitt to be named amongst Christians, by which the name of our holy God is much dishonored, and the churches of Christ in these parts much reproached . . ."

Pledged to contribute more than twice as many men and more than twice as much money as any of her allies, Massachusetts was disposed to treat her smaller partners with a good deal of condescension, impatiently brushing aside whatever suggestions and criticisms they offered.

Contrary to the articles of agreement, the Bay insisted that the commissioners meet twice as often in Boston as elsewhere. She demanded that in seating the commissioners, her representatives "should have the first place" and that they should be the first to sign documents, which her partners reluctantly granted—not "as a matter of right," they said, but merely as an act of courtesy.

But when Massachusetts reached out to grab Seekonk and other territory along Plymouth's western limits, the smaller confederates gave her a sharp rap on the knuckles.

2. Ruling Elder Thomas Cushman

CHURCH RECORDS — Not longe after the decease of our Reverend Elder Mr. William Brewster, and the Reverend Mr. John Reyner left alone in the minnestrey, the Church saw cause to adde unto him another Ruling Elder and pitched their thoughts on Mr. Thomas Cushman, who was the son of that worthy servant of Christ, Mr. Robert Cushman, . . . the said Mr. Cushman Junior being by generall consent approved, elected, and ordained to that worthy office and function for which he was competently fitted and prepared by the Lord.*

And longe after his election, it appeared that there was great necessetie of this gracious healp, for . . . troubles came on apace . . .

There arose a perverse sect called Quakers, whose tenetts and principles (if I may soe call them) are and may ezely be demonstrated to be herettical and abominable . . .

But the Lord healped us unanimously to withstand these Incendiarys of mischiffe. Soe as by the mutuall and faithfull healp of this our worthy and beloved Elder, with the concurrance of severall other of the bretheren, it pleased the Lord to uphold us in our Integrety and in a constant withstanding and opposeing of those horred and damnable tenetts . . .

And we desire this specialty of God's good providence and protextion may never be forgotten, but that the Lord may have all the praise and Glory thereof.

For how ezely might these wolves in sheep clotheing have ruined this poor flock of Christ if the Lord had not interposed with his Almighty power and Goodnes, improving this our good Elder as a speciall instrument in this worthy worke, both by teaching the will of God every Lord's day for a considerable time, both plainly, pouerfully, and profittable, and seconding the same by a blamles life and Conversation.

Blessed be his holy Name forever and ever.

In a word, this blessed servant of Christ is a good man (as was said of Barnabas) & full of the holy Goast . . .

3. Left Like an Ancient Widow

BRADFORD'S HISTORY Also, about these times, now that cattle & other things begane greatly to fall from their former rates, and many persons begane to fall into more

---

*As remarked before, the younger Cushman, who had arrived as a boy of fourteen on the *Fortune*, was virtually a Bradford, having been brought up in the governor's household after his father's untimely death in 1625.

straits, and many being allready gone from them (as is before noted), both to Duxberie, Marshfeeld, and other pleaces, & those of ye cheefe sorte—as Mr. Winslow, Captaine Standish, Mr. Alden, and many others—and still some dropping away dayly, . . . and many more unsettled, it did greatly weaken ye place.

And by reason of ye straitnes and barrenes of ye place, it sett ye thoughts of many upon removall . . .

Mr. Edward Winslow was chosen governor this year [1644].

Many having left this place, . . . and sundrie others still, upon every occasion, desiring their dismissions, the church begane seriously to thinke whether it were not better joyntly to remove to some other place than to be thus weakened and, as it were, insensibly dissolved.

Many meetings and much consultation were held hereaboute, and diverse were men's minds and opinions.

Some were still for staying togeather in this place, alledging men might here live if they would be contente with their condition, and that it was not for wante or necessitie so much that they removed, as for ye enriching of themselves.

Others were resolute upon removall, and so signified that here they would not stay. But if ye church did not remove, they must.

Insomuch as many were swayed, rather than there should be a dissolution, to condescend to a removall if a fitt place could be found that might more conveniently and comfortably receive ye whole, with such accession of others as might come to them for their better strength & subsistence—and some such like cautions and limitations.

So as, with ye afforesaid provissos, ye greater parte consented to a removall to a place called Nawsett,* which had been superficially viewed, and ye good will of ye purchasers (to whom it belonged) obtained, with some addition thereto from ye Court.

But now they begane to see their errour, that they had given away already the best & most commodious places to others, and now wanted themselves. For this place was about 50 myles from

---

*At Nauset, halfway up Cape Cod, where the Pilgrims had had their First Encounter with the Indians almost twenty-five years before.

hence, and at an outside of ye countrie, remote from all society.

Also, that it would prove so strait as it would not be compe-tente to receive ye whole body, much less be capable of any addition or increase, so as (at least, in a shorte time) they should be worse there than they are now here.

The which, with sundery other like considerations and incon-veniences, made them change their resolutions.

But such as were before resolved upon removall tooke advan-tage of this agreemente & went on notwithstanding. Neither could ye rest hinder them, they having made some beginning.

And thus was this poore church left, like an anciente mother, growne olde and forsaken of her children—though not in their affections, yett in regarde to their bodily presence and personall helpfullnes—her anciente members being, most of them, worne away by death and these of later time being, like children, trans-lated into other families, and she, like a widow, left only to trust in God.

Thus she, that had made many rich, became herselfe poore.

CHURCH RECORDS The principall of the members that then removed was that honorable Gentleman, Mr. Thomas Prence, who went away with severall others of the church who were very desirable, and they became a body of themselves, destinct from the Church of Plymouth, and settled at Nawsett—by them, named Eastham.*

In these years, reviewing his manuscript volume, perhaps with an eye to see where sin and weakness and error had first crept in, Bradford came upon his transcription of a letter written many years before, back in 1617, when the congregation at Leyden was negotiating with the Virginia Company. In that letter, the Leyden leaders had assured Sir Edwin Sandys for his "encouragemente

---

*"The third Church which came forth, as it were, out of our bowells."—Morton's marginal note as he wrote this part of the record.

The preceding two were the churches at Duxbury and Marshfield. There were still other congregations in the colony—at Scituate, Barnstable, Taunton, Rehoboth, and elsewhere. But the members of these, for the most part, had not come from Plymouth, being new additions to the colony. It was the breakup of Mother Plymouth's "church-children" that so distressed Bradford, Morton, and others.

in ye worke" that those at the Green Gate had not only the will but the required unity and strength to make a success of the venture they contemplated.

Among other "instances of indusmente," Robinson and Brewster had proudly cited this:

"We are knite togeather as a body in a most stricte and sacred bond and covenante of the Lord, of the violation whereof we make great conscience, and by vertue whereof we doe hould ourselves straitly tied to all care of each other's good, and of ye whole by every one, and so mutually."

Turning over the page, Bradford disconsolately noted:

O sacred bond, whilst inviollably preserved, how sweete and precious were the fruits that flowed from ye same! But when this fidelity decayed, then their ruine approached.

O, that these anciente members had not dyed or been dissipated (if it had been the will of God). Or els, that this holy care and constante faithfulnes had still lived, and remained with those that survived and were in times afterwards added unto them.

But (alass) that subtill serpente hath slylie wound in himselfe, under faire pretences of necessitie and ye like, to untwiste these sacred bonds and tyes and, as it were, insensibly by degrees to dissolve, or in great measure to weaken, ye same.

I have been happy, in my first times, to see, and with much comforte to injoye, the blessed fruits of this sweete communion.

But it is now a parte of my miserie in old age to find and feele ye decay and wante thereof (in a great measure), and with greefe and sorrow of hart to lamente & bewaile ye same.

And for others' warning and admonnition, and my owne humiliation, doe I here note the same.

4. Saved by Pirates Again

BRADFORD'S HISTORY   Aboute ye middle of May this year [1646] came 3 ships into this harbor in warrlike order. They were found to be men-of-warr. The captain's name was Crumwell [Thomas Cromwell] . . .

WINTHROP'S JOURNAL   One Captain Cromwell (about ten years since, a common seaman in the Massachusetts) had been out . . . in a man-of-war by commission of the Earl of Warwick*, . . . and had taken four or five Spanish vessels and, in some of them, great riches . . .

He and all his men had much money, and great store of plate and jewels of great value . . .

And being bound hither [to Boston] with three ships . . . they were forced into Plymouth (divine providence so directing for the comfort and help of that town, which was now almost deserted), where . . . they spent liberally and gave freely to many of the poorer sort . . .

BRADFORD'S HISTORY   He had abord his vessels aboute 80 lustie men (but very unruly), who, after they came ashore, did so distemper themselves with drinke as they became like madd-men.

And though some of them were punished & imprisoned, yet they could hardly be restrained. Yet in ye ende, they became more moderate & orderly.

They continued here aboute a month or six weeks, . . . in which time they spent and scattered a great deale of money among ye people, and yet more sin (I fear) than money, notwithstanding all ye care & watchfullnes that was used towards them to prevente what might be.

In which time, one sadd accidente fell out. A desperate fellow of ye company fell a-quarling with some of his company. His

---

*It will be recalled that another of Warwick's pirate captains, Thomas Jones, had been master of the *Discovery*, which providentially put in and saved Plymouth in 1622, bringing John Pory and the trading commodities which enabled the Pilgrims to go on when they were at the end of their resources.

Incidentally, another of Warwick's marauders has a place in our history. Sailing from Virginia in 1619 on a "roving voyage" in the Spanish West Indies, the *Treasurer* soon returned with another pirate craft, both loaded with stolen or kidnaped Negro slaves, twenty of whom were sold in Virginia, being the first Negroes in the colony and the base upon which Southern slavocracy was built.

At that time, Warwick, always a crafty schemer, was merely a "designing" noble on the make. Always a Puritan, at least politically, he was now Lord High Admiral of the Parliamentary Navy and chasing the King's ships.

captaine commanded him to be quiet & surcease his quarelling.

But he would not, but reviled his captaine with base language, & in ye end drew his rapier & intended to run at his captain. But he closed with him and wrasted his rapier from him, and gave him a boxe on ye earr.

But he would not give over, but still assaulted his captaine. Whereupon, he tooke ye same rapier, as it was in ye scaberd, and gave him a blow with ye hilt. But it lit on his head, & ye small end of ye bar of ye rapier's hilt peirct his scull, & he dyed a few days after . . .

WINTHROP'S JOURNAL   It was then the General Court at Plymouth. And a jury being empannelled, they found that he died of the wound received from the captain. Whereupon, the captain was sent for on shore.

He offered to put himself upon trial, so as he might not be imprisoned, and that he might be tried by a council of war, both which were granted.

And one of Plymouth—one of their chief men, but no magistrate—undertook for him, body for body, and some of the magistrates and other military officers were chosen a council of war, who, upon the evidence and sight of his commission, by which he had power of martial law, &c., acquitted him.

The trained band accompanied the body to the grave, and the captain gave every one of them an ell of black taffeta for a mourning robe.

After this, he came with three ships to Boston, . . . [where] he took up his lodging in a poor thatched house. And when he was offered the best in town, his answer was, that in his mean estate that poor man entertained him when others would not, and therefore he would not leave him now, when he might do him good.

A conscientious and kindhearted pirate—it would seem, a very Saint. And for all the sin scattered by his lusty and drunken crew, Plymouth, almost a ghost town, had reason to be grateful too.

5. Halleluiah!

While Mother Plymouth's fortunes were at a low ebb, the lowest they would ever be, there was a light in the sky that lifted the spirits of all Saints.

The fortunes of the King had gone from bad to worse. In 1644, Cromwell had routed the Cavaliers with great slaughter at Marston Moor. "God made them as stubble before our swords," said he piously.

The next year was decisive. The New Model Army smashed the King's forces at Naseby; Archbishop Laud was beheaded. Parliament had overturned the episcopacy; Charles was well on his way to the executioner's block. All of this inspired Bradford to the most exclamatory passage he ever wrote:

A late observation, as it were by the way, worthy to be noted:
Full little did I thinke that the downfall of ye Bishops, with their courts, cannons, & ceremonies, &c., had been so neare when I first begane these scribled writings (which was aboute ye year 1630 and so peeced up at times of leasure afterward), or that I should have lived to have seene or heard of ye same.

But it is ye Lord's doing and ought to be marvelous in our eyes!

Every plante which mine heavenly father hath not planted (saith our Saviour) shall be rooted up. Mat. 15. 13. I have snared thee, and thou art taken, O Babell (Bishops), and thou wast not aware; thou art found, and also caught, because thou hast striven against the Lord. Jer. 50. 24.

But will they needs strive against ye truth, against ye servants of God? What, & against the Lord himselfe? Doe they provoke the Lord to anger? Are they stronger than he? 1. Cor. 10. 22.

No, no, they have mete with their match.

Behold, I come unto ye, O proud man, saith the Lord God of hosts; for thy day is come, even the time that I will visite thee. Jer. 50. 31.

May not the people of God now say (and these pore people among ye rest) the Lord hath brought forth our righteousness; come, let us declare in Sion the work of the Lord our God. Jer. 51. 10. Let all flesh be still before the Lord, for he is raised up out of his holy place. Zach. 2. 13.

In this case, these poore people may say (among ye thousands of Israel), *When the Lord brought againe the captivitie of Zion, we were like them that dreame.* Psa. 126. 1. *The Lord hath done greate things for us, whereof we rejoyce.* v. 3. *They that sow in teares, shall reap in joye. They wente weeping, and carried precious seede, but they shall returne with joye, and bring their sheaves.* v. 5, 6.

Doe you not now see ye fruits of your labours, O all ye servants of ye Lord that have suffered for his truth, and have been faithfull witnesses of ye same, and ye litle handfull amongst ye rest, ye least amongst ye thousands of Israll?

You have not only had a seede time, but many of you have seene ye joyefull harvest. Should you not then rejoyce—yea, and againe rejoyce—and say Hallelu-iah, salvation, and glorie, and honour, and power, be to ye Lord our God, for true and righteous are his judgments. Rev. 1, 2.

But thou wilte aske, what is ye mater? What is done?

Why, art thou a stranger in Israll, that thou shouldest not know what is done?

Are not those Jebusites overcome that have vexed the people of Israll so long, even holding Jerusalem till David's days and been as thorns in their sides so many ages, and now begane to scorne that any David should meadle with them. They begane to fortifie their tower, as that of the old Babelonians.

But those proud Anakimes are throwne downe, and their glory laid in ye dust. The tiranous bishops are ejected, their courts dissolved, their cannons forceless, their service cashiered, their ceremonies uselesse and despised, their plots for popery prevented, and all their superstitions discarded & returned to Rome from whence they came, and ye monuments of idolatrie rooted out of ye land. And the proud and profane supporters and cruell defenders of these (as bloody papists & wicked atheists, and their malignante consorts) marvelously overthrowne.

And are not these greate things? Who can deney it?

But who hath done it? Who? Even he that sitteth on ye white horse, who is called faithfull & true, and judgeth and fighteth righteously, Rev. 19. 11., whose garments are dipte in blood, and his name was called the word of God, v. 13., for he shall rule them with a rode of iron.

For it is he that treadeth the winepress of the feircenes and wrath of God almighty. And he hath upon his garmente, and upon his thigh, a name written, The King of Kings, and Lord of Lords. v. 15, 16.

Hallelu-iah!

Anno Dom. 1646.

XXIX

Departure and Death of the Old Standards

What will be the issue of these things, our all-ordering God only knows. Only we know, without him it shall not be, and that's our greatest comfort.

—Edward Winslow

But the revolution in England, welcome as it was, brought its problems too.

With the Anglican church and its bishops overthrown, a general toleration of all Christian faiths had become established in practice, though the Presbyterians were trying hard to erect another state church, with themselves as masters and arbiters in all religious matters.

But many felt that "new Presbyter is but old Priest writ large," as remarked by the great poet and brilliant pamphleteer, John Milton, later one of Cromwell's chief secretaries. Already, in 1644, Milton had published *Areopagitica*, his immortal plea for freedom of the press, freedom of speech, freedom of thought and belief.

Opposition to the Presbyterians, still the majority party, centered in the rapidly growing Independents, of whom Cromwell was one. In recruiting his famous Ironsides, he drew no sectarian lines, and it was charged against his army that it harbored all kinds of "heretics"—Anabaptists or worse.

"You would respect them, did you see them," Cromwell told the frightened Presbyterians. "They are no Anabaptists. They are honest, sober Christians. They expect to be used as men." They were "godly" men who went into battle singing psalms.

Yes, there were differences of religious opinion among them.

But "the State, in choosing men to serve it, takes no notice of these opinions. If they be willing faithfully to serve it, that satisfies," wrote Cromwell before Marston Moor, later urging Parliament to write toleration into law.

These Independents were the spiritual descendants of Robert Browne, more immediately of the Pilgrim's former pastor, their own beloved John Robinson, who "first struck out the Congregational or Independent form of church government," as all contemporaries agreed. Robinson's works went through many editions in these years and exerted great influence—his later works, especially.

As early as 1617, a friend noted, Robinson "so far came back [from the Separation] that he approved of communion with the Church of England, in the hearing of the word and prayer (though not in sacraments and discipline), and so occasioned the rise of such as are called Semists, that is Semi-Separatists, or Independents."

Robinson wrote a treatise on this point entitled *The Lawfullnesse of Hearing Ministers in the Church of England*. At his death, this manuscript was found on his desk. Their pastor's new and expanding liberal views so outraged the stiffer brethren at the Green Gate that they suppressed the work, keeping it from publication for nine years. The Saints at Plymouth stood equally stiff against any "innovation," as events now disclosed.

The greater toleration practiced in England raised a disturbing question on the matter of "libertie of conscience."

Did that liberty belong to all, or just to the Saints, as the latter contended?

It should be extended to all believers, answered many both in the Old Colony and in the Bay. In both colonies there was a large and growing number of non-Saints, who were deprived of all religious services and many civil rights because they did not choose to embrace the Holy Discipline.

While in London, Roger Williams had published *The Bloody Tenent of Persecution for the Cause of Conscience* (1644), a plea for toleration as practiced in neighboring Rhode Island, which added to the agitation.

1. Toleration Scuttled

The question of removing religious discrimination and the civil disabilities based upon it was brought to a head in 1645 by William Vassall, a man of wealth and of influence in both colonies. He had arrived with Winthrop as one of the assistant governors, but soon returned home. In 1635, he came again to New England and settled in the Old Colony, at Scituate. One of his daughters was the wife of Edward Winslow's stepson, Resolved White.

In dealing with the many sharp and specific complaints made by Vassall and others, the Saints had to move warily. The complainants had strong friends at home. Vassall's brother Samuel was a member of the new Commission for the Government of Foreign Plantations, established by Parliament. This new commission, quite as much as the old royal commission, was bent on exercising a controlling hand in the colonies. It had already decreed that all of the American colonies should allow "libertie of conscience," which was worse than poison to the Saints.

WINTHROP'S
JOURNAL One Mr. William Vassall, sometimes one of the assistants of the Massachusetts, but now of Scituate in Plymouth jurisdiction, a man of a busy and factious spirit, and always opposite to the civil governments of this country and the way of our churches, had practised with such as were not members of our churches to take some course—first, by petitioning the courts of the Massachusetts and of Plymouth, and (if that succeeded not) then to the parliament in England, that the distinctions which were maintained here both in civil and church estate might be taken away, and that we might be wholly governed by the laws of England.

And accordingly, a petition was drawn up to the parliament, pretending that they, being freeborn subjects of England, were denied the liberty of subjects both in church and commonwealth; themselves and their children debarred from the seals of the covenant, except they would submit to such a way of entrance and church covenant as their consciences could not admit; and take such a civil oath as would not stand with their oath of allegiance, or else they must be deprived of all power and interest in civil affairs; and were subjected to an arbitrary government and extra-judicial proceedings, etc.

And now at this Court at Boston [in May 1646] a petition to the same effect, much enlarged, was delivered to the deputies under the hands of Doctor [Robert] Child, Mr. Thomas Fowle, Mr. Samuel Maverick, Mr. Thomas Burton, Mr. John Smith, Mr. David Yale, and Mr. John Dand, in the name of themselves and many others in the country, whereto they pressed to have present answer.

But the Court being then near an end and the matter being very weighty, they referred the further consideration thereof to the next session.

And whereas a law was drawn up and ready to pass for allowing non-freemen equal power with the freemen in all town affairs, and to some freemen of such estate, etc., their votes in election of magistrates, it was thought fit to defer this also to the next session.

By this maneuver, the Bay Saint leaders avoided passing a law that was anathema to them, and found time to gather support and arguments to justify them in a subsequent summary rejection of the petition.

By a like maneuver, the petition to the Plymouth authorities was also ditched. But there is not a word about this in Bradford, in Morton's Memorial, or in the colony records. On the matter of toleration, the Pilgrims evidently did not wish to be officially on record. But Winslow wrote Winthrop about it.

[Plymouth
November 24, 1645]

WINSLOW'S
LETTER*

Honored Sir,
    Yours I long since received . . .
    Sir, I had written to you long since, but the truth

*This letter is from Thomas Hutchinson's *Collection of Papers* (1769).

is I could neither have content in silence or writing by reason of some unworthy passages in our last General Court, to the great offence of our Governor [Bradford], Mr. Prence, myselfe, and sundry others . . .

[After other proceedings critical of an action by the Court], the first excepter* having been observed to tender the view of a scroule [Vassall's petition] from man to man, it came at length to be tendered to myselfe. And withall, said he, it may be you will not like this.

Having read it, I told him I utterly abhorred it as such as would make us odious to all christian commonweales.

But, at length, he told the Governor he had a written proposition to be propounded to the Court, which he desired the Court to take into consideration and, according to order, if thought meet, to be allowed.

To this, the Deputies were most made beforehand,† and the other three assistants, who applauded it as their Diana.

And the sum of it was: To allow and maintaine full and free tollerance of religion to all men that would preserve the civill peace and submit unto government: and there was no limitation or exception against Turke, Jew, Papist, Arian, Socinian, Nicholayton, Familist, or any other, etc.

But our Governor and divers of us having expressed the sad consequences would follow, especially myselfe and Mr. Prence, yet notwithstanding it was required, according to order, to be voted.

But the Governor would not suffer it to come to vote, as being that indeed would eate out the power of godlines, &c.

By this you may see that all the troubles of N. E. are not at the Massachusetts. The Lord in mercy looke upon us and allay this spirit of division that is creeping in amongst us.

*The "excepter" was probably Timothy Hatherly, formerly a merchant adventurer and London Undertaker, now a neighbor of Vassall's in Scituate. An assistant governor since 1636, Hatherly was later deprived of office and disenfranchised for opposing the Saints' persecutions of Quakers and Baptists.

†In modern parlance, the deputies had been "lined up" to vote for the measure.

You would have admired to have seen how sweet this carrion relished to the pallate of most of the Deputies!*

What will be the issue of these things, our all-ordering God only knows. Only we know, without him it shall not be, and that's our greatest comfort.

But if he have such a judgment for this place, I trust we shall finde (I speake for many of us that groane under these things) a resting place amongst you for the soales of our feet.†

I had not thought to have been so long. But if you have heard of the particulars and the persons, especially the ringleader of this rout (if a rout might be in lawfull assembly), by this generall you may gather the more insight into the particulars.

Thus, saluting you and all yours, . . .

Your ever loveing friend,
Edward Winslow

2. Winslow's Last Mission to London

BRADFORD'S
HISTORY
 This year [1646], Mr. Edward Winslow went into England upon this occasion: some discontented persons under ye governmente of the Massachusetts sought to trouble their peace and disturbe, if not innovate, their governmente by laying many scandals upon

---

*The "carrion" of toleration was sweet not only to the deputies, it appears, but to half of the chief magistrates, who were equally divided about it.

Governor Bradford and Assistant Governors Winslow, Prence, and Collier were opposed to giving way on strict conformity.

Those favoring greater toleration were these—Timothy Hatherly; Edmund Freeman, John Beauchamp's brother-in-law, who with ten others had founded Sandwich on Cape Cod, "to worship God and make money"; John Browne, a Leyden Saint and an assistant governor since 1636; and Captain Myles Standish, who, with his wife Barbara, had never joined the church.

†Feeling must have run deep if Winslow really meant what he says here—that if God willed toleration for the Old Colony, many of the Saints there would migrate to the Bay, where the Lord could be expected to be of a different mind and deal roundly with all who did not walk strictly in the Holy Discipline.

them, and intended to prosecute against them in England by
petitioning & complaining to the Parlemente.*

Allso, Samuel Gorton & his company made complaints against
them,† so as they made choyse of Mr. Winslow to be their
agente, to make their defence, and gave him commission & instructions for that end, in which he so carried himselfe as did
well answer their ends and cleared them from any blame or dishonour, to the shame of their adversaries.

But by reason of the great alterations in the State, he was
detained longer than was expected. And afterwards, fell into
other imployments there, so as he hath now bene absente this 4
years, which hath been much to the weakening of this govermente, without whose consente he tooke these imployments
upon him.

On this discouraged note, entered in 1650, seven years before
his death, Bradford ended his history, perhaps tired of recording
nothing but losses and crosses, feeling more and more lonesome

---

*The Massachusetts petitioners for more equal rights were fined, jailed, and
generally harassed by the Bay authorities in a most arbitrary and high-handed
manner, with three members of the General Court stoutly dissenting—Richard
Bellingham, Simon Bradstreet, and Richard Saltonstall.

Though they lie outside the Pilgrim story, the toleration petition and the
magistrates' reply are most revealing documents—the latter, especially, illumi-
nates the sophistries of the day in defense of the indefensible. Both appear in
Thomas Hutchinson's *Collection of Papers*.

William Vassall had already gone to England with his complaints.

†Several years before, in 1643, on various pretexts and pretenses, the Massachusetts magistrates, with their usual arrogance and easy assumption of authority, had sent soldiers into Rhode Island to arrest and disposses Gorton and his
people, dragging the leaders to Boston and locking them up.

They were charged with "practising" with the Narragansett Indians against
the United Colonies and with trespassing on Massachusetts lands, which was
not true in the sense alleged.

Their real offense was that they were not Saints and called "baptism an
abomination, and the Lord's supper the juice of a poor silly grape turned into
the blood of Christ by the skill of our magicians, etc.," as John Winthrop
irately noted.

Such was the rage and bigoted fury against Gorton that he and his friends
narrowly escaped hanging for blasphemy, though Massachusetts had only the
flimsiest grounds of jurisdiction over them.

Gorton had since gone to England to seek redress and protection against
being further molested by the bigots in the Bay.

as death and circumstance further dispersed the Pilgrim band, his friends and fellow workers in the early heroic days when Plymouth was not a sleepy country village living on its memories, but a pulsing center of life and high adventure, the hope of the world, the one bright light in Zion.

WINTHROP'S
JOURNAL
The court had made choice of Mr. Edward Winslow (one of the magistrates of Plymouth) as a fit man to be employed in our present affairs in England, both in regard of his abilities of presence, speech, courage, and understanding, as also being well known to the commissioners, having suffered a few years before divers months' imprisonment, by means of the last arch-prelate, in the cause of New England.

But it was now moved by one of the elders to send one of our own magistrates and one of our elders. The motion and the reasons of it were well apprehended, so as the governor [Winthrop] and Mr. Norton, teacher of the church at Ipswich, were named and in a manner agreed upon.

But upon second thoughts, it was let fall, chiefly for these reasons:

1, it was feared, in regard that Mr. [the Reverend Hugh] Peter had written to the governor to come over and assist in the parliament's cause, etc., that if he were there, he would be called into the parliament and so detained:

2, many were here upon the wing [leaving for England and other places], and his departure would occasion more new thoughts and apprehensions, etc.;

3, it was feared what changes his absence might produce, etc.

The governor was very averse to a voyage into England. Yet he declared himself ready to accept the service if he should be called, though he were then fifty-nine years of age, wanting one month.* But he was very glad when he saw the mind of the Lord to be otherwise . . .

---

*Winthrop had less than three years to live, dying at Boston in the spring of 1649.

Mr. Winslow being now to go for England, etc., the court was troubled how to furnish him with money or beaver, for there was nothing in the treasury, the country being in debt £1,000. And what comes in by levies, is corn and cattle. But the Lord stirred up the hearts of some few persons to lend £100 [$5,000] to be repaid by the next levy.

Next, we went in hand to draw up his commissions and instructions, and a remonstrance and a petition to the commissioners in England . . .

In London, Gorton had set forth his case in *Simplicitie's Defence against Seven-Headed Policie* (1646). Upon his arrival, Winslow immediately struck back at him with *Hypocrisie Unmasked*.

But victory went to Gorton. Under the protection of the Earl of Warwick, he soon returned to his lands at Shawomet on the western shore of Narragansett Bay and lived there unmolested, renaming his settlement Warwick for the Lord High Admiral.

WINTHROP'S JOURNAL [May, 1648.] Here arrived three ships from London in one day. By the passengers we understood, as also by letters from Mr. Winslow, etc., how the hopes and endeavors of Dr. Child and other petitioners, etc., had been blasted by the special providence of the Lord, who still wrought for us.

Dr. Child had a brother, a major of a regiment in Kent, who, being set on by his brother and William Vassall (who went from Scituate to petition against the country, etc.), set out a pamphlet, wherein he published their petition exhibited to our General Court, and other proceedings of the Court.

This was answered by Mr. Winslow in a book entitled *Salamander* (pointing therein at Mr. Vassall, a man never at rest but when he was in the fire of contention), wherein he cleared the justice of our proceedings.

As for those who went over to procure us trouble, God met with them all. Mr. Vassall, finding no entertainment for his petitions, went to Barbados.

Major John Child's tract was *New England's Jonas cast up in London* (1647). Winslow's was *New England's Salamander Discovered*. In it, Winslow took very high ground, as secretly instructed by the Bay. But these instructions must have paralleled his own opinions, or he would not so freely have expressed them.

It was right that only the Saints enjoyed full liberty in New Canaan, Winslow argued. Far from being an injustice, that was obviously the will of God.

As to Massachusetts in particular, its charter limited the franchise "expressly to the freemen only," and the proper authorities had decided that only communicants in good standing could be freemen.

The Bay colony, in short, was a closed corporation, and none could join it but those invited into "fellowship." It was the duty of non-Saints to help support it by paying taxes and performing military service, of course, but that did not qualify them as freemen.

As for regulation from London or the appointment of a governor general, declared the Bay, "our charter gives us absolute power of government." There was nothing about regulation or a governor general in the charter, either expressed or implied, and they had not transported themselves and their families upon any such understanding.* Nor was there any appeal from Boston to London. In its own affairs, Massachusetts—and by inference, each of the United Colonies—was to have the last word, which was not subject to any review.

The narrow intolerant views of the New England Saints were most embarrassing to their brethren in England, the Independents, in their struggle against the Presbyterians, who had had their credo proclaimed the only official and legal one in the realm. When the Independents pleaded for "libertie of conscience" as their God-given right, the Presbyterians pointed to the practice in New England to justify their own course in denying toleration.

But the questions raised by Vassall and others—important questions touching not only religion but the constitutional relationship between the colonies and the mother country—were now lost in the press of grave and dramatic events at home.

*For Winslow's secret instructions, see Winthrop's Journal for 1646.

Charles I had been caught in correspondence with the Catholic Irish, whom he had invited to invade England and reduce his people to obedience—"a more prodigious treason" could not be imagined, said Cromwell.

Purging the Parliament of appeasers, expelling those Presbyterians disposed to compromise with the King, Cromwell and his Independents proclaimed that the "people, under God, are the original of all just power," appointing a court to try Charles for high treason.

When the House of Lords objected, they abolished that House as a "useless and dangerous" thing and proclaimed England a Commonwealth, stripped of feudal trimmings in Church and State, sending the King to the block early in 1649.

Faced with all too many perplexing problems at home, the Commonwealth had little time for the colonies. Left to themselves, the Saints continued to rule the United Colonies as they chose, though their years of exclusive rule were numbered.

3. Another Breach: Teacher Reyner Resigns

CHURCH RECORDS

Concerning that worthy servant of Jesus Christ, Mr. John Reyner . . .

He served Christ in the office of Teacher about eighteen years [1636–54] . . . in great faithfulnes and much industry, being largely indowed with Gifts suitable to soe worthy a worke, and might have continewed much longer therein, to the Glory of Christ and Comfort of the Saints, had not sin and Sathan's malice hindered.

The unhappy difference that fell out in the Church of Barnstable had such an ill influence in the Church at Plymouth as that it, together with the unsettlednes of the Church and going away of divers of this Church—yea, of the eminentest of them—, was a means of unsettlement of this holy man of God. And althoe much blame may be layed to the people about his removall, yett himselfe cannot be wholy excused.

But the breach was soe great by the leaving of the Church as it is to be feared will never be made up againe, especially considering the insensible ffraun [frown?] at that time on those who were concerned therein, both in respect of sin that caused it, and in respect of our losse of him, which ought to have bin more layed to hart than it was.

He left Plymouth in the month of November, 1654, and went to Boston, where he continewed that winter, and came the spring following, in a way of visitt, and would have bin ezely perswaded to come againe if the people would have condecended to a proposition made by him.

But they, then having a prize, had not a hart, but added to former sin by their neglect of this tender of mercye, being divers of them tainted with the then epidemicall disease of some parte of the country about that time: viz., a slight esteem of an able minnestry.

The summer following, he was invited to Dover, on Pascattaqua River, and thither went, and was called to minnesteriall office there, where he continewed until his death.

He was an able, faithfull, laboriouse preacher of the Gospell, and a wise orderer of the affaires of the Church. He was singularly indowed with a Gift and propence upon his sperrit to traine up children in a Cattikettical way in the grounds of Christian religion. So that by losse of him, ignorance insewed in the towne of Plymouth amongst the voulgare, and alsoe much lysensiousness and prophanes amongst the younger sort . . .

Soon after whose departure to Dover, and noe hopes of his returne to take place amongst this poor forlorne fflock of Christ groning under the want of Gospell ordinances, we made many tryalls for a supply, improving therein the healpe of the Reverend Elders of the churches of Christ in the Massachusetts Bay.

And by divers sollisitations att sundry times, severall messengers were sent to them and the said Church, craving theire best healp for a supply, but could not obtaine any healp notwithstanding theire said indeavers, which were also accompanied with fasting and prayer, frequently, continuing in this condition for the space of nine years . . .

4. Sheep without Shepherds

Except for two brief periods, Plymouth did not have a pastor again for thirteen years, not until 1667, when it acquired the son and namesake of the great John Cotton, a name that had a particular odor of sanctity throughout New England. The younger Cotton brought solace and comfort for a time, though in the end he departed under a heavy cloud, being dismissed for "Notorious Breaches of the Seventh Commandment." He had spent a great deal of time with his women parishioners—or "female ch-children," as he liked to call them—having a natural fondness for them and their charms, to his disgrace and undoing.

After Reyner's departure, Plymouth was not alone in being without a minister. The pulpits were empty at Barnstable, Eastham, Marshfield, and other places. Tired of hardship and poverty, the "larned Mr. Channcy" now abandoned his flock at Scituate. He packed up, planning to return home, but, much to his surprise, became president of Harvard College.[1]

At this time, the congregations in so many Pilgrim towns were "sheep without a Shepard" that the Bay took notice of this, writing to the commissioners of the United Colonies about it:

Boston
Sept. 2, 1656

MASSACHUSETTS' Honoured Gentlemen,
LETTER* The remembrance of the solemne covenants and promises the United Colonies (in the beginning of their combination) made one with another, not only to strengthen the hearts and hands each of other in appointing and maintaining of religion in its purity, but also to be assisting each to other where any deficiency in such respects may appear, hath putt us upon the pursuance of our endeavours to discharge our duties in desiring you to consider of some such meete way and expedient as where any defect appears in any

*This letter and the commissioners' recommendations appear in Hutchinson's Collection of Papers.

colony in the right improvement of such meanes and ordinances as the Lord hath appointed all his to use and improve for the edification of the body, whereof Christ is the head, till his second coming.

Having heard some time since that our neighbour colony of Plymouth, our beloved brethren, in great part seeme to be wanting to themselves in a due acknowledgment and incouragement to the ministry of the gospell, so as many pyous ministers of the gospell have (how justly, we know not) deserted their stations, callings, and relations: Our desire is that some such course may be taken as that a pyous orthodox ministry may be reinstated amongst them, that so the flood of errors and principles of anarchy (which will not long be kept out where Satan and his instruments are so prevalent as to prevaile to the crying downe of ministry and ministers) may be prevented.

Here hath arrived amongst us severall persons professing themselves Quakers, fitt instruments to propagate the kingdom of Satan. For the securing of ourselves and our neighbors from such pests, we have imprisoned them till they be dispatched away to the place from whence they came . . .

Gentlemen,

Your assured friends,
Edward Rawson, Secretary
In the name and by the order
of the General Court

Delivered to the assembled commissioners, this letter of rather officious concern and scarcely disguised censure of their "beloved brethren" in the Old Colony was opened and read by Governor Bradford, who was in the chair.

What a humiliation—to be lectured on want of zeal by the novice Saints in the Bay! Yet the grounds of the complaint could not be denied.

And what a blow to Pilgrim pride—and what a bitter pill for the old governor to swallow in the last year of his life.

5. Winslow's Death

MORTON'S
MEMORIAL This year [1655] that worthy and honourable Gentleman, Mr. Edward Winslow, deceased, . . . being a very worthy and usefull instrument amongst them, both in the place of Government and otherwise until his last voyage for England, being sent on special imployment for the government of the Massachusetts . . .

And afterwards, was imployed as one of the Grand Commissioners in that unhappy design against Domingo in Hispaniola, who, taking grief for the ill success of that enterprize, . . . together with some other infirmities that were upon him, fell sick at sea betwixt Domingo and Jamaica and died the eighth day of May, which was about the sixty-first year of his life.

And his body was honourably committed to the sea, with the usual solemnity of the discharge of fourty-two pieces of ordnance.

One of the company who was imployed in taking notice of the particulars of that tragedy gave such testimony of the said Mr. Winslow as followeth in this poem:

> The Eighth of May, west from 'Spaniola shore,
> God took from us our Grand Commissioner,
> Winslow by name, a man of Chiefest Trust,
> Whose Life was sweet, and Conversation just;
> Whose Parts and Wisdome most men's did excell:
> An honour to his Place, as all can tell.

After his labors in behalf of Massachusetts, Winslow had interested himself in promoting Christianity among the heathen. Though it had been one of the Pilgrims' professed aims to spread the glad tidings of salvation among the Indians, they had done little or nothing about this, making few converts—only Squanto, and perhaps Hobomok, who appeared at his death to have "some good hopes" of going to heaven.

Roger Williams had early interested himself in the Indians, mastering their tongue, publishing a very useful *Key* to their language in 1643. But Williams, with his individualistic "Seeker" views, did not proselytize among them.

That work was first systematically undertaken in the Bay, initiated by the Reverend John Eliot, teacher at Roxbury,[2] who in 1647 published *The Day-breaking, if not the Sun-rising, of the Gospell with the Indians in New England*, designed to give "a true relation of our beginnings with the Indians."

Two years later, to aid the work of making more "praying Indians," Winslow published *The Glorious Progress of the Gospell among the Indeans in New England*, dedicating it to Parliament, and through his influence persuaded that body to incorporate the Society for the Propagation of the Gospel in New England, with himself as one of its directors. The Society's subsidies financed much work in the Old Colony, where it was perhaps most successful, particularly among the weak tribes on Cape Cod.

After the quiet of life at Marshfield and the dwindling importance of affairs at Plymouth, Winslow appears to have liked the bustle of London and the larger stage there, becoming more and more a man of the world, though no less zealous as a Saint. In 1651, in a moment of vanity, he sat for his portrait, which is of interest for several reasons.

This is the sole authentic Pilgrim portrait. And in more than one sense it is our only one. In his pen portrait of Brewster after the latter's death, Bradford gives us a fine likeness of the man in all but one respect—what did he look like in the flesh? Was he tall or short, thin or fat, fair or dark, handsome or plain?

We shall never know. This is true of all the Saints but Winslow, for in all the Pilgrim records there is not a word about their personal appearance or physical characteristics, with this signal exception—when the Reverend Richard Clyfton arrived at Amsterdam in flight from Scrooby, he was a venerable figure with a "great white beard." That is all.

As for Winslow, he certainly does not answer the popular conception of what the Pilgrims were like as he sits before us, a pleasant-looking man, serious but far from solemn, dressed in doublet with gold buttons, ruffled wristbands, and a wide starched collar secured by a looped gold cord with tassels. He might easily be mistaken for a prosperous and amiable Dutch burgher—such a one as Van Dyck liked to paint.

Continuing in London, Winslow tried unsuccessfully to obtain a new charter for Plymouth, but performed many useful services for the New England colonies. His abilities coming to Cromwell's attention, he was appointed in 1654 as chairman of a joint English-Dutch commission to assess damages against the Dutch for attacks on English shipping.

At a salary of £1,000 ($50,000) a year, he was then made chief of three commissioners in command of a force dispatched to drive Spain from the West Indies. One of his fellow commissioners was testy old Admiral William Penn, father of a more famous William.

Attacking Santo Domingo, the force was repulsed with heavy loss. As the ships pulled away for Jamaica, Winslow died, evidently of a tropical fever, and his body went over the side with full military honors, including a salvo of forty-four guns.

Winslow had come a long way since those days at Leyden when he had been an apprentice in Brewster's printing shop. But perhaps it was just as well for his fame and fortune that he died when he did. If he had survived and returned to England, he would have been sent to prison again, locked up in the Tower of London, as were his two colleagues, Admiral Penn and General Venables, for their part in mismanaging the expedition.

6. Standish Dies

MORTON'S MEMORIAL — This year [1656] Captain Miles Standish expired his mortal life. He was a Gentleman, born in Lancashire, and was heir-apparent unto a great estate of lands and livings, surreptitiously detained from him, his great-grandfather being a second or younger brother of the House of Standish.[3]

In his younger time, he went over into the Low Countreys, and was a souldier there, and came acquainted with the Church at Leyden, and came over into New England with such of them as at the first set out for the planting of the plantation of New Plimouth, and bare a deep share of their first difficulties, and was alwayes very faithfull to their interest.

He, growing ancient, became sick of the Stone, or Strangullion, whereof, after his suffering of much dolorous pain, he fell asleep in the Lord and was honourably buried at Duxbury.

For thirty-three years, from the day of the first landing down to 1653, when age and ill health forced his retirement, Standish had been commander-in-chief of the Pilgrim army. For years it was ridiculously small, yet always an effective instrument in his hands, never suffering a defeat. Standish showed great resolution in the field and on all occasions was the bravest of the brave.

In his later years, from 1644 to 1649, Standish was treasurer of the colony, collecting taxes, signing vouchers, keeping books, which must have been tedious and unpleasantly confining business to one used to more wholesome and exciting pursuits.

In the New World, the captain had done rather well for himself, leaving an estate of £258 ($13,000), which was considerable for the time. His assets included five horses, two saddles, a bridle and pillion, fourteen head of cattle, a flock of sheep, some swine, assorted weapons, a warming pan, a dozen trenchers, three beer casks, a malt mill, a churn, and a small library.

This library was, in its way, as interesting as Brewster's. It reflected the tastes of a man of the world. There were few books on religion, and none on purely Separatist doctrine. Among other things, the library contained "three old Bibles," the *Iliad* in translation, a history of the world, a chronicle of England, a history of Queen Elizabeth's reign, a history of Turkey, another of Germany, a book on farming, *The Physician's Practice*, Bariffe's *Artillery*, and Caesar's *Commentaries*.

In his will, Standish directed that he be laid away "as neare as conveniente to my two dear daughters, Lora Standish, my daughter, and Mary Standish, my daughter-in-law," and he was buried beside them in the now historic Old Burying Ground at Duxbury, where their graves have been identified and marked.

His "dearly beloved wife Barbara" survived him, as did four sons—Alexander, Myles, Josiah, and Charles. While Standish and his wife never joined the church, they had no objection to their children doing so. Alexander was a deacon at Duxbury, and the town clerk, too, and soon opened a store in his father's house.

It is significant that, as executors of his will, the captain chose none of the Saints, none of his old friends and neighbors, but two more recent arrivals, Timothy Hatherly and James Cudworth, both of Scituate. They were two of the most liberal men in the colony and a few years later, in 1658, were deprived of office as assistant governors and disenfranchised for speaking out against the persecution of Quakers and Baptists.

Standish was one whose palate relished the "sweet carrion" of toleration, and he evidently remembered that fateful day when Hatherly and Cudworth had stood with him in support of it, to the fear and anguish of the leading Saints.

7. Death of Bradford

MORTON'S MEMORIAL
This year [1657] it pleased God to put a period to the life of his precious servant, Mr. William Bradford, who was the second governour of the jurisdiction of Plimouth and continued in the same place for the most part of his time, with little intermission.

Concerning whom, the following poems made—the one by himself, and the others by such as were well acquainted with his Worth and Excellency—will give a large testimony thereof: Certain verses left by the Honoured William Bradford, Esq., . . . penned by his own hand, declaring the gracious dispensation of God's Providence towards him in the time of his life, and his preparation and fittednes for death.

> From my years young in dayes of youth,
> God did make known to me his Truth,
> And call'd me from my native place
> For to enjoy the Means of Grace.
> In wilderness he did me guide,
> And in strange lands for me provide.

In fears and wants, through weal and woe,
As Pilgrim passed I to and fro,
Oft left of them whom I did trust.
How vain it is to rest on Dust!
A man of sorrows I have been,
And many changes I have seen . . .

Faint not, poor Soul, in God still trust.
Fear not the things thou suffer must . . .
Farewell, dear Children, whom I love,
Your better Father is above . . .
Fear him in Truth, walk in his Wayes,
And he will bless you all your dayes.

My dayes are spent, old age is come,
My strength it fails, my glass near run.
Now, I shall wait when work is done
Untill my happy change shall come,
When from my labours I shall rest
With Christ above for to be blest . . .

A few verses more added by one that was well acquainted with the worth of the said Mr. Bradford:

The ninth of May, about nine of the clock,
A precious one God out of Plimouth took, . . .
A man approv'd in Town, in Church, in Court, . . .

Sweet Brewster, he is gone some time before.
Wise Winslow, whose death we lament so sore.
And faithful Standish, freed from horrid pain,
To be with Christ—in truth, the greatest gain.

Now blessed holy Bradford, a successor
Of blessed holy Bradford, the Confessor,
Is gone to place of rest, with many more
Of precious ones, whom I might name, great store . . .

This worthy gentleman was interred with the greatest solemnities that the jurisdiction to which he belonged was in a capacity to perform—many deep sighs, as well as loud volleys of shot, declaring that the people were no less sensible of their loss who were surviving, than mindful of the worth and honour of him that was deceased.

Striving to the last to keep the ship of state and the ark of the covenant afloat in choppy seas, with perils looming in every quarter, Bradford had been in failing health for some months, but "felt himself not what he counted sick" until he had a resplendent vision in the night. "The next morning he told his friends that the good Spirit of God had given him a pledge of his happiness in another world and the first-fruits of his eternal glory; and on the day following he died . . . in the sixty-ninth year of his age."

In spite of the fact that he had labored continuously in the public service since 1621, at first without payment and later on a niggardly salary, Bradford amassed a relatively large fortune, both from farming and trading, and died one of the richest men in the colony, leaving an estate of £900 ($45,000). The governor's personal effects included "2 hattes, a blacke one & a coulered one, and 4 fine shirts"; a "stuffe" suit and a "lead coullered cloth suit," both with silver buttons; a turkey-red grogram suit and cloak; another cloak, "faced with taffety"; and an "old violet coullered cloake, and an old green gowne."

The estate was left in varying proportions to his wife Alice, "a blessed mother in Israell," and their three children—William, Joseph, and their daughter Mercy. Portions also went to Bradford's two stepsons, Thomas and Constant Southworth; to his former ward, Thomas Cushman, now the Ruling Elder; and to his son John by his first wife, Dorothy May. Left behind at Leyden as a small boy and sent for in 1627, John lived his life in almost complete obscurity, first at Plymouth, later at Duxbury and Marshfield, eventually moving to Connecticut, where he died in 1678.

Of Plimoth Plantation fell to Bradford's elder son by his second marriage, Major William Bradford, and was handed down in the latter's family for several generations, as attested by this rather illiterate notation on a flyleaf of the manuscript:

"This book was rit by goefner William Bradford, and gifen to his son majer William Bradford, and by him to his son majer John Bradford, rit by me [his son] Samuel Bradford, Mach 20, 1705."

Bradford's history, still in manuscript, disappeared during the American Revolution and was long missing, having a curious history of its own.[4] But Bradford laid rather more store by his other writings, for he had not laid down his pen when he abandoned his magnificent chronicle. He most prized his poetry, or "sundrie usefull verses," as he called them. Also, he had penned three dialogues "betweene some yonge-men borne in New-England and some Anciente men which came out of Holand and old England, concerning the Church."

The first dialogue was, in large part, a very disingenuous defense of Francis Johnson and the scandalous Ancient Brethren—lecherous Ruling Elder Studley and all. Evidently stories about them had reached Plymouth to pique the curiosity of the younger Saints. To protect the good name of the Separatists, Bradford held the Amsterdam congregation up to view as very pious folk.

The second dialogue has been lost, while the third was a sharp attack upon the "corrupte" Roman and Anglican churches, a mild criticism of the Presbyterian, and a complete vindication of the "Congregationall Way."

In his later years also, thinking to have missed something in the schooling denied him as a youth, Bradford began reading philosophy and studying the ancient languages, Latin and Greek, but especially Hebrew, having a desire, he said, to know the language of God and the angels, and "how the words and phrases lye in the holy texte . . . and what names were given to things from the creation."

Variously gifted, a man of purpose and intelligence, unselfishly devoted to the welfare of New Plimoth, blessed with seemingly inexhaustible energy and strength, Bradford was, beyond question, the greatest of the Pilgrims. More, he was one of the first of the really great Americans.

His passing marked the close of a critical era. More than any other he had opened and secured a new frontier, and he went to his grave, as Cotton Mather declared with none of his usual extravagance, "lamented by all the colonies of New England, as a common blessing and father to them all."

8. Intimations of Immortality

MORTON'S   You might now easily discern a heavy heart in
MEMORIAL   the mournful countenance of every sober-minded
                 and considerate man. For, as you have heard, in
the three or four years last past God was pleased greatly to
weaken this poor tottering colony of Plimouth by taking away
several of the most usefull props thereof, both in Church and
Civil State.

Some others who had been of singular use, now stooping under
the infirmities of old age, could not be so serviceable as in times
past. And others removed so far from the center of the Government that they could not, without great difficulties, attend their
publick concerns, nor could possibly so constantly as our necessities required, which did greatly aggravate our troubles.

We were become weak, when we had need of greatest
strength; had lost many of our chieftains, when we stood in need
of the best conduct and guidance.

For besides the troubles and changes that then attended our
native country and might call for great circumspection in our
walking in relation unto them, we had also, at this very time,
some amongst us that, growing weary of the long peace and
concord that we had enjoyed, and hoping to fish better in
troubled waters when their bait might be taken in and the hook
not easily discerned, would willingly have been ringing changes
in this jurisdiction also, pretending a great zeal for liberty of
conscience, but endeavoring to introduce such a liberty of will
as would have proved prejudicial, if not destructive, to civil and
church societies . . .

But the Lord, many times, delighteth to appear in the mount
of his people's miseries, distresses, and troubles, that his power
and wisdom may appear when they are weakest, and that they
may know their salvation is from him.

At such a time, & when the condition of this colony was such as hath been declared, God was pleased to minde it, even in its low estate. And when he had taken to himself not only our Moses, but many of the Elders and Worthies of our Israel, he hath not hitherto left us without a Joshua to lead us in the remaining part of our pilgrimage.

When the usual time for the renewing of our election of such as should govern us came, Mr. Thomas Prence was by unanimous vote chosen governour.

And although men's spirits were so distempered, as I have related, and it might have been expected that they would have been much divided in their choice, yet God (who disposeth the lot that is cast into the lap) so disposed that all their votes centered there—a good demonstration that he was chosen of God for us, and by his blessing made an instrument of much peace and settlement in this place, and to this people, in these times of trouble and confusion.

The Lord also directing the freemen of this jurisdiction at the same time in their election to the choice of a discreet and able Council to be assistant unto the said honoured Governor in this so weighty work—divers of them being descended of several of the honoured magistrates deceased, not only bearing their names, but having a large measure of their spirit bestowed on them, befitting them for such work.

So as through the goodness of God, those storms that seemed to threaten the subversion of all and did at first prevaile to the disturbing and shaking of many towns and churches, and to the great discouragement of the ministers in divers places, do seem to be pretty well blown over.*

Such uncomfortable jarrs (as have been sometimes thought uncureable) seem to be thoroughly reconciled and healed. Our towns, for the most part, supplied with godly and able ministers. And we sit under our vines and fig trees in peace, enjoying both civil and religious liberties.

For which goodness of the Lord, let his holy Name be praised . . .

*Morton's Memorial was published in 1669. The lines here were probably written a few years earlier.

Afterword

BRADFORD'S SUCCESSOR, Thomas Prence, continued as governor for sixteen years, till his death in 1673. Now in his late fifties, a man of considerable ability but little or no education, he had been governor twice before, in 1634 and 1638, and for more than twenty years had been a member of the General Court. Bradford had probably recommended him as his successor.

Arriving as a Stranger on the *Fortune*, Prence had become one of the narrowest and most bigoted of the Saints, being very harsh and overbearing as a magistrate. The colony was seething with dissensions and discontent, but Prence would not listen to grievances or make any attempt to redress them.

On Prence's council sat John Alden, nearing sixty, but still actively plying his carpenter's trade. He had succeeded Standish as treasurer and held that post until 1659, at which time he was so "low in his estate" that the colony voted him a grant of £10 ($500) for his public services. Alden continued to be an assistant governor down to his death almost thirty years later.

Several younger men appear among the assistants at this time— Winslow's oldest son, Captain Josiah Winslow, and three of the Bradford family—the old governor's elder son, William, "eminente in grace," and his two stepsons, Thomas and Constant Southworth.

Events at home soon placed Prence and his colleagues in a very difficult and delicate position. With the restoration of the Stuarts in 1660, the Anglican bishops were again riding high and tracking down their enemies. Reporting this from London, a Massachusetts agent exclaimed, "The Lord keep and preserve his churches, that there may not be fainting in the day of trial."

To assure Charles II of Plymouth's utter devotion, Prence drew up a "hombel petishon" and enclosed it in a letter to a friend in London, entreating him "with all exspideton to present the inclosed to my Lord [Say and Sele], as also the vewe of our hombel petishon, craving his lordship's help and furtheranc ther in . . .

"I hop you will not find anything in it which will be offensive, exsep our rude expreshons, for which we crave your helpp, also to ecskuse us . . . We would not be to tedios, but leav our case with you, and count both you and it, and all other pore waighty ocations, to the blessing of the Lord our God, who is our hop, and in hom we ever desir to rest."

Making peace with the new monarch did not prove to be too difficult. While Bradford and his brethren had cried "Halleluiah!" when Cromwell's forces crushed the King's and decreed a "day of public thanksgiving" to celebrate the victory, yet they had cannily kept a discreet official silence on the execution of Charles I and the virtual crowning of Cromwell as Protector. If there were laments for Cromwell's death, they were kept off the record. Besides, Charles had too much to do at home in consolidating his own position to be concerned about the colonies for the moment, and therefore graciously received Prence's "hombel petishon."

While still uneasy about the King's intentions, as there was cause, the Saints had more immediate and vexing problems to worry them. Vassall's petition for toleration, which almost passed the General Court, prompted them to become more intolerant. Demanding stricter conformity, they now began to follow the Bay in calling upon the constables to act where the ministers had failed, substituting force for persuasion, always a confession of weakness. Here was the first certain sign that the rule of the Saints was doomed.

A law was passed imposing a fine of 10s. ($25) for neglect of public service for any reason whatsoever. Another threatened corporal punishment for "such as shall deney the Scriptures to bee the rule of life." Still another threatened to take away the citizenship of all, whether freemen or not, who were "opposers of the good and wholesome lawes of the colony, or manifeste opposers of the true worship of God, . . . or such as shall speak contemptuously of the lawes."

These measures, of course, did not increase the popularity of the meetinghouse. To silence growing criticism, a law was aimed at those who "shall villifie by approbrious tearmes or speaches any church, or minestry, or ordinance."

This, in turn, did nothing to increase the popularity of the General Court, which necessitated still another law, one imposing a fine of 20s. ($50) "for speaking evill of one of the magistrates."

Later, after Massachusetts' officious complaint about the many empty pulpits in the Old Colony, the Pilgrims took an unprecedented step, reversing a historic policy. The "true" church, they had always contended, was a purely voluntary fellowship, a free association of like-minded Christians, to which each contributed what he would or could.

Abandoning this fundamental tenet, they now made support of the church compulsory, a legal obligation upon all—one of the "tyrannies" they had so objected to in the Anglican church. This measure caused much groaning, not only among the Strangers, but among the Saints. Dr. Matthew Fuller of Duxbury spoke for many of the latter when he declared, paying a 50s. fine as a consequence, that surely the "Divill sat in the stern" when this "wicked" law establishing a virtual tithe system was passed.

Though otherwise pleased, the ministers found that the law contained a mean joker. While the civil authorities set the rates, pastors had to collect their own salaries, which, as one of them plaintively remarked, "was attended with much trouble and often impaired their usefulness." Parishioners were often in arrears, sometimes for many years together, and when they saw the minister coming to call, they did not know just how to greet him, having a natural aversion to being dunned.

Yet the poor pastor could not be expected to sit idly at home and watch his usually numerous family starve. And it must be said that the General Court, for all its pious professions, was of not much practical help.

It took only one immediate step to ease the ministers' hard lot, recommending that it would be a "thing very commendable and beneficial" if the seashore towns would set aside, for the "Incurragement of an able Godly Minnestry amongst them," a small part of the oil and flesh taken from all drift whales washed up on the beach within their bounds.

In his *Cape Cod*, Thoreau has left us a touching picture of a poor Pilgrim pastor sitting forlornly on a high bleak sand dune, with the wind whistling around him, intently watching the sea to the far horizon for sight of some expired leviathan that might possibly drift his way and provide a little something for his hungry ones at home.

Such vigils were pretty hopeless, to be sure. And yet, "for my part," said Thoreau, "if I were a minister, I would rather trust to the bowels of the billows, on the back side of Cape Cod, to cast up a whale for me, than to the generosity of many a country parish I know."

These troubles within the church were complicated by others, both civil and religious, brought on by a "swarm of Notoriouse heretiques," chiefly Quaker, who began to appear in New England in 1656.

In the Friends, the Saints for the first time met a people as courageous and stubbornly determined as themselves, possessed of the same death-defying devotion to their beliefs and principles, which infuriated the Saints and left them puzzled, not knowing just how to deal with these "pests."

The Quakers stood at the extreme left of the Separation, representing its final revulsion against a religion of sacrament and spectacle. They went beyond the Saints in their aversion to Romanesque and Gothic churches, which they scorned as "idoltemples" and "Steeple-houses." They rejected all formal ritual. They had as scant respect for magistrates, the Pilgrims' included, as the Saints had had for those in England when they lived there. They even allowed women to speak in meeting, not only a dangerous innovation in itself, but a violation of Scripture, as the Saints pointed out.

Altogether, the Friends were "madmen, lunaticks, daemoniacks," and in 1657 the United Colonies decided to drive them into the wilderness, warning Rhode Island not to give them refuge there. As the Confederation refused to admit Rhode Island and constantly snubbed it, this was sheer impudence, and that colony, true to Roger Williams' principles, rejected the "request," adding an observation that might have given the commissioners pause.

Rhode Island had no law "whereby to punish any for only declaring by words, &c., their minds and understandings concerning the things and ways of God, as to salvation and an external condition." And experience had proved that where these people "are most of all suffered to declare themselves freely, . . . there they least of all desire to come . . . They begin to loathe this place."

But the United Colonies were not convinced and recommended even more violent measures for its members. Quakers and all other heretics in each jurisdiction were to be banished "under pain of death, and if afterwards they presume to come again into that jurisdiction, then to be put to death as presumptuously incorrigible." All of the commissioners signed this—Governor Prence and Josiah Winslow for Plymouth. All of the United Colonies adopted the resolution, but only Massachusetts acted upon it.

In 1659, when six Friends were banished from the Old Colony on pain of death, John Alden nodded assent as Prence declared that, "in his conscience," all Quakers deserved "to be destroyed, both they, their wives and children, without pity or mercy"—a sad commentary on what "libertie of conscience" meant to some of the Saints.

But the Old Colony, for the most part, did not share Prence's view. Nor did it follow the Bay in branding Quakers with hot irons, slicing off their ears, flaying them with tarred ropes, beating them senseless with iron rods, burning their books, and confiscating everything they owned in guise of fines.

Still, the Pilgrims feared "these wolves in sheep clotheing" and locked up any found within the colony. After some months in jail, one William Leddra and a Quaker friend were offered their release if they would promise "without any sinestery reservation . . . to depart, and to come into this Collonie noe more, and pay their fees to the jaylor."

They refused to give any such promise. Nor would they pay the jailer. What could one do with such people?

Leddra had remarked, however, "It is like if I were at libertie out of prison, I might depart in the will of God ere long."

Seeing nothing better to do than make trial of this, they set Leddra free. And sure enough, he soon departed, going to Salem, where he was promptly seized and carried to Boston. The authorities there offered him his freedom if he would go to England. Leddra replied that he had no reason to go there. Brought to trial, he was sentenced to death.

Massachusetts had already hanged three Quakers for "rebellion, sedition, and presumptuous obtruding themselves," including gentle Mary Dyer, wife of the secretary of Rhode Island, once a Bay Saint herself. The trials of the condemned had been marked by the most revolting scenes, with Governor Endecott and most of the ministers crying for blood, led by John Wilson, pastor of Boston's First Church.

"I would carry fire in one hand, and fagots in the other, to burn all the Quakers in the world," cried Wilson. "Hang them! Or else——" And he drew a finger across his throat.

His colleague at the First Church, John Norton, who had been in Plymouth for a time, rushed into print to celebrate these proceedings, but there were deep and growing revulsion and indignation among the people. Leddra went to the gallows, but he was the last Quaker to be hanged in Massachusetts for heresy. Another was condemned to die, but the authorities did not dare to proceed. The theocrats of the Bay met a significant reverse here, beating their first retreat before the humanity and good sense of the common people.

Opposition to the crusade against "heretics" was even stronger and more articulate in the Old Colony, among Saints and Strangers alike. Nathaniel Morton and others tried to make out that the Quakers had little or no influence in the colony, that few were "leavened with their fixions and fantacyes."

The truth is, as the records reveal, that throughout the colony there was much open sympathy for the poor harassed Friends. The latter made a number of converts by their patience in adversity, their fearless spirit, their devotion to their cause, qualities the Pilgrims always admired.

In Barnstable, Sandwich, and other towns, their neighbors often went to great lengths to shield them from the authorities and self-appointing guardians of the state. Prence's policy met stout opposition at Duxbury, which harbored not only Quakers but Baptists. The opposition was led by John Howland's brother Arthur, and by the sons of Joseph Rogers, of the *Mayflower* group, and was seconded by the local pastor, John Holmes, who was not an inquisitor.

To his consternation and almost apoplexy, Governor Prence now discovered that his chief enemy's son, young Arthur Howland, was surreptitiously courting his daughter Elizabeth. As the law forbade "making motion of marriage" to a girl without her parents' consent, the irascible old governor summoned the "impudent" youth into court and fined him £5 ($250) for "inveighling" his daughter.

But the young lovers were not discouraged, and seven years later Arthur was again in court for having "disorderlie and unrighteously endeavored to obtain the affections of Mistress Elizabeth Prence." He had already obtained her affections, it is plain, wanting only those of her father, who again fined him and placed him under a £50 bond "to refrain and desist."

But the younger Saints could be quite as stubborn as their fathers. The couple went right on behaving "disorderlie and unrighteously" until they broke the iron will of the old governor, and in good time the names of Thomas Howland and Prence Howland were added to the baptismal roll.

The stoutest resistance to intolerance came from Scituate, directed by Assistant Governors Timothy Hatherly and James Cudworth, executors of Standish's estate.

"Our Civil Powers," Cudworth complained, "are so exercised in matters of religion and conscience that we have no time to effect anything that tends to the promotion of the civil weal; but must have a State religion, and a State ministry, and a State way of maintenance."

Angered by this, the General Court called Cudworth to explain his presence at Quaker meetings.

"I thought it better so to do," he replied, "than with the blind World to Censure, Rail at, and Revile them, when they neither saw their Persons, nor knew any of their Principles. But the Quakers and myself cannot close in divers things. And so I signify to the Court that I am no Quaker . . . But withal I tell you that I am no Quaker, so I will be no Persecutor."

Cudworth and Hatherly were deprived of office and disenfranchised. More and more dissenting Saints were similarly punished. As this did nothing but swell the chorus of protest, the authorities drew back a bit and decided to try a more reasonable policy.

They would overpower the Quakers by showing them the evil and error of their ways. In every town several reliable Saints were appointed "to repair to their meetings, together with the marshal or constable of the town, and to use their best endeavors by argument and discourse to convince or hinder them."

Whether these "truth" squads made any converts among the "heretics" does not appear. In any case, the scheme was soon abandoned, for in several places it backfired in a quite surprising manner.

One of the deacons at Barnstable was John Cooke, formerly a deacon at Plymouth for many years. His father had been Francis Cooke, of the *Mayflower* group, one of the Saints from Scrooby. Appointed to spy on the Baptists at Barnstable, Deacon

Cooke became one. Denounced and excommunicated, he withdrew to Dartmouth along the western limits of the colony, being followed by several of the Howlands.

One of the four men appointed to reason with the Quakers at Sandwich was Isaac Robinson. As the son of John Robinson, he was regarded as eminently sound and could certainly be expected to bring them to their senses. But Quaker doctrine evidently made more sense to him, and he now embraced it. Dismissed from office and disenfranchised for "sundrie scandels and falsehoods," Robinson crossed the Cape with a group of Quakers and settled at Succanesett (Falmouth), where he ran a tavern for many years, later crossing to Martha's Vineyard.

In Plymouth, as in Massachusetts, the Friends in the end defeated the Saints and forced them to grant "libertie of conscience"—*de facto*, if not *de jure*. Plymouth finally let it be known that if Quakers and other "rantors" would remove to the western limits of the colony along Narragansett Bay, they would not be molested.

In 1681 the town of Sandwich granted heretics the right to vote in the disposal of town lands and assessment of taxes, "soe long as they carry themselves civilly and not abuse their libertie." Other towns granted them similar privileges, though all disabilities were not removed for some time.

Charles II had intervened in the conflict, ordering the colonies to cease their persecutions—an order that was blandly ignored, though it did something to discourage official violence. As complaints of injustice continued to pour into London, the King appointed a commission to visit New England and look into affairs there—a step which rightly alarmed all the colonies.

Four ships of the line put in at Boston, the first appearance of the Royal Navy in the harbor, and four royal commissioners came ashore. Though their mere presence was a nuisance, they were not very officious. They found Plymouth the most tractable of the United Colonies, largely because the Pilgrims now were, as Governor Prence confessed, "the meanest & weakest, least able to stand of ourselves, and litle able to contribute any helpfullnes to others, and we know it, though none should tell us of it."

As seen by one of the commissioners in 1664, Plymouth was "a poor small Towne now, the People being removed into Farmes in the country." In all the colony there were "about twelve small townes, one sawmill for boards, one bloomary for iron, neither good river nor good harbour, nor any place of strength. They are so poor they are not able to maintain scholars to their ministers, but are necessitated to make use of a gifted brother in some places."

Three years earlier, in 1661, Massasoit had died, having always faithfully kept the peace that he had signed with the Pilgrims exactly forty years before. He was succeeded by his older son, Wamsutta, who soon came to Plymouth with his brother Metacom to confirm the peace treaty. On their visit they asked the Pilgrims to give them English names. The older became Alexander; the younger, Philip.

Soon the rumor ran that Alexander was plotting against the Pilgrims. When he failed to answer a summons, an armed force was dispatched to bring him in. Dragged from Sowams at pistol point, as if he were a common felon, whereas he and his father had always regarded themselves as sovereign allies, Alexander was sharply questioned by Governor Prence and finally released, being desperately sick of a fever—brought on, said some of the Saints, by a guilty conscience and "inward fury." A few days later he died at Plymouth, and his braves carried his body back to Sowams in solemn procession to be buried next to his father there.

This was not an auspicious beginning of a new regime, and it soon became evident that a storm was brewing. Both the Wampanoag and the Pilgrims were restless, full of complaints against each other. The old mutual trust had given way to brooding suspicion. The conflict stemmed basically from their very different and incompatible ways of life. What was good for the one was not good for the other. The more the English settlements grew and expanded, the more they impinged upon the

Indians' hunting grounds. In spite of every effort to Christianize and "civilize" them, the Indians preferred their old nomadic life —not because they were ignorant and perverse, but because, like most of us, they preferred the old and familiar ways handed down to them by their fathers. As we have since learned, culture patterns cannot be changed overnight.

Governor Prence died in 1673, in his seventy-third year, being succeeded by Josiah Winslow, now forty-four, "a worthie and well-accomplished gentleman, deservedly beloved by the people, being a true friend of their just liberties, generous, facetious, affable, and sincere, qualities incident to the family."

Winslow was far more liberal than Prence. He immediately restored the civil rights of those who had been deprived of them during the Quaker troubles. But his short regime is less remembered for this than for the great conflict and tragedy that ensued shortly after he took office.

Relations between the Indians and the whites had now reached the point where no compromise or accommodation of interest was possible. It was war to the death, and Massasoit's son, King Philip, was busily engaged in building up against the white intruders as grand an alliance as an Indian chief ever conceived, rallying to his banner almost all the Indians of New England, uniting them in one last desperate fight for their lands and their heritage—all the more desperate because their opportunity had almost passed.

After many frontier incidents, fighting broke out in the summer of 1675 in what became famed as King Philip's War, one of the great Indian conflicts in our history. At the insistence of Plymouth, the United Colonies raised a joint force to stop Philip, who had struck deep into the Old Colony, razing many towns, sweeping into the outskirts of Plymouth, sacking and burning Scituate. The flames of war quickly spread throughout New England as one tribe after another joined Philip.

With Governor Winslow as commander-in-chief, the forces of the United Colonies surprised and smashed the Narragansett. This was the decisive blow, for if the powerful Narragansett had joined Philip, as they were preparing to do, the Indians would have been triumphant everywhere from the Penobscot to Long Island Sound, as all informed contemporaries agreed.

As it was, the issue hung in the balance for some time, with Philip and his allies plundering and burning town after town, taking a heavy toll of life. As disaster piled upon disaster, Plymouth decreed a solemn day of prayer and humiliation, and then another, and another.

Seeking the cause of the trouble, the root of all the Saints' woes and reverses, the Plymouth pastor, John Cotton, found it in the unconscionable ways of New England youth, who were "haughty in spirit, in countenance, in garbe & fashion, . . . stubborne and rebellious against God & disobedient to parents, . . . very dull & sloathfull & irreverent in the time of worship."

There was no unanimity about this, however. Old John Eliot, "the Apostle to the Indians," attributed the scourge to the new fashion of wearing wigs, "an Abhomination unseemlie in the sight of God."

The pastor at Duxbury, John Holmes, was of still another mind and profoundly shocked many by saying the Saints' troubles were of their own making, a just punishment "for our dealing with the Quakers," a bold opinion he repeated on his deathbed.

In any case, the tide of battle began to turn in the spring of 1676.* As one after another of his allies deserted him, Philip returned to his homelands around Sowams. Surprising him there, a Plymouth force trapped and killed him, chopped off his head, and carried it in triumph to Plymouth. The bloody head of the "blasphemous leviathan" was posted on a pike on Fort Hill, where the bleaching skull remained for many years, a favorite nesting place for wrens.

Plymouth proclaimed a "day of publick Thanksgiving for the beginning of revenge upon the enemy." And the revenge was terrible. Indians who had declined to join Philip and placed

*Virginia, too, was having serious Indian troubles at this time, which occasioned the disturbances that erupted in Bacon's Rebellion and forced the royal governor, Sir William Berkeley, to run for his life.

themselves under Plymouth's protection were shipped off to Tangiers to be sold as slaves. Others who had surrendered on promise of their lives were shot or beheaded. As captives—men, women, and children—continued to pour into Plymouth, they were all sold as slaves, some locally, but most in the West Indies.

A likely Indian boy was picked out by the Plymouth pastor and sent as a present to the Reverend Increase Mather, soon to be president of Harvard, who declared himself delighted with such kindness in the form of so useful a gift. After some talk of executing him for his father's action, King Philip's son, a boy of nine, was shipped off and lived his life in chains, a slave in Bermuda.

As old John Eliot growled in bitter protest against these and like proceedings throughout the United Colonies, "The design of Christ in these last days is not to extirpate nations, but to gospelize them. To sell souls for money seemeth to me a dangerous merchandise."

All Wampanoag lands were seized and sold to pay the costs of the war, which were heavy. Almost every family in the colony was grieving for someone lost in Indian raids or on the battlefield. Losses of cattle, houses, and other possessions had left many in dire straits. Part of the proceeds from the sale of Wampanoag lands went to build a new meetinghouse at Plymouth.

Only one part of New England escaped devastation. Most of the Rhode Island towns escaped without any hurt though the bitterest fighting raged around them. Throughout the war, Roger Williams lived quietly and unmolested at his trading post in the heart of the Indian country, dying there eight years later, a "seeker" to the last.

The Old Colony had weathered its worst storm, but currents were already in motion that would extinguish its existence as a separate colony.

King Philip was no sooner disposed of than King Charles raised his head, and Plymouth could scarcely hope to post his on Fort Hill. Charles sent over a special royal agent, Edward Randolph, to see that Massachusetts walked the line laid down in London and to inspect the colonies generally.

As usual with royal agents, Randolph got little satisfaction at Boston. He was pleased with Plymouth, however, finding Josiah Winslow a "gentleman of loyal principles" and critical of Massachusetts' carriage toward "his Majestie's royal person." As Plymouth was anxious to have a proper charter, Randolph promised to do all he could on their behalf for such a "loyal colony."

Winslow suspected that the Bay, with its grasping ways, had designs on Plymouth. It had just put in a most impertinent claim to some of the best of the Wampanoag lands, always accepted as lying within Plymouth's bounds. Plymouth feared the fate of the small New Haven colony, which had been gobbled up by Connecticut some ten years before.

Agents were sent to London to prosecute the charter business, one of them being Ichabod Wiswall, pastor at Duxbury, married to one of John Alden's granddaughters. Wiswall got many promises of favorable action. But little had been accomplished by 1685, when things took a sharp turn for the worse, with the death of the Merry Monarch and the succession of his glum brother.

James II came to the throne with the scarcely concealed design of restoring Catholicism and returning the kingdom to the tutelage of Rome. This was alarming enough, but one of the first steps taken by the deluded King, the most wrongheaded of all the Stuarts, caused utter consternation in New England, among Saints and non-Saints alike. He appointed a former governor of New York, Sir Edmund Andros, a pliant tool, to be "Governor-in-chief in and over the territory and dominion of New England."

Andros entered Boston in ducal style late in 1686, accompanied by sixty redcoats—"to keep the country in awe; a crew that began to teach New England to drab, drink, blaspheme, curse, and damn," the outraged inhabitants exclaimed, "committing insufferable riots amongst a quiet and peaceable people."

The new governor general summarily scrapped the existing machinery of government, deposing the chief magistrates in all the colonies, inviting a few of them to sit with him on his council. There were to be no more elections. All authority centered in Boston, in the person of Andros, who disposed of things as he saw fit, arbitrarily increasing taxes and levying special assessments.

Sir Edmund requested the use of a meetinghouse where he and his friends might hold Anglican services. The Saints could not have been more shocked if he had asked to bring the Pope in—or Satan himself. The Boston ministers refused his request, declaring that they could not "in good conscience" allow any meetinghouse to be used "for the Common-Prayer worship."

Andros therefore ordered Anglican services in the Third Church, later renowned as the Old South, while the pious spat and fumed at having their church defiled with "leeks, garlic, and trash."

Saints were required to "kiss the Book" when taking an oath—howling all the while about the tyranny and injustice of it all, forgetting their own practices upon the Quakers and others. Non-communicants may have enjoyed a grim smile at the irony of this. But even they were alarmed and profoundly disturbed when Andros challenged the colonists' title to their lands, refusing to recognize the validity of any Indian deeds—of "no more worth," said he, "than a scratch with a bear's paw."

Things went on in this painful course for two years, until the spring of 1689, when Boston learned that James had been deposed. Andros and fifty friends were soon in jail, to be shipped home to answer for "high crimes and misdemeanors." The former governments in the colonies were reinstituted. In Plymouth, Governor Thomas Hinckley was restored to office, with Major William Bradford as deputy. The Old Colony was more anxious than ever to procure a charter. And with such good Protestants as William and Mary on the throne, the prospect looked more promising than for a long time.

During Andros' reign, Increase Mather had slipped away from

Boston at night and in disguise to carry the colonists' complaints to England. Plymouth now returned Wiswall to London as its agent. All the colonies now lacked charters and in the race for favors, as Wiswall soon discovered, Mather had the inside track, thanks to a fat purse. On his mission he spent £1,700 ($85,000), finding it "necessarie to gratifie severall persons, some with £20, some with £30, some with £50, some with 50 guineas, &c. . . ."

Massachusetts, as usual, was seeking everything within reach— New Hampshire, Maine, and even Nova Scotia. Learning that New York had included Plymouth in its patent, Mather "procured the dropping of it." Then, with no authorization whatever, he included it in the Massachusetts charter on the pretext that the Old Colony had no hopes of obtaining one of its own.

The clause was angrily stricken out by Wiswall—"the Weasel," snapped Mather, annoyed to have been balked in his design. Wiswall kept writing for funds. The Plymouth pastor, John Cotton, Mather's brother-in-law and originally from the Bay himself, urged Governor Hinckley to go over, saying that all men "of wisdome, prudence, and pietie" were opposed to any scheme of union with Massachusetts.

But the governor was halfhearted and discouraged, declaring that there was no likelihood of obtaining a charter unless William and Mary, "out of their Royal bounty and clemencie, graciously please to grant it, *sub forma pauperis*, to their poor and loyal Subjects of this collonie."

It was not so granted, and in October 1691, Massachusetts was given a patent with New Plimoth included within its bounds— largely through the "rashness and impudence," said Wiswall, "of one at least who went from New England in disguise by night."

Perhaps Mather could not have saved Plymouth. It was small and weak, thinly populated and having few resources. Yet Rhode Island, even smaller and quite as weak, obtained a charter and retained its independence.

In any case, the Old Colony had been thrown by the Bay Horse. It expired in its seventy-third year, less than the span of many a life. Two members of the *Mayflower* party survived it—

John Cooke, the former deacon, now a Baptist minister at Dartmouth; and Mary (Allerton) Cushman, widow of Ruling Elder Thomas Cushman. The Elder had died just a short time before, at the age of eighty-four, and "much of God's presence went away from this Church when this blessed pillar was removed."

John Alden narrowly missed the final debacle, dying four years earlier, in his eighty-ninth year, having outlived many of his children, being buried beside Priscilla on his farm in Duxbury, near Eagle Tree Pond.

Early in July 1692, the Plymouth General Court met once more, for the last time. As its final act, it set aside the last Wednesday in August "to be kept as a day of sollemne fasting and humiliation."

The Saints had kept many such days, but never one so deeply humiliating.

And yet as they looked around, despondent as they were, they glimpsed a ray of hope. It might have been worse, much worse. And some months later, they proclaimed a Thanksgiving "for the preservation of the King & Queen, &c.; for our Gospel-mercies, health, harvest, destroying caterpillars last summer, saving ours in storms, & for that the Governmente over us is yet in the hands of Saincts."

Falling suddenly from its exalted position as the poor but proud capital of the Pilgrim empire, Plymouth became a mere county seat—and not of much importance at that. For a century or more, it remained just another sleepy country town of no special distinction, lying quite outside the main currents of history, its heroic beginnings all but forgotten and of interest to few.

But historically and spiritually, it would enjoy a glorious resurrection. The essentially democratic concepts that underlay the Pilgrim meetinghouse would exert an influence second to none in shaping the ideas, manners, customs, ways of life, and moral values of millions of Americans.

In time, Plymouth and Plymouth Rock[1] would become a national shrine.

APPENDIX

The Pilgrim Company

Who should properly be included in the Pilgrim Company? The question is almost wholly one of definition. Many lists have been drawn, some more inclusive than others. By the criteria I have chosen to use, which are as broad as they can reasonably be made, the company includes:

a) all "saincts," "strangers," hired hands, and indentured servants who came on any of the Pilgrims' ships—*Mayflower, Fortune, Anne, Little James, Talbot, Handmaid,* or second *Mayflower;*

b) all members of the Green Gate congregation who came at any other time, either soon or late;

c) those of the merchant adventurers who settled in the colony;

d) all others who settled at Plymouth and were granted land there before 1631 (such as Phineas Pratt, a refugee from Wessagusset, and those who came with John Oldham "on their perticuler").

With the exception of the "Straggling Saints" and "Merchant Adventurers," the several groups are listed under the name of the ship on which each came.

An asterisk (*) indicates the remarkably few Pilgrims from Scrooby.

Those addressed as "Master" (sometimes written "Mister," occasionally "Mr.") were relatively the aristocrats of the company—in general, those with means to bring indentured servants.

I. *MAYFLOWER* — of Harwich (180 tons); Christopher Jones, master; out of London, mid-July, 1620, dropping anchor off tip of Cape Cod, November 11, Old Style, with 102 passengers, including Oceanus Hopkins, born at sea.

(Names in italics are of those who died in General Sickness or within six months of landing.)

A. SAINTS

(17 men, 10 women, 14 children)

Allerton, Master Isaac (c. 1586–1659) —of London, tailor "the first Yankee trader" Probably one of Ancient Brethren, Amsterdam; citizen, Leyden, 1614; asst. governor, Plymouth, 1621–c. 1631; married, 1626, to 2nd wife, Fear Brewster (see *Anne* Saints); 1 child; Purchaser, 1626; Undertaker and London business agent, 1627–c. 1631; dis-

missed in disgrace, went to Marblehead, operating fishing fleet until
asked to leave by Massachusetts authorities, c.1635; merchant, New Amsterdam, c.1636-46; married, c.1644, to
3rd wife, Joanna ——; merchant, New
Haven, c.1647-59, making fortune in
Virginia and West Indian trade; died
insolvent.

——, Mrs. Mary (Morris) (c.1588-
1621)—of Newbury, Berks. Married,
Leyden, 1611; died on Mayflower in
Plymouth Harbor several days after
being delivered of stillborn child at
height of winter gale.

> Bartholomew (c.1612-   )
> After father's disgrace, returned to
> England, becoming minister there.
> Remember (c.1614-c.1655)
> Married, c.1633, to Moses Maver-
> ick, pastor at Marblehead; 6 chil-
> dren.
> Mary (c.1616-99)
> Married, c.1635, to Thomas Cush-
> man (see Fortune Saints); last sur-
> vivor of Mayflower company; 4
> children.

*Bradford, Master William (1590-
1657)—of Austerfield, Yorks.; fustian maker
"a commone blessing and father to
them all"
Early orphaned and virtually adopted
by Brewster, c.1602; silkworker, Amsterdam, 1607-09; citizen, Leyden,
1612; governor or asst. governor,
Plymouth, 1621-57; Purchaser, 1626;
Undertaker, 1627-41; leader in opposing attempt to establish toleration,
1646; presiding officer of United Colonies, 1648 and 1656; left £900 estate.

——, Mrs. Dorothy (May) (1597-
1620)—of Wisbeach, Cambridge-
shire; daughter of Henry May,
elder of Ancient Brethren and later

of Ainsworthians, subsequently
joining Leyden church
Married, Leyden, 1613; drowned at
tip of Cape Cod, "falling" from Mayflower while at anchor; 1 child, John
(see Straggling Saints).

*Brewster, Master William (c.1566-
1643)—probably born in Scrooby or
vicinity
"wise and discreete and well spoken
. . . qualified above many"
Peterhouse   College,   Cambridge,
1580-c.1583; employ of Sir William
Davison, c.1583-89; postmaster and
bailiff-receiver, Scrooby, 1590-1607;
instrumental in organizing Scrooby
congregation, 1606-07; Amsterdam,
1608-09; tutoring and odd jobs, Leyden, 1609-16; Ruling Elder, 1609-43;
operated Choir Alley press, 1616-19;
flight and hiding in England, 1619-20;
Purchaser, 1626; Undertaker, 1627-41;
argues against Roger Williams' reten-
tion as "teacher," 1633.

*——, Mrs. Mary (Wentworth?)
(c.1568-1627)—perhaps daughter of
Thomas   Wentworth,   Brewster's
predecessor at Scrooby Manor
Married, Scrooby, 1591; died Plymouth; 5 children.

> Love (1611-50)
> Married Sarah Collier (see Mer-
> chant Adventurers), 1634, and early
> removed to Duxbury where he
> died.
> Wrestling (1614-c.1635)
> Went to Piscataqua (Portsmouth),
> N.H., as young man and soon died
> there.

Carver, John (c.1566-1621)—of Doncaster, Yorks.; merchant
"Of singular piety, and rare for humilitie"
First appears in Leyden records as
connected with church, 1616; negotiations with merchant adventurers and

purchasing of supplies, 1617-20; deacon, c.1617-21; died of sunstroke while toiling in cornfields.

———, Mrs. Catherine (White) c.1580-1621)—of Sturton-le-Steeple, eldest sister of Bridget, John Robinson's wife

Married George Leggatt, 1596; 1 child, Marie, who evidently died young; married Carver, c.1600; died "of a broken heart" soon after husband; no children.

    Minter, Desire (c.1600–)—daughter of Thomas Minter, member of Green Gate congregation, citizen of Leyden

    Returned to England, c.1625, and died there.

*Cooke, Francis (1577-1633)—wool comber, of Blyth, Notts.

Amsterdam, 1607-09; Leyden, 1609-20; Purchaser, 1626; died Plymouth (for family, see Anne Saints).

    John (1612-95)

Married Sarah Warren (see Anne Strangers), 1634; deacon, c.1634; deprived of office and excommunicated for turning Baptist during religious troubles, 1657; removed to Dartmouth (New Bedford) and became occasional Baptist preacher there.

Crackston, John ( )—of Colchester

    John (–1628)

Lost himself in woods and froze feet, dying of gangrene.

Fletcher, Moses ( )—smith, of Sandwich

Married Mrs. Sarah Dingby, Leyden, 1613.

Fuller, Master Samuel (c.1585-1633) —say maker, of Redenhall, Norfolk; Pilgrims' "physition & chirurgeon" "a great help & comforte unto them" Leader of seceding Ancient Brethren, 1609; deacon, c.1609-33; married Agnes Carpenter, 1613; married Bridget Lee, 1617; Purchaser, 1626; "bled" and converted Puritans at Salem and Boston, 1628-30 (for wife, see Anne Saints).

Goodman, John (c.1595-1621)—linen weaver

Married, Leyden, 1619, to Sarah Hooper. Brought only dogs on ship, large mastiff bitch and small spaniel; Peter Browne's companion on deer and "lyon" hunt.

Priest, Degory (c.1580-1621)—hatter, of London

Married, Leyden, 1611, to Mrs. Sarah (Allerton) Vincent; citizen, Leyden, 1615.

Rogers, Thomas ( )—camlet merchant

Citizen, Leyden, 1618.

    Joseph (c. 1608-78)

Married Hannah —— and removed to Eastham, 1644; 7 children.

Tilley, Edward (–1621)—cloth maker, of London

Joined with Captain Standish "for counsel and advice" on First Discovery; almost froze on "Thievish Harbor" exploration.

———, Mrs. Anne (——) (–1621)

Brought along two small "cousins," Humility Cooper and "Henery" Samson (see Strangers below).

Tilley, John (–1621)—silkworker, of London

On Third Discovery, probably on First and Second as well.

———, Mrs. Elizabeth (Comyngs) (c.1585-1621)—of St. Andrew Undershaft, London

Married, London, 1605

    Elizabeth (1606-87)—once presumed to be Carver's daughter

Married John Howland (see Servants below), c.1624; died at Swansea; 9 children.

Tinker, Thomas (–1621)–wood
sawyer
Citizen, Leyden, 1617.
——, *Mrs.* (——) (–1621).
——*(son)* (–1621).
Turner, John (–1621)–merchant
Citizen, Leyden, 1610.
——*(son)* (–1621).
——*(son)* (–1621).
White, Master William (c.1592–1621)
–wool carder
Perhaps related to White family of
Sturton-le-Steeple, into which Carver
and Robinson married.
——, *Mrs.* Susanna (Fuller) (c.1594–
1680)–sister of Deacon Samuel
Fuller (see above)
Married, Leyden, 1612; became 2nd
wife of Edward Winslow (see below), 1621.
  Resolved (c.1615–c.1690)
  Married Judith Vassall of Scituate,
  1640, and settled there, removing to
  Marshfield, 1662; later at Salem,
  where he married Mrs. Abigail
  (——). Lord; returned to Marshfield
  and died there; 5 children.
  Peregrine (1620–1703)
  Born on *Mayflower* month after arrival; 1648, married Sarah Bassett
  (see *Fortune* Saints); granted 200
  acres by General Court, 1665, "in
  respect that he was the first of the
  English that was born in these
  parts"; captain of militia, 1673; did
  not join church till 1698, in 78th
  year; died at Marshfield; 6 children.
Winslow, Master Edward (1595–
1655)–of Droitwich, Worcestershire; printer
Assistant printer at Choir Alley press,
1617–19; member of parties sent out
to explore Cape Cod and environs;
married, Plymouth, 1621, to Mrs. Susanna (Fuller) White (see above);

diplomatic mission to Massasoit, 1621;
author of "come-on" literature to attract settlers; agent to England, 1623;
opened trade along Kennebec, 1625;
member of General Court as governor
or asst. governor, 1624–46; Purchaser,
1626; Undertaker, 1627–41; jailed in
London by Archbishop Laud, 1635;
removed to Marshfield, 1637; commissioner to New England Confederacy, 1643–44; sailed for London, 1646,
and never returned; chairman of joint
English-Dutch commission to assess
damage done English ships by Dutch
in neutral Danish ports; chief of 3
commissioners appointed by Oliver
Cromwell to conquer Spanish West
Indies; died of tropical fever on flagship off Jamaica; buried at sea with
salvo of cannon.
——, *Mrs. Elizabeth (Barker)* (c.1597–
  (1621)–of Chattisham, Suffolk
Married, Leyden, 1618; no children.

B. STRANGERS
(17 men, 9 women, 14 children)
Billington, John (c.1590–1630)–of
London
"one of ye profanest families amongst
them"
Tied up by neck and heels for curs-
ing Standish when called to perform
military duty, 1622; mixed up in Lyford-Oldham "mutiny," 1624; Purchaser, 1626; hanged for murder, 1630.
——, Mrs. Ellen (c.1592–   )–of
London
Married, Plymouth, 1638, to Gregory
Armstrong.
  Francis (c.1612–   )
  Almost blew up *Mayflower* by
  shooting off squibs near powder
  kegs; discovered Billington Sea,
  small lake behind Plymouth; married, Plymouth, 1634, to Mrs. Christian (Penn) Eaton (see *Anne*

Strangers); removed to Yarmouth and died there; 9 children.

John (c.1614–c.28)
Lost himself in woods and turned up on Cape Cod, 1621, leading to first acquaintance with Cape tribes.

Britteridge, Richard (–1620)

Browne, Peter (c.1600–33)–of Great Burstead, Essex
John Goodman's companion on deer and "lyon" hunt; married, Plymouth, 1623, to Mrs. Martha Ford (see *Fortune* Strangers); Purchaser, 1626; married to Mary ——, 1628; 2 children by 1st marriage and 3 by second.

Chilton, James (c.1563–1620)–of Canterbury, tailor

——, Mrs. —— (——) (–1621).

Mary (c.1605–79)
Reputedly first Pilgrim to step foot on Plymouth Rock; married, Plymouth, 1624, to John Winslow (see *Fortune* Strangers); removed to Boston, 1655, and died there; 10 children.

Clarke, Richard (–1621).

Cooper, Humility (c.1612–   )–of London
One of two small "cousins" brought along by Edward Tilleys (see above); "was sent for into England, and dyed there."

Eaton, Francis (c.1595–1633)–of Bristol, carpenter and shipwright
Married, Plymouth, c.1622, to 2nd wife, —— ——; married Christian Penn (see *Anne* Strangers), c.1626; 4 children.

——, Mrs. Sarah (——) (c.1590–1621)
–presumably of Bristol
Samuel (1620–   )–arrived in mother's arms, "a suckling child"
Married, Plymouth, to Elizabeth (——), c.1647; in 1661, to Martha Billington, daughter of father's

third wife by her second husband, Francis Billington (see above).

Fuller, Edward (–1621)–of Redenhall, Norfolk
Probably Deacon Samuel Fuller's brother, but apparently not of the Leyden congregation.

——, Mrs. Ann (——) (–1621).

Samuel (c.1616–83)
Removed to Barnstable, c.1640, and married Jane Lothrop, local pastor's daughter; 3 or more children.

Gardiner, Richard (c.1600–21)–of Harwich, Essex, John Alden's home town

Hopkins, Master Stephen (c.1585–1644) – of Wotton-under-Edge, Gloucestershire
Shipwrecked on Bermuda while on way to Virginia and condemned to death for leading mutiny there, 1609–10; joined to Captain Standish for "counsel and advice" on First Discovery, being only one of passengers with any knowledge of New World; accompanies Winslow on visit to Massasoit at Sowams, 1621; Purchaser, 1626; asst. governor, 1633–36, and probably 1624–32; frequently in conflict with authorities in later years.

——, Mrs. Elizabeth (——) (–c. 1640)–Hopkins' second wife
Bore 5 more children at Plymouth (Giles and Constance were Hopkins' children by 1st wife).

Giles (c.1607–c.1690)
Married, Plymouth, 1639, to Catharine Wheldon, and removed to Yarmouth; died, Eastham; 7 children.

Constance (c.1605–77)
Married, Plymouth, c.1627, to Nicholas Snow (see *Anne* Strangers); died at Eastham.

Damaris (c.1617–c.1627)

Oceanus (1620–   )

Born at sea on *Mayflower*, dying before 1627.

Margeson, Edmund (–1621)

Martin, Master Christopher (c.1575–1621)–of Great Burstead, Essex "he so insulteth over our poore people, with shuch scorne & contempte, as if they were not good enough to wipe his shoes"

Named by merchant adventurers to represent Strangers in purchase of provisions for voyage, 1619–20; treasurer of emigrant company and "governour" of passengers on *Mayflower;* accounts found to be in great disorder, the beginning of Pilgrims' extended financial troubles.

———, *Mrs.* —— (——) (–1621)

Prower, Solomon (–1620) Martin's stepson.

Mullins, Master William (c.1580–1621)–shopkeeper, of Dorking, Surrey

———, *Mrs. Alice* (——) (–1621) Probably Mullins' 2nd or 3rd wife.

Priscilla (c.1602–c.1685) Married John Alden (see Hired Hands below), c.1622; 9 children.

Joseph (c.1614–21)

Rigdale, John (–1621)–of London

———, *Mrs. Alice* (——) (–1621)

Samson, Henry (–1684)–of London Married Ann Plummer and removed to Duxbury; 8 children.

Standish, Captain Myles (c.1584–1656) –probably of Chorley, Lancashire "a little chimney is quickly fired"

Soldier in English forces sent to aid Dutch, c. 1600–02; leader of First Discovery, 1620; saves Pilgrim party in "huggery" at Eastham, 1620; organizes Pilgrim army and explores Massachusetts Bay, 1621; brings Wituwamat's head home in triumph from Wes-

sagusset, 1623; married, Plymouth, 1623, to 2nd wife, Barbara —— (see *Anne* Strangers); vainly attempts to recover Cape Ann, 1625; sent to England and returns with news of Robinson's death, 1626; Purchaser, 1626; Undertaker, 1627–41; arrests Thomas Morton at Merry Mount, 1629; removed to Duxbury, c.1632; asst. governor almost continuously from 1633, and probably from 1624; favors religious toleration, 1645; left estate of £258 ($12,900); alone of Pilgrim leaders, never joined church.

———, *Mrs. Rose* (——) (–1621) Nothing whatever is known of Standish's wife.

Warren, Master Richard (c.1580–1628)–of London, merchant "a usefull instrumente"

Member of exploration parties along Cape Cod; probably asst. governor, 1624–28 (for family, see *Anne* Strangers).

Williams, Thomas (–1621)–of Yarmouth, Norfolk

Winslow, Gilbert (1600–)–Edward Winslow's 3rd brother Returned to England, c.1646, and died there.

C. HIRED HANDS
(5 men)

Alden, John (1599–1686)–cooper of Harwich, Essex "a hopfull yong man"

Married, c.1622, to Priscilla Mullins (see Strangers above); removed to Duxbury, c.1632; asst. governor, 1633–39, 1651–86, and probably 1631–32; arrested at Boston for murder, 1634; opposes religious toleration, 1645; leader in Quaker and Baptist persecutions, 1657; treasurer, 1656–58; being "low in his estate," granted £10 in consideration of his public services, 1660.

Allerton, John (-1621)—mariner
Hired to go back for those at Leyden.

Ellis, — ( )—sailor
Engaged to remain a year in colony; returned to England on *Fortune.*

English, Thomas (-1621)—mariner
Hired to take charge of Pilgrim shallop.

Trevore, William ( )—sailor
Returned to England with Ellis and spread lavish tales about richness of Plimoth Plantation.

D. SERVANTS
(11 men, 1 woman, 6 children)
Allerton's—
  Hooke, John (-1621)—"a servante boy"
Brewster's—
  More, Richard (c.1613-c.1684)—of London
One of family of orphaned waifs forced, as was common practice at the time, to become indentured servants under auspices of church and Lord Mayor of London; was living with one of adventurers, Thomas Weston, when "transported"; migrated to Massachusetts; married Christian Hunt and Jane Hollingsworth; died Salem; 4 children.
  More, — (-1621)—Richard's brother
Carver's—
  More, Jasper, (-1620)
  Wilder, Roger (-1621)—"Manservant"
  —, — ( )—"Maid-Servant"
Catherine Carver's "maid servant maried, & dyed a year or two after, here in this place."
  Latham, William (-c.1645)—servant boy

After more than 20 years at Plymouth, returned to England and thence to Bahamas, where, "with some others, was starved for want of food."

Howland, John (1592-1672)—of London
"a plaine-hearted Christian"
Evidently inherited Carver's estate and immediately bought his freedom; married Elizabeth Tilley (see Saints above), c.1624; Purchaser, 1626; Undertaker, 1627-41; asst. governor, 1633-35, and probably 1629-32; in charge of Kennebec trading post at time of Hocking murder, 1634; apparently held somewhat to blame, for never again entrusted with public office; died Swansea; 9 children.

Fuller's—
  Butten, William (1598-1620)—of Austerfield
Died before land was sighted, and buried at sea.

Hopkins'—
  Dotey, Edward (c.1600-55)—of London
Perhaps one of leaders of mutiny on *Mayflower;* with Leister (see below), fought first and last duel in colony, 1621; Purchaser, 1626; married — — and then Faith (Clarke), c.1635; died at Yarmouth; 9 children.
  Leister, Edward (c.1600-)—of London
". . . after he was at liberty, went to Virginia, & there dyed."

Martin's—
  Langemore, John (-1620)

Mullins'—
  Carter, Robert (-1621)

White's—
  Holbeck, William (-1621)
  Thompson, Edward (-1620).

Winslow's—

More, Ellen (-1621)—"a little girle that was put to this family."

Story, Elias (-1621)—manservant, of London

Soule, George (c.1600–1680)—of Eckington, Worcestershire

Married Mary Becket (see *Anne Strangers*), c.1627; died Duxbury; 7 children.

II. *FORTUNE*—of London (55 tons); Thomas Barton, master; out of London early July, 1621, arriving Plymouth, November 11, with "35 persons to remaine & live in ye plantation."

A. SAINTS
(9 men, 2 women, 1 child)

Bassett, William (c.1590–c.1655)— master mason, of Bethnal Green, Middlesex

Married, Leyden, 1611, to 2nd wife, Margaret Oldham; later married 3rd wife; Purchaser, 1626; removed to Bridgewater, 1649.

———, Mrs. Elizabeth (——) (   )

Bompass, Edward (-1693)—native Leydener

Removed to Duxbury; married Hannah ——; later to Marshfield; 8 children.

*Brewster, Jonathan (1593–1659)— ribbon maker, of Scrooby.

Amsterdam, 1608–09; Leyden, 1609–21; married, c.1615, to —— ——, losing wife and child four years later; citizen, Leyden, 1617; married, Plymouth, 1624, to Lucretia Oldham (see *Anne Strangers*); Purchaser, 1626; removed to Duxbury, c.1632; agent at trading post on Connecticut River, 1635–36; removed to New London, Conn., 1649, founding trading post by Thames River on present site of Gro-

ton; deputy to Connecticut General Court, 1650, 1655, 1658; 8 children; 2 oldest sons returned to England, c.1656, and Brewster seriously contemplated going with them.

Cushman, Robert (1578–1625)—wool comber, of Canterbury

"their right hand with their freinds, ye adventurers"

Married, Canterbury, 1606, to Sarah Reder; deacon, c.1609–25; married, Leyden, 1617, to Mrs. Mary (Clarke) Singleton, widow of Canterbury shoemaker; negotiations in London for removal to New World, 1617–20; sailed on *Speedwell*, 1620, but abandoned voyage when vessel put back 3rd time; sermonized on "Danger of Self-Love" soon after arrival of *Fortune;* returning to England to compose quarrel about amended articles of agreement, captured by French pirates; planning to settle in colony, died suddenly, London, 1625, probably of plague.

Thomas (1607–91)

"very studious & sollicitous for the peace & prosperity of the church, & to prevent & heale all breaches" Left with Bradford during father's absence and adopted by him after latter's death; married, Plymouth, c.1636, to Mary Allerton (see *Mayflower* Saints); Brewster's successor as Ruling Elder, 1649–91; 7 children.

De la Noye, Phillipe (Delano) (1602– c.1680)

"born of French parents, . . . and proving himself to be come of such parents as were in full communion with the French churches, was hereupon admitted by the Church of Plymouth"

Removed to Duxbury, c.1632; married, 1634, to Esther Dewbury; removed to Bridgewater, 1649; married,

1657, to Mrs. Mary (Pontus) Glass (see Straggling Saints); 9 children.

*Morton, Thomas ( )—of Harworth, Notts; brother of George Morton (see *Anne* Saints)
Died or left colony before 1627.

Nicholas, Austin ( )
Died or left colony before 1627.

Symonson, Moses (Simmons) ( )
"a child of one that was in communion with the Dutch church at Leyden"
Removed to Duxbury, c.1632; married — —; 2 children.

Wright, William (–1633)
Purchaser, 1626.

———, Mrs. Priscilla (Carpenter) (1597–1689)—sister of Mrs. Juliana Morton (see *Anne* Saints)
Married, Leyden, 1619; died, Duxbury; 1 child.

B. STRANGERS

(17 men, 2 women, 4 children)

Adams, John (–1633)
Married, c.1625, to Ellen Newton (see *Anne* Strangers); Purchaser, 1626; 3 children.

Beale, William ( )
Died or left colony before 1627.

Briggs, Clement (–1649)—of Southwark, fellmonger
Married Joan Allen, c.1630, and removed to Dorchester; 5 children.

Cannon, John ( )
Died or left colony before 1627.

Conner, William ( )

Deane, Stephen (–c.1636)—of Southwark, miller
Married Elizabeth Ring (see Straggling Saints); Purchaser, 1626; granted leave to build Plymouth's first mill, but died before work began; 3 children.

Flavell, Thomas ( )—of London

Died or left colony before 1627.
——(son) ( )
Died or left colony before 1627.

Ford, Mrs. Martha (—) (–c. 1626)—probably of London
"delivered of a sonne the first night she landed, & both are doing very well"
Widow of leather dresser, of Southwark, who evidently died at sea; married, 1623, to Peter Browne (see *Mayflower* Strangers); 5 children.

William ( )
Returned to England but came back to settle at Duxbury, c.1632; married Ann —; 4 children.

Martha ( )

John (1621–93)
Married Hanna —; died, Marshfield.

Hicks, Robert (–1648—of Southwark, dealer in hides.
Purchaser, 1626 (for family, see *Anne* Strangers).

Hilton, William (c.1600–75)—vintner, of Northwich, Cheshire
Left colony at time of Lyford-Oldham troubles, 1624, going to New Hampshire and there founding Dover with brother, Edward, fishmonger, of London; removed to York, Me., c. 1648, and died there (for family, see *Anne* Strangers).

Morgan, Benedict ( )—of London, mariner
Died or left colony before 1627.

Palmer, William (–1638)—of London, nailer
Purchaser, 1626; removed to Duxbury, c.1632; 3 children (for wife, see *Anne* Strangers).

William (–c.1661)
Married, Scituate, 1633, to Elizabeth Hodgkins; removed to Yarmouth, c. 1640; to Dartmouth, 1652; to New-

ton, R.I., 1656, where he died a member of Baptist church.

Pitt, William ( )—of London, armorer
Died or left colony before 1627.

Prence, Thomas (1600–73)—carriage maker, of London
"a terrour to evill-doers"
Married, 1624, to Patience Brewster (see *Anne* Saints); 5 children; Purchaser, 1626; Undertaker, 1627–41; married, 1635, to Mary Collier (see Merchant Adventurers); 4 children; member of General Court, 1633–73; governor, 1634, 1638, 1657–73; removed to Eastham, 1644; opposed religious toleration, 1645; leader in Quaker and Baptist persecutions, 1657; married, Eastham, 1662, to Mrs. Apphia (——) Freeman; induced to move back to Plymouth by gift of large farm at "Plain Dealing"; married Mrs. Mary (——) Howes, c.1667.

Stacey, Hugh ( )
Removed to Dedham, then Salem, finally returning to England.

Steward, James ( )
Died or left colony before 1627.

Tench, William ( )
Died or left colony before 1627.

Winslow, John (1597–1674)—of Droitwich, Worcestershire; Edward Winslow's 2nd brother.
Married, Plymouth, c.1627, to Mary Chilton (see *Mayflower* Strangers); agent at Kennebec, 1651–54; removed to Boston, 1655, and died there; 10 children, daughter Sarah marrying Myles Standish, Jr.

III. *SHALLOP FROM SPARROW*, arriving early in 1622, bringing seven men who joined those sent out later by Weston on *Charity* and *Swan* and went north with them to found Wessagusset.

Pratt, Phineas (1593–1680)—probably of London.
Fled Wessagusset to Plymouth before Standish's liquidation of Weston's "disorderly" colony, 1623; Purchaser, 1626; married, Plymouth, 1630, to Mary Priest (see *Anne* Saints); removed to Massachusetts, c.1650; died, Charlestown; 9 children.

Joshua (–c.1656)
Removed to Dartmouth, 1652; married Bathsheba ——; 3 children.

IV. *ANNE*—of London (140 tons); William Peirce, master; and *LITTLE JAMES* (44 tons); John Bridges, master, arriving July-August, 1623, with "about 60 persons for ye generall, some of them being very usefull persons, . . . and some were so bad as they were faine to be at charge to send them home againe ye next year."

A. SAINTS
(5 men, 9 women, 18 children)

*Brewster, Patience (1600–33)—Ruling Elder's oldest daughter
Amsterdam, 1608–09; Leyden, 1609–23, probably living with Robinsons, 1620–23; married, 1624, to Thomas Prence (see *Fortune* Strangers); died, Plymouth, in smallpox epidemic; 5 children.

*Brewster, Fear (1606–33)—born on eve of flight from Scrooby
Amsterdam, 1608–09; Leyden, 1609–23; married, 1626, to Isaac Allerton (see *Mayflower* Saints); died, Plymouth, of smallpox; 1 child, Isaac Allerton, Jr., first Plymouth student at Harvard, who later migrated to Virginia.

Cooke, Mrs. Hester (Mayhieu) (c.

1592–1675)—Walloon; wife of Francis Cooke (see *Mayflower* Saints)
Married, Leyden, c.1613.

Jane (c.1615–66)
Married, Plymouth, c.1638, to Experience Mitchell (see below); died, Bridgewater; 7 children.

Hester (c.1616–c.1666)
Married, Plymouth, 1644, to Richard, son of William Wright (see *Fortune* Saints); 3 children.

Jacob (1618–75)
Married, 1646, to Damaris Hopkins; 1669, to Mrs. Elizabeth (Lettice) Shurtleff; 6 children.

Godbertson, Godbert (Cuthbert Cuthbertson) (c.1590–1633)—Walloon; hat maker, of Leyden
Married, Leyden, 1617, to Elizabeth Kendall; Purchaser, 1626; died Plymouth, "of infectious fever."

———, Mrs. Sarah (Allerton) (c.1590–1633)—of London; widow of John Vincent, of London, and Degory Priest (see *Mayflower* Saints)
Married, Leyden, 1621; 5 children by her husband's two and her own three marriages.

Mary Priest (   )
Married, Plymouth, 1630, to Phineas Pratt (see *Sparrow* above).

Sarah Priest (   )
Married John Coombs.

Samuel Godbertson (   )
Removed to Dartmouth, c.1652.

———
———

Fuller, Mrs. Bridget (Lee) (–1664)—3rd wife of Deacon Samuel Fuller (see *Mayflower* Saints)
Married, Leyden, 1617; opened small private school, 1634; donated lot for parsonage on the Street, 1663; 2 children.

Jenney, John (c.1594–1644)—of Norwich, brewery worker

Granted "libertie to erect a mill for grinding and beating of corne upon the brook at Plimoth," 1636; asst. governor, 1637–40.

———, Mrs. Sarah (Carey) (–c.1655)—of "Moncksoon"
Married Ann Lettice; 2 children.

Samuel (–c.1690)
Removed to Dartmouth, c.1652; Married Ann Lettice; 2 children.

Abigail (   )
Married Henry Wood.

Sarah (   )
Married Thomas Pope.

Mitchell, Experience (1609–89)—Purchaser, 1626; married, c.1628, to Jane Cooke (see above); removed to Bridgewater, 1649, and died there; 7 children.

*Morton, George (1585–1624)—merchant, of well-to-do Roman Catholic family of Harworth, near Scrooby
"a pious gracious servante of God"
As "G. Mourt," signed Bradford and Winslow's *Relation* (1622); organized *Anne* and *Little James* company; died impoverished not long after landing, his brother-in-law Bradford providing for his family.

———, Mrs. Juliana (Carpenter) (1584–1665)—of Wrington, near Bath, Somersetshire; daughter of Alexander Carpenter, member of Ancient Brethren
Amsterdam,   –1609; married Leyden, 1612; married, Plymouth, 1627, to Menassah Kempton (see Strangers below).

Nathaniel (1616–85)
"very religiously tender & carefull in his observations of the Sabbath day & of speaking truth"
Brought up by uncles Bradford and Fuller, becoming former's clerk and agent, 1634; married Lydia Cooper,

1635; secretary of Old Colony, 1647–85; town clerk, 1674–79; *New England's Memoriall*, 1669; secretary of Pilgrim church, copying many passages of Bradford's *Of Plimoth Plantation* into church records; granted many tracts of land for services and died one of wealthiest men in colony; 8 children.

Patience, (1616–91)
Married, 1634, to John Faunce (see Strangers below); 9 children, including Ruling Elder Thomas Faunce.

John (1616–73)
Married, c.1636, to —— Lettice; removed to Middleborough, c.1670; 8 children.

Sarah (1618–94).
Married, 1644 to George Bonum, or Bonham; 4 children.

Ephraim (1623–93)
Born on voyage; married, 1644, to Ann Cooper; deacon, 1669–93; 8 children.

Morton, Thomas, Jr. (   )—young son of Thomas Morton (see *Fortune* Saints)
Died or left colony before 1627.

Southworth, Mrs. Alice (Carpenter) (c.1590–1670)—of Wrington, near Bath, Somersetshire; sister of Mrs. Juliana Morton (see above)
"a godlie matron"
Amsterdam,   –1609; married Leyden, c.1610, to Edward Southworth of Sturton-le-Steeple, silkworker; 2 children, Constant and Thomas Southworth (see Straggling Saints); married, Plymouth, 1624, to William Bradford; 3 children by second marriage—William, Mercy, and Joseph.

Tracy, Stephen (   )—of Great Yarmouth, Norfolk; say maker Purchaser, 1626; removed to Dartmouth, c.1652; returned to England, 1654.

——, Mrs. Tryphosa (Lee) (   )
Married, Leyden, 1620; 5 children.

Sarah (1621–   )
Married, Duxbury, 1638, to George Partridge, brother of local pastor; 6 children.

B. STRANGERS
(23 men, 18 women, 17 children)

——, Barbara (–c.1650)
Married, 1623, to Captain Standish; nothing is known of her antecedents, though by family tradition she was younger sister of Rose, Standish's 1st wife; 5 children.

Annable, Anthony (–c.1655)—of Cambridge
Purchaser, 1626; removed to Scituate, c.1632; to Barnstable, 1639; 3 wives and 5 children.

——, Mrs. Jane (Momford) (– 1643)
Married, Cambridge, 1619.

Sarah (c.1620–   )
Married, 1638, to Henry Ewell.

Hannah (c.1622–   )
Married, 1645, to Thomas Freeman.

Bangs, Edward (c.1592–1678)—shipwright, of Panfield, Essex
Purchaser, 1626; married, c.1627, to Lydia Hicks (see below); later married Rebecca ——; removed to Eastham, 1644; 10 children.

Bartlett, Robert (1603–76)—cooper
Married, c.1627, to Mary Warren (see below); 8 children.

Becket, Mary (c.1605–76)
Married, c.1627, to George Soule (see *Mayflower* Servants); died, Duxbury; 7 children.

Burcher, Edward (   )—of Southwark.

——, Mrs. —— (——) (   )
Burchers died or left colony before 1627.

Clarke, Thomas (1599–1697)—carpenter
Married, c.1630, to Susanna Ring (see Straggling Saints); to Mrs. Alice (Hallet) Nichols, 1664; to Mrs. Elizabeth (——) Crow, 1670; 6 children; grave probably oldest on Burial Hill.
Conant, Christopher (c.1596–   )— of London, grocer; brother of Roger Conant (see below)
Left colony at time of Lyford-Oldham troubles, 1624, withdrawing to Nantasket (Hull).
Conant, Roger (c.1592–1679)—of London, salter
"a pious, sober, and prudent gentleman"
One of those who came "on their perticuler" with Oldham (see below); withdrew to Nantasket (Hull) with Oldham, 1624; governor of Pilgrims' rival settlement on Cape Ann, 1625; founded Naumkeag (Salem), 1626; supplanted as governor by John Endecott, 1628; withdrew to found Beverly, 1636; son and namesake married, 1644, Elizabeth, daughter of Thomas Weston, merchant adventurer.
——, Mrs. Sarah (Horton) (c.1600–c.1642)
Married, London, 1618; 9 children.
Caleb, (c.1620–   )
Returned to England, c.1644, and died there.
Dix, Anthony (–1638)
Left colony before 1627, probably in Lyford-Oldham exodus, 1624; shipmaster, Charlestown, c.1630; drowned in shipwreck off Cape Cod, 1638.
——, Mrs. Tabitha (——) (   )
Married, c.1640, to Nathaniel Pitman.
Faunce, John (c.1610–87)—probably of Purleigh, Essex
Married, 1634, to Patience Morton (see Saints above); 9 children, including Ruling Elder Thomas Faunce

Flavell, Mrs. Elizabeth (——) (   ) —wife of Thomas Flavell (see *Fortune* Strangers)
Died or left colony before 1627.
Flood, Edmund (   )
Died or left colony before 1627.
Heard, Thomas (   )
Died or left colony before 1627.
Hicks, Mrs. Margaret (Morgan) (   )—wife of Robert Hicks (see *Fortune* Strangers)
Married, Southwark, c.1606; 4 children.
Lydia (c.1608–   )
Married, c.1627, to Edward Bangs (see above); 1 child.
Phebe (c. 1610–63)
Married, c.1635, to George Watson; 2 children.
Samuel (c.1615–c.1675)
Removed to Eastham, 1644; married, 1645, to Lydia, daughter of Deacon John Doane; removed to Barnstable, c.1650; to Dartmouth, c.1670; 2 children.
Hilton, Mrs. Mary (——) (c.1600–   )—wife of William Hilton (see *Fortune* Strangers)
Left colony with family, 1624; 5 children, one born at Plymouth, its baptism by Anglican rite precipitating Lyford-Oldham rumpus.
William (c.1618–   )
Removed from Dover, N.H., to Newbury, Mass., c.1648; to Charlestown, c.1667; twice married; 10 children.
Mary (c.1620–   )
Holman, Edward (   )—of Clapham, Surrey
Returned to England, coming back in 1632; removed to Dartmouth, 1652.
Kempton, Menassah (c.1600–63)—of Colchester, Essex

Purchaser, 1626; married, 1627, to Mrs. Juliana Morton (see Saints above); removed to Dartmouth, 1652; no children.

Newton, Ellen (1598–1681)
Married, Plymouth, c.1625, to John Adams (see *Fortune* Strangers); 3 children; married, 1634, to Kenelm Winslow (see 2nd *Mayflower* Strangers); 4 children.

Oldham, John (–1636)—probably of Lancaster.
"a mad jack in his mood"
Organized group to come not as partners in settlement, but "on their perticuler" (see Oldham's Company below); expelled with Reverend Lyford for trying to establish Anglican rite and incite insurrection, 1624, retiring to Nantasket (Hull); returned and again driven out "with a bob upon the bumme," 1625; trading agent of group which seized Pilgrims' fishing stage on Cape Ann, 1625, later making peace with Saints; Thomas Morton of Merry Mount sent to England in his charge, 1628; settled Watertown, Mass., 1630, and grew rich in Indian and coastal trade; representative in Massachusetts General Court, 1632, 1634; overseer of shot and powder for colony, 1633; one of committee to consider problem raised when Asst. Governor John Endecott cut red cross of St. George out of English flag, 1635; killed by Indians while on trading expedition to Block Island, 1636, precipitating Pequot War.
——, Mrs. Lucretia (——) (   )
Lucretia (c.1606–   )
Married, 1624, to Jonathan Brewster (see *Fortune* Saints); 8 children.
Christian (   )
Oldham's Company—granted 10 acres in assignment of lands, 1623, presumably one each for every person

in Oldham's family and for the following:
Conant, Roger (see above)
Penn, Christian (see below)
——
——
——
——
Palmer, Mrs. Frances (——) (   )— wife of William Palmer (see *Fortune* Strangers.
Penn, Christian (c.1608–   )—one of those who came with Oldham "on their perticuler"
Married, c.1626, to Francis Eaton (see *Mayflower* Strangers); 4 children; married, 1634, to Francis Billington (see *Mayflower* Strangers); died Yarmouth; 9 children by 2nd marriage.
Rande, James (   )—of Southwark Died or left colony before 1627.
Ratcliffe, Robert (   )
——, Mrs. —— (——) (   ). Ratcliffes died or left colony before 1627.
Snow, Nicholas (c.1605–77)—of Hoxton, Middlesex
Married, c.1626, to Constance Hopkins (see *Mayflower* Strangers); removed to Eastham, 1644; town clerk, 1646–62; 11 children.
Sprague, Francis (c.1600–76)
Licensed to "keepe a victualling on the Duxburrow side," 1638; ran tavern till 1669, when succeeded by son John.
——, Mrs. Anna (——) (c.1602–c.1660)
Four children; died Duxbury.
Mercy (   )
Married William Tubbs.
Tilden, Thomas (   )—of London Left colony before 1627, probably returning to England.
——, Mrs. —— (——) (   )
—— (child) (   )
Wallen, Ralph (   )—of London
——, Mrs. Joyce (——) (   )

Warren, Mrs. Elizabeth (March) (c.1583-1673)—wife of Richard Warren (see *Mayflower* Strangers) Married, London, c.1605; 7 children.
Mary (c.1608-80)
Married, c.1627, to Robert Bartlett (see Strangers above); 8 children.
Ann (c.1612–)
Married, 1633, to Thomas Little; 8 children.
Sarah (c.1614-c.1676)
Married, 1634, to John Cooke (see *Mayflower* Saints); 5 children.
Elizabeth (c.1616-70)
Married, 1636, to Richard Church; 12 children, including Benjamin Church, Plymouth's captain-general in King Philip's War.
Abigail (c.1618–)
Married, 1639, to Anthony Snow; 6 children.

C. SERVANTS
(1 man, 2 unidentified)
Brewster's—
Long, Robert ( )
Captain Peirce's—
———
———

V. *MAYFLOWER* (not the original Pilgrim ship); William Peirce, master; out of London, March, 1629; arriving Salem, May 15, with many Puritans for Bay colony and a few passengers for Plymouth.

A. SAINTS
(3 men, 2 women, 4 children)
Blossom, Thomas (–1633)—of Cambridge
"a holy man & experienced sainct"
Shipped on *Speedwell*, 1620, turning back with Cushman, discouraged by mishaps; deacon, 1629-33.

———, Mrs. Ann (Elson, or Alston) ( ) of Cambridge
Accompanied husband on *Speedwell*; married, 1633, to Henry Rowley.
Thomas, Jr. ( )
Married, 1645, to Sarah Ewer of Charlestown; 2 children.
Elizabeth ( )
Married, 1637, to Edward Fitz-Randolph.
Masterson, Richard (c.1590–1633) of Sandwich, wool carder
"a second Stephen"
Citizen, Leyden, 1612; deacon, 1629-33.
———, Mrs. Mary (Goodall) (c.1600-c.1650)—of Leicester
Married, Leyden, 1619; married, Plymouth, 1634, to Pastor Ralph Smith; died Boston.
Nathaniel (c.1620–)
Removed to Salem, later to Boston, c.1660, being sheriff there, 1665.
Sarah (c.1622–)
Married, c.1640, to Henry Atwood (subsequently Wood).
Willet, Thomas (c.1610-74)—born, Leyden, son of Thomas Willet of Yarmouth, Norfolk
"an honest yonge man"
Agent at Kennebec, 1629-34; agent at trading post on Penobscot, 1635; married, Plymouth, 1636, to Mary Browne (see Straggling Saints below); at New Amsterdam, 1650, acting as agent for Peter Stuyvesant; asst. governor, 1651-64; in command of company on expediton against Dutch along Hudson River, becoming first English mayor of New York City, 1664-67; died Swansea; 12 children.

B. STRANGERS
(1 man)
Winslow, Kenelm (1599-1672)—carpenter and cabinetmaker, of Droit-

wich, Worcestershire; brother of Edward Winslow (see *Mayflower* Saints)

Married, 1634, to Mrs. Ellen (Newton) Adams (see *Anne* Strangers); official coffin maker; designer and builder of only fine furniture in early colony, many pieces being preserved in Metropolitan and other museums; removed to Marshfield, 1641; encouraged settlement of Yarmouth and other Cape Cod towns; jailed 4 weeks, 1646, "for opprobrious words against the church of Marshfield, saying they were all lyars, &c." Died, Salem; 4 children.

VI. *TALBOT*—of London; Thomas Beecher, master; out of London, mid-May, 1629; arriving Salem, July 29, with company of servants for Plymouth, "being 35 persons." None of this group can be identified.

VII. *HANDMAID*—of London; out of London, mid-August, 1630; arriving Plymouth, Oct. 29, with some 60 passengers, chiefly from Leyden, "of ye weakest & poorest sort." While none of the Leyden Saints in this company can be identified, there were two Puritan "gentlemen" on board Boston-bound. Having sampled the rigors of Boston, one promptly returned to Plymouth and settled there as a Stranger:

Eddy, Samuel (1608–87)—son of the Rev. William Eddy, vicar at Cranbrook, Kent; tailor

Married Elizabeth (Savory?), c.1630; freeman, 1633; helped found Middleboro, 1640; died, Swansea; 5 children.

VIII. *STRAGGLING SAINTS*
      (8 men, 4 women, 6 children)
Bradford, John (c.1615–78)—born,

Leyden, only child of William and Dorothy (May) Bradford (see *Mayflower* Saints)

Arrived, c.1627; married, c.1640, to Martha Bourne; removed to Duxbury, 1645; to Marshfield, 1653; to Norwich, Conn., 1660; no children.

Browne, John (–1662)—brother of Peter Browne (see *Mayflower* Strangers)

Arrived and settled Duxbury, 1632; asst. governor, 1636–55; removed to Taunton, 1643; commissioner to New England Confederacy, 1644–55; died Rehoboth.

———, Mrs. Dorothy (——) (–1674)
Died, Swansea; 4 children.

Mary (c.1616–c.1670)
Married, 1636, to Thomas Willet (see 2nd *Mayflower* Saints); 12 children.

Carpenter, Mary (1577–1667)—sister of Mrs. Alice (Carpenter) Southworth (see *Anne* Saints)

"a godlie old maid, never married" Amsterdam, c.1600–09; Leyden, 1609–c.1635; living in England, 1646, when sent for by William and Alice Bradford, arriving Plymouth, c.1647.

Chandler, Edmund (c.1582–1662)—say weaver, probably of Colchester, Essex.

Citizen of Leyden, 1613, and married there; arrived Plymouth, c.1633; removed to Duxbury, then Scituate: 7 children.

Chandler, Roger ( )—say weaver, probably of Colchester, Essex.

Married at Leyden to Isabella Chilton, 1615; arrived Plymouth, c.1630; 2 children.

Pontus, William (c.1583–c.1653)—of Dover, fustian maker.

Arrived, Plymouth, c.1633, settling

along Eel River several miles south of town.

———, Mrs. Wybra (Hanson) (c.1590–)—perhaps of Austerfield
Married, Leyden, 1610; 2 children
Mary (c.1612–)
Married, Plymouth, 1644, to William Glass; married, Duxbury, 1657, to Philip Delano (see *Fortune* Saints); 4 children.
Hannah (c.1614–90)
Married, 1644, to John Churchill; to Giles Rickard, 1669.
Ring, Mrs. (Mary? ——) (–1631)
Widow of William Ring, say weaver and citizen of Leyden, who turned back with Cushman after misadventures with *Speedwell* in 1620; arrived Plymouth, c.1630, with 3 children.
Andrew (c.1616–c.1693)
Married Deborah Hopkins, then Mrs. Lettice (——) Morton; 6 children.
Elizabeth (–1687).
Married Stephen Deane (see *Fortune* Strangers); 3 children; married Josiah Cooke, 1635.
Susanna (–c.1664)
Married, c.1630, to Thomas Clarke (see *Anne* Strangers).
Robinson, Isaac (c.1610–1704)—born, Leyden, son of John and Bridget Robinson, only one of pastor's family to come to New World
Arrived, Scituate, c.1632; married, 1636, to Margaret Hanford, niece of Timothy Hatherly (see Merchant Adventurers below); removed to Barnstable, 1639; married, c.1650, to ——; disenfranchised for opposing Quaker and Baptist persecutions, 1659–72; licensed to keep tavern at Succanesett (Falmouth), 1665; removed to Tisbury, Martha's Vineyard,

1673; returned to Barnstable, 1701, and died there; 10 children.
Southworth, Constant (c.1615–79)—born, Leyden, son of Alice (Carpenter) Southworth (see .*Anne* Saints)
Arrived, Plymouth, c.1628; married, 1637, to Elizabeth Collier (see Merchant Adventurers below); treasurer of colony, 1659–79; asst. governor, 1670–78; died, Duxbury, "of feavor & jaundice"; 8 children.
Southworth, Thomas (c.1616–69)—born, Leyden, brother of Constant (see above)
"rarely Indowed both in Sacred and Civill Respects"
Arrived, Plymouth, c.1628; married, c.1637, to Elizabeth, daughter of Pastor Reyner; agent at Kennebec, 1651–54, representing stepfather Bradford's interests; asst. governor, 1652–53; 1657–69; commissioner to New England Confederacy, 1659–61, 1664, 1667–69; 1 child.

IX. MERCHANT ADVENTURERS
(3 men, 1 woman, 5 children)

Collier, William (c.1585–1670)—of London, brewer
"lived a godly and holy life until old age"
Arrived 1633; asst. governor, 1634–37, 1639–51, 1654–65; commissioner to New England Confederacy, 1643; took liberal side in attempt to establish religious toleration, 1645.
———, Mrs. Jane (——) (c.1590–)—presumably of London.
Rebecca (c.1610–98)
Married father's apprentice, Job Cole.
Sarah (c.1612–91)
Married, 1634, to Love Brewster (see *Mayflower* Saints); married,

c.1652, to Richard Parks of Cambridge, and removed there; 4 children.

Mary (c.1614–c.1662)
Married, 1636, to Thomas Prence (see *Fortune* Strangers); died Eastham; 5 children.

Elizabeth (c.1616–   )
Married, 1637, to Constant Southworth (see Straggling Saints); 8 children.

Hatherly, Timothy (–1666)—of Southwark, felt maker
Came on *Anne*, 1623, returning to London when house burned down; settled at Scituate, 1632; married, 1642, to Mrs. Lydia (——) Tilden; asst. governor, 1636–57; deprived of office and disenfranchised for opposing Quaker and Baptist persecutions, 1658; died, Scituate; no children.

Thomas, William (c.1573–1651)—of Yarmouth, Norfolk; merchant
"a well-approved and well-grounded Christian"
Arrived 1637, settling at Marshfield; asst. governor, 1642–44, 1647–50; 1 son.

Nathaniel (c.1608–   )

SUMMARY

		Saints	Strangers	Hired Hands	Servants	Unidentified	Total	Summary
MAYFLOWER	Men	17	17	5	11	—	50	
	Women	10	9	—	1	—	20	
	Children	14	14	—	6	—	34	
		41	40	5	18	—	104	104
FORTUNE	Men	9	17	—	—	—	26	
	Women	2	2	—	—	—	4	
	Children	1	4	—	—	—	5	
		12	23	—	—	—	35	35
SHALLOP from SPARROW	Men	—	1	—	—	—	1	
	Women	—	—	—	—	—	—	
	Children	—	1	—	—	—	1	
		—	2	—	—	—	2	2
ANNE and LITTLE JAMES	Men	5	23	—	3	—	31	
	Women	9	18	—	—	—	27	
	Children	18	17	—	—	—	35	
		32	58	—	3	—	93	93
Second MAYFLOWER	Men	3	1	—	—	—	4	
	Women	2	—	—	—	—	2	
	Children	4	—	—	—	—	4	
		9	1	—	—	—	10	10
TALBOT	Men	—	—	—	?	—	—	
	Women	—	—	—	?	—	—	
	Children	—	—	—	?	—	—	
		—	—	—	35	—	35	35
HANDMAID	Men	—	1	—	—	?	1	
	Women	—	—	—	—	?	—	
	Children	—	—	—	—	?	—	
		—	1	—	—	60	61	61
STRAGGLING SAINTS	Men	8	—	—	—	—	8	
	Women	4	—	—	—	—	4	
	Children	6	—	—	—	—	6	
		18	—	—	—	—	18	18
MERCHANT ADVENTURERS	Men	—	3	—	—	—	3	
	Women	—	1	—	—	—	1	
	Children	—	5	—	—	—	5	
		—	9	—	—	—	9	9
TOTALS		112	134	5	56	60	—	367

*Of these, only nine Saints came from Scrooby, and four were children at the time.

NOTES

Chapter III

(1) If the elusive Elder had been caught, the consequences would have been serious, as Brewster well knew. His classmate at Peterhouse College, John Penry, had been hanged as operator of the secret, wandering Martinist press, printer of the celebrated Martin Mar-prelate tracts, the first great satires in our language, aimed at the "proud, Popish, presumptuous, profane, paultrie, pestilent, and pernicious Prelates."

If not hanged, Brewster might well have suffered the fate of the Reverend Alexander Leighton, a Scottish minister, who a few years later published in Holland and smuggled back a "libellous" attack upon the Anglican church. His work was not half as sharp and "libellous" as *Perth Assembly* from Brewster's shop.

Apprehended, Leighton was sentenced by the notorious Star Chamber to pay a fine of £100,000, to be whipped and pilloried in the presence of the Court, to have one ear sliced off and his nose split, to have branded upon his forehead the letters "SS" (stirrer of sedition), to be whipped and pilloried again "at some conveniente later time," to have his other ear sliced off, and to suffer imprisonment for life.

It is no wonder, then, that "Mr. B." was not feeling well at this time.

Chapter VI

(1) The conflict on the *Mayflower* bears a striking resemblance in a most curious way to a mutiny that had occurred on the island of Bermuda about ten years before, also among a company Virginia-bound.

In 1609, a fleet of nine vessels sailed from England for Jamestown, under the command of Sir Thomas Gates, who was going out to become governor of Virginia. Off the Bahamas, a terrible hurricane struck the fleet and dispersed it, piling up the flagship on the rocks of Bermuda, fortunately without loss of life.

The survivors found Bermuda a fertile and delightful place, with the great advantage of being under no government, not yet having been claimed. When Governor Gates ordered the company to start building pinnaces to carry them on to Virginia, there was much grumbling, with growing resistance on every hand.

If they were forced to go on to Virginia, the argument ran, they "might well feare to be detained in that countrie by the authority of the Commander thereof, and their whole life to serve the turnes of the Adventurers with their travailes and labours." The records report some "Brownists" among the dissidents. But that term may merely have been used there as the term "Red" so often is today, to signify anyone not wholly orthodox down to the last particular.

The center of resistance, it transpired, lay in Governor Gates' own household, in the suite of his chaplain, the Reverend Richard Buck, who had brought with him "a Clarke to read the Psalms and Chapters on Sundays, . . . a fellow who had much knowledge of the Scriptures and could reason well therein."

It was this humble clerk who, insidiously at first, then more openly, began "to advance substantial arguments, both civill and divine (the Scriptures false quoted), that it was no breach of honesty, conscience, nor Religion to decline from the obedience of the Governor or to refuse to go further, . . . since the authority ceased when the wracke was committed. And with it, they were all then freed from the government of any man."

This was precisely what some on the *Mayflower* were contending under essentially similar circumstances—that Virginia writ did not run in New England, and that when they came ashore, "they would use their owne libertie, for none had power to command them."

When the clerk began to advocate organized resistance, he was seized and tried for "Mutinie and Rebellion," along with three or four of his lieutenants in these "divellish disquiets."

All were convicted and sentenced to die. All were executed with the exception of the chief rebel, who "made so much moane, alleadging the Ruine of his wife and children in this his Trespasse," that he was finally pardoned.

The name of the rebellious, Scripture-quoting clerk was Stephen Hopkins, and if he were not the Stephen Hopkins on the *Mayflower*, one of the Stranger group, then several other curious things need explaining.

The matter of name may be mere coincidence, but not the fact that the *Mayflower* rebels echoed the arguments, even the very phrases, of the Bermuda mutineers.

Also, it is plain that Stephen Hopkins, perhaps alone of the passengers on board, had been in the New World before. When the Pilgrims sent ashore their first exploring party, he was one of three named to assist Captain Standish with "counsel and advice." As the Saints exercised command and were not disposed to share it, Hopkins was the only Stranger chosen, presumably because he knew something about the wilderness and the ways of the Indians.

And he obviously did. Tramping through the woods, the exploring party came upon an ingenious contrivance which none could puzzle out until Hopkins came up and illustrated how it worked, explaining that it was an Indian trap "to catch some deer."

How did he know this if he had not been one of those who finally got from Bermuda to Virginia?

Only three men on board had been in America before—Hopkins and two of the mates, John Clarke and Robert Coppin. During the long weeks at sea they must have whiled away many an hour telling a goggle-eyed audience about the wonders of the wilderness and their own adventures in the great mysterious land toward which they were bound, for better or for worse.

And what a story Hopkins could have made of the hurricane, the shipwreck on Bermuda, Gates' tyranny, the boiling resentment of the men, his own part in the conflict, the court-martial, his last-minute reprieve!

Nor would Hopkins have apologized for any of this, for he was the most democratically inclined of the more prominent Pilgrim Fathers. Although he served as assistant governor for many years, he had no blind respect for authority as such, being heavily fined on one occasion for "allowing servants and such to sit in his house drinking and playing shovelboard."

But this is not to suggest that Hopkins led the rebels on the *Mayflower* as he had those in Bermuda. He had come up in the world. He was no longer a humble clerk, perhaps even a servant, but a master in his own right, with servants of his own. And he would certainly not have been pleased to hear them talking of using "their owne libertie" when they came ashore.

But it is likely that rebellion centered in his household. As he told his stories, there were many to listen reflectively. Poorer and humbler freemen ("goodmen," as they were called) had no more desire than those at Bermuda "to serve the turnes of the Adventurers with their travailes and labours." Indentured servants, too, were only too eager to be free of their bonds. And none can have listened more attentively than Hopkins' own bond servants, Edward Dotey and Edward Leister.

Both were ambitious, high-spirited, and rather violent youths. It was they who, soon after the landing, fought Plymouth's first and last duel, armed with cutlasses in one hand, knives in the other, for which they were tied together by their heads and their heels until their tempers cooled off.

It would be ironic if these two led the mutineers, using the arguments given them inadvertently by their master.

When Bradford came to write of the incident more than ten years later, in the 1630s, Hopkins was an assistant governor. Having served his indenture, Dotey was a rapidly rising freeman of substance. Both had long since become Saints.

Bradford's diffidence about identifying the mutinous "strangers" by name doubtless came from a desire not to reopen an old conflict.

(2) The original of this document signed here on the *Mayflower* has been lost. Bradford's nephew, Nathaniel Morton, may have seen and used it in preparing his *New England's Memoriall* (1669), in which he published the covenant, followed by a list of forty-one names. While it is not certain, it seems likely that these were the names on the document and that they were inscribed in the following order (the names of those from Leyden are marked with an asterisk):

John Carver*	Edward Tilley*	Degory Priest*
William Bradford*	John Tilley*	Thomas Williams
Edward Winslow*	Francis Cooke*	Gilbert Winslow
William Brewster*	Thomas Rogers*	Edmund Margeson
Isaac Allerton*	Thomas Tinker*	Peter Browne
Myles Standish	John Rigdale	Richard Britteridge
John Alden	Edward Fuller	George Soule
Samuel Fuller*	John Turner*	Richard Clarke
Christopher Martin	Francis Eaton	Richard Gardiner
William Mullins	James Chilton	John Allerton
William White*	John Crackston*	Thomas English
Richard Warren	John Billington	Edward Dotey
John Howland	Moses Fletcher*	Edward Leister
Stephen Hopkins	John Goodman*	

It is quite extraordinary that Dotey and Leister, Hopkins' bond servants, were asked to sign at the bottom of the list. It may have been as an afterthought. If they were two of the mutineers, it would serve as a reminder and a pledge of their prescribed loyalty to their superiors, for bond slaves did not ordinarily set their hands to such a document.

The high significance of the Mayflower Compact was first pointed out in 1802 by John Quincy Adams, who hailed it as an example of the original social contract, a then popular concept hypothecated by Rousseau. Though its promise of "just & equall lawes" was not always performed, the Compact was a great charter of freedom, a remarkable statement of revolutionary new principles, the foundation stone upon which the Pilgrims built a distinctive society, self-governing from the start.

Chapter VII

(1) It is strange that there is no mention of this tragedy in the otherwise detailed Pilgrim chronicles of these days. If Dorothy had accidentally fallen overboard, one would expect at least a few words about her terrified cries and her frantic struggle for life as attempts to rescue her failed —some expression of regret and sorrow.

In his pocket book, under the heading of "Deaths," Bradford made this laconic entry: "Dec. 7. Dorothy, Wife to Mr. William Bradford."

There was some reason for this general silence, and there would have been reason enough if Dorothy had jumped overboard. In those days, no offense against the laws of God and man was as heinous as suicide.

Many women, before her and since, cracked in fear and terror of the "hideous & desolate wildernes." It is impossible for anyone today to image the forlorn lot and soul-searing experience of the pioneer women who first came to our wild shores.

Chapter VIII

(1) The adventurers were John Goodman, of Leyden, and Peter Browne, one of the Strangers. Moving off to cut more thatch, they had two dogs with them, a large mastiff bitch and a small spaniel. Near a pond, the dogs raised a deer, a large buck, which went bounding away through the woods with the dogs barking after him and men puffing along behind, hoping they could somehow manage to cut the deer down with their sickles.

They were soon winded and lost, wandering around all afternoon in a cold drizzle that later changed to snow. Tired, hungry, and cold, they stretched out on the frozen ground to sleep.

Suddenly they were terrified to hear "two lyons roaring exceedingly, for a long time together." Leaping up, they dashed for the nearest tree, intending to climb it if they were attacked, though they knew it would be "intollerable cold lodging."

Expecting to be pounced on any minute and torn limb from limb, the Nimrods paced up and down and around the tree all night, having a difficult time with the mastiff bitch. She was not at all impressed by the "lyons" and kept trying to break away and go for them.

The next day, after much aimless wandering in the snow, the hunters spied the harbor from a hill and came stumbling into the "randevue" after dark, "readie to faint with travail & wante of victuals, and almost famished with cold." Goodman's shoes—and shoes were worth their weight in gold—had to be cut from his swollen, frostbitten feet.

Not long after, to exercise his lame feet, Goodman called his spaniel and wandered off again. As he was limping along the edge of the clearing, two wolves jumped out from the woods and ran for the dog, which escaped, yelping, to take refuge between his master's legs. Picking up a stick, Goodman threw it and hit one of the beasts, which sent both trotting off into the forest.

But they immediately circled round and came back, advancing quite close in the boldest manner. Snatching up a heavy stake, Goodman stood ready, whereupon the wolves "sat both on their tayles, grinning at him a good while"—perhaps remembering their success as "lyons."

Still grinning, they "wente their way & left him," which is our last glimpse of "Goodman" John Goodman, who soon died with so many of his friends.

Chapter XI

(1) Later, in his *Good Newes from New England* (1624), Winslow corrected his mistaken view that the Indians had no religion or knowledge of God, and gave a good and tempered account of their religious beliefs as he understood them and of their rites as he had observed them.

Chapter XIII

(1) This incident, as later maliciously elaborated by Thomas Morton of Merry Mount, gave rise to a story that long plagued all of the Saints in New England. The man condemned for stealing from the Indians, so the story ran, was a strong able-bodied young man, a cobbler. As Wessagusset could ill afford to spare him, an old man was substituted for him on the gallows.

Ignorant of the difference between Plymouth and Wessagusset, assuming that both were Separatist settlements, the early satirist Samuel Butler seized upon the story and in his *Hudibras* blasted the Saints:

> Our brethren in New England use
> Choice malefactors to excuse,
> And hang the guiltless in their steed [stead],
> Of whom the churches have less need . . .

Chapter XIX

(1) Brokenhearted as they were by the loss of Robinson, the Pilgrims would have been even more upset if they had known—which they evidently did not—that in his last years the Leyden pastor had changed his mind about coming to Plymouth if opportunity offered.

The older he grew, the broader and more tolerant he became in his views, being increasingly distressed by the contentiousness and narrow sectarian spirit in the churches of the Separation. He even came to believe that it was "lawfull" to take communion with the Church of England, "in the hearing of the word and prayer (though not in sacraments and discipline)."

Documents unearthed in Leyden in recent years disclose that Robinson wished to lessen schism among Christians, and to that end hoped to have his son educated for "ministry in the Dutch churches."

But as things stood at Leyden, Robinson was not hopeful of accomplishing anything at all, for he "found in his congregation so many difficulties . . . that he, with a good part of his congregation, was resolved to remove to the West Indies, where he doubted not that he should be able to accomplish his desires."

It was well for the Pilgrims' peace of mind that they did not know of Robinson's final resolve not to come to them, but to go elsewhere, when means offered.

Chapter XXIV

(1) The founding of new communities raised problems of another kind. The new towns were soon demanding representation in the colony's government, which consisted of the General Assembly of all freemen and the annually elected General Court, composed of the governor and his seven assistants. How were the new towns to be governed locally?

Technically, all of Plimoth Plantation belonged to Bradford, for the patent of 1630 stood in his name. In 1640, when requested to do so, he surrendered it to "ye freemen of this corporation of New Plimoth."

Previously, a committee had been appointed to revise the frame of government and draw up a general code of laws. Up to this time, law had been improvised as occasion warranted, with only a few scattered enactments written into the books.

Many changes were made in the hitherto unwritten constitution. Annual elections were confirmed. To other officers were now added a treasurer and a secretary. For the first time, the governor was paid a salary, £20 a year. Other officers received their living expenses while on duty.

To represent them in the government and on the General Court, each incorporated town elected two deputies—Mother Plymouth demanded and obtained four for herself—who were "to join with the Bench to enact and make such laws and ordinances as shall be judged to be good and wholesome for the whole."

Only freemen could vote, and it was difficult to attain that status. Massachusetts had early decreed that only "members of some of the churches within the lymits of the same" could become freemen. While not so explicit, Plymouth accomplished the same end by allowing no one to become a freeman until he had proved to the magistrates that he was of sober carriage and "orthodox in religion."

In 1643, when the Old Colony contained some 3,000 people, there were just 232 freemen. And not all of these could vote. The franchise was limited to those with a ratable estate of at least £20 ($1,000).

In the beginning, Plymouth kept a sharp eye on the new towns and interfered in local affairs frequently. No one could own land or build a house in them without the approval of the General Court. No one could live in the colony "without the leave and liking of the Governor, or two of the Assistants, at least."

For some years, in fact, the new towns were not civil communities at all, but private corporations run by the principal stockholders—the local proprietors, to whom the General Court had granted the land. Except at Plymouth, there was no representative local government until 1651, when Sandwich won the right to govern itself by an annually elected board of selectmen, an institution soon established in all the Pilgrim towns.

In making the changes earlier described, the Pilgrims took occasion to draw up a Declaration of Rights, stating that they would recognize only such laws as were enacted "by the consent of the body of freemen or associates, or their representatives legally assembled, which is according to the free liberties of the free-born people of England."

At the same time, they adopted a criminal code, which was quite simple and, for its day, extraordinarily humane, especially in the matter of capital offenses. England exacted the death penalty for scores of offenses, down to relatively small thefts. Plymouth limited the number to seven— treason, murder, witchcraft, adultery, rape, sodomy, and arson.

Actually, it took life for only one, murder, though there was the case of an unhappy youth executed for sodomy.

Chapter XXVI

(1) Massachusetts' chief emissary at this time, Hugh Peter, Roger Williams' successor as pastor at Salem, never returned to the colony, becoming a man of great influence and large affairs in England, serving as Cromwell's chaplain, walking with the poet John Milton at the Protector's funeral. In 1660, at the Restoration, Peter was beheaded for alleged complicity in the execution of Charles I, charged with being one of the masked men on the scaffold when the axe fell upon the King— even that he was the man who wielded it.

Among others who returned to England during these years and rose to positions of high responsibility were Edward Hopkins, governor of Connecticut; Stephen, Governor Winthrop's son; George Fenwick, of Saybrook; John Leverett, later a governor of the Bay; and George Downing, Governor Winthrop's nephew, one of nine in Harvard's first class of graduates, who agilely changed sides after the Restoration, betrayed some of his earlier friends to their death, and won a title and a fortune. He gave his name to the street in London long famed because of the address, "10 Downing Street," the official residence of British prime ministers.

Later, as will be seen, Edward Winslow left Plymouth and spent his last years serving the cause of the Rebellion, dying at sea in its service.

During these years, as the tide of immigration not only ceased but began to reverse itself, New England had to populate itself by internal generation, so to speak. This continued to be true for decade after decade, giving New England a remarkably homogeneous population. There was not another large migration to New England for two hundred years, not until the Irish began to come after potato famines at home.

Chapter XXVIII

(1) In the United Colonies' articles of confederation, the chief operative clauses were these:

"3. It is further agreed that the plantations which at presente are, or hereafter shall be, settled within ye limites of ye Massachusetts shall be forever under ye Massachusetts, and shall have peculiar jurisdiction amongst themselves in all cases, as an intire body.

"And that Plimoth, Conightecutt, and New Haven shall, each of them, have like peculiar jurisdiction and governmente within their limits . . .

"4. It is by these conffederats agreed that the charge of all just warrs, whether offencive or defencive, upon what parte or member of this confederation soever they fall, shall—both in men, provissions, and all other disbursements—be borne by all ye parts of this confederation in differente proportions, according to their differente abillities, in the manner following:

"Namely, that the commissioners for each jurisdiction, from time to time, as there shall be occasion, shall bring a true accounte and number of all the males in their plantations, . . . of what qualitie or condition soever they be, from 16 years old to 60, being inhabitants there.

"And that according to ye differente numbers which from time to time shall be found in each jurisdiction upon a true & just accounte, the service of men and all charges of ye warr be borne by ye poll [this occasional census], each jurisdiction or plantation being left to their owne just course & custome of rating themselves and their people according to their different estates, with due respecte to their qualities and exemptions amongst themselves, though the confederats take no notice of any such privilege . . .

"5. It is further agreed that if these jurisdictions . . . be invaded by any enemie whomsoever, upon notice & requeste of any 3 magistrates of the jurisdiction so invaded, ye rest of ye confederats, without any further meeting or expostulation, shall forthwith send aide to ye confederate in danger, but in differente proportion—namely, ye Massachusetts, a hundred men sufficiently armed & provided for such a service and journey; and each of ye rest, forty-five so armed & provided—or any lesser number, if less be required, according to this proportion . . .

"6. It is also agreed that for ye managing & concluding of all affairs proper & concerning the whole confederation, two commissioners shall be chosen by & out of each of the 4 jurisdictions, . . . being all in church membership with us, who shall bring full power from their severall Generall Courts respectively to hear, examene, waigh, and detirmine all affairs of warr, or peace, aids, charges, numbers of men for warr, divisions of spoyles, . . . and all things of like nature which are ye proper concomitants or consequences of such a confederation, . . . not intermeddling with ye governmente of any of ye jurisdictions, which by ye 3rd article is preserved entirely to themselves.

"But if these 8 commissioners, when they meete, shall not all agree, . . . any 6 of the 8 agreeing shall have power to settle & determine ye bussines in question.

"But if 6 doe not agree, that then such propositions . . . be sente and referred to ye 4 Generall Courts, and if at ye said Generall Courts ye

business so referred be concluded, then to be prosecuted by ye confederats and all their members.

"It was further agreed that these 8 commissioners shall meete once
every year, besides extraordinarie meetings, to consider, treate, & conclude of all affairs belonging to this confederation . . .

"8. It is also agreed that the commissioners . . . doe indeavor to frame
and establish agreements & orders in generall cases of a civill nature
wherein all ye plantations are interested for ye preserving peace amongst
themselves and preventing, as much as may be, all occasions of warr or
difference with others—as aboute ye free & speedy passage of justice in
every jurisdiction to all confederats equally as to their owne; not receiving those that remove from one plantation to another without due
certificate; how all ye jurisdictions may carry towards ye Indeans, that
they neither grow insolente, nor be injured without due satisfaction, lest
warr break in upon the confederacy through such miscarriage.

"It is also agreed that if any servante run away from his maister into
another of these confederated jurisdictions, that . . . upon due proofe,
the said servante shall be delivered either to his maister or any other that
pursues & brings such certificate or proofe [and similarly, for escaped
prisoners and fugitives from justice] . . .

"9. And for that ye justest warrs may be of dangerous consequence,
. . . it is agreed that neither ye Massachusetts, Plimoth, Conightecutt, nor
New Haven, nor any member of them, shall at any time hereafter begine,
undertake, or ingage themselves or this confederation, or any parte
thereof, in any warr whatsoever (sudden exegents with ye necessary
consequents thereof excepted, which are also to be moderated as much
as ye case will permitte), without ye consente and agreemente of ye
forementioned 8 commissioners, or at ye least 6 of them . . .

"And that no charge be required of any of the confederats in case of
a defensive warr till ye said commissioners have mett and approved ye
justice of ye warr, and have agreed upon ye summe of money to be
levied . . ."

At their first meeting, the commissioners had to weigh a problem laid
in their laps by Uncas, sachem of the Mohegan, long-time allies of the
English, who had captured a Narragansett chief, Miantonomo. Not
knowing what to do with him, Uncas said he would do nothing "without
the advice" of the English. Considering the problem and deciding that
Uncas "could not be safe whilst Miantonomo lived," the commissioners
thought that Uncas might justly put him to death, "but in his own jurisdiction, and not in the English plantations," and without cruelty or
torture.

"And Uncas followed this advice," wrote Bradford, "and accordingly executed him in a very fair manner"—splitting his skull from behind with a hatchet, "some English being present." And that the Indians might know "that the English did approve of it," wrote John Winthrop, "they sent 12 or 14 musketeers home with Onkus to abide a time with him for his defense, if need should be."

An engaging figure, Canonicus' nephew, Miantonomo had served the English well, declining to be drawn into the Pequot War against the whites. The latter would doubtless have been seriously injured or even wiped out if the powerful Narragansett, as frequently urged, had joined the Pequot.

Miantonomo's chief offense, it seems, was his friendship and help to Roger Williams, Anne Hutchinson, Samuel Gorton, and other "heretics" who had settled in Rhode Island. The Saints violently objected that he sold such people lands. It was to be discouraged.

Chapter XXIX

(1) While awaiting shipping in Boston for passage to England, Chauncy was approached by a committee appointed by the Harvard Overseers to find a president for the college to succeed Henry Dunster, who had been forced out for holding "anti-paedobaptistical principles"—which, in the unacademic, meant simply that he had come to the views of John Smyth, Roger Williams, and others on the "unlawfullness" of infant baptism.

As Harvard was the temple of orthodoxy, the consistory of the Holy Discipline, Dunster's "heresy" was a great shock. Fearing the wrath of the Bay authorities, he fled to the Old Colony, to Scituate, where in time he succeeded to Chauncy's place in the pulpit there.

Meantime, at Boston, acting for the Harvard Overseers, John Norton and Richard Mather came to terms with Chauncy, demanding a promise of him that he would "forbear to disseminate or publish any tenets concerning the necessity of immersion in baptism and celebration of the Lord's Supper at evening."

Chauncy had left Plymouth because he could not, in conscience, forbear insisting upon such tenets, but he now yielded "without reluctance." Becoming Harvard's second president at a salary of £100 ($5,000) a year, he directed its affairs for seventeen years, introducing a strenuous regime of prayers and devotion, even delivering an occasional sermon himself to the "nasty salvages" in the Indian College, originally planned as a principal part of the College.

(2) John Eliot, "the Apostle to the Indians," was one of the authors of

the *Bay Psalm Book*, collaborating with the Reverends Thomas Weld and Richard Mather.

Later the Saints at Plymouth, abandoning the Psalms of Ainsworth used since Leyden days, adopted the *Bay Psalm Book* and did their distracted best to sing such verses as these, the Bay's "improved" version of the 137th Psalm:

> The rivers on of Babilon
>   there when we did sit downe:
> Yea even then we mourned, when
>   wee remembered Sion.
> Our harpe wee did hang it amid,
>   upon the willow tree,
> Because there they that us away
>   led in captivitee,
> Requir'd of us a song, thus
>   askt mirth: us waste who laid,
> Sing us among a Sions song
>   unto us then they said.

It is small wonder that some of the Saints in both the Bay and Plymouth got into trouble "for speaking contemptuously of singing psalms."

The *Bay Psalm Book* was the first book published in the colonies, being issued at Cambridge in 1640 from the press of Stephen Daye, a locksmith, who had arrived two years before. The book went through many editions.

At New York in 1947, one of the eleven known surviving copies of the first edition of 1,700 fetched a price of $151,000, believed to be the highest price ever paid for a book—and certainly not deserved for its contents.

(3) The large estates to which Standish asserted his claim lay in Lancashire and the Isle of Man. In his *Captain Myles Standish* (London, 1920), T. C. Porteus disclosed after much research that the House of Standish did not own any properties in the parishes which the captain named, and that he had only the remotest connection with this family of rich landed gentry.

(4) Having disappeared during the American Revolution and long since been given up as lost, Bradford's manuscript history was found in London in 1855 and first published in full the next year at Boston. It was found on the shelves of the Bishop of London's library at Fulham Palace. How it got there, or to London at all, no one knows exactly, though there are several likely surmises.

Parts of Bradford had previously been published. The governor's nephew, Nathaniel Morton, used the manuscript in preparing his *New England's Memoriall* (1669), transcribing and paraphrasing parts of it for incorporation in his work. Subsequently, Morton copied into the church records most of the material in Bradford's early chapters, down to the arrival of the *Mayflower* in Cape Cod Bay, and parts of later chapters. What Morton copied of the early chapters was published in 1841 by Alexander Young in his *Chronicles of the Pilgrim Fathers*.

Later, Increase Mather borrowed the Bradford manuscript, and it was seen and used by others who were writing on early New England. It then passed into the hands of Judge Samuel Sewall, who had it in 1728, as was learned at the time by a collector of old manuscripts and memorabilia, the Reverend Thomas Prince, minister of Boston's Old South.

Prince wished to add it to his New England Library of Prints & Manuscripts, which he kept in the "steeple room" of the old South. The owner of the manuscript, Major John Bradford, "signified his willingness —only that He might have the perusal of it while he lived."

Having used it in compiling his own brief *Annals* on early New England, Prince placed *Of Plimoth Plantation* on the library shelves in the Old South, where it remained many years. For his *History of Massachusetts Bay* (1767) it was consulted by Governor Thomas Hutchinson, soon to flee the country as a Tory refugee. From this point to its discovery in London, nothing of its pilgrimage is known, but there are grounds for conjecture.

At the outbreak of the American Revolution, the Old South had been commandeered by the British and used as a riding rink by the Queen's Light Dragoons. After the royal forces evacuated Boston, sailing to Halifax with hundreds of native Tories in tow, it was found that Prince's library had been looted. Among other things, Bradford's history and other of his manuscripts were missing.

One of these, Bradford's "Letter-Book," suddenly came to light at Halifax in 1793 in a grocer's shop, where its precious pages were being used to wrap up purchases. Fortunately, it was rescued before it was altogether destroyed.

The hope lingered that *Of Plimoth Plantation* would also turn up in the town. But as the years passed, this hope faded and died, and the manuscript was written off as a casualty of the Revolution.

In compiling material for his *History of the Colonial Church* (1848), the Reverend James S. M. Anderson used manuscript sources in the Bishop of London's library, including Bradford's history, which he identified as such. But this was the end of the matter. It would almost seem that no one read the book. For quite inexplicably, no scholar on either side of the Atlantic picked up this plain lead, nor did Anderson himself appreciate the importance of his find.

Four years earlier, Samuel Wilberforce, Bishop of Oxford, had published his *History of the Protestant Episcopal Church in America*. He, too, had used unpublished sources in the Bishop of London's library in Fulham Palace. The book was sufficiently well received so that it was reprinted in New York in 1849.

But the clues it contained escaped notice for eleven years—until 1855, when John W. Thornton, thumbing through a copy of Wilberforce in an old Boston bookshop, came upon several passages attributed to a "MS. History of the Plantation of Plymouth," and surmised that they could have been written only by Bradford.

Thornton brought this to the attention of the Reverend John S. Barry, a writer on Massachusetts history. Others were interested, and excited inquiries to London brought the news that it was Bradford's history, in his "own autograph . . . The written pages are 270, the number named by Prince . . . as the number of pages in the long-lost volume."

How did it get to London and into the bishop's library?

Perhaps Governor Hutchinson still had it in his possession when he left Boston in 1774. Two other manuscript volumes from Prince's collection were found in the Fulham Palace library, with marginal notes in Hutchinson's handwriting. But these may have been put in when Hutchinson was using the volumes, and he may have returned them and Bradford's manuscript to the Old South before he departed.

Perhaps some British soldier of a literary or historical turn of mind helped himself to the manuscripts while the Old South was being used as a riding school.

Curiously, there is no record at Fulham Palace on how the pilfered manuscripts got into the bishop's library.

In any case, the Lord Bishop was graciously pleased to allow a transcript of Bradford's history to be made, and it appeared in print at Boston the next year, in 1856.

But the Lord Bishop was not disposed to return the original manuscript, raising many legalistic objections when such a move was suggested as the right thing to do—first by an English clergyman, the Reverend John Waddington.

The question of its return was raised by interested Americans and others in 1860, in 1867, in 1877, and again in 1881, but to no avail. Finally, as a result of concerted efforts by several societies and many distinguished Americans, our ambassador in Britain, Thomas F. Bayard, was officially instructed to see what he could do in the matter. After some discussion, the church authorities suggested a plea to the Consistory Court of the Diocese of London. Such a plea was framed, with the usual legalistic abracadabra, and the court was much impressed.

"Had this Mss. been solely of historical value," the chancellor adumbrated, it would have been very difficult indeed to see any reason for its removal. Fortunately, there was a most compelling argument for granting the plea. That was the "necessity of protecting the pecuniary interests of the descendants of the families named in it, in tracing and establishing their rights to succession of property."

And so, in 1897, *Of Plimoth Plantation* returned at last to our shores—not as a superlative historical and human document, but as a mere title deed.

And it did not go home to Plymouth, but into the Bay, to Boston, where it was presented to the governor and later placed in a glass case in the State House, where its neatly inscribed pages are still to be seen.

Afterword

(1) As observed before, there is no mention whatever of Plymouth Rock in the Pilgrim records. The story of the landing there, in the form in which it has come down to us, was first publicly told almost a century and a half after the Pilgrims initially entered Plymouth Harbor and came ashore there, staying a day or two before those on the Third Discovery returned to the *Mayflower* anchored at the tip of Cape Cod.

Deacon Ephraim Spooner, on fourth-hand authority, was the one who made the story known in 1769 to the young blades of the Old Colony Club at Plymouth, who held that year the first celebration of the landing on the Rock.

Whether or not the initial landing was made there late in 1620—on December 11 (Old Style), or December 21 (New Style), now commemorated as Forefathers' Day—Plymouth Rock serves very well as a symbol of a great adventure and as a useful pivot for the whole Pilgrim story.

The career of the Rock after its "discovery"—especially its long and bruising pilgrimage to the point where it now lies—is a significant and fascinating story of its own, related at some length in the last chapter of my *Saints and Strangers*.

BIBLIOGRAPHY
AND
SELECTED READING LIST

The chief original materials appearing in this book come from the following sources, listed more or less in order of importance (the editions I have used are indicated in parentheses after the title):

WILLIAM BRADFORD. *Of Plimoth Plantation*. Boston, 1856. (Worthington C. Ford's two-volume edition of 1912.)
This is the basic Pilgrim document, which has appeared in many editions. The latest has just appeared with the text subjected to modern usage, excellently edited by Samuel Eliot Morison.

"G. MOURT" (BRADFORD and EDWARD WINSLOW). *A Relation, or Journall, of the Beginnings and Proceedings of the English Plantation settled at Plimoth, in New England*. London, 1622. (Original edition.)
A detailed and almost day-by-day account of the Pilgrims' first year ashore in the New World.

EDWARD WINSLOW. *Good Newes from New-England*. London, 1624. (Original edition.)
This relates the Pilgrim story in considerable detail from late in 1621 to late in 1623. It has appeared in many reprints.

NATHANIEL MORTON. *New England's Memoriall*. Cambridge, 1669. (Facsimile reproduction by the Club of Odd Volumes, Boston, 1903, with an introduction by Arthur Lord.)
For the earlier years, it consists largely of passages copied from Bradford's history, but it contains some material not found elsewhere. It was Morton who first gave us the names of the original Pilgrim ships a half century after they had sailed—the *Speedwell* and the *Mayflower*.

WILLIAM BRADFORD. *Letter-Book*. In Series I Mass. Hist. Soc. Coll., Vols. 3–4. Boston, 1794. (There is another Bradford letter of importance, written in 1623, in the *American Historical Review*, Vol. 8.)

EDWARD WINSLOW. *Hypocrisie Unmasked*. London, 1646. (Facsimile reproduction by the Club for Colonial Reprints, Providence, 1916.)
Presents several graphic Pilgrim scenes not pictured elsewhere.

ROBERT CUSHMAN. *The Danger of Self-Love, and the Sweetnesse of True Friendship*. London, 1622. (Reprint, New York, 1858.)

Plymouth Church Records, 1620–1859. 2 vols. Boston, 1920.
Contains some interesting material on the early churches and their troubles. Also, Nathaniel Morton copied into the records William Bradford's *A Dialogue, or the Sum of a Conference betweene some Yonge-men, born in New England, and sundry Ancient-men that came out of Holand and Old England*, written in 1648.

John Pory's Lost Description of Plymouth Colony, ed. by Champlin Burrage. Boston, 1918.

JOHN WINTHROP. *The History of New England from 1630 to 1649*, now better known as *Winthrop's Journal*, ed. by James Savage. Boston, 1825–26. (Reprint, ed. by J. K. Hosmer. New York, 1908.)

PRINCE, THOMAS. *A Chronological History of New England in the form of Annals*. Boston, 1736.

In addition to other early Pilgrim writings, Prince had the use of and made entries from Bradford's "Pocket-Book," which has been lost.

THOMAS MORTON OF MERRY MOUNT. *New English Canaan*. Amsterdam, 1637. (Prince Society's edition, Boston, 1883, with an introduction by Charles Francis Adams, Jr.)

THOMAS HUTCHINSON. *A Collection of Original Papers Relative to the History of the Colony of Massachu-* *setts Bay*. Boston, 1769. (Original edition.)
Among other Pilgrim documents, this collection contains Winslow's letter on his outrage in discovering that half the General Court and most of the deputies, his own brethren, were eager to swallow the "sweet carrion" of religious toleration.

ISAACK DE RASIERES. Letter on Plymouth in 1627, in *Narratives of New Netherland*, ed. by J. Franklin Jameson. New York, 1909.

The selective reading list which follows may be of some help to the general reader with a desire to explore further in the Pilgrim and related fields.

ADAMS, BROOKS. *Emancipation of Massachusetts*. Boston, 1887.

ADAMS, CHARLES FRANCIS. *Three Episodes in Massachusetts History*. Boston, 1892.
For a somewhat different view of the affairs at Wessagusset and Merry Mount.

AINSWORTH, HENRY. *The Book of Psalms: Englished both in Prose and Metre*. Amsterdam, 1612. Reprinted in Waldo Seldon Pratt (see below).

ANDREWS, C. M. *The Fathers of New England*. New Haven, 1919.

ARBER, EDWARD. *The Story of the Pilgrim Fathers, 1606-1623*. London, 1897.

BANKS, CHARLES EDWARD. *The English Ancestry and Homes of the Pilgrim Fathers*. Boston, 1929.

———. *The Planters of the Commonwealth*. Boston, 1930.

Bay Psalm Book. Cambridge, 1640. (Facsimile reprint, with introduction by Wilberforce Eames. New York, 1903.)

BISHOP, GEORGE. *New England Judged by the Spirit of the Lord*. London, 1667.
Quaker account of their persecutions at the hands of the Saints.

BENÉT, STEPHEN VINCENT. *Western Star*. New York, 1943.

There is more about the Pilgrims in a dozen pages of this unfinished masterpiece than in a dozen volumes of conventional history.

BLISS, WILLIAM R. *Old Colony Town*. Boston, 1893.

———. *Side Glimpses from the Colonial Meeting House*. Boston, 1894.

BURGESS, WALTER H. *John Robinson, the Pastor of the Pilgrims*. London, 1920.

———. *John Smith, the Sebaptist . . . with fresh light upon the Pilgrims Father's Church*. London, 1911.

BURRAGE, CHAMPLIN. *The Church Covenant Idea*. Philadelphia, 1904.

———. *The True Story of Robert Browne*. Oxford, 1906.

———. *Early English Dissenters*. 2 vols. Cambridge, 1912.

CUCKSON, JOHN. *First Church at Plymouth*. Boston, 1902.

DAVIS, WILLIAM T. *Ancient Landmarks of Plymouth*. Boston, 1889.

———. *Plymouth Memories of an Octogenarian*. Plymouth, 1906.

———. *History of the Town of Plymouth*. Philadelphia, 1885.

DEXTER, HENRY MARTYN. *The Congregationalism of the Last Three Hundred Years*. New York, 1880.

———. *Congregationalism as Seen in its Literature*. Boston, 1880.

————. and DEXTER, MORTON. *The England and Holland of the Pilgrims.* Boston, 1905

DIGGES, JEREMIAH. *Cape Cod Pilot.* Provincetown and New York, 1937. The story of the Cape from the early days down to the intrusion of those strangest of "strangers," the summer tourists—a book with a rare sparkle.

DOW, G. F. *Domestic Life in New England in the Seventeenth Century.* Topsfield, Mass., 1925.

————. *Every Day Life in the Massachusetts Bay Colony.* Boston, 1935.

DRAKE, S. G. *The Witchcraft Delusion in New England.* Roxbury, 1866.

DUNHAM, H. C. *Old Houses in Plymouth.* Plymouth, 1893.

EARLE, ALICE MORSE. *The Sabbath in Puritan New England.* New York, 1893.

ERNST, JAMES. *Roger Williams.* New York, 1932.

GARÇON, MAURICE, and VINCHON, JEAN. *The Devil. An historical, critical, and medical study.* London, 1929. Witchcraft down the ages.

GOODWIN, J. A. *The Pilgrim Republic.* Boston, 1888.

HARRINGTON, THOMAS. *Dr. Samuel Fuller of the Mayflower.* Baltimore, 1903.

HART, ALBERT BUSHNELL. *Commonwealth History of Massachusetts.* 5 vols. New York, 1927–30. Latest and most inclusive history of the Commonwealth.

HILL, H. A. *History of the Old South Church.* Boston, 1890.

HARRIS, JAMES RENDEL. *Finding of the Mayflower.* London, 1920.

————. *Last of the Mayflower.* London, 1920. Harris believes the first and second *Mayflower* to be the same.

———— and JONES, STEPHEN. *The Pilgrim Press.* Cambridge, 1922. Excellent account of the Choir Alley press and its publications, with facsimiles of title pages.

HUNTER, JOSEPH. *Collections Concerning the Church or Congregation of Protestant Separatists formed at Scrooby,* etc. London, 1854.

HUTCHINSON, T. *History of the Province of Massachusetts Bay.* 3 vols. London, 1765–1828. A Tory view of early New England.

KITTREDGE, GEORGE LYMAN. *Witchcraft in Old and New England.* Boston, 1929.

JOHNSON, EDWARD. *Wonder-Working Providence.* London, 1654.

JOSSELYN, J. *Account of Two Voyages to New England, 1638 and 1663.* London, 1665.

LEVETT, CHRISTOPHER. *A Voyage into New England.* London, 1628.

Leyden Documents Relating to the Pilgrim Fathers, ed. by D. Plooij and J. R. Harris. Leyden, 1920.

LORD, ARTHUR. *Plymouth and the Pilgrims.* Boston, 1920.

MATHER, COTTON. *Magnalia Christi Americana.* London, 1702. Adulatory biographies of the more eminent Saints at Plymouth and in the Bay, etc.

MORISON, SAMUEL ELIOT. *Builders of the Bay Colony.* Boston, 1930.

————. *Three Centuries of Harvard.* Cambridge, 1936.

New England's First Fruits. London, 1643.

NUTTING, WALLACE. *Furniture of the Pilgrim Century.* Framingham, Mass., 1924.

PARRINGTON, VERNON LOUIS. *The Colonial Mind.* (Vol. I in *Main Currents in American Thought.*) New York, 1927. The best and sharpest analysis of the ideas and temper of early New England, though not without bias.

PATTEN, E. B. *Isaac Allerton.* Minneapolis, 1908.

PERRY, RALPH BARTON. *Puritanism and Democracy.* New York, 1944.

PHILLEO, C. W. "A Pilgrimage to Plymouth," in *Harper's New*

Monthly Magazine, Dec., 1853, and May, 1854.

PIERCE, WILLIAM. *John Penry.* London, 1923.
Interesting not only for its exciting story but for the Elizabethan background.

PLOOIJ, D. *The Pilgrim Fathers from a Dutch Point of View.* New York, 1932.

PORTEUS, T. C. *Captain Myles Standish.* London, 1920.

POWICKE, F. J. *John Robinson.* London, 1920.

PRATT, ENOCH. *History of Eastham.* Yarmouth, 1844.

PRATT, HARVEY H. *Early Planters of Scituate.* Scituate, 1929.

PRATT, PHINEAS. *A Declaration of the Affairs of the English People that first Inhabited New England.* In Series IV Mass. Hist. Soc. Coll., Vol. 4.
The story of Wessagusset by one of Weston's men.

PRATT, WALDO SELDON. *The Music of the Pilgrims.* Boston, 1921.

RUSSELL, WILLIAM S. *Pilgrim Memorials, etc.* Boston, 1864.

SCHOLES, PERCY A. *The Puritans and Music in England and New England.* Oxford, 1934.

SMITH, BRADFORD. *Bradford of Plymouth.* New York, 1951.
The only good biography of any Plymouth Saint.

STRAUS, OSCAR SOLOMON. *Roger Williams.* New York, 1894.

SWIFT, CHARLES E. *History of Old Yarmouth.* Yarmouthport, 1884.

TAWNEY, R. H. *Religion and the Rise of Capitalism.* London, 1926.
The economic motives in the Reformation.

THACHER, JAMES, *History of the Town of Plymouth.* Boston, 1832.

THOMAS, M. A. *Memorials of Marshfield.* Boston, 1854.

THOREAU, HENRY DAVID. *Cape Cod.* Boston, 1865.
Altogether charming account of the old and then still remote Cape about 1850.

Three Unknown Documents concerning the Pilgrim Fathers in Holland, ed. by Albert Eekhof. The Hague, 1920.

USHER, ROLAND. *The Pilgrims and Their History.* New York, 1918.
The best conventional history but, in my opinion, not without Anglican bias.

WALKER, WILLISTON. *History of the Congregational Churches in the United States.* New York, 1894.

WAYMAN, DOROTHY G. *Suckanesset, a History of Falmouth.* Falmouth, 1930.

WEEDEN, WILLIAM B. *Economic and Social History of New England,* 1620–1789. Boston, 1890.

WELDE, THOMAS. *A Brief Narration of the Practices of the Churches in New England.* London, 1645.

WINSOR, JUSTIN. *A History of Duxbury.* Boston, 1849.

WINTHROP, R. C. *Life and Letters of John Winthrop.* 2 vols. Boston, 1867.

WOOD, WILLIAM. *New England's Prospect.* London, 1635.

WRIGHT, THOMAS GODDARD. *Literary Culture in Early New England,* 1620–1730. New Haven, Conn., 1920.

YOUNG, ALEXANDER. *Chronicles of the First Planters of the Massachusetts Bay.* Boston, 1846.

———. *Chronicles of the Pilgrim Fathers.* Boston, 1844.

INDEX

For complete listing of Pilgrim Company, see Appendix